A HISTORY

THE PUBLIC

POLICIE

J. M. HODG

WHARTON C

FOREWORD

Nineteen hundred and twenty-four was a year of more than ordinary importance to historians of the American West for it was then that Frederick Jackson Turner ended his great teaching career at Wisconsin and Harvard to finish some long-contemplated writing on western history, that two books of major importance on public land policies and the frontier were published, and that Robert Marion La Follette's Progressive party had its brief but exciting career in western agrarian politics.

It was in the University of Wisconsin that Richard Ely and Frederick Jackson Turner built brilliant careers in teaching and writing in agricultural economics and the history of the American West. Both men deeply influenced each other and in turn their students profited from both scholars. From the seminars of Ely and Turner came a series of significant monographs and scores of teachers who were inspired by these men to teach the new fields of learning at other institutions. Soon courses in the history of the American frontier were being offered in most colleges and universities, and agricultural economics came to be taught at every land grant institution. Students of Ely who carved out great careers for themselves in land and agricultural economics included Thomas Nixon Carver, Henry C. Taylor, Benjamin H. Hibbard, O. E. Baker, L. C. Gray, and M. L. Wilson, while Turner inspired such prominent historians of the American West as Carl Becker, Solon J. Buck, Frederick Merk, Marcus Lee Hansen, James B. Hedges, and Carl Wittke.

Turner's hope of producing a magnum opus on the West was dashed by ill health which made it difficult for him to write; but had he done little more than to give to America his brilliant essay, "The Significance of the Frontier in American History," his role in creating a school of interpretation would have been established.* For a generation the Turner school of frontier historians held its own with other schools built around such masters as Bolton who stressed the Spanish background of the Southwest, Osgood and Andrews with their emphasis on institutional and colonial history, Dunning who was obsessed with the wickedness of reconstruction, Phillips who loved the plantation system, Dodd and Beard who feared lest powerful economic interests overwhelm the true democracy.

The Turner school was concerned, among other things, with western agrarianism, its reaction to monopolies, excessive railroad capitalization and rates, currency problems, the incidence of taxes, and the turning of the Republican party from its earlier idealism to the conservatism of McKinley, Taft, Harding, and Coolidge. The nefarious activities of the robber barons, the railroad magnates, the cattle kings, the bankers and usurers were being laid bare, with an assist from Charles A. Beard. Western progressives such as Norris, La Follette, and Johnson and, at times, the easterner, Theodore Roosevelt, breathed the spirit of the frontier with its willingness to experiment, its belief in democracy, its dislike of the cant of old-line professional politicians. La Follette's 1924 campaign seemed an exemplification of the continuing spirit of Turner's West, a glorious effort of the West to free itself and the country from the shackles of plutocratic conservativism. Though La Follette was defeated, his advocacy of effective railroad regulation, of curbing the trusts, of revivifying democracy, of conserving natural resources, and of the need to use government powers for the relief of

---

*Ray A. Billington, "Why Some Historians Rarely Write History: A Case Study of Frederick Jackson Turner," *Mississippi Valley Historical Review*, L (June, 1963), 36.

heavily mortgaged farmers and other underprivileged or depressed groups contributed to the movement for reform that flowered in the New Deal. Ely, John R. Commons, and E. A. Ross all had their part in the growth of Wisconsin progressivism and in contributing to the intellectual climate of opinion that made possible La Follette progressivism and the Franklin D. Roosevelt New Deal.

Nineteen hundred and twenty-four was also exciting to students of western history for the appearance of two books by Wisconsin men, both followers of Turner. Frederick Logan Paxson, who succeeded Turner at Wisconsin when he was drawn away to Harvard, built upon his earlier teaching experience in Colorado by familiarizing himself with western geography, routes through the mountains, disputed boundaries, the process of state making, and a variety of other questions concerned with the growth of the West, and out of this knowledge he compiled his *History of the American Frontier*. In the words of a follower, Paxson "picked up, added to, and carried on the interpretation of the frontier influence that Turner first made famous." Strong on the democratic process of western growth but weaker on the social and economic side, this manual at once became a convenient text for courses in western history. For years, until it was replaced by Riegel, Hafen and Rister, Billington and Clark, it was extensively used for its systematic coverage, its logical arrangement, its general accuracy, its usefulness. True, its story began in 1763, which made little sense, and ended in 1893, which made less, though I hasten to add that other writers seem to have followed these limitations. But Paxson was interested in the "frontier" and, since the Superintendent of the Census had said in 1893 that the frontier was gone, its influence, but not the influence of the West which comprehended the frontier, was gone.

While Paxson may have lacked the philosophical and imaginative insight that Turner had in such abundance, he had the same curiosity about and understanding of all things relating to the West. Turner's students were now reinforced by the men and women whom Paxson interested in populism, railroads, territory making, and land policy. Paxson's *History of the American Frontier* is a product of the best work of Turner, of Paxson himself, and of their numerous students.

In one of his numerous bibliographical footnotes Paxson declared there was "great need for a general historian of the public lands," apparently being unaware that his colleague Benjamin Horace Hibbard was completing his *History of the Public Land Policies* at precisely the same time that Paxson's *History of the American Frontier* was being published. In 1904, Hibbard, who was soon to become one of the leaders in the newly developing field of agricultural economics, first at Ames and then at Madison, had written his doctoral dissertation, entitled "A History of Agriculture in Dane County," under the supervision of Ely and Turner. Here he first touched upon public land policies in studying the selection of land by early settlers, the role of speculators, and the process of making land entries under federal law. He made use of local newspapers from which he collected stories of pioneers and the problems they met in securing title to their land. Despite some errors which use of the statutes and of the *Congressional Globe* and more rigorous inspection by his teachers might have enabled him to avoid, he produced a useful local history that anticipated some of the results later elaborated by Frederick Merk and Joseph Schafer. It was doubtless the writing of these chapters on land policies and the encouragement of Ely and Turner that interested Hibbard in making a systematic study of federal land policies, and to this task he next turned.

Internal evidence suggests that the early chapters of *A History of the Public Land Policies* were completed before 1914, possibly before 1910 when Turner, who had a profound influence on Hibbard, went to Harvard. In his preface Hibbard states: "this piece of work was begun a long time ago under the auspices of the Carnegie Institution and was designed to be a part of the history of American Agri-

culture." From this it may be deduced that it was to be one
of that great series of studies in economic history which this
institution financed, including Bidwell and Falconer, *History
of Agriculture in the Northern United States, 1620–1860*,
and Lewis C. Gray, *History of Agriculture in the Southern
United States to 1860*. As with some other volumes in the
series, other obligations intruded and it was long years before
Hibbard had completed study for publication. This delay of
many years from the time Hibbard's first chapters were
written until publication in 1924 doubtless accounts for the
fact that these chapters show no evidence of the use of two
studies prepared under Turner and published in 1914 and
1917: Raynor G. Wellington, *The Political and Sectional
Influence of the Public Lands, 1828–1842*, and George M.
Stephenson, *The Political History of the Public Lands from
1840 to 1862*. Like them, Hibbard devoted much space to
summarizing the Congressional discussions which preceded
the adoption of measures providing for sales, preemption,
graduation, distribution, and homestead. His close reliance
upon these discussions led him at times to fail to make clear
what features actually were included in the measures when
they finally passed.

Hibbard was too much of an economist and westerner to
be altogether concerned with what congressmen said in
Washington about proposed measures. He wanted to know
how these congressmen reflected western sentiment and, even
more, what were western views and how the land laws
actually worked; consequently he searched western newspapers, particularly those of Wisconsin and Iowa, for information which — with his feel for the land, for farmers,
and particularly for pioneer farmers — gave him a keen
insight into the way the land system was operating in the
West, with all its weaknesses and errors, its strength and
successes. Furthermore, Hibbard knew that any discussion
of land policies would be sterile if it was not accompanied by
statistics, tables, charts, and maps showing the creation of

the public domain and the grants, sales, donations, and other transfers of land. He therefore included thirty-six tables and eleven charts and maps which added immeasurably to the usefulness of his work. True, the tables, charts, and maps were compiled from data readily available in published documents, for Hibbard used no manuscript materials, save for the research of a student of his in the entry volumes of the Iowa land offices. Nor, for that matter, had other students of land policy used at the time any considerable amount of the enormous quantity of manuscript materials relating to public land administration. Hibbard was attempting a task for which there were few guidelines, other than studies essentially political. Historians of later generations will have a much easier task because of the great amount of preparatory work which has now been done for them.

Notwithstanding the lack of regional and special studies that might have aided him in analyzing the effect of public land policies, even for the early period, Hibbard offers useful analyses and criticisms of the various measures. His writing reflects the period in which La Follette progressivism was strongly critical of the devices used by special interests to acquire possession of great natural resources. A follower of Ely and somewhat influenced by Henry George, Hibbard was deeply concerned with speculation in land in which all classes of western society, from pioneer farmers to powerful capitalists, indulged. He was aware that the rapid rise of values must have brought profits to many but at the same time he knew that many holders, large and small, never realized their dreams of fortune making. All speculative purchases he reprobated but he directed his scorn most at the large capitalists whose investments he found to be "socially reprehensible." His sympathies were always with the settlers though he seemed somewhat troubled by the poor investor in land who had to unload his holdings at less than cost.

For the period after Homestead, Hibbard was striking into new territory where studies only of limited fields had been accomplished. John Ise had published his excellent *United States Forest Policy* in 1920 and Ray Palmer Teele had brought out his *Irrigation in the United States* in 1915, neither of which did Hibbard appear to use. Ise, like Hibbard, was a conservationist and public control advocate and may have been unduly disturbed by the exaggerations of some "denudiacs" of the time, but his work remains today as the standard treatment of our forest policy. Teele, as in his later *Economics of Land Reclamation,* published in 1927, did not pull his punches in revealing how both private and public reclamation-irrigation activity had not been well planned, how expensive projects had been undertaken without proper preliminary studies and soon fell into arrears in payments. The substance of the work of Ise and Teele was certainly familiar to Hibbard and appears in his study.

Hibbard was uniquely prepared to discuss the operation of the Homestead laws because he had lived on a farm in O'Brien County in Northwestern Iowa, when homesteading was still going on in the neighborhood, though doubtless on land long since passed over for its poor quality by early land seekers. His account of homesteading shows neither the carping, ill-balanced criticism of the officials of the General Land Office nor the unbounded praise bestowed upon it by some western politicians who were anxious to cover up its weaknesses. Free land was inevitable and, though the Homestead Law made possible large ownerships of timber and grazing land and lacked essential safeguards that might have confined its bounty to pioneer settlers, nevertheless a million homesteads were created, a great many of which were family farms. "East of the hundredth meridian the Homestead was a success," Hibbard rightly concluded. He might have added that west of that line the original Homestead unit was the nucleus of many larger farms and ranches.

Hibbard was aware that our public land policies, including the Homestead Law with its offer of free land, had "failed to keep the land permanently in the hands of tillers of the soil."

Within a generation or two economic forces governing prices sent land values to hundreds of dollars an acre and produced the rapid emergence of tenancy. Giving land away did not assure permanent family farm ownership.

One of the most useful chapters of Hibbard's work is "The Public Land Policies Reviewed and Criticized." Here the agricultural economist with a fine training in history, and experience in the research of its sources, examined from the point of view of an enlightened person of 1924 the whole gamut of policies, modifications, new tacks, reversals, and oddities of the American land administration. He raised many questions, suggested alternatives, considered the Wakefield concept of a "sufficient" price to prevent speculation, and urged a decade before the adoption of the Taylor Grazing Act, that the remaining grazing lands of the government should be kept under organized public control. He showed that the weakness of government policy was owing to public opinion and its willingness to condone corruption and mismanagement, the laxity of Congress in drafting laws and its refusal to give adequate financial aid to administer them, and to unimaginative administrators who rarely attempted to use the full powers granted them to eliminate abusive practices.

Errors there are in *A History of the Public Land Policies* (see the review by Raynor G. Wellington in the *American Historical Review*, XXX [July, 1925], 837–38). One that has bothered me for years is on page 29. In a table purporting to show the private land claims Hibbard gives an inaccurate reference (in note 3, the page reference should be to 140 and 159), a caption for the second column of statistics is misleading, and without any documentation for it a reader cannot determine what is actually included. All one can say is that somewhere Hibbard found the column, misunderstood precisely what it contained, lost the reference, and leaves the reader with an inaccurate picture of the total acreage included with the claims. Furthermore, he carried over from this table the wrong column for the table on page 31.

Donaldson estimated the total acreage included within the private land claims to be 80,000,000 acres. Another example of Hibbard's carelessness is seen in his discussion of the grant to the Pacific Railroad. He does not distinguish between the ten section to the mile grant of 1862 and the twenty section to the mile grant of 1864. But in a work of such extensive coverage and so fresh in character, at least for much of the story after 1860, errors of this sort can be excused.

The real test of a reference book is the frequency with which satisfied readers return to it for information. In the Cornell University Library the original 1924 copy has long since been worn out and discarded and the three copies of the reprint edition of 1939 have been checked out at least 126 times since 1953 (the earlier charge slips are missing). In addition three copies in other libraries on the Cornell campus have been charged out 39 times since 1953. Surely any scholarly author could feel proud that a work of this kind is in such extensive use a generation after it first appeared. The reasons for this long-sustained use are clear. Hibbard produced a synthesis of public land policies which was much needed in 1924 and, though parts have been displaced by Roy M. Robbins' fine *Our Landed Heritage,* by E. Louise Peffer, *Closing of the Public Domain,* and by scattered articles of other writers, the synthesis still stands because of Hibbard's penetrating understanding of land problems, his critical and clearly defined judgments, the data he presents so graphically, the concise summaries at the end of each chapter, and by his advocacy of the changes he deemed essential for a modern and constructive program of land management.

PAUL W. GATES.

Ithaca, New York.

PREFACE

The piece of work was begun a long time ago under the auspices of the Carnegie Institution and was designed to be a part of the history of American Agriculture. With the reorganization of the institution, it seemed hardly practicable to make use of this part of the work as originally planned. The result was a considerable period of years during which no progress was made on the manuscript. Recently the Institute for Research in Land Economics and Public Utilities has provided a great deal of help toward the completion of the work, and a means of publication.

The author wishes to acknowledge his indebtedness to a considerable number of people who have helped in the gathering and preparation of material. Only those who have worked with the sources of information on the land subject can fully appreciate the enormous amount of time and patience involved in getting together and sifting the material to be used. In making original search for data, the following should be mentioned: Miss Stella G. Hibbard, Leonard Paulson, Asher Hobson and Charles Deshler. From time to time the various chapters have been used as topics in seminar work and in this manner revised, and during one semester the manuscript was made the main basis of a seminar. Several chapters are left in much the same form they were given at that time. The members of this special seminar were Dr. O. E. Baker, Dr. P. A. Eke, Professor Eric Englund, Professor P. E. McNall, Dr. G. S. Wehrwein, and Dr. B. Youngblood. Several of the chapters were radically revised by members of the class, and have been changed comparatively little. The chapter on Land

Classification was made anew by Dr. Baker. Special credit
is due Dr. V. P. Lee, whose services were made available
by the Institute for Research in Land Economics and Public
Utilities, for much faithful, high-grade work in helping with
a radical revision of the whole book, the writing of many
paragraphs and pages, and the checking of footnotes and
figures. A great deal of work was done on the chapter dealing with educational grants by M. H. Greene. The entire
manuscript was read by Dr. Mary L. Shine, who made
numerous and valuable criticisms, many of which were complied with. Professor F. J. Turner read a considerable part
of the manuscript in one of its earlier stages and made
helpful criticisms. Professor Ely has read the manuscript
in its present form and given much valuable advice. The
plan of Chart I was made by Dr. Wehrwein. The author's
wife, Mrs. Jeannette B. Hibbard, has read the manuscript
and made improvements in the style. Much credit is due
to the painstaking work of Miss Florence Rasmussen in
preparing the manuscript with respect to accuracy and
clearness.

The aim has been to put into one moderate-sized volume,
a sketch of the historical development and operations of our
federal land policies. No doubt some special students will
wonder how so many important things have been omitted,
while the more casual reader will wonder at the inclusion
of so many details. Nearly all data are from original
sources, though occasionally, where the ground seemed to
have been well covered by some previous writer, the findings
have been accepted. There should be, and will be without
doubt, many monographs written on the general subject of
American land policies. Among the few already in existence are several of distinct merit. If it seems that scant
attention has been paid to them, it is not because of lack
of appreciation, but rather because the aim of this volume
is a complete sketch which precludes the possibility of a
complete treatment of each and every phase.

No attempt has been made to account for every acre of

land. The data available are not such as to lend themselves easily to such an exhibit. However, an approximation of the original amount of the public domain, and the dispositions made of it is presented, and it is believed that for all practical purposes the discrepancies will not appear formidable.

B. H. HIBBARD.

University of Wisconsin.
June, 1924.

CONTENTS

TABLES

MAPS AND CHARTS

CHAPTER I

THE weakness of the Federal government in the matter of finances during its early years is well known. It was so extreme that an exaggerated statement of the case is hardly possible. Under the Confederation the States could not, and would not, raise the apportioned shares of government revenue. Thus to the leaders charged with the stern duty of raising the money with which to pay necessary national expenses, were the nation to continue to exist, it was little wonder that the land belonging to the nation should be viewed as the most promising asset. The debts owed by the new republic were in large measure owed to European creditors, the interest was not being paid and embarrassment was not only painful, it was apparently without prospect of relief unless money could be raised by means other than taxes. The only other source of any importance was the public domain.

Never was a new country confronted with a more serious duty than that which faced the Confederation. It had the opportunity and the duty, of providing a financial policy for a newly constituted state, and fully as important, of deciding upon a colonization plan. The case was decided, as most frequently is done, by letting the more immediate considerations dominate. Clearly this does not mean that the weightier one of two alternatives is given its proper place viewed in the abstract. It is not viewed in the abstract; it is viewed in the concrete. And the concrete, immediate question of raising revenue was the one that demanded attention. Hamilton had a lively imagination respecting the income and outgo of the young Republic. He was not devoid of ideas regarding the settlement of the great stretch of country between the Alleghanies and the Mississippi. Nevertheless, he is bound to be remembered as a financier and praised as such. He will be remembered, likewise, as one of the leading influences in framing a plan for the disposition of the public domain, but there will be little occasion for praise. Hamilton was more than willing that the Western pioneer should be treated fairly; he had no plan that comprehended the herculean task of absorbing the vast unoccupied territory and making it, together with its inhabitants, a part of a symmetrical unit.

Substantially Hamilton's whole doctrine, one of expediency, is summed up in a paragraph of his well-known report. The financial and colonization aspects were to him questions of primary and secondary importance respectively: "That, in the formation of a plan for the disposition of the vacant lands of the United States there appear to be two leading objects of consideration: one the facility of advantageous sales, according to the probable course of circumstances; the other the accommodation of individuals now inhabiting the western country, or who may hereafter emigrate thither. The former as an operation of finance claims primary attention; the latter is important, as it relates to the satisfaction of the inhabitants of the western country." [1] He believed that the two objects were not necessarily in conflict and could both be satisfactorily taken care of.

Jefferson, and many others, had strong convictions on the necessity for some sort of plan by which the western country might be settled. It must be admitted that these plans, granting that they can be called by so dignified a name, were not characterized by clearness except in one respect: the land was to be sold at a very low figure, to the settler, or to be given away outright. But such plans as these, based on social views or theories, have a hard time making headway against the supposedly feasible, practical, means of raising

---

[1] *American State Papers, Public Lands* (Duff Green Edition), I, p. 4.

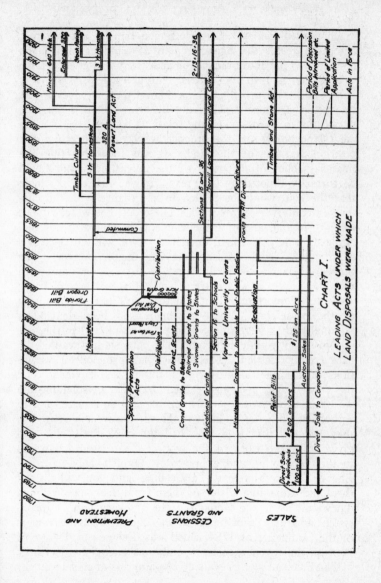

CHART I.

LEADING ACTS UNDER WHICH
LAND DISPOSALS WERE MADE

much needed money. Even Jefferson himself surrendered, and as a result the financial plan of handling the public domain was put into practice, or at least it was given a trial.

It is one thing to vote a policy through a legislature; it is quite another to provide for its administration. Never was this principal more conclusively illustrated than during the period under discussion in the relations between the government land policy and the practice respecting the actual disposition and use of the land. It was inevitable that the financial policy of disposing of the unoccupied land should be formally adopted by Congress. It was just as inevitable that the land would be settled in accordance with the customs, already well established. These customs were without legal form and void of embellishments in the nature of recognized, widely accepted, doctrines. Not without doctrines stoutly defended by those practicing them, however. The pioneer looked upon vacant land as a free good, and with reason. Surely it was no-rent land; it was superabundant; and, more important still, it had for years been the property of the possessor. Where payments had been demanded, nominally, they were in the first place small, and in the second place not rigidly collected. The colonies had wanted the back country settled. The settlers had pronounced convictions on the questions of rights, duties, and payments due the government, and one of them was that in subduing the wilderness they were performing a patriotic service, and in agreement with the findings of H. C. Carey at a later day, they believed that wild land had no value until such was given it by the work of the pioneer. Jefferson acquiesced in this conception and expressed it unmistakably in referring to the frontiersman: "By selling land you will disgust them and cause an avulsion of them from the common union. They will settle the lands in spite of everybody." Inconsistent as it may seem Jefferson was one of the main framers of the Ordinance of 1784 which was designed to dispose of land on the revenue basis. Conditions outweight doctrines.

The financial plan prevailed. As a means of raising money

it was a failure. Congress pledged the returns from land sales toward the payment of the public debt,[2] but the receipts from this source were so small as to be of secondary importance until after the early years of embarrassment were passed. It must be remembered that the receipts were by no means net, and even when there was a considerable income it was erratic, falling and rising in no predictable manner.

When the financial plan was replaced by that of development is not an easy question to answer. To begin with the financial plan was never accepted by the people most concerned, the settlers. Neither was it unanimously accepted by those in the older settlements more responsible for the conduct of the affairs of government. Justice was always tempered with mercy, or to change the figure, the alloy frequently appeared as the predominating ingredient. The pioneers were settling the wilderness; the government wanted it settled. Hence the long list of acts condoning the violation of the newly enacted land laws. The pioneer won, and was destined to win, every encounter, sooner or later, with the cold business calculations of the East. Financiers could make paper requirements providing for a handsome payment by settlers for land. The settlers did not have the money, were destined not to have it, but settle the land they would. And back of every demand for revenue and obedience to law, from Hamilton to Jackson, was the stronger desire to make the government secure and great through the spread of people over the millions of acres of the great central valley of the United States, beyond which the imaginations of the early statesmen hardly reached. When Jackson in 1832 expressed the view that as soon as the public debt was paid the land should cease to be a source of revenue, he failed just a little, and pardonably, of comprehending that the attempted revenue régime was then about past, and that its demise did not depend on the final payment of the public debt. The spirit of national development had gradually

[2] Proceeds of Sales of Public Land now belonging or which may belong to the United States pledged "solely to that use (i.e. payment of debt) until the said debts shall be fully satisfied." *U. S. Statutes at Large*, I, pp. 144, 1700.

overshadowed the desire to make the land, popularly considered the most fundamental basis of economic life, a source of immediate income. The settlers were taking the land; yet for a score of years the sales, on a credit basis, did not correspond with receipts in cash due to delinquencies. When the government most needed the revenue, lands did not sell; when revenues could be raised otherwise, land brought in considerable cash. In the fitful years preceding the panic of 1837, the surplus in the treasury, over which Congress wrangled interminably, was due in no small part to receipts from land. Thus more clearly than before proving that as a regular source of income the receipts from the sales of public land are about as bad as possible. They cannot be forced, limited, or predicted in any normal way corresponding with the needs of a well-ordered government. It was patent to the frontiersman that the public domain was not properly to be viewed as a great source of revenue; the more conservative portions of the population took a half century in comprehending and acknowledging the principle.

CHAPTER II

THE ACQUISITION OF THE PUBLIC DOMAIN

The *public domain* included all lands that were at any time owned by the United States and subject to sale or other transfer of ownership under the laws of the Federal Government. The *national domain,* on the other hand, consists of the total area, both land and water, under the jurisdiction of the United States. Hence, the difference between the public domain and the national domain is one of property rights in the land itself and not one of sovereignty. The Federal Government has, or has had, both ownership in and jurisdiction over the former while it exercises only jurisdiction over the latter.

This definition of the public domain excludes all lands rightfully claimed by individuals or other private interests on the basis of occupancy or grants by other governments prior to the accession of the territory by the United States. Many private claims were contested in the courts, and where it was decided that the land in question belonged to the claimant, it followed that it was not the property of the United States, and therefore, not a part of the public domain. Considerable areas of the western lands (back lands) of the original thirteen states never became a part of the public domain, as will be shown later, because under the terms of cession by the various land owning states the central government did not acquire property rights in all land included in the ceded territory.

Cessions of Land by the States

At the close of the Revolutionary War, the new nation found itself in possession of the territory lying east of the

7

Mississippi, south of the Great Lakes and north of the thirty-first parallel, the present northern boundary of Florida. To the northeast there was some vagueness as to boundary, likewise to the northwest, but the general outline of this district was never essentially different from its present form.

The portion of the above described territory lying west of the present western boundary of the Original Thirteen States became the nucleus of the public domain, with the exception of Kentucky, Tennessee and some minor areas reserved in the deeds of cession. Aside from the two states mentioned, this territory is embraced in the present states of Ohio, Indiana, Illinois, Michigan, Wisconsin, that portion of Minnesota lying east of the Mississippi River, and the portion of Alabama and Mississippi lying north of the thirty-first parallel. It is difficult to determine exactly what portion of this vast area of land became public domain because private claims were many, widely scattered, and required much litigation extending over a long time for their final settlement. For instance it required thirty-four acts of Congress, aside from special legislation, to provide for the bounty claims of Virginia alone.[1]

Within this wide domain there was much controversy as to jurisdiction and ownership. The lands westward to the Mississippi River were claimed by Massachusetts, Connecticut, New York, Virginia, North Carolina, South Carolina, and Georgia on the basis of the terms of their colonial charters. The boundaries of these claims were very indefinite and consequently settlement could not be made without engendering serious controversies. The extreme difficulty of adjusting these conflicting claims undoubtedly aided in bringing about the final cession of the land to the central government.

Under the leadership of Maryland, the six states that

[1] P. J. Treat, *The National Land System*, p. 338.

did not have western claims demanded that the Western
Lands "wrested from the common enemy by blood and
treasure of the Thirteen States, should be considered as
common property."[2] These six states also feared the
strength which the rival states would gain should they be
allowed to retain their claims. Maryland even refused to
sign the Articles of Confederation unless these claims were
abandoned, and the force of her stand is indicated by the
fact that the first act of cession (New York, March 1,
1781), was by its own wording an act "to facilitate the
completion of the Articles of Confederation." The same
day, March 1, 1781, Maryland signed the Articles on
promises to the effect that the entire seven states having
western claims would relinquish them. In pursuance of
these promises[3] the seven claimants to the Western lands
surrendered their claims at various times from 1781 to 1802,
with the understanding that when the territory was settled
it should be divided into states and admitted to the Union.[4]
Thus the wide western domain became the common property
of the states and a bond of union at a time when the life of
the new nation depended upon a harmonious relation of its
parts.

In view of the purpose of this work, it is not necessary
to go into the details of the cession by each of the seven
states, but since it is the aim to show how the public domain
was acquired it seems desirable to mention the reservations
made by the four states whose deeds of cession were con-
ditional and to determine as far as possible the extent of
these reservations and the amount of land actually added

[2] Maryland's instructions to her delegates in Congress, Dec. 15, 1778. See
Johns Hopkins University Studies, III, No. 1, p. 26.
[3] Resolution of the Congress of the Confederation. Oct. 10, 1780, *Journal
of Congress,* VI, pp. 146, 147.
[4] The Continental Congress decided on October 10, 1780, that the states to
be formed out of this territory should be of suitable size, not less than 100 nor
more than 150 miles square. This was later found to be impracticable and,
at the time of the Virginia session, it was finally provided that not more than
five nor less than three states should be formed out of the ceded territory.

to the public domain by the cessions. Only three deeds of cession were unconditional, those of New York, Massachusetts, and South Carolina, while four contained important reservations, some of which were not finally met till after 1870.[5]

Virginia's claim to Western lands was based on her colonial charter and on the conquest of a portion of the Northwest by General George Rogers Clark and his Virginia troops. Her entire claim included Kentucky, Ohio, Indiana, Illinois, Wisconsin, Michigan, and the portion of Minnesota east of the Mississippi River. On March 1, 1784, she ceded to the central government all the territory claimed by her northwest of the Ohio River, and later she consented to the erection of Kentucky into a state and ceded the land within its boundaries to that state. Hence, the territory embraced in the present state of Kentucky never became a part of the public domain because it was not ceded by Virginia to the national government.

The Virginia deed of cession contained other important reservations. It required that those who had been recognized as citizens of Virginia or had been granted land by her for military service or otherwise should have their possessions and deeds confirmed to them. All the land not thus excepted became a part of the public domain. The reservations included 150,000 acres near the falls of the Ohio River given to General Clark and his command composing the expedition to Illinois. It also included the holdings of the French and Canadian settlers at Kaskaskia and St. Vincennes, and the so-called "Virginia military lands" to meet the bounty claims of Virginia soldiers of the Revolution. Some of the land set aside for this purpose lay between the Green and Tennessee rivers in Kentucky, but,

[5] In 1871, 76,735.44 acres of Virginia land were unappropriated. It was ceded to Ohio by Act of Congress, February 18, 1871, and later turned over to the Ohio College of Agriculture and Mechanic Arts. (Thomas Donaldson, *The Public Domain*, p. 83.)

if this area were not sufficient to satisfy the claims, the deficiency was to be met in land north of the Ohio River. These lands were located in twenty-three counties and embraced an area of 6,570 square miles or 4,204,800 acres.[6] Aside from these stipulations, the deed of cession also provided for compensation to Virginia for expenses incurred in the defense of this territory.

Connecticut ceded her claim to Western lands September 13, 1786, but her deed was not without reservations. She retained both ownership of, and jurisdiction over, an area of land between the western boundary of Pennsylvania and the eastern boundary of her cession, "being a point 120 miles west of Pennsylvania's western boundary, comprising a strip of land between the above boundaries 120 miles long and irregular in width, lying between the parallel 41° and 42° 2' north, being the northeastern portion of the present state of Ohio and known as the Western Reserve of Connecticut in Ohio."[7] This area, together with the "Firelands," contained about 3,800,000 acres.[8] Land lying between these two parallels (41° and 42° 2') in the present State of Pennsylvania was claimed by Connecticut, but in 1782 a Federal Court under the Confederation decided that it rightfully belonged to Pennsylvania.

The reservations made by North Carolina, February 25, 1790, were more detailed and far reaching than those made by any other state. She first reserved land for her own Continental and state soldiers to be selected by each claimant wherever he should desire to select it. Secondly, she required confirmation of all grants of land to individuals under state law, and of all rights whether acquired by formal entry or by occupancy. Entries conflicting with prior claims were to be located on other land. According to a report by

---

[6] Donaldson, p. 82.

[7] *Ibid*, p. 73.

[8] The "Fire lands" were grants made by Connecticut to her citizens who had suffered by fire and raids of British troops durng the Revolution.

Thomas Jefferson to Congress, November 10, 1791, these claims amounted to 8,118,601½ acres. The thoroughness of North Carolina's reservation is illustrated by the following sentence from the deed of cession: "All and every right of occupancy and preëmption, and every other right reserved by any act or acts to persons settled on and occupying lands within the limits of the lands hereby intended to be ceded as aforesaid shall continue in full force, in the same manner as if the cession had not been made, and as conditions upon which the said lands are ceded to the United States." [9]

The State of Tennessee was erected out of the territory ceded by North Carolina. It was, however, almost entirely covered by claims and was consequently not an addition to the public domain, thus accounting for the fact that this state is not one of the "public land states." In 1841 Congress made Tennessee its agent to dispose of the unappropriated lands within her boundaries, and gave her all land that remained after satisfying the claims under the deed of cession.

Georgia was the fourth state to include reservations in her deed of cession and the last to cede her claims to western lands to the central government. The cession was made April 24, 1802, and included all the territory between the present western boundary of Georgia and the Mississippi River, and between the 31st parallel and 34° 40′ north latitude.

The conditions of the Georgia cession were: First, payment by the national government of $1,200,000 to Georgia from the sale of public lands in the cession; second, the reservation of 500,000 acres, or the proceeds of sales thereof, to satisfy claims against land in the ceded territory; third, extinguishment of Indian titles to certain portions of the cession; and fourth, agreement that all persons who actually settled within the territory ceded "shall be con-

[9] It was also provided that land belonging to absentee owners should not be taxed more than other land.

TABLE I. — SUMMARY OF CESSIONS BY STATES

STATE	DATE OF CESSION	CONDITIONAL OR UNCONDITIONAL	AREA ADDED TO THE PUBLIC DOMAIN	
			Sq. mi	Acres
Massachusetts claim (disputed) [10]	April 19, 1785	Unconditional	54,000 [11]	34,550,000
Connecticut (disputed) and Western reserve and "fire lands" [12]	September 13, 1786	Conditional	40,000	25,600,000
New York and Massachusetts, actual cession	March 1, 1781 (N. Y.)	Unconditional	315.91	202,187
Virginia (exclusive of Kentucky "Western reserve" and "Fire lands")	March 1, 1784	Conditional	253,054.50	161,959,680
South Carolina	August 9, 1787	Unconditional	4,900	3,136,000
North Carolina [13]	February 25, 1790	Conditional	—	
Georgia	April 24, 1802	Conditional	88,578	56,689,920
Total area to public domain [14]			346,848.41	221,987,787

[10] Area included in Virginia cession.
[11] Estimated.
[12] Estimated.
[13] Tennessee, once a part of North Carolina, is not a "public land state" because its area was covered with reservations.
[14] This table is largely based on the table in Donaldson, p. 11. Areas of reservations mentioned in this chapter have been subtracted from the total cessions in order to arrive at the area that actually became a part of the public domain.

firmed in all grants legally and fully executed" prior to the date of cession. [15]

THE LOUISIANA PURCHASE

The purchase of Louisiana from France in 1803, which added 827,987 [16] square miles to the national domain, was not brought about by preconceived plans on the part of the United States to acquire that vast territory, but rather by the determination of President Jefferson and other American statesmen to secure the use of the Mississippi River as an outlet to the sea for the portion of the United States lying between that river and the Alleghany Mountains. The immediate object of the American mission to France in 1803 was to purchase the Island of New Orleans in order to secure control of the mouth of the Mississippi. Our representatives in Paris, Robert R. Livingston and James Monroe, were not instructed to buy the whole province, but decided to do so upon Napoleon's refusal to sell a part of it.

In 1660 La Salle descended the Mississippi and took possession of the adjacent territory in the name of Louis XIV, and named it "Louisiana." This territory came to include not only what is known as the province of Louisiana but also Texas which France claimed on the basis of discovery by La Salle in 1682 and of colonization at Matagorda Bay in 1685. France never ceded this claim to Spain and consequently it was considered a part of Louisiana. The southwest boundary of the United States was definitely established only in 1828 by a treaty with Mexico based on the Florida treaty with Spain in 1819, as will be pointed out more in detail later. France held this entire territory from 1680 to 1762 when it was ceded to the King of Spain by royal order of the King of France. Spain held Louisiana for thirty-eight years and transferred it back to France in 1800.

The acquisition of Louisiana by Napoleon raised apprehension in America. On April 18, 1802, President Jef-

[15] Donaldson, p. 83.
[16] *United States Thirteenth Census, Abstract,* p. 28.

ferson wrote to Mr. Livingston in Paris: "There is on the globe one single spot the possessor of which is our natural and habitual enemy. It is New Orleans—through which the produce of three-eighths of our territory must pass to market; and from its fertility it will ere long yield more than half of our produce and contain more than half of our inhabitants."

Due no doubt in some measure to the ease with which the great area to the west had been transferred from one European prince to another by royal orders, as well as to a vision of the ultimate greatness of America, Jefferson considered that the future of the country depended upon our getting rid of aggressive and province-trading neighbors and securing control of the territory from sea to sea and from the Gulf to the Great Lakes. However, as has already been mentioned, the immediate cause for accrediting James Monroe to France, January 10, 1803, was to negotiate a treaty to guarantee to the United States the right of way through the Mississippi River. The navigation privileges, not too good at best, had been in danger for some time, for under Spanish control of the province, the authorities of Louisiana made it understood that the privileges enjoyed by the United States up to that time must cease on account of changed relations between this country and Spain. Since French possession of New Orleans was considered a greater menace than Spanish possession, the transfer of the province to France only intensified the danger. Monroe went to Paris to negotiate for the cession of the Island of New Orleans and Florida, thinking that Florida had been ceded to France, but, upon learning that the Spanish cession of 1800 did not include that province, the American representatives at Paris confined their efforts to securing control of the mouth of the Mississippi.

Napoleon realized the value of Louisiana perhaps better than most Europeans of his time, and he is reported to have said that the nation that controls the Mississippi Valley would eventually be the strongest of nations. Although he refused to sell the island of New Orleans and with it the control of the Mississippi, he expressed his willingness to sell the entire province. There appear to have been two main reasons for his decision. In the first place, he was greatly in need of money to conduct his extensive wars. Secondly, the combinations led by England that were then being formed against him in Europe made it seem difficult to protect this over-seas province. To these may be added the failure of his San Domingo plans, and the possibility of the United States joining his European enemies if navigation rights on the Mississippi were not secured. Regarding the United States as more friendly than the nations of Europe, he preferred to sell Louisiana to a friendly power than to risk its capture by his enemies.

Without specific authorization from their government, Monroe and Livingston negotiated for the purchase of the entire province. The cession was made April 30, 1803, and the treaty was ratified by Congress, October 17 of that year. The following is the area and cost of the Louisiana purchase:

Area [17] ....827,987 sq. mi., or 529,911,680 acres
Cost: [18]

    Principal sum $15,000,000
    Interest to Redemption 8,529,000
    Claims of citizens of the United States due from
        France and assumed by the United States........ 3,738,000

        Total cost $27,267,000

THE PURCHASE OF FLORIDA

Spain acquired the right to Florida by the discovery of that peninsula in 1512 and by various expeditions into its interior. In 1736 she ceded this possession to Great Britain in exchange for Cuba, but both East and West Florida were ceded back to Spain at the time of the treaty of peace between Great Britain and the United States in 1783. In this cession the boundaries were left indefinite, as were the boundaries

[17] *Thirteenth Census, Abstract*, p. 28.
[18] Donaldson, p. 105.

of Louisiana, resulting in the dispute between the United States and Spain over West Florida. Great Britain had held that the 31st parallel marked the northern limit of Spanish possessions, while Spain claimed more territory on the basis of a proclamation in regard to boundaries by the King of England in 1763. This matter was settled in 1795 when Spain waived her claims to the territory north of the 31st parallel.

Following the acquisition of Louisiana, President Jefferson took steps to purchase Florida, but his early attempts at negotiations were rejected by the Spanish king in 1805, and James Monroe, whose mission it was to negotiate for the purchase, left Spain. Both East and West Florida were a source of trouble to Spain. In 1810 the people of West Florida declared themselves independent of Spanish rule. By act of Congress, March 31, 1811, the United States occupied West Florida on the alleged ground that it was a part of the Louisiana purchase, and did not withdraw her claims notwithstanding the protests of France and Spain.[19] An Indian war resulting in the invasion of Florida by United States troops under Andrew Jackson in 1818, and boundary disputes and similar difficulties continued until John Quincy Adams and the Spanish minister signed the treaty by which the Floridas were ceded to the United States, February 22, 1819.

This treaty was important, not only because it gave the United States possession of Florida, but also because it definitely fixed the Southwestern boundary between the United States and the Spanish possessions in Mexico. The boundary by the treaty was from the mouth of the Sabine River along its west bank to the 32° north latitude; thence by a line north to the Red River and along its course to the 100th meridian; thence due north to the Arkansas River and following its south bank to its source; thence north to latitude 42° north, and thence due west to the Pacific Ocean. This latter parallel now marks the boundary

between Oregon and California. The area and the cost of
the Floridas were:

Area ..,..........................72,101 sq. mi., or 46,144,640 acres
Cost:
    Purchase price in bonds.............................$5,000,000
    Interest on bonds.................................... 1,490,000
                                                             ————
      Total $6,490,000

The Annexation of Texas and the Texas Purchase

The United States claimed as a part of the Louisiana
purchase the territory to the southwest as far as the Rio
Grande, but finally yielded her claim by the treaty with
Spain in 1819 when the Sabine River became the southwestern boundary of American territory. Texas became
closely allied with the United States largely on account of
the fact that a great number of Americans removed to that
territory. In 1827 and again in 1829 the United States
made unsuccessful attempts to purchase Texas. The sums
offered were $1,000,000 and $5,000,000.

In 1837, one year after freeing herself from Mexico,
Texas applied for annexation to the United States, but
without immediate favorable response. This question became a national political issue in 1844, and in that year
the annexation treaty was rejected by the Senate with a
vote of 16 to 35. This was, indeed, only a temporary
defeat of the annexationists, for Texas was admitted to
the Union the following year.

The Republic of Texas comprised an area of 389,166
square miles,[20] but only the land lying outside of the state
as now constituted became a part of the public domain.
This area was purchased from the State of Texas in 1850

[20] *Thirteenth Census, Abstract,* p. 28. See *The Public Land System of
Texas,* Reuben McKitrick, *Bulletin* University of Wisconsin No. 905, which
treats of the land belonging to that state.

and includes 123,270 square miles.[21] The unoccupied and unappropriated lands within the present borders of Texas became, not part of the federal public lands, but became public lands of that state, subject to disposition under her own laws.

The Texas purchase includes what is now the southwestern corner of Kansas, southeastern Colorado, the eastern portion of New Mexico, a portion of Wyoming and central Colorado, and the public land strip north of the "panhandle" of Texas, now the panhandle of Oklahoma. Cost of the purchase:[22]

Principal sum	\$ 5,000,000
Interest on bonds....................................	3,500,000
Act of February 28, 1855............................	7,500,000
Total cost	**\$16,000,000**

THE ACQUISITION OF THE OREGON TERRITORY

The Oregon Territory which embraces the present states of Oregon, Washington and Idaho, the northwestern corner of Montana, and the southwestern portion of Wyoming has been considered a part of the Louisiana purchase, but since there were other grounds for the claim to that region it can be regarded as a separate acquisition.

In the negotiations with Great Britain in 1846 regarding the boundary in the northwest, the United States based the claim to the Oregon Territory on three main contentions. The first of these was discovery and prior occupation. In 1791 Captain Gray, of Boston, discovered the mouth of the Columbia River while sailing his ship, *The Columbia,* after which the river was named, and in 1805 the Lewis and Clarke expedition descended the Columbia River and spent the winter near its mouth. Furthermore those who had settled in the "Oregon Country" prior to 1846 were mostly

[21] This figure is obtained by taking the difference between the area of the Texas annex and the area of the present state of Texas, as given in the *Thirteenth Census, Abstract,* p. 28.
[22] Donaldson, p. 135.

American citizens. The second ground for the claim of America to this territory was that Spain had ceded her claim to the Pacific Northwest to the United States by the treaty of 1819, which made the 42° of latitude the northern boundary of Spanish possessions in the West. The third ground was the contention that the area in question was a part of the Louisiana purchase. Settlement was made with England in 1846 establishing the present boundaries.

The acquisition of the Oregon Territory added 286,541 square miles to the national domain and the greater share of this area also became a part of the public domain.

The Acquisition of Territory from Mexico

The territory embraced in the present state of California was in part claimed by Russia by reason of her having established there in 1802 the fishing and fur-trading colony of Badega with the permission of Spain. The Russian settlers gradually took up agriculture and the colony began to assume some characteristics of permanence. In 1842 these colonists constituted one-sixth of the white population of California, but when the United States gained possession the colony was withdrawn, thus ending Russian claims in California.

In 1846, representatives of England, France, and the United States tried to encourage in the people of California a desire for annexation to their respective countries, and in the meantime rival British and American fleets were maneuvering off the coast of California. It has been claimed that Great Britain intended to seize the province as payment for debts owed by Mexicans to British subjects, and that the American fleet was there to prevent any foreign power from taking possession of the coast territory.

In 1835 President Jackson proposed to purchase from Mexico the territory then in her possession north of the 37th parallel. Had this negotiation succeeded the United

States would have secured San Francisco Bay. When the terms of the annexation of Texas had been agreed upon in 1845, President Polk ordered the United States army to occupy western Texas between the Nueces and Rio Grande rivers, and sent the fleet to coöperate with the army. In the meantime, through a secret agent, an attempt was made to offer $5,000,000 and to assume responsibility of claims of American citizens against Mexico in return for the cession of New Mexico and the adjustment of the boundary line on the Rio Grande and thence north to the 42nd parallel. At the same time $25,000,000 and the assumption of the claim of American citizens against Mexico was to be offered for the province of California. A third offer of $20,000,000 was to have been made for San Francisco Bay and the territory north of it.[23] These negotiations did not succeed, and on May 13, 1846, Congress declared that "war existed by the act of Mexico," and American troops invaded that country.

The war came to a close with the treaty of Guadalupe Hidalgo, February 2, 1848. By this treaty the present southwestern boundary of the United States was established with the exception of the Gadsden Purchase, and 529,189 square miles [24] were added to the national domain. This area with the exception of private claims became a part of the public domain. [25]

The area acquired by the cession includes the states of California, Nevada, Utah, and Arizona (except the Gadsden purchase), also that part of New Mexico west of the Rio Grande and north of the Gadsden Purchase, Colorado west of the Continental Divide (the Rocky Mountains), and the southwestern portion of Wyoming. In the treaty it was provided that a sum of $15,000,000 be paid for this territory.

[23] John B. McMaster, *History of the People of the United States from the Revolution to the Civil War*, VII, 436; *United States Senate Documents*, No. 52, 30th Congress, 1st Sess.

[24] *Thirteenth Census, Abstract*, p. 28.

[25] See Private Claims in tabulated summary at the end of this chapter.

The Gadsden Purchase

In 1853 a treaty was negotiated with Mexico by James Gadsden, American minister, for the purchase of the territory now constituting the southern part of New Mexico and Arizona, "lying south of the River Gila and from the Rio Grande on the east to a point twenty miles below the mouth of the Gila on the Colorado River." The professed purpose of this purchase was to secure a more regular boundary between the United States and Mexico. It established the boundary as it is to-day. This area includes 29,670 square miles [26] and was purchased for $10,000,000.

The Purchase of Alaska

Russia claimed Alaska by reason of discovery by Captains Behring and Tschirikow in 1741, who were sent by Empress Ann to explore the extreme northwest of the American continent. For some time the extent of Russia's claim on the Pacific coast was very indefinite, but its boundaries were finally determined by a treaty between Russia and Great Britain in 1825.

Alaska was first offered for sale to the United States in 1854. This was at the time of the Crimean War and Russia was undoubtedly in great need of money, as Napoleon had been in 1803. President Pierce, however, declined the offer. Negotiations were reopened during Buchanan's administration and a price of $5,000,000 was offered, but Russia expected more than this amount. Official Washington became more anxious to secure Alaska when it became known that the Hudson Bay Company's lease of the franchise of the Russo-American Fur Company was to expire in 1867. Fear of the renewal of this franchise and petition by the legislature of the territory of Washington for the acquisition of Alaska intensified the desire of the Government to close the deal. Negotiations for the purchase were continued,

[26] *Thirteenth Census, Abstract,* p. 28.

terms agreed upon, and ratifications exchanged June 20, 1867. The United States paid $7,200,000 for Alaska, which comprises an area of 590,884 square miles. [27]

PRIVATE CLAIMS

Confirmed Private Claims. "Private land claims are a class of titles situated in different sections of the country, now constituting a part of the Union, having their origin under the governments preceding the United States in sovereignty." [28] The first private land claims that came up for consideration were within the national domain as established by the treaty with Great Britain in 1783. [29] They were in the Northwest Territory, and were made by French and British military commanders prior to 1783. [30] These claims were granted wherever it could be shown that they were rightfully founded. They prevailed wherever settlements had been made. For example, there were French settlements with their "ribbon" [31] farms near Detroit, Green Bay, Prairie du Chien, Vincennes, and elsewhere. There were many French and Spanish claims in Louisiana and Florida, and in the southwestern and western parts of the United States there were many claims based on grants by the Spanish and Mexican governments. "The claims have been recognized and confirmed by the various boards of commissioners acting under authority of Congress, by the courts and by acts of Congress." [32]

The area added to both the national and the public domain by the various acquisitions included many individual titles based on written grants or settlement before the

[27] *Thirteenth Census, Abstract,* p. 28.

[28] Donaldson, p. 365.

[29] *Ibid,* p. 370.

[30] For specific provision see Articles V and VI of the treaty with Great Britain, Sept. 3, 1783.

[31] A "ribbon" farm is a farm between parallel lines running back usually from a water front. The name comes from the fact that through subdivisions the farms become narrow, at times too narrow to be of much use.

[32] United States General Land Office. *Report* of the Commissioner, 1910, p. 12.

change of government, and the observance of these rights was provided for in the treaties of acquisition. Congress has pursued a liberal policy in carrying out treaty stipulations and in meeting the requirements of public law, to secure to individuals rights that originated under governments prior to the United States in sovereignty. The new government merely took the place of the old and the change did not alter private rights within the territory concerned. "We have acknowledged and carried out the principle that, although sovereignty changes, private property is unaffected by the change, and that all claims in this relation are to be maintained sacred, including those in contract, those executory, as well as those executed. The courts in their rulings, show how zealously private rights have been vindicated and confirmed." [33-34]

The Supreme Court of the United States clearly took the position that the right of private property in land in the acquired territories should not be affected by the change of sovereignty regardless of treaty stipulations. The following quotations from the decision of the Supreme Court will illustrate this point:

"The modern usage of nations, which has become law, would be violated; that sense of justice and of right, which is acknowledged and felt by the whole civilized world, would be outraged if private property should be generally confiscated, and private rights annulled, on a change in the sovereignty of the country by the Florida treaty. The people change their allegiance, their relation to their ancient Sovereign is dissolved, but their relation to each other, and their right of property remain undisturbed. Had Florida changed its sovereign by an act containing no stipulation respecting the property of individuals, the right of property in all those who became subjects or citizens of the new

---

[33-34] Donaldson, p. 365. There has been a great deal of litigation over the question of private land claims. For example, *United States Senate Miscellaneous Documents*, 45th Congress, 3rd Sessions, IV, contains 1492 pages of private land claims documents.

government would have been unaffected by the change. It would have remained the same as under the ancient sovereign." [35]

"The right of property is protected and secured by the treaty [treaty with France in 1803] and no principle is better settled in this country than that an inchoate title to land is property. This right would have been sacred, independent of the treaty. The sovereign who acquires an inhabited country, acquires full dominion over it; but this dominion is never supposed to divest the vested rights of individuals to property." [36]

To facilitate the handling of private claims the Court of Private Land Claims was created by Act of Congress in 1891. It was created to pass on all claims not otherwise taken care of, within the area ceded by Mexico in 1848 and 1853. Through this court the confirmation of private land claims was removed from political influence. Its work was completed in 1894.

Up to June 30, 1904, 28,492 private land claims had been confirmed.[37] On June 30, 1910, about 5,000 confirmed claims were unpatented, but were entitled to patents, and these had, for the most part, been confirmed many years previously. It can therefore be concluded that the total acreage (33,440,482) of private land claims confirmed up to June 30, 1904, represents with fair accuracy the main area of private claims on the original public domain. The work of the General Land Office pertaining to private claims is constantly diminishing, owing to the fact that these claims are, on the whole, close to final settlement. "The force of this office working on private land claims," says Commissioner Fred Dennett in his annual report in 1910, "has dwindled from a division to one clerk, and only a portion of the time of this clerk is taken up with the work."

[35] *United States v. Percheman.* 7 Peters, p. 51.
[36] Delassus v. The United States. 9 Peters, p. 117.
[37] *L. O. R.*, 1904, p. 140. *Sen. Doc.*, 189, 58 Cong., 3 Sess.

Private Scrip Claims

The term "scrip," when used in connection with private land claims, literally means a piece of paper entitling the person to whom it is issued to a prescribed amount of land on the public domain. The right to a "private scrip claim" was based on confirmed private land claims. If the claim was for any reason not located where the right originated, the scrip entitled the person in whose favor the private land claim had been confirmed, to a piece of land to be located somewhere else on the public domain. For example, there were no private claims *confirmed and located* in Kansas, but claims amounting to 147,364.9 acres that had been confirmed elsewhere were *located* in that state. (See Table II.)

"Congress, in 1806, began the practice of ordering the issuing of indemnity scrip for confirmed private land and other land claims, which had been left entirely or partially unsatisfied as to location, by reason of non-location, conflict with other claims or grants, entries, or reduced by deficient surveys." [38] The private claims summarized under the head of "private scrip claims" in Table II, were granted to the claimants under general acts of Congress June 2, 1858, and June 22, 1860, and under a few special individual acts. The act of 1858 made provisions for the claims already confirmed, and the act of 1860 was, by its title, "an act for the final adjustment of private land claims in the states of Florida, Louisiana, and Missouri and for other purposes." It aimed to afford settlement of the confirmed but unsatisfied private land claims, according to regulations prescribed by the General Land Commission.

The accompanying map of "The Original Public Domain" will be helpful in holding the facts in mind. The boundaries of the several acquisitions to the national domain shown in this map are drawn according to the map of the General Land Office published in 1912. It will be noted that the southwestern, western and northeastern boundaries of the

[38] Donaldson, p. 289.

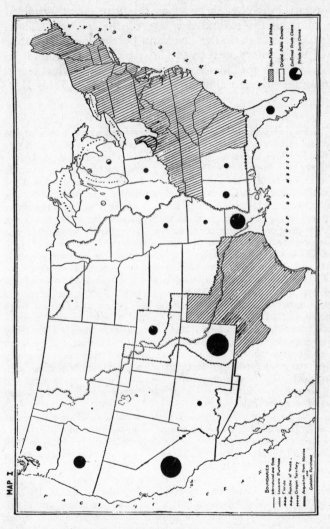

ORIGINAL PUBLIC DOMAIN

MAP I

BOUNDARIES
———— International and State
······· Louisiana Purchase
✦✦✦ Florida
✦✦✦ Republic of Texas
✦✦✦✦ Oregon Territory
———— Acquisition from Mexico
———— Gadsden Purchase

Non-Public Land States
Original Public Domain
Confirmed Private Claims
Private Scrip Claims

Louisiana Purchase, as given on this map, are determined according to the natural drainage of the country. These boundaries include in the Louisiana Purchase approximately all of the territory west of the Mississippi draining into the Missouri and the Mississippi rivers. The circles representing the private claims by states are based on Table II.

SUMMARY

The idea of a public domain was firmly fixed in the minds of the colonists, particularly those living in colonies with a claim to extensive territory. This sense of proprietorship over unoccupied land very promptly extended to the Confederacy, even antedating any tangible claim to the back lands. A controversy between the colonies and the new national government regarding jurisdiction was inevitable. The colonies having claims to western land, no matter how flimsy the claim, were not disposed to give them up without something in the semblance of compensation. The principle on which the dispute was settled was at least clear, even though not altogether logical; the western land was obtained by common sacrifices, hence should be common property. Such a principle might have been applied so as to have cut down the claim to a great deal of unsettled land within the boundaries of the new states as they were later established. Just what were the logical territorial limits of such states as Virginia and Georgia there was no way of saying. Maryland claimed a share in the "western lands," but just what western lands were nobody knew. Like many other disputes a settlement was more important than the basis on which it was made. The states, even before they were properly called states, in order to form the Confederation, beginning with New York, 1781, and ending with Georgia, thirteen years after the adoption of the Constitution, ceded their western claims. Thus was formed a great public domain.

In 1803 by the purchase of Louisiana almost a third of the present area of the United States was added. The payment was $15,000,000 plus enough more eventually to make $27,000,000. Florida in 1819 with 72,000 square miles, cost $5,000,000 plus another million and a half, Texas in 1845 annexed added 389,000 square miles. Oregon with 287,000 square miles, though at one time believed to be a part of the Louisiana Purchase, was acquired by treaty in 1846. By conquest California, in 1848, with half a million square miles, was added. The Gadsden Purchase added a mere trifle, about the size of South Carolina, in 1853. This completes the acquisitions, outside of Alaska, of continental territory. From the gross amount of land ceded to,

TABLE II. — PRIVATE LAND CLAIMS

STATE [1]	LAND SURFACE OF STATE (ACRES) [2]	TOTAL PRIVATE CLAIMS			CONFIRMED PRIVATE CLAIMS [3]			PRIVATE SCRIP CLAIMS [3]	
		Acres	Per cent of total private claims	Per cent of land surface of state	Number of claims	Acres	Per cent of confirmed claims	Acres	Per cent of scrip claims
Alabama	32,818,560	252,963.16	.74	.77	448	251,602.04	.75	1,361.12	.11
Arizona	72,848,400	295,732.19	.85	.40	95	295,212.19	.87	520.00	.04
Arkansas	33,616,000	135,363.76	.39	.40	248	110,090.39	.32	25,273.37	2.17
California	99,617,280	8,877,548.73	25.66	8.91	588	8,850,143.56	26.74	27,405.17	2.35
Colorado	66,341,120	1,464,085.10	4.25	2.20	6	1,397,883.78	4.16	66,199.32	5.68
Florida	35,111,040	2,778,942.58	8.04	7.91	869	2,711,290.57	8.08	67,652.01	5.98
Idaho	53,346,560	920.00	.00	.00				920.00	.08
Illinois	35,867,520	185,854.37	.53	.51	936	185,774.37	.55	80.00	.00
Indiana	23,068,800	188,383.62	.54	.81	862	188,303.62	.56	80.00	.00
Iowa	35,575,040	26,368.68	.07	.07	1	5,760.00	.01	20,608.68	1.77
Kansas	52,335,360	147,364.91	.42	.24				147,364.91	12.64
Louisiana	29,061,760	4,397,555.38	12.71	15.13	9,302	4,347,891.31	13.00	49,664.07	4.26
Michigan	36,787,200	500,514.15	1.47	1.36	942	280,762.83	.83	219,841.32	18.86
Minnesota	51,749,120	99,724.93	.29	.19				99,724.93	8.56
Mississippi	29,671,680	776,713.02	2.24	2.61	1,154	773,087.14	2.29	3,625.88	.31
Missouri	43,985,280	1,136,656.13	3.29	2.58	3,748	1,130,051.62	3.35	6,604.51	.56
Montana	93,568,640	3,214.09	.00	.00				3,214.09	.27
Nebraska	49,157,120	84,270.73	.24	.17				84,270.73	7.23
New Mexico	78,401,920	9,900,063.62	28.62	12.62	504	9,899,021.67	29.55	1,041.95	.08
North Dakota	44,917,120	46,935.70	.13	.10				46,935.70	4.03
Ohio	26,073,600	51,161.14	.15	.19	111	51,161.14	.15		
Oregon	61,188,480	2,619,282.24	7.56	4.28	7,432	2,614,082.24	7.78	5,200.00	.44
South Dakota	49,195,520	81,586.79	.23	.16				81,586.79	7.00
Utah	52,597,760	14,876.80	.04	.02	60	8,876.80	.02	6,000.00	.51
Washington	42,775,040	317,314.51	.91	.74	1,011	306,795.91	.92	10,518.60	.90
Wisconsin	35,363,840	220,791.51	.63	.62	175	32,778.82	.09	188,012.69	16.13
Wyoming	62,460,160	640.00	.00	.00				640.00	.05
Total	1,327,489,920	34,604,327.84	100.	2.60	28,492	33,440,482.00	100.	1,164,345.84	100.
Square miles	2,074,302	53,070.04				52,250.75		1,819.29	

[1] The states of Nevada and Oklahoma with a land surface area of 109,821 and 69,414 square miles respectively, are the only public land states not included in the above table.

[2] *L. O. R.*, 1923, p. 32.

[3] Based on *report* of the United States Public Lands Commission, 1904, covering private land claims to June 30, 1904. *Sen. Doc.* 58 Cong., 3 Sess., No. 189, p. 40. According to letter by the Commissioner of the General Land Office of Nov. 24, 1920, to the author, the 1905 report contains the last compilation of its kind.

or purchased by, the United States must be subtracted 34,600,000 acres of private claims. The total extent of public domain acquired by the government was approximately 1,400,000,000 acres of land. The cost in money payment, including interest, was $59,758,000, or about four and a quarter cents an acre.

Table III. — Summary of the Acquisition of the Public Domain [1]

Acquisitions [2]	Date	Land Surface Area Added to the National Domain		Private Claims		Land Surface Added to the Public Domain		Purchase Price [4]	Purchase Price in Cents per Acre of Public Domain
		Sq. miles	Per cent of present land surface area of U.S.	Sq. m.	Acres	Sq. miles	Acres		
Cession by States	1781 to 1802	406,219 [3]	13.4	3,515	2,249,711.3	402,704	267,730,560	—	—
Louisiana Purchase	1803	842,760	28.4	9,967	6,379,007.8	832,793	432,987,520	$27,267,621.98	6.5
Purchase of the Floridas	1819	54,861	1.8	4,342	2,778,942.6	50,519	32,332,160	6,489,768	20.
Annexation of Texas and the Texas Purchase	1845 and 1850	383,463	12.9	10,197	6,525,712.2	110,868	70,955,520	15,000,000	21.
Acquisition of the Oregon Territory	1846	264,096	8.9	4,590	2,937,636.7	259,506	166,083,840	—	00.
Acquisition of the Territory from Mexico	1848	529,169	17.8	21,367	13,674,670.8	507,802	324,993,280	15,000,000	4.6
Gadsden Purchase	1853	22,762	.8	92	59,146.4	22,670	14,508,800	10,000,000	68.5
Total		2,503,330	84.	54,070	34,604,827.8	2,186,862	1,309,591,680	73,757,389.98	5.7

[1] The land surface area of acquisition is based on the land surface area of states, as given in the *Report of the General Land Office*, 1919, and the private claims in the acquisitions are based on Table II. In case of a state divided by boundaries between two or more acquisitions (See map page 27), the land surface area and the private claims of the state are divided according to the estimated portion of the state lying in each acquisition concerned. Hence, the figures here given for each acquisition may not be absolutely accurate, but it does not affect the total for the public domain. Where the boundary of the Louisiana Purchase includes a portion of the Republic of Texas, the area concerned has been included in the latter. The whole of the states of Louisiana and Montana have been included in the Louisiana Purchase.

[2] Exclusive of Alaska and insular possessions.

[3] Exclusive of Kentucky and Tennessee, the Virginia military lands and the Connecticut reserve in Ohio, and the "Fire lands." These reserves in Ohio amounted to 6,570 square miles (See p. 11.) This figure includes the drainage basin of the Red River of the north, not a part of any acquisition.

[4] Includes only the purchase price with interest on bonds, and does not include any other expense of acquisition.

CHAPTER III

THE ORIGIN AND FEATURES OF THE PUBLIC LAND SYSTEM

There were certain conditions that influenced Congress very materially in the formation of a land policy. It is necessary to think of the country as consisting of thirteen independent states held together by a mere "league of nations" agreement. Congress had induced the various states to cede their claims to the western lands to the Confederation to be held and used for the common good. These lands formed a bond of union among the states and was a major factor in holding them together. It soon became necessary to devise some means of handling and disposing of these common lands. There were urgent reasons for acting quickly.

First of all, Congress had promised lands to Revolutionary soldiers and officers early in the struggle at a time when the colonial group did not have a foot of territory, but now it could make good its promise.[1] After the war the soldiers were anxious to make use of their land warrants and the correspondence of Washington in this period is indicative of the dissatisfaction among the officers.[2] Also the certificates of the governmental indebtedness were "selling at no more

[1] In August, 1776, Congress began by offering land to deserters from the British army with a special bonus to officers who should induce soldiers to desert with them. On September 15, 1776, grants were made to soldiers and officers in the American army ranging from 500 acres to a colonel to 100 acres to non-commissioned officers and soldiers. In 1780 Congress added grants of 1100 acres to a major general and 850 to a brigadier general. *Public Lands, General Public Acts of Congress, Respecting the Sale and Disposition of the Public Lands*, Part I, pp. 5-8.

[2] Wm. P. and Julia P. Cutler, *Life, Journals and Correspondence of the Reverend Manasseh Cutler, LL.D.*, I, pp. 137-178.

32

than 3 sh. 6 pence or 4 sh. on the pound" and Putnam expressed the anxiety of the soldiers when he wrote Washington in 1784 wanting to know what Congress would do about the western lands. If Congress would receive the certificates in exchange for western lands their value might in his opinion double.[3]

Secondly, Congress was without means to secure revenue. It had no taxing power and quite naturally came to look upon this great public domain as a source of income. This is shown in the correspondence and the official reports of this period. A committee reporting September 5, 1782, favored the ceding of the western lands, to be sold to "discharge the national debt."[4] This was a new departure, since land selling had not been a feature of the land policy of the colonies or the British government, and within a few years preceding the lands of Kentucky and Tennessee had been alienated, without yielding a revenue to either state or national government. However, the states after independence was declared, began to charge for land.[5] Jefferson changed his opinion concerning the advisability of selling land. He was opposed to it at first but in 1784 he incorporated the plan of selling lands to meet public expenditures in the ordinance of that year.[6]

Thirdly, Congress was confronted with the question of the defense of the Northwest against the Indians. Putnam suggested to Washington the need of attaching the Indians to the United States through commercial relations but he also advised military posts on the Great Lakes, a chain of forts through Ohio and settlements at Oswego and in Ohio. If Congress should act favorably, the Ohio country would be filled with faithful subjects of the United States "so as

[3] Putnam to Washington, Rutland, April 5, 1784, in Charles M. Walker, *History of Athens County, Ohio,* p. 37.
[4] Cutler, I, p. 129.
[5] Amelia Clewley Ford, Colonial Precedents of Our National Land System as it Existed in 1800. *Bulletin.* University of Wisconsin, 352 (1908), pp. 85-89; Cutler, I, p. 128.

to banish forever the idea of our western territory falling under the dominion of any European power."[7]

Fourthly, as just intimated, the western settlements in Kentucky and Tennessee were but loosely connected with the eastern states and there was great danger that their commercial relations would link them more closely with Spain to the south or England to the north than to the new republic across the Alleghanies. Washington was fully aware of the situation. "The western states," he said, "(I speak now from my own observation) stand as it were, upon a pivot. A touch of a feather would turn them either way."[8]

Fifthly, Congress had to decide upon a form of government for the new territory. Here it was confronted with such problems as the methods to be employed in carving out new states, whether large or small, their admission to the Union and the danger of having them outweigh the older section of the country in political power.

Sixthly, there was also the problem of disposing of the land as property for the public benefit. "It was the occasion for maturing and applying upon the vast interior a system of land surveys, locations and entries, securing perfect titles with the least possible expense such as had never before been attempted on such a magnificent scale."[9]

Seventhly, the country was confronted with the pressure of immigration to the West. In 1769 Zane's settlement was made at Wheeling and in 1774 Fort Henry was established there. The best lands on the Ohio side were probably being cultivated by people who lived on the Virginia side of the river. In 1778-9 illegal settlements were being made in Ohio and in 1780 those that wished to be law abiding, and wanted Ohio land, petitioned Congress for

---

[7] Putnam to Washington, New Windsor, June 16, 1783, in Walker, pp. 30-36; or Cutler, I, pp. 167-172.

[8] Ellen Churchill Semple, *American History and its Geographic Conditions*, pp. 84-92; Washington to Governor Harrison of Virginia, October 10, 1784, quoted in Cutler, pp. 134-135.

[9] Cutler, I, p. 123.

permission to cross the river.[10] "The spirit of immigration is great," wrote Washington in 1784. "People have got impatient and though you cannot stop the road it is yet in your power to mark the way."[11]

THE FORMATION OF A LAND POLICY

With these forces bringing pressure upon Congress an act was passed October 10, 1780, that foreshadowed a land policy. It provided for the disposal for the common benefit of the United States of the territories ceded to the United States; for the formation of states out of these territories; and for the regulation by Congress of the granting and selling of these lands.[12]

In 1783 a petition signed by some 200 officers at Newburgh again called the attention of Congress to the promise of lands made during the Revolution and asked for a grant of land in Ohio. This prompted Congress to appoint a committee in the spring of 1784 consisting of Jefferson, Williamson, of North Carolina; Howell, of Rhode Island; Gerry, of Massachusetts, and Reach, of South Carolina, to prepare an ordinance for ascertaining and disposing of the lands in the western territory. Jefferson was the leading member. The committee on May 7, 1784, presented its report which, though not accepted at the time, became the basis for the Land Ordinance of 1785.[13]

Before proceeding with the details of the various land ordinances notice should be taken of the precedents that existed in the colonies upon which a national land policy could be built. None of the features incorporated in the land system of the Confederation, or even in later land systems were evolved out of the inner consciousness of the men who drew up the measures, but "a handful of clear-

[10] *The Records of the Original Proceedings of the Ohio Company* ed. with introduction and notes by Archer Butler Hulbert in *Marietta College Historical Collections,* I, p. 23.

[11] Shosuke Sato, "History of the Land Question in the United States," *Johns Hopkins University Studies,* Fourth Series IX, p. 86.

[12] *Ibid,* p. 77.

[13] *Ibid,* pp. 80-86.

visioned statesmen drew upon the experience of a dozen states to form one national system." [14]

There were two systems in vogue in the colonies, the New England and the Southern. The former was a scheme of "township planting" in which a new area was laid out, surveyed, plats prepared and recorded by the colony before any one could obtain a foot of land in the new tract. An illustration is afforded by the method employed on June 17, 1732, when the general court of Massachusetts granted six miles square for a new township to be laid off by a surveyor and chairman under oath. Certain conditions were laid down. Sixty New England families had to be settled on this tract within five years; each settler had to build a house at least eighteen feet square and one story high, improve at least four acres, and have three acres in grass. There were sixty-three shares, one to each of the settlers and one to be applied to the support of a school, one for the ministry and one for a minister who had to be a "learned and Orthodox" man. They were also pledged to build a convenient meeting house. [15]

Such towns were always laid out with reference to neighboring allotments. Under this plan no one could engross the best lands for himself and as the town grew the people shared in each division of the unappropriated land. This system tended toward compactness, protection against savages and mutual help during the severe winters, a product "adapted to a free population, loving community life and forced to it." [16] "Little republics—townships—of convenient size were organized, placing the civil and political power in the hands of those who own the country, at the same time making provision for the moral and educational wants." [17]

In the South the more favorable climate, the less hostile Indians and large scale agriculture favored scattering settle-

[14] P. J. Treat, "Origin of the National Land System under the Confederation," *Annual Report of the American Historical Association for* 1905, I, p. 239.
[15] Cutler, I, pp. 123, 124.
[16] Treat, pp. 25, 26.
[17] Cutler, I, p. 123.

ments. Land was taken up by the location of warrants giving the holder a right to select his parcel on any part of the unappropriated area. Surveys did not usually precede location, claims often overlapped and errors were common, causing endless litigation. Men often went out and got a virtual monoply of the choicest lands. With all its disadvantages this practice expressed the spirit of the frontiersman and, in spite of logic, persisted as an important incident, even assuming the dignity of a policy.

Another feature later incorporated into the land policies, and one of the most permanent features of all, was the method of surveying and dividing the land. The peculiar division of the land into squares (townships) which were further divided into "lots" or sections is to be found in part in the practices of many of the colonies, even in the South.[18] It was suggested by Pelatia Webster, by Putnam in his letter to Washington, June 16, 1783,[19] and in the Financiers' Plan.[20]

The Ordinances of 1784, 1785 and 1787

The Ordinance of 1784 was a combination of the New England and Southern systems. The former prevailed in that the surveys had to be made before the land was sold and all grants carefully recorded. The land was to be purchased from the Indians, surveyed by being divided into "hundreds" of ten geographical miles square, and the hundreds into square mile "lots,' all lines to run due north and south, east and west. Surveyors and registers were to be appointed by Congress.

The Ordinance deviated from the New England plan in that it did not insist upon township settlement with the usual conditions as to settlers, clearings and building of houses. There were no reservations for schools or re-

[18] Ford, Chs. I-IV; Sato, pp. 133-8.
[19] Walker, p. 34. Putnam suggested townships six miles square, or six by twelve or six by eighteen, to be subdivided by the proprietors into townships six by six miles.
[20] Treat. Both Ford and Treat discuss the origins quite at length.

ligious purposes nor was the price per acre mentioned. The land was to be sold in exchange for warrants, by "lots" or by "hundreds" and the settler could locate his holdings where he chose. These provisions resembled the Virginia practice.[21]

The Ordinance of 1784 was carried over to 1785 when Congress had it read twice and referred to a committee consisting of one member from each state. Jefferson was in Europe at the time and Grayson was appointed in his place. The committee reported a new ordinance on April 14, 1785, which was debated and amended and finally passed May 20 of the same year.

The original draft of the Ordinance again provided that surveys should precede sales. The system of surveying was modified to provide for townships seven statute miles square. In each township were reserved section 16 for schools, one section for religious purposes and sections 8, 11, 26 and 29 for the future disposition of Congress. One third part of all gold, silver, and lead mines was also reserved. Lands were to be sold at auction with a minimum price of one dollar per acre, but the purchaser of the land had to pay for the surveying and the deed was made out for a specific tract of land. The Secretary of War was first to draw one-seventh of the whole area for the Continental Army, after which the rest was to be sold in the various states (instead of at the seat of Congress, for instance), "in proportion to the last preceding requisition."[2] Land was to be sold by whole townships, the sales to begin as soon as five ranges were surveyed (later changed to seven) without reference to the formation of states.

In the course of the debate the reservation for religion was stricken out, rather by the way in which the vote was taken, than by design. The main fight was on the size of the tracts to be sold and the New England method of settle-

---

[21] P. J. Treat, "Origin of the National Land System Under the Confederation," *Annual Report of the American Historical Association*, I, p. 236.
[22] This refers to soldiers furnished to the Continental Army.

ment. This method had the support of the best minds of the country. Jefferson incorporated it in modified form in the report of 1784, and in general the southern members on the committee favored it. Washington said that settlement "ought not be too diffusive. Compact and progressive settling will give strength to the Union, admit law and good government, and federal aids at an early period. Sparse settlements in the several new states, or a large territory for one, will have direct contrary effects; and whilst it opens a large field to land jobbers and speculators, who are prowling about like wolves in many shapes, will injure the real occupiers and useful citizens and consequently the public interest." [23] In another letter he also notes the danger of disputes with the Indians and the overrunning of the country by a "parcel of banditti" who would skim and dispose of the country before the soldiers and officers could get their reward. [24] But in 1785 there was considerable opposition to the plan and the first aim was to get the size of the tracts reduced. To sell in full townships would mean sale to a speculator, or a group, and not to an individual settler. A compromise was effected. The size of the township was reduced to six miles square. An amendment was lost which provided for the sale of lands in sections, but to secure the desired compactness of settlement all the land had to be disposed of in the first township before a second one was to be opened for sale. The plan agreed upon was that one half of the townships were to be sold entire, the other half in sections of 640 acres, these two types to alternate. An attempt to reduce the lots to be sold to 320 acres failed. Thus the New England idea prevailed even though it postponed the procuring of revenue till after surveys could be made. [25]

The New England idea triumphed only for a time. The Northwest did not appear to need such a system, and within a lifetime the frontier showed that the plan did not fit the

---

[23] Washington to Hugh Williamson, March 15, 1785, in Cutler, I, p. 131.
[24] Cutler, I, p. 132.
[25] The Ordinance also set aside three townships for Canadian and Nova Scotian refugees and another three townships for Christian Indians in Ohio.

disposition of the pioneer. Attempts were made to change the Ordinance in this respect in 1786 and again in 1787 when it was proposed to introduce "indiscriminate locations," but prior discriminate surveys triumphed decisively.[26] In fact the system of surveying, the recording of titles and the provision for schools have been retained, though practically all other parts of the original system have been modified. The Ordinance did indeed lay down great general principles which have run through our entire land policy. "The lands were not to be lavished on favorites. No one could obtain an acre except for 'value received' or service rendered." [27]

The Ordinance of 1787 was enacted to provide for a government of the territory of the United States in which lands to be sold were situated. The members of the incipient Ohio Company were anxious to have this matter made very definite before they purchased their lands, and the Ordinance and the sale of land to them came during the summer of 1787. Cutler was connected with both and there is a good deal of discussion as to just how much he had to do with the wording of the Ordinance.[28]

The Ordinance of 1787 has little to do with the practical problems of land purchase and land sales. It was on the Ordinance of 1785 that all the operations of the Ohio Company were based. "There is but a single mention of the Ordinance of 1787 in the entire records of the Ohio Company from 1787 to 1796. . . . The Ordinance of 1787 was written on another plane; with its abolishment of slavery and the Bill of Rights it was the law of inspired idealists." [29]

Since the Ordinance of 1787 does not relate to the direct disposal of the public domain it need not be discussed any further here. However, it may be remarked in passing

---

[26] *Public Lands, General Public Acts of Congress, Respecting the Sale and Disposition of the Public Lands,* I, 28, pp. 33-35.
[27] Treat, "Origin of the National Land System under the Confederation," *Annual Report of the American Historical Association,* I, p. 239.
[28] *Marietta College Collections,* I. Introduction, pp. 42, 46.
[29] *Ibid,* pp. 95, 96.

that its provisions relating to the property conceptions of land are noteworthy.[30]

THE SALE OF LAND UNDER THE CONFEDERATION

Congress followed out the Ordinance of 1785 in appointing one surveyor from each state who operated under the direction of the Geographer. The first Geographer was Thomas Hutchins, appointed in 1781, who began the surveys of the seven ranges in 1786, and between July and the following February four ranges were surveyed. The work was resumed in 1788 but Hutchins died the next year.

After four ranges were surveyed sales began, Congress not caring to wait till the seven ranges were completed. The plan of holding sales within the several states was abandoned and all sales concentrated at the seat of Congress after the required land had been drawn for the soldiers.[31] The original provision for cash sales was replaced by an amendment in 1787, providing for the payment of one-third cash and the rest in three months. Failure to pay the balance caused the settler to lose the first payment. This was the first step toward the "credit system."

Under these provisions some 108,431 acres were sold between September 21 and October 9, 1787 at auction in New York for $176,090. But 35,457 acres valued at $88,764 were forfeited, involving a loss of $29,782, leaving as the net amount of the sale 72,974 acres for $117,108.[32] No entire townships were sold. Later the delinquent purchasers petitioned Congress for relief and in 1828 new certificates were issued for sums forfeited in these sales.[33]

The reasons for the slow sales of public land were several. The Indians were always a menace and were holding settlements back, till after their defeat by Wayne. Also the sale of land through large land companies had begun and for

[30] Donaldson, pp. 156-160.
[31] *Public Lands. General Public Acts of Congress, Respecting the Sale and Disposition of the Public Lands,* I, pp. 17, 18.
[32] Donaldson, p. 17.
[33] *U. S. Stat. at Large,* IV, p. 287.

a while this was the popular method of disposing of the public lands.   Another reason was that a great deal of land was being taken up by "squatters" in defiance of the Ordinance of 1785 which called for prior surveys and the sale of land to settlers.   In 1785 the Indians were complaining that the whites were entering their lands.   Congress in 1785, 1804 and 1807, warned squatters and forbade their entering the public domain.   In 1787 the militia was instructed twice to move against the settlers, burn their cabins and destroy their improvements, but the settlers generally returned when they thought it safe to do so.[34]   In 1791 a statement was made on the floor of Congress that the number of families seated without right or license south of the French Broad and Big Pigeon amounted to three hundred, settled upon a tract of Indian land of about 300,000 acres.[35]

These settlers were mostly of southern origin and brought with them the customs and laws of Virginia and North Carolina which were very favorable to the squatter, allowing him to make good his right to land by "tomahawk improvements," "cabin rights," "corn rights" and "sugar camp rights."   Maine, Pennsylvania and other colonies also came to adopt the squatter point of view, but Massachusetts considered such settlers mere trespassers and illegal possessors and never adopted a lenient view toward them.[36]   In the early days Congress held the Massachusetts point of view as is shown by the acts of 1785, 1804 and 1807.

Lastly there was the sale of land in the original states. Maine was still unsettled and Massachusetts was anxious to dispose of the lands there.   New York was actively "inviting the eastern people to settle in her state."[37]   The states did not begin to sell lands until after independence was declared.   Practices varied among states but it is interesting

[34] Cutler, I, p. 133; Donaldson.
[35] Annals of Congress, 2nd Congress, 1st Session, Appendix, p. 1038.
[36] Ford, Ch. VII (a discussion of squatters and preëmption, the growth of this practice and the justification and incorporation into the national land system).
[37] Putnam to Washington, Walker, pp. 38, 39.

to note how these practices were incorporated into the national system from time to time.[38] Naturally these states found in the national land sales an unwelcome competitor. Massachusetts expressly stated in the preamble to one of her land laws that this act was for the purpose of preventing emigration into other states and to help settlement within her own borders.[39] In general, the terms in the states were more liberal than those of Congress. Cutler speaks of lands being sold by several states at half a dollar an acre; a price which would outweigh the greater fertility of Ohio lands if distance and hazards were also considered.[40]

These factors account for the small sales during the period of the Confederation. One sale which is not of the usual type needs to be mentioned here, however. Lying in the triangle between New York, Lake Erie and Pennsylvania as then bounded, was a tract of 200,000 acres which was part of the public domain. Congress sold this at a private sale to Pennsylvania for 75 cents an acre, giving this state an increased frontage on Lake Erie. Letters patent were issued in 1792.[41]

SALES TO PRIVATE COMPANIES

The granting of land by the government to a private company which in turn undertook the management of settlement was not new at the time of the Confederacy. In fact much of the early settlement of America by the English was conducted on that plan, the most conspicuous examples of which were the London and Plymouth companies. A similar attempt to colonize the interior of the continent was made about the middle of the eighteenth century by Thomas Lee and Lawrence and Augustine Washington. They obtained from the crown a grant of 500,000 acres of land in the Ohio valley and organized the "Ohio Company." Their efforts to open a road into the West was presumably a

---

[38] Ford, Ch. V.
[39] Ibid., p. 88.
[40] Cutler, I, pp. 126, 194.
[41] Ann. of Cong., 3 Cong., p. 1328.

factor in precipitating the French and Indian War.[42]   In 1766 Franklin engineered a land company composed of thirty-two Americans and two Londoners of which Thomas Walpole, a London Banker, was the figurehead. They petitioned for 2,500,000 acres east of the Scioto but the petition was not granted till 1772 and the Revolution broke out before the legal titles were finally perfected. This was known as the "Vandalia" or "Walpole Company." A third company called the Mississippi Company in which three Lees of Virginia and George Washington were interested asked for the same amount of land in 1769, but the petition was referred to the Board of Trade and was never heard from.[43]

Another company, in which Rufus Putnam was one of the prime movers, was styled the "Military Company of Adventurers" and was composed of men who had served in the provincial army during the French and Indian War. This company expected to obtain grants in West Florida, and in 1773 Putnam sailed with a group to Pensacola only to find that the governor had no authority to grant land. After losing time in explorations and negotiations they abandoned the enterprise.[44]

During the Confederation three actual sales were made and two applications which did not result in sales. Congress at first passed special acts for each sale but later laid down general rules to apply to the sale of land to companies. The Board of Treasury was authorized to contract with any person for the sale of land free of Indian claims, in lots of 1,000,000 acres or more not to extend more than one-third of its depth along the Ohio, Mississippi, Wabash, or Illinois Rivers.

The two applications that failed were that of Royal Flint and Joseph Parker and their associates for 2,000,000 acres on the Ohio and another 1,000,000 acres on the Mississippi

[42] H. B. Adams, "Maryland's Influence upon the Land Cessions to the U. S." in *Johns Hopkins University Studies,* Third Series (1885), I, p. 12.

[43] *Ibid.* See also *Thesis* by C. G. Jones (1896 B. S.), University of Wisconsin: The Ohio and Indiana Land Companies.

[44] Walker, footnote p. 52.

and that of George Morgan and his associates for a tract on the Mississippi south of the Flint and Parker grant.[45]

THE OHIO COMPANY

The outstanding one of the private land companies attempting to act as intermediaries between government and people was one engineered by Reverend Manasseh Cutler, and known as the Ohio Company. The Revolutionary War had left among the people a measure of restlessness, one manifestation of which was a disposition to move into the unsettled West. The officers of the Continental Line were especially interested in the possibilities of settling the wilderness to the end of bettering their own fortunes. It must be remembered that society was simply organized in regard to industry in those days and men who had lost touch with business of any sort on account of absence during the war found few opportunities of reinstatement. The desirable land east of the Appalachians was nearly all in private hands. Hence opportunities to move to the West onto land reported to be first class, and obtainable at a low price, were favorably received. The soldiers had been showing much discontent due to the poor pay, in poorer money, which they had received. Land was the one asset the government assumed to have, and nothing was more natural than an attempt to assuage the rising discontent by the liberal use of the public land.[46] At the same time the government was willing to take a small payment for land particularly since the idea of a colonization company had taken strong hold in the minds of most of the leaders. The demand of the soldiers in general for liberal treatment respecting land was stimulated by the action of Virginia toward her veterans.[47]

General Rufus Putnam in his letter to Washington in 1783 had estimated that 2,160,000 acres of land had been granted through resolutions to the army.[48] The Newburgh

[45] *Journals of the American Congress*, IV, p. 823.
[46] H. Z. Williams *History of Washington County*, Ohio, p. 30.
[47] *Marietta College Collections* I, Introduction, p. 18.
[48] Putnam to Washington, in Walker, p. 34.

addresses, and near mutiny were another indication of the psychology of the times.[49] The prime object of Putnam and his colleagues was to go to the West as a body where they could take up new lands and pay for them with certificates of indebtedness which were of very little value as currency. Here they could start on a plane of equality and together retrieve their fortunes. Though primarily formed, at least ostensibly so, for the purpose of helping the individual soldier, the element of land speculation was not entirely absent from the plan. Reverend Manasseh Cutler himself "was not above turning an honest penny in a land speculation which bade fair to be remunerative as well as interesting." [50]

The officers of the Continental line had become close friends and were bound together through the Order of Cincinnati. Fully 90 per cent of the signers of the Newburgh petition belonged to this order. The Masonic order was another tie among them, and both of these had the effect of making the Ohio Company an interstate and not merely a local association. [51]

Putnam had been engaged in the surveying of the western land under Hutchins and now suggested Benjamin Tupper in his place while he went to survey the Maine lands for Massachusetts, perhaps designedly, in order that he could compare them with the lands in the West, since the officers always had the choice of buying from one of the states if they could not obtain terms from Congress.[52]

In 1786 Putnam and Tupper compared notes and began active promotion by advertising in the papers of Massachusetts January 25, 1786, calling county meetings of officers and others who were willing to "adventure" in a land settlement in Ohio. At these county gatherings delegates were elected to meet in Boston on March 1. By March 3 a plan of operation was reported and the sale of stock opened. A

[49] McMaster, I, pp. 180-183.
[50] *Marietta College Collections*, I, Introduction, p. 58.
[51] *Ibid*, p. 40.
[52] *Ibid*, p. 58.

year afterward it was considered that a sufficient number of
shares had been sold to justify the completion of the plan.
Meanwhile General Parsons, General Putnam and Reverend
Manasseh Cutler were sent as a committee to purchase a
suitable tract from Congress. Cutler worked with Congress during most of June and July, 1787, and finally,
October 27, 1787, the contract was executed.[53]

At other times Congress might not have acted favorably
upon the proposal made by Cutler since acceptance really
suspended the Ordinance of 1785 before it was actually
tried. It meant the alienation of an immense tract at a few
cents an acre, as offered by Cutler, a price below that set by
law. However, conditions were not normal. Shay's rebellion
was fresh in everybody's mind and the new Constitutional
Convention was already in session. The old Congress was
meeting in a desultory fashion and for months a quorum
failed to be present. Cutler, however, knew the situation
of the country and with an adroitness which would have
been a credit to Benjamin Franklin placed his arguments
before Congress as a body of individuals "in their lodgings."
He called attention to the prospect of reducing the public
debt by $4,000,000 and of further enhancing the value of
the other Federal lands. The intention of the company was
"an actual, a large and immediate settlement of the most
robust and industrious people in America," men "who had
no intention other than the Federal Government," thus off-
setting the secessional tendencies of the West and affording
a compact systematic settlement as provided for by the
Ordinance of 1785.[54]

But Congress was slow to act and he became impatient.
As a last resort it was proposed to have Winthrop Sargent,
the secretary of the new company, go to Maryland while
Cutler himself should visit Rhode Island and Connecticut,
which were not represented at this time, in order to solicit

[53] For the details and narrative of the formation of the Ohio Company see
Williams, Walker, and the *Marietta College Collections*, Vols. I and II.
[54] Cutler, I, Chs. V-VII.

these members to come to New York on which occasion the circumstances for renewing the application might be favorable.[55] Cutler's most telling argument seems to have been the alternative of buying land from one of the states. He pretended indifference, proposing "to leave the city immediately" and talking much of the advantages of a contract with one of the states. He says, "This I found had the desired effect."[56]

Cutler found his warmest support in the southern states. Virginia saw in the new settlement a protective "buffer state" for her old settlements as well as for the military reserve on the Ohio.[57] Washington gave the plan his support because he wanted the army rewarded and later (1788) praised the type of men and their method of settlement on the Muskingum.[58] A little "log rolling," proposing St. Clair for the first governor, which pleased the southern members and tended to conciliate the eastern states, had a good effect. But it was only after Cutler agreed to enlarge the scope of speculation by organizing the Scioto Company, that the deal was finally accomplished. Cutler says in his Journal (July 27) that they obtained nearly 5,000,000 acres of land. "One million and a half are for the Ohio Company, the remainder for a private speculation in which many of the principal characters of America are concerned. Without connecting this speculation, similar terms and advantages could not have been obtained for the Ohio Company."[59]

It is not necessary here to outline the meager facts known about the Scioto Company. An account of it is given in Cutler's Journal.[60] Suffice it to say that it was one of the first, and most ambitious, of all the land speculating schemes attempted in connection with the public domain. Through

[55] Walker, p. 66.
[56] *Ibid*, pp. 58, 59, 60, 67.
[57] Cutler, I, p. 136.
[58] *Ibid*, pp. 137, 138.
[59] Walker, p. 68. Cutler, I, p. 305.
[60] Also a very full account in an article by A. B. Hulbert in the *Mississippi Valley Historical Review*, I, No. 4, and II, No. 1.

the enterprise of Cutler and the mission to France of Joel Barlow the fiasco of the French settlement at Galliopolis was engineered. The Scioto Company, so-called, never really existed. No land was patented to it, though 25,200 acres were granted to the French immigrants brought over in connection with the project.

The tract of 1,500,000 acres purchased for the Ohio Company lay west of the seven ranges and along the Ohio River. According to the contract with Congress, the exterior lines were to be run by the Government but the interior lines by the company itself. In each township section 16 was reserved for schools, sections 8, 11, and 26 for the future disposition of Congress and 29 for religion, the latter provision being found only in the Ohio Company and Symmes tracts. Two townships were also contributed for a university. The price was fixed at one dollar an acre with one third off for bad lands and incidental charges. Since the land could be paid for in government paper worth about twelve cents on the dollar, the actual price was only eight or nine cents an acre. Military bounty rights could be offered in payment up to one seventh of the whole amount.

In order to protect the legitimate Ohio Company from the speculative Scioto Company whose lands were contracted for at the same time, Cutler and Sargent voluntarily proposed to Congress that $500,000 should be paid down when the contract was completed, $500,000 when the survey was completed and the rest in six equal yearly payments. Not until $1,000,000 was paid should a deed be given for the land represented by this amount. As further payments were made deeds for proportional areas of land should be given. In the meantime a right of entry and occupancy should be allowed the company on land not yet paid for.[61]

This liability, however, proved to be harder to meet than the company had expected, the second $500,000 payment could not be met, and the grant was lost. But in 1792,

[61] *Public Lands, General Public Acts of Congress Respecting Sale and Disposition of the Public Lands*, I, p. 26.

almost immediately after the time limit for payment had expired, Cutler and Robert Owen journeyed to Philadelphia to ask for a new grant.

Congress took a lenient view of the situation of the company and granted in a Relief Act of the same year[62] first of all, 750,000 acres of land with definite boundaries between the eighth and fifteenth ranges of townships for the $500,000 actually paid in. Another grant was authorized, a tract of 214,285 acres if within six months warrants "issued for army bounty rights sufficient for the purpose" were received, —"A large amount of which had been turned over by Colonel Platt." [63] During the Indian troubles the company had given lands to actual settlers and to those performing military duty, and had spent considerable sums for defense. To reimburse the company for this outlay another 100,000 acres was petitioned for and granted, but this tract was to be held in trust to be given to actual settlers 18 years of age, or over, in 100 acre tracts. After five years all grants not so conveyed were void. This last grant had been considered a national concession for the encouragement of settlement on the border, the Company merely holding it in trust. Taken altogether they received, or might have received, a little over two thirds of the original amount contemplated in the purchase. However, only 142,900 acres of the 214,285 acres available through bounty land warrants were actually called for, leaving the amount actually patented to the company at less than a million acres.

The Symmes Purchase—John Cleve Symmes of New Jersey was inspired by the Ohio Company to ask for a similar grant and organize another company. He proposed to a number of army friends to purchase 2,000,000 acres between the two Miamis, to which several agreed, "if the plan were safe." He had seen the country, was pleased with the fertility of the land, and with the thousands of immi-

[62] *Public Lands, General Public Acts of Congress Respecting Sale and Disposition of the Public Lands,* I, pp. 26, 44; *Marietta College Collections,* I, Introduction, p. 115.
[63] Williams, p. 91.

grants coming into it. He saw a fortune in store for "the lucky speculator who should buy lands from Congress for five shillings an acre and sell it to the immigrants at twenty." [64]

On August 29, 1787, he petitioned Congress, but before the contract was made started, in 1788, for the West. Rumors spread that he had gone to seize lands in defiance of Congress, and Dayton and Marsh, two associates, journeyed after him and overtook him at Pittsburgh. He delegated these two to go back and act in his behalf. The contract was completed October 14, 1788.

The Board of Treasury granted 1,000,000 acres at 66⅔ cents an acre payable in certificates of indebtedness of the United States—in fact the terms were similar to those given to Cutler and Sargent but no donation was made for a seminary. A payment of $82,198, one seventh in military rights was made, a similar sum was to be due within a month after the survey of the external lines was completed and the rest in six semi-annual payments. The total payment, exclusive of military rights, was estimated at $571,438. [65]

About 40,000 acres were set aside for Symmes "for attending to the general purpose." For this tract he was to pay personally but was to receive all the profits. Everybody was invited to come in at the contract price until May 1, 1788, when the price was to go up to $1.00 per acre. All the money above the contract price was to be deposited with the Register and used for the opening of roads, and for their improvements. [66] Under the contract Symmes was to have a long narrow strip bordering the Great Miami, but before the survey was completed he was granting lands beyond his limits. St. Clair, Governor of the Northwest territory, warned prospective buyers and prohibited further

[64] McMaster, I, p. 516.
[65] *Journals of the American Congress*, IV, p. 371.
[66] C. H. Winfield, Life and Public Serevices of John Cleve Symmes in New Jersey Historical Society *Proceedings*, Vol. V, 2nd Ser. (1879), p. 34.

location on the lands under dispute. In 1792 Congress granted Symmes terms similar to those given to the Ohio Company. He was granted a patent for as much land as he had paid for and it was made to cover all the lands between the two Miamis. He was, in addition, granted 106,857 acres to be taken up under military rights and a township for an academy was also included. In 1794 letters patent were issued for 311,682 acres including the reserved sections in each township and one whole township for the academy. Symmes quit-claimed all his rights to lands remaining in his former contract.

But the matter was not settled as yet. In amending the contract Congress assumed that 1,000,000 acres lay between the two rivers, whereas only 543,950 acres were within the area. There was misunderstanding about what was quit-claimed and forfeited and Symmes thought he still had the right to make payments and complete his original contract for 1,000,000 acres and so kept on granting land in antici-pation of this in parts of Ohio where he had no title. Congress did not accept his point of view and in 1796 definitely refused to grant him any more land. His financial affairs were on a poor footing. The judgments against him made it difficult to perfect title even within his boundaries. Grantees brought suit to recover, and in 1802 he was arrested on three counts. He had been appointed as a judge of the Northwest Territory in 1788, and since land disputes were brought before him he could exercise a good deal of power, at which people protested.[67]

It fell to Congress to look after those who had purchased lands from Symmes outside of his limits. These, however, were not dealt with in the same spirit as were the French at Galliopolis. They were granted preëmption of their lands at $2.00 an acre but were given two years in which to make the payments instead of but one which was then the practice. It took additional acts in 1801, 1802, 1803 and 1804 to take

[67] New Jersey Historical Society *Proceedings*, 2 Ser., Vol. V, No. 1, p. 37.

care of those to whom Symmes continued to make sales. Four years of credit were allowed as under the amended land system.[68]

MAP II

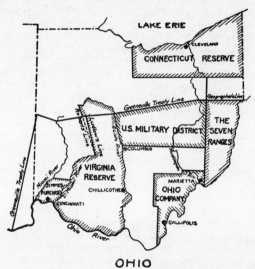

OHIO

SPECIAL GRANTS AND RESERVES

Summary

Congress was not free to devise a land policy in a quiet, philosophical, manner. On the contrary it had been necessary to make promises in advance involving the disposition of land in satisfaction of services. Furthermore Congress was in desperate straights regarding income. And finally, the hold of the newly created Republic on the territory and settlers of the West was none too secure. All these facts conditioned the action of Congress in its plans for disposing of the newly acquired domain.

There were two main systems in vogue in the colonies, the New England and the Southern. The New England system required compact settlement in "towns" under the direction of the parent colony. In the South the individual was allowed the utmost freedom in

[68] Treat, pp. 60-62. *Public Lands,* I, pp. 62, 80, 86, 108.

selecting land, with no reference to the establishment of a compact settlement. One very distinctive feature of the new federal system was the adoption of the rectangular survey.

The ordinances of 1784 and 1785 embodied features from both the New England and the Southern system, yet it must be admitted that, as the years went by, the latter became dominant. Surveys always preceded sales, as in the New England plan, but they need not precede settlement as came to be the practice. Under the early land ordinances sales began. Following the completion of survey of a few ranges of land in eastern Ohio sales were undertaken. The sales were at auction at the seat of government and were distinctly disappointing. But 73,000 acres were sold at a price of about $1.60 per acre.

Congress seems to have welcomed the idea of selling land through land companies. It meant reduction of the debt in large blocks and they were anxious for sales in as large tracts as possible, large enough to compare with the Western Reserve or the Military Reserve of Virginia.[69] It relieved the nation of dealing with the individual small buyer and allowed it to make a contract with well known business men who promised responsibility. The method of compact settlement was in line with the Ordinance of 1785 and the ideals of the times.

The government, however, was doomed to financial disappointment as were the promoters and adventurers themselves. Instead of the increasing sales so sanguinely expected, Congress was obliged as time went on to relieve the distress of the companies and also that of the innocent purchasers from the companies in relief acts from 1792 to 1804. The Ohio Company was the only one of the three managed in a commendable manner. Even though the prime movers of this company, and above all Mr. Cutler, were willing to make money by speculating on land, they at the same time undertook to treat their settlers well, and do the country at large a good turn.[70] Not so much can be said for Mr. Symmes, much less of the Scioto Company.

The experience of the Confederacy served to convince Congress, following the adoption of the Constitution, that there were grave dangers in this wholesale method of disposing of the public lands. Besides, when the price of land was raised to $2.00 an acre more

[69] *Marietta College Collections*, I, Introduction, pp. 70-71. Hamilton's Plan made provisions for the investor (speculator), the colonization company and the individual. See Sato, p. 141.

[70] In spite of his connection with the Scioto Company not a writer accuses the Reverend Manasseh Cutler of being an active member of this group. He worked with them to obtain the grant to the Ohio Company; he was careful to separate the affairs of the two companies and seems enirely ignorant of what the Scioto speculators were doing "beneath the surface, as was the rest of mankind."

revenue was to be obtained from private sales than from sales to companies. To have granted Symmes further lands in 1794 would in the opinion of Congress have meant a contribution of $2.000 land instead of land worth 66⅔ cents, the price at which he had obtained his grant.

Finally it was recognized that company settlement could not succeed alongside the "Daniel Boone manner—shotgun settlement on an enormous scale." [71]

TABLE IV

LAND DISPOSED OF UNDER THE CONFEDERATION [72]

Sales	Acres
1787 Sales at New York	72,974
1787 Ohio Company	822,900
1788 Symmes (Patented 1794)	248,540
Pennsylvania	202,187

Donations:

Canadian refugees	69,120 [73]
Arnold H. Dorham	22,040 [74]
Bounties to British deserters [75]	

[71] P. S. Lovejoy, "The Promised Land," *The Country Gentleman,* Jan. 15, 1921, pp. 4, 5.

[72] Donaldson, pp. 196-210.

[73] This amount was set aside but not all of it was granted to these refugees.

[74] Dorham was at Lisbon during the Revolutionary war and at his own cost befriended American sailors captured by British cruisers. Congress granted this tract of land to reward him.

[75] By the acts of August 14 and 17, 1776. Amount transferred unknown.

CHAPTER IV

THE PUBLIC LAND SITUATION, 1789

It was a clear case that something must be done to improve the system of handling the public domain. Within six weeks after the first Congress under the Federal Constitution began its deliberations, it reached the second economic question to be considered, that of western lands. Thomas Scott, of Pennsylvania, was the first to introduce the subject in the House. On May 28, 1789, he made a speech setting forth the situation: the Congress of the Confederation had sold land by the million acres; the surveys had not kept pace with the sales; the money was not yet paid in for the land; it was doubtful whether the selling price would exceed the cost of survey and transfer; land should be sold in small tracts; a land office should be created. Mr. Scott went on to inform Congress that there was already a large number, some 7,000 persons, settled on unsurveyed public land; they were waiting an opportunity to buy; they were willing to pay an equitable price, but they wanted a preëmption right granted them in order to secure the claim until such a time as the land came regularly into the market. The previous Congress, it will be remembered, had dealt harshly with these pioneers, who had, as Congress put it, settled upon land in defiance of the authority of the government.[1] Mr. Scott was much concerned over the relation of these settlers to the government. He goes on to state that the settlers—squatters, as they soon after were called—had gone onto the land with

[1] *Ann. of Cong.*, 1 Cong., 1 Sess., pp. 412, 413.

the intention of purchasing it from the government; they were willing to pay a fair price. He pointed to the danger of offers to these people of land by a foreign power; hopes had already been held out to them of such offer; they would be led to think their interests different from those of the Atlantic shore; to refuse to sell land in less than million acre lots would be a cause of disgust, if not of separation. If the object was to prevent the settlement of the country, it would be another thing. He advocated the establishment of a land office in the vicinity of the land, as settlers could not afford long journeys in making purchase and securing title.

Objection to the creation of a district federal land office was raised on the ground that it would injure the interests of the men who had bought land in large amounts expecting to sell in small parcels. A motion to appoint a committee to investigate this carried.[2] The committee brought in its report on July 13, 1789, recommending the establishment of a land office. Mr. Scott, the leading member of the committee, showed a comprehensive knowledge of the West and an appreciation of its possibilities. He estimated that the land under consideration, the Old Northwest, would contain 2,000,000 farms, or "for great caution, say it will contain 1,000,000."[3] It was noted that already land had been sold to the amount of five million dollars' worth, an amount equal to more than one-sixth of the domestic debt of the United States. Should any one fear that a liberal land policy would result in depopulation of the Atlantic States, it might be stated that settlers disposed to go would do so whether the United States made them a good offer or not, for Spain would give them land free, together with a guarantee of political and religious liberty. Here was a man familiar with the frontier who described the men who seek homes in advance of civilization in clear cut terms: "The forming settlements in a wilderness upon the frontiers, be-

[2] *Ann. of Cong.*, 1 Cong., 1 Sess., p. 414.
[3] It contains now 1,084,744 farms. See *Fourteenth Census of the United States*, VI, Part 1.

tween the savages and the least populated of the civilized parts of the United States, requires men of enterprising, violent, nay, discontented and turbulent spirits. Such always are our first settlers in the ruthless and savage wild; they serve as pioneers to clear the way for the more laborious and careful farmer." [4]

He believed it impossible to keep such men out of the wilderness, and asked whether anyone would have the hardihood to point out a class of citizens "who ought to be the servants of the community," yet, unless that were done, they could not be denied the right to settle on the western lands. It would be feasible to sell land in small quantities to actual settlers and sell in million acre tracts to companies at the same time.

The effort to revise the method of disposing of the western land ran through the first three sessions of Congress; a committee was appointed and a report favoring action was brought in; a bill was prepared and a day set for its consideration, but nothing appears in the minutes of that day to indicate that it was again brought before the House. It is of more than passing interest to note that the friend of a new policy favorable to the pioneers,—the sale of small tracts at low prices, the establishment of a land office in the West,—was Mr. Scott, of Pittsburg, probably more closely in touch with the West than any other Congressman of the time. It was the fear of reduced receipts from the sales that prevented action. [5]

DISCUSSION IN CONGRESS, 1789-1804

Although no action was reached, there were some important discussions during these early Congresses. For example: Should there be one price for all land, or should it be graded in price to fit the quality? Sedgwick, of Massachusetts, and Lawrence, of New York, favored gradation of prices. White, of Virginia, and Bloodworth, of North Caro-

[4] *Ann. of Cong.*, 1 Cong., 1 Sess., p. 624 *et seq.*
[5] *Ibid*, p. 625.

lina, favored one fixed price.[6] The danger of speculation;
the advisability of selling for cash or for credit; of selling
in large or in small amounts; of having one land office or
several; the question of alien ownership of land; all these
were threshed over.[7] But on the whole subject hardly a
man other than Mr. Scott, of Pennsylvania, seemed to have
convictions; it was a conundrum. The one item on which a
common sentiment prevailed was that the land must in some
way furnish the funds for paying the public debt.[8] The
petition of a foreigner, one H. W. Dobbyn, for the purchase of a tract of land on credit led to a request on
the part of Congress that the Secretary of the Treasury
submit a general plan for the disposition of the public
domain.[9] This was January 20, 1790; on July 22 of the
same year Mr. Alexander Hamilton made his well-known
report.[10]

In this report the secretary recognized two main objects
to be kept in view: First, "the facility of advantageous
sales, according to the probable course of purchases"; second, "the accommodation of individuals now inhabiting the
western country, or who may hereafter emigrate thither."
There was no question in Mr. Hamilton's mind as to the
relative importance of the two considerations; he was a
financier, and the "moneyed individuals" and "association of
persons" that is to say the buyers who would take wholesale
amounts,—came first in importance; however, he did not for-
get the small settler, but believed it possible to accommodate
him and still gain all the advantage to be derived from the
large purchasers. He proposed that evidences of indebtedness of the United States be receivable for land in quantities
of not less than five hundred acres; that actual settlers be

[6] *Ann. of Cong.*, 2 Sess., p. 1835 *et seq.*
[7] *Ibid*, 1 Sess., pp. 622-632; 2 Sess., pp. 1068-1072; 3 Sess., p. 1833 *et seq.*
[8] Even Jefferson, who was probably the first to propose giving land to settlers, was by 1785 so impressed with the need of revenue as to say: "I am
sanguine in my expectations of lessening our debts by this fund." *The Writings of Thomas Jefferson*. Monticello Ed. Washington, D. C., 1904.
[9] *Ann. of Cong.*, 1 Cong., 2 Sess., p. 1068.
[10] *Pub. Lands*, I, p. 4 *et seq.*; Donaldson, p. 198.

provided with tracts of not over one hundred acres; that townships of ten miles square be sold as units; that the price should be thirty cents per acre; that credit should be given, not to exceed three-fourths the purchase money, and on tracts not under ten miles square; and that security other than land itself be required as a pledge for back payments. Mr. Hamilton recommended that the main land office be established at the capital, with branch offices within the territory where the land was located; that a surveyor general be appointed and given power to appoint deputies for the western governments; that three commissioners, either *ex officio* or appointed, be given general charge of the whole matter.

In the language of Mr. Donaldson, the report "forms in its several leading features the basis of the prior and existing methods of administration for the sale and disposition of the public domain."[11]

Though deeply concerned about the disposition of western land, Congress for years was unable to act; again and again some member, at the critical time, would suggest that the subject was too large and too important to be acted upon on such short notice.[12] Yet during these years an occasional memorial or petition from the frontier reminded Congress that its duty was not yet done respecting the western country and those looking for new homes.[13]

Size of Tracts

In the early months of 1796 Congress took up seriously the question of disposing of the public domain. It is hard to determine which idea was uppermost, that of accommodating settlers, or that of filling the public treasury. Almost the first remark reported in the discussion of the bill was in the interest of the small purchaser. Mr. Rutherford, of Virginia, who claimed the distinction of having been a

---

[11] Donaldson, p. 200; *Pub. Lands,* I, p. 4.
[12] *Ann. of Cong.,* 1 Cong., 1 Sess., pp. 414, 623.
[13] *Pub. Lands,* I. See table of contents.

pioneer for half a century himself, "hoped that they would destroy that Hydra speculation, which had done the country great harm." "Let us," he said, "dispose of the land to original settlers." Rutherford did not like the bill as proposed, since it would favor speculators.[14] Findley, of Pennsylvania, presumably also familiar with frontier conditions, since he lived in Pittsburg, objected to the proposal to sell land in quarter-township lots, which apparently was the smallest lot proposed in the bill, and suggested that part of it be divided into one-hundred-sixty acre tracts. He believed men already on the land would purchase small pieces, but were too poor to buy large tracts. "Speculation," said he, "seems to have no bounds," and it was his wish to set bounds beyond which the speculator could not well go. This view was supported by a large number of members of the House,[15] and the amendment providing for the sale of part of the land in one-hundred-sixty-acre lots passed the Committee of the Whole.[16]

The most consistent and the most analytical supporter of the small divisions was Albert Gallatin. He appreciated the fact that land must ultimately be paid for by cultivators of the soil. If speculators should buy the land first, prosperity would be impaired; possibly more land would sell the first year to speculators than to settlers, but that was a minor matter; the added price which the speculator would get from the next purchaser might just as well go to the government, provided only that the government wait a little longer for the sale. Mr. Gallatin showed his appreciation of the public domain unmistakably: "If the cause of the happiness of this country was examined into it would be found to arise as much from the great plenty of land in proportion to the inhabitants which their citizens enjoyed as from the wisdom of their political institutions. It is because

---

[14] *Ann. of Cong.*, 4 Cong., 1 Sess., 328. "Speculaton and money-making are seldom found in a more raging extreme; *Ibid*, pp. 402, 403.

[15] *Ibid*, pp. 340, 408, 414, 856, 864.

[16] *Ibid*, p. 865.

the poor man has been able always to attain his portion of land." [17]

There were widely differing opinions as to the effect likely to result from selling small pieces. It would cost all the land was worth to survey it into such tiny squares. It would result in culling out the good land and leaving the poor land unsold. It would scatter the settlers over too wide a territory and increase the danger from Indians. It would reduce the price by excluding the moneyed men from bidding. It would even prevent the small purchaser from finding land to suit him since he could not afford to go so far to locate land and then go back to the land office to buy it. Mr. Cooper, of New York, thought it just as reasonable to lay out garden plots for the settlers as to survey such little farms as a quarter-section; he urged that no bidders interested in small purchases appeared at the sales in his state. This testimony was offset by reports from Pennsylvania where the small purchasers predominated. [18]

The supporters of the smaller tract plan were quite clearly the members of the House representing districts nearest the frontier. For example, both representatives from Kentucky were unqualifiedly on that side. The Pennsylvania members, so far as they went on record, were all but unanimously in favor of the same. Strong support was given by members from Virginia, though there was also opposition from that state. New York, North Carolina, and South Carolina furnished partisans for the smaller divisions, favoring the actual settlers.

Settlement Requirements

Alongside the question of the size of tracts offered came that of a settlement requirement. Such a practice had long obtained in New England, New York, and in fact in most of the old states. Thus far no such requirement had been made by the United States for the western lands. An

[17] *Ann. of Cong.*, 4 Cong., 1 Sess., p. 411.
[18] *Ibid*, pp. 348, 863.

amendment was proposed providing that there should be "a settler for every —— acres," and though it failed to pass, it brought out some views showing the knowledge and lack of knowledge on the public land question possessed by the members of Congress. Mr. Gallatin referred to the experience of a century in which settlement had always been required; the happiness of the country had thus been promoted; would it be wise to throw away this experience and replace it by mere theory? [19] As to the workings of a settlement proviso there were many skeptics: "There was not rigor sufficient in government to carry such a clause with effect. Besides, in order to avoid the forfeiture, a purchaser might build a hut, put in a person for a time, and then go off again." Another objection offered was that pioneers would organize themselves against the non-resident and tax the latter enough to compel the use of the land. [20] Some feared that a settlement requirement would cause too much emigration from the Atlantic states, a calamity which they kept ever in mind in dealing with the land question. It was also feared that requiring a man to settle his land would depress the price which he would be willing to pay for it. [21]

Another favorite plan was the limitation of the amount of land to be put upon the market during a year. This was in order to keep settlements compact, to hold the price up, and to prevent settlers from getting beyond the pale of government. It was suggested that in case the price of two dollars was not high enough to prevent the sale of over 500,000 or 800,000 acres a year, it should be increased. [22] However, this motion failed to pass the committee.

The Minimum Price

On the important question of the price, no debate is reported. The committee which drafted the bill proposed the

[19] *Ann. of Cong.,* 4 Cong., 1 Sess., p. 411.
[20] *Ibid,* p. 408.
[21] *Ibid,* p. 412.
[22] *Ibid,* pp. 350, 353, 404, 405, 411, 413.

minimum price of two dollars per acre, and the House accepted it with no opposition. Incidentally it appears that this price, which was double the former price asked, three times the price obtained in previous large sales, and seven times the price proposed by Hamilton in his report, was expected to discourage speculation. By charging a figure approaching the true value to start with, and increasing that by means of the auction, it was believed that there could be left only a reasonable margin between the price received by the government and that paid by the actual settler.[23] But withal, the prime object seems to have been to get money for the treasury, after which consideration the settler and his wants received attention.[24] Speculation, always a subject of apprehension, it was held, could not thrive at this particular time in Ohio, since land was already selling at four to six dollars, a price too high to be attractive to the land jobber. Therefore, two dollars was really low, a mere nominal price, yet a safeguard against selling too far below real value. The fact that New York, Pennsylvania, and Massachusetts were selling land nearer by and at a price as low as or lower than the new figure for the western land did not seem to attract much attention.[25] Mr. Cooper, of New York, one of the largest land holders of his time, objected to the price of two dollars since "many millions of acres were now selling . . . on the Ohio for three shillings, on long credit."[26] Objection to the new price was made also by a man from Virginia.[27] It was generally believed that the land would sell in great quantities at a figure much above the two dollar minimum. Only five years before this time the House had spent some hours on a land bill which it passed, but which did not pass the Senate and in which the question was whether or not thirty cents was too high a minimum price. It was at the end of the debate agreed

[23] *Ann. of Cong.*, 4 Cong., 1 Sess., pp. 331, 346, 348, 405.
[24] *Ibid*, pp. 330, 334, 404.
[25] *Ibid*, p. 863.
[26] *Ibid*, p. 405.
[27] *Ibid*.

that the minimum should be "twenty-five cents hard money." [28]

Cash or Credit

Should the land be paid for in cash at the time of purchase, or should credit be allowed? It will be remembered that credit had been allowed in the case of the big sales, such as those to the Ohio Company and to Symmes. Credit had been given by certain of the states also, but it had been found difficult to make collections on the delinquent payments. [29]

In a report of the House committee on Public Lands in January, 1791, it was provided that no credit be given on less than a township six miles square, and that in every instance at least one-fourth of the purchase price be cash, with the longest term of credit not to exceed two years. The Committee further showed its appreciation of some of the complications sure to arise in connection with credit on cheap land by providing that security other than the land itself should be required on the time payments. [30]

In the bill brought before Congress in 1796 provision was made for the payment of half the purchase money in cash and a credit of one year on the balance. During the debate in the Committee of the Whole a motion was made to extend the time of payment, requiring but one-quarter cash in hand and putting the balance into three successive annual payments. [31] This motion passed the committee but failed to pass the House, the original wording being retained. Congress therefore went on record against extending very liberal credit to land buyers. Mr. Gallatin remarked that poor men would be given long time credit by the speculators. This was the only way in his opinion the "poorer classes" could hope to get land, since the "Govern-

[28] *Ann. of Cong.*, 1 Cong., 3 Sess., pp. 1840, 1964.
[29] *Ibid*, 1 Sess., p. 411.
[30] *Ibid*, 3 Sess., p. 1841.
[31] *Ibid*, 4 Cong., 1 Sess., p. 416.

ment would not be inclined to give the credit necessary to be given to these purchasers." [32]

A hard problem was found in the land office controversy. Should all land be sold at the seat of government, at offices to be established on the frontier, or should certain tracts be sold at Washington and other tracts on the frontier? The last suggestion prevailed. The question was brought before the House by Mr. Gallatin, who moved that the large tracts be sold at the capital and the small ones in the Western Territory, [33] although it was his judgment that the whole should be sold in the Western Territory; subsequently he proposed the latter as his motion, the other part of the original motion being added by a member from Virginia. In the discussion the idea prevailed that small purchasers could not well go to the capital. As to the large purchaser, there was not a full agreement: could he be best accommodated at a local land office or at the central one? Would it be fair to bring all purchasers into competition for the small pieces? These were matters of disagreement. Yet after a brief discussion the motion providing for the double system of sale on the ground and at the seat of government carried, the members from the westernmost districts favoring the exclusive sale in the West. [34]

The Location of Land Offices

The land ordinance of 1785 had provided for the rectangular system of surveys, and under this system the "seven ranges" had been surveyed. However, it was by no means acceptable to everyone. During the debate of 1796 the first bit of satire brought out was, "if the country was not square, the lines could not be run in squares." Even Mr. Findley, who seems eminently practical and who lived a near neighbor to the seven ranges is quoted as saying: "Survey . . . should not destroy natural boundaries; and the fewer parallel lines,

[32] *Ann. of Cong.*, 4 Cong., 1 Sess., p. 349.
[33] *Ibid*, p. 406.
[34] *Ibid*, p. 406, *et seq.*

the less destruction of this kind." [35]   Mr. Gallatin was of the opinion that a compromise between parallel lines and natural boundaries might be made, the surveyor to put the land into "such lots as may be the most convenient"—"The lines may be run parallel on by rivers." [36]   It was feared that the lines run on the rectangular plan would not be permanent; that is to say, they would not be easy to relocate, owing to the variation of compasses and other complications. [37]

Surveying was not held in high esteem as a difficult science by all members, one of them remarking that the art could be "taught to a surveyor of moderate capacity in one evening."   The criticism of the magnetic survey did not assume serious proportions and the original wording of the bill, a virtual copy of the plan of survey in the land ordinance of 1785, was allowed to stand.   In this we had established once for all the rectangular survey.

From the administrative standpoint the creation of the office of surveyor general put the matter of surveying on a definite and permanent basis.   It was expected that the survey would always precede settlement and the hope was expressed that the surveyors might make notes on the value and quality of the land and that these might be of great value in effecting sales.

The Act of 1796, and Its Failure

The law of May 18, 1796, provided for a Surveyor General who should appoint a corps of surveyors.   It adopted definitely the rectangular system of survey and gave directions for applying it.   Half of the townships were to be divided into sections of 640 acres each and offered for sale in the local land districts in 640 acre tracts.   The remaining half of the townships were to be left undivided and sold in

[35] *Ann. of Cong.*, 4 Cong., 1 Sess., p. 339.
[36] *Ibid*, p. 336.
[37] Mr. Gallatin, not appreciating the possibilities of mathematics, supposed it "impossible to survey exactly by the magnet as they varied from each other, and from year to year." *Ann. of Cong.*, 4 Cong., 1 Sess., p. 422.

quarters, excluding always the four sections at the center which were reserved. The quarter-township sales were to be at the seat of government. However, the remaining entire townships in the "seven ranges" were to be sold entire as originally planned. The price set was two dollars per acre as a minimum, the land to be offered at auction and sold to the highest bidder above that amount. The purchaser was required to pay one-twentieth cash, allowed a credit of thirty days on the balance of the first half, and a year on the second half. In case of default in any payments as they became due after the purchase was made, all money previously paid was to be forfeited and the land taken back by the government and treated as though it had never been sold. A deduction of ten per cent was allowed on payment of the second half of the purchase money if made at the same time with the first. Four sections of land in each township were reserved for future disposition, also all salt springs, together with the section of land in which they were situated.[38] It was provided that in payment for land evidences of public debt bearing six per cent interest should be received at face value, and other evidences of debt at market value.[39]

As to the operation of the new act nothing could have been more disappointing from the financial standpoint, and hardly anything from the standpoint of settling the wilderness. Less than fifty thousand acres were sold between 1796 and 1800. Forty-three thousand acres were sold at Pittsburg at about two dollars and thirty-three cents per acre, while at Philadelphia, where the large scale sales were to take place, but a single quarter township was sold and that at the bare minimum. "The sections and quarter townships in the seven ranges have been repeatedly offered for sale [at Pittsburg] without success." As early as January, 1797, Oliver Wolcott, Treasurer of the United States, was ready to say, "Indeed, it is now certain that none of the quarter townships will be

[38] *U. S. Stat. at Large*, I, p. 464.
[39] *Ann. of Cong.*, 4 Cong., 2 Sess., p. 2954.

sold." [40]   In June, 1797, Mr. Gallatin reported a petition to
the House: one hundred persons in the Ohio country complained that they could not become purchasers of land at the
sales owing to conspiracies on the part of speculators. [41] Yet
the rage of speculation was apparently unable to rise above
the two-dollar barrier.

Attempts at Readjustment—1800-1804

By the year 1800 it was thoroughly evident that the land
riddle had not been solved. Four years had passed and the
sales which were to have been reckoned in terms of millions
of acres had hardly reached five per cent of a single million.
The great stream of gold which was to flow into the treasury
had turned out to be, not a stream at all, but a few inter-
mittent drops. The settlers who had received such solicitous
consideration had bought at a lower figure from the Ohio
Company, or from Symmes, or in the Western Reserve, or
just as often had settled without authority on unsurveyed
land, hoping that some lucky turn of the wheel of fortune
would bring them a prize in the form of cheaper land. The
repeated reports of no sales and no prospect of sales; the
memorials and advice from the frontier, all meant that the
work of forming a public land policy must be done over.

Harrison's Frontier Bill, 1800

The most important event in the remolding of the public
domain policy was the advent of William Henry Harrison
into the counsels of Congress. [42] Mr. Harrison took the oath
as delegate to Congress from Indiana on December 2, 1799,
and on December 24 [43] he introduced a resolution asking "that
a committee be appointed to inquire . . . what alterations are
necessary in the laws authorizing the sale of the lands of

---

[40] Report by Gallatin on sales of land June 13, 1798, *Pub. Lands,* I, pp.
65, 73.
[41] *Ann. of Cong.,* 5 Cong., 1 Sess., p. 377.
[42] B. A. Hinsdale, *The Old Northwest,* p. 306.
[43] McMaster, III, p. 124. Date erroneously given as December 4.

the United States northwest of the Ohio." [44] The resolution was passed at once and Mr. Harrison was named as chairman of the committee. The occasion for action was emphasized by the presentation of a petition from settlers in the Northwest on the same day by Mr. Gallatin. The import of the petition was to the effect that a law might be passed preventing speculators from getting land already improved by settlers, and making it possible for the settlers themselves to buy.

About three months later, March 31, 1800, the committee reported a bill. It was manifestly a frontiersman's bill. While the debate within the committee is not available, the committee was made up of men from the extreme West together with eastern men who had shown themselves friendly to the pioneers. This bill was in all its important innovations, a concession to the western farmer, and with no radical changes it became a law. It began with the provision for four definite land districts in the Northwest Territory. An office in each district was to be established in charge of a "register of the land office" who should reside at the place where the office was to be kept. This arrangement has hardly been changed to the present time.

The size of tracts offered was a major consideration, though it was coupled with the question of receipts. No sooner had the bill been introduced than a motion was made to strike out the provision for survey into half-sections: it would cost too much. Gallatin, Harrison and others came promptly to the rescue defending the half-section plan "because it prevented speculators receiving the advantages resulting from offering the lands in large quantities for sale." [45] Mr. J. Brown, of Rhode Island, wanted to go further than had the committee in parcelling the land and moved to insert "quarter-sections" in place of "half-sections" but the motion was lost. [46] Soon afterward an amendment was passed pro-

[44] *Ann. of Cong.*, 6 Cong., 1 Sess., p. 209.
[45] *Ibid*, p. 651.

viding that land east of the Muskingum should be sold in sections instead of half-sections. This affected scarcely any land outside the old "seven ranges." [47]

Another major consideration was that of time payments. The credit allowed in the act of 1796 was not credit at all so far as the small purchaser was concerned. It gave but a year's postponement of pay day, though the most superficial acquaintance with the frontier would make it plain that the settler who could not pay cash at the time of purchase would hardly be able to produce it in another twelve-month. It was during the first year that important initial expenses must be met, while receipts above living expenses could hardly begin during the period, or during a period five times as long for that matter.

Hardly more than half a year had elapsed after the passage of the act of 1796 before petitions for extension of time began to come in. A committee appointed to consider the subject reported on January 30, 1797, in favor of extension of time. It was suggested that one-fifth be required at the time of sale and the balance paid in four annual installments. [48]

A genuine credit system was adopted in 1800 and for twenty years was destined to make trouble such as Congress had seldom encountered in domestic affairs. Whether the subject of prices of land was much discussed at this time, there is no certainty; but at least it hardly got outside the committee which drew the bill, and on this committee was Mr. Gallatin who saw in the western lands the means of paying the public debt. It was believed that reducing the size of tracts would increase the auction price, and more complaints had come on the question of size than on that of price, although there were not wanting petitions praying for reduction in price: the privilege had been asked of buy-

[46] *Ann. of Cong.*, 6 Cong., 1 Sess., p. 652.
[47] A "range" is a tier of townships running north and south.
[48] Credit provisions discussed in Chapter V.

ing "on terms different from those prescribed by the law.[49] These requests were promptly refused.

There was no respite for Congress regarding western lands. By 1803 a committee was appointed "to inquire into the expediency of amending the several laws providing for the sale of public lands." The immediate cause of the appointment of this committee was the receipt of two petitions asking that the land laws be so amended "as to enable industrious residents or emigrants to purchase a quantity of land proportionate to their capital." [50]   On this committee of five, the states of Georgia, Kentucky and Ohio were represented, which may be something of an explanation of the report brought in.   On January 23, 1804, the committee reported a series of resolutions which amounted to a bill.[51] These resolutions were made the order of the day for the "next Monday," but the next Monday came and the scribe failed to record any action on the resolutions.

The committee had sent a set of questions to Mr. Gallatin, then Secretary of the Treasury, asking: "Will the sales of land be retarded or accelerated, and how will the revenue be affected:

1. By selling the land in smaller tracts?
2. By charging no interest on the amount of sales, until after the purchaser has made default in payment?
3. By selling for cash instead of credit now authorized by law?
4. By reducing the price of the public lands?
5. By making grants of small tracts to actual settlers and improvers?" [52]

In these questions, with the exception of the third, we have a reflection of the sentiments of the frontier. All of the suggested changes of the other four were embodied in petitions received by Congress..[53]

[49] Pub. Lands, I, pp. 71, 73.
[50] Ann. of Cong., 8 Cong., 1 Sess., p. 616; Pub. Lands, I, p. 149.
[51] Ann. of Cong., 8 Cong., 2 Sess., p. 1582.
[52] Ibid, p. 1584.
[53] Pub. Lands, I, p. 149.

Mr. Gallatin's Report on the Deficiencies of the Land System

Mr. Gallatin, replying to the questions, recounted the provisions of the law of 1800 and explained the purpose of fixing the minimum price so much above the usual terms on which vacant lands had previously been granted in the several states, as "a wish to prevent monopolies and large speculations, and at the same time to secure a permanent revenue to the Union. The first object has been fully attained." The receipts had not been so satisfactory owing to the competition of lands in the Connecticut Reserve, in the military tracts and in Kentucky, which might generally be purchased at a lower price. Mr. Gallatin was apprehensive as to the collection of the money due on land already sold. Speculation, he said, had been shut off by the two dollar minimum, yet 2,000 persons owed $1,100,000 on the land which at the highest calculation was only one-fourth paid for. Thus these 2,000 purchasers held over 360 acres each, on an average, and the conclusion is inevitable that they held it for speculation, as few were farming a quarter of that amount. In fact a petition had asked that sections be cut into sixths, a little over a hundred acres, in order that settlers might be accommodated with land in proportion to their needs.[54] It was the opinion of the secretary that no credit, beyond forty days, should be allowed on future sales, and in the same connection he favored a reduction in price and in the size of tracts sold. He suggested the offering of tracts of half-sections instead of sections, and of quarter-sections instead of half-sections, and the reduction of the price to a dollar and a quarter and a dollar and a half per acre for these tracts respectively.

It was pointed out by Mr. Gallatin that these changes would permit a man to buy land for a farm with two hundred and forty dollars, whereas under the arrangement in operation he must pay one hundred and sixty dollars in cash and go in debt four hundred and eighty more—and with small prospect of being able to meet the obligation. More-

[54] *Pub. Lands*, I, p. 149.

over, the interests of the purchasers for cash would become identified with those of the United States. As to revenue the secretary believed that it would be easier to sell a given number of dollars' worth of land at the reduced price than at the old, so that the revenue would not only not suffer but would gain, and the government would merely give a little more land for the money, a trifling difference. Mr. Gallatin had the squatters in mind, and believed the proposed changes would enable them to purchase, but he was opposed to allowing them the right of preëmption on land appropriated without due legal process.

This was the most comprehensive discussion of the land question since the report by Hamilton, if not since the beginning of deliberations on the public domain, and the committee accepted almost every point, incorporating them in the resolutions presented to the House. The resolutions conformed to the views of the people upon the land; of those who wished to go onto the land, and of the representatives of this class of people in Congress; of the Secretary of the Treasury, a man fully acquainted with the question from the standpoint of both government and settler; and finally it was the expression of the views of a select committee which had given it careful study. With all of this it might seem that the enactment of a law embodying these features would be inevitable, yet the bill that passed contained only two of the five suggestions made by the committee.

The Act of 1804

Interest on Land Debt

On March 26, 1804, an act providing for the disposal of public land in the state of Indiana and "for other purposes" was approved. It is within the "other purposes" that the fundamental changes in the land policy are found. In this act Congress acceded to the demand that no interest be charged until payments became delinquent. This changed the cash price of the land from one dollar eighty-four cents to one dollar sixty-four cents, since under the new arrangement the eight per cent discount was reckoned on the face value of the deferred payment instead of on that sum increased by the interest charges at six per cent.

Reduction of Size of Tract

The other concession made to the popular demand was the reduction of the size of tract offered, provision being made for the sale of land in quarter-sections. This was an important advance step so far as settlement was concerned. The minimum amount offered had dropped from the whole townships, and whole sections in alternate townships, provided by the Land Ordinance of 1785, step by step, with quarter townships (eight sections), and single sections in 1796, half sections, quarter sections,[55] eighty-acre tracts,[56] and finally, in 1832, to forty-acre tracts,[57] The quarter section provision was achieved in 1804—while the eighty was allowed in part in 1817 and universally in 1820.

Minimum Prices and Selling Prices to 1820

One of the outstanding features of the discussions and legislation on the public land question during the period from 1787 to 1840, and for much longer, for that matter, was that of the price at which public lands were to be sold. This was an important consideration from the standpoint of those in charge of government financing as well as that of the settler. Those looking to the sale of land as a source of revenue desired to set a price which, on the whole, would give a maximum net return, whereas the settler was of course interested in getting land at the lowest figure.

As previously noted, the price fixed by the Land Ordinance of 1785 was one dollar per acre. This was, however, so

[55] *U. S. Stat. at Large*, II, p. 281.
[56] *Ibid*, III, p. 346, six designated sections of each township to be sold in eighty-acre tracts.
[57] *Ibid*, IV, p. 503.

administered as to result in a payment very much less than a dollar. For example, in the dealings with Cutler, Symmes and the state of Pennsylvania, a deduction of 33⅓ per cent was made to offset worthless land included within the boundaries. This was not altogether unreasonable, since a tract of a million acres taken as an entirety was on a different basis from sales of a section, or even a township, which would in most cases be inspected individually, thus giving an opportunity to reject undesirable tracts. Of much more importance than the reduction of one-third of the price was the privilege allowed of presenting evidences of the public debt in payment. Such paper was so depreciated that the actual price, in hard money, received for the land was sometimes less than a tenth of a dollar.

In the law of 1796 the minimum price was set at two dollars per acre, was left at the same figure in the law of 1800, and so remained the basis of transaction till 1820.

In setting the price in 1796 at two dollars Congress made a bold move, since much state land was selling for from thirty cents to a dollar an acre. Congress, however, was determined to set a figure that would at one stroke shut out speculators and increase the revenue.[58] This move was made for the West, not by it. There was no organized opposition to the two dollar minimum; the plan was clearly a revenue plan primarily. As already noted, the demand for a reduction in the price came promptly and persistently from the frontier, but just as promptly the petitions were refused. A question, destined later to occupy front rank, that of graduation of the price to fit the quality of the land, had received attention in 1790.[59] In this discussion the merits and demerits of the price graded to fit the varying qualities of the land received as keen notice as the same subject brought out half a century later, but the consensus of opinion was that a fixed price was preferable because simpler, and because the

[58] *Ann. of Cong.*, 8 Cong., 2 Sess., p. 1585.
[59] *Ibid*, 4 Cong., 2 Sess., App., p. 2907; also, 1 Cong., 2 Sess., p. 1834.

poorer land would rise in value as soon as adjacent tracts were improved. Thus was shown an appreciation of the principle of the unearned increment, and a feeling that it might as well accrue to the government.

In a very real sense the two dollar minimum, like the earlier minimum of one dollar, was only nominal, since evidences of the public debt were receivable on terms such that the land cost was reduced to a dollar and a half,[60] while the direct cash payment was but one dollar eighty-four cents in the first years of the law, and but one dollar sixty-four cents after 1804.

It was feared that a lower price would stimulate too far the emigration from the older states; also that to reduce the price of government land would injure the private land owner by bringing the price of his land down. Just why this should be the case while the privately owned land was already selling at half the price of government land does not appear.[61] Mr. Gallatin had been in favor of a small reduction in connection with a cash system, but believed a great lowering of the price would throw the land "into the hands of a few individuals," and "prevent that gradual and equal distribution of property, which is the result of the present system." But he continues: "To reduce it only to what may be considered as the market price which actual settlers give for small tracts in similar situations, would only satisfy the demand for land created by the existing population, and without promoting migrations or speculations on a large scale, would increase the receipts in the Treasury."[62]   The price had clearly prevented sales to a considerable extent, for the cheaper land above referred to, sold also on credit, had attracted buyers. Mr. Lyon of Kentucky, speaking of debts due the government for land, doubted whether a single member of Congress had ever bought land of the government,—he had not, because he was able to buy elsewhere

[60] Ann. of Cong., 8 Cong., 2 Sess., p. 1586.
[61] Ibid, 11 Cong., Part II, p. 2003.
[62] Ibid, 8 Cong., 2 Sess., p. 1586.

on better terms, other land, just as good, being in the market at a dollar an acre. This was in 1810.[63] In his own state land had been selling at thirty to sixty cents an acre, and was even granted free of charge in some cases.[64] In fact, for many years the government was obliged in all its land sales to compete against the states which had land of their own on the market. Massachusetts, for example, sold, between the years 1783 and 1821, nearly 5,000,000 acres of land at about seventeen cents an acre.[65] Much of this was not desirable agricultural land, but a similar situation was found in the West, where the quality of land offered by the states was not different from the government land. Such was the case in the military tracts and the Connecticut Reserve.[66]

On the frontier the sentiment in favor of cheaper land never abated. In 1812 a petition reached Congress from a company of men styling themselves the "True American Society." They complained that they were poor and suffering, and that thousands of acres of land, the property of the United States, were lying unoccupied, and that they considered every man entitled "by nature to a portion of the soil of the country." Here was a proposal to reduce the price to nothing. The petition was referred to a committee and was not afterward heard of.[67] Two years later a petition signed by over seven hundred men from the same section asked that land be sold at twelve and a half cents an acre. During these years the auction price of land was a mere trifle above the required price of two dollars. It is reported that in 1816 the average price on all land sold under the two dollar limit had averaged two dollars, ten and a half cents.[68]

[63] *Ann. of Cong.*, 11 Cong., Part II, p. 2003.
[64] M. Butler, *History of the Commonwealth of Kentucky*, pp. 258-262.
[65] *Massachusetts Senate Documents*, No. 4, p. 13.
[66] *Pub. Lands*, I, p. 167.
[67] *Ann of Cong.*, 12 Cong., 1 Sess., 1031. Mr. Morrow in presenting this petition states that the members of the "True American Society" are numerous, and are found in Illinois, Ohio and Pennsylvania. The writer has not been able to find further trace of the society.
[68] *Pub. Lands*, III, p. 149.

With the revival of business following the War of 1812 came rapid sales and higher prices for land. In Ohio, sales were brisk and for the most part in small quantities to actual settlers. In the fall of 1815 some two townships per month were being sold in each of several land districts, and for the most part in quarter-section tracts. "The main road through the state . . . had been almost literally covered with wagons moving out families." [69] The following year at Jefferson-ville, Missouri, land sold as high as thirty-two dollars per acre,[70] but the top notch was reached in Alabama when in March, 1818, wild land sold, not in a few isolated instances but quantities of it, for almost as much as it has brought in recent years. Speaking of these sales a correspondent for an Ohio paper says: "There were about 42 townships offered; and the quantity which would not bring the government price was very considerable; on the other hand, many, indeed very many places have been purchased, by the practical farmer for agricultural purposes, at rates, which although the fact may astonish our tramontane brethren, and perhaps stagger their credulity, yet afford the most convincing evidence of the unexampled prosperity of this important section of the union. From 40 to 70 dollars per acre were repeatedly paid for choice places, estimated for their intrinsic worth, calculated only for cultivation and bought by practical farmers." [71] Senator Walker of Alabama speaking of the sales said that they "seemed to have been made under a sort of delirium—the most prudent, calculating men in the country were swept away by the delusion of the moment. It was the most discreet men sometimes who gave the highest prices; he had known, for example, as high as seventy-eight dollars per acre given for land by those who bought it with the full intention themselves to cultivate it—he was satisfied himself that if the lands were now set up, they would not produce as much as had been already paid on the

[69] *Niles Register*, VII, p. 350.
[70] *Ibid*, XI, p. 107.
[71] *Western Spy* (Cincinnati), Apr. 4, 1818.

first installment," [72] *i.e.,* one-fourth the selling price. On account of these high prices which had already been paid, it was argued that relief of some kind should be accorded these purchasers before the regular price should be lowered, for "it would be found that lands would follow the government price, and would consequently fall." However, it was impossible to get any favorable action of this character. Taking the period 1800-1820 as a whole the average price at which the Ohio land sold was very close to the two dollar minimum. In Alabama it was four dollars and forty cents, but this was materially reduced by relinquishments of much land bid off at a high figure.

By an act passed in 1820 the minimum price was reduced to one dollar and twenty-five cents. In neither house was the change in price made a primary issue; it was merely a concomitant of the change from credit to cash, a further discount as it were, in favor of immediate payment. Thus the price which for a hundred years since has remained the government price "was fixed upon as a mere incident in the adjustment of a more vexatious matter." Experience had shown that a dollar and a quarter could not be too high and there were few indeed who contended that it was too low. It was stoutly maintained that the cash system with the lower price was favorable to the poor man. [73] The only serious attempt to establish a different price was embodied in an amendment providing for graduating the price to fit the quality of the land. "The motion was negatived by a large majority." [74] The West had insisted that the price of land be lowered; Congress acquiesced. [75]

Summary

The experience in land disposal under the Confederation was not looked upon as a good precedent to follow, hence it was readily

[72] *Ann. of Cong.,* 16 Cong., 1 Sess., p. 445; McMaster says that one cotton planter paid $127.00 an acre for a quarter section. IV, p. 396.
[73] *Ibid,* p. 1880.
[74] *Ibid,* p. 486.
[75] *Pub. Lands,* III, p. 365.

recognized that a change must be made. Preliminary discussions in Congress lasted through several years, the main points at issue being the size of tracts; the settlement requirements, if any; whether cash or credit was to be the basis of sales; and the place of sale, whether at the capital or in western land offices. The question of speculation received attention, and arguments against settling in large tracts presented.

In 1796 a land act was passed This act provided for the rectangular survey, the division of half of the townships into sections of 640 acres each to be sold at local land offices, the other half of the townships to be sold in quarters at the seat of government. In all cases four sections of land at the center of the township were to be reserved. One twentieth of the price, two dollars per acre, was to be paid in cash, and credit of varying lengths of time allowed on the balance, the final payment to be made in one year. The plan met with little success.

Another land bill was passed in 1800. In this act the frontiersmen had a voice. Land was to be sold at local land offices, mainly in half section tracts at a minimum of two dollars per acre. The most prominent feature of this act was the credit provision by which the purchaser was required to pay a fourth down with four annual installments for the balance. The act was not satisfactory to most people concerned. A report by Gallatin was made the basis of a revision in 1804. Interest, which had been charged previously was now not to be charged until payments became delinquent; the size of the tract offered was again reduced.

CHAPTER V

THE CREDIT SYSTEM

THE CREDIT FEATURES OF THE ACTS OF 1796, 1800, AND 1804 SUMMARIZED

To counteract the effects of the increase in price of lands provided in the act of 1796 the same law, as noted above, extended a limited amount of credit to purchasers. This marks the beginning of a credit system of land sales which, with various changes, lasted until 1820. According to the law of 1796 one half the purchase price was to be paid within thirty days after sale and the remainder by the end of twelve months. A discount of ten per cent for cash was allowed. It was quite evident to most Congressmen that the average settler could not pay cash at two dollars per acre for a whole section of land, and this was the minimum amount that could be bought.

It was soon discovered that lands were not selling as rapidly as had been expected. The new two-dollar minimum price, the minimum size of tract of 640 acres, and the limited credit offered by the federal government seemed to have swelled the land sales, not of federal land, but of that of states and private companies. This situation was indicated in 1797 by the report of a committee in Congress, appointed "to inquire into the progress of the sales of land." [1] The act was given further trial yet it proved so unsatisfactory that in 1800 it was amended and superseded by the act of May 10 of that year.

According to the law of 1800, the credit allowed the settler

[1] *Pub. Lands,* I, p. 73.

was much more liberal,—one-fourth within forty days and another fourth within two years from date of the sale and all to be paid within four years after sale.[2] The indebtedness thus incurred bore interest at 6 per cent from the date of sale. Discounts were allowed for prompt payment, whereas in case any installment with interest was not paid within one year after the last installment was due, the land was again offered at auction for a sum not less than the amount still due plus the expenses of the sale. Any surplus above this price went to the original purchaser. If no bids were made the lands reverted to the United States to be resold in the regular manner.

A law passed in 1803 applying to lands acquired from Georgia in 1802 contained the same provisions with regard to credit. Both the act of 1800 and that of 1803 made the further concession to the settler of reducing the size of tract from 640 to 320 acres.

In the preëmption acts of 1801 and 1803 some concessions were made to persons who had purchased lands from Symmes,[3] but which were not located within his grant. The main concession was that no interest would be charged on deferred payments until they became due. As a result of this legislation two systems were in operation in Ohio. If a cash payment were made according to one, the price, with the discount deducted, amounted to $1.84 per acre, and according to the other $1.64 per acre. This caused a demand for a revision of the act of 1800 in this respect. In 1804 an act providing for the sale of land in the Indiana Territory and "for other purposes" was passed. Under the head of "other purposes" the law of 1800 was amended so that if cash payment were made the actual purchase price would amount in all cases to $1.64 per acre. We see in this act one of the first indications of favoring the purchasers of land at the expense of the treasury. Another notable gain

---

[2] *U. S. Stat. at Large,* II, p. 74. If such lands were not paid for within five years after sale they were to be resold.
[3] *Pub. Lands,* I, pp. 75, 128.

for the settlers was the provision for the sale of quarter sections rather than half sections.[4]

So much for the legislation which created the credit system of land sales. However, before going into the details of the administration of this system it is well to take notice of the two, three and five per cent fund grants made to the public land states beginning with Ohio in 1803. The policy of making such grants was in close relation and, in part, an outgrowth of the credit system. Congress, being anxious to hasten land sales, sought to relieve the burden of purchasers by obtaining tax exemption from the states. It was argued by Congressmen that, since under the credit system the deed to the land was really not handed over to the settler until the end of his four year credit period,[5] the state could not force him to pay taxes by selling the land which in reality still belonged to the United States.[6] Since the right of the state to sell land for taxes is the only assurance that collections can and will be made the proposed interpretation on the part of the federal government meant that purchasers on credit would be exempt from a state land tax until the patent was issued.

The Three and Five Per Cent Fund Grants

It was self-evident that the state would not relish the idea of having within its borders a group of citizens possessing property and at the same time paying nothing to the support of the state. As an offset to this condition, Congress voted to give to Ohio three per cent of the net receipts from the sales of public lands, stipulating that the lands sold by the United States were to be free from state and local taxes for a period of five years; and that the money so paid to the state was to be used in road building and for no other purpose.[7]

---

[4] This quarter-section provision did not apply to territory south of the Ohio.
[5] *U. S. Stat. at Large*, II, p. 74.
[6] *Ann. of Cong.*, 7 Cong., 1 Sess., p. 1100.
[7] *U. S. Stat. at Large*, II, p. 226.

In 1811 Louisiana was admitted under the same terms, essentially, but with the added requirement that lands of non-resident citizens should never be taxed higher than those of the resident citizens of the state. This seems to have been a stroke in favor of speculators, the belief no doubt being that a contrary policy would discourage the sale of public lands. The same requirement respecting taxation was imposed on seventeen states.[8]

When Indiana was admitted the same specifications were laid down with the exceptions that five per cent of receipts from sales of government land was granted and that the state was directed to expend three-fifths of the money for roads and canals, while two-fifths was to be expended under direction of Congress for a road to the state.[9] Mississippi in 1817, Alabama in 1819, and Missouri in 1820 were admitted with almost exactly the same conditions and requirements as Indiana. The amount of the two per cent funds out of which Congress was to build roads to the states within which the land was sold equalled $1,343,000, but a sum more than twice as great was expended in national highways leading from Maryland to Ohio, Indiana, Illinois, and Missouri. Thus these states really received directly but three per cent of the net proceeds of the public lands within their borders.[10]

The state of Illinois[11] received the same treatment as Indiana, except that the expenditures were to be two-fifths for making a road to the state and three-fifths for educational purposes.

The grant of five per cent has been made to all the states admitted in recent years. There has, however, been a considerable change in the stipulations as to the use to be made of the funds. Kansas was allowed to use the money for

---

[8] Louisiana, Iowa, Illinois, Alabama, Mississippi, Missouri, Michigan, Arkansas, Wisconsin, Minnesota, Oregon, Nebraska, Colorado, Utah, Arizona, New Mexico, Nevada. See *Sen. Reports,* 46 Cong., 2 Sess., No. 121; for Colorado, Utah, Arizona and New Mexico, see enabling acts.

[9] *U. S. Stat. at Large,* III, p. 290.

[10] *House Misc. Doc.,* 30 Cong., 2 Sess., No. 19.

[11] *U. S. Stat. at Large,* III, p. 430.

"roads, internal improvements, or for other purposes."[12] Colorado for "internal improvements." In all the more recently created states the five per cent has been given with the requirement that the money so obtained be kept as a permanent common school fund, the interest only to be spent. To June 30, 1922, the total amount paid to the states, under these provisions, was $16,883,661.75.[13]

The Taxation of Land Sold on Credit

By 1825, the conditions having changed, Congress took up anew the question of exemption from taxation of lands sold by the United States. Five years had elapsed since the last sales of land on credit. The states were beginning to demur against the exemptions, and a bill was introduced in Congress repealing the exemption provisions.[14] The bill was lost, although the Committee on Public Lands to which the subject was referred, brought in a favorable report.[15] The Committee expressed a belief that in the past the exemption had promoted sales and made the collections on time sales easier. Neither of these reasons for continuing the plan longer existed. An interesting observation bearing on taxation was made: "In most of the new states with the greatest abundance of real estate, there is very little personal property, and that little requires to be fostered; the consequence of this has been, and must continue to be, that the revenue of their governments has been derived almost exclusively from land taxation."

Memorials continued for twenty years to come from the states asking for the right to tax land as soon as it became private property.[16] However, the years passed and nothing was done to relieve the situation, until Congress recognized the justice of the principle involved by passing an act cov-

---

[12] *U. S. Stat. at Large*, XII, p. 127.
[13] *L. O. R.*, 1923, p. 49.
[14] *Cong. Deb.*, 19 Cong., 1 Sess., pp. 802-803.
[15] *Sen. Doc.*, 29 Cong., 2 Sess., No. 16.
[16] *Pub. Lands*, VI, p. 298; *Sen. Doc.*, 29 Cong., 2 Sess., No. 16.

ering the case in 1847.[17] It had for some time been delayed by being tied to the "Graduation" bill. The Senate Committee in recommending the bill, called attention to the fact that the occasion for requiring the states to exempt federal land from taxation had passed with the credit system of sales. Some years before this several new states had been admitted to the Union. To these states had been granted the usual five per cent of receipts from land sales, but they were not required to exempt land from taxation for any period after its sale. The question of exemption of land from taxation for the five years subsequent to sale by the federal government became unimportant as time passed, since about all the land in the states so restricted was sold and the five year period was over long before these later attempts to have the restriction removed. Thus the problem solved itself.

DIFFICULTIES IN MAKING PAYMENTS

In spite of the assistance Congress had given the settlers through securing tax exemptions, they had great difficulty in keeping up their payments. The chief worry of the settler seemed to be caused by his inability to raise the original purchase price. It had been pointed out at the time of the adoption of the credit system by those opposing the plan that the laws had certain inherent tendencies that would cause trouble in the future. The predicted trouble was not long in making its appearance. In a report to the House by Gallatin in 1806 a statement was made concerning delinquent payments on Ohio land. The amounts on October 1 for the different years were as follows: $1,092,390 in 1803; $1,434,212 in 1804 and $2,094,305 in 1805. Some of this land would be forfeited in 1806 if something were not done.

Before the year 1803 petitions had begun to come in from the Northwest asking for changes in the plan of land disposal. The House Committee on Public Lands summarized these petitions and referred them to Gallatin, then

[17] *U. S. Stat. at Large,* IX, 118.

Secretary of the Treasury, for suggestions. Among other things they asked his advice as to the effect on land sales and on revenue of substituting cash sales for the credit system then prevailing. It was his opinion that all sales should be strictly cash.[18] The House Committee reported [19] in 1806 that the enforcement of the forfeiture feature of the credit law was impracticable since no neighbor of the debtor would want to bid for the property at public vendue, and that, therefore, the lands would revert to the government, encumbered by a tenant who must be evicted before resale.

The committee, however, did not feel that the credit system should be repealed. It had resulted in a great increase in the sale of land: "but by the accumulation of debts the evils which were dreaded now begin to unfold themselves, and certainly wear an unpleasant aspect." Accompanying the report was a letter from Gallatin wherein he once more recommended that a cash system be substituted for the credit system and thus put an end to the situation that was becoming worse as time passed. He feared that too great a number of debtors for public lands would create a hostile interest, which would endanger the whole value of the land.

TABLE V

OPERATION OF THE CREDIT SYSTEM FROM 1803 TO 1811 [20]

Year	Acres Sold	Due from Individuals	Arrearages
1803	199,080	$1,092,390.17	$40,218.35
1804	373,611	1,434,212.50	176,778.02
1805	619,266	6,094,305.85	384,799.11
1806	473,211	2,245,557.58	243,933.18
1807	358,372	2,265,219.92	315,312.12
1808	213,472	2,180,425.86	586,817.05
1809	231,044	2,186,186.71	886,841.92
1810	235,879	2,036,837.37	702,557.91
1811	288,930	1,970,912.91	656,603.64

This table covers sales south as well as north of the Ohio. There were no sales in the South before 1803, since the land was not acquired

[18] Pub. Lands, I, pp. 167-169.
[19] Ann. of Cong., 9 Cong., 2 Sess., p. 1033.
[20] Ann. of Cong., 1 Cong., pp. 1069, 1070; Ibid, 4 Cong., 2 Sess., pp. 2209, 2210; C. F. Emerick, The Credit System and the Public Domain, p. 2.

from Georgia until 1802, and no statements of sales were made before 1807 when all previous sales were included.

TABLE VI
SALES OF LAND SOUTH OF THE OHIO[21]

Year	Acres Sold	Due from Individuals	Arrearages
1807	74,192	$111,993.50	
1808	17,892	138,752.85	
1809	87,635	273,482.85	$36,166.88
1810	77,035	390,195.33	80,413.13
1811	81,913	474,541.23	148,190.72

REASONS FOR FAILURE OF CREDIT SYSTEM

During the years immediately following the inauguration of the credit system, times were good, money was plentiful, and the call for land was increasing. Under these conditions the system had a chance to survive, but, as already noted, the amount of arrears was steadily growing. With the advent of a financial depression nothing short of disaster could be expected. Within the next few years several forces over which the purchasers of land had no control, followed one another in a manner that absolutely blasted the hopes of many of these credit purchasers to meet their obligations. The Napoleonic Wars had made a good market in the West for all kinds of produce, considering the rude systems of transportation, but during the period between 1808 and 1812, while Jefferson's Embargo Act was in effect, trade was greatly retarded, and money became scarce, especially in the newly settled districts. The value of the exports of agricultural products from the United States in the years 1802 to 1807 amounted annually to about $30,000,000, but in 1808 it dropped to about $5,000,000.[22]

Following closely upon the Embargo Act, came the War of 1812. Many of the settlers joined the army and payments could not be expected to be made promptly under such conditions. Added to the difficulties of the land purchaser was

[21] Emerick, p. 2.
[22] E. L. Bogart, *Economic History of the United States*, p. 144.

the passage about this time of certain very lenient laws in several states in regard to the collection of debts. Many could not now collect debts on which they had counted to make land payments.

Furthermore, after the War of 1812 the country was flooded with depreciated bank notes,[23] and the government made the mistake of accepting these for payment on public land. This caused unprecedented speculation in land, and when the government decided in 1817 to accept payment in specie only, it worked a great hardship on the debtor class of settlers. Relief laws granting extensions of time seemed to be the only solution for the situation.

It was the intention of Congress when it instituted the credit system, to prevent speculation, but as a matter of fact it thus put a premium on the practice. A report by a special Senate committee in 1812 set forth very effectively the defects of the system. The committee showed a keen under-standing of the psychology of the land speculator, even the speculator who becomes at the same time a settler. He has rosy hopes concerning the ease of making subsequent pay-ments. He has failed to count in all the costs involved; has overestimated his income; and is almost sure to find him-self, when pay day arrives, without the money. Five years of his life has been squandered. He has, however, culti-vated some portion of his land and so added to its ultimate value. From the standpoint of the government the pros-pect of resale is poor, if for no other reason, because of agreements and associations among settlers whereby outsiders are not allowed to bid on land under these circumstances.[24]

In December, 1812, the House Committee on Public Lands reported that the credit system was bad and recom-mended some radical changes which were set forth as fol-lows: "that the present system cannot be continued, and the laws rigidly executed without occasionally producing

[23] Emerick, pp. 8, 9.
[24] *Pub. Lands*, II, p. 440.

great injury to the purchasers. Men are seduced by the temptation, which the credit held out to them, to extend their purchase beyond their means of making payment; the unfavorable fluctuations of commerce cannot be foreseen, and the pretty general disposition in men to anticipate the most favorable results from the produce of their labor, are the general causes of the failure of purchasers in making their payments, . . . by abolishing the credit in future sales, every subsequent purchaser would, without any liability to error, be able to calculate his means of making payment. If his purchase should not be so extensive, he will at once be secure and quiet in his possession. In the future those fertile sources of discontent and disquietude, which arise from disappointment, and from the exercise of the measures necessary to enforce the payments, as also the frequent distress, occasioned by the forfeiture of lands, on which settlements have been made, would be removed." [25] The committee recommended also that the cash price be $1.25 per acre, but it took eight years more of discouraging experience to prove the wisdom of this recommendation. The East still considered the public land as a source of revenue, and was not willing to encourage further migration to the West, since this movement threatened the serious depopulation of the older states. The Inland Navigation Committee of North Carolina in its report in 1815 says: "It is mortifying to see that thousands of rich respectable citizens are still moving west each year to be followed by thousands of poorer citizens who are literally driven away by the prospect of poverty." [26] This was a plea for internal improvements at home. Petitions from the land purchasers and recommendations from the western state legislatures came in asking for changes that would relieve the credit situation which was steadily growing worse. The Indiana,[27] Ohio,[28] and Mississippi,[29] legisla-

[25] *Pub. Lands*, II, p. 604.
[26] McMaster, IV, pp. 384, 385.
[27] *Pub. Lands*, II, p. 745.
[28] *Ibid*, p. 252.
[29] *Ibid*, p. 898.

tures sent in pleas for relief. Even the western states which in former years had practically unanimously favored credit, were now ready to vote for a change. Congress, however, was not ready to act upon the insistent recommendations, The day of reckoning was merely delayed by the passage of temporary relief laws.

The Relief Laws, 1806-1832

The last payments on lands sold in 1802 were due in 1806.[30] The next year this land, if still not completely paid for, would have to be forfeited and resold. Men acquainted with the situation in the West were doubtful as to whether or not the law could be enforced, especially with regard to settlers actually upon the land. In February, 1806, Albert Gallatin sent a communication to the House in which he stated: "I will only add that if credits shall not be allowed hereafter, some indulgence in point of time may be given to those former purchasers whose lands will otherwise be sold during the course of this year, on account of their payment not having been completed within five years of the time of purchase. Should the present system be continued, a more rigid enforcement of the law will be necessary." [31] Congress, however, did not change the credit system, but in an act of April 15, 1806, extended the time of payment to those settlers whose lands would have been forfeited within the year. The law applied to 309 persons,—actual settlers on the land,—owing the United States $229,000. The time for forfeiture was extended to October 1, 1806. The reason for this step has been shown in the above discussion. This act was a precedent for the passage of eleven more such relief laws before 1820.

The manner in which these relief laws operated can be very well illustrated by reviewing the first general law of this character passed on March 2, 1809.[32] The law applied

[30] *U. S. Stat. at Large*, II, p. 74.
[31] *Ann. of Cong.*, 9 Cong., 2 Sess., App., pp. 1032-1036.
[32] *U. S. Stat. at Large*, II, p. 533.

to all purchasers of land (not exceeding 640 acres) from the United States which had not reverted or already been resold for non-payment of purchase price, or which might have expired or would expire on or before January 1, 1810. Two years' extension of time was granted from one year after the last payment fell due. Provision was made, however, that the arrears of interest due be paid in full, and that one half of the remaining debt be paid with interest within one year after the two-year extension began and the other one half before the two-year extension ended. Failure to comply with any of these provisions would result in forfeiture and resale. This act purported to have been passed to relieve the situation created by the Embargo Act, but it really was an effort to save the credit system from collapse. As with the relief laws that followed, it is interesting to note that they were for the relief of the small purchaser, or actual settler. The large speculator presented a different problem because he could be dispossessed without awakening the resentment of the neighborhood and without imposing much suffering and injustice, since he did not usually live on the land and did not have it partially improved as did the settler.

It might appear at the first glance that relief laws came to the rescue of the settler from year to year, and that there was no reason, except the interest charges, for him to try to pay his debt. Upon a closer examination it will be found that a large number of purchasers forfeited their lands. To begin with, no relief law was passed from 1806 to 1809, so that all those whose last payments became due or whose extension of time ran out before 1809 were obliged to take their chances. Another extension applying to all actual cultivators was made in 1810, but in 1812 the relief law applied only to purchasers northwest of the Ohio, and of course did not prevent forfeitures in the Mississippi Territory. After 1812 no relief was granted to the territory northwest of the Ohio, till 1814, and even then did not apply to purchases made prior to 1809. The relief law of 1815 applied only to those who had become purchasers between

April 1, 1810, and April 1, 1811. From the passage of the law of 1815 until April, 1818, no further relief was granted northwest of the Ohio, and then only to those whose land had not before this time been forfeited for non-payment. The relief laws of 1818, 1819 and 1820 simply extended the time of forfeiture on land from time to time until it was finally extended to March 31, 1821. The Mississippi Territory was favored with more uniform extensions of time especially after 1812. The relief law of that year, as noted, applied only to settlers northwest of Ohio. The result of these laws as stated by Representative Sloan[33] of Ohio in April, 1820, was that extensions had not been granted to the same purchaser from year to year, and that in 1812 all purchasers of land prior to, and including that year, had either paid in full or forfeited their land. So in spite of the numerous relief laws, much land had been forfeited to the United States. In a large number of cases the land had not been resold but was still encumbered by the settler as a tenant. As will be shown later this resulted in a series of relief laws passed from 1820 to 1832. Up to September 30, 1819 the sum of $412,678[34] had been forfeited to the United States. Under the credit system, which ended in 1820, the gross acreage sold was 19,399,153; this, however, "was scaled down by acts of Congress, by reversions and relinquishments, so that the government parted title to 13,642,536 acres."[35]

The credit system of land sales was abolished in 1820 but this law did not provide relief for those who had purchased land on credit. Attempts were made to include a relief clause in the law but this was defeated. Purchasers of public land owed the government at that time over $21,000,-000. The problem resolved itself into the question of how to collect this amount with the minimum of forfeiture. Congress was already beginning to think of the public lands less as a source of revenue and more from the standpoint of promoting settlement. Furthermore, the West was be-

---

[33] *Ann. of Cong.*, 16 Cong., 1 Sess., pp. 1889, 1890.
[34] *Pub. Lands*, III, p. 371.
[35] Donaldson, pp. 202, 203.

coming a political force. The Democrats were in power, and since a great deal of their support came from the western and southern states it was natural that the land purchasers should receive every consideration. Congress itself began to feel that in a measure at least it was responsible for the size of the debt. The purchaser had been allowed five years credit by the act of 1800, and Congress had refused to correct this unfortunate method of sale. Moreover other factors had come in, due to acts passed by Congress which further complicated the matter.

An act very favorable to the debtors was passed on March 2, 1821. It provided for relinquishment of a portion of the land in payment of the balance due, 37½ per cent discount for prompt payment, remission of accrued interest, and for a further extension of time of from 4 to 8 years, depending upon the amount already paid.

As may readily be understood, the news of this relief act did not reach every land debtor promptly, hence the next year the time for filing an application for relief was extended to September 30, 1822, and a few months later it was again extended to September 30, 1823, in case delay was due to causes beyond their control.

It was hoped that the liberal provisions of the law of 1821 would greatly reduce the debt, and in a measure this hope was realized. By September 30, 1821, the land debt had been reduced from $21,173,489.87 on December 3, 1820, to $11,997,430.39. But after the first big reduction the decline was much slower, and on September 30, 1822, it was still $10,544,454.16.[36]

Even under the liberal terms now offered many forfeitures were taking place. Special credit had been extended under the law of 1821 to cover some 3,588,558[37] acres of land. However, still further leniency was required or some of this land must have been forfeited, consequently on February 28, 1824, a new relief law passed which allowed all persons holding certificates of further credit to file relinquishment of

[36] *Pub. Lands,* III, p. 561.
[37] *Ibid,* p. 549.

part of the land before April 10, 1825, or in case of complete payment before that date a reduction was allowed of 37½ per cent on the balance due. This law resulted in a reduction of the land debt to the extent of $10,221,274, so that on June 30, 1825, only $6,322,766 [38] remained. In 1826 the terms of the act of 1824 were reënacted and extended to July 4, 1827. Permission was given those whose lands had been forfeited since 1820 to reënter them, if they had not been resold, upon paying the amount due with 37½ per cent discount exclusive of all interest due on the same. Again on March 21, 1828, an extension of time to July 4, 1829, was made.

Since the law of 1828 did not apply to debtors taking advantage of certificates of further credit, Congress passed an act March 31, 1830, allowing a preëmption to such purchasers up to July 4, 1831, to purchase their land at the minimum price of $1.25 per acre above what had been previously paid, the sum not to exceed $3.50 per acre. Or, they might obtain scrip with which they could locate land offered for sale within their respective states or territories. Cash payments of balances due were accepted at 37½ per cent discount.

Finally, on July 9, 1832, the last relief law was passed. It applied to all purchasers who had taken advantage of the extension laws of 1821 to 1828. These purchasers could draw scrip for the amount paid down on any land which had been forfeited, the scrip to be used in exchange for lands within the state or territory in which it was issued.

At last, twelve years after credit sales were abolished, the whole debt on public lands was liquidated. It was done in this way: 4,602,573 acres were relinquished, liquidating seventy per cent of the debt; cash and discounts were received amounting to fifteen and two-tenths per cent; abatements, six and four-tenths per cent; [39] and the remainder in one or another of the following ways: [40] (1) cancellation of indebtedness on land upon which certificates for forfeitures were

[38] *Pub. Lands,* IV, p. 795.
[39] *Ibid,* VI, p. 456; for statement of balance due from purchase prior to July 1, 1920, see *Ibid,* IV, p. 795.
[40] Emerick, p. 14.

issued; (2) cash incidental to abatement; (3) cash without discount on installments.[41]

THE REPEAL OF THE CREDIT LAWS

On December 31, 1820, as already stated, the United States was creditor to individual purchasers of lands to the amount of $21,000,000.[42] Almost annually, for a decade or more, the committee on public lands had reported in favor of discontinuing the credit system. The only people in favor of the continuance of it were those who expected to buy land on the terms provided for, who, mistakenly, thought the credit system worked for the benefit of the poor settler.

Both the Northwest and Southwest required a change. Especially in the Southwest where land speculation had reached its greatest height was there need of relief from the obligations incurred. The auction system, mushroom banks, and the prospects of great gain in cotton culture by use of slaves, combined to induce men to make extravagant offers. The sale of land during the four years preceding 1820 increased by leaps and bounds. Debts on public land were increasing rapidly as were also the arrears which resulted in many forfeitures. During the four years from 1815 to 1818, inclusive, the amount due the government increased from $3,042,613.89 to $16,794,795.14.[44] The panic of 1819 found the land debtors, therefore, in bad circumstances. The price of produce fell, wheat selling for only 20 cents a bushel in Kentucky. At Pittsburg flour was one dollar per barrel, and sheep were one dollar per head.[45] The price of cotton fell more than fifty per cent.[46] In Alabama, where cotton was the sole cash crop, it meant ruin, "many banks, too tedious to mention, [shut] up shop, leaving the little circle in which their

---

[41] Pub. Lands, VI, p. 11.
[42] Ibid, III, p. 561.
[43] Ann. of Cong., 16 Cong., 1 Sess., pp. 445, 446.
[44] American State Papers, Finance, III, p. 718.
[45] W. G. Sumner, History of American Currency, p. 82.
[46] Pub. Lands, IV, 805.

notes were received in a state of wonderment that a bank should break. . . . Begotten in iniquity, they died in corruption." [47] All this was disastrous to the land debtors. In February, 1819, the Senate Committee on Public Lands brought in a report showing unusual care and thought. [48] Senator Morrow, of Ohio, who had been concerned with the public land question ever since Ohio became a state, was chairman. The men with one exception were from the West and of course were vitally interested in the settlers' problems. The committee reviewed the workings of the credit system and recommended that it be abolished and that a new system founded on a cash basis be substituted.

According to the recommendations, a bill was introduced in 1819 which proposed to abolish credit and reduce the size of tracts offered to 80 acres. The minimum price was reduced to a dollar and a half an acre. There was a spirited debate over the bill, the West favoring the price reduction, the East opposing it. Some western Senators wanted a preëmption clause in the bill, even so it passed the Senate without any important change, but was lost in the House, due to the lateness of the time at which it arrived. A year later another bill providing cash payments in place of the credit system was introduced in the Senate. The same concessions and amendments were sought as were debated the previous year. The West wanted a liberal treatment of the settlers, but was not unanimous as to substituting the cash payments for the credit system. In the House the western states, as Indiana, Illinois and Mississippi, were against the cash payments, but Ohio with longer experience voted solidly for the change, while the votes of Kentucky and Tennessee were about equally divided. Therefore, on April 2, 1820, was passed the most important piece of land legislation since the passing of the Ordinance of 1785. In short, the new law provided for the sale of tracts as small as 80 acres at a cash payment of $1.25 per acre. So ended the ill-starred system of selling government land on time.

[47] *Niles Register*, XVIII, p. 364.
[48] *Ann. of Cong.*, 15 Cong., 2 Sess., p. 216.

The sales under the credit system, from the opening of the land offices in the territory northwest of the Ohio to June 30, 1820, were as follows:[49]

TABLE VII

SALES BY STATES FROM OPENING OF LOCAL LAND OFFICES TO JUNE 30, 1820

Location	Acres	Amount
Ohio	8,848,152.31	$17,226,186.95
Indiana	2,490,736.17	5,137,350.20
Illinois	1,593,347.53	3,227,805.20
Missouri	1,249,113.91	3,349,465.70
Alabama	3,957,281.00	16,182,147.67
Mississippi	1,147,988.10	2,297,652.91
Louisiana	45,277.00	90,554.00
Michigan	67,362.02	178,400.46
Total	19,399,158.04	$47,689,563.09

SUMMARY

The credit system had been in operation for the twenty-four years from 1796 to 1820. Very little land was sold before 1800. From that time on a few hundred thousand acres were sold each year, reaching the highest figure before the War of 1812 of 619,000 acres in 1805. Not much was sold during the early part of the war. In 1814, over a million acres were sold, after which date not less than that amount was disposed of annually until the end of the period. The record sale was made the last year of the credit system, 1819, when over 5,000,000 acres were sold. Nearly half of the sales under the credit system were made in Ohio, the next largest, not half as great, was made in Alabama. During the period of the credit system a total of 19,339,158 acres had been sold, but due to reversions only 13,649,641.10[50] acres had passed from the hands of the government. The land had sold for $47,689,563 of which only $27,663,964[51] had been received. Between four and five hundred thousand dollars had been forfeited by purchasers where land had reverted to the government.

Starting with a debt due from purchasers of over $21,000,000 in 1820, it took twelve years, and eleven separate relief laws, to bring the matter to a successful conclusion. Land speculation reached its height in Alabama and Mississippi and within these states one-half of the debt of 1820 was due. Under the relief laws most of the

[49] Donaldson, p. 203.
[50] Pub. Lands, VIII, p. 424.
[51] Ibid.

relinquishments occurred, as could be expected, in Alabama where the selling price had gone to such heights. In Ohio most debts were met by paying cash, taking advantage of the 37½ per cent discount, thus showing that the land was worth the selling price and that some money was to be had. In Missouri and Illinois a large proportion was reliquished.

The credit system had proved a failure. It had not been a source of great revenue for the treasury, it had not promoted the interests of the settlers, and it had not prevented speculation. It had created a large class of land holders so hopelessly in debt to the government that it took the government twelve full years to clear away the wreckage of the credit system.

The following table shows the amount of land sold and the amount received for the same before June 30, 1800, and amounts from June 30, 1800 to June 30, 1820, including reversions and relinquishments. [52]

TABLE VIII

SALES AND RECEIPTS TO JUNE 30, 1820

Year	Acres	Dollars
Prior to opening of land office	1,281,860.00	$1,050,085.43
1800	67,750.93	135,501.86
1801	497,939.36	1,031,893.26
1802	271,080.77	532.160.74
1803	174,156.04	349,292.18
1804	398,155.99	817,270.50
1805	581,971.91	1,186,562.09
1806	506,018.67	1,053,792.34
1807	320,945.79	659,709.17
1808	209,167.34	490,080.35
1809	275,004.09	605,970.20
1810	285,795.55	607,867.77
1811	575,067.18	1,216,447.28
1812	386,077.36	829,404.10
1813	505,647.82	1,066,372.33
1814	1,176,141.67	2,462,914.88
1815	1,306,368.33	2,713,414.36
1816	1,742,523.63	3,692,738.39
1817	1,886,163.96	4,478,820.40
1818	3,491,014.79	13,122,836.41
1819	2,968,390.80	8,238,309.21
June 30, 1820	491,916.46	1,348,119.84
Total	19,399,158.04	$47,689,563.09

[52] *Sen. Doc.*, 27 Cong., 3 Sess., No. 246, p. 6.

CHAPTER VI

THE CASH SALES SYSTEM AFTER 1820

The act of 1820 was a very simple one, but nevertheless, very significant. In the first place, it freed the future purchaser from the evils of the credit system; secondly, it reduced the minimum price to $1.25 and, thirdly, it retained the eighty-acre minimum size of farm offered. [1] Thus it was a return to a low minimum price and the cash sales system of the Ordinance of 1785, but was a great improvement over the system established in 1785 in that tracts of eighty acres instead of a minimum of 640 acres were offered. After all, a farm was what the settler wanted and eighty acres served the purpose in many cases about as well as a larger tract. In any case the eighty-acre tract was the minimum, though as many such tracts might be bought as were desired. The eighty-acre farm could now be had for $100 cash, while under the Ordinance of 1785 a tract of 640 acres cost a little over $400 cash, and under the acts of 1796 and 1800 the settler paid eighty dollars as one of four installments, or $320 for 160 acres.

Extent and Geographical Distribution of Sales

With the advent of the new system sales fell off greatly. This was due not to the system, but to the financial conditions following the crisis of 1819. In 1820 only about three hundred thousand acres were sold. Not until 1829 was the million mark, so common from 1814 to 1819, again reached. From 1829 to 1832 the annual amount disposed of grew steadily and rapidly but failed to reach the figure of 1819.

[1] The eighty-acre minimum, according to a law passed in 1817, applied to only certain specified sections of the township.

Then came the boom period just preceding the crash of 1837. During the four years from 1834 to 1837, inclusive, over forty-two million acres were sold, the peak of sales being reached in 1836 when twenty million acres of land passed from the Government into private hands.

Although the amount of land sold fell off very greatly after the crisis of 1837, the average for the four years, 1838-1841 inclusive was approximately three million acres. Of the 12,000,000 acres, about two-fifths were sold in two states, Illinois and Missouri. From July 1, 1820, to September 30, 1842, 74,755,000 acres, an area almost equal in extent to the combined areas of Michigan and Wisconsin, were sold.[2] Approximately 30,478,000 acres of this land were sold in the three states of Ohio, Illinois and Indiana; 20,579,000 acres in Mississippi, Alabama and Louisiana; 9,184,000 in Michigan; 7,639,000 in Missouri,—just coming into prominence at the opening of the period; and 1,252,000 acres in Iowa,—just coming into prominence at the close of the period.[3]

The table on page 103 shows the net quantity of land sold and the amount paid for it, after deducting reversions and relinquishments, from the earliest period of sales to June 30, 1820; also acres sold and amount received for it from July 1, 1820, to September 30, 1842.[4]

In almost no case did the price paid appreciably exceed the $1.25 minimum on any considerable acreage, though in many exceptional instances an eighty-acre tract or a quarter-section brought ten, twenty or even thirty dollars per acre. The average price for the period was approximately $1.28 per acre, or three cents per acre more than the minimum.[5] The amount of money received during this period was $95,351,-000.[6] This was over 11 per cent of the total federal revenues. For the year 1835 alone the land office receipts

[2] Sen. Doc., 27 Cong., 3 Sess., No. 246.
[3] Ibid, p. 10.
[4] Ibid.
[5] Ibid.
[6] Ibid.

TABLE IX

SALES AND RECEIPTS 1796 TO 1841

Year	Acres	Dollars
Net sales 1796 to June 30, 1820......	13,647,536.19	$27,900,379.29
From July 1, 1820...................	312,147.52	435,078.79
1821...................	782,459.39	1,123,392.52
1822...................	709,997.68	908,817.25
1823...................	652,093.85	847,607.99
1824...................	737,048.40	947,086.67
1825...................	998,985.33	1,392,324.55
1826...................	848,082.26	1,128,617.27
1827...................	926,727.76	1,318,005.36
1828...................	965,600.36	1,221,357.99
1829...................	1,244,860.01	1,572,863.54
1830...................	1,929,733.79	2,433,432.94
1831...................	2,777,856.55	3,557,023.76
1832...................	2,462,342.16	3,115,376.09
1833...................	3,856,227.56	4,972,284.84
1834...................	4,658,218.71	6,099,981.04
1835...................	12,564,478.85	15,999,804.11
1836...................	20,074,870.92	25,167,833.06
1837...................	5,601,103.12	7,007,523.04
1838...................	3,414,907.42	4,305,564.64
1839...................	4,976,382.87	6,464,556.78
1840...................	2,236,889.74	2,789,637.53
1841...................	1,164,796.11	1,463,364.06
Grand Total to 1842.............	87,538,346.88	$122,172,013.11

exceeded custom house receipts by a small margin. Although cash sales have continued even to the present the importance of the system was greatly modified by the passages of the general Preëmption Act of 1841 and subsequent acts favoring the settlers, the Homestead Act of 1862 nearly supplanting the sales system.

DECREASED SALES FROM 1841 TO 1862

Since the Land Office made no distinction in its reports between the regular cash sales and the sales under the Preemption Act, the total annual sales reported include both. Even though sales were greatly below the figures of the decade preceding 1841 they remained above the million-acre mark until the passage of the Homestead Act in 1862. During the first few years following 1841 no pronounced change occurred in the amount of land sold or in the prices received for it. There was a gradual increase from but little over a million acres in 1841 to two and a half million in 1847, followed by a decrease back almost to the million mark in 1853, just before the passage of the Graduation Act. No important change occurred in the price, and none was to have been expected. True the Preëmption Act made it certain that a great deal of land would sell at the minimum price, but that was the usual price, and had been for years previously.

Speculation was presumably given a body blow by the Preëmption Act, yet great quantities of land were sold during the fifties to speculators.[7]

With the passage of the Graduation Act of 1854, which provided for the sale of certain lands for less than the old minimum of $1.25, sales ran up very considerably. In the first place, there was great demand for all types of land due to the prosperity of the period; secondly, large areas could be bought for less than half the original minimum. Thus, in the fiscal year ending June 30, 1855, 7,009,050.34 acres were sold for $1.25 or more per acre, while 8,720,474.54 acres were sold at an average of approximately twenty-seven cents, making a total amount of more than fifteen million acres sold during the year. The next year, while the sales were much less, 5,230,584.50 acres were sold at $1.25 or more, and 3,997,294.48 acres at about forty cents.[8]

Beginning with 1857, when the sales fell off over 50 per cent as compared with the previous year, there was a decrease each year till the passage of the Homestead Act of 1862. Thus, during the fiscal year ending June 30, 1857, only 1,622,729.93 acres were sold at $1.25 or more per acre, and 2,520,014.55 acres were disposed of at about $.40 per acre.

[7] See chapters on Speculation and Graduation of the Price of Land.
[8] *L. O. R.*, 1855 and 1856.

By 1860 the acreage sold at $1.25 or more was cut to 601,-159.05, while that sold on the graduated scale was increased to 2,860,044.61 acres, the average price per acre for the latter being reduced to about $.33. For 1861 the acreage for both types of land sales was cut to 380,527.21 and 1,085,076.36, respectively. This decrease from 1857 to 1861 can be accounted for in part by the hasty disappearance of lands which could be bought at a figure below $1.25, and in part by the fact that it seemed more and more probable that Congress would soon pass a law providing homesteads for settlers free of charge. Sentiment had almost entirely changed since the early part of the century and the public domain was no longer looked upon as a source of revenue but as a place to establish homes for homeless citizens. The panic of 1857 was no doubt an important factor in the decline in land sales. However, the failure to recover within the next few years would suggest that the causes noted were of more fundamental importance.

The table on page 106 shows the total number of acres of public lands sold per year from 1842 to 1862, inclusive. [9]

METHODS OF SALE

Almost from the first it was the belief of Congress that the most feasible and equitable way of putting land on the market was by auction sales. Under the direction of Congress land was "proclaimed" by the President for sale. Notwithstanding a few spectacular exceptions the auction method failed of its main purpose, which was to raise prices above the minimum.

It was provided by the Act of 1796 that public land should be sold at auction, [10] the lowest acceptable bid being fixed by the provision of a minimum price. The plan was continued under the several subsequent acts providing for the sale of land until after the passage of the Homestead Act in 1862. This method of offering land was not an innovation on the

[9] A. B. Hart, *Practical Essays on American Government*, p. 257.
[10] The Ordinance of 1785 also had provided for sale by auction.

TABLE X

SALES AND RECEIPTS, 1842 TO 1862

Year	Acres	Dollars
1842	1,129,218	$1,417,972
1843	1,605,264	2,016,044
1844	1,754,763	2,207,678
1845	1,843,527	2,470,303
1846	2,263,731	665,248
1847	2,521,306	3,296,404
1848	1,887,553	2,621,615
1849	1,329,903	1,756,890
1850	1,405,839	1,778,151
1851	1,846,847	2,370,947
1852	1,553,071	1,975,658
1853	1,083,495	1,804,653
1854	7,035,735	9,285,534
1855	15,729,525	11,485,385
1856	9,227,879	8,903,064
1857	4,142,744	3,471,523
1858	3,804,908	2,116,768
1859	3,961,581	1,628,187
1860	3,461,204	1,843,630
1861	1,465,604	884,887
1862	144,850	125,048
Total	69,198,547	$64,125,589

part of the federal government, but had been in use by the states. In the state of New York the law provided that state land should be sold in quarter-township lots at auction. The surveyor general was required to advertise land from thirty to forty days by publication in at least three newspapers of the state and to offer for sale at public vendue and "strike off to the highest bidder" the lands so advertised. [11]

During the period of regular auction sales the land was surveyed, and under the general direction of Congress proclaimed for sale by the President. These proclamations were issued through the General Land Office, and were required to be "advertised" i. e., published, not less than three months nor

---

[11] *Laws of New York*, 1778-1797, 2nd Ed., pp. 280, 281.

more than six months before the date set for the opening of the sales. [12] This exact requirement came into vogue in 1834. Previously to that time there had been various regulations.

Under the cash system, as under the credit system, the land was sold at auction to the highest bidder, the minimum bid conforming to the new price of $1.25, or twice that amount in case of "double minimum," in place of the $2.00 minimum of the preceding twenty years. Each auction sale was to be kept open for a period of two weeks, during which time all of the land was offered, providing bidders appeared. Land not sold the first time it was offered could be offered again in case any bidder wished an opportunity to bid on it. After the auction period had passed, the land remaining unsold was kept on sale indefinitely at the minimum price.

Not much could be said in favor of the auction system of sales. It was a legacy handed down from the time when the public domain was viewed as a source of revenue. It had been hoped that it would result in higher prices and more ready sales than could be effected under the system of private entry. It also carried the appearance of fairness, but the results were disappointing. The cost of selling at auction was a little higher than at private sale on account of the employment of an auctioneer and a special clerk. The results in the form of higher prices were trifling, the three cents or such a matter, obtained over the minimum price not compensating for the extra expense entailed. [13]

The auction system of selling land was not in favor with the people of the West, especially of the Southwest. Alabama was continually remonstrating against it. [14] The petition of the legislature in 1832 is a fair sample. They say: "Your memorialists would again press upon the consideration of Congress the propriety of abandoning the present mode of disposing of the public lands at auction. This system is believed not to be beneficial to the government, and, in practice,

[12] U. S. Stat. at Large, IV, p. 702.
[13] Cong. Globe, 26 Cong., 2 Sess., App., p. 19.
[14] Pub. Lands, VI, 12, p. 657.

is found to operate injuriously and oppressively upon the purchasers." [15] Believing that the auction was especially favorable to the buyer of large tracts for speculation, but detrimental to the buyer of a small piece of land for cultivation, it was proposed by Senator Walker, of Mississippi, to change the land laws so as to let actual settlers bid at auction for tracts of limited size, but to exclude from such bidding the buyer who wished larger tracts or who could not give evidence that he intended to reside on the land. [16] By this means, it was believed that the government would receive the maximum price the settler could afford to pay and, at the same time, avoid a repetition of the evils of speculation experienced in 1836 and following. The bill did not pass.

The makers of the land laws expected competition to be free and untrammelled among purchasers, thereby guaranteeing the highest price which any buyer would pay. But there were interferences with this ideal operation of competition before any considerable quantity of land had been sold. An example of such action is related in connection with the sales of land in Alabama in 1819. About forty speculators, presumably the whole number present, agreed among themselves not to bid over the minimum price for any land offered at the Cahaba district sale. They bought two townships at that figure when the register of the office decided to stop the sales. "We presume," said the writer describing the affair, "that the gentlemen speculators formed their plans on the commonly received principle that the public is a goose, and that while its enchanting plumage offered so many temptations to pluck a few feathers, no other danger was to be apprehended than that of being hissed at!" [17]

A land sale in pioneer days was by no means an uneventful affair. Since it was held on the frontier, it was almost of necessity in a small town where hotel accommodations were inadequate for the occasion, and where land was the one

[15] *Pub. Lands,* VI, p. 12, p. 384.
[16] *Cong. Globe,* 24 Cong., 2 Sess., App., p. 118 *et seq.*
[17] *Niles Register,* XVI, p. 192.

abundant commodity. The abundance precluded the higher price which had been coveted by the government, or rather the abundance of land and the temper of the settlers together made bidding above the minimum price illogical and well-nigh improbable. The scene on one of these occasions is pictured by a western editor:

"Since the last issue of the *Democrat,* a great excitement has prevailed throughout our town. At 6 o'clock, Saturday evening, many of our prominent citizens seated themselves at the door of the Land Office, that they might secure, in season, the door for the Monday morning following. Before break of day on Sunday morning, some fifty had gathered upon the steps and registered their names in a book. This little band continued to hold its own till afternoon, when many more were added. Evening came, and still larger numbers gathered. During the day, however, the speculators had been laboring to enforce the number system, which gave each man (settlers excepted) an opportunity of registering his chance to enter the Land Office and enter two quarter-sections of land.

"Outsiders, finding themselves thwarted on every hand, resolved to make one general rally, and if possible, crowd those at the door up so hard that they would yield their positions. At one time scores would rush up against them in front, then on the sides, then upon the front and side at the same time.

"These operations were continued, and were for the most part unsuccessful, from about five till nearly eight A.M., when more harsh means were used. We passed the office at about seven, and saw many who were nearly exhausted from fatigue, having stood upon their feet thirty-six hours. A constant agitation and clamor was kept up by the crowd on the outside, and a continual pushing inside, until many were so crushed that they fainted, and were thought to be dying.

"Window panes were broken out from a tier of lights above the door, and several buckets of water thrown upon the fainting ones below. The Register, seeing many were likely to be killed, and others badly injured, went upon the roof of the building, and declared that none who pushed or crowded should be served that day. This served to produce the desired effect upon many; others were so much wrought up that they almost felt desperate.

"At 9 o'clock the door opened, and many fell prostrate and nearly helpless upon the floor. To sum the matter in brief, we have never seen a more distracted and desperate set of men than were about that office. All were armed, and resolved to defend themselves to the last. Mr. E. M. Downs of this place had a leg broken; a gentleman from Ohio had some two or three of his ribs broken, besides a large number of persons who were badly injured, but were fortunate enough to have no limbs broken." [18]

After the passage of the Homestead Act in 1862 which provided homesteads of 160 acres free of charge, it was taken for granted that sales in a large way were to cease, and as a result the amounts sold, independent of the preëmption law, at once fell to an insignificant figure. Referring to the acts pertaining to settlement as a condition of obtaining title to land, the Commissioner of the General Land Office said: "This policy, thus enlarged, indicates the design of Congress not to look to the public lands as a source of direct revenue, but, rather, by encouraging actual settlement and important works of internal improvement, to quicken the settlement of the country, and, by increasing individual wealth, secure national riches and prosperity. The result is, that for the year ending June 30, 1863, the aggregate cash sales amounted to 91,354.10 acres and $136,077.95." [19] Whereas, the cash sales for 1835 and 1836 had averaged sixteen millions of acres per year.

In 1868 a resolution passed the House concerning the sale of agricultural lands, and although it was not enacted into law

[18] Dubuque (Iowa) *Daily Republican*, June 19, 1857.
[19] *L. O. R.*, 1863, p. 3.

until twenty-three years later, it apparently had virtually the same effect as though such had been done. The resolution reads: "Resolved, That in order to carry into full and complete effect the spirit and policy of the preëmption and homestead laws of the United States, the further sale of the agricultural public lands ought to be prohibited by law." [20] Since no land could be proclaimed for sale without action of Congress, it was evident that the settled conviction on the part of Congress was tantamount to a law. At least, there was no subsequent disposition to open up the public domain by the auction method, and in 1891 the policy was put into definite legal form.[21] An exception to the restricted privilege of purchase of public lands was made for five southern states. In these states land was purchasable in any amounts at public auction after 1876, whereas, from 1862 to that date, it had been subject to homestead entry only.[22]

An interesting variation from the auction system is seen in the "drawings" of recent years. Where the amount of land is very limited and at the same time desirable as in the case, for example, of an Indian Reservation left for years in a settled country, or a promising irrigation tract, the rush of settlers would be out of all proportion to the amount of available land. For meeting such emergencies the government has devised the plan, involving the chance feature of the lottery, of putting the names, or corresponding numbers, of applicants into a cage and drawing out as many as there are tracts of land. At times the prizes have been very attractive. The main advantage of the lottery is to determine who of the aspirants shall have the most desirable locations.

In a very limited way the auction is still in use, but the various methods of taking land under some sort of settlement requirement have made ordinary sales the exception instead of the rule. An act of 1891 prescribed that ordinary public sales such as had been held for many years should be

[20] *Cong. Globe,* 40 Cong., 2 Sess., p. 1861.
[21] *U. S. Stat. at Large,* XXVI, p. 1095.
[22] *Ibid,* XIX, p. 73.

discontinued except in case of abandoned military sites, and other similar tracts.

Sales After 1862

Congress was not clear as to intentions respecting cash sales following the enactment of the Homestead Law. Without a definite provision to that effect, it was not possible to discontinue old laws. Therefore, sales continued, though only in connection with preëmption and miscellaneous parcels of land, the preëmptions covering by far the larger part of the operations. Land sales were no longer generally proclaimed. That is to say, offerings of the tracts newly surveyed and now subject to homestead were not put on the market at a price. Auctions were confined to a few special tracts, and ceased to be the regular manner of disposing of public land. In all reason, the Preëmption Act should have been repealed at the time of the passage of the Homestead Act. As it was, many millions of acres were taken from the government at $1.25 per acre, by the same people who were getting the homesteads. For a time, three quarter sections could be obtained by the same person by a payment of little over $200. He could take one quarter under the Homestead Act, another under Preëmption, and a third under the Timber Culture Act.

Summary

The change from the credit to the cash sales system was a radical move in the way of policy. It was accompanied by a change in price from $2.00 to $1.25. The eighty-acre size of tract offered was retained. Thus for $100 a piece of land large enough for a farm could be purchased. For nearly a decade sales were very limited in amount. Not only was the payment of cash a deterrent, but a reaction from the boom following the War of 1812 was inevitable. The speculators were already loaded with land far in advance of settlement. By 1834 another feverish period of speculation was begun which carried the sales, in 1836, beyond the 20,000,000 mark in acres sold within a year. The price of land was barely above the minimum.

With the passage of the preëmption act of 1841 a positive step in advance was taken in favor of the settler as opposed to the speculator. Sales went little beyond two and a half million acres a year at any time between 1841 and the time of the graduation of the price downward in 1854.

There was much sentiment against selling land after the adoption of the homestead policy in 1862, but no legislation on the subject till 1891, at which time it was provided that ordinary sales at auction should be discontinued except in certain very limited instances. However, in one way or another sales continued in considerable quantities. Counting under the head of sales land disposed of as Timber and Stone land, commuted homestead entries, and the like, the receipts were above a million dollars a year from 1867 to 1922 with but three exceptions. Thus, though not a recognized, leading method of disposing of land for over a half century, there have been disposed of at cash sale many millions of acres.

TABLE XI

ACRES SOLD, AND RECEIPTS, 1863-1922 [23]

Year	Acres	Dollars
1863	91,354	$136,078
1864	432,773	687,007
1865	557,212	748,427
1866	388,294	546,979
1867	756,620	1,071,706
1868	914,941	1,285,451
1869	2,899,544	5,495,717
1870	2,159,516	3,123,677
1871	1,389,982	2,262,844
1872	1,370,320	2,444,695
1873	1,626,266	2,918,104
1874	1,041,345	1,865,179
1875	745,061	1,382,282

[23] About 1880 the character of the cash sales report underwent a considerable change. Instead of representing sales of the more ordinary character there were included sales under the Desert Act, Commuted Homestead, Timber and Stone Act, and from time to time various other items, such as coal and mineral lands. The Land Office reported, however, an acreage under sales until 1906. From 1907 to date the above table was compiled from the reports by adding for each year the items that appear to have been used by the office for this purpose previously. As a result this table includes considerable land reported in other chapters of this book. The significance of the cash sales item becomes much less after, say 1880 or 1890, with the disappearance of land suitable for the more usual types of farming, or at least it becomes more and more difficult to draw conclusions concerning the occasion for the purchases.

TABLE XI (*Continued*)

Year	Acres	Dollars
1876	640,692	1,136,693
1877	740,687	969,317
1878	877,555	1,130,752
1879	622,574	894,841
1880	850,741	1,255,584
1881	1,587,617	3,534,551
1882	4,728,238	6,628,776
1883	5,547,610	9,657,032
1884	6,317,847	10,302,582
1885	3,912,450	6,223,927
1886	3,773,498	5,757,891
1887	5,587,910	9,246,321
1888	7,980,181	11,203,072
1889	5,291,228	8,018,255
1890	3,302,847	6,349,174
1891	2,143,091	4,160,099
1892	1,571,478	3,322,865
1893	1,401,959	3,193,281
1894	615,827	1,653,081
1895	416,878	1,116,090
1896	465,026	1,053,906
1897	419,052	917,911
1898	632,736	1,291,076
1899	629,857	1,703,988
1900	1,178,982	2,899,732
1901	1,301,669	2,966,543
1902	1,757,593	4,139,268
1903	3,073,897	8,960,471
1904	2,307,345	7,445,903
1905	1,646,652	4,849,766
1906	1,774,342	4,885,989
1907	3,997,213	7,728,114
1908	5,199,091	9,760,570
1909	4,489,032	7,698,337
1910	5,066,018	6,342,745
1911	3,549,206	5,783,693
1912	3,479,232	5,437,502
1913	1,449,094	2,746,447
1914	1,328,674	2,650,762
1915	747,297	2,331,368
1916	817,210	1,769,860
1917	731,481	1,935,955

TABLE XI (*Continued*)

Year	Acres	Dollars
1918	762,813	2,050,576
1919	640,181	1,464,719
1920	817,243	1,990,764
1921	700,327	1,546,706
1922	894,289	906,545
1923	394,842	605,506

CHAPTER VII

Lands Offered by Colonies to Induce Enlistments

Like some other elements in our national land system, the practice of giving land bounties to reward military services had its beginnings in the colonial period. Virginia, as early as 1646, donated one hundred acres to the commander of the palisaded settlement at Middle Plantation. Ingle's Insurrection and the "Pequot War" led to similar gifts from Lord Baltimore and from Connecticut. The main idea in these cases was one of mere compensation for services. As a motive for granting bounties this idea later came to be overshadowed by a policy of securing protection through the promotion of compact settlements on the frontier of men able to defend it.

Virginia was the first to inaugurate this defensive policy. In 1679 an act was passed granting large tracts to Major Lawrence Smith and Captain William Byrd on condition that they settle on the land two hundred and fifty men, fifty of whom should be well armed and in constant readiness. The same privilege, open to all, was further extended in 1701. Large quantities of land, between 10,000 and 30,000 acres, were made available to companies of persons who would settle together on the frontier and maintain one warlike Christian man completely armed and equipped for every five hundred acres granted. Connecticut, in an effort to settle its frontier lands, especially those near disputed boundaries, in 1733 granted nine townships to the officers and soldiers, or to the heirs of such, who had served in King Philip's War. Land was granted, also, to the men who participated in Philip's expedition to Canada in 1690. Liberal grants, usually two hundred acres, were made to individual sufferers from the wars—disabled soldiers, widows or children of soldiers, and those who had endured captivity. The offer of lands on the frontier to all persons who would join in an expedition to expel the French, extended by Pennsylvania in 1755, was calculated to strengthen the frontier as well as to attract military aid.

During the time of trouble between England and France over the possession of North American territory England made very free use of land as an inducement to the soldier to enlist and serve during war. The most important act of this nature is the Proclamation of 1763 by which King George III granted to soldiers who had served in the war just ended tracts of land, from 50 to 5,000 acres, according to rank. The warrants for these lands might be located on any unoccupied crown land.[1] Some of the colonies of their own accord made similar grants.[2]

THE REVOLUTIONARY WAR AND LAND BOUNTIES

With the opening of the Revolutionary War Congress turned almost at once to the unoccupied land as a means of inducing enlistments in the army.

Washington was convinced that land was likely to be a temptation worth while setting before the recruit. He said, "I cannot find that the bounty of ten dollars is likely to produce the desired effect. . . . The addition of land might have a considerable influence on a permanent enlistment."[3] It was by no means a new method of paying the soldier, and although Congress had no land it was believed that the several states would aid in procuring such land, and hence Congress was willing to sell itself short, as it were, in order to deal successfully with the question of enlistment. To begin with, land was offered to deserters from the British army.[4] To reach the Hessians these offers

[1] *Land Laws* (1810), p. 17.
[2] Ford, p. 105.
[3] Letter to the President of Congress. *American Archives*, 5th series, II, p. 121.
[4] Donaldson, p. 209; *Journal of Continental Congress*, V, p. 654.

were rendered in German and printed on the backs of tobacco wrappers.[5] Very soon, however, a more positive use of the public lands, if they may be so called, was made in the grants offered to men to induce enlistment in the continental army. A colonel was promised 500 acres; a lieutenant-colonel 450 acres; a major 400 acres; a captain 300 acres; a lieutenant 200 acres; an ensign 150 acres; non-commissioned officers and privates 100 acres each. It was the intention that the soldier should serve out his time before this addition to his pay should become available, and with that end in view an act was passed providing that no assignment of a land warrant during the war should be valid.[6]

In 1780 the land resolution was extended so as to give a major-general 1,100 acres and a brigadier-general 850 acres. And in 1783 Congress resolved that whenever it could consistently make grants of land it would "reward in this way the officers, men and others, refugees from Canada."

Many of the states—Massachusetts, New York, Pennsylvania, Maryland, Virginia, North Carolina, and South Carolina—also granted military bounties. Virginia was especially liberal, being in possession of a large amount of unoccupied territory. In the spring of 1779 one hundred acres were promised to every private at the end of the war, and as much to the officers as was given to those of the same rank in the continental army. Later in the year the donation to soldiers was raised to two hundred acres, and the quantity given to officers increased ten-fold. By acts passed in 1780 and 1782 the bounties were further increased; the settlers of the Vincennes section in Illinois who had helped Clark each received four hundred acres.

Bounties and the War of 1812

Even before the opening of the War of 1812 Congress, in an effort to strengthen the army, offered 160 acres of

[5] *Jol. of Cont. Cong.*, V, p. 708, note.
[6] *Ibid*, pp. 763, 788.

land to non-commissioned officers and private soldiers who should serve five years, or until discharged, in the United States Army.[7] It will be observed that no land was offered to the officers of this war. Furthermore, no bounties were available for a soldier under eighteen or over forty-five years of age. This defect respecting both classes was remedied by an act passed April 16, 1816.

The land bounty acts during and following the War of 1812 show a complete lack of understanding of the proper use of land, assuming that there is a proper use as a reward for military service and the proper way of administering it. To begin with, the limitation of the grants to privates was on the supposition that officers, being better paid, did not deserve a bonus. However, this meant that a man might be a private till the war was about over, receive a commission for distinguished service, and so lose all claim to a land bounty. This would imply that a title of Lieutenant was worth at least a quarter section of land. Probably there was no sinister intention involved in the provision of bounties for soldiers between the ages of eighteen and forty-five only, but it developed, as, indeed, it always would, that some privates were under eighteen and some over forty-five. Why, forsooth, should not these patriots be located as well as those of regular army age? To this question there was no answer.

The privates, who had served in the regular army, and who were entitled to land, were obliged to apply for it within five years, and to take it within one of several military districts, the particular assignment to be chosen by lot. Thus the applicant was greatly restricted in his choice of land in the general matter of the part of the country into which he might wish to emigrate, and again in the particular tract on which he might settle. The choice by lot often gave poor land miles from desirable sites, and for no good reason. This detail was remedied, but not for more than ten years after the war. The reason for providing military reserves

7 *U. S. Stat. at Large,* II, pp. 669, 672.

and requiring soldier bounty land to be located within their boundaries was in order to provide a screen of veterans between the older settlements and the Indians.

A feature which would now meet with general approval was at the time viewed as a great hardship. The land warrant was not transferable, and as a result the beneficiary was obliged to make use of it to the extent of locating upon it and getting a patent before he could sell it. Since a large majority of the soldiers have always looked upon the land bounty as so much additional pay for service in the army, it is no wonder that they favored the transferable warrant or scrip. This provision did not directly harm the man who preferred to settle on the land, though it did, subsequently, keep the value of his land down to an unnecessarily low figure when soldier scrip flooded the land offices about the middle of the century.

BOUNTIES AND THE MEXICAN WAR

Promptly on the outbreak of hostilities between this country and Mexico, Congress set about the organization of a larger army and at once resorted to the well-established custom of offering a land bounty.[8] It was at first proposed to provide the bounty for non-commissioned officers and private soldiers only, but the law as passed in February, 1847, included all soldiers. An option was offered in connection with this bounty whereby a soldier might take, instead of his land warrant, a treasury scrip for $100, the scrip to be receivable by the government in payment for land.

GENERAL BOUNTY GRANTS OF 1850 AND FOLLOWING

A series of acts beginning with 1850[9] put the land bounty on a different footing. Before that time there had been a strong tendency to keep the land gratuities to soldiers down to a minimum. Now it was clearly the plan to be liberal. Bounty lands were offered to men of every rank, in every

[8] *U. S. Stat. at Large,* IX, p. 125.
[9] *Ibid,* p. 520.

branch of the service, and the act was made to apply to substantially all wars from 1790 to and including the Mexican War.

Another act, in 1852,[10] made all land warrants assignable. This was a much disputed point. It was undoubtedly the intention of Congress to make land warrants useful in settling the frontier with a class of men able to help in defense against Indians, or other enemies. Also, there was the idea of giving the soldiers homes of their own. It was evident to those concerned in the administration of the bounty land laws that the majority of the soldiers, and others who became entitled to the bounty, did not care to go to the pioneer country and make use of the land as a home.[11]

This was the case through the years preceding 1852, and in that year the situation was relieved by the passage of an act making all military land warrants assignable. At one time there had been an attempt in Congress to make these warrants commutable, that is, receivable by the government, at the rate of $1.40 for each acre represented.[12] This was while land was still selling at a minimum of $2.00 per acre. But nothing was done to enable the soldier to realize on his land in any other way than by locating it with his warrant until 1852. The Commissioner of Pensions the preceding year recommended the passage of an act making warrants assignable in order that all entitled to the bounty might in some manner receive it.[13] It was supported by the members of Congress and enacted March 22, 1852.

In 1855 a thoroughly general act gave a bounty of 160 acres of land to any soldier or his heirs who had served in any war after 1790, and a year later it was made to include Revolutionary soldiers. The service for which this bounty was given need not have been for a longer period than fourteen days.

[10] *U. S. Stat. at Large*, X, p. 3.
[11] *Ann. of Cong.*, 16 Cong., 1 Sess., p. 1490.
[12] *Ibid*, 15 Cong., 1 Sess., p. 409.
[13] *Cong. Globe*, 32 Cong., 1 Sess., App., p. 9.

In the early years of land bounties they were given as an inducement to men to enlist. During the fifties they were granted as a reward for services long past and evidently in a spirit of generosity as additional pay.

With few exceptions the state grants were to be located in tracts exclusively devoted to the satisfaction of military claims. When Virginia ceded her western territory to the National Government, she retained a contingent claim to the right to use a tract supposed to contain 4,204,800 acres in what is now the state of Ohio for the purpose of making good her promises to the soldiers and sailors of the Continental Army and Navy. It was provided that lands to the south of the Ohio, which never became federal public domain, but belonging to Virginia, should first be exhausted before the reserve north of the Ohio should become subject to the disposal of Virginia. Much difficulty arose over the boundaries of the Reserve, also concerning the contention of Virginia that state troops as well as Continental troops were entitled to land under the deed of cession. By the Ordinance of May 20, 1785, which provided for "ascertaining the mode of disposing of lands in the Western Territory," it was ordained:

"That no part of the land included between the rivers called Little Miami and Scioto, on the northwest side of the river Ohio, be sold, or in any manner alienated, until there shall first have been laid off and appropriated for the said officers and soldiers, and persons claiming under them, the lands they are entitled to, agreeable to the said deed of Session and act of Congress accepting the same." [14]

Congress followed the example set by the states, in the creation of the "United States Military District," June 1, 1796.[15] This was laid out in Ohio and embraced about 2,560,000 acres. The land warrants issued by the Government in accordance with the legislation of 1796 were restricted exclusively to this district until after the passage

14 *Land Laws* (1810), p. 133.
15 *Ibid*, p. 196.

of the Scrip Act of May 30, 1830. Thereafter, Revolutionary warrants issued either by the general government or
by Virginia could be exchanged for scrip which might be
located either in Ohio, Indiana, or Illinois. In 1832 the
vacant lands in the district were made subject to sale at
private entry, and by that mode of disposition went into
private hands. After this provision two methods of satisfying bounty warrants were possible—exchange for scrip,
or location upon any of the public lands subject to private
sale.[16]

The State of Virginia, December 9, 1852, in response to
the Scrip Act by Congress of August 31, 1852,[17] ceded all
the lands in the Virginia Military district to the United
States. In satisfaction of outstanding military warrants,
fairly and justly issued by the authorities of that state,
the United States issued land scrip which was made receivable in payment for any public land subject to sale at private
entry. Under the provisions of the Act of 1852, scrip has
been issued for more than a million acres of land (1,114,525
acres)—an area much greater than that surrendered by
Virginia in yielding her claim to the unoccupied portions
of the Military Reserve.[18] In 1871, when the unappropriated lands in the District had shrunk to 76,735.44 acres, they
were ceded by the federal government to the State of Ohio,
which in turn appropriated them to the Ohio Agricultural
and Mechanical College.

Bounty Land Designated and Located

In 1812 an act was passed providing for the administration
of the land bounties just voted.[19] A quantity of land not
exceeding 6,000,000 acres was directed to be surveyed,

[16] Donaldson, p. 233.
[17] *U. S. Stat. at Large*, X, p. 143. For a very complete account of the Virginia military bounty lands see Treat, Chap. XIII.
[18] The total amount of land granted on account of Virginia bounties was approximately 6,363,000 acres. The amount in the Virginia Military Reserve in
Ohio was actually about 3,770,000 acres; under early scrip acts, 1830-1835,
1,478,000 acres were granted; and under the act of 1852, 1,115,000 acres.
[19] *U. S. Stat. at Large*, IV, p. 425.

reserved, and set apart; 2,000,000 acres in what was then included in the Territory of Michigan; 2,000,000 acres in the Illinois Territory, and 2,000,000 acres in the Territory of Louisiana, between the St. Francis and Arkansas Rivers. In 1816 these arrangements were changed by authorizing the survey of 1,500,000 acres in the Illinois Territory, and 500,000 acres in the Missouri Territory north of the Missouri River. This change was made as a result of President Madison's report that the lands set aside in Michigan were covered with lakes and swamps and unfit for cultivation.

Before 1842 warrants for services in the War of 1812 could be located only within the reserved districts, the selections being made by drawing lots from the territory designated by the person in whose favor they were issued. In virtue of the Act of 1842, renewed in 1848 and 1854, all military land warrants could be located upon any of the public lands subject to sale at private entry. On June 25, 1858, in accordance with previous legislation, they ceased being issued and on June 22, 1863, even the right to locate them expired.

The use of the public domain as an inducement to military enlistment was a most natural, no doubt an inevitable one. Whatever use it served as a means of securing needed soldiers is a matter for another inquiry, but its influence as a means of putting public land into private hands requires a brief treatment here.

So long as warrants were not assignable, they were likely to result in what they were designed to be, insofar as they were used at all. That is to say, they would result in putting men on land on the frontier, and yet the rapidity with which they were located, even when not assignable, makes it highly probable that by some means or other they were used for speculation rather than as a means of obtaining land for cultivation.[20] As soon as they were made assignable another result was inevitable.

[20] *L. O. R.,* 1850.

The assignable warrant was the most tempting means of its time for land speculation. This was bound to be true so long as there were people possessing such warrants who preferred the money to the land. Throughout the whole period during which bounty warrants were important there was land to be had for $1.25, or, earlier, $2.00 an acre. This fact determined the upper limit of the value of the warrant. The lower value was determined by the lack of desire, or the inability of the possessor of the warrant to use it for the purpose for which it was intended.

The soldier took whatever competition among speculators was able to afford.[21] This was little enough, though the testimony concerning prices for the early grants is not abundant. A writer in 1837 says that military warrants very much retarded the settlement of Illinois; that the titles to the land had long since passed out of the hands of soldiers; and that the land was largely in the hands of companies which held it at three to ten dollars an acre. In 1841 it was reported that scrip obtained in exchange for military warrants was bought "for a mere song."[22] Promptly following the act of 1830 providing that scrip, virtually land-office money, since it was receivable in payment for land, was to be had in place of land warrants, traffic in warrants began. Single companies of men dealt in scrip by the hundred thousand dollars' worth.

With the issue of Mexican War warrants, another lot of unassignable warrants came into the field. But in one way or another they were used to get land out of the hands of the government and into private possession at a rate vastly beyond that of settlement. For the years 1849 and 1850 the locations by warrants issued to Mexican War soldiers exceeded the sales, the former amounting to 5,573,000 acres, the latter to 2,735,000 acres.[23] In 1855 the sales were unusually large, nine and a quarter million acres, but the warrants were not far behind with eight and a third millions.

[21] *Ann. of Cong.*, 16 Cong., 1 Sess., p. 1491.
[22] *Ohio Statesman* (Weekly), Sept. 8, 1841.
[23] *L. O. R.*, 1851, p. 2.

In 1857 the warrants were again in the lead by over two million acres.

The Military Warrants and Speculation

The years between 1848 and 1858 were the big years for the military bounty locations. Warrants were quoted in the stock exchange reports along with stocks and bonds. They were at times dull and again in demand. The people of the West, near where they were used, had a keen appreciation of their significance. An Iowa paper in 1851 predicted that, should the bill pass Congress making all warrants assignable, "20,000,000 acres of land would soon pass from the United States into the hands of speculators and into the market." [24] In 1852 Mexican land warrants were reported dull, selling at $110 to $115, whereas they would have been worth $200 on the basis of $1.25 an acre. [25] Just after the passage of the Act of 1855 giving every ex-soldier for wars since 1790, or his heirs, 160 acres of land, it was predicted that the warrants would be purchased at wholesale by speculators, the land located in large tracts and sold out at an advance of four or five hundred per cent, the main benefits of the act going to land jobbers, while many attendant evils would result. [26]

Horace Greeley commented on the matter in one of his characteristically sarcastic editorials in which he said : "By these Bills, a little money has been secured to the discharged soldiers, and a great deal more to claim agents, warrant speculators, attorneys, brokers, etc., all at the expense of the future pioneers of our new states." [27] Again: "The rewards of that glorious patriotism so . . . shamefully inadequate, and the love for that species of employment [*i.e.* service in the army] may be expected to dwindle and die if no more determined efforts are made to encourage the occupation." [28]

[24] *Des Moines Valley Whig*, Dec. 18, 1851.
[25] *Western Democrat* (Iowa), Feb. 25, 1852.
[26] *Des Moines Valley Whig*, Mar. 21, 1855.
[27] *New York Semi-Weekly Tribune*, Mar. 6, 1855.
[28] *New York Weekly Tribune*, May 10, 1856.

The predictions were not more spectacular than the realization. At times the warrants were so numerous that there was danger of trouble concerning precedence in the right to enter them in such quantities, and an agreement was arrived at whereby a lottery plan was used to settle the case. Numbers were drawn and in the order so determined each man was allowed to locate 640 acres. Hence the man with warrants representing many thousands of acres had a chance at 640 acres only on the basis of one number. On one occasion warrants for 115,000 acres, almost a third of a county, were so handled at the land office at Fort Dodge, Iowa. [29]

An examination of the books at the state land office in Iowa shows that land warrants were used by the speculators in a thoroughly wholesale manner. Following the bounty enactments of 1847, 1850, 1852 and 1855 a few men entered many thousands of acres of land at the western land offices. Very clearly these men were all speculators as were thousands more who entered smaller tracts. [30] The real farmer in few instances needed over a quarter or half section. Of course the military warrant had to be purchased by the speculator, but he got it for less than it was worth to him on the basis of dollar and a quarter land. In 1857 warrants were quoted by New York City brokers as low as 60 cents per acre, or less than half price. The highest quotation on one day, taken as a sample, was 85 cents per acre. [31] The broker usually handled them on a margin of ten cents per acre. The Commissioner of the General Land Office, who had every opportunity to know all the facts, wrote concerning the relation of the military warrant to the soldier: "The files and records of this office show that not one in five hundred of the land warrants issued and placed in the hands of the soldiers or their heirs have been located by them, or for

[29] *Fort Dodge Sentinel*, July 17, 1858.
[30] *Green Bay Advocate*, Wisconsin, June 12, 1856. Speaking of land purchased with warrants: "We know of parties in this city who have over 20,000 acres of good farming land which they are anxious to dispose of to actual settlers." See also C. C. Andrews, *Minnesota and Dakota*, p. 129.
[31] *N. Y. Weekly Tribune*, Oct. 24, 1857.

their use and benefit; . . . the most part having been used by persons to acquire title to the public lands for speculation purposes."[32] The House Committee on Public Lands at about the same time reported that Mexican land warrants were selling at about one dollar per acre.[33]

Bounty warrants were used as the basis of farm loans, money was often hard to find at any price in the West, and preëmptors were frequently in desperate need of it for payment to the government. Holders of warrants could, under these circumstances, sell them to preëmptors at a big advance and take a note from the purchaser, sometimes at 3 to 5 per cent interest per month.[34]

There is hardly need of further evidence. The military land warrant, whatever its use as a war measure, was a boon to speculators and helped marvelously in putting land into their hands. By these warrants an area of land larger than the State of Oregon was taken from the public domain and made private property. From the standpoint of settlement the best that can be said for it is that the speculators were ready to sell within a comparatively few years and so held the settler up for but a few dollars per acre. In fact, everything counted, many of the speculators lost money. They had taxes and perhaps interest to pay. They were in competition with cheap government land, and sometimes with cheap railroad land. Worst of all, after 1862, they were in competition with *free* government land. They were doing a legitimate, but, in most cases, a socially reprehensible business, and little sympathy was offered to those who failed to realize their dreams.

Had the government actually given the land to the soldier who cared to live on it, all would have been well, but that plan would have at least appeared to be unfair to the soldier, or perhaps his widow, who could not make personal use of the soil. This argument resulted in making warrants trans-

[32] *Cong. Globe*, 40 Cong., 2 Sess., App., p. 424. See also *Ibid,* 37 Cong., 2 Sess., p. 135.
[33] *Ibid.*
[34] *Quindaro Chin-Do-Wan*, Kansas, Mar. 27, 1858.

ferable. The whole matter grew out of the patent fact that the government had the land which was not proving to be a valuable asset so far as finance was concerned. It found the raising of money through taxation a hard matter, while parting with land was easy, relatively, and since there was no policy developed for making the best and most logical use of the public domain, much of it was destined to be thus frittered away, becoming an easy mark for the speculator and bringing hardship to the farmer. As an example of how not to dispose of public land it was excellent.

The Homestead Act Supersedes Military Bounty

By the time the Civil War began, the homestead idea had so far progressed as to be practically assured. Hence military bounties were hardly in point. However, there were not wanting warm advocates of military bounties as a means of partial payment for military services. Almost at the very beginning of the war soldiers enlisting for at least two years were promised a bounty of $100 in cash. A prolonged and rather weighty debate took place in the House of Representatives in December, 1861, on the question of land for soldiers.[35] An amendment to the Homestead Bill reviving the bounty provisions of the act of 1855 was proposed by a representative from Indiana. He stated that soldiers who had already enlisted in his state had done so with the belief that the Mexican Bounty Acts would be extended to them. The amendment was supported by some other western men, but was also strenuously opposed by men from that section. A phase of opposition to bounties not previously made conspicuous was brought out by Morrill of Vermont, and Fessenden of Maine. They felt that at a time when the federal finances were under a strain it would be unwise to part with public property which was viewed as an asset in the nature of a guarantee that the debt would be paid. The amendment was lost, and the war was finished without any land bounty, or any favor of any sort with

[35] *Cong. Globe,* 37 Cong., 2 Sess., p. 133.

respect to land acquisition being offered the soldier. The principles of the Homestead bill predominated.

Although the Homestead policy predominated, the bounty idea died hard. In one way or another it made its appearance on several occasions. A very remarkable instance was in the form of a bill proposing to confiscate land within the seceding states and turn it over to the Union soldiers. The bill providing for bounties was reported favorably by the House Committee on Public Lands and after a keen debate passed the House by a vote of 75 to 64.[36]

On some occasions the soldiers themselves asked that the land bounty policy be restored, and from time to time some Congressman brought forward the proposition to return to the usual policy.[37] In 1868 the question was debated at length, but no action was taken.[38] In 1870 a concession of some importance was made to the soldier. The Homestead Law provided that a homesteader within the limits of railway grants, that is to say, on the alternate sections, the price of which had in all cases been doubled, should be allowed but 80 acres instead of 160 acres as elsewhere. By an act of that year the soldier was allowed, under these circumstances, as under others, to take 160 acres.[39] This was a privilege of no small weight, since land within these limits was usually salable property.

A more sweeping act followed in 1872, by which soldiers were allowed a deduction from the time required in gaining title to a Homestead of the amount of time served in the army, the time of residence, however, not to be less than one year.[40] This action had been recommended by the Commissioner of the General Land Office in the report for 1871. There was no great opposition to the bill in Congress, the debate being almost altogether on details and not on the principle. Probably it went through easily, partly because

[36] *Cong. Globe,* 38 Cong., 1 Sess., pp. 2233, 2235, 2249 *et seq.*
[37] *Ibid,* 40 *Cong.,* 2 Sess., App. p. 422.
[38] *Ibid.*
[39] *U. S. Stat. at Large,* XVI, p. 321.
[40] *Ibid,* XVII, 49, p. 333.

it cost the government nothing in money, and very little in land, and also partly because soldiers were by this time exerting a powerful influence in politics. Great numbers of soldiers availed themselves of the shortened residence period, and the privilege unquestionably resulted in a more rapid settlement of the public lands.

The most extravagant proposals have been brought forward in the name of liberality to the soldier. For instance, in 1873 a bill was introduced in the House providing for the donation to a soldier, or his heirs, of a quarter-section of land, to be entered either in person or by an agent. The residence requirements were vague and uncertain and in the opinion of the Commissioner of the General Land Office the inevitable outcome would have been the issue of assignable warrants in volume sufficient to cover all the valuable public domain then remaining.[41] The bill passed the House but failed in the Senate. The only show of strength it had was based on its alleged relation to the soldiers' bounties which many Congressmen believed required equalization.[42] Attention was called to the undoubted fact that the privileges conceded to the soldiers with reference to the public domain had no real effect so far as the great majority of soldiers was concerned. The bill proposed in 1873 would very probably have annulled all the important laws then in operation under which land was granted to settlers and would have put land warrants on the market at a few cents per acre, given to the soldiers a sum of money amounting to a few months' pay, and put the land into the hands of speculators at a rate never known before or since. It was a plan which the country was extremely fortunate in escaping.

Altogether, it cannot be said that the military bounty sentiment in connection with the Civil War had a very great effect on the land policies of the country. Free land under the Homestead Act was the undoubted safeguard preventing a

---

[41] *Senate Reports,* 42 Cong., 3 Sess., p. 482.
[42] See discussion of bill, *Cong. Globe,* 42 Cong., 3 Sess., p. 105 *et seq.*

flood of military warrants which would have dissipated the remaining stock of desirable lands, and put them on the market at speculative prices long before they were needed in the natural development of the country.

TABLE XII

BOUNTY LAND WARRANTS ISSUED TO JUNE 30, 1907[43]

	Number	Acres
War of the Revolution, acts prior to 1800 [44]	16,663	2,165,000
War of 1812	29,186	4,845,920
Act of 1847	88,274	13,213,640
Act of 1850	189,145	13,168,480
Act of 1852	11,992	694,400
Act of 1855	263,100	34,151,590
		68,239,030

PROPOSED LEGISLATION FOR SOLDIER SETTLEMENT SINCE THE WORLD WAR

While the World War was yet in progress the Department of the Interior prepared a draft of a bill providing rural homes for returning soldiers. The plan was for the different states to provide the land while the federal government should finance the reclamation, clearing and preparation of the land for farming by providing buildings, implements and live stock. The total cost of land and improvements with 4 per cent interest on the capital invested to be repaid by the settler over a period of forty years.

In October, 1918, a bill, supported by the Department of the Interior, was introduced in Congress by Senator Meyers, providing for a survey and classification by that department of all unentered public lands and all privately owned unused lands for the purpose of finding out what

---

[43] The *Land Office Report* of 1907 gives the latest summary available, covering the acts from 1812 to the last bounty legislation. There have been very few additional warrants issued since 1907.

[44] Donaldson, p. 236.

lands could be reclaimed and put to use by returning soldiers.[45]

Several bills have been introduced since the war was over. Senator Kenyon [46] of Iowa and Representative Kelly [47] of Pennsylvania introduced bills which, among other things, provided for the systematic development of rural districts. The chief feature of these bills was, however, to provide employment for returning soldiers on public construction work.

A bill was introduced into the house by Taylor of Colorado on February 15, 1919, providing "for employment and securing of rural homes for the promotion of the reclamation of land for cultivation under the direction of the Secretary of the Interior." [48] The bill provided also for short-term loans to settlers. If this bill had passed it would have involved the Reclamation Service in the new functions of colonization work and in making loans to settlers.

Representative Mondell of Wyoming introduced a bill May 19, 1919,[49] providing for employment and rural homes for returned soldiers through reclamation of lands under the direction of the Secretary of the Interior. An appropriation of five hundred thousand dollars for the purpose was proposed. This bill carries a provision for safeguarding the settler's holdings against speculation, and for liberal loans to settlers.

On May 27, 1919, Representative Knutson introduced a bill [50] which proposed to create in the Treasury Department a National Colonization Board with local colonization commissions for the purpose of providing capital for the development of colonization of the remaining agricultural lands of the nation, with certain privileges to soldier settlers. The main aims of the bill were to standardize private land coloni-

[45] Sen Rep. 4947, 65 Cong., 3 Sess.
[46] Ibid, 5397, 65 Cong., 3 Sess.
[47] House Report 15672, 65 Cong., 3 Sess.
[48] P. A. Speek, A Stake in the Land, p. 101.
[49] Ibid, p. 102.
[50] Ibid, pp. 102, 103.

zation companies, to facilitate the extension of credit to them, and to make loans to soldier settlers.

A soldier relief bill introduced by Senator Borah, May 12, 1920, provided that a loan aggregating $300,000,000 be made to ex-soldiers for the coming ten years, not more than $50,000,000 to be loaned in one year. Two alternative plans of loan were proposed, one of which provided employment for ex-soldiers on reclamation construction work and their acquisition of some of this land "at a reasonable price." The other plan was to furnish a long-time loan for the purchase of suburban homes or farms, the amount of the loans being limited to $3,000.

Ex-soldiers of the Spanish-American War and the World War have been granted the privilege of counting the period of service on the regular time and residence requirements of the Homestead Law. However, the amount of time so deducted may not be less than 90 days or more than two years. Thus a soldier homesteader must live on the land at least one year. In the case of a soldier dying in the service after having made entry upon a homestead and leaving a widow or children, the residence requirements shall be viewed as having been fulfilled, and the patent issued to the heirs. With this exception, nothing of significance has been done in the way of granting special concessions to returned soldiers in recent years.

SUMMARY

The use of land as military bounty was not new. The occasion for it in the days of the Revolution was extreme. Thus several of the colonies, and the Continental Congress, adopted the plan at once. Washington favored it, and the result was a liberal offer of land to the soldiers and sailors of the Revolution. The same policy, with various modifications, was followed in the War of 1812, and again in the Mexican War.

One of the outstanding features of land as a military bounty is the lack of interest in land as such by a great number, in recent years the majority, of the soldiers. After some vacillation Congress decided to make military bounty warrants transferable. By this means the easiest possible road to speculation was opened. The holders of the warrants would sell at a very low figure. There were always buyers at some price, and at these low prices the land passed into private hands.

The enactment of the Homestead Law with its lenient soldier provisions made military warrants unnecessary during the Civil War. The same is true of the more recent wars. Whatever may have been the excuse for granting land to soldiers as a reward for service in the early days of the Republic there is little occasion for continuing the practice now. Soldier settlement on land certainly has its limitations also, but in any case it can hardly be a question pertaining to the public domain in any vital way.

CHAPTER VIII

THE PUBLIC DOMAIN A BASIS OF NATIONAL DEVELOPMENT, 1841 TO 1900

FREE LAND FOR THE SETTLER

No doubt the leading men in Congress, and out, during the period of attempted use of the public domain as a source of revenue would have insisted that they were undertaking to promote national development through their land policies. In the perspective of a century and a half, however, it appears that a much clearer and more comprehensive outlook upon national development characterized the actions of 1841 than had been discernible a half century before. True, this outlook was not gained by the instantaneous falling of the scales from the eyes of the men in charge of affairs at that time. Washington and Jefferson had held progressive and liberal ideas. Benton and John Quincy Adams, in different ways, had tried to link the new West to the older settlements by internal improvements, fostered and supported by federal liberality and expenditure. The long succession of preëmption acts were but the premonitions of a free land policy, a policy destined to come, but hindered by sectional interests and differences for many years.

LAND FOR PUBLIC AND QUASI-PUBLIC IMPROVEMENTS

The primary question of political strength and unity had been settled by the occupation of the central portion of the country before 1841. Four states of the Old Northwest, together with Louisiana and Missouri beyond the Mississippi, had been admitted into the Union, while several Territories were manifestly approaching statehood. It was a sparse population scattered over a vast stretch of country. The demand for national aid in the building of highways, canals and railroads was irresistible. The West was producing crops, but had no market.

How to get a market was uppermost in the minds of the whole population of the West. The older idea of self-sufficiency was breaking down. In the main the pioneer community was self-sufficient. The foodstuff was nearly all locally produced. The meat was all but wholly home grown and home cured. Grists of "rye and Indian" were taken to the local mills in the East, and wheat was similarly handled in the West. While water transportation had been developed to a remarkable degree, it was manifestly inadequate as a solution of the question. Faith in canals persisted for several decades, even to the middle of the nineteenth century, yet the interest in railroads all but obscured the canal enthusiasm within a short time after 1840, and by 1850 the railroads were thoroughly established and recognized as the means of connecting the eastern ports and business centers with the interior of the country. The western farmers and dwellers of the small towns were no longer content to live on the fat of the land, locally produced. The fare was too limited and too monotonous. Furthermore, it was not altogether a matter of taste; it was in addition a question of business. The farmers were as a class in debt. The debts were carried in an awkward and painful manner. They had been incurred for the payment of the amount due the government on the occasion of closing the preëmption period and securing a title to the land. The rates of interest were high, often 24 per cent a year, and now and then 100 per cent.

Thus a market was the all-essential desideratum. Without it the peopling of the West would, of necessity, cease to progress at the rate attained during the early years of the century. In fact, it was freely predicted that much progress already achieved would be lost. As settlements spread

back from the rivers marketing became more and more difficult, even impossible. Prices were so low as hardly to be
expressed in positive terms. Cereals were frequently 10 or
12 cents a bushel, merely nominal figures, and no sales
feasible again and again. Dressed pork was reported as low
as two cents a pound at lumber camps, which meant virtually
no price at all at the farm. There could be little exchange
of goods because what one farmer had they all had; what
one lacked they all lacked; while people who wanted farm
produce and had something to exchange for it were inac-
cessibly far away. The stage was in a sense adequate for
carrying passengers and mail; as a freight carrier it was
soon taxed beyond its power. Thus to the accepted plan of
using land as the reward of the pioneer farmer it became
the lure, or a lure, of the railroad builder. Added to this,
perhaps as often preceding it, was the program of using the
public lands in the promotion of internal improvements,
broadly construed, but centering mainly in transportation
facilities.

Land for Settlement

For a half century, or more, following 1841 the policy
of using the public domain in the promotion of settlement,
the very basis of national strength and security, of civilization itself, was accepted and furthered in the disposition of
the western lands. It was the fruition of the work and
teachings of such men as Gallatin, Jefferson and Benton. In
1826 Benton had said regarding a liberal treatment of the
western pioneer: "I speak to Senators who know this to
be a Republic, not a Monarchy, who know that the public
lands belong to the People and not to the Federal Government." Thus debts were to be forgiven, preëmption was
to be granted, land was to be made easy of access and of
acquisition, indeed free as soon as the East could be converted to the view.

Every new Territory and State wanted people to take up
and use the vacant lands. Immigration agents were em-

ployed by the state. Advertising campaigns were adroitly conducted by the railroads. The private land agent became an institution, offering to conduct land seekers to the best locations. All forces combined to get the land into the hands of settlers. The government helped the campaign along. With the transportation lines established, the ownership of land assumed a new aspect; values were expected to increase. In the early years of the development of farms on the frontier the settler was looking for room, for a chance to support himself and family. With a market assured, not by going around half a continent by water, taking weeks for the trip, but going with speed directly toward the eastern seaboard with its cities, meant a price for product which would soon reflect itself in land values of the West. Thus the farmer, not altogether for the first time, but with a new emphasis, began to look upon the land as a prize in itself, easily obtained, and likely to increase rapidly in value. With this optimism permeating the imaginations of the on-coming waves of settlers it was inevitable that more enterprising adventurers should precede them and profit by the optimism by taking the first advance in price over the government minimum. The Preëmption Act was designed to preclude, at least to restrict this practice.

Grants for Internal Improvements

With such a demand on the part of the settler for an outlet to the East, and a demand hardly less keen in the East for connection with the West, the almost unrestrained indulgence in an orgy of appropriation of land for internal improvements, mainly transportation facilities, can easily be understood. The land as it lay was worth little to the government; the hope of getting revenue out of it was well past; the program of settling the land was accepted and under way. Thus the use of land as an indirect aid to settlement by making the settlements feasible, making life endurable after the settlement was accomplished, took first place in the minds of many Congressmen and other influential leaders of the day. While sentiment against granting land lavishly for the promotion of internal improvements was prevalent at the time the movement was at its height, a great deal stronger sentiment against the policy grew up during the years following. At the time of the enactment of the laws the opposition concerned itself with questions of fairness as between old and new states, and the policy of granting federal aid for what should be state responsibility. The abstract question of centralized power was uppermost in the minds of many concerned. Later it was not so much a question of the theory of government, or a balance of accounts among the states. It was rather a question of its effect on the people directly concerned as settlers of the new territory. This land was not offered as promptly and freely to settlers as was the public domain held as such until taken by the settler. The social and economic status of the settler appealed to the majority of those concerned. Organized labor took a pronounced stand. The Free Soil party voiced a sentiment becoming popular, and the merging of the preëmption doctrines and practices into the Homestead Acts became inevitable. The West itself took sides against the granting of land to states or corporations, and demanded a distribution to the settler direct.

THE ATTITUDE OF ORGANIZED LABOR

The West, with its cheap or free land, was the outlet for the energy and the discontent of the East. Union labor early discovered the importance of the Public Domain and used its influence in making it free to the settler. Many of the petitions sent to Congress by western state legislators bear unmistakable evidence of a common origin and without doubt the origin was organized labor. The National Labor Union Convention in 1867 passed a series of drastic resolutions on the subject of the public domain, denouncing Congress for having allowed speculators to buy land, and demanding that it be made free to settlers. Grants to railways were denounced roundly, and Congress was asked to take measures to put land into the hands of cultivators as speedily as possible.

The attitude of labor toward the land question was part and parcel of the doctrine of natural rights which a decade later was voiced by Henry George in *Progress and Poverty*. It was suggested by the labor leaders that all unimproved land should be taxed the same as improved land. The whole question of unemployment was to be solved by allowing free access to land. The National Labor Union believed that the solution to the problem of distributing wealth in the interest of humanity lay in the union of labor and agriculture. A petition in Congress in 1864 asked for an appropriation with which to move poor people from the city to the public lands. It can hardly be said that labor exerted any great influence on the public land policies, though to some extent their ideas were embodied in legislation.[1]

FREE LAND FOR SETTLEMENT

With transportation facilities assured, the demand for free land in small tracts for settlers obtained not only in the West, but found many advocates among leaders of thought in the East. For example, Horace Greeley kept the subject before his readers constantly. With him, the belief in the distribution of land among the people of small fortunes was hardly short of a religion. It was the way, virtually the one way, of advancing human welfare, and preventing social disaster. Galusha Grow of Pennsylvania was likewise as enthusiastic on the subject as any westerner. Others of lesser note in this respect were ready at all times to lend their support to the plan of using the public domain as the means ready at hand to aid in spreading people over the wilderness. A settled country appealed to the imagination of those ambitious with respect to national strength and security. An unsettled country was at least a problem and more likely a menace. Thus humane considerations, politics, and a sense of security all contributed to the feeling that the land should

[1] On the attitude of labor see *The Working Man's Advocate* 1867 to 1876.

be put to some use, and the use that appealed to the great majority of those involved was that of the small, independent farmer.

Thus the Homestead period logically followed the period of appropriation of great tracts of land toward the promotion of roads, canals and railways. At no time had it been forgotten that the ultimate use to be made of the land was primarily agricultural, and that the small holding was the most desirable. For many years the possibility of exhausting such a vast supply of land was not appreciated. After many millions of acres had been bestowed lavishly on states and companies it dawned slowly upon those responsible for plans that the supply was not inexhaustible. This feeling favored the sentiment looking toward free land to settlers, and by the end of the century the easily accessible land, that is to say, land which could be turned into farms with no great expense, was about gone. The vision of a farm family on every quarter or half section had become a reality more nearly than most visions are turned into tangible form. While perhaps still sparsely settled, the country was in a real sense settled. With this done, many were inclined to think the land question a thing of the past, not understanding that giving land away will settle the problems involved in the management of landed property for a few short years only.

One of the main hopes of the friends of free land was that the plan would result in a succession of generations of land-owning farmers. Before the beginning of the period here designated by the term national development the dominant idea was expressed as vigorously as at any subsequent time. The following words are from a speech by Senator Benton: "Tenantry is unfavorable to freedom. It lays the foundation for separate orders in society, annihilates the love of country, and weakens the spirit of independence. The tenant has, in fact, no country, no hearth, no domestic altar, no household god. The freeholder, on the contrary, is the national supporter of a free government, and it should be the policy of republics to multiply their freeholders as it is the policy of monarchies to multiply tenants. We are a republic, and we wish to continue so: then multiply the class of freeholders; pass the public lands cheaply and easily into the hands of the People; sell for a reasonable price to those who are able to pay; and give without price to those who are not. I say give without price to those who are not able to pay; and that which is so given I consider as sold for the best of prices; for a price above gold and silver; a price which cannot be carried away by delinquent officers, nor lost in failing banks, nor stolen by thieves, nor squandered by an improvident and extravagant administration. It brings a price above rubies—a race of virtuous and independent farmers, the true supporters of their country, and the stock from which its best defenders must be drawn." [2]

Quite in keeping with these sentiments was the oft-quoted view of Jefferson expressed during the earlier period: "Whenever there are in any country uncultivated lands and unemployed poor, it is clear that the laws of property have been so far extended as to violate natural right. The earth is given as a common stock for man to labor and live on. If for the encouragement of industry we allow it to be appropriated, we must take care that other employment be provided to those excluded from the appropriation. If we do not, the fundamental right to labor the earth returns to the unemployed. It is too soon yet in our country to say that every man who cannot find employment, but who can find uncultivated land, shall be at liberty to cultivate it, paying a moderate rent. But it is not too soon to provide by every possible means that as few as possible shall be without a little portion of land. The small landholders are the most precious part of the state." [3]

[2] Cong. Deb., 119 Cong., 1 Sess., pp. 727, 728.
[3] Jefferson, *Writings*, (Monticello Ed.) XIX, 18.

CHAPTER IX

PREËMPTION RIGHTS

EARLY PRECEDENTS FOR TAKING PUBLIC LAND WITHOUT AUTHORITY

The right of preëmption, that is, the right to settle on and improve unappropriated public lands and later buy them at the minimum price without competition, was gained first in a general way in 1841. However, such privilege was granted in many individual cases before that time. Long before such privileges were officially obtained the practice of settling on government land without permission had been quite common. Complaint is made in the Declaration of Independence that England discouraged the appropriation of the back lands. Before the inauguration of President Washington, intrusions on unoccupied land were numerous, and in a special message to the Senate Washington speaks of a proclamation issued in 1788 against trespasses of this sort.[1] In fact, Washington had had personal experience with squatters on his own land west of the Alleghanies as recorded in his diary in 1784.[2]

No sooner was the Revolutionary War at an end than thousands of emigrants started for the West; some went to western New York, some to Pennsylvania, others into the newly acquired domain of the Confederation. Without authority, land was located and improvements begun.[3] Indian titles had not been extinguished, and the intruders complicated matters in this regard. Commissioners, in making a

[1] J. D. Richardson, *Messages and Papers of the Presidents*, I, p. 79.
[2] A. B. Hullbert, *Washington and the West*, p. 46 *et seq.*; George Bancroft, *History of the Formation of the Constitution of the United States*, I, pp. 387, 388.
[3] *Ibid.*

144

treaty with the Indians, promised redress and sent Colonel
Harmar to remove the intruders; this he did to a great
degree, and reported the situation to Congress.[4] On receipt
of the report Congress acted, passing a law which, in vigorous terms, provided for the removal of all trespassers.[5] The
Secretary of War was commanded to furnish troops on
request of two Commissioners of the Treasury for removing
such settlers from the public land. Harmar was ordered to
establish himself on the Ohio River and keep the intruders
off. He drove them off again and again, but the love for
land was strong while the respect for the Confederation
was weak, so back came the settlers even more rapidly
than they were dislodged.[6]

EARLY PROPOSALS IN CONGRESS FOR PREËMPTION—
ALLOWED IN SPECIFIC CASES

During the first session of Congress under the Constitution
Mr. Scott of western Pennsylvania, in his notable efforts
toward securing action on the question of western lands,
gave a clear-cut picture of the settlers who were going by
the thousands to the Ohio country, and spoke strongly in
favor of a preëmption indulgence toward those already occupying land. "The emigrants who reach the Western country," said he, "will not stop until they find a place where
they can securely seat themselves," and "they must have a
well grounded hope that the lands they cultivate may become
their own."[7] But Congress was not ready to act, although it
was shown that Spain was offering "lands without charge,
exemption from taxes, protection in civil and religious liber-
ties, besides provisions and the implements of husbandry,"
to induce Americans to cross the Mississippi.[8] Seven years
passed before the public land question received further
attention.

[4] *St. Clair Papers*, II, pp. 3, 4.
[5] *Jol. of Cong.* X, pp. 148, 149.
[6] *St. Clair Papers*, II, p. 2; McMaster, III, p. 105 *et seq.; Ann. of Cong.*,
1 Cong., 1 Sess., p. 412.
[7] *Ann. of Cong.*, 1 Cong., 1 Sess., p. 413.
[8] *Ibid*, p. 624.

In the resolutions which passed the House January 4, 1791,[9] it was proposed that a preference, virtually a preëmption, be given to actual settlers on public land where title had not been secured by a former government or by the acts of Congress. In 1796, however, the idea of revenue was too prominent to permit such a liberal plan to gain recognition. Although no general action concerning the intruder was taken for some years afterwards, Congress, in 1799, passed an act of indulgence toward settlers on land claimed, but not owned, by Judge Symmes. These men had bargained with Symmes, but, finding him unable to fulfill his part of the contract, they petitioned Congress for the privilege of purchasing direct from the government. They had agreed with Symmes' agent to pay one dollar an acre, but Congress could see no reason why they should not pay the newly established minimum of two dollars, and so gave them the preëmption right on that basis.[10] There was hardly a recognition of the principle of preëmption in this act, since the settlers had presumably purchased of Symmes in good faith, and were therefore not to blame in finding themselves on government land without the knowledge or consent of the government.

In fact, several years previously Congress had refused to recognize any right of the settler to land taken without authority. A petition had been submitted claiming preëmption rights on the grounds of settlement and improvement. This petition was referred to a committee which reported adversely, since "illegal settlements on the lands of the United States ought not to be encouraged . . . yielding to the said claims would interfere with the general provisions for the sale of said lands." [11]

Governor St. Clair reported from the Northwest Territory in 1799 that there was then a squatter [12] population of

---

[9] *Ann. of Cong.*, 1 Cong., 3 Sess., p. 1841.

[10] *Pub. Lands*, I, p. 68; *Ann. of Cong.*, 5 Cong. 3 Sess., p. 3018; *Ibid*, p. 3937, (Text of the act).

[11] *Pub. Lands*, I, p. 60.

[12] Apparently the first use of the term "squatter" in Congress was by Mr. Morrow of Ohio: "There are some small tracts of land on which what are called 'squatters' are settled." *Ann. of Cong.*, 9 Cong., 1 Sess., p. 469.

upward of two thousand in the vicinity of the Scioto and Miami rivers, and expressed the fear that there would be trouble in removing these settlers, yet few would be able to purchase even a quarter-section at two dollars per acre; they were, however, willing to purchase.[13]

In 1801 came from the settlers on government land in Ohio a plea stating that "with much labor and difficulty, they have settled upon, cultivated, and improved certain lands, the property of the United States . . . and have thereby not only enhanced the value of the lands upon which they have respectively settled but of other lands in the vicinity of the same to the great benefit of the United States, and pray for a Preëmption right to those lands at two dollars per acre, and such credit as Congress may think proper to extend to them, clear of interest."[14]

In 1806 a petition from settlers in Indiana asked for the grant of the land on which they were located, and also that the system of rectangular survey be not extended into their settlement. They took great credit to themselves for having rejected the offers of Spain to settle across the Mississippi, and through attachment to their own country begun a settlement on government land in Indiana Territory. This petition, like the preceding, failed to pass the Committee of the House on public lands.

UNAUTHORIZED SETTLEMENT PROHIBITED BY THE ACT OF 1807

On March 3, 1807, an act was passed "to prevent settlements being made on lands ceded to the United States, until authorized by law."[15] This act ran the gauntlet of a heated, not to say acrimonious, debate.[16] For the first time sectional lines are fairly well defined, the North and West favoring the squatter—the small farmer—and the South taking a stand against him.[17] It was evident that the squatter would

[13] *Pub. Lands,* I, pp. 80, 81.
[14] *Ibid,* p. 100.
[15] *Ann. of Cong.,* 9 Cong., 2 Sess., p. 1288.
[16] *Ibid,* pp. 664, 672.
[17] *Ibid,* p. 672.

be in the way of plantation development. In the Senate the lines were not so closely drawn, though the general aspect of the case was the same as in the House.

The act was a drastic one, providing that "it shall be lawful for the President of the United States to direct the marshall or other person acting as marshall, . . . and also to take such other measures and to employ such military force as he may judge necessary and proper to remove from lands . . . any person or persons who shall hereafter take possession of the same, or make, or attempt to make a settlement thereon, until thereunto authorized by law." [18] It was further provided that any squatter not heeding the first warning to move (and this meant leaving his improvements) would be liable to a fine of one hundred dollars, and on conviction, at the discretion of the court, to imprisonment not to exceed six months. In the debate preliminary to the passage of this act it was stated that the purpose of the squatter was not to buy the land at all, but to make improvements, sell out, and do the same thing again on other land.[19] Such an argument indicated not merely a lack of sympathy but a lack of information respecting the frontier.

"Strict construction" ran a curious course during the debate, the New England Federalists contending for a rigid compliance with the Constitution, while the members from South Carolina and Virginia did not seem disposed to let a little matter of technical consequence stand in the way of a law which was to their liking.[20] This act was in force nominally for a quarter of a century. However, the interested parties were not at all inclined to accept the action as final. The House of Representatives of the Territory of Mississippi in a memorial addressed to the government set forth the views of the frontiersmen of the Southwest. Many, it was stated, had emigrated to Mississippi expecting to find land on sale, only to be disappointed; they could go

---

[18] *Ann. of Cong.*, 9 Cong., 2 Sess., p. 1288.
[19] *Ibid*, p. 665.
[20] *Ibid*, pp. 664-666. The constitutional objections here set forth seem rather far-fetched, and vague. The bill in its earlier form is not to be found.

to Spanish territory or settle on the lands of the United
States; they chose the latter; "Wherefore your memorialists pray that a law be passed, extending to such settlers
the preference in becoming the purchasers of such lands,
or so much thereof as may be proper, as they may have
settled and improved." [21] But the Public Lands Committee
was inexorable: "The Committee do not impute to these
settlers the improper intention of violating the laws of their
country," but believe that granting the request "would be
offering an inducement to future intrusion, and be giving
support to a practice liable to many abuses, and which, if
encouraged, must destroy all competition in the public sales,
and eventually defeat the object of drawing a revenue from
the sale of lands." [22] Similar sentiment came from the committee, as from time to time some community of western
squatters presented a similar petition. In 1824 the Committee on Public Lands submitted a report to the House setting
forth at length its views on the treatment due to squatters.
Mention is made of the fact that settlers on land at the
time of its cession to the United States had been treated
leniently, being permitted a preëmption right. In fact, this
leniency resulted in many abuses, later settlers claiming to
have been in possession before the cession. [23]

Apropos of the general subject of preëmption, the committee says: "It cannot be perceived by what principle persons having no color of title, should, after lands on which
they were settled were known to belong to the United States
at the time of making such settlement, claim the preëmption
right to these lands." The committee further stated that in
all probability, were preëmption grants freely made, squatters would precede the surveyors systematically, choose the
choice tracts, and thus get them at the minimum price;
competition at the regular sales would be precluded, but
"competition would be excited among a certain description
of our population to locate themselves upon the public lands

[21] *Pub. Lands,* I, p. 545.
[22] *Ibid,* p. 546.
[23] Treat, Ch. IX.

without much regard to lines or boundaries, and with very little respect for the rights either of the Government or their Indian neighbors." [24] The opinion was expressed that preëmption would result in perplexity to the government, and in injury to those who were concerned in settling on western lands.

In the act of 1820 abolishing the credit system, provision was made for certain preëmption rights, but these related only to settlers who had made payment on land and later relinquished some part of it. The merits of the preëmption principle seem to have been brought before Congress but seldom, and to have received scant support until after 1830. In 1824 on the occasion of an adverse Senate report on a petition asking for the privilege of preëmption, Johnson of Louisiana moved a reversal of the report, arguing that the act of 1807 prohibiting unauthorized settlements had been passed to meet one or two extraordinary cases; that Congress had recognized the rights of occupants again and again. Mr. Johnson maintained that the best policy was to encourage the settlement of the vacant land: the frontier would be safer from Indian attack; the price of surrounding lands would be enhanced. Mr. King of New York thought it the best policy to prohibit an unlawful settlement and used the well-known argument that the nation had been at great expense in acquiring the land; that the minimum price was low and the terms easy. He feared for the very stability of government, since men who had gained property by disregarding law would perhaps themselves be elected to sit in Congress with the law-abiding. The yeas and nays were taken and eleven votes were cast in favor of preëmption, seven of them being from public land states. [25] This, in the language of Senator Benton, shows "the low point at which

[24] *Pub. Lands,* III, p. 619.

[25] *Ann. of Cong.,* 18 Cong., 1 Sess., pp. 121, 123, 130. As to the purpose of the act of 1807 see *Senate Proceedings* Jan. 4, 1830. Barton of Missouri says it was to prohibit settlement on the *batture* at New Orleans. Again it was claimed that the law was to prevent the location of a class of French and Spanish grants in the Southwest. See also *Congressional Debates,* 22 Cong., 1 Sess., p. 3529.

the preêmption system stood at that time in Congress," though it afterwards "was fought up into general popularity" and became a "most beneficial part of the public land system." [26]

A resolution presented to the House providing for the privilege of occupancy of land by the squatter for a period sufficient to permit him to mature and gather his crop before yielding possession to a purchaser was voted down without debate.[27] A short time later a similar resolution was introduced, debated, and passed, the support in this debate coming wholly from the public land states and Tennessee.[28] Nothing came of the resolution.

And yet, with all this show of rigid adherence to the letter of a law, embodying presumably justice in the abstract, Congress over and over when confronted by the responsibility of enforcement of the act of 1807 tempered its justice with mercy. Preêmptions were allowed in state after state on one pretext or another.[29]

FAVORABLE REPORT OF PUBLIC LANDS COMMITTEE, 1828

In 1828 the Public Lands Committee in a report to the House was unequivocal in its expression of opinions concerning the relation of squatters to the government. "It may be contended that the laws interdict settlement on the public lands. But it is impossible to prevent settlements on the public lands. Wherever land is expected to be brought into market, the people in other parts of the same State, whose lands are exhausted, and those who are the owners of none, will remove to the new settlement and select a new home. It is right and proper that the first settlers, who have made roads and bridges over the public lands at their own expense and with great labor and toil, should be allowed a privilege greater than other purchasers. It cannot be denied that these settlers increase the value of

[26] *Debates of Congress,* 16 Cong., 2 Sess., p. 489, note.
[27] *Ann. of Cong.,* 18 Cong., 1 Sess., p. 1680.
[28] *Ibid,* p. 1832.
[29] *Pub. Lands,* III, p. 619.

contiguous lands of the United States. By this means an additional amount on sales of the public land is realized to the government. It is just and proper that he who renders a benefit to the public, who by his enterprise and industry has created to himself and his family a home in the wilderness, should be entitled to his reward. He has afforded facilities to the sale of the public lands, and brought into competition lands which otherwise would have commanded no price and for which there would have been no bidders, unless for his improvements."[30] One could well believe the above words penned by a committee at some squatters' meeting in Illinois or an enthusiastic editor in a frontier village.

PREËMPTION ACTS OF 1830 TO 1838

The above was western defense by advocates who were finally admitted to court, and, though a mere preliminary, the case was docketed, and two years later was given a hearing. The legislatures of Indiana, Louisiana,[31] Alabama and Arkansas[32] passed resolutions asking for preëmption laws; petitions were numerous; a general in place of special action was demanded, and in 1830 the demands produced results. A bill originating in the Senate called out the expression of opinions on the merits and demerits of preëmption. The committee report was favorable. Samuel Bell of New Hampshire took the negative; the bill would defeat the revenue feature of the land system; it would even extend credit again. To him the squatters were intruders. He concluded his remarks with: "It would be better to repeal all laws on this subject, and to permit a general scramble, than to pass the present law." Messrs. Barton of Missouri, Noble of Indiana and Hayne of South Carolina took the affirmative and gave all the familiar arguments of the West: The settlers had risked much, had made valuable land improve-

[30] *Pub. Lands,* V, p. 401.
[31] *Ibid,* p. 582.
[32] *Ibid,* VI, pp. 10, 33.

ments, had raised the value of government land.[33] The bill passed Congress and became a law. Provision was made for the preëmption of a quarter section by a settler who had occupied and cultivated it during the preceding year; the preëmption right was not to delay the sale beyond the time when it should regularly occur; the act was to continue in force one year. It was not provided in this act that the right of preëmption was available only to those settling on land already surveyed, hence a right could be claimed by a settler who had preceded the survey. This was a distinct advance in the principle of favor to squatters. In an argument for an extension of this act a year later Joseph M. White of Florida asserted that the "act of 1807 concerning intruders had not been in force for many years; it was practically repealed in 1814 and had never been considered, by the government nor the occupants, in force since. Hence the settlers provided for in this bill are not trespassers or violators of law."[34] Certainly the squatter was not classed with lawbreakers in the West, but, on the contrary, the petitions speak again and again of "a very respectable class of citizens," "a sturdy class of pioneers," "the hardy yeomanry," or "the meritorious and industrious citizens." While a few in the older states continued to retain the old prejudice, with the act of 1830 the squatters had 'won. It remained only to confirm the victory. White in the connection above mentioned put the matter in good form by saying: "It is too late . . . to question the preëmption policy."

The interested parties were not slow to follow up the advantage gained and the legislatures of the public land states continued their vigorous memorials and the settlers their petitions.[35]

During these years both Presidents Jackson and Van Buren took sides with the settlers.[36] Van Buren in his first annual message recommended a preëmption law, though

[33] *Cong. Debates*, 21 Cong., 1 Sess., pp. 830, 831 *et seq.*
[34] *Ibid*, 22 Cong., 1 Sess., p. 3529.
[35] *Pub. Lands*, VI, Index.
[36] Richardson, II, p. 601.

at the same time favoring some means of preventing further unauthorized settlement.[37]

The law of 1830 was reënacted in 1834, failed of further extension in 1837, was reënacted in a modified form in 1838, and brought out in the last-named year the most interesting, lengthy, and vitriolic debate held in the history of the preëmption question. The bill, which was essentially the one left over from the preceding year, was brought up in the Senate. The conspicuous leaders on the opposing sides were, respectively, Thomas H. Benton and Henry Clay. Benton had been hammering away on the subject for eighteen years in Congress and had worked for the same principle in Tennessee long before that.[38] Benton defined preëmption in a very clever way: "It is nothing but a right of first purchase. It is no donation . . . it is no gift . . . it is no gratuitous distribution of the land. . . . The preëmption merely exempts the settler from the competition of speculators at the auction sales, and these auction sales have in reality produced nothing for the public treasury." The receipts above the minimum price had varied from one cent to a few cents an acre, averaging, up to this time, about six cents for the period 1823 to 1837. Benton eulogized agriculture; the banks had suspended; the customs receipts had fallen off; "but the farmers, the cultivators of the soil, have poured out hard money to the government." Yet commerce and manufacturers had been fostered and favored, and banks petted, but agriculture, the foundation of all industry, had not received justice, much less favor.

Clay had never been in favor of preëmption laws. To him the squatters were a "lawless horde"; he supposed there would be a demand for preëmption till the end of time, till settlements reached the Pacific Ocean; preëmptioners did not stay on the land they bought—they were frequently hired to preëmpt for some moneyed speculator

[37] Richardson, III, pp. 388, 389.
[38] T. H. Benton, *Thirty Years View*, I, p. 102.

who thus got land worth ten to forty dollars an acre for one and a quarter dollars; the "intruders" interfered with the government surveyors; a preëmptioner might as well "squat" in the East Room of the White House; he might as well rob the public treasury as to rob the public of possessions in lands. Mr. Clay wished the Senate would consider the Union and its interests rather than a few western states, and charged that the general preëmption scheme was one of "a fatal system of experiments which grew up under the late administration," and freely characterized the plan as "democratic." He introduced an amendment proposing to make criminal all intrusions on public land, and thus revive the law of 1807.[39]

Clay two years before had introduced a resolution providing for the sale of the land and the distribution of the proceeds among the states. He still favored that plan. Calhoun proposed the cession to the states of the land lying within their borders. Thus the fight was a three-cornered one and in the final vote many of those favoring either the Clay or the Calhoun view voted against preëmption. The vote stood 30 to 18 for the bill. This was primarily a sectional vote but tempered with partisanship. Clay had hoped to hold the Whigs to the "distribution" program; Benton expected the Democrats to vote for preëmption; both were disappointed, in a measure.

Such a furore as had not been known before out in the land states was stirred up by this debate, or rather by the debate of 1838 and this one together. Taking land ahead of the surveyors was by no means on the decline. In fact, there were by 1838 twenty to thirty thousand people living in what is now Iowa, yet no land had even been offered for sale; they were all squatters.[40] They fully expected Congress to grant them the first right to buy the land on which they were settled, and the same sentiment prevailed on the frontier from Wisconsin to Alabama. They were ready to

[39] Cong. Globe, 25 Cong., 2 Sess., App., pp. 129-143.
[40] Ibid, 26 Cong., 2 Sess., App., p. 28.

resist any effort on the part of the government, or outside purchasers, to conduct an auction at which their interests were not safeguarded. "Refuse to our hardy settlers the privileges heretofore granted and you create a necessity for combinations among them. They will combine to protect their fields and their homes. . . . If the Honorable H. Clay would conciliate the New England people by his hostility to preëmption laws, he will fail in his object." [41] Similar expressions are abundant in the western newspapers throughout the period preceding 1841. [42] State legislatures renewed their zeal in demanding recognition of squatter rights. Especially noticeable is the plea of the new states and territories in this regard. Michigan asks for "the usual preëmption rights." Wisconsin relied on the "liberal policy," "the humane system," "the wisdom and patriotism of Congress" in dealing with all settlers on the public lands. Missouri, Illinois, Alabama and Mississippi held to the position taken years before and "instructed the Senators, and requested the Representatives" to exert themselves in favor of a general preëmption law. [43]

THE PASSAGE OF THE ACT OF 1841

The demand of the West was irresistible; the Whigs must carry the northwestern states, and to do so meant that the squatters and their friends must be held in line. Harrison always had favored preëmption; now the party nominating him endorsed it. The Democrats were committed to the measure. Therefore, when Benton introduced this hardy perennial in the Senate, it was destined to pass. With a humor savored with shrewdness he designated the bill the "Log Cabin Bill." The official title served as a table of contents: it was a "Permanent Prospective Pre-

---

[41] *Iowa News*, Feb. 24, 1838. This was a good prophecy, for New England cast but four votes against the preëmption bill a few months later. On the same subject see also same publication for April 21 and May 26, 1838.

[42] For example, *Dubuque Visitor*, Iowa, Sept. 28, 1836; *Niles Intelligencer*, Michigan, June 27, 1838.

[43] *Pub. Lands*, VIII, Index; *Illinois Senate Journal*, 1836-7, p. 80.

emption Law." [44] The debate in the Senate in comparison with former occasions was a mere love feast, even Clay, submitting to the inevitable, made but few remarks. The vote stood 31 to 19, the opposition coming, as two years before, from the old states, the original thirteen furnishing, in fact, all but three of the nineteen negative votes. Mr. Clay did himself the honor of voting against the bill, as did also his colleague, Mr. Crittenden.

The debate in the House was voluminous, yet a great part of it was on the questions of distribution and graduation rather than preëmption. It was charged by the friends of preëmption that a great part of the opposition coming from the Whigs was counterbalanced only by inserting in the program of land legislation the provision for distribution among the states of a large portion of the proceeds of land sales. [45] And further it was held that the distribution was desirable in order that the surplus produced by the tariff might not be augmented by receipts from the public domain. After the Whig campaign of 1840 was projected, it became expedient for the members of that party to cease their opposition to preëmption, and many became its warm advocates. Webster had always been friendly to preëmption; Clay had always been hostile to it. During the year 1841 comparatively few members of the party opposed the measure as such, although under cover of alleged objections to details several representatives from the old states, both North and South, and of both parties, maintained their opposition to the end.

The vote in the House on the passage of the bill—preëmption and distribution combined—stood 116 to 108. This was a close party division, the great majority of the Whigs voting for the bill and the Democrats almost solidly against it. This must not be taken as the expression of sentiment on the preëmption bill. The Democrats wanted to vote for such a measure in some form or other, but refused to take

[44] *Cong. Globe*, 26 Cong., 2 Sess., XX, p. 14.
[45] *Ibid*, 27 Cong., 1 Sess., App., p. 313.

the distribution pill along with it. The Whigs were in the majority, however, and the opposition of the Democrats was unavailing. This vote was in marked contrast with that on the preëmption bill of 1838 when 92 out of 98 Democrats voted in the affirmative and 68 Whigs, a great majority of the whole number, voted against it. In the Senate the vote in 1841 was not drawn so rigidly on party lines, due, doubtless, to the fact that many Senators who had long been committed to the cause of preëmption refused to take an opposite stand even though it became necessary to accept the distribution plan along with it. For example, the two Democratic representatives from Missouri voted against the bill, while the Senators, both Democrats, voted for it, although both had consistently opposed the principle of distribution.

The right of preëmption was open to the head of a family, to a man over twenty-one years of age, to a widow, —these to be citizens of the United States—or to aliens who had declared their intention of becoming such. The applicant was required to swear that he had not to exceed 320 acres of land other than his preëmption claim. To such persons the preëmption act gave the right to settle on a piece of land, 160 acres in extent, and at a subsequent date to buy the same free from competitive bids, at the minimum government price.

The Act of 1841 Characterized

The fight was won against heavy odds. It was a triumph of the West over the prejudices of the older states, although paradoxical as it may seem, in this case western Democrats in the House voted against the measure which had always been known as both western and Democratic. It was a case of the progressives against the standpatters, and finally the standpatters voted the progressive program through in order to carry their own.

One western paper [46] contained the following editorial on

[46] *Hawk-Eye and Iowa Patriot*, Feb. 25, 1841.

the subject: "The Preëmption Bill has passed the Senate. To be sure, it is far better to have the law on many accounts, as it legalizes a course which, although universally in vogue, was in fact unlawful. But that is not the principle about which we have been contending. All we have ever attempted to prove was that the settler stood just as good a chance of securing his land without as with the existence of a pre-emption law. All who live in this country know this. It is true that the bill passed the Senate, as has been stated, under the influence of the argument that it is better to legalize what is incurable and inevitable, than to keep on the statute book a provision which is a dead letter. 'If this was the motive, then all must consider Mr. Clay's views acquiesced in to a very considerable extent.'"

The arguments advanced against the principle of pre-emption as embodied in this law were political, sociologic and economic. From the political standpoint, it was urged that the government would be unable to assert its authority over the lawless rabble that would occupy the public domain in advance even of the surveyors.[47] As clearly pointed out by White of Florida, this was a manifest begging of the question, for how could men be trespassers in settling on land after being invited to do so?

There was danger that the internal peace of the nation might suffer; the new states and the old states would take, indeed, they had taken, different views and attitudes, and so one could predict the outcome should a great number of men be coaxed, as it were, to leave their homes in the East and become citizens, under these circumstances, of the wilderness? Preëmption was looked upon as a privilege, a bounty, offered to new states, and therefore partial and unjust in its operations with respect to the old states.[48]

The sociological objections were quite similar in character: the labor supply of the established centers would be decimated since great numbers of the "operatives" would

---

[47] *Cong. Globe*, 26 Cong., 2 Sess., App., p. 30.
[48] *Ibid*, p. 75.

be induced to go west. This attitude was resented by the people of the new states, who accused the manufacturers and farmers of the East of a desire to retain among themselves a laboring class at low wages instead of permitting an emigration to new land and independence. No doubt the men from the West were ready to charge the East with selfish motives, but it is clear that there was a deep-seated fear in the old settled districts that the better lands of the West would, under the favorable conditions of the preëmption law, become so attractive to eastern farmers, and even to non-farmers, as to induce them to leave their old farms uncultivated and the towns with a dearth of labor supply.

The arguments from the economic standpoint were the most extended of any. It was held that preëmption would reduce the selling price; that it would result in selling best land first and leaving the government in possession of all the poor, unsalable land; that it would reduce the price of land already in private hands; that it would encourage speculation and fraud; that it would help to make the rich richer and the poor poorer; that it would revive credit.

The claim that the price would be reduced has been noted above. Since the selling price under the auction system was but a very few cents above the minimum, the claim that preëmption could effect a pronounced decrease was preposterous. Whether or not it would result in the settlement of the best land first was not so easily disposed of since no accurate information was available, or ever has been, on the subject of land entry according to quality. There were many factors to be taken into account in choosing land, and it is fair to presume that the purchasers were exercising their best judgment in this respect. That they were able to choose, in most instances, the land which was eventually the best, however, is open to doubt. Moreover, the speculator was always attempting to choose the best land first, and while he was permitted to choose without limit as to amount, the preëmptor was restricted to a single quarter section. This argument would seem, therefore, to have been used mainly for declamatory purposes.

Of a little more genuine nature was the argument that preëmption would reduce the price of land already sold. Yet the importance of the view admitted of easy exaggeration. It was a nightmare of the speculator, who frequently waited a long time for an increase over the price he had paid. Manifestly, preëmption could not reduce the price of land, which had been sold at $1.25 per acre, to a lower value, and since that was the prevailing figure at which most of it had actually sold, it was only in those scattered spots where the minimum had been exceeded that damage could result; or, perhaps, in addition to this possibility, was that of land still unsold in proximity to land held by speculators, which might, when offered, bring a figure well above the minimum and so aid the speculator in realizing a profit. These were rather remote contingencies, especially as viewed in the light of subsequent events. To devise some plan by which land should rise above the minimum price, while there was an abundance of it to be had at that figure, was a problem for which many anxious landholders of the first half of the nineteenth century sought in vain.

Another favorite argument against preëmption was that it would encourage speculation and fraud, these terms being as a rule coupled together. How it could encourage speculation in any large way passes understanding. Speculation had been running riot for years. Every man so disposed could, with a single hundred dollars—and, until 1836, it mattered not whether it was a hundred dollars or a hundred depreciated paper dollars—become a land speculator. Now he could undoubtedly make some use of the preëmption privilege, but to do so would mean moving his lares and penates to the frontier, building a habitation, improving some portion of the soil, and waiting till the day set for the land sale before paying his $1.25 an acre, and this on a paltry quarter section. Surely this was aiding speculation on a petty and not a grand scale. To repeat the process on other pieces of land would necessarily mean months, or even years, of waiting between ventures. A little less absurd was the prediction that the requirements in respect to cultivation and improvement would not be carried out in good faith. It was stated that the settler would come and go in a night; he would cut down a single tree, build one rod of fence, and yet claim the privileges of preëmption.[50] To prevent the use of the right of preëmption by speculators the bill as first introduced was amended so as to exclude from its benefits all persons who had previously made use of a preëmption right, all who owned 320 acres of land, and all who left land which they owned in the same state or territory in order to preëmpt more from the public domain.

In the minds of some of the leaders of Congress preëmption meant a return to the credit system of sales with all of its attendant and almost interminable evils. "Whether the term be one, two or three years," said Henry Clay, "it changes our land system from a sale for cash to a sale for credit."[51] The answer to this charge was put very clearly by Senator Sevier of Arkansas, and, although it was still held by several of the old enemies of preëmption, it apparently was seriously considered by very few of the men in Congress or in the country at large.

It was a case of half a loaf rather than no bread, so far as the West was concerned. Although many features of the act as passed were objectionable, it had the redeeming merit of being general in its application, and, above all, in being prospective instead of retrospective. The pioneer wanted the right to settle on land before it came into the market, not merely the tardy, though certain, forgiveness of a trespass. The tried friends of preëmption were entirely justified in accepting the garbled form in which the bill finally passed rather than in holding out for something more to their liking, since it was comparatively easy to remedy its defects after the main principle was established.

The bill was destined to become a law, if for no other

---

[50] *Cong. Globe*, 26 Cong., 2 Sess., App., pp. 36-38.
[51] *Ibid*, p. 29.

reason than because, as expressed by Senator Smith of Indiana, it was merely "declaratory of the custom of common law of the settlers."[52] From the standpoint of men far from the frontier and its conditions, the privilege of buying land at the minimum price instead of running the risk of getting it at about the same price at public auction, was tantamount to a gift. By men familiar with the West, it was conceded that the pioneer paid dearly for his purchase in privations and hardships. The land, it was repeatedly said, was worth no more than it cost.[53] Moreover, the fact that land was settled before being sold meant that it was improved more or less before the day for selling at auction arrived. A serious question was bound up in the matter of right to these improvements. The speculator who outbid the settler had a legal title to the improvements. The settlers were always determined that the speculator should not get improvements for which he paid nothing, and, furthermore, that the United States should not receive in the price of the land an equivalent for the improvements made by them. Repeatedly it was declared in Congress that the pioneers would, if driven to it, defend their interests and supposed rights in their lands by the use of force. Senator Smith of Indiana declared that "no honest man would take from a poor man the improvements he had made on a piece of land, and no dishonest man would dare to do so." [54] Senator Linn of Missouri put the whole question tersely, thus: "The whole body of Missouri had been settled by a hardy and enterprising band long before the lands were thought of being surveyed. It had always been so, and always would be so; and if, after these people had settled on the public lands, and made their improvements, any attempt was made to put these lands up at auction because they had not been surveyed, it would compel these people to combine and drive off intruders with their rifles." [55]

It seems that since there was no longer any hope of

[52] *Cong. Globe*, 26 Cong., 2 Sess., App., p. 70
[53] *Ibid*, 25, p. 44.
[54] *Ibid*, App., p. 70.
[55] *Ibid*, 27 Cong., 1 Sess., p. 317.

defeating the whole bill, the old-time enemies of preëmption were determined to make all the trouble that could be made with respect to some of its provisions. Attempts were made by Clay and other opponents of the bill to restrict the act by making amendments to prohibit all aliens from taking advantage of it. Such amendments, however, were not adopted since an alien could get the full benefit of the law by declaring his intention of becoming a citizen of the United States.

Another attempt to restrict the application of the act of 1841 was made by Senator Crittenden of Kentucky in a proposed amendment to restrict the act to those settlers whose estate was worth less than $500. This amendment failed, however, as did a similar amendment, proposed by the same senator, making the maximum value of the preëmptor's estate $1,000.

CHANGES MADE IN THE PREËMPTION ACT

Although the principle of preëmption was established by the passage of the act of 1841 the West was not content to let the matter rest, since the conditions of the act were not altogether satisfactory. The pioneers had never taken kindly to the restriction of the act pertaining to settlement on land subsequent to survey.

An Iowa paper expresses the prevailing sentiment: "The preëmption sections that were tacked by the Whigs, at the Extra Session of Congress, to the Distribution Bill, for the purpose of making that act more palatable to the western people, were, as our readers will well recollect, unpopular with the great mass of the citizens of the valley of the Mississippi." The Democrats used their untiring efforts to give more liberal features to the law, but were overpowered by the Whig majority in Congress.

The Preëmption law, however liberal it may look in retrospect, fell far short of pleasing all parties concerned. The West wanted free land, and wanted it free for all, or substantially so. Since the act had been passed by a Whig

Congress it was quite naturally the press of the Democratic party that was most outspoken in criticism. One item of severe complaint was centered on the provision of the act restricting the privileges to citizens or those having declared their intentions of becoming such. Would not the alien who had taken no steps toward citizenship eventually become a good citizen? A more general complaint pertained to the restriction of preëmption privileges to those settling on surveyed land. The pioneer demanded the extension of the act to settlers on unsurveyed land. To him the running of the surveyor's lines was a mere detail of convenience. The land and all essential qualities and relationships pertaining to it were there in advance of the survey.

Third, and almost equally important in the minds of the western settlers, was the exclusion from the preëmption right of those having in their possession 320 or more acres of land in any state or territory. It was contended that many might own barren, or at least worthless, land somewhere else and because of it, and the great difficulty in disposing of such land, be unable to preëmpt land in the fertile West.[56]

A bill in the nature of an amendment was introduced in the United States Senate in 1842 designed to remove these restrictions. Although the measure was quite warmly supported by several senators, particularly those from Illinois, it passed the Senate by the narrow margin of 20 to 23 votes,[57] and failed in the House.

It should be remembered that the most formidable of these complaints as to the operation of the preëmption law was directed against the restriction of its operation to surveyed land. It had been the custom for years for the pioneer settlers to occupy land ahead of the surveyors. Congress was familiar with this fact, but while wishing to favor the first settlers, was not willing to offer a premium to the settlers who took land before it was in any sense ready for the

[56] *Lee County Democrat*, Iowa, Apr. 23, 1842.
[57] *Cong. Globe*, 27 Cong., 2 Sess., p. 352.

market. Such action was still looked upon as trespass. Nevertheless, men in authority in the administration of the public domain were not blind to the hardship which was unintentionally worked by the provision of the law. Four years after the passage of the act the commissioner of the general land office reported:

"I consider the spirit of the preëmption principle violated, when the first settlers, who open the way for succeeding emigration, are deprived of the benefit of their settlements because they have been made on unsurveyed public land; and despoiled of their homes, perhaps, by the very men whom they have pioneered into the country, merely because the latter happened to become the first settlers on the land after it is surveyed. The law in this respect tends to reward cupidity and favor spoliation, and ought to be modified at once, in such a manner as to prevent the commission of such flagrant injustice." [58]

Other weaknesses soon manifested themselves, the most prominent one being the advantage taken by purchasers of the opportunity to file on a piece of land, and, without payment, hold it off the market. This made it possible for the holder of such a claim to sell a relinquishment, and in that way profit by whatever increase in value there might be within the year. The commissioner of the general land office reported in 1847 that such entries were common. [59] The remedy suggested was that proof be required of persons holding these claims that settlement and improvement had actually been made. In the act of 1843 it was provided that one person could not, after once exercising the right of preëmption, file on a second tract. It was later found, however, that several different men could each, in succession, hold a given tract until eventually the actual settler would be required to pay a high price for it. Prior to 1843 it had been possible for two men to exchange courtesies by filing on each other's claims, each giving the other a relinquish-

[58] *Executive Doc.*, 29 Cong., 1 Sess., No. 12.
[59] *Cong. Globe*, 30 Cong., 1 Sess., App., p. 37.

ment at the end of the year and so put off for an additional year the day of payment. This was obviated by the act of 1843, but it was still possible for a limited amount of speculation to take place. In the Milwaukee land district, for example, 6,441 preëmption declarations were made prior to October 1, 1847, yet, although six years had elapsed since the first of them were made, only forty had been paid for. This was a clear case of speculation such as Congress hoped to prevent.[60]

Had Congress seen fit to permit preëmption claims to be established on unsurveyed land, the greater part of the difficulties would have been overcome, as in that case no real pretension to a claim could have been made without settlement, since possession was the main basis on which such claim could be defended. Although these facts were patent to the people of the West, and to those administering the laws, it was about a decade from the time of the first amendment, 1843, until the next one. By that time the preëmption of unsurveyed land had ceased, in several states, to be an issue, since the land was in the meantime surveyed. In 1853 and 1854 acts were passed providing for the preëmption of land previously to surveys. These acts were at the same time retroactive, but applied only to the newer states, six in number.[61]

In 1849 Horace Greeley, then a member of the House, introduced a bill which embodied the leading ideas of both preëmption and homestead.[62] This bill proposed to give a right of preëmption to *bona fide* settlers for a period of seven years, during which period the preëmptor might at any time, on proof of settlement and improvement, receive free the title to forty or eighty acres. The settlers must not, however, own any other land. Furthermore, these homesteads could not be inherited by any heir who possessed enough land to make, together with the inheritance, over

[60] *Cong. Globe,* 30 Cong., 1 Sess., App., p. 37.
[61] *Ibid,* 32 Cong., 2 Sess., 1020; *Ibid,* 33 Cong., 1 Sess., p. 2204 *et seq.*
[62] *Ibid,* 30 Cong., 2 Sess., p. 605.

one hundred and sixty acres. The preëmption might cover a hundred and sixty acres and the person entering it should have the privilege of buying the amount not included in the homestead, forty or eighty acres, at the minimum price. Any person wishing to buy more land might, on affidavit that it was for his own use, have it at the same price, but otherwise the minimum was to be raised to $5.00 per acre. In the language of Mr. Greeley this was the only bill of the winter recognizing the right of a man, even though without money, "to live *somewhere*." This bill was named, "A bill to discourage speculation in the public lands, and to secure homes thereon to actual settlers and cultivators." It went through the Committee on Public Lands, but was tabled in the House.

Not many fundamental changes were made in the preëmption law after 1854. In 1862 it was made generally applicable, whereas, up to that time it had been necessary to designate the states and territories to which it applied. In 1866 the preëmption privilege was withdrawn from operation in Mississippi, Louisiana, Arkansas and Florida in order that the homestead law might have fuller application.[63] The principle of the preëmption law had much in common with that of the homestead law, the main difference being the payment in the one case of $1.25 per acre at the end of about fourteen months' residence, and the free grant following five years of residence in the other. However, there was nothing to prevent a man from taking advantage of the privileges of each law and so getting 320 acres on terms somewhat better than that of the open market. The commissioner of the General Land Office recommended in 1870 that the exercise of the right of preëmption should be a bar to the homestead right, and *vice versa*. The commissioner praised both laws, but believed it unwise to extend both privileges to the same person. The following year the commissioner advised the repeal of the preëmption law and stated it as his conviction that, "The provisions of the home-

[63] *L. O. R.*, 1870, p. 177.

stead law were undoubtedly sufficient at the date of its passage for a measure of complete substitution for the preëmption system, if we except the omission of the single feature of priority of settlement [*i.e.* "preëmption" settlements], which failed to be recognized.[64] Apparently the recommendation was taken seriously by Congress, for a bill repealing the law passed both houses during the following year, though it was crowded to the end of the session and lost because of a failure to agree on some minor amendments.

The Commissioner of the General Land Office in 1877 made bold to call in question the advisability of continuing to give away land under either the preëmption act or the homestead act. Was it not true that the acts were intended to aid in settling the West and was not the West largely settled? At least, he believed that non-agricultural lands should not be donated to settlers under the guise of agricultural improvement. Mild criticisms were offered nearly every year, but again in 1882 the commissioner declared positively in favor of repeal of the preëmption law on the ground that it was not needed and that it was the cause of frauds "which have approached great magnitudes—a material portion of the preëmption entries now made are fraudulent in character, being chiefly placed upon valuable timber or mineral lands, or water rights, and made in the interest and by the procurement of others, and not for the purpose of residence and improvement, by the professed preëmptor."[65] From this time until the law was repealed the land office made a constant recommendation that it be done. In 1888 an important mass of evidence was submitted substantiating the position taken.

REPEAL OF THE PREËMPTION ACT IN 1891

The charge was made that the commissioner during these years was over-impressed by the fraudulent entries, and

----

[64] *L. O. R.*, 1871, p. 29.
[65] *Ibid*, 1882, p. 8.

hence exaggerated the matter. At all events he made his point, and Congress, in 1891, repealed the law.[66]

That the preëmption act was a very important one up to the time of the homestead act there is no room for doubt. It secured the settler in his rights. Since, however, the amount of land purchased under this right was not kept as a separate record, but included with cash sales indiscriminately, it is impossible to give its importance in terms of acres.

Preëmption Requirements Summarized

The preëmption right was mainly a possessory right, established by the construction of a dwelling house and the making of improvements. For many years the preëmption privilege secured the settler in his right to purchase, at the minimum price, before the date of the general sale of the tract of which his claim was a part. After the passage of the homestead law and the discontinuance of the general sales, this provision was hardly applicable. Hence it was provided that the preëmptor should file his declaration of intent to purchase within three months after settlement upon the land, or, in case it was not surveyed at time of settlement, within three months after the filing of the survey plat, and should make payment within eighteen months after filing his declaration. Thus he could hold land in possession for twenty-one months before being required to pay for it.[67] Payments were received in cash, in military bounty warrants, or in agricultural college scrip. Many minor changes in the preëmption law were made from time to time, but the facts just mentioned give the substance of the requirement with respect to settlement, improvements, and time of payment.

[66] *U. S. Stat. at Large*, XXVI, p. 1097.
[67] *Ibid*, XVI, p. 279.

CHAPTER X

THE DISTRIBUTION OF THE PROCEEDS FROM THE SALE OF LANDS AND THE CESSION OF LANDS TO THE STATES

(A) DISTRIBUTION OF THE PROCEEDS FROM PUBLIC LANDS

When the states possessing western lands ceded them to the United States it was, among other reasons, in order that the general government might, from the proceeds, be enabled to pay its debts. Nearly a half century passed, and it seemed that the debt was soon to be extinguished, but the land was not all sold. Thus it was somewhat natural that the question of the right of the government to retain for its own use the funds still to be realized should be raised. The states which never had any western domain were always particularly jealous of their rights to the public lands and the returns from the same. These states were active in the distribution controversy.

PROPOSALS, RESOLUTIONS AND INVESTIGATIONS, 1824 TO 1832

Perhaps the first suggestion of a distribution of the proceeds of the public lands among the states was made by Mr. Johnston of Louisiana, who, in 1824, proposed that the money from land sales be invested by the United States in bank or other stock, and the interest therefrom be distributed among the states. The suggestion met with little favor.

In December 1825 a resolution was introduced in the House instructing the committee on public lands "to inquire into the expediency of appropriating a portion of the net annual proceeds of the sales and entries of the public lands exclusively for the support of the common schools, and of

[1] *Cong. Deb.*, 18 Cong., 2 Sess., p. 42.

apportioning the same among the several states in proportion to the representation of each in the House of Representatives." [2]

On the 24th of the following February the committee brought in an elaborate and favorable report. Arguments were marshalled to prove that the federal government had a right to make a disposition of this kind of the proceeds of public land, but especially was the advisability urged of aiding in the support of common schools. Moreover, such action, it was held, would have a salutary effect in respect to the public domain itself. While there was a feeling on the part of some that this measure might result in forcing the land into the market too rapidly, the committee was enthusiastic in its support: "Our burdens are light. We have money to meet all the engagements and exigencies of the government, and some to spare. . . . Believing, therefore, that a portion of the proceeds of the public lands may be spared; that the diffusion of common education among the people is demanded by the highest considerations of national glory and safety; and that Congress possesses both the power and the right to appropriate them for this purpose, the committee submit a bill." [3] Thus was launched a program which was destined to be bitterly fought through four presidential administrations.

One of the first notices from the states showing an interest in this subject came from Maryland. In 1826 the legislature of this state voted on the project, but the motion to sanction it failed to pass. [4] The next year Senator Dickerson of New Jersey introduced in the Senate of the United States a bill providing for the distribution of the surplus revenue among the states. [5] True, the bill related to the general surplus, and not specifically to that obtained from the sale of land, but the same senator, a few weeks later, opposed in vigorous terms the graduation of the price of refuse lands, because, as

[2] *Pub. Lands*, IV, p. 750.
[3] *Ibid*, p. 753.
[4] *Maryland Senate Journal*, 1826, p. 26.
[5] *Cong. Deb.*, 19 Con., 2 Sess., p. 209.

he put it: "New Jersey has a vested right to a share of those lands from which she did hope to obtain some remuneration from her heavy losses and expenses in carrying on the Revolutionary War." [6] Thus the inference is clear that Mr. Dickerson expected the revenue from land to swell the surplus which he proposed to distribute among the states, and as a representative of the sentiments of New Jersey, he was bound to prevent the depletion of the fund to be so distributed. Such a view involved the right of the federal government to raise, either by sale of land or by taxes, money to be given to the states.

HENRY CLAY AS A PROMOTER OF DISTRIBUTION

Not much more was done until 1832, when the Senate referred the subject of distribution of the public land proceeds to the committee on manufactures. This committee, with Henry Clay as chairman, reported in favor of the distribution. [7] According to Senator Benton, Clay was the author of the whole scheme. [8] The report of the Committee on Manufactures made its way to the Committee on Public Lands, the logical committee to consider such subjects, and from this committee came a drastic counter-report. [9] The case went over to the next session of Congress, at which time a bill embodying for the most part the ideas of Mr. Clay and the Whig party was passed and presented to the President for his signature. But President Jackson vetoed the bill and returned it with his objections the following autumn. Again Mr. Clay introduced it in the Senate. It made little progress and was introduced by him again a year later. Then came the bill for "depositing" the general surplus with the states, and in this measure the special cause of distributing the land surplus was obscured, but was presumably included. In 1841 the distribution project was coupled with the Preëmption Act and passed. The Whigs

[6] *Cong. Deb.,* 20 Cong., 1 Sess., p. 675; 22 Cong., 1 Sess., p. 786.
[7] *Pub. Lands,* VI, p. 441.
[8] Benton, I, p. 649.
[9] *Pub. Lands,* VI, p. 478.

had come into power; the preëmption principle had established itself. Hence, with the combination of party fortunes and legislative predestination, the bill was bound to pass. It remained in effect after passing fewer months than it had been years in the making, although nominally it lasted till 1862.

THE ARGUMENTS FOR AND AGAINST DISTRIBUTION

The path of the distribution measure in becoming a law was long and tortuous. It was not only partisan, but sectional. Sooner or later at least eight states on the Atlantic seaboard petitioned in favor of it, while to the west of the Alleghanies two states, Indiana and Kentucky, were insistent in its favor.[10] The states claimed a right to the proceeds either on the basis of the deed of cession by Virginia, on which many generalizations were made,[11] or, more often on the plea that the state, and not the general government, is competent to enter the field of internal improvements; that the money could advantageously be used for establishing public schools; or, negatively, that a surplus in the United States treasury was dangerous, and that distribution would enable the states to decrease their taxes.[12] It was assumed that a large part of the surplus came from the sale of public land, an assumption subject to much interpretation. Perhaps the most insistent of all the states in the demand for distribution was Indiana. In 1832 the Governor, in his annual message, discussed the subject at length. It would yield enough money to provide schooling for fifty thousand children; it would not become an obstacle in the way of reduction of price or donation of land; it would counteract the draining process by which seven to eight hundred thousand dollars are withdrawn from the state, in the price paid by settlers for land.[13] A member of the legislature, in the argument attending the passage of the memorial sent to

---

[10] These petitions were scattered over a considerable number of years, but a large part of them are to be found in *Pub. Lands,* VI, VIII.
[11] *Cong. Globe,* 25 Cong., 3 Sess., p. 98.
[12] For example, see memorial from Pennsylvania, *Pub. Lands,* VIII, p. 555.
[13] Indiana House Journal, 1832, p. 19 *et seq.*

Congress, voiced the sentiment of one class of pioneers respecting distribution:

"But if the present population are to cast from them the benefits they may derive from this distribution, in the means it will afford them to improve their condition, the undersigned would ask who is to be benefited by it? Surely none but those who may be attracted to our state by the lures and bounties thus held out to them. And is it the duty of this House solely to legislate for the future population, without regard to the interest of the present whose representatives its members are? Is the present population willing to yield up their whole share of this common fund to those who may come after them? Or, rather, is it not their interest, would it not be their wish, and is it not the duty of this House to hold on to it for the general improvement of the condition of the whole people? Those who settle the new territory will be equally benefited by this course. Imagine them located in the wilderness without a fund to make a road or establish a school; and contrast it with their situation when, as fast as population increases, roads of the most perfect and durable construction may be made—their rivers improved, so that whatever they may have to export can be easily and cheaply taken to market; and when they can behold the certainty of their offspring being educated at the charge of the public. Surely these would be inducements to emigration far more powerful than any system of bounties that could be devised." [14]

But the above sentiment was not allowed to go unchallenged. There was in the West a feeling that the distribution of public land money would, through its reaction on land sales, do more harm than good. In the same debate from which the above extract is taken occurs also a remonstrance.

It was declared that to distribute the proceeds of the public land money to the several states would soon result in a feeling on the part of the states in which public lands lay that something belonging to them personally was being offered whenever land was sold. This would lead such

[14] Indiana House Journal, 1832, p. 146.

states to favor any measures promising higher prices, if possible, for all government land sold within their borders. Thus the settler might not be treated so liberally. Surveys might very likely be retarded, so as to hold land for higher prices. Speculators would benefit. Emigration would be retarded, and Indiana would fail to make progress.[15]

In two states remonstrances against distribution preceded the passage of the act. The first was by Alabama in 1836.[16] The basis of this remonstrance was: first, it was inimical to state rights and would result in one consolidated government; second, prices of land would not be reduced, "and it will be the interest of the states to wring from the persevering and meritorious emigrant the last dollar, without the prospect of relief." Furthermore, it was held that the government should not hold land or try to make money out of it. Four years later, New Hampshire protests against the policy of distribution in a similar remonstrance.[17]

Clearly sentiment among the states, though divided, was preponderantly favorable to distribution. A scheme somewhat similar to the distribution demanded by so many states was embodied in a petition sent to Congress by a group of citizens of Philadelphia. The request was that Congress issue $200,000,000 in currency and pledge the public domain for its redemption, the money so issued to be distributed to the states.

From the partisan standpoint the lines were clearly drawn. During these years of diminution of the public debt, and increased revenues, sentiment regarding the policies of land disposition was taking definite form. In the early hours of the debate on Foote's Resolution, Senator Hayne gave a clear statement of the case as he understood it, showing that from the standpoint of party politics there were the most divergent views: "On the one side it is contended that the public land ought to be reserved as a permanent

[15] Indiana House Journal, 1832, p. 108.
[16] Pub. Lands, VIII, pp. 434, 512.
[17] Ex. Doc., 26 Cong., 1 Sess., No. 174.

fund for revenue and future distribution among the states; while on the other it is insisted that the whole of these lands of right belong to, and ought to belong to, the states in which they lie." [18] A considerable debate had already taken place on the subject, hence this clear understanding respecting the situation within the ranks of the two great parties. The Whigs wanted to sell the land and give the money to the states, that is, to all the states. The Democrats wanted to give the land itself, not to all the states, but to those in which it lay. These views were developed in the course of the debates on the subject during the year 1829, following the favorable report of a special committee on the subject of distributing the proceeds of the public lands.

President Jackson announced early in his presidency that it was his belief that the public lands should, as soon as possible, cease to be a source of revenue. Henry Clay had always emphasized the revenue side, and began an active campaign in favor of distribution during Jackson's first administration. In the report of the Committee on Manufactures in 1832 favoring distribution the arguments supporting the measure were set forth at length.[19] To begin with, the familiar arguments against reducing the price of public land were enumerated, and it was stated that Ohio, Kentucky and Tennessee would suffer most through loss of men and money. The view that the price paid for public land was a drain on the resources of the new states was denied; it was rather a drain on the resources of the old states. The new states were growing fast enough. They did not need the added stimulus of cheaper land. Next came an analysis of the proposition to cede the land to the states in which it lay. To this the committee was unalterably opposed.

This report must have been the result of previous views and judgments rather than of deliberations within the com-

[18] *Cong. Deb.*, 21 Cong., 1 Sess., p. 33.
[19] *Pub. Lands*, VI, p. 441.

mittee, since the elaborate document was ready within a few weeks after its reference to the committee. The same must also have been true of the counter-report presented by the Committee on Public Lands, since but a month intervened between the times of the two reports. The reference of the report of the Manufacturers' Committee to the Public Lands Committee was in a sense a defeat, since the Democrats dominated the one committee, the Whigs the other. The report of the Committee on Public Lands was in the nature of a heated discussion.[20] Every one of the elaborate points set forth by the other committee was met with denial, objection or refutation. With these reports before the Senate the fight was on. Clay, in presenting the report of his committee, had introduced a bill providing for the distribution to the states, for a limited time, of the proceeds of public land sales. One matter especially resented by the opponents of distribution was the fact that the question referred to the Committee on Manufactures was merely that of reduction of price; hence this committee should have reported on that subject alone instead of going out of its way to introduce another plan altogether. The occasion for submitting the land question to the Committee on Manufactures is explained by *The Tribune:* "The Jackson majority of the Senate thought it would be a clever trick to refer these petitions to a committee of which Mr. Clay should be chairman, with a majority of his friends as associates, and so subject him to the odium of reporting against graduation. He promptly accepted the post, proceeded to the consideration of the important subject involved, and in due time reported against Graduation or Cession, yet in favor of preserving and selling the lands as before, but distributing their cash proceeds equitably among the states, to form a perpetual fund sacredly devoted to the furtherance of education and internal improvement. This proposition was, of course, not approved by that nor any other Jackson Congress."[21]

[20] *Pub. Lands,* VI, p. 478 *et seq.*
[21] *N. Y. Weekly Tribune,* Feb. 23, 1856.

This committee was made up of eastern men with the exception of Henry Clay. The Committee on Public Lands was, as usual, composed mainly of men from the public land states. Contrary to the above version of Mr. Clay's attitude, he objected, or, at least, put up a show of objection, to the reference of the question to his committee; the Senate insisted upon it.[22] No sooner had the report been presented than a reference of it to the land committee was demanded, and the same body which a few weeks before had refused to send the matter to the land committee now did so.[23]

Mr. Clay had presented to the Senate a bill providing for the distribution of the land proceeds, for a period of five years, to the states. The public land states were to receive twelve and a half per cent of the proceeds of sales within their respective borders, after which the net proceeds were to be shared by all states in proportion to their representation in Congress. In support of this measure, Mr. Clay made a lengthy address in the Senate, setting forth, no doubt, as ably as could any man in Congress, the merits of the bill.[24] His arguments were based primarily on the doctrine of a strong federal government as contrasted with the states' rights ideas of the Democrats. He held that it was clear that Congress should use the lands for the benefit of all the people of all states. Whether this was to be done by paying out the money received directly from the federal treasury or by granting it to the states for commendable purposes was a matter of *modus* only, not a matter of principle. His closing paragraph shows the temper of his whole speech:

"And now, Mr. President, I have a few words more to say, and shall be done. We are admonished by all our reflections, and by existing signs, of the duty of communicating strength and energy to the glorious Union which now encircles our favored country. Among the ties which bind us together, the public domain merits high consideration. And

[22] A motion was made from a quarter unfriendly to him to refer the subject to the Committee on Manufactures. *Cong. Globe,* 24 Cong., 1 Sess., p. 57.

[23] *Cong. Deb.,* 22 Cong., 1 Sess., p. 1096 *et seq.*

[24] *Ibid.* Much material on this subject is to be found in *Pub. Lands,* VI.

if we appropriate, for a limited time, the proceeds of that great resource, among the several states, for the important objects which have been enumerated, a new and powerful bond of affection and of interest will be added. The States will feel and recognize the operation of the General Government, not merely in power and burdens, but in benefactions and blessings. And the General Government, in its turn, will feel, from the expenditure of the money which it dispenses to the states, the benefits of moral and intellectual improvement of the people, of greater facility in social and commercial intercourse, and of the purification of the population of our country, themselves the best parental sources of national character, national union, and national greatness. Whatever may be the fate of the particular proposition now under consideration, I sincerely hope that the attention of the nation may be attracted to this most interesting subject; that it may justly appreciate the value of this immense national property; and that, preserving the regulation of it by the will of the whole, for the advantage of the whole, it may be transmitted, as a sacred and inestimable succession, to posterity, for its benefit and blessing for ages to come." [25]

The brunt of the opposition was borne by Senator Benton. He said that Clay had quibbled, that he had refused to meet the real arguments against distribution, that he had juggled his figures:

"The Senator from Kentucky, in skipping all the arguments of the Committee on Public Lands, had been equally adverse to the use of arguments on his own side. Song, anecdote, metaphor; many exhibitions and flourishes to entertain the ladies and by-standers; but very few arguments to enlighten the Senate. The cash argument was the only one which he condescended to use. The table of dividends was the Alpha and Omega of his argument, and that table was constructed upon a principle of error, which exhibits to each state about four or five times more spoil than it would

[25] *Cong. Deb.*, 22 Cong., 1 Sess., p. 1117.

ever get. Instead of an average of a series of years, which would give a million and three-quarters in place of three millions, for the gross receipts from the public lands, instead of the net proceeds, which would require about a million to be deducted for expenses in administering the public lands, buying them from the Indians, paying the annuities incurred on account of them, and effecting the removal of the Indians; instead of the remainder which these deductions would leave, and which in some years would be nothing, and in others perhaps half a million of dollars, the Senator from Kentucky takes the gross proceeds of the last year, swelled, as it was, with payments due for lands sold before the year 1820, with military and forfeited land scrip, and constructs his table upon that fallacious sum, and then exhibits to the states these large and seductive dividends. But this argument will do upon paper alone. An amendment to confine the distribution to the net proceeds will detect its fallacy, and leave those empty handed who supposed they were to become rich on the spoils of the new states." [26] Mr. Benton believed that underneath the exterior so adroitly covered the major motive was a strengthening of the tariff position.[27] The bill passed the Senate by a close party vote, 26 to 18.[28] The House postponed action until the following December.

JACKSON'S VETO OF THE DISTRIBUTION BILL OF 1833

When December 1832 arrived, Mr. Clay, without awaiting the action of the House, re-introduced his bill in the Senate, and it passed promptly by a vote of 24 to 20. In the House it passed by a vote of 96 to 40.[29] Curiously enough, Mr. Clay of Alabama was the main opponent of the bill in the House. He denounced distribution as a plan likely to corrupt the states receiving it, and advocated reduction of the price as a counter measure. The bill passed the two houses, but Jackson was ready with a pocket veto. He had, in his

[26] *Cong. Deb.*, 22 Cong., 1 Sess., p. 1150.
[27] *Ibid*, p. 1162.
[28] *Ibid*, p. 1174.
[29] *Ibid*, 2 Sess., 1920.

annual message of December 1832, expressed his belief that
the public land should, as soon as practicable, cease to be a
source of revenue to the United States, but instead be "sold
to settlers in limited parcels at a price barely sufficient to
reimburse to the United States the expense of the present
system and the cost arising under our Indian compacts." [30]
This was understood by the Democrats, and most properly
so, as an indication of Jackson's attitude respecting the distribution of the net proceeds from the sales of public lands ;
there were to be none.   In the same message he stated
it as his conviction that it was unconstitutional for the federal government to furnish funds for the financing of
projects of internal improvements not national in character
within the states.   Clearly, then, he could not approve the
bills so warmly championed by Mr. Clay for the distribution
of money from the sale of lands.   But Congress was not
to give up a pet project merely because the President was
not likely to acquiesce.   The bill was held over by Jackson
during the summer of 1833 and returned in December with
his objections. [31]   This veto message was replete with the
history of the public domain ; eloquent and sarcastic in its
objections to the bill.   It was contrary to the compact made
with the states which had ceded land to the government.
It was not a plan to distribute money incidentally in possession of the federal government, but a scheme to create
a surplus in order that it might be distributed.   It meant
that money must first be paid to the general government
in order that it might again be paid out by that government.
This meant that the customs duties must be burdened with
the task of paying the expenses of government.   The new
states were to receive a bounty at the expense of the old
states.   To the old states it was a dead loss, and the new
states would not find their interests promoted by the plan.
What the new states wanted was reduction of the price of
land and more settlers.   But the paramount objection, after

[30] Richardson, II, p. 601.
[31] *Pub. Lands*, VI, p. 616.

all, seemed to be the relation of the states to the Union. Thus he says:

"It appears to me that a more direct road to consolidation cannot be devised. Money is power, and in that government which pays the public officers of the states will all political power be substantially concentrated. The state governments, if governments they might be called, would lose all their independence and dignity. The economy which now distinguishes them would be converted into a profusion, limited only by the extent of the supply. Being the dependents of the general government, and looking to its treasury as the source of all their emoluments, the state officers, under whatever names they might pass, and by whatever forms their duties might be prescribed, would, in effect, be the mere stipendiaries and instruments of the central power.

"I am quite sure that the intelligent people of our several states will be satisfied, on a little reflection, that it is neither wise nor safe to release the members of their local legislatures from the responsibility of levying the taxes necessary to support their state governments and vest it in Congress, over most of whose members they have no control. They will not think it expedient that Congress shall be the tax-gatherer and paymaster of all their state governments, thus amalgamating all their officers into one mass of common interest and common feeling. It is too obvious that such a course would subvert our well balanced system of government, and ultimately deprive us of all the blessings now derived from our happy union." [32]

Mr. Clay was furious. "He arose and animadverted with severity upon the course pursued by the President." The "incidental debate" of which this was a part was promised by the reporter, but is not to be found.

The next important struggle came in 1835 and 1836. Mr. Clay was on hand with his bill. [33] It was modified a little, providing for a ten per cent share in place of twelve

[32] *Pub. Lands,* VI, p. 620.
[33] *Cong. Globe,* 24 Cong., 1 Sess., p. 56.

and a half per cent for the new states, and the act was to continue for ten years instead of for five. But though the Democrats had objected to a distribution of the proceeds of the public lands, they, as well as the Whigs, wished to dispose of the surplus revenue. Moreover, the Democrats wished to mollify the feelings of the states on the matter of their claim to this surplus. As a result of this complexity of motives, Mr. Calhoun, who had so vigorously and persistently opposed Mr. Clay's land distribution bills, himself brought forward a bill providing for the "deposit" of the surplus with the states. In vain was it shown that a deposit was a distribution; in vain was it shown that the money distributed must first be raised by taxation. The dominant party had had trouble to satisfy its constituents on the question of distributing the land proceeds, but now, under the guise of a deposit, they could at once favor the states with the largess and at the same time ease their consciences, and answer their critics with the claim that the money still belonged to the federal government and was subject to its call. Mr. Clay's land bill was lost by the wayside, and the deposit bill was passed June 23, 1836. Senator Benton characterized the act thus: "It is, in name, a deposit; in form, a loan; in essence and design a distribution. All this verbiage about a deposit is nothing but the device and contrivance of those who have been for years endeavoring to distribute the revenues, sometimes by the land bill, sometimes by direct propositions, and sometimes by proposed amendments to the constitution." [34]. Although the land distribution bill was brought before the Senate again in the following December, it failed to pass.

DISTRIBUTION, PREËMPTION AND THE WHIGS 1840-1841

Nothing was done further until after the presidential election of 1840. In that year the Democrats in their party platform declared against the distributing of the proceeds

[34] Benton, I, p. 652.

of the public lands.[35] The Whigs had no platform, but distribution of the proceeds of the public land was one of the issues on which they fought their campaign.[36]

When the measure came up in 1840, it was coupled with the preëmption bill. The Whigs were in power. The bill, so long delayed, had now a chance to become a law. It had powerful support. Representatives of the great banking houses of England were present in the Washington lobbies urging the passage. It would help them in collecting state bonds, now below par. It was coupled with other Whig measures and by common practice it must share the fate of these. It was in tow of a measure justly popular with the people of the West, *i.e.,* the preëmption bill. There was a loan bill before Congress at the same time; a plan to borrow in order that they might distribute. The Whigs were in need of a popular measure and in this they believed they had it; but they were doomed to early disappointment. In the language of Senator Benton: "The very men that passed the bill had to repeal it, under the sneaking term of suspension, before their terms of service were out—within less than one year from the time it was passed; to be precise, within eleven calendar months and twelve days from the day of its passage—counting from the days, inclusive of both, on which John Tyler, President, approved and disapproved it."[37] In passing the Senate this double bill received the Whig vote, lacking one.[38] In the House it had but a narrow margin to spare, the vote standing 116 to 108.[39] Not all the Democrats supported it. Mr. Calhoun, the author of the deposit bill, denounced this as destined, if passed, to make a wider breach in the Constitution than had ever been made since its adoption. It was profligate, wicked, hideous. "It . . . would do more to defeat the ends for which this government was instituted, and to sub-

[35] E. Stanwood, *History of Presidential Elections,* p. 149.
[36] *Cong. Globe,* 27 Cong., 2 Sess., App., p. 771.
[37] Benton, II, p. 245.
[38] *Cong. Globe,* 27 Cong., 1 Sess., p. 388.
[39] *Ibid,* p. 156.

vert the Constitution and destroy the liberty of the country, than any which has ever been proposed." [40] These were strange words from the champion of the deposit law, especially in view of the fact that he felt sure that the "deposits" once made would not be withdrawn.

The debate was long and bitter, and while most of the arguments were identical with those of previous years, the relation of the distribution of federal money to the collection of tariff received special attention. It was, as it had been before, the claim of the Democrats that to distribute land proceeds meant the necessity of a high tariff. Such a view had been taken by Benton all along. It was brought vigorously into the debate at this time.[41] Mr. Calhoun appealed to the senators of the southern states, "on whose constituents this increased burden would principally fall. Are they willing to give their sanction to a measure which must necessarily terminate in the violation of the compromise act, and reopen the tariff controversy?" [42] In favor of the bill were not only all the arguments previously urged, but, in addition, the argument that distribution to all states was the alternative to cession of the land to the states in which it lay. Apparently this consideration turned several votes in favor of the bill. Tyler favored the bill. In his first message to Congress he stated that distribution "would act as an efficient remedial measure." It would emancipate the states "from the situation to which the pressure of their finances now subjects them." [43] Mr. Tyler was further hopeful of using the public lands as the basis of credit.[44] These were his ideas during the hopeful days of the first two years of his administration. In his third annual message he regarded it, under the circumstances, as suicidal to alienate the public lands or the proceeds arising from their sale.[45]

[40] *Cong. Globe,* 27 Cong., 1 Sess., App., p. 337.
[41] *Ibid,* p. 314.
[42] *Ibid,* pp. 313, 314.
[43] Richardson, IV, p. 47.
[44] *Ibid,* pp. 110, 185, 208.
[45] *Ibid,* p. 265.

THE 500,000 ACRE GRANT FOR INTERNAL IMPROVEMENTS

The act providing for distribution carried with it a donation of 500,000 acres of land to each new state for the support of internal improvements, and also the apportionment of ten per cent of the proceeds of sales in addition to the five per cent previously allowed. These were strong bids for the votes from the public land states. The Whigs were obliged to accept one distasteful amendment. It provided that the distribution should cease whenever customs duties were above twenty per cent. This was intended as a check on the increase in duties, which the Whigs had promised. A year later this provision of the bill was repealed.[46] The President, who had so earnestly recommended the passage of the distribution act in 1841, was equally emphatic in 1842 that its operation should be suspended. He says: "When the distribution law was passed there was reason to anticipate that there would soon be a real surplus to distribute. . . . But to continue it in force while there is no such surplus to distribute, and when it is manifestly necessary not only to increase the duties, but at the same time to borrow money . . . would cause it to be regarded as an unwise alienation of the best security of the public creditor which would with difficulty be excused and could not·be justified."[47] The real difficulty in 1842 was that there was no surplus to distribute. In the wild days of 1836 Mr. Clay had estimated the surplus subject to distribution at more than twenty millions.[48] At that time land was selling as never before; bank notes, good and bad, were received at the land offices. This was abnormal. The specie circular of 1836; the collapse of the speculative craze in the crisis of 1837; the reduction of customs duties under the compromise act of 1833; the repudiation of state debts; the pressure of foreign creditors for payment—all these conspired to turn the surplus of the Jackson period into the

[46] U. S. Stat. at Large, V, p. 567.
[47] Richardson, IV, p. 109.
[48] Cong. Globe, 24 Cong., 1 Sess., p. 56.

deficit of the ill-starred Whig administration of the early forties.

It was clearly a case of much cry and little wool. The many millions for which the states had hoped proved, on realization, to be less than three-quarters of a million. The distribution was to be made quarterly. Three installments were paid, amounting in the aggregate to $691,000.[49] The states were beginning to view the matter with disgust. New Hampshire, always opposed to distribution, refused to accept the money.[50] South Carolina, which had never favored distribution, refused to accept it and sarcastically referred to the offer as that of a bribe. Alabama and a few other states likewise refused to accept the funds.[51] Other states urged the repeal of the law. The governor of Maine in a message to the legislature assumed that the "policy of distribution is fully repudiated by both government and people," [52] and so it became the style for the states to refuse the money. Mr. Clay proposed to give to the assenting states the sums refused by the dissenting states.

The Distribution Act Suspended, 1842

On the 27th of August, 1842, the Senate, and on the 29th the House, passed the tariff act which contained, as one of its sections, a suspension of the land distribution act. There had been a demand for its repeal, but to suspend it was as much as the dignity of those who had stood sponsor for it could be expected to stand. Even Mr. Clay was moved to declare that he had never wanted to distribute land sale proceeds when there was a deficit in the treasury. The friends of the measure were, however, though baffled, not beaten. They submitted to the inevitable for the moment, but adhered to the principle. They still hoped for better times and distribution of a real surplus. But regret it as they might, the finances of the country demanded immediate

[49] Donaldson, p. 753.
[50] *Niles Register*, LXIII, p. 244.
[51] *Sen. Doc.*, 27 Cong., 2 Sess., No. 54.
[52] *Niles Register*, LXV, p. 340.

action. Twice the tariff legislation had been blocked by Tyler's veto. In the language of Senator Benton: "The compromise and the land distribution were the stumbling-blocks: it was determined to sacrifice them together, but without seeming to do so. A contrivance was fallen upon; duties were raised above twenty per centum; and that breach of the mutual assurance in relation to the compromise, immediately in terms of the assurance, suspended the land revenue distribution—to continue it suspended while duties above the compromise limit continued to be levied. And as that has been the case ever since, the distribution of the revenue has been suspended ever since. Such were the contrivances, ridiculous inventions, and absurd circumlocutions which Congress had recourse to, to get rid of that land distribution which was to gain popularity for its authors." [53]

In 1844 the House, being Democraitc, voted to repeal the bill outright, but a Whig majority in the Senate saved it. So the shell of it was retained though the kernel was gone. Not often has the same Congress been obliged to repeal its own measures, but the twenty-seventh Congress officiated at the beginning and at the end of the distribution episode.

The sentiment in favor of distribution was widespread and showed itself to be persistent even after Congress was forced to abandon it. The Whig press was hopeful that circumstances would again favor the measure. [54] Mr. Clay, as late as 1844, was still firm in the faith that distribution was sound in principle and expedient in practice. He feared that a failure to distribute the proceeds would result eventually in a complete loss to the federal government of the whole public domain. It would be ceded to the states in which it lay. [55] In fact, the question of cession of the public lands to the states had been before Congress a number of times prior to the passage of the distribution act, but it was inde-

[53] Benton, II, p. 417.
[54] For example, several quotations are to be found in *Niles Register*, See Vol. LXV, p. 223, and Vol. LXVI, pp. 8, 283.
[55] *Niles Register*, LXVI, p. 299. ˙

pendent of the distribution question, being fostered naturally by the congressmen from the public land states.

(B) CEDING THE PUBLIC LANDS TO THE STATES
REDUCING THE TREASURY SURPLUS

As the payment of the public debt became almost a certainty, and the prospect of a surplus in the treasury almost another certainty, the effort to cut off revenue assumed serious, though varying, proportions. In addition to the plan to distribute the proceeds from the sale of lands it was proposed to cede the land to the states—sometimes the plan was to cede the land to the states in which it lay, sometimes to cede it to all the states of the Union in proportion to population. But, in one form or another, the question was before Congress for over a quarter of a century, with an occasional out-cropping in more recent years.

COUPLED WITH THE GRADUATION BILL

One of the first proposals to cede all public land to the states in which it lay was made by Senator Tazewell in 1826.[56] This was without any reference to its value at the time, or to length of time over which it had been offered for sale. The more acceptable plan of cession was that of Senator Benton, who in 1828 proposed in his graduation bill to cede the land which did not sell, after a long time and at a very low price, to the states. This, it was made to appear, was a gift without value; one which the federal government could make without loss, but which furnished a means by which the land could be made to serve the best purpose of which it was capable.[57] In the House this bill was referred to the Committee on Public Lands, and it reported favorably, especially concerning the cession of refuse lands to the states in which they were situated.[58]

It was a plan which immediately met with favor in the states that were to receive the land. From time to time the

[56] *Sen. Doc.*, No. 99, 19 Cong., 1 Sess.
[57] *Cong. Deb.*, 20 Cong., 1 Sess., p. 609 *et seq.*
[58] *Pub. Lands*, V, p. 449.

states were even so anxious to receive land as to offer to pay for it. Alabama anticipated by a few months the proposition of Senator Benton in asking that the government sell to her the entire amount of public domain within her borders. To begin with, it was suggested that the state simply could not pay the full price at which the land was to be sold. "The idea of purchase, however, is founded on the liberality of Congress in adjusting the terms." [59] The purpose was to obviate the inconvenience of having land within the state owned by the federal government, and to aid the state in making internal improvements and supporting education.

The House referred the matter of change in the methods of disposition of the public lands to the Committee on Public Lands, and among other projects considered by the committee was that of ceding of the land to the states. They reported: "A division of the public land among the states has been suggested to the committee. This measure, they believe, would be injurious. There would be an impossibility so to locate the several divisions as to attach to them an equal value. Each state would have a system of sales differing from that of the other states. Struggles would take place in Congress for measures to advance the value of the possessions of some of the locations over that of others. Serious collisions would necessarily occur; speculation, fraud and corruption would be attempted in the state legislatures; all which and other serious evils would be avoided and the greatest possible benefits derived to the states from the sale of these lands by the general government agreeably to the present organized system, and from directing by law the distribution of the proceeds of sales among the several states." [60]

Thus, in no uncertain terms, the first official judgment of Congress was clearly against a wholesale cession of land to the states. It was never favorable, as a whole, to such a

[59] *Pub. Lands,* V, p. 445.
[60] *Ibid,* p. 797.

cession, yet the question figured prominently in the debates concerning graduation, distribution and homesteads.

Nevertheless, the mere mention of the matter encouraged state after state to declare itself a willing recipient of land, should Congress, by any means, decided favorably regarding the cessions. During the year 1829, under one pretext or another, five of the public land states petitioned Congress to grant them public lands remaining within their respective borders. Not always did they ask for all such lands. Some modestly expressed themselves as favorable to Senator Benton's bill; others hoped the "refuse" lands would become state property; while still others boldly asked for a donation of all public land within their borders. Indiana even discovered that the land within her borders did, as a matter of fact, on the basis of the Virginia cession, belong to her, and asked Congress to look into the matter.[61]

CESSION OF LANDS AND STATES' RIGHTS

The next year, 1830, the states' rights idea embodied in the cession in question was espoused by Senator Hayne in the debate on Foote's resolution. His remarks summed up the case admirably: "Giving up the plan of using these lands forever as a fund either for revenue or distribution, ceasing to hug them as a great treasure, renouncing the idea of administering them with a view to regulate and control the industry and population of the states or of keeping in subjection and dependence the states or the people of any portion of the Union, the task will be comparatively easy of striking out a plan for the final adjustment of the land question on just and equitable principles. . . . In short, our whole policy in relation to the public lands may perhaps be summed up in the declaration with which I set out, that they ought not to be kept and retained forever as a great treasure, but that they should be administered chiefly with a view to the creation, within reasonable periods, of great and flourishing communities to be formed into free and inde-

[61] For all these state claims see *Pub. Lands,* VI.

pendent states; to be invested in due season with the control of all the lands within their respective limits." [62]

The Committee on Manufactures, in its famous report on the public lands, had given the subject prominent consideration and had reported adversely on every point: It could not be justified without first proving that the federal management had been bad, but this was not the case. It would establish a dangerous relation between state and government, that of debtor and creditor, *i.e.*, assuming that a price was to be paid by the states. In any case, it would establish many policies in place of one policy . . . would promote speculation. Were the price paid by the states merely nominal, it would be manifestly unfair, for example . . . Missouri, with a population of 140,000, would receive thirty-eight million acres of land, while Ohio, with 936,000 in population, would receive less than six million acres. The Committee on Public Lands, in its counter-report, favored the reduction of price and also a relinquishment of federal land to the states. [63]

At this time Mr. Calhoun was apprehensive concerning the distribution of the proceeds of the public lands; he feared the precedent. In 1836 he introduced a bill providing for the deposit of the surplus revenue with the states; in 1837 he introduced a bill providing for the cession of all public land to the states in which it was located.

President Jackson had been converted to the state's rights side of the land question sufficiently to lead him to say in his annual message of 1832: "It is desirable, however, that in convenient time this machinery [*i.e.*, of the federal government] be withdrawn from the states, and that the rights of soil and the future disposition of it be surrendered to the states respectively in which it lies." [64]   In similar language he expressed himself in his veto message regarding the distribution bill, passed in 1833, as favorable to a cession, ultimately, of refuse lands to the states. [65]   Mr. Calhoun's

[62] *Cong. Deb.*, 21 Cong., 1 Sess., p. 35.
[63] *Pub. Lands*, VI, pp. 445-447.
[64] Richardson, II, p. 601.
[65] *Ibid*, III, p. 69.

bill was tabled in the Senate, so it never got to the House, but in 1840 he introduced it again. This was undoubtedly a counter-move against Clay and his distribution bill. He acknowledged that his purpose was a vindication of states' rights. Mr. Clay prayed to be delivered from such rights and from such advocates, since it meant robbing seventeen states in order to benefit eight or nine.[66] Mr. Calhoun's bill proposed a cession to the states with the stipulation that half the proceeds of sales should be paid to the federal government. The bill was referred to the Committee on Public Lands, and was never reported out.

In December, 1840, the same senator introduced substantially the same bill. It was referred to the Committee on Public Lands and reported to the Senate. The argument against it was mainly that it would eventually mean the complete loss of the public domain and all proceeds from it to the federal government.[67] It came to a vote and was lost, the vote standing 20 to 31. Of eighteen senators from the nine new states, fourteen voted for the measure.[68]

PARTIAL CESSION THROUGH THE 500,000-ACRE GRANT

Although the cession of the land to the states was hopelessly defeated as a whole, the bill of 1841 granted 500,000 acres to each new state. The larger scheme of cession was not forgotten. It was kept in mind, for example, by Illinois, which state, in 1846, again asked Congress for a grant of her remaining lands.[69] In 1851, when a bill was before the Senate providing for the equalization of grants to new states, Senator Hale of New Hampshire proposed an amendment by which the half-million-acre grant should be extended to include the old as well as the new states.[70]

[66] Cong. Globe, 26 Cong., 1 Sess., p. 97.
[67] Ibid, 2 Sess., App., p. 76 et seq.
[68] Ibid, p. 140.
[69] Ibid, 29 Cong., 2 Sess., p. 334. And again in 1847 Illinois asked that the price of land be reduced or the land given to the states. Ill. Sen. Jol. 1847, p. 45.
[70] Cong. Globe, 31 Cong., 2 Sess., p. 331.

Again Coupled with Graduation Bill, 1850

Senator Benton again, in 1850, made the cession of refuse lands a part of his Graduation bill. The importance of extinguishing finally the claim by the federal government to land within the states had evidently grown on him. In support of his bill, he says: "The first object of the bill is to pay the public debt; the second, to extinguish the federal title to lands within the states. This second object is itself a great one and consistent with the first, and accomplished by the same means. Accelerated sales, while rapidly putting money into the Federal Treasury, will be rapidly extinguishing the federal government *as a land holder* in the new states; and, to complete the good work, all the lands remaining unsold at the end of the operation of the bill are to be ceded to the states in which they lie for public purposes; and where the lands in any state have been sold down to a refuse of three million of acres or less in any state, the same shall be ceded to the state. . . . So that the commencement of the year 1860 should see every new state released from the presence and dominion of a federal landlord and elevated to an equality with the old states in the great essential requisites of state sovereignty—that of having all the lands within its limits subject to state jurisdiction and available for all the purposes of settlement, improvement and taxation." [71]

However, the Senate Committee on Public Lands reported adversely on the measure in 1852, and this feature of the Graduation Bill was eventually lost. [72]

During these years the Democratic press had taken much interest in the subject. An Iowa paper expressed the sentiment thus: "Besides, it is sound Democratic doctrine that the United States should cede the lands within each State to the Government thereof, to be disposed of as they deem proper. If there is any one particular reason why our members of Congress have not had better success in their

[71] *Cong. Globe*, 31 Cong., 2 Sess., p. 134.
[72] *Ibid*, 32 Cong., 1 Sess., p. 2100.

advocacy of the land grants, it is because they have, like honest and consistent men, refused to sell their principles, and the dearest interests of their constituents, to the manufacturing capitalists of the East. And for this course, which should and will entitle them to the respect and gratitude of every honest man in Iowa, these Whig Committee-men seek to break them down." [73]

The Charleston Mercury in stronger terms expresses itself with the words: "Land grants are becoming the great feature and the great pest of congressional legislation. They loom up on every side and spread their darkening wings over every question. Good projects and bad are hurried forward pell-mell and have equal chance of success, because there is neither time nor means of discrimination; and, in despair of succeeding in any other way, the friends of any one grant are driven to pledge their support to every other." [74]

STATES ULTIMATELY RECEIVE MUCH PUBLIC LAND

About 1852 and afterward, the demand for a cession of land to the states was merged in the homestead discussion, or in the various measures by which the states demanded, and received, vast grants for internal improvements, for railroads, or, as in the case of the swamp land grant, on the pretext of the public good. As a project in itself, the demand for the cession to the states failed, but the idea persisted and bore fruit. The states did not receive the gift of all the land outright, nor what was intended to be virtually the same as a gift: the opportunity to buy the land within their borders at a mere nominal price. They did eventually, however, receive princely portions of it. This was brought to pass through grants for internal improvements, education, and the swamp land cessions.

[73] *Democratic Banner* (Iowa), Apr. 30, 1852. See also the *Weekly Ohio Statesman*, Apr. 27 and July 13, 1852.
[74] Quoted in the *Miners' Express* (Iowa), June 28, 1854.

SUMMARY

Distribution of the Proceeds from the Sale of Land: For about twenty years there was a constant, and at times, violent struggle over the distribution to be made of the money received from the sale of land to the states, that is to all the states. Few questions were more severely partisan. The party in favor of protective tariff, as the payment of the public debt neared completion, feared a piling up of revenue, making the tariff unimportant as a source of income. The opposition wanted to reduce the price of land, or even make it free, and so opposed creating a demand on the part of states for an income from this source.

A bill providing for distribution was passed in 1833 and vetoed by President Jackson. It was passed again in substantially the same form in 1841 under the Whig administration. Within a year a deficit in the treasury led to the suspension of the act, and although it was not repealed outright, it remained a dead letter.

Ceding Public Lands to the States: Not unlike the distribution of money to the states was the proposal to cede the land to the states in which it lay. This plan was proposed as early as 1826, and continued to be an issue for a quarter of a century. At times it was proposed to cede all land to the states, at other times to cede that which had been on the market for some years, but found no buyers. At times it was proposed to cede the land free of charge, and at other times the states were to pay a nominal price for it. The purposes involved in the plan were mainly to allow the states full jurisdiction over the lands within their borders, and to give them the income from sales as a revenue useful and necessary in developing a new commonwealth.

Although the proposal to cede the land to the states failed as a whole, it succeeded in part. In 1844 the half-million-acre grants were inaugurated, and continued for forty years. The grants for internal improvements outside the half-million-acre grants were liberal, and became more and more so as time passed. Thus great areas of land were granted to the states, more than was for many years intended, though never has the policy been adopted of turning over the remaining government land to the respective states.

CHAPTER XI

CLAIM ASSOCIATIONS

Throughout the whole period during which preëmptions were allowed, the settler rarely hesitated to take possession of government land either before or after it was surveyed. He did this apparently with a clear conscience. The great number of precedents, the attitude of the government toward the squatter, the apparent justice of the case—all these played their part in strengthening the feeling that the first comer had a rightful claim to the soil. These conditions not only developed feelings and habits, but from them were evolved also institutions. The laws of the federal government and of the states and territories lagged behind the needs of the people on the frontier, and as a result the spirit of "popular" or "squatter sovereignty" manifested itself.

EXTRA-LEGAL NATURE OF "CLAIM ASSOCIATIONS"

These actions, while not legal, were extra-legal rather than illegal. The law did not protect the squatter in his right to the soil. He must first preëmpt or buy, before the law recognized him. Moreover, the preëmption right was not adequate protection in all cases, since he might not be able to fulfill all its conditions. To cover these defects in the defense of what the squatters considered their undoubted rights they banded themselves together into "claim associations." Just when these associations were first formed is hard to say, since they were less formal during the early periods than later. A letter addressed to the Secretary of War in 1830 by a resident of Alabama, who felt much aggrieved at the settlers on the public domain, explains the situation very well:

"Sir: I take the liberty to inform you of an outrage that is perpetrated in this county against the laws of the United States, and the peaceable and good citizens thereof. There are five valuable townships of public land in this [the Cahaba] district, that are now offered for sale by the President's proclamation, on the fourth Monday in May. This land is thickly populated by farmers, as wealthy in general, as in any part of South Alabama. The citizens occupying this land, together with a few others, have held a meeting or convention, and entered into written and solemn resolutions to prevent all, and every person, whatsoever, from viewing or exploring the land previous to the day of sale. They have pledged themselves to do this by force of arms. They have further resolved for one individual in each township to bid off the whole of the land that they or any of their body may wish to buy, and the balance of their company to be armed with their rifles and muskets before the land office door, and shoot, instantly, any man that may bid for any land that they want.

"In pursuance of these resolutions, a number of men who wish to buy farms of this land have been met by companies of armed men, and driven from the townships. They have surrounded a house (where three men had put up) at the hour of twelve at night, and compelled the landlord to drive them off.

"In consequence of the large body that is united, and their determined violence, they have, and will keep every individual from examining or buying the land, and, unless the public authority interpose, a man will not, unless he joins their mob, be safe in entering any land after the sale. They have resolved, that, inasmuch as Congress has refused to give them preëmption rights at the minimum price, to obtain those rights by the force of arms. As public sentiment in Alabama is so strong in favor of preëmption rights, I do not believe that these proceedings will be noticed by public authority, inasmuch as it is to the interest of the State for the land to sell at a low price.

"These five townships constitute what is known in Alabama by the Big Cane Brake: it is the best body of land by far in South Alabama, and would sell, in a fair market, at from five to ten dollars per acre.

"I make this statement to you, sir, and if you conceive the matter to be an object that should be noticed by you, or the Government, it can, and will be vouched for by hundreds of individuals of as good standing as any in Alabama." [1]

ATTITUDE OF SQUATTERS TOWARD PREEMPTION

From the standpoint of the settler the case was wholly different. As he saw it, the value of the land was due in no small measure to his efforts and expenditures. Hence he was protecting himself in his own right, while to him the bidder from the outside was a thief and a pirate. Organizations of the same kind became the usual practice. Squatters' meetings were held in what is now Iowa on the first arrival of settlers. [2] In these associations, in 1833, restrictions were put upon the right of choice of land, no one settler being allowed more than half a mile frontage on any river or prairie. A similar restriction in Wisconsin limited a settler's right to claim no more than forty acres of "good timber." [3] In Kansas claim associations in some instances undertook to secure to the settler a claim of 240 acres, 80 acres of which might be woodland. Thus the settlers allowed one another a preemption right of 80 acres more than the legal amount. [4]

Not only did the squatter assume the right to protect himself, but he was aided and abetted in such action by

[1] *House Document, State Papers,* 21 Cong., 1 Sess., No. 109. Letter dated April 14, 1830. Signed, "Jabez Curry."
[2] *Wisconsin Territorial Gazette* (Burlington, Ia.), Sept. 7, 1837.
[3] *Madison City Express,* Wisconsin, March 20, 1845.
[4] *The Garden of the World, or the Great West,* p. 196.

the other people of influence in the community. An editorial in a Chicago paper refers to the custom of self-protection among squatters as an old one. It voices the prevalent spirit of the day:

"As the time approaches when there is to be a large sale of public lands at this place, and as there will doubtless be many here who are unacquainted with the situation of the settlers on the tracts of land and with the local customs of this western country, we feel it our duty to allude to this subject at this time. Custom, as well as the acts of the General Government, has sanctioned the location of settlements on the unsurveyed public lands, and the Government has encouraged the settlers in such lands, by granting them a preëmption right to a sufficiency for a small farm. Many of the settlers on the tract now offered, and to be sold on the 15th inst., came to the West and made their locations under the implied pledge of the Government by its past acts: that they should have a preference and a right to purchase the lots on which they located, when the same came into market, and at the minimum price. Government was then morally bound to provide for these settlers, and have been guilty of an act of injustice in bringing these lands into market without making such provision. 'Public opinion is stronger than law,' it has well been said, and we trust it may prove so in this case, and that the strangers who come among us, and especially our own citizens, will not attempt to commit so gross an act of injustice as to interfere with the purchase of the quarter section, on which improvements have been made by the actual settler. We trust for the peace and quietness of our town that these local customs, to which long usage has given the force of law . . . which have been repeatedly sanctioned by the general government . . . and which are so strongly sustained by the principles of justice and equity, will not be outraged at the coming sales." [5]

[5] Chicago *Democrat*, June 4, 1835.

METHODS OF CLAIM ASSOCIATIONS

It was far from the thoughts of the squatters to violate law. On the contrary, they urged their fellow-claimants to fulfill the requirements of the law to the letter. A committee chosen to adjudicate differences relative to claims in a township of eastern Iowa published a signed statement that claimholders could be protected only on condition of making "such improvements as is required by the by-laws of the self-protecting confederacy." [6] However, the determination of the squatters was of a type not to bear trifling with. A committee representing a group of squatters near Peoria, Illinois, addressed a memorial to Congress setting forth in vigorous terms the squatter's side of the case. They asked Congress to protect them, and it was done insofar as pre-emption law affecting surveyed land could accomplish it. A strong hint was dropped concerning the inclination of the squatter to take the matter into his own hands unless the government took care of his interests. They say: "A sad alternative is likely to be presented, viz: either that there will be such violence used in defence of the rights of the settlers as we must seriously deplore, or that many a settler will be driven from his present pleasant and beautiful abode, and his well cultivated fields, by the more opulent capitalist or the greedy and merciless speculator." [7]

PROCEDURE OF ASSOCIATIONS AT FEDERAL LAND AUCTIONS

The failure of Congress to pass and enforce laws adequate for the protection of these settlers resulted in a series of claim associations covering a great portion of the frontier country. They were brought into existence in a manner much like the establishment of a government, there frequently being a vote of the citizens, a meeting of elected delegates, a formal adoption of a constitution, and the election of officers to put the measures adopted into effect.

"Perhaps no country has ever exhibited a spectacle like

[6] *Iowa Sun*, March 27, 1839 (Possibly 1838).
[7] *Iowa News*, Sept. 16, 1837.

Iowa, previous to the public land coming into market, where a social compact has been formed so strong, or the spirit of its requirements so honorably adhered to."

The regular order of procedure is thus described by the same writer: "In order to prevent unpleasant litigation, and to keep up a spirit of harmony amongst neighbors, and the better to protect them in their equitable rights of 'claim' purchase, each township has its own organization generally throughout the territory and announces by public notice a 'call meeting,' thus: 'The citizens of township 72 north, range 5 west, are requested to meet at Squire B——'s. Hickory Grove (or as the place and time may be) to adopt the necessary measures for securing their homes at the approaching land sale at B——, or D——.' After a short preamble and set of resolutions, suited to the occasion, a 'register' is appointed, whose duty it shall be to record the name of each claimant to his respective 'claim.' A 'bidder' is also appointed, whose duty it shall be, on the day of sale, to bid off all the land previously registered in the name of each respective claimant. These associations are formed mutually, to sustain and protect each other in their claim-rights. Thus, everything moves along at the land sales with the harmony and regularity of clockwork; and should any-one present be found bidding over the minimum price ($1.25) on land registered in the township book, woe be unto him. Although 'claim-law' is no law derived from the United States, or from the statute book of the territory, yet it nevertheless is the law, made by and derived from the sovereigns themselves, and its mandates are imperative.

"When any controversy arises between two neighbors relative to trespassing (in common parlance 'jumping a claim'), it is arbitrated by a committee appointed for that purpose, and their decision is considered final." [8]

There was much similarity in type in these organizations, although some had long and elaborate constitutions, while some had but a simple statement of principle and purpose.

[8] J. B. Newhall, *Sketches of Iowa*, pp. 54-58.

The rules and regulations of a Kansas association serve as a good illustration:

"In view of existing difficulties in the neighborhood in reference to Claims, and hoping by a judicious management to be able to reconcile all contending parties, and in the end secure and maintain justice; we, therefore, the citizens of Bloomington neighborhood, hereby form ourselves into an association for the purposes above mentioned. The association to be called Club of Honor, hoping that no other principle will be recognized or permitted to influence any member in any way whatever; and in order to insure success satisfactory to all, we further agree to adopt the following rules and regulations as landmarks to guide us through all intricacies to the fair and open truth.

"First—That no person be permitted to cross the line of the survey in making out his or her claim, where, by so doing, he or she will come in conflict with an actual settler on the claim when the survey is made; nor will the privilege be granted to anyone except for the express purpose of securing improvements made by him or her prior to the survey and where no one is settled on the quarter to which the improvement belonged.

"Second—That the quarter section shall be regarded in every case as settled, when there is a house on it, or other demonstrations made which are usually permitted to hold claims.

"Third—That each member of this association shall be protected in the possession of his claim as well when he is absent from the Territory on business expecting to return, as when here. Recognizing as we do the right of property in claims, we will permit our members to buy and hold an additional 80 or 160 acres, if necessary to secure an improvement.

"Fourth—We will elect by ballot *nine jurymen,* whose duty it shall be to try, impartially, every case where the parties cannot agree among themselves, the plaintiff and defendant in every case before going into trial may each challenge any two jurymen without giving cause, and more, if they can show good cause for so doing, and their vacancies shall be filled by ballot by the remaining jurymen; after which the parties may try their case before the jury as made out, and be in honor bound to abide the verdict.

"Fifth—That the trials shall be in every case public; the plaintiff and defendant may appear in person or by attorney.

"Sixth—That the jury shall hold courts whenever notified that a suit will be brought; said jury shall fix the time and place for holding courts.

"Seventh—That the jury may adjourn from time to time as the necessities of the case may dictate.

"Eighth—That in case of absence of any juryman, the vacancy may be filled by the parties to the suit and the jurymen present—all voting by ballot.

"Ninth—That no person holding a disputed claim shall cut or sell any timber off it until such dispute shall be settled.

"Tenth—That we will remove any person or persons who may intrude on the claim of any settler and live upon the same, peaceably if we can, forcibly if we must; being compelled so to do for our common interest and safety, that we may not be driven from our homes and farms by dishonest men, to gain their ends by dishonest means." [9]

The most complete account available of any claim association is for that of Johnson County, Iowa. [10] A description is given in this connection of the method of conducting a land sale where the association had, in reality, charge of the procedure. A large company of squatters had gone from Johnson County to the land office at Dubuque. From among their number they had chosen a "bidder" and an "assistant bidder." The assistant bidder has left a description of the sale:

"The bidder and assistant bidder had furnished themselves with large plats of the two townships to be sold, with each

[9] *Herald of Freedom* (Lawrence, Kansas), Jan. 12, 1856.
[10] B. F. Shambaugh, *Constitution and Records of the Claim Association of Johnson County, Iowa.*

claimant's name plainly written on the subdivision which he wished to purchase. When the time came for the sale to begin, the crier stepped out on the platform, and inviting the bidder and assistant to take places on the platform beside him, took hold of one side of the plat, and began at section No. 1, and called out each eighty-acre subdivision as rapidly as he could speak. When he came to a tract with a name written on it, he would strike his hammer down, and give the name to the clerk. He thus proceeded, taking the sections in numerical order. The two townships were offered in less than thirty minutes. During this time the claimants stood in a compact semicircle in front of the platform in breathless silence, not a sound being heard except the crier's voice." [11]

Yet this, remember, was, from the standpoint of the government, an auction.

The man who had the hardihood to defy the claim association and attempt to gain possession of land in a manner contrary to their code, was, to say the least, vigorous. Few, if any, lost their lives, and this speaks well for the squatter, but it was due in no small measure to the discretion of the offender, since the settlers were determined, at almost any cost, to enforce their regulations. Whipping was not unknown; threats of drowning are recorded; destruction of improvements common. [12]

TREATMENT OF "CLAIM JUMPERS"

In Wisconsin one claim association, *"Resolved,* That in case any person or persons should violate the sense of this meeting and deprive claimants of their just expectations, that we will not fail to rebuke his conduct with such severity as has been common in the settlement of this western country." [13]

The sense of the meeting was occasionally violated and

[11] Shambaugh, Introduction, p. 17.
[12] *Ibid,* p. 15.
[13] B. H. Hibbard, *History of Agriculture in Dane County, Wisconsin,* p. 96.

the traditions and customs of the western country were carried out, apparently in good faith.

"The usual mode of procedure in case a claim was bought by a 'land pirate' was to visit the purchaser in case he were not too far distant, taking along a justice of the peace armed with a 'warranty' deed ready for the offender's signature, which would constitute his conveyance of the land in question to the aggrieved squatter; the justice would then acknowledge the instrument. It was not unusual for the members of this committee to carry guns and ropes and to indulge in remarks calculated to stimulate the claim-jumper in his tendency toward a speedy and amicable settlement. Very rarely did he resist vigorously, but once in a while it required heroic measures to overbalance his greed. The story is told of one 'jumper' who resisted, and addressed the committee in irreverent terms, daring them to do him physical injury, and threatening to bring the strong arm of the law down violently upon their heads. The committee exhausted their verbal arguments in vain; then, putting a rope around the waist of the culprit, led him to a pond, cut a hole in the ice, and immersed him. He was soon drawn out, but, being still in a combative and profane frame of mind, was treated to another ducking, and on his second coming out was unable to continue his side of the debate; so the negative was declared closed, and, after returning to the house, the dripping defender of that side set his signature to the papers and with uplifted right hand swore that it was his 'voluntary act and deed.' The squatter usually agreed to refund the money advanced by the 'jumper,' but custom allowed him to take his time to it and no interest was paid." [14]

In all of these matters the squatters were looking out for their own rights, their natural rights, as they believed. They were literally violating law, of course, but they believed the law gave an advantage to the outside bidder which was not intended by the lawmakers. The settlers were making a

[14] Hibbard, pp. 97, 98.

new law, no doubt, but when it is remembered that they were often many miles from even a territorial capital, beyond the reach of organized courts, and substantially beyond the pale of organized government, it cannot be charged that their methods were unfair or unwarranted. The squatter law was, in the light of subsequent development, as good as the law made in Washington. Moreover, the squatter law fitted the conditions it was designed to meet; the federal law often failed to do so.

SUMMARY

From the beginning there was a disagreement in official circles as to the propriety of allowing settlers to take possession of land in advance of the survey. The majority in these circles was inclined to take sides against such action, such presumption, as it was termed. Out on the frontier the sentiment was quite the opposite. Early in the history of settlement the pioneers began to band themselves in "claim associations" for the protection of their rights against every "speculator" who should undertake to buy at the public sales land already claimed by the settlers, or *squatters,* as they soon came to be called.

The squatter was both sincere and earnest. He believed that whatever value the land had he had given it; that the men who came to the sales from a distance, not having resided upon the land, were interlopers. With these views firmly established it can be easily understood that a group of pioneers would put up a formidable defense of their supposed rights. This they did. Their procedure while extra-legal was orderly. The land was listed; a bidder was appointed who bid off the land for the claimants as it was offered. It was hardly possible for an outsider to buy land wanted by settlers. The price of land under these circumstances was rarely above the minimum.

CHAPTER XII

SPECULATION

LAND SPECULATION DURING THE COLONIAL AND THE CONFEDERATION PERIOD

There were in the early days of the Republic comparatively few opportunities for speculation. The stock exchange was unknown; mining was little developed; neither speculation in, nor betting on, future prices of grain was a regular business. However, there was a chance, fairly legitimate, to invest money in western lands and wait for them to rise in value. There was under the credit system an opportunity to deal in margins, as it were, the buyer making a deposit of one-fourth of the full price and, before another payment was required, selling out, if possible, at a profit. Had not too many attempted the game, more would have won; it was too attractive.

The hope of making money out of a rise in the value of land did not originate west of the Alleghanies. The possibilities of settlement in that country, however, resulted in a revival of speculation which developed to proportions all but incredible. Going a little back of the period under consideration, it may be noted that Washington was early interested in the new country, and while it was still a part of the British possessions selected fifteen thousand acres as officers' bounty land, besides buying out the claims of several other officers. Altogether he owned over 49,000 acres of western land. Washington had visited the Ohio Valley and was sanguine as to its future. His land had cost him but little, yet he considered it worth about $8.00 per acre.[1]

[1] Hulbert, A. B., *Washington and the West*, pp. 11-12.

There were numerous and gigantic frauds, one of the worst being an attempt on the part of the court established in the Ohio country by the Colony of Virginia to grant the land to itself and then dispose of it. William Henry Harrison, writing of this to James Madison, says: "The price at which land is sold enables anybody to become a purchaser; one thousand acres being given for an indifferent horse or a rifle gun." [2] Of course, the titles were not recognized by the United States, but the settlers who came to claim the land had nevertheless to be reckoned with.

The land sales mentioned in a preceding chapter made by the Congress of the Confederation were instances of speculation. Another transaction quite similar in character, though dealing with other than federal land, was made in 1795 when the North American Land Company was formed with Robert Morris as the moving spirit. This company obtained vast tracts of land, about six million acres, situated in several different states, principally from Pennsylvania south to Georgia.

During the year 1795 Connecticut sold her claim to the lands of the Western Reserve to the Connecticut Land Company for a million two hundred thousand dollars, or about forty cents an acre; [3] half a million acres had previously been given to Connecticut citizens who had suffered losses during the Revolutionary War, this grant being known as the Fire Lands. The main body of Western Reserve land was disposed of by lottery, the first drawing being in 1798.

Effect of Speculation on Sale to Settlers

With the lands of these great speculators in the market,—some ten millions of acres, which had cost from ten cents to two-thirds of a dollar per acre,—it is easy to understand that land at two dollars was not tempting. During the years 1798 to 1800, inclusive, the United States did not sell land to the value of an average farm in Ohio to-day. Gallatin

[2] *Pub. Lands*, I, p. 3.
[3] *Ibid*, p. 87. See also J. H. Perkins, *Annals of the West*, p. 457.

believed, in 1804, that the wish on the part of Congress to
prevent monopolies and large speculations had been fully
attained, though he had to admit that it was at the expense
of sales and revenue.[4] Out on the frontier there was a
different opinion: it was there reported that speculators by
forming conspiracies prevented the small farmer from
buying.[5]

In 1803, Mr. Gallatin expressed the view that some
reduction in price might be made, without stimulating speculation.[6] Again, in 1806, the Committee on Public Lands
was of the opinion that unless the price should be greatly
reduced moneyed capitalists would not be induced to engage
in that extensive speculation in land, which some years since
prevailed so generally in every part of the country, and
from which so many mischiefs had resulted.[7] By "extensive
speculations" the committee undoubtedly referred to the
purchases like that of the Ohio Company, Symmes, and
the North American Land Company, in which the term
million figures constantly. No company of this kind chose
to pay the two-dollar price.

SETTLERS SPECULATE ON SMALL SCALE

Speculation was of a different type from that of the
earlier period. Instead of the great company there was a
large number of small purchasers who, perhaps involun-
tarily, became speculators in just as true a sense. These
were purchasers of the minimum amount: at times a section,
at other times a half-section. But these adventurers were
of two classes: either they were men with a little or with
much money buying land for the sake of the margin between
the government price and what an actual settler would give,
or they were actual settlers buying more than they could
farm in the hope of selling part of it before the deferred

[4] *Ann. of Cong.*, 8 Cong., 2 Sess., p. 1585.
[5] *Ibid*, 5 Cong., 1 Sess., p. 377.
[6] *Pub. Lands*, I, p. 168.
[7] *Ann. of Cong.*, 9 Cong., 2 Sess., p. 1034.

payments came due. Mr. Johnson of Kentucky, speaking in defense of the settlers, in a plea for extension of time, refers to those who were struggling to pay for "five or six hundred acres on which they have settled," and exclaims: "Are these men speculators? No, sir." [8] A few lines later he calls their purchases "little farms." He therefore had in mind the latter of the two classes mentioned, which the land system by its nature decreed should be numerous.

The first real craze of speculation came just after the War of 1812, induced largely by the bargain made by the Treasury Department with western banks. The banks were to receive and reissue the Treasury notes and in turn the Treasury would receive the notes of the banks in payment for land. The result was a rage for land, encouraged by the fact that bank notes were cheap and easily obtained. The credit system permitted the purchaser to go in debt for the major part of the price, and the prospect of making subsequent payments with cheap money seemed good. Everybody bought land. Then came an order of the Treasury refusing to take depreciated money in payment, with the result that great numbers of purchasers were unable to pay at all, and the land was forfeited. In many instances leniency on the part of the government was all that prevented wholesale forfeiture. [9]

OPPOSITION TO SPECULATION BY WESTERN STATES

The larger speculator was by no means unknown, not even in the Northwest. A petition presented to Congress from Ohio prayed "that additional regulations may be adopted in relation to the sale of public lands, in order to prevent speculations, and to protect the rights of poor men." [10] An Ohio editor speaks of "those mushroom speculators who have infested this western country by buying at a credit, and holding land to the prejudice of the com-

[8] *Ann. of Cong.*, 11 Cong., 2 Sess., p. 2001.
[9] McMaster, V, pp. 171, 172.
[10] *Ann. of Cong.*, 16 Cong., 1 Sess., p. 939.

munity." [11] Another Ohio paper bears similar testimony: "This mode, now proposed, would not only put at rest, forever, these vexatious appeals to Congress for relief, but would nearly annihilate those speculative and high prices which have been bid to the great injury of the community, but in reality never intended to be paid. Should a bill [providing for cash sales] . . . be carried through Congress, it would be a means of benefiting the states of Ohio, Indiana, and Illinois particularly, as large entries have been made, not for settlement, but for resale." [12]

Mr. Sloan, a representative from Ohio, in an extended speech in the House, said: "Your best land is generally purchased by speculators who have money, not with a view of cultivating it themselves, but to keep it until the settlement of the country enhances its value, and then to sell it to some person at an advanced price. Companies are formed in various parts of the Union who send their agents to the Western Country, who enter whole townships merely with a view to speculation." [13]

The testimony from Kentucky was similar, with the additional charge that the hard times of 1819 were attributed in large measure to speculation in land. [14]

THE YAZOO AFFAIR

Among the most spectacular of all land speculation within the pioneer portion of America may be mentioned the "Yazoo Affair" within what is now Alabama and Mississippi. This territory, at least the greater part of it, was claimed by Georgia. The first attempt at getting rich quick out of these lands was made in 1789 when a sale at a few cents an acre of a great amount of this land was made, the purchasing company planning a colony outside the jurisdiction of the federal government, to be governed by Spain. This

[11] *Ohio Monitor*, May 11, 1820.
[12] *Western Spy and Literary Cadet* (Cincinnati), Sept. 7, 1820.
[13] *Ann. of Cong.*, 16 Cong., 1 Sess., 1895.
[14] *Kentucky Reporter* quoted in *Niles Register*, XVII, p. 10.

was thwarted. In 1795 the Georgia legislature sold over half the western territory to which she laid claim, to four land companies. It transpired that the sellers were also the buyers and a great scandal resulted. The legislature rescinded its action promptly, but not until much of the land had passed into the hands of third parties. The outcome was a long series of controversies over the right to the land so transferred, resulting in a recognition of the claims of the innocent purchasers. The case was not settled until 1814 and at a cost to the United States of over six million dollars.[15]

Fraudulent Combinations at Auctions

Speculation in the Southwest was at times accompanied by fraud. For example, a group of about forty men in Alabama in 1819 agreed among themselves not to bid above the minimum price for a certain township of land. They got the land at two dollars and immediately offered it at auction and realized nineteen dollars per acre for it,—not a bad day's work.[16] A similar combination of speculators some fifteen years later is described by an aggrieved party.[17]

A little earlier, in the year 1819, in a carefully prepared report to the House, the Committee on Public Lands speaks emphatically on the subject of speculation: "Experience," says the committee, "has exploded the opinion that injurious speculators might be discouraged and monopolies prevented by simply fixing a high price on the sale of public lands; . . . the industrious class with small capital have been prevented from becoming purchasers with a view to settlement and cultivation."[18] The only remedy suggested was the sale of land in smaller tracts, thereby permitting the

---

[15] C. H. Haskins, American History Association *Report* 1890, p. 83, Donaldson, pp. 83-85. *Pub. Lands,* I. McMaster, III, pp. 131-133.

[16] *Alabama Courier,* quoted in *Ohio Monitor,* May 20, 1819.

[17] *Niles Register,* XLVI, p. 326.

[18] *Pub. Lands,* III, p. 366. In 1812 the same committee with Mr. Morrow of Ohio, chairman, as in 1819, was positive that speculators could do no harm with land at two dollars, or even at a lower price, so long as it was uniform, and offerings were in small tracts. *Pub. Lands,* II, p. 730.

man with a hundred dollars to buy direct from the government.

SPECULATION BECOMES A CRAZE

The next great period of speculation was that just preceding the panic of 1837. The sales of land during 1835 and 1836 were in large measure to men who bought in order to sell again at an advanced price. This fact is so patent as to need little or no proof. There is no evidence even to suggest that additions to the farming area of the West kept pace with the land sales; no such amount of land could have been assimilated in so short a time. Conditions were, however, ripe for speculation. The Erie Canal, steamboat navigation, highways, and, above all, the railroads, led or gave promise of leading from the cities of the East with their markets to the plains of the West with their fertility. Thousands of men, with little or much money, had a vision of settlement, wheat, prosperity and profits. There was an undue amount of zeal in attempts to help the vision to come true. The condition of the currency was such as greatly to facilitate the speculation. "As the market value of land frequently rose to much above the government selling-price, there was an eager contest on the part of those who could borrow money to buy for speedy sale at an advanced price or hold the land for future profit. Borrowers found ready accommodation at local banks, and with the loans thus secured made their purchases from the land receiver; the purchase money in many instances was thereupon re-deposited by the government in the bank whence it came, where it once more served as a loan to another or even to the same land speculator. These local banks and the government surplus thus became involved in a common network of credits; banks were established to meet this temporary demand, so that the lender leaned upon the borrower." [19]

The West was fully aware of the nature of the sales. An Iowa paper describes the condition of a new state:

[19] D. R. Dewey, *Financial History of the United States*, p. 225.

"The rage for speculation in wild lands, though natural enough in the present state of things, and, indeed, unavoidable to some extent, is, notwithstanding, a great impediment to the pursuit of agriculture. Men come to this country to make money by speculating, not by steadily pursuing a course of tilling the fertile soil, of which they become the temporary proprietors, and which soon passes into the hands of others, who are equally disposed to sell out at an advance. Hence the low state of the agricultural art everywhere to be seen in this state; and until all the public land is sold, we despair of seeing even a beginning to a regular system of cultivation.

"There is another view to be taken of this subject. The present mode of speculations is a species of gambling, leading men to rely upon uncertain events for the completion of their grasping and eager wishes for wealth. It puts a stop to the pursuit of every object worth the attainment of good and virtuous citizens. It operates as an essential check to efforts to arrive at moral and intellectual excellence. It impedes the progress of science and literature, and of every species of moral culture. It leaves the mind a barren waste, unprepared for the reception either of moral or religious impressions. It is the moral upas which taints, with the poison of its influence, every aspiration of the mind after purity of thought and integrity of conduct. Happy is the man who escapes unscathed the enticing vortex." [20]

A Boston paper complained that money was going over the mountains as fast as railroads and steamboats could carry it, and yet nothing was heard of increased agriculture. "The land is not transferred to those who cultivate, but to those who speculate." [21] A southern paper gives a description of the speculator and his operations. Probably the chances of success were somewhat lessened by the events of the year 1837, but in the main it unquestionably describes one type of speculator with fidelity. Unlike most of the accounts of speculation, much credit is here given the speculator for

[20] *Dubuque Visitor* (Iowa), Nov. 9, 1836.
[21] *Boston Daily Courier*, Aug. 13, 1836.

his work as a prospector. This he undoubtedly deserves. Whether his services were, or were not, worth what they cost depended on the information and integrity of the man. Again the value of these services could easily be overestimated from the fact that the first venturer very often sold to a second man of the same class except that often the latter had not been on the frontier. Hence the services of the prospector were likely to lose greatly in the process of percolating through several strata of owners before reaching the farmer. The account reads:

"The western country is full of men, wandering from place to place, for the purpose of inspecting public lands, and entering them, when found sufficiently fertile and well situated to be tempting to real settlers. The land speculator goes forth with a guide and a pack horse; and for weeks perambulates the uninhabited forests—he pitches his tent every evening, builds his fire, and prepares the frugal meal which has been afforded him by his unerring rifle. When he has selected some tracts of virgin soil, shaded with oaks, interspersed with natural prairies and watered by some deep, broad stream, he returns to the land office and pours forth his *all* into the coffers of the government. He talks loudly of the unexampled prosperity of the western country, of inexhaustible resources, and finally points out a particular section of the country, which, he says, is selling fast, and is superior to anything *he* knows of. He meets the tide of emigration and endeavors to direct it toward this spot of his predilection. If he succeeds, he realizes in a short time a ten-fold profit, and begins again, with enlarged capital. Hardly ever does it happen that he fails—he may have to wait more or less long, but the spreading sea of emigration finally covers the district in which he made his location—his lands, being choice tracts, command a preference, and are bought at ten or twenty dollars an acre, when government lands alongside are rejected at ten bits.

"A great many fine things may be said against this species of trade. It cuts off and forestalls the real *bona fide* settler—

prevents this trade and we are satisfied; but, since it is permitted and encouraged, we cannot blame those who turn it to profit. In fact, it is doubtful whether our western wilds would be colonized half so fast without these speculators. They stimulate and keep up the spirit of emigration and enterprise—they seek out and find favorable places for making settlements which otherwise would remain undiscovered—they encourage the European emigrant to the cultivation of the soil, and guide him to a fertile and well situated spot—without the land speculator many would remain vagabonds in our cities who are drawn off to the country, and at last become rich and respectable planters.

"Oh! but our city banks; what will become of them? All their cash is drawn from them; our commerce will be ruined! Pooh! Where would be your commerce were it not for the produce of the West? On the contrary, as the settlement and agriculture of the West increase, so will your commerce; and as to your cash, never fear—it will come back—it cannot stay long in the woods, and once the come-and-go rotation is established everything will wag along smoothly." [22]

Not so flattering was the version of the register and receiver of a Land Office in a Michigan district:

"The undersigned, deeply regretting the nefarious transactions which are daily practiced and repeated by certain individuals in the vicinity of this land office, and impelled by a sense of duty, both to the public and themselves, feel bound to state that, from facts and circumstances within their knowledge, they are thoroughly convinced that numerous individuals, without capital, and without integrity, are in the constant practice of making applications to the register of this office for large quantities of land for the purpose of imposing upon the honest purchaser, by inducing him to pay them for what they are pleased to call their right, thereby assuming and exercising a partial control over numerous lots of land, without either the intention or ability to pay for it, and in many instances with no knowledge of its quality. This practice, so dastardly in itself, and so injurious in its consequences, is, nevertheless, beyond the power of the officers wholly to prevent. Many instances have therefore occurred where these gentry have taken applications for land and, being unable to sell their *right*, have failed to complete them—thus leaving the land marked on the plats as sold until the arrears of business could be brought up and the fraud detected. Other individuals may have honestly applied in the meantime for the same land and been answered that it was taken, when an application, subsequent to the detection of this fraud, may have purchased it; thereby causing, on the part of the intermediate applicants, just indignation, and inducing them in some instances to reproach the officers and charge them with exercising partiality among purchasers. It is, therefore, confidently hoped that real and honest purchasers will aid in suppressing this species of swindling by treating every effort of the kind with merited contempt." [23]

SPECULATION HOLDS LAND OUT OF MARKET

One of the worst effects of speculation was that it held land out of the market for at least a time and so compelled settlement to pass around or across it. Such would be in the natural course of events, and testimony that it happened is abundant. [24] Agriculture necessarily remained for an unnecessarily long time in a backward condition under these circumstances.

It was an open secret that many members of Congress were deeply involved in land speculation. For example, Daniel Webster bought several sections of land in Wisconsin and other tracts in Illinois. He is said to have invested $60,000 in lots in Rock Island, Illinois. [25] He also once owned the section of land on which Stoughton, Wis-

[23] *Niles Register*, L, p. 228.
[24] *Belmont Gazette* (Wisconsin), Nov. 2, 1836; *Dubuque Visitor*, Sept. 7, 1836; *Miners' Express* (Iowa), Jan. 16, 1850.
[25] *Iowa News*, July 15, 1837.

consin, now stands. These were perfectly open and honorable transactions so far as is known. However, the relation of Congress as a body to the banks, with their paper money and the use of the same in land speculation, was in question. On June 20th, 1836, the House appointed a committee to inquire into the matter. In due time the committee reported tentatively asking that its membership be enlarged and that the inquiry proceed. The House refused to acquiesce and the committee was discharged.[26]

SPECULATION LESSENED BY SPECIE CIRCULAR OF 1836

The specie circular of 1836 and the panic of 1837 brought a sudden end to the work of speculators so far as purchases from the government were concerned. The land previously bought could not be resold advantageously and much of it which had been bought with borrowed money proved bad property to the buyer. In a desperate effort to hold such land exorbitant rates of interest were paid.[27] Much land was sold for taxes; much was traded off and gotten rid of in any and every possible way. Some years ago the writer made an attempt to trace the transfers of some of the great tracts of land held by speculators in Wisconsin, but with indifferent success. A brief account was, however, ventured: "Greedy as were the statesmen and other wealthy men who invested their money in western land during the palmy days in 1836, the very fact that they were unable to form anything approaching a monopoly in land rendered them almost as helpless as their unfortunate friends whose capital went down in mercantile disasters of the older states. . . . It is impossible to tell from the records much about the sums realized by these large holders when they finally parted with their land. The greater share of it was held by firms of several members and the number of quit-claim deeds with 'consideration one dollar' fill many pages of the register's

---

[26] *Niles Register*, L, p. 434.
[27] *Lee County Democrat* (Iowa), Dec. 9, 1843; *Miners' Express* (Iowa), Jan. 16, 1850.

books. Nor is this all the difficulty; the most of these firms owned land in different counties and even different states, and very frequently transfers were made of one-fourth, or one-tenth, or even one-nineteenth of these widely scattered acres, and exchanges of various kinds of property for land again complicate matters hopelessly. Occasionally, where the sale was made directly to a *bona fide* purchaser previous to about 1850, the price was a little more than the original figure—one and a quarter dollars." [28] Contemporary testimony confirms the conclusion.[29]

Although speculation never has entirely ceased, even to the present time, there was a decided lull during the early part of the twenty years between 1837 and 1857, with a perfect rage of speculation again during the latter years of this period. By this time the speculators were no longer free to buy any land in sight on account of the settlers and their organizations, since, as noted in Chapter IX, the squatters and preëmptors were in a position to defend themselves. In one instance, at a government auction, neither settlers nor speculators were able to buy. They could not, during the first few days, agree, and whenever a representative of one party made a bid some one of the opposition raised it, some tracts being bid off for as much as $140.00 per acre. A transaction of this sort would be recorded on the books, but no money paid, therefore, on closing the books for the day, the entry "no sale" completed the burlesque. The next day the same land could be, and frequently was, offered again, and with similar results. Finally the speculators gave up and

---

[28] Hibbard, p. 100.

[29] "Lands have been entered in this country at one dollar and twenty-five cents per acre, and after paying taxes on them for years their owners have sold them for one dollar per acre to avoid further taxation. Show us a non-resident who has made much money speculating in western land, and we will show you a rare bird, more rare by far than a successful gold hunter. . . . Large investments in land always defeat their own object. . . . We need no national reform to punish speculators. The only way in which anything can be made by buying western lands is to locate in small tracts remote from each other so as not to interfere in the general settlement, and even then the settlers skin the speculator out of his profits by taxation." *Madison Argus,* October 22, 1850. See also *Cong. Globe,* 26 Cong., 2 Sess., App. p. 99.

the settlers bought what they wanted. The observer of this scene added: "For my part, I am wholly for the settler, and I am convinced that every one must be who has ridden over those vast and beautiful prairies—wholly uncultivated for miles because held by speculators, who keep the land for a rise. I cannot but believe that it would be better for the whole country if there would never be another acre of land sold at auction, but to let any man who would go and live on the land and cultivate it for one or two years have 160 acres at $1.25 per acre, and give none to any one else at any price." [30]

Testimony is abundant to the effect that speculators ran ahead of settlers and bought up a large portion of the public domain throughout the Mississippi Valley. Except in the panic periods there was hope of making money. The normal trend of events is thus described: "What is western land speculation in reality? It is simply this: One man buys land at $1.25, sells it at $2.50 or $3.00, and invests again 'further west.' The second purchaser makes some improvements upon the lands and sells for $5.00 per acre. In the meantime some other 'speculator' has built a mill nearby and lays out a village, and the third purchaser sells the tract of land of which we have been speaking at $15 or $20 per acre. In a year or two 'a railroad comes along,' which is built by some other 'speculator,' because it will pay, and the fourth buyer sells for $25 per acre, to a purchaser who wishes to put on improvements and occupy it himself, to whom the same property will be worth $50 per acre in a few years.

"Here are four men who have doubled and trebled their money within a year or two from the day of investment, and this is the simple history of land speculation in the fertile West." [31]

The professional speculators who "produce more poverty

[30] *N. Y. Weekly Tribune,* May 23, 1857. An account of a similar case is given in the Charles City (Iowa) *Intelligencer,* May 7, 1857.
[31] *Charles City Intelligencer* (Iowa), Aug. 20, 1857.

than potatoes and consume more midnight oil in playing poker than of God's sunshine in the game of raising wheat and corn" did their share of buying and holding for a higher price. At the same time the farmer himself became a speculator to the extent of his means.[32] It would be impossible to trace the speculation of the latter class, if for no other reason than that it cannot be identified in the records, and because no one knows whether the first, third or fifth eighty acres owned by a farmer was held for speculation or for farming purposes. However, when the acreage runs into the thousands there is no room for controversy.

The greatest wave of speculation preceded the panic of 1857 and swamped many a venturer in the catastrophe of that year. The quieter times following gave agriculture a much needed opportunity to develop.

The people of the West were not unaware of the situation. "During this period [from 1854 up to the fall of 1857]," writes an Iowa editor, "it is amazing how completely our citizens were filled with the desire of sudden riches. Credit was easily had—eastern currency flooded the country —imaginary towns sprung up everywhere—lands were fictitiously high—usury was unscrupulously asked and willingly promised—farms were neglected—debts were left to run on unasked about, goods and groceries being bought on credit, lands alone selling for ready money at exorbitant rates. In short, every one was a professed speculator, and the good results which always flow from a proper division of labor, skill and capital were entirely dried up. Then followed the wrecks of fortunes and the crash of business. It was natural—it could not have been otherwise. Many men have sunk, doubtless, who will never rise again, some of whom are entitled to pity, and others not. But it must be seen that the effects of the hard times, as now plainly visible, are of unmixed benefit to real progress and prosperity." [33]

Within the next few years great quantities of land were

---

[32] *Dubuque Daily Republic*, Aug. 14, 1857.
[33] *Charles City Intelligencer* (Iowa), Sept. 1, 1859.

advertised and sold for taxes. At one time almost one-half of the land of Hamilton County, Iowa, was so advertised, the taxes being delinquent for two and three years on the greater share of it.[34]

SPECULATION AND MILITARY SCRIP

It would be an endless task to trace the land sales for any considerable area with a view to determining the extent of speculation. However, the records of sales of land in Iowa have been searched for such information covering a period of some forty years, during which time the bulk of the sales were made. It appears that more big purchases were made with military scrip than with cash. The 140 largest purchases with this scrip amounted to 1,381,000 acres, or about 9860 acres each on an average. Very few of these reached a hundred thousand acres each, though one exceeded a quarter of a million acres and another very nearly reached 200,000 acres.

Of cash purchases there were 54 that exceeded one thousand acres each. These covered an aggregate of 752,550 acres, or 13,936 acres on an average for each buyer, or eighty-seven farms of one hundred sixty acres each. The very largest purchaser, made in part by military scrip and in part by cash, was 344,578 acres, or almost fifteen townships in extent.

It has not been found feasible to follow the records of sales minutely enough to determine what became of these big purchases or how well the purchasers fared. An examination in one case showed heavy sales at about the same price that had been paid. It is evident that in almost all instances the land was sold within a comparatively few years, since for many years there have been no holdings in the state that compare in size with these early purchases. When it is remembered that most of this land was bought

[34] *Hamilton County Freeman* (Iowa), July 7, 1860. A similar condition prevailed in Buchanan County. See *The Guardian* (Manchester, Iowa), Sept. 4, 1860.

from the government before 1860; that there was land open to homestead in the northwestern part of the state from 1862 till well into the seventies, it is plain that land could not rise very high or very rapidly until after these conditions passed. The result was that the big speculators, who were always opposed to the homestead act, sold out long before land reached twenty or even ten dollars per acre. The result was that a series of smaller speculators often intervened between the first buyer and the first farmer. This series of speculators managed to get several dollars per acre—several times government price—out of the tillers of the soil before the latter got a chance at the productive operations. Competition among these forerunners of agriculture prevented the great majority of them from reaping immense fortunes. Nothing short of minute studies by townships, counties or perhaps of individual speculations will serve to show the full importance of this phase of passing the land down from the government to the farmer.

Preëmption and Homestead Acts as Remedies; Large Grants a Stimulus

Speculation had a few favorable aspects, yet on the whole it was a way to make, and often to lose, money without adding materially to the development of the country. The remedy most frequently proposed was the sale of land to settlers only. This was the natural and, on the whole, the most promising remedy. True, there were bound to be evasions—no laws pertaining to the public domain have been proof against evasion; but even in spite of this fact the preëmption laws and later the homestead laws succeeded in the main in putting land into the hands of farmers rather than of land jobbers. Nevertheless, there was already a vast amount of land held by speculators. It must also be admitted that lands disposed of under the preëmption or the homestead laws—in the case of the latter the part "commuted" especially—were easily obtainable at second hand by speculators. Last, but by no means least, the great grants of land to the railroads, grants to the states for educational purposes, the swamp land grants, and the like, put an empire of territory within reach of the speculator. The unearned increment was more attractive than the earned increment, and a vast number of people attempted to reap it.

The case against the speculator seems clear and severe. However, it should be remembered that he was doing the natural and legitimate thing in buying land on which there was a prospect of making a gain. The damage done by these transactions, damage just as often to the speculator as to the subsequent buyer, serves but to show the folly of handling such a vast business as that of disposing of the public domain with so little plan. To offer land freely in any quantity was to invite speculation. The land was so offered and the invitation was accepted. Merely holding land as private property in advance of its final occupancy and full use may be a public service, contributing to the building of roads, schools and communities. This may be seen by contrasting such holdings with land still in the hands of the government on which no taxes are paid. The retention of much land in the hands of the government is no doubt desirable, but it should be done in accordance with a plan, and not in a haphazard manner.

SUMMARY

Speculation in land is as old as history. At least as old as the history of private property in land. Speculation in land was prevalent during colonial times. Many of the leading men of that period, notably Washington, were heavy speculators. Land companies organized for speculation played a considerable part in the settlement of much territory west of the Alleghanies soon after the Revolution.

The complaint was made early in the westward movement that speculators were robbing the real settlers. At the same time the settlers were themselves speculators on a small scale. They usually bought more land than they could use. Speculation in a large way cropped out on certain occasions. These were mainly the period following the War of 1812; the years preceding the panic of 1837, and again in the late fifties. On two of these occasions cheap money played a large rôle in the deals. On the third it was the military scrip that made speculation unduly easy. While there are many individual instances to the contrary it is safe to say that for the most part speculation led to disappointment much more often than to affluence.

CHAPTER XIII

FEDERAL LAND GRANTS FOR INTERNAL IMPROVEMENTS

GRANTS FOR GENERAL INTERNAL IMPROVEMENTS

Following the passage of the enabling act for the State of Ohio, in 1802, providing for a donation of five per cent of the proceeds from public lands sold in that state, for building public roads, the question of the expediency of distributing the public lands among the several states became a subject of Congressional inquiry. The need and desirability of improved transportation in connecting the East with the newly developing Middle West furnished a primary incentive for the legislation of 1841, which provided, (1) for distribution of the Treasury surplus—due largely to the extensive sale of public lands, (2) for the land grants for internal improvements, and (3) rather incidentally for preëmption rights of settlers.

The Act of 1841 and Internal Improvements

The passage of the Act of 1841 was preceded, as shown in Chapter IX, by many long debates. In the first place it was not quite clear that such land grants were constitutional. Secondly, the South came to oppose such grants, since it would give the North the advantage in development. Thirdly, the land grant legislation became tied up with the question of distribution of the Treasury surplus among the states. Nevertheless, Congressmen favoring such grants for internal improvements found precedent in the donation to Ebenezer Zane of three sctions of land as a bonus for a wagon road;[1] in the five and three per cent fund grants to Ohio and other states for road building and other purposes;

---

[1] *Laws of the United States*, II, p. 533.

and in the land grant to Ohio in 1823 on condition that a road be built. Hence, in 1829, with a view to realizing the maximum benefit from the public lands, Hunt of Vermont submitted a resolution in the House instructing the Committee on Public Lands "to inquire into the expediency of appropriating the net annual proceeds of the sales of public lands among the several states for the purposes of education and internal improvements."[2] Three years later Senator Clayton of Delaware proposed a similar inquiry relative to the "public lands or the proceeds thereof."[3] A plan to cede public lands to the states in which they were situated was recommended during the session 1831-1832 by the Secretary of the Treasury, but rejected by the Public Lands Committees in both Houses.[4] The Senate Committee proposed an assignment of fifteen per cent of the net proceeds to the new states and nothing to the old.[5] It will be remembered that one of the main objects in the proposed distribution to the states of land, or the proceeds of sales of land, was the promotion of internal improvements.

During the Congressional session of 1831-32 Senator Benton came forward with a bill providing for a grant of five hundred thousand acres of public land to Missouri for the purpose of internal improvements within that state.[6] Amendments were later offered to give similar amounts to Louisiana and Mississippi. Then came the initial move to tie up this land grant bill with Clay's distribution bill. When the latter came up for discussion Poindexter of Mississippi moved an amendment "giving five hundred thousand acres to each of the states of Missouri, Mississippi and Louisiana." Other amendments were made, but the entire bill was rejected by the House.

At the next session of Congress Clay's land bill, which had failed in the House, as noted in Chapter X, was again in-

[2] *Cong. Deb.*, 22 Cong., 1 Sess., p. 477.
[3] *Ibid*, pp. 638, 639.
[4] *Ibid*, App., p. 117.
[5] *Ibid*, 22 Cong., 1 Sess., p. 931.
[6] *Ibid*, p. 592.

troduced in the Senate. The land-grant feature was retained and read in part as follows: "To the states of Mississippi, Louisiana and Missouri a quantity of five hundred thousand acres of land, and to the state of Indiana one hundred and fifteen thousand two hundred and seventy-two acres; to the state of Illinois twenty thousand acres, and to the state of Alabama one hundred thousand acres of land, lying within the limits of said states, respectively, to be selected in such manner as the legislatures thereof shall direct, and located in parcels conformable to sectional divisions and subdivisions, of not less than three hundred and twenty acres in any one location.

"The net proceeds of the sales of the lands so granted are to be faithfully applied to works of internal improvement within the aforesaid States, respectively."[7] This was the bill vetoed by President Jackson, one of his main objections being the provision of federal aid for internal improvements.

During the session of 1836-1837 the land bill reappeared in a form only slightly revised. It provided for the new State of Arkansas her 500,000 acres of land as proposed for the other states and made provision for a similar grant to Michigan, when she should enter the Union. The application of the fund was again restricted to the "great objects of education, internal improvement and colonization."[8] The select Senate committee to which the bill was referred reported it with an amendment, striking out the whole excepting the enacting clause, and changing its object. It became "a bill to prohibit the sales of public lands except to actual settlers in limited quantities." Opposed by Clay and his friends, and defended by Benton, it passed the Senate. In the House it was tabled.

For several years the matter virtually slumbered, although propositions for specific grants of various kinds as well as for the cession of the entire public domain to the states continued to be brought forward. A bill introduced by

[7] *Cong. Deb.*, 22 Cong., 2 Sess., p. 146.
[8] *Ibid*, 24 Cong., 2 Sess., pp. 20, 21.

Senator Norvell of Michigan during the session of 1839-40, granting lands to the other new states equal in quantity to those which had been granted to Ohio, for purposes of internal improvement, was laid on the table. As noted in the chapter on the distribution of land sale proceeds among the states the granting of land for internal improvements was passed by the Whig Congress as part of the Distribution Act. While the question of distribution of money was the primary issue, the granting of land attracted a measure of attention.

In the House the land grant proposal was characterized by its enemies as "a bribe which was thrown out to the states for nothing unless to be available at the next election." [9] Wise of Virginia was opposed to it, since it involved an inequality in its provisions among the new states themselves, and was "especially inequitable as between the new states and the old." Winthrop of Massachusetts, who did not "begrudge" the western states "the half million of acres which it proposes to make up to them," nevertheless believed that "the contemplated cession would be a fatal dowry to them, as well as a measure full of injustice to us." In spite of determined opposition the bill came to a vote within two weeks after being reported, and was passed—yeas 116, nays 108. [10]

By a Senate amendment the scope of the grant was enlarged to include any new states that might thereafter be admitted. An attempt was made by several western senators to make the grant to each state equivalent to the total quantity of land granted to Ohio for the encouragement of internal improvements—1,142,000 acres. The change was advocated on the basis of equality; and Calhoun, whose opinion of the bill was that it was "a most unconstitutional measure . . . the most odious measure that could be presented," gave his support because the amendment involved an approach toward giving the whole of the land to the

[9] *Cong. Globe,* 27 Cong., 1 Sess., p. 131.
[10] *Ibid,* p. 156.

states.[11] The bill passed the Senate and was approved by Tyler, September 4, 1841.

According to the terms of the act the selections were to be made within the limits of the states "in such manner as the legislature thereof may direct and in parcels of not less than 320 acres. A minimum price of one dollar and twenty-five cents was stipulated and the proceeds were to be "faithfully applied to objects of internal improvement, namely: roads, railways, bridges, canals and improvement of water courses, and draining of swamps." Such means of communication thus made or improved were then to be "free for the transportation of the United States mail and munitions of war, and for the passage of their troops without the payment of any toll whatever." [12]

Subsequent Application of the Act

The original bill, as it passed the House, limited the grant to nine states—Ohio, Indiana, Illinois, Alabama, Missouri, Mississippi, Louisiana, Arkansas and Michigan. By the amendment attached in the Senate, it was extended to the new states that might later be admitted into the Union. In either case, grants for internal improvements previously made were to be considered as part of the five hundred thousand acres. In accordance with these provisions Ohio and Indiana received no further donation, Illinois received 209,000 acres and Alabama 97,000 acres. The nine states above mentioned and those admitted between 1841 and 1889 (with the exception of Texas and West Virginia)—Florida, Iowa, Wisconsin, California, Minnesota, Oregon, Kansas, Nevada, Nebraska and Colorado—nineteen in all, received at least their full 500,000 acres. Up to 1880 a total of 7,806,554.67 acres,[13] distributed through seventeen states, had passed from the public domain. These lands were used in five instances exclusively for school purposes.[14]

[11] Cong. Globe, 27 Cong., 1 Sess., p. 332.
[12] Laws of the U. S., X, pp. 157, 158.
[13] Donaldson, p. 22. There was no further legislation affecting the grant until 1889.
[14] Wisconsin, Alabama, Iowa, Nevada, Oregon.

With the admission into the Union of the two Dakotas, Montana and Washington in 1889, a change in at least the form of land grants was inaugurated. Technically the act of 1841 ceased to operate altogether, being repealed with regard to these states along with the swamp land and saline land grant acts. However, definite donations to specified state institutions were given in lieu of these grants, making the total quantity of land given to these six states—the four admitted in 1889 and Idaho and Wyoming, admitted in 1890 —in each case 500,000 acres. Such specific donations may collectively be considered the lineal descendants of the grant for internal improvement.

The idea expressed in the new legislation seems to have originated with Springer, a Representative from Illinois and Chairman of the House Committee on Territories in 1889.[15] It was unanimously approved by that committee, and, although different land grant plans were presented, it met with no opposition. The question of land endowments for new states was no longer an issue on which partisan spirit came into evidence. From the close of the Civil War until 1889 only two new states were admitted, Nebraska in 1867 and Colorado in 1876. During this period the habit of looking toward the national government for assistance in the construction of "roads, railways, bridges, canals and improvement of watercourses and draining of swamps" largely ceased. State institutions not possessing the same direct appeal to the economic interests as did these verifiable necessities were, however, still objects suitable for national bounty. In the older established states these had been given definite shape; and it was recognized that the establishment of comparable institutions in the newer states would require considerable outlay.

GRANTS FOR SPECIFIC INTERNAL IMPROVEMENTS

In a separate class of legislation is found a series of federal land grants made for certain specific internal improve-

[15] *Cong. Rec.*, 50 Cong., 2 Sess., p. 900.

ments rather than for general internal improvements. In Washington liberal grants were made for a scientific school, public buildings, penal and reform institutions. In Montana provision was made specifically also for a school of mines, an agricultural college, and a deaf and dumb asylum. In North and South Dakota the State University received 40,000 out of the 500,000 acres. Wyoming received specific grants for an insane asylum, a penitentiary, a fish hatchery, a poor farm, and a hospital for injured miners, besides grants for most of the other objects mentioned in relation to the other states. A similar list of institutions was provided for in Idaho.

In the acts admitting the last four states—Utah, Oklahoma, Arizona and New Mexico—into the Union, it was declared that the internal improvement and swamp land grants should not be made to Arizona and New Mexico. The saline grant to the latter state was repealed.[16] In lieu of these a number of grants more liberal than those discontinued were given to the state institutions. In Utah the aggregate area of such grants was 1,150,000 acres; in Oklahoma, 1,050,000 acres; in New Mexico, 2,250,00 acres; and in Arizona, 2,150,000 acres. New Mexico and Arizona received, in addition, a million acres each for help in paying off state bonds. The last feature of the act of 1841 to die— the half-million-acre limit—had thus completely disappeared.

Some of the specific grants, especially the canal grants, came before the law of 1841, but most of the specific grants were made subsequently to that date. These donations, although made for the same general purpose, differed from the grants made by the act of 1841 chiefly in that they were designed to meet certain well defined needs for improvement of the transportation system rather than serving primarily as a means of just distribution of an over-abundant supply of public lands.

Wagon Road Grants, 1823-1869.—In 1823 Ohio received

[16] *U. S. Stat. at Large,* XXVIII, pp. 109, 110; XXXVI, p. 562; XXXVI, p. 573.

a grant to be applied toward the construction of a highway from the lower rapids of the Miami of Lake Erie to the western boundary of the Connecticut Western Reserve. The grant included the equivalent of two strips, a mile in width, one on each side of the projected road, in addition to a right of way 120 feet wide." Under the provisions of this act and a similar one in 1827, providing for a road from Columbus to Sandusky, 80,773.54 acres were certified or patented and $10,206.41 paid to the state in lieu of lands previously sold.

It was provided that none of the grant should be sold for less than $1.25 per acre, and in the case of the Columbus-Sandusky road, it was provided that "no toll shall at any time be collected of any mail coach, nor of any troops, or property of the United States"—a provision that was attached not only to grants for wagon roads, but also, on a much larger scale, to those for subsidized canals, and later for railroads. In 1827 a grant was made to the State of Indiana for a road to connect Lake Michigan with some convenient point on the Ohio River by way of Indianapolis.

From 1827 to 1863, excepting for some minor legislation directed mainly toward facilitating the administration of the grants already made, no positive action involving the construction of wagon roads was taken by Congress in the disposition of the public domain. By the act of March 3, 1863, however, Michigan and Wisconsin were given the even numbered sections for three miles on each side of a road to be built from Fort Wilkins, Copper Harbor, Michigan, to Green Bay, Wisconsin. The limits upon the area available for indemnity selections were set at fifteen miles on each side of the road." Eight similar acts were passed within the following six years, the indemnity limits being fixed at eight or ten miles, and freedom of government traffic

---

17 *U. S. Stat. at Large*, III, p. 727.

18 "Indemnity selections" or "lieu lands" were lands selected in lieu of land which would have been included in the first assignment but for some circumstances such as previous occupation.

from toll stipulated in all. Two of these acts never became operative since Michigan and Wisconsin, in whose favor they were drafted, failed to avail themselves of the grants for which they provided.

The amount of the grants for wagon road purposes is shown in the following table:[19]

TABLE XIII

GRANTS FOR WAGON ROAD PURPOSES

The Road	State Receiving Grant	Date of Grant	Acres Granted
From Lake Erie to Connecticut Western Reserve	Ohio	1823	80,773.54
From Lake Michigan to Ohio River	Indiana	1827	170,580.24
From Ft. Wilkins, Copper Harbor, Mich., to Green Bay, Wisconsin	Michigan and Wisconsin	1863	302,930.96
From Ft. Wilkins, Copper Harbor, Mich., to Wisconsin State Line	Michigan and Wisconsin	1863	221,013.35
Oregon Central Military Co. (Now California & Oregon Land Co.)	Oregon	1864	859,937.29
Corvallis and Yaquina Bay	Oregon	1856	83,716.76
Willamette Valley and Cascade Mountains	Oregon	1866	861,511.86
Dalles Military Road	Oregon	1867	590,942.10
Coos Bay Military Road	Oregon	1869	105,240.11
Total			3,276,646.21

All of the acts by which the grants made to Michigan, Wisconsin and Oregon were effected contained provisions for their administration. The states were permitted to sell thirty sections with the completion of each successive ten-mile portion of the road, these thirty sections to be coterminous with the finished portion. The original acts imposed a time limit of five years, all unsold lands to revert to the government whenever the construction of a highway was still incomplete at the end of this period. But in a number of instances the time was extended, Wisconsin and Michigan receiving several such extensions.

[19] L. O. R., 1923, p. 38.

Oregon, which received the largest grant, disposed of its title to five road-building companies by which the actual work of construction was done. Portions of the land have been sold to private individuals, but the greater part was still in the hands of the companies in 1920.[20]

Canal Grants, 1824-1866.—In 1824, only a year after the date of the first wagon road subsidy, Congress passed an act authorizing Indiana to locate a canal to connect for navigation the Wabash River and Lake Erie, granting a right of way ninety feet in width on each side of the canal.[21] The law was not utilized, and in 1827 it was followed by another which gave to the state "a quantity of land equal to one-half of five sections in width and reserving each alternate section for the United States." As in the wagon road grant made at the same time, freedom from tolls for government use was stipulated. The clause providing for the reservation of each alternate section incorporated a principle that later became of much importance in the legislation concerning railway grants. It was urged that the donation was advisable because of the increase in value of the remaining public lands in the neighborhood of the canal.[22]

Additional legislation was from time to time directed toward the settlement of the grant, until, in 1848, when the state was given authority to select as indemnity land any lands subject to private entry, fulfilling the terms of the original act.[23] The same authority was, within four years, extended to two other states which had received canal grants—Ohio and Illinois. In Ohio two canals were involved—one being a portion of the Erie and Wabash Canal, Indiana having yielded in 1834 its rights and obligations so far as the portion lying without its boundaries was concerned; the other, the Miami Canal. In Illinois, the Illinois-

---

[20] Letter from the clerk of the Oregon State Land Board.
[21] *U. S. Stat. at Large*, IV, p. 47.
[22] *Cong. Deb.*, 19 Cong., 2 Sess., p. 310 *et seq. Ibid*, 20 Cong., 1 Sess., p. 2742.
[23] *U. S. at Large*, IX, p. 219.

Michigan Canal had been subsidized on the same date as the Wabash-Erie, March 2, 1827. In each of these cases the extent of the donation had been "a quantity of land equal to five sections in width on each side."

In all, eight other canal grants were made after 1827; one to Ohio in 1828 for the Miami Canal, to which allusion has already been made, two to Wisconsin in 1838 and 1866; and four to Michigan, one in 1852, another in 1865, and two in 1866. Wisconsin, however, failed to construct the canal provided for in the grant of 1838, and the land reverted to the government. The proceeds of the canal lands sold by the state, aggregating more than 125,000 acres, were charged against her five per cent fund; the lands certified to the state, but not sold, were charged to her internal improvement allotment. These grants differed from those of 1827 and subsequent similar enactments, in no important detail, until the grant was made to Wisconsin for aid in constructing the Wisconsin-Fox River Canal in 1846. The states had received a definite amount of land to be sold as they chose, and not affecting changes in the prices of remaining government land. In the case of the Wisconsin-Fox River Canal grant provision was made for the sale of the alternate sections of government land to be sold at $2.50. Thus was inaugurated the "double minimum" program.

In many respects the most interesting grant of all was one made in 1828 to Ohio. Congress granted a half million acres to Ohio for "canals generally," the state to determine the locations and complete the work, which must be undertaken within seven years. But the turning point between interest in canals and in railroads had just been reached and it was not strange that the generous grant was not utilized for canal purposes. When the half-million-acre grant was made in 1841 to the western states this canal grant to Ohio was considered to be her allotment. The later subsidized canals were relatively short, uniting such bodies of water with the Great Lakes as were sufficiently large to accommodate the larger vessels.[24]

The distribution of the canal grants is shown in the following table:[25]

Indiana	1,480,408.87 acres
Ohio	1,204,113.89 acres
Michigan	1,251,235.85 acres
Wisconsin	338,626.97 acres
Illinois	324,282.74 acres

Total 4,598,668.32 acres

Canals were, from the beginning, owned largely by the states. In 1817 the New York Legislature authorized a group of "canal commissioners to begin the construction of the middle section of the Erie—to raise $250,000 by taxing the lands and farms lying along the routes of the waterway and within twenty-five miles of it. Moreover, a canal fund was created and given in charge of the commissioners, who were to borrow money on the credit of the state. . . ."[26] The money to pay for the undertaking was to be raised in part also by a duty on salt in the eastern district of New York, a tax of one dollar on each person who traveled more than one hundred miles on the canal, the proceeds of lotteries in the state, and the commissioners were permitted to hire out convicts of the state prison to the contractors.

Likewise, in 1827 the Pennsylvania legislature granted authority to a board of canal commissioners to "proceed at once to build 'the Pennsylvania Canal' at state expense,"[27] and made a first appropriation of money.

[24] There were four canals of this type: (1) the ship canal around the falls of the St. Mary's River; (2) the ship canal through "the Portage" in Michigan; (3) the Green Bay Canal; (4) the ship canal connecting Lake Superior with Lac La Belle in Michigan. Of an entirely different type were the long overland canals subsidized in 1827 and 1828; these were designed for distinctly inland traffic to be carried on by canal craft.

[25] *L. O. R.*, 1907, p. 84.

[26] McMaster, IV, pp. 417, 418.

[27] *Ibid*, V, p. 142.

A few noteworthy gifts were made by individuals and in some of the earlier undertakings private companies held shares of stock in canals, but in general the states administered the canal building program, whereas the federal government furnished the most substantial aid through land grants.

Canals as a means of transportation fill an important place in the development and unification of the United States during the period from 1825 to 1850, just before the railroads came into their own. Canal building meant the rapid development of such cities as Rochester, Buffalo, Utica and Troy. It meant much to people west of the Alleghanies in the way of reduced costs on goods shipped from the East and increased prices for their raw products. A Columbus paper said, after the completion of the Erie Canal, "It takes thirty days and costs five dollars a hundred to transport goods from Philadelphia to this city; but the same articles may be brought in twenty days from New York by the Hudson and the canal at a cost of two dollars and fifty cents a hundred." [28]

River Improvement Grants.—In the three grants made to promote river improvements were embodied the same principles as in the canal grants. The first relevant legislation was passed in 1828, only a year after provision had been made for the construction of the Illinois and the Wabash and Erie canals. By its terms, Alabama became the recipient of 400,000 acres to be used for the improvement of navigation on the Tennessee River. The second act, approved August 8, 1846, granted to Wisconsin the equivalent of three sections on each side of the Fox and Wisconsin Rivers to be devoted to the improvement of the navigation of these streams, and in the construction of a canal uniting them at or near the Portage. The third and largest subsidy was granted to Iowa in 1846 for the improvement of the Des Moines River; it embraced "an equal moiety of alternate sections of land in a strip

[28] McMaster, V, p. 136.

five miles in width on each side of the river." The final
extent of the river improvement grants was as follows: [29]

Alabama	400,016.19 acres
Wisconsin	683,722.43 acres
Iowa	1,161,513.69 acres

2,245,252.31 acres

Granting land to aid in river improvement was a dismal
failure. Little or no improvement was accomplished and
the land was therefore given away to no purpose. In Iowa
the river land cases were the subject of litigation for many
years.

Railroad Grants.—Of the land grants made to promote internal improvements, those applying to railways completely
overshadow all the rest in importance. The principle of governmental aid for wagon roads and canals had been advocated
early in the nineteenth century, and during the first three decades national aid was frequently solicited in the interest of
various projects; but no very important results were obtained.
The right of Congress to make money grants was long disputed; and although by the beginning of Jackson's administration this right had come to be quite generally accepted, its exercise was checked in 1830 by the veto of the Maysville road
bill. Thereafter, attention was drawn more and more to the
public lands, portions of which had already been given to
the states for roads, canals and river improvements.

It should be observed that railways were, from the beginning, for the most part privately owned. Canals and roads
belonged to the states and the lands granted in their behalf
were disposed of by the states, but railroad grants were
made directly to private railway companies themselves, or
indirectly through the states, who in turn granted them to
the private companies.

The Illinois Grant, 1833.—The belief in the propriety of
land grants for railways was slow in maturing and did not

become positively effective until more than a quarter of a century had elapsed after the passage of the first wagon road measure. In 1833 the grant to Illinois for the construction of the Illinois and Michigan Canal was so modified that the state received the right to use it in building a railroad, but advantage was not taken of the privilege and consequently this more or less accidental circumstance produced no further results.

Beginning with 1835, Congress frequently granted to railroads the right of way through public lands. The right of way privilege was made general by an act passed in 1852.[30] In addition the roads were given land for depot sites and terminals, together with the privilege of taking stone, timber and earth from adjoining government land for building or repair purposes.[31] The system of actual land grants for railways was not inaugurated until a change in industrial conditions had prepared the way for successful political action.

The West and Railroads.—The stream of emigration into the Mississippi Valley which had made itself felt in the distribution of population as early as 1810 continued. By 1830 Indiana, Illinois and Missouri had each passed the 100,000 mark. In 1850 Indiana was seventh among the states in population and Illinois was eleventh. Settlements which had first been confined to the vicinity of large rivers were now filling up the unoccupied spaces and beginning to appear west of the Mississippi.

The increasing demands for transportation soon exceeded the facilities afforded by navigable rivers. When further national aid for turnpike roads and canals was refused, the states themselves, following the example set by New York in the construction of the Erie Canal, took up the work. However, in the West the projects terminated in almost complete failure.

[30] *Cong. Globe*, 32 Cong., 1 Sess., p. 1949.
[31] L. H. Haney, *Congressional History of Railways in the U. S. to* 1850, p. 338.

Railroad building, which had commenced in 1830, increased rapidly within the next two decades. By 1850 the railway system of New England had in large measure taken on its present form, while in the Middle and South Atlantic states enough had been completed to indicate the direction of further development. In the Mississippi Valley, however, the construction of railroads was still experimental and incipient. The idea that railroads for some years were looked upon as feeders to river transportation is partly erroneous. Some early railroads supplemented river traffic, but just as many, such as the Baltimore and Ohio, were clearly independent of such connection.[32]

Trunk lines centering in New York deflected the trade of the West to the East, the change of trade routes being expressed in the loss of freight business sustained by the Mississippi River just prior to 1850. And with this came a rearrangement of economic and political ties; the union of the East and the West was more firmly established, the South at the same time tending toward separation from the upper Mississippi Valley.

Although every attempt made between 1835 and 1850 to secure lands for railways (other than right of way) resulted in failure, this period, nevertheless, was a formative one. The debates in Congress clearly defined the principles involved in the question. The main argument of those advocating grants, which had been advanced as early as 1827 in connection with the discussion on the Indiana Canal, rested upon the position of the government as a landholder whose possessions might be increased in value by the improvements proposed. By retaining and doubling the price of each alternate section, it was held that the government would be able to sell its lands readily and still secure the same amount of money as otherwise it would secure for the whole, and possibly secure it more promptly. This view, among others, was voiced in 1846 by Mr. Calhoun, who was

[32] Haney, p. 227.

very hopeful with respect to treasury receipts.[33] Four years later, when the debate was on concerning the Illinois Central grant, Mr. Walker of Wisconsin objected to the proposal to fix a price of $2.50 an acre for the alternate sections sold to settlers on the ground that the settlers would hardly be willing to pay for the railroad by bearing a 100 per cent tax on the price of government land.[34] Mr. Walker announced that a bill providing for a free homestead of land would meet with favor in his state, whereas he believed a bill granting land to railroads would not. The argument for grants to railroads found its best application in relation to railroads projected beyond populated sections; and such projects were at the time generally believed to be quite commendable.

Opposition to the grants during this period was based mainly on the general unconstitutionality of national support for internal improvements. The soundness of this objection was not admitted by the advocates of the plan, who argued that the provision of the Constitution that "Congress shall have power to dispose of and make all needful rules and regulations respecting the territory or other property belonging to the United States," gave ample authority for their measures.

The Illinois Central Grant of 1850.—With 1850, the date of the passage of the Illinois Central grant, begins a new epoch in land grant legislation. The attitude of the House on previous bills promised little favorable action. The success of this bill depended largely on a happy combination of provisions that reduced opposition and enlisted the support of many who had formerly cast their votes against similar proposals. The East was conciliated by the provision for a branch line which was to unite the old Central road project from Galena to Cairo with Chicago, thereby connecting the Mississippi traffic with the trade of the East

[33] *Cong. Globe,* 29 Cong., 1 Sess., p. 752. The same idea had been brought forward much earlier. (See *Sen. Doc.,* No. 409, 25 Cong., 2 Sess.)
[34] *Cong. Globe,* 31 Cong., 1 Sess., p. 845.

by way of the Great Lakes and the railroads which were just being constructed. An amendment extending the grant to Alabama and Mississippi with a view to the southward extension of the same railroad system, secured the support of those Southern States likely to be benefited. To the comprehensiveness of the proposed railroad system, connecting as it did the Northwest, South and East, and to the energy and political astuteness of its friends, chief of whom was Senator Douglas of Illinois, must be attributed the success of the measure.

The terms of the grant provided that alternate sections of land for six miles on each side of a line of railroad extending from Chicago, Illinois, to Mobile, Alabama, and from the mouth of the Ohio River to Dubuque, Iowa, should be given to the states within which public land lay, *i.e.*, Illinois, Alabama and Mississippi, and through which the road should pass. This land was to be handled by the state legislatures and sold, the money to be used in building a railroad. The law did not say whether the states should build and own the road or not, but it was understood that a private road might receive the proceeds as a subsidy. On this latter plan the states very promptly acted.

The remaining public land, intervening between the alternate railway sections, was to be sold at not less than $2.50 per acre, a provision which characterized nearly all subsequent grants. In much of the territory through which the road was to pass the government land had already been sold. As an offset to this situation the state was allowed to select "lieu" lands, in alternate sections, within a distance not to exceed fifteen miles from the road.

United States troops were to be transported over such roads as should be built under these provisions, free of charge, and United States mails at rates to be fixed by Congress.[35]

The arguments for and against railway land grants had now been definitely formulated. The advocates of the grants

[35] *U. S. Stat. at Large*, IX, p. 466.

based their contentions not on the power of the government as a sovereign state, but on its prerogatives as a landed proprietor. They held that the grant of a portion of the domain to make the rest more valuable was sound business policy; and that the new states were entitled to a share of the government lands on account of the exemption of such from taxation. Opposed to this, besides the constitutional argument, was the objection from the standpoint of the settler, to the higher price of the lands—an objection that was to lead to important consequences.

A period of about three years following the passage of the Illinois Central grant was marked by much unsuccessful activity concerning railroad land grants in Congress. Many bills that passed the Senate were rejected by the House, where the majorities from the hostile eastern and southern states made themselves felt. Only two were successful. After the lull which followed this agitation, however, came a flood of grants, some 14,599,000 acres being donated to railways in 1856, and 5,118,000 acres in 1857. The explanation for this change must be sought in the activity of the railroads, which could now point out as precedents previous grants made by the government; in the increasing strength of the new states; and probably, too, in the pressure brought to bear by eastern capital invested in the West on members of Congress, some of whom were not at all above suspicion.[36] Opposition to land grants had, indeed, almost ceased. New grants continued to be made, and old ones were renewed quietly and without arousing much interest.

From the standpoint of land disposal it was rather the growing agitation for homesteads and the dispute concerning the route of the proposed Pacific railway that gave color to public opinion during the years preceding the Civil War. The South opposed both the Homestead bill and the Pacific road projects, and it was not until after the secession of the southern states that favorable action was secured. The Homestead Act was passed in 1862, encountering little oppo-

[36] J. B. Sanborn, *Congressional Grants of Land in Aid of Railways*, p. 55.

sition in either house, and the same year, under the stress of military necessity, the first bill for a Pacific railroad was also passed.

Liberal Grants to the Pacific Roads.—The idea of a railway from the valley of the Mississippi to the Pacific coast had suggested itself as early as 1832, when a plan was presented for a railroad from Lake Michigan to the mouth of the Columbia and to San Francisco.[37] During the early forties a transcontinental railway involving a grant of alternate sections on each side was proposed. Asa Whitney presented several plans to Congress, one of which, in 1850, secured a favorable report from the House committee. The bill accompanying the report authorized Whitney to construct a road from Lake Michigan to the Pacific, giving him the right to purchase the lands for thirty miles on each side at ten cents an acre. It was opposed by a faction that advocated the construction of a road by the government on the grounds that the project was too great for private management, and that individuals could not treat with Indians.[38]

Neither Whitney's nor the "National" plan received much attention from Congress. With the addition of California to the national territory in 1848, a new difficulty was introduced. Up to this time a terminus in California was out of the question; now it was not only possible, but had many points of advantage over the northern termini. With the schism between the North and the South continually becoming wider, neither side would readily assent to a project which would give an economic advantage to the other. Several bills, a few of which were attempts to satisfy the conflicting interests, were introduced in 1853 and 1855, but without success. In 1861 a bill for two roads on the central and southern routes passed both houses, but some amendments by the Senate, providing for a third line, deferred positive action until the secession of the southern states and the exigencies of war changed the face of the situation.

[37] H. H. Bancroft, *History of California,* VII, p. 498.
[38] *Cong. Globe,* 30 Cong., 2 Sess., p. 472.

In 1862, with the virtual unanimity given Congress by the withdrawal of the Southern representatives and senators, a bill was passed providing for a grant of land in behalf of the Union Pacific and Central Pacific roads. It was provided in this grant that these roads should receive alternate sections of land for twenty miles on each side of the road; and that three years after completion of the road any land remaining unsold should be subject to preëmption by settlers and should be sold to them by the road for not to exceed $1.25 per acre. Mineral land was excluded from the grant, but the roads were to have a right to all timber on the regular railroad lands within a ten-mile limit from the road.[39]

The Northern Pacific received a grant in 1864 which was equally liberal and more extensive than that to the Union Pacific, twenty sections per mile on each side being granted within all territories traversed, and half that amount within states. Here lieu lands might be chosen within ten miles of the outer line of the regular alternate section grant. Mineral lands were excluded from all the Pacific grants, a reservation which loses most of its significance in view of the exclusion from the lists of minerals of both iron and coal.[40]

The grants to the other Pacific roads, *i.e.*, the Atlantic and Pacific in 1866, now the Atchison, Topeka and Santa Fe, and the Southern Pacific were similar to the Northern Pacific grants in amount of land granted per mile.

Whereas, the Union Pacific road was required to sell land at $1.25 per acre after three years following the completion of the road, the Northern Pacific was required to sell all lands not previously sold or mortgaged for a price not to exceed $2.50 after five years following the completion of the road. In the case of the Union Pacific grant the government did not provide that the price of intervening sections remaining in its possession should be raised to $2.50, as in most instances was done.[41] The unprecedented liberality

[39] *U. S. Stat. at Large*, XII, p. 492; *Ibid*, XIII, p. 356.
[40] *Ibid*, XIII, p. 365.
[41] *Ibid*, XVI, p. 378.

in the grants to the Pacific roads was due largely to the nature of the country through which the roads were to pass. To begin with, the grant was made directly to the company instead of to the states which in turn should subsidize the companies, and this made it possible for the interested parties to present their claims in a strong manner.

The magnitude of these donations, removing large tracts from the operation of the settlement laws, made the demand for their discontinuance increasingly insistent. And the year 1871 saw the passage of the last railway grant.

The Interests of the Settlers and the Roads Conflict.—Conflict between the interests of the roads and the interests of the settlers assumed two forms. The first manifested itself in opposition to any and all grants of land to railways or other great companies, since the settlers were the ones entitled to the land while railroads could be built and supported without such princely gifts. The other cause of friction was the manner of allowing the railroad companies the advantage of a first claim to indemnity lands many miles back from the road. The government had withdrawn these lands from settlement pending the choice by the railroads, and the choices were slow in the making, thus holding settlers off from great and desirable tracts of land which would otherwise have been open to homesteaders. A case in the courts upheld the railroads' contention that a settler could acquire no rights while the railway privilege of selection within a prescribed area was pending.[42] Out of this controversy came an executive order from President Cleveland in compliance with which the Secretary of the Interior withdrew over 21,000,000 acres of land from the contingent indemnity lists and reopened it to settlement.[43]

The more radical demand that no more land be granted to railroads was met not by positive action, but by a discontinuance of the policy following the grants of 1871. Closely connected with the above conflicts in interests was

---

[42] *Report of Secretary of the Interior,* 1887, pp. 9, 10.
[43] *L. O. R.,* 1888, p. 41.

a demand that railway companies forfeit unearned land grants, *i.e.*, grants for lines not built within the specified time. The courts had been favorably inclined toward the contention that roads might subsequently earn the right to receive land after the time set for the completion of the road. Accordingly Congress took the matter up and in 1890 passed an act declaring that all lands granted to corporations or states in aid of railways which were not then built should be forfeited to the United States and restored to the public domain.[44] The railways, however, were successful in the courts contesting such restoration of lands until 1913, when 2,008,772 acres were restored to the United States from a grant made to the Oregon and California Railroad Company.[45] Little seems to have been done in restoring such lands since that time.

It is a significant fact that the last of the railway land grants were made in 1871. This is the date of the first "Granger legislation" of the West. In that year the Illinois legislature, in accordance with powers conferred upon it by the constitution of 1870, passed acts regulating passenger and freight charges over railways within the state. This was the first of a long series of legislative acts by state and nation dealing with railway rights and charges. The roads were called "monopolies" and their demands were set over against the supposed rights of the people. It is, therefore, clear that the granting of bonuses to railways out of the public treasury was no longer to receive such undivided support from the people of the West. It was now the rights of the settlers and farmers which came to the front.[46]

It must not be supposed, however, that there had been no earlier protest against the granting of land, destined eventually for the use of farmers, to railroad companies. Editors, both west and east, reflected a strong undercurrent of opposition. "The sooner this land-grant business for railroads is now stopped the better," said the *New York Tribune* in

[44] *U. S. Stat. at Large*, XXVI, p. 496.
[45] *L. O. R.*, 1913, pp. 18, 19.
[46] S. J. Buck, *The Granger Movement*, Ch. IV and V.

1870,[47] and this was a mere reiteration of what it had been saying for many years.[48]

The Railroad Grants and the Homestead Act.—Not only was the sentiment toward railroads undergoing a profound change, but the demand for land under the Homestead Act was at its height and every friend of the West was anxious to see actual settlers take possession as rapidly as possible. Thus the advocates of the free gift of land to actual farmers opposed such gift to transportation companies, particularly after the need for transportation facilities was no longer pressing.[49]

A long line of difficulties arose on account of the interference, mutually, of the railroad grants and the federal disposition of land direct to settlers. For example, a railroad grant would give a certain number of sections of land on each side of the road, but on the land so granted were, in innumerable instances, settlers already located. Where such settlers were in possession of a patent to the land, there was, of course, no disposition to go back of that in the interest of the railroad, but where the settler had the claim of a preëmptor, or a homesteader with no final title, there was much room for quibbling. The railroad insisted on claiming land not yet patented, and to settle the matter once for all, Congress, in 1876, passed an act protecting the settler.[50] A year prior to this Congress had passed a law permitting railways to select lieu lands in place of those claimed by settlers within the limits of the grants. Such lands were ordinarily to be located within fifteen miles of the road.

The question has been asked, were railway grants contrary to the homestead principle? Opposite answers of a positive nature have been given by students of the case.[51] Both answers are in a measure right, and hence neither one

[47] *N. Y. Semi-Weekly Tribune,* June 24, 1870.
[48] *Ibid,* Feb. 28, 1854.
[49] *Ibid.*
[50] *U. S. Stat. at Large,* XIX, p. 35.
[51] Sanborn takes the affirmative; Haney takes the negative.

wholly so. In the minds of such men as Horace Greeley the two measures were sharply opposed in principle. Greeley looked upon the land as a source of production sacred to the tiller of the soil. Hence he was opposed early and late to any plan for granting it to big corporations, and in favor of a homestead measure.[52] However, such strong advocates of the use of the public domain for settlement as Benton of Missouri and Hendricks of Indiana were in favor of donations of land to both railroads and settlers. Speaking of the two projects, Mr. Hendricks, in 1852, said, "They will sustain and strengthen each other." He believed it would not be fair to the railroads to encourage them to build into a country without, at the same time, promoting its settlement; that it would be unfair to go on promoting settlement without providing means of transportation.[53] It is true that a few Congressmen considered the two plans incompatible, but they were men from the eastern states who did not understand the West, where the belief prevailed that there was land enough for both purposes.[54] The claim was put forward repeatedly that the land which would be granted to the railroads was land which had been in the market for years at $1.25 an acre without being sold. Thus it had little value. The settlers could better afford to pay the double minimum for the remaining half of the land near the roads than go into the wilderness and buy it at the smaller price.[55] In view of this testimony, somewhat conflicting though it be, it seems safe to conclude that in the early fifties the granting of land to railroads was not viewed by the majority of the people interested as antagonistic to the principle of free land for settlement.

But after twenty years had elapsed and principalities had been granted to railways, much sentiment had developed against this railway subsidization. It was evident that the

[52] N. Y. Semi-Weekly Tribune, July 4, 1856; N. Y. Weekly Tribune, Feb. 13, 1859, with very many other similar references intervening.
[53] Cong. Globe, 32 Cong., 1 Sess., App., p. 482.
[54] Ibid, p. 737.
[55] Ibid, p. 273.

change was due to the fact that relatively little inexpensive desirable land was left for settlement. Pennsylvania opposed further donations on this ground,[56] likewise Indiana.[57] At the same time Indiana was passing resolutions asking for further homestead concessions to soldiers.[58] Nevertheless, Mississippi still wanted grants, since the land in question "was of little or no value," but would, by this means, become useful.[59] Even earlier than this the encroachment of great grants on the homestead privileges was recognized by the House committee on public lands and made the subject of a report in which grants to railroads are referred to as "inaugurating further and fearful monopolies of the public domain" and "no one will need to be told that, should this policy be continued, the opportunities of settlement and tillage under the preëmption and homestead laws must constantly diminish." [60]

On March 5, 1869, the legislature of Wisconsin passed a resolution asking Congress to discontinue the practice of railway land grants, believing that such legislation was opposed to the national interest of the country "and in violation of the spirit and interest of the national homestead law, and manifestly in bad faith toward the landless." [61]

Congress passed an act, approved April 10, 1869, providing that three different lines of railroad, to which extensions were made of the time limit allowed for earning grants of land, must sell to settlers only, in tracts of not over 160 acres each and for prices not over $2.50 per acre.[62]

These acts passed Congress with little debate, but what there was, was significant. For example, Mr. Julian of Indiana in reporting the bill from the public lands committee said that the provisions in question were made in order "to conform to the views of this House in regard

[56] *House Miscellaneous Documents,* 42 Cong., 1 Sess., No. 9.
[57] *Ibid,* No. 25.
[58] *Ibid,* No. 23.
[59] *Ibid,* No. 39.
[60] *Reports of Committees,* 40 Cong., 2 Sess., No. 25.
[61] *House Misc. Docs.,* 41 Cong., 1 Sess., No. 9.
[62] *U. S. Stat. at Large,* XVI, p. 46.

to the rights of settlers." [63] The Senate concurred cheerfully, Mr. Warner of Alabama stating that the amendments "were in the interest of the Government and the settlers." [64] This is in marked contrast with the provisions made thirty to forty years earlier, that land granted to states for use in financing internal improvements should not be sold for less than $1.25 per acre. [65] The earlier provision was mainly in the interest of government receipts from land sales; the latter in the interest of the farmers. [66] This is a strong testimony reflecting the actual facts of the case. It is plain that one undertaking through deductive reasoning to state the relations of the two principles of disposing of land must almost of necessity arrive at the correct solution. While public land was abundant, even superabundant, it was dispensed lavishly; when it became scarce, it was recognized that if used for one purpose it would not be available for another. Hence, under the latter conditions those interested in the homesteading of land opposed the grants of it to corporations.

POLICIES OF RAILROADS IN SELLING LAND

The most vital question connecting itself with the railway land situation is the disposition made of such gifts by the companies. In the case of several canal grants it was stipulated that the land should be put on the market at not less than $1.25 per acre. The act granting land to Illinois, Mississippi, and Alabama to aid in construction of the Illinois Central provided that no land should be sold except as the work of building the road progressed and at a price not less than the double minimum price. The price restriction was apparently in the interest of further government sales, and also in order that privately owned land should not be decreased unduly in selling value.

[63] *Cong. Globe*, 41 Cong., 1 Sess., p. 588.
[64] *Ibid*, p. 582.
[65] For example see *U. S. Stat. at Large*, III, p. 728; IV, p. 588; and V, p. 455.
[66] For protest against railroad grants in view of effect on homestead, see *Iowa Northwest*, Mar. 2, 1871.

While the different roads had different policies for disposing of their lands, it may in the main be said that they
wanted to sell them all as wild land to actual settlers, and
within relatively few years. The policies of a few representative roads will make this clear:

The Illinois Central, having been granted over two and
a half million acres by the state of Illinois, set about making
plans to realize ready cash from the gift as promptly as
possible, and at the same time undertook to provide for
the future prosperity of the road.

A land department was organized and the lands were
advertised far and wide. Out of the entire grant about
four-fifths of the area was designated "mortgage lands"
and the other fifth "free lands." Against the "mortgage
lands," bonds had been issued and sold to the extent of
$17,000,000, with which to prosecute the road building.
These lands were thus mortgaged to the amount of $8.50
per acre. The land department of the road issued a pamphlet setting forth the leading facts relating to the lands
for sale and the terms and conditions under which they
were offered.[67] The mortgaged lands were offered at $5.00
to $20.00 on six years time, no payment the first year,
after which time one-fifth of the amount was to be paid
annually. During a short period, in order to induce sales,
interest was charged at the rate of two per cent. Later it
was set at six per cent and remained almost uniformly at
that figure. On the mortgage lands it was stipulated that
improvements should be made, one-half to be fenced and
brought under cultivation at the rate of one-tenth of the
tract each year, before the deed should be issued. The
"free lands" were sold at twenty per cent less, but one-
fourth of the price was demanded at once and the balance
within three years. Interest rates were six per cent and no
cultivation requirements imposed. In all cases interest had
to be paid annually in advance.

The pamphlet gives a brief survey of Illinois as an agri-

[67] *Guide to Illinois Central Railroad Lands.* (1861.)

cultural state and presents hypothetical results to be obtained by farmers on the lands offered. One very interesting feature of this prospectus is the advice given concerning prairie land. Until about the time it was issued, timber land had always been sought diligently by the pioneer. The land department of the road now very earnestly recommends prairie land. "Let the settler avoid the shelter of groves; . . . dig wells instead of resorting to surface water; . . . erect a comfortable frame house instead of the common log cabin." [68] Without doubt the railroad was the greatest influence in bringing enterprise into the wilderness and making the broad prairies habitable.

The requirement that part of the land should be put under cultivation within the first six years after being sold was in the interest of rail traffic, of course. It was the plan to sell mainly to settlers and in small tracts. Nevertheless, the company had hopes of reaching all possible classes of land buyers. The patronage of three distinct grades of purchasers was solicited: [69] First, "the poor man with nothing but youth and industry; the middling farmer; or the mechanics-men who can look forward in the older states to nothing but a life of labor." To these the railway land department suggested the plan of working on farms in Illinois for a few years in order to get acquainted and get money for the first payment on a quarter section of land. They show that such a man might easily be worth four or five thousand dollars within a very few years. Second, the man of moderate means. He was to buy a section of land at ten dollars per acre, and spend an equal sum putting it into shape for use. For him they predicted an income of forty per cent on the sum invested. Third, the capitalist with a big sum of money to invest: For him they suggested a purchase of nine sections of land, or 5,760 acres at $7.00 per acre. This expenditure, plus improvement and equipment, involved the outlay of $82,000. A farm with its equipment was said to rent on

[68] *Guide to Illinois Central R. R. Lands* (1861), p. 29.
[69] *Guide to Illinois Central R. R. Lands* (1861), pp. 37-41.

halves, and handled in this manner an income of 45 per cent
was postulated. It was stated that such a thing as this grand
scale investment was actually in practice. The prediction
was made that cultivation and the accompanying influences
would soon quadruple the value of the land, thus enriching
the owner.

The company was not a little disappointed in the slowness
of the sales; advertising matter was printed in several lan-
guages and agents sent to Europe to induce foreigners to
immigrate and purchase. But the results were small and
sales were made principally to people from the East and
from adjoining states.

The country did not fill up as rapidly as the railroad
promoters had hoped, yet prices rose so that the intervening
sections of government land sold readily at the double minimum price, although it had been offered for thirty years
previously at $1.25 with no takers.[70]

Little land was sold by the Illinois Central road prior to
1855. By 1864 somewhat over half of the whole amount
had been disposed of at an average price of $10.77. Sales
were fairly brisk till about 1871 at which time all but a
third of a million acres had been sold. The price remained
about as usual, the average for the two million acres sold
before 1871 being $10.61. The small amount of land remain-
ing was a long time on the market, but by 1890 an unimportant area was left. The price rose a little, despite the fact
that much of the later sales was of land not very high in
quality, making the average price on the total sales up to
that date, 2,457,000 acres, $11.70.[71] Thus the gross receipts
from the land were not far from thirty million dollars, or
about six-sevenths the first cost of the road. According to
Mr. Ackerman's estimate, the average amount of land sold
to one settler was but little over 80 acres.

The Chicago and Northwestern Railway sold to each of
its purchasers in Iowa from 73.65 to 111.98 acres from the

[70] W. K. Ackerman, *Illinois Central Railroad, Historical Sketch.*
[71] *Ibid.*

year 1873 to 1885.[72] During this period it is clearly noticeable that for the first few years the sales were heaviest in
the central part of the state and along the line of road
then built to the west, while later the heavy sales were in
the newer section to the northwest. From this it may be
gathered that the railroads did not push sales while government land was open for homesteads or on sale at a dollar
and a quarter or two dollars and a half an acre, but they
waited till the government land was gone and then sold at
a figure two to four times as great. Along the line of
the Chicago and Northwestern Railway across the state of
Iowa it was found by a study of the government land entries
and the sales of railway land that the latter followed the
former by twenty to twenty-five years.[73] This indicates
strongly that the railway understood very well the practical
meaning of the unearned increment. At the same time, the
company was awake to the fact that its business depended
upon settlement and cultivation of the land, and with this
in view favored the farmer buyer as against the speculator.[74]

The policy of the Chicago, Milwaukee and St. Paul Railway may be observed by the way it disposed of lands
acquired from the McGregor Western. The policy of the
road was perhaps the most liberal of any. The line was
built through northwestern Iowa in 1879, and much of the
land so earned was put upon the market within the next
five or six years. For example, about all the land in Clay
County, Iowa, belonging to this road was sold before 1885.
The usual prices of wild land there at that time were $5.00
and $10.00 per acre, and the railroad sold at these figures.
However, the real spirit of the transactions is to be found
in the rebate of $2.50 allowed on all land put under cultiva-
tion within a specified time.[75] The price even then was above
that of government land, which had about all been bought

[72] *Annual Reports of the Iowa Railroad Land Company.* This company took
over the entire Northwestern Railway grant in 1867.
[73] Leonard Paulson. *Thesis.* The Disposal of the Public Domain of the
State of Iowa. Iowa State College, 1908.
[74] *Ibid.*
[75] *Ibid.*

or homesteaded some ten or fifteen years earlier, but the advantage of the railroad to the settlers much more than made up the difference in the cost of the land.

The Burlington and Missouri River Railroad Company may be taken as an instance of the methods of putting land on the market. Their sales began in 1870 and up to 1879 the average size of tract sold to each settler was 130 acres.[76] Prices were $10.00 to $30.00 an acre for land in Iowa and $1.00 to $10.00 in Nebraska. Terms were liberal, from two to ten years' time being given with interest at six per cent. Discounts ranging from ten to twenty-five per cent were allowed on cash payments. This company maintained a system of elaborate agencies for the sale of land. A general agent was put in charge of the land department; sub-agents were stationed in Burlington, Iowa; Lincoln, Nebraska; New York City, Glasgow, Liverpool, and London; with a general agent over the European offices. Advertising matter was published liberally. Not finding sales as easy as had been hoped, added inducements of one kind and another were offered from time to time. Transportation of the land seeker and his freight was furnished at half rates, or for nothing. Ten per cent was deducted from purchase price to settlers who invested an amount equal to one-fourth the purchase price of the land or put one-fourth of the area under cultivation and continued to cultivate it for four years. The company undertook to help the settler get started by furnishing architect's sketches and prices of farmhouses.[77] It furnished at Burlington and Lincoln, free of charge, rooms in which immigrants might keep house while looking for land. It is not too much to say that it was the unmistakable intention of this, as of other roads, to settle the country as rapidly as possible with actual farmers.[78]

[76] *The Great North Platte Region of the B. & M. Railroad lands*, 1879.
[77] *The Great South Platte Regions of the B. & M. Railroad Lands*, 1879.
[78] Officials of the Burlington Railway Company have recently expressed a desire to have a study made of the disposition of their lands with a view to devising a plan for handling their remaining lands in the best manner possible.

The Northern Pacific Land Grant Dispute.—During the past few years a contest between the Northern Pacific Railway Company and the government has been waged concerning indemnity land. The railroad company claims the right to locate land within what is now a national forest reserve on the ground that it still has a lawful claim to some 3,900,000 acres, largely in lieu of land classified as mineral land by government authority and so according to the terms of the grant excluded from the railway holdings. The Forest Service contends that the Northern Pacific has, in the first place, received all the land to which it is entitled, and in the second place that a "mistake" was made in the classification of a great deal of land as mineral land.

The case passed through one phase in 1917 to 1921 when it was decided by the Supreme Court that the government might not refuse to allow the railway company to locate land to which it was entitled merely on the ground that it was within the forest reserves. Now, in 1924, the matter comes up for further consideration, with, however, different points of issue. Is the railway entitled to any more land? Is it even entitled to all which it holds, or to the proceeds from all it has sold? These latter questions hinge on the interpretation of the "mistakes" in connection with the classification of worthless land as mineral land, and the right of the company to receive valuable land in place of it. The matter rests, in the first instance, in Congress. Any act of Congress adverse to the railway company will undoubtedly be taken promptly to the courts.

Incidentally, some interesting evidence has come to light. The railway company admits that the sales of land have returned to the company in cash a sum approximating $136,000,000, whereas the road cost about $70,000,000. Thus the land brought 94 per cent more than the original cost of the road. It is by no means clear that this fact should be construed as an argument against the claims of the road for more land. When the grant was made it was through what "then consisted of great stretches of homeless prairies, trackless forests, and unexplored mountains." The value has developed during recent years, and, moreover, it happens that the original Northern Pacific passed through bankruptcy. Thus the question as to the value of the land as an offset to the original cost of the road becomes a very remote one. The decision must rest entirely on the legality of the claim.

The questions at issue are too complex and involved for the lay mind to answer. Thus far the case has been handled in a very calm manner. The government is basing its contention against allowing the claim for more land on questions of fact pertaining to the fulfillment of the original agreement with the road, not on views relating to the rights or wrongs of the original grant, or the good luck and good management on the part of the road in getting money out of the grant. Against the claim of the railroad for an additional 3,900,000 acres the government holds that the railway company received more land than the amounts to which it was entitled in several instances, which, all counted, amounts to more than the acreage now claimed to be still due.

Résumé of Prices at Which Railway Lands Were Sold.— It is all but impossible to assemble the information for all sales, but a close approximation may be made from the reports of several roads which in the aggregate represent the bulk of land grants within the area readily available for agriculture. The average price of substantially all railroad land sold prior to 1881 was $4.76 per acre.[79] Until that time most sales consisted of land to be used for ordinary farming within the humid district. The sales of the Illinois Central road were about all of the kind to take place in Illinois, and, as stated above, these lands brought about $11.70 per acre.

For the state of Iowa a very complete report is at hand, from which it appears that 3,724,801 acres were granted

[79] Donaldson, p. 783.

to nine roads. This land was substantially all sold prior to 1893 at an average price of $5.50 per acre.[80]

The Union Pacific was one of the greatest land grant beneficiaries, and its sales up to and including 1894 were 7,141,000 acres, at an average price of $3.14 per acre.[81] Later sales have been such as three-quarters of a million acres in 1905 at $3.44 per acre; a million and a quarter acres at $2.72 in 1906, and a very small amount in 1911 at $4.08.[82]

The Chicago, St. Paul, Minneapolis and Omaha between the years 1882 and 1907 sold 1,502,000 acres of land at $5.23 per acre. The Northern Pacific between 1875 and 1895 sold 4,352,000 acres of land, largely in North Dakota, at an average price of $3.90 per acre.[83]

Much as the policy of granting public lands to the railroads has been criticized, it hardly appears that it resulted in immense fortunes to the builders. The Illinois Central received an unusually high price for its land, situated as it was within a district pretty well surrounded with settlements. To be sure, it did not amount to enough to pay for the road, but it did amount to the major part of the cost. On the other hand, Illinois made a bargain with the road by which the company is paying seven per cent of its annual gross income to the state as a tax, and by this arrangement the value of the land has been recovered by the state several times over. Concessions presumably favorable to the public were made by other roads,—for example, the transportation of the mails at rates to be set by Congress. However, it has never been shown that the rates set by Congress were such that the railroads earned any part of the value of the lands by such service.

Nevertheless, what actually did take place in general was

[80] Iowa R. R. Commissioner's *Report*, 1893, pp. 12, 13. (The sales of 444,000 acres of land granted to the Dubuque and Sioux City R. R. not included in computing the average price.)
[81] H. K. White, *History of the Union Pacific Railway*, p. 121.
[82] *Annual Reports of the Union Pacific Railway Company*
[83] *Ibid.*

the rapid disposal of government land in the vicinity of the projected railway lines; the rapid disposal of railroad land a little later; the overdevelopment of railways and of grain growing; the bankruptcy of many roads; the loss of public confidence in the roads; and the clash of interest which resulted in railway rate regulation.

In some instances the railroad grants have resulted in concentrated holdings by the purchasers. Some immense ranches are to be found in California where undoubtedly smaller holdings would have predominated had the government disposed of the land direct to settlers. There is one farm of seven thousand acres in Iowa which was bought from the railroad land company. It is hardly likely that this particular block of land would have been brought under one control had it been distributed to many owners through the usual process. There has been in recent years one other farm equally large in the state. Numerous timber holdings trace their lineage directly to the railroad grants. Even yet important tracts of railroad land are held off the market awaiting higher prices.

Had the land not been granted to the roads, what disposition would have been made of it? Speculation on this point is idle. Had we developed a land policy wise and adequate, a great deal of good might have grown out of it. Having no such policy, and believing as the majority of people at the time did that the primary desideratum was to get settlers on the land at the earliest possible moment, it must be admitted that the granting of land to railway companies was in keeping with the views of the time. The general agricultural depression covering the West throughout the greater part of the period from the early seventies till the later nineties was attributable in great measure to the too rapid development of farms which resulted from the phenomenal spread of the railway network and the overproduction of cereals. A sordid phase of land grants is the political corruption which seemed an inevitable concomitant of it; but that is another story.

TABLE XIV

GRANTS TO STATES AND CORPORATIONS FOR RAILROAD PURPOSES—1850
TO JUNE 30, 1923 [84]

State Grants		Corporation Grants	
Illinois	2,595,133.00	Union Pacific	11,935,121.46
Mississippi	1,075,345.12	Central Pacific	6,891,404.94
Alabama	2,746,560.81	Central Pacific (successor by	
Florida	2,217,619.39	consolidation with Western	
Louisiana	372,092.34	Pacific)	458,786.66
Arkansas	2,562,161.89	Central Branch Union Pacific	223,080.50
Missouri	1,837,968.17	Union Pacific (Kansas Divi-	
Iowa	4,929,849.44	sion)	6,175,660.63
Michigan	3,133,231.58	Union Pacific (successor to	
Wisconsin	3,649,869.15	Denver Pacific Ry. Co.)	821,164.15
Minnesota	8,035,577.61	Burlington & Missouri River	
Kansas	4,633,760.73	in Nebraska	2,374,090.77
		Sioux City & Pacific (now Mis-	
Total	37,789,169.23	souri Valley Land Co.)	42,610.95
		Northern Pacific	38,916,338.61
		Oregon Branch of Central Pa-	
		cific (California & Oregon)	3,172,610.48
		Oregon & California	2,777,591.96
		Atlanta & Pacific (now Santa	
		Fe Pacific)	9,878,352.14
		Southern Pacific (main line)	4,323,794.01
		Southern Pacific (branch line)	2,118,220.48
		Oregon Central	128,618.13
		New Orleans Pacific	1,001,943.40
		Total	91,239,389.27
			37,789,169.23
		Grand Total	129,028,558.50

MISCELLANEOUS MINOR LAND GRANTS

A number of minor grants coming largely under the head of internal improvements should be mentioned here. Most of these grants were made to individuals for services rendered or to be rendered. It is specified in some cases that the grants should be used for improvements. This summary of minor land grants is largely taken from Donaldson's *Public Domain:*

[84] *L. O. R.*, 1923, pp. 37-38

In recognition of services rendered by Dohrman, an agent of the United States at Lisbon, the Dohrman Grant was made. It consisted of a township of land in the state of Ohio.

As a bonus for establishing ferries on the road from Wheeling to Limestone, Ebenezer Zane was granted three sections of land in 1796. In 1802 a similar grant was made to Isaac Zane.

In addition to Section No. 29 reserved in the Ohio Company and Symmes grants, for religious purposes, a few grants were made outright to missionaries.

A fifty-acre grant per man was offered to British deserters in 1776, but very little land was ever so claimed.

In 1787 Congress granted three townships in Ohio to certain Canadian refugees in this country.

The Ohio Company located certain French settlers on lands to which it had no title and to avoid more difficulties Congress confirmed their titles to the land.

In 1803 in appreciation of services rendered—during the Revolutionary War,—Congress granted land to La Fayette to the amount of 11,520 acres, and in 1824 he was presented with a township of land in Florida, making a total of 33,920 acres.

In 1807 Congress granted to Lewis and Clark 1,600 acres each, and to each of their thirty-one followers 300 acres,— in all 12,500 acres.

Land was given in 1815 to sufferers from an earthquake a few years before at New Madrid, Missouri. This was an absurd bit of philanthropy on the part of Congress. The damage done by the earthquake was greatly exaggerated; but, worst of all, the act was so drawn that fraud was all but openly invited. A great deal of land, relatively, was granted to the undeserving, and subsequent acts were required down to 1866 in attempts to set things right.[85]

Congress granted land to two parishes in Louisiana in 1824 on condition that they keep levees built along the Mississippi.

[85] *Pub. Lands,* IV, p. 46.

In 1788 Congress granted 12,000 acres of land for the use of Christian Indians in three towns in Ohio. Later most of this land was surrendered to the United States.

By an act of 1826 land, eventually amounting to 22,509 acres, was given for the purpose of supporting a deaf and dumb asylum in Kentucky.

Thirty-six sections (23,040 acres) were granted in 1812 for the support of Jefferson College in Mississippi.

Congress granted to the different public land states quantities of land varying in amount from 1,280 to 274,000 acres for use in the erection of public buildings. The total amount so granted approximated 500,000 acres.[86]

Under the saline grants twelve states received land aggregating 560,593 acres.[87]

A great many schemes were presented to Congress involving grants or, more often, sales on special credit arrangements. These involved the plans of emigration societies; of coffee, tea, grape, and silk cultivators; of religious and social reformers; of educational enthusiasts. But while Congress was guilty of many faults in regard to the disposition of the public domain, it was for the most part deaf to the importunities of dreamers and schemers. Many of the general acts of Congress were twisted to meet the plans of selfish private individuals, but few indeed were the occasions on which Congress helped out such plans directly. This safe policy was in no small measure due to the wisdom of a few men. Such men as Morrow of Ohio, President Monroe with his veto of a bill to grant land for a church site, Benton of Missouri, and Grow of Pennsylvania were powerful factors in keeping Congress headed right respecting public land.

Beginning with the act of 1796 and continuing till 1867, Congress made special disposition of lands containing salt springs. At first they were to be reserved for federal use,

---

[86] M. N. Orfield, *Federal Land Grants to the States*, p. 75.

[87] Donaldson, pp. 217, 218. This figure includes the grant of 1628 acres to Mexico.

but with the admission of Ohio, the precedent was set giving them to the states in which they lay. This was continued with the admission of each state up to and including Nebraska, and once later, New Mexico having been allowed saline lands as part of a grant in support of a university.

During all the early years lands designated as saline were excluded from entry under the Preëmption and Homestead Acts, but after 1877 they were subject to such entry. However, if on a hearing it was established that they were really saline, they were offered for sale at not less than $1.25 per acre.

SUMMARY

The use of land grants for internal improvement purposes was a part, indeed a major part, of the whole episode of conscious development of the nation through public action. It was believed that private action was likely to be too uncertain and too slow. The only known alternative was public action. Beginning with wagon road and canal grants in the twenties, followed closely by river improvement grants, the plan of granting the land to the states was devised. These specific grants extended over a period of about forty-five years, from 1823 to 1869. A more general plan was embodied in the half-million-acre grants, mainly for the same, or at least similar purposes, in the act of 1841. These grants were extended to eighteen states, in a few of which it did not appear as a half million acre item merely because the grants had already exceeded that figure. The newer states received still more liberal grants but not this particular one after 1876, when Colorado was admitted to the Union, and allowed this item.

The grants for railroads, the most liberal donations ever made for the encouragement of private enterprise, reached the figure of 129,000,000 acres, and even this is somewhat short since other lands granted to states, not specifically for railroads, were turned over to them nevertheless.

Minor grants, and grants to states for miscellaneous purposes, run well into the millions, but the interest in internal improvements had undergone a profound change by 1889 when a new group of states was admitted, and no longer was there a disposition to appropriate land for such projects.

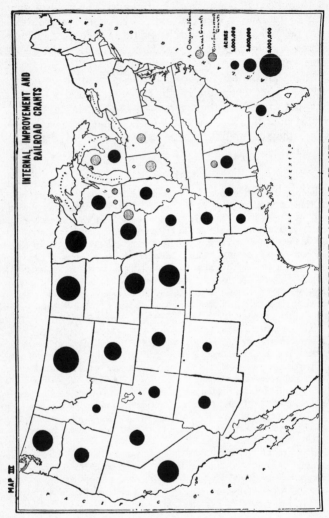

MAP III

INTERNAL IMPROVEMENT AND RAILROAD GRANTS

THE BLACK DOTS REPRESENT RAILROAD GRANTS

CHAPTER XIV

SWAMP LAND GRANTS

SWAMP LAND ACTS OF 1849-1850

The earliest effort to make swamp lands the subject of national legislation occurred in 1826.[1] A resolution was passed by the Senate providing for a report showing the quantities and locations of wet, marshy, and inundated public lands in Missouri and Illinois; and upon the information thus obtained, measures were proposed for ceding these lands to the two states. The attempt, though unsuccessful, was renewed from time to time, till it culminated in the Act of 1849.[2]

Congress at that time granted to Louisiana "the whole of those swamps or overflowed lands, which may be, or are, found unfit for cultivation." In order to prevent the inundation of the Mississippi, Louisiana had resorted to a system of artificial embankment, embracing approximately 1,400 miles of levees, and constructed at a cost of at least twenty million dollars. This expenditure by the state had resulted in the reclamation of over three million acres of public land which the Government had sold, the proceeds going into the National Treasury.[3] More money was required to complete the work; and it was this immediate need which led Congress to adopt the policy which contemplated not only the prevention of destructive inundations, but also the draining of swamps.

The policy thus begun was made general with the grant

[1] *Cong. Globe,* 31 Cong., 1 Sess., p. 1849. See *Senate Journal,* 19 Cong., 1 Sess., p. 217.
[2] Donaldson, p. 219; *L. O. R.,* 1867, p. 97.
[3] *Cong. Globe,* 30 Cong., 2 Sess., p. 592.

of September 28, 1850, under which the larger portions of territory classed as swamp or overflow land were ceded to the several states. The act provided that "the proceeds of said lands shall be applied, exclusively, so far as necessary, to the purpose of reclaiming said lands by means of levees and drains." The main reasons assigned for the donation were:[4]

1. The alleged worthless character of the premises in their natural condition and the inexpediency of an attempt to reclaim them by national interposition.

2. The great sanitary improvement to be derived from the reclamation of extensive districts notoriously malarial, and the probable occupancy and cultivation that would follow.

3. The enhancement in value, and readier sale, of adjoining government property.

The measure as originally reported and passed by the Senate granted only such tracts as were designated on the plats of the government surveys as swamp and unfit for cultivation. As the plats of the Land Office, however, were found to be based on surveys made in many instances in the dry seasons and which consequently reported as "swamp lands" only such as were mostly irreclaimable, including little of the areas subject to annual overflow,[5] amendments were made at the instigation of the Commissioner, adding overflowed lands and conveying to the states the swamp or inundated lands, without reference to their description on the plats of survey.[6] It was held, too, that the amendments would make the grant more definite and that by the insertion of terms precisely defined in surveyors' parlance, the executive department would be enabled specifically to designate the lands transferred.

By a decision of the Secretary of the Interior rendered in 1851, the act became effective at the date of its passage.

[4] L. O. R., 1867, p. 97.
[5] Ibid, 1851, p. 18.
[6] Cong. Globe, 31 Cong., 1 Sess., p. 1999

Although the work of segregating the lands was immediately undertaken, in most states several years elapsed before even a considerable portion of the selections had been made and approved. Meanwhile the laws for the private and public sales and locations of the public lands remained operative, and the local government offices disposed of tracts which afterwards were selected and claimed as swamp. In many cases the state also sold the same land, and granted its title. A large number of conflicts arose. As early as 1856 over 700,000 acres were in dispute, and the trouble continued for years afterwards.[7]

To protect the interests of the government alienees, Congress, by act approved March 2, 1855,[8] provided for the settlement of these conflicts and indemnification for the states. For swamp lands sold by the government the state was to receive the purchase money; in case of an existing claim the privilege was given of making a selection of a similar quantity from any of the public lands subject to entry at $1.25 or less per acre.

The grant was extended to Minnesota and Oregon, which had been admitted into the Union since 1850, by the act of March 12, 1860. Two wholesome conditions were imposed, obviating the difficulties that had grown out of the original acts: No land having been disposed of by the United States was included in the grant; and the period for making selections in all states was limited to two years.

The purpose of the legislation directed toward swamp land since 1860 has been to decide the questions arising from the shortcomings of the statutes by which the grants were made rather than to extend their scope. In 1866 measures were adopted "to quiet land titles in California"; in 1872 Congress intervened in behalf of several counties in Iowa, and passed an act "to quiet certain land titles in the state of Missouri." In 1874, 1875 and 1877 further laws were passed for the benefit of Missouri, supplementing the

[7] *Sen. Doc.*, 34 Cong., 1 & 2 Sess., No. 86.
[8] *U. S. Stat. at Large*, X, p. 634.

statutes as construed and followed by the Land Office. Numerous bills have since been introduced proposing to quiet swamp-land titles, but the general attitude of Congress has been to discourage further legislation. Existing laws have been considered adequate to guide the executive officers in deciding claims. This attitude, while not expediting the settlement of disputes, has been effectual in preventing any increase in the potential source of conflicts.

With the beginning of the twentieth century there has, moreover, been brought about a complete revolution in the national swamp-land policy. The failure of the states to carry on the work of reclamation as intended by the acts of 1849 and 1850, contrasted with successful performances of the government in promoting irrigation works in the arid regions of the West, has turned attention toward national rather than state enterprise.

A number of serious attempts have been made in Congress to initiate a comprehensive program of drainage and levee construction. Though so far unsuccessful, they have been energetically supported in both Houses; and a considerable amount of interest has been aroused. The advocates of national intervention argue that the control of the navigable rivers would enable the government to plan a system of reclamation that, by being comprehensive, would obviate the injustice that one state acting for itself might inflict upon another. It has also been argued that the states would be powerless to act in any proposed scheme of reclamation involving public lands, since the constitutional grant of power to Congress excludes all other authority that could interfere with its exercise; and that the states are hampered by the Constitution in any action involving tidewater lands.

"The proportion of swamp lands that could be reclaimed without Federal intervention is comparatively insignificant when compared with large areas connected with navigable rivers or tidewaters, or which involve the control of the interstate waters. Thus we see that the Federal Government is the only power that can do the work without hindrance. The expenditure and work to be done under this act are public and governmental in character."

Such, in brief, has been the course and development of national legislation regarding swamp lands. The areas that have been disposed of under the grant, in the aggregate, have been enormous. Yet neither the older states in the East, in which naturally no public land was located, nor any states admitted into the Union since 1850, except Minnesota and Oregon, were directly concerned. Fifteen members of the Union—Louisiana, Michigan, Wisconsin, Minnesota, Alabama, Arkansas, Florida, Illinois, Indiana, Iowa, Mississippi, Missouri, Ohio, Oregon, and California—alone were benefited.

The Land Office promptly set about the administration of the grants. A few months after the passage of the act of 1850, the Commissioner submitted to the several state authorities two methods for the purpose of designating the swamp lands: (1) The field notes of government survey could be taken as a basis for selections, and all lands shown by them to be swamp or overflowed within the meaning of the act, which were vacant and unappropriated September 28, 1850, would pass to the states. (2) The states could select the lands by their own agents and report them to the Surveyor General with proofs as to their character.[9]

Conflicting Claims

Louisiana, Michigan, Wisconsin, and Minnesota chose to use the field notes of survey. Alabama, Arkansas, Indiana, Mississippi, Ohio, Florida, Illinois, Missouri, and Oregon elected to make selections by their own agents, the first five, however, changing to the former method some time before 1893. The authorities of California did not adopt either method, the passage of the act of 1866 rendering this unnecessary. This act provided for a comparison of the government plats and the segregation maps made by the

⁹ *Sen. Doc.*, 34 Cong., 1 and 2 Sess., No. 86.

state surveyors; if these were found to conform, the selections were at once approved; if they failed to conform, the character of the land was determined by the collection of evidence, and the title settled accordingly.[10]

Thus provided with the machinery for making selections, the states lost no time in availing themselves of the bounty of the government. When the donations were made, Congress held that the extent of the grant would not exceed a few million acres. It was not intended to include any lands that were merely wet or occasionally overflowed, but only such as were so wet or so frequently overflowed as to make them worthless for agricultural purposes in their natural state.

The administration of the acts was no sooner under way than these tacit limits were overstepped. The agents employed by the states that had rejected the government plats of survey were generally compensated at a certain rate per acre of land segregated. Actuated by self-interest, these agents returned large quantities of dry land as inuring to the states under the granting acts. Only six years after the passage of the act of 1850 the amount of land selected already exceeded the enormous figure of 52,000,000 acres, of which more than 38,000,000 acres were approved and almost 18,000,000 patented. During the Civil War relatively few locations were reported, though the issuing of patents went on at a normal rate; in the states which seceded, all action was naturally suspended. Since then the amount of swamp land annually selected has gradually declined, until recently it has ceased to be of much significance in the transactions of the Land Office.

AMOUNT OF LAND GRANTED

The total amount of land covered by the claims reported under the swamp land grant is over 83,000,000 acres, nearly 64,000,000 of which have been patented. The distribution among the several states is given in the following tables:

[10] *U. S Stat. at Large,* XIV, p. 218.

TABLE XV

SWAMP LANDS PATENTED TO THE STATES TO JUNE 30, 1922[11]

	Acres
Alabama	418,633.53
Arkansas	7,686,335.37
California	2,159,303.92
Florida	20,202,327.78
Illinois	1,457,399.20
Indiana	1,254,270.73
Iowa	874,094.33
Louisiana	9,384,626.29
Michigan	5,655,816.13
Minnesota	4,663,007.10
Mississippi	3,286,305.56
Missouri	3,346,936.01
Ohio	26,251.95
Oregon	264,069.01
Wisconsin	3,251,683.94
Total	63,931,060.85[12]

In addition to these lands in place, cash, and land indemnity have been given to the same states to June 30, 1922, as shown in Table XVI on page 276.

The business of transferring swamp lands to the states is practically finished. The grand total to June 30, 1922, is approximately 64,685,000.

Table XVI indicates the amount of cash and land given to states as indemnity to cover claims of the states against the federal government (1) for the sale of lands to which the states had claim under the Swamp Lands Act of 1850, (2) for lands "located" or purchased with military warrants or scrip. In the former case the states were to receive the purchase money for the land sold, indicated in the first column of Table XVI. In the latter case the states were permitted to select a similar quantity of land from the public lands subject to entry at $1.25 or less per acre.

The accompanying map, based on Table XV, will indicate the location and relative size of swamp-land grants to

[11] *L. O. R.*, 1922, pp. 36-39.
[12] *Ibid*, p. 16; gives 63,931,169.54 acres.

TABLE XVI

INDEMNITY SWAMP LAND

	Cash [13]	Land (Acres) [14]
Alabama	$ 27,691.50	20,920.08
Arkansas	374,450.00	....
Florida	67,221.69	94,782.85
Illinois	473,875.99	2,309.07
Indiana	39,080.14	4,880.20
Iowa	587,477.59	321,976.98
Louisiana	53,118.65	32,630.97
Michigan	15,922.06	24,038.69
Mississippi	46,449.62	56,781.76
Missouri	195,874.82	81,016.69
Ohio	29,027.76	....
Wisconsin	185,278.97	105,047.99
Total	$2,095,468.79	754,385.28

the different states. It will be observed that Florida, Louisiana, and Arkansas have approximately three-fifths of all the swamp lands, and that most of the remaining grants are clustered about the Great Lakes, in Minnesota, Wisconsin, and Michigan.

The reasons for the magnitude of this area, many times larger than was contemplated by Congress at the time the grant was made, lie partly in the liberal construction placed upon the somewhat indefinite terms of the acts, and more largely in the persistent and extensive frauds perpetrated in the administration of the law. Success in the prosecution of fraudulent claims was rewarded by the acquisition of alleged swamp land in place, or by a land or cash indemnity, as provided by the acts of 1855 and 1857. No limit was imposed on the time during which indemnity claims might be preferred. The quantities of land granted to satisfy these claims are not included in Table XV. By June 30, 1922, they aggregated 754,385 acres patented to the states. The money paid from the United States Treasury in sat-

[13] *L. O R.*, 1915, p. 48.
[14] *Ibid*, 1922, pp. 34-39.

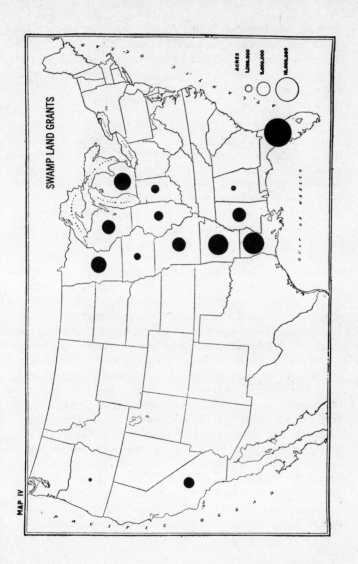

MAP IV

SWAMP LAND GRANTS

ACRES
100,000
1,000,000
5,000,000
10,000,000

GULF OF MEXICO

PACIFIC OCEAN

isfaction of claims on lands located under the national laws up to that date amounts to $2,095,469.[15] The generosity of the government was abused to such an extent that the commissioners repeatedly took occasion to protest against the action of the states.

SWAMP-LAND SELECTIONS

It was a general practice in selecting swamp land for agents, appointed to act in behalf of states, to select great areas along creeks and rivers without reference to the notes made by the government surveyors. Time and again it was found on examination that 75 per cent of the land claimed was not in any sense swampy or subject to serious overflow. For example, in Champaign County, Illinois, the state agent had listed 22,000 acres as swamp, while a representative of the Land Office found that over half the amount was dry land. In Piatt County, of the same state, one hundred and sixty-six tracts were claimed for the state, while a special agent from the government saw fit to reject the classification in all but six of the selections.[16]

The states were aggressive and insistent in enforcing these claims, fraudulent though they were. Particularly shameless were the cases made out in the form of demands for indemnity land, even though the claim involved the question as to why the land claimed to be swamp had been purchased by private parties voluntarily while good land was still available. Members of Congress were involved in the scandal, appearing on commissions in support of the claims made by the states, even though the claims were not borne out by the available information and facts. The game was to get as much land as possible. Taking advantage of the great extent of actual swamp in Florida, the state agents selected as swamp land whole townships which upon investigation were found to be substantially all dry land.[17]

---

[15] *L. O R.*, 1915, pp. 47-48.
[16] *Ibid*, 1886, p. 42.
[17] *Ibid*, 1888, p. 45.

These instances of patent fraud could readily be multi-plied.[18] They are in no way exceptional, but may be regarded as a fair index of claims approved for years. In California the most valuable lands, the valleys of the Sacramento and other principal streams, were claimed as overflowed, because of an occasional inundation; at two places irrigation works were found on areas claimed as swamp. Frequently the swamp-land selections embraced the finest and most available agricultural lands in a locality. In numerous instances indemnity claims were preferred against tracts that had been sold as agricultural land between the years 1850 and 1857 and had since been incorporated into thriving farms, on the grounds that in 1850 they had been swamp. False and corrupt surveys of extensive tracts were resorted to; fraudulent representations and perjury were devices only too frequently employed.

That this condition was due entirely to the rapacity of the state authorities, or to a demoralized public conscience, would be difficult to imagine. It is true the states took no active measure to check the corrupt practices of their agents, and many even connived in promoting them. Thus the governor of Missouri in 1855 was charged with having used his influence to obtain the grant of a large tract of false claims; a charge in which the President of the United States was also involved.[19] The basis adopted by most of the states

[18] A symposium of swamp land fraud is presented in *Sen. Doc.*, 50 Cong., 1 Sess., No. 249. The Commissioner says: "Instances of fraudulent and unlawful claims in nearly every State to which this grant has been extended could be cited almost without number."

[19] "How were the lands in Monroe County and other counties in Northeast Missouri approved? The agent for Monroe County selected thirty-one thousand acres where there were not three hundred acres of swamp land, and then repaired to Washington City. Through the instrumentality of a member of Congress, and the late commissioner of the general land office, his selection of lands under the act of 1850 was submitted to the Secretary of the Interior and approved in forty-eight hours afterwards."

Again: "More than three hundred individuals from the Palmyra land district—the yeomanry of this country, men who want homes; hard-working men have filed affidavits since the approval of these lands, and before Governor Price's visit to Washington, setting forth that the lands specified by them, and selected under the act of 1850 are and always were, dry and rolling, and fit for cultivation.

"Now, I ask the people of the United States whether the policy of adminis-

for remunerating their agents—that of a fixed sum per acre of land selected—in itself, as we have seen, stimulated individual dishonesty. An entirely similar condition was brought about in the indemnity transactions, the state prosecutors being paid a certain part of the proceeds. That this type of personal interest on the part of the administrative authorities of the states remained of no little importance may be gathered from a speech made in Congress in 1890 apropos of a bill to relieve settlers on swamp lands, and to indemnify certain states:

"In Louisiana one-half of these swamp lands, so-called, for which patents are secured to Louisiana, or one-half that can be got from the Treasury on account of these for Louisiana under an act of the State Legislature and under a contract made by the governor of that state inure to the benefit of an agent who is interested in the bill. It is not quite so bad in Illinois, and not quite so bad in Iowa, but pretty nearly so.

"There has been a grabbing of the public lands under these laws which has been thoroughly discreditable." [20]

FRAUD AND SPECULATION

No better bait was ever thrown to speculators than the swamp lands of the various states. True, they had been on sale at a dollar and a quarter an acre before, but now they were for sale at greatly reduced figures. Speculation in swamp lands commenced as soon as the act of 1850 became operative. The legislation of 1855 and 1857 was, in large measure, necessitated by the multitude of conflicting titles which such dealings brought about. Speculators entered claims in the state land offices knowing that the same lands

tration shall prevail and Missouri steal more than two hundred thousand acres of land under the act of 1850, or whether a half million of dollars shall be paid into the public treasury for these so-called swamp lands? Thousands of acres in this land district, worth from five to ten dollars per acre, would be contested, but for the decision of the commissioner refusing to give the contestant the preference right at the ordinary cash price over the speculator."—*N. Y. Semi-Weekly Tribune*, Nov. 20, 1855.

[20] *Congressional Record*, 51 Cong., 2 Sess., App., p. 9.

had previously been located by settlers under the homestead or preëmption laws. Prior to 1855, disputes of this kind were settled by determining the character of the land, each party presenting its evidence; after that year, which marked also the inception of the indemnity principle, the United States claimants were granted the title.

In some of the states the lands were sold to speculative purchasers in advance of selection. These advance purchasers, or their attorneys, armed with the authority of the state, appeared before the General Land Office in the character of state agents, made selections in the name of the state and insisted upon their approval as the dues of the state, arraying the influence of state representations in support of the demands of what had become mere private speculation.

No doubt, in many cases speculators honestly acquired their titles, following the same procedure as the settler who purchased in perfectly good faith. By keeping informed of the land dealings of the state they were enabled to make an occasional *coup* without actually transgressing any laws. A statement made by an Iowa official in 1858 after certain lands had been restored to market indicates the avidity with which this class sought possession of them:

"There can be but little doubt that within a very short time after the date of their being offered for sale, the most, if not the whole, will be entered by speculators who have flooded the state with warrants for this purpose." [21]

The Disposition of Swamp Land

Some of the states gave the grant to railroad corporations. In the northeastern part of Minnesota, when railroad and mining companies had acquired by purchase or grant the title to large tracts of swamp land, fraudulent reports were returned by the surveyors in which extensive

[21] *L. O. R.*, 1887, and especially 1888. The House Committee on Public Lands in 1868 estimated that half of the swamp land grant was in the hands of speculators. *House Repts. of Committees*, 40 Cong., 2 Sess., No. 25.

areas of valuable land were included as wet lands. In those states in which the counties were given possession, corporations necessarily were compelled to make arrangements with the county,[22] arrangements which were by no means always above suspicion.

Three states—Missouri, Iowa, and Illinois—transferred their swamp-land claims to the counties. By the national government, the counties were considered merely the agents of the states for administering the grant. The position of the ultimate grantees, in these states, consequently was no stronger in the case of doubtful titles than those of locators in other states. A record from Bureau County, Illinois, dated 1855, states that "many of our philanthropic citizens were disposed, for a small consideration, to take charge of these lands from our counties, and drain them for use; but recently they have become patriotic and have thought it prudent to wait until the counties obtained the title." [23]

Since here, as elsewhere, the size and value of the grant depends on the vigor with which the claims were prosecuted, it was not surprising that the counties took steps to make themselves heard. An extract from a newspaper of 1861 is illuminating in this respect:

"W. P. Hepburn, the District Attorney for this judicial district, has recently visited Washington City for the purpose of prosecuting the *Swamp land claims* of several counties against the government, and . . . we learn has been very successful." [24]

The administration of the grant by the counties commended itself to many as a measure leading to local improvement. In Wisconsin, efforts were made merely to benefit

[22] "The swamp land election in Wright County last week, resulted in favor of transferring the swamp lands and the swamp land interests to the I. M. & N. P. and the St. P. & I. S. W. railroad companies—the same being divided equally between the two companies, we believe. From our best information the majority will be nearly or quite 100—the vote standing in the ratio of about three 'for' to one against the proposition "—*The Boone Standard* (Iowa), Jan. 18, 1873.

[23] *N. Y. Semi-Weekly Tribune*, Dec. 11, 1855.

[24] *Fort Dodge Republican* (*Iowa*), April 2, 1861.

the counties, although in this state the swamp lands were never turned over to be disposed of by the counties. These efforts nevertheless met with much approval.[25]

The transactions of the counties were characterized by all the doubtful practices countenanced by the states. The inexperience of the boards of supervisors, moreover, enabled unscrupulous individuals to add swindle to corruption and perjury as a means to attain their end. A record of as late a date as 1872 suggests the ingenuity with which fraud was projected:

"Most Iowans are only too familiar with the swamp land swindles that disgraced the state some years ago, and we had hoped that the day of such things was over, but we are credibly informed that a certain ring has been formed to reopen these old swindles with variations. The plan of operation is this: Believing that the old sales of swamp and indemnity lands were in many cases irregular and may be set aside by the courts, they combine with the County Supervisors, where they can find inexperienced men, and get up a second sale for a small consideration; then they intend to carry the matter into the Courts where they will attempt to have the old sale set aside, and if successful, share the profits of the speculation.

"This might be well enough if the title to the lands was still vested in the old purchasers, but unfortunately these

[25] "We see that the 'gentleman from Brown,' Mr. Day, is chairman of the committee on Public Lands. We hope he will introduce a bill, at an early day, to give the swamp lands to the counties in which they lay, for county purposes, and for the building of roads and other necessary improvements. Such a disposition of these lands we are satisfied would meet the wishes of a large majority of the tax payers of the State."—*Green Bay Advocate*, Wisconsin, Jan. 24, 1856.

"We have received a copy of a bill, through the favor of Senator Loy, which has been introduced by him, for the disposition of the swamp lands, and from the very casual glance at it which our time has permitted, we are inclined to believe that it embodies the best plan yet presented to the Legislature for that purpose. The counties are charged with the duty of managing and reclaiming the lands, and each county is required to elect a Drainage Commissioner. One-half of the lands are granted to counties for the purpose of reclamation, and for building roads, etc., and the other half is to be devoted to paying off the state indebtedness for the various public institutions, *Lunatic*, and others."—*Green Bay Advocate*, Wisconsin, March 15, 1855.

lands are nearly all in the hands of innocent parties and settlers who will be ruined by the defeat of their title. They have in most cases paid taxes for eight or ten years and their lands are now worth from five to fifteen dollars per acre." [26]

The general policy of the states in regard to overflowed lands encouraged their immediate disposal. [27] The prospective settler, or the speculator, merely had to make his selection and await the announcement of the date on which the sales were to commence. In Iowa the land was ceded to the counties and variously disposed of by them. The board of supervisors in each county was given authority to appraise these lands with the condition that those "not lying in, along or contiguous to navigable streams," and not subject to periodic overflows during the summer months, should not be sold for less than one dollar per acre. [28] In Wisconsin lists of the available land were issued from time to time, with a little information concerning their character and appraised value. In this state, until about 1874, they were sold on credit, the buyer paying at least ten per cent at the time of purchase, the remainder being left for subsequent payments with interest at seven per cent. The price was usually determined by previous appraisal. Some states established a minimum price varying from fifty cents to one dollar and a quarter per acre, although in certain states tracts were sold for as little as ten cents per acre. In more recent years, however, owing to the general increase in

[26] *Iowa State Register,* April 17, 1872.

[27] Exceptions to this general rule, though few, may nevertheless be found. That the withholding of these lands from sale was not calculated to court popularity may be gathered from the following indignant extract: "There are thousands of acres of land scattered all over this section of the state known as indemnity swamp lands. They are owned by the older and wealthier counties for purposes of speculation, and are exempt from taxation and withheld from sale or settlement. There is no reason why they should not be taxed the same as lands owned by individuals, and we trust the legislature will make provisions for such taxation. It is high time that the legislature looked after the interest of the people in all of these matters pertaining to land grants, remembering that corporations are generally able to take care of themselves."—*Montana Standard* (Iowa), Feb. 27, 1868.

[28] *Laws of Iowa,* 1864, p. 74.

value of lands and timber, a higher price has been placed on them.

The original purpose of the grant was to enable the states to reclaim their wet lands by the construction of levees and drains. Its primary object was not to enrich the states, but to enable them to carry out a program of reclamation that should on the one hand lessen the destruction wrought by extensive inundations, and, on the other, eliminate the malaria-breeding swamp. However, no stipulation was made whereby this form of improvement became a necessary condition for the acquisition of titles by the states. And it is not improbable that if this stipulation had been made, few states would have accepted the grant.

In 1853 a bill was introduced in Congress providing for the repeal of that clause in the act of 1850 in which the purpose of the grant was stated. It was not passed, nor was a similar bill again introduced. In a few states plans of some sort were, nevertheless, made by which the funds derived from the sale of the lands should be directed toward the fulfillment of the purposes intended. Later, however, the proceeds were deflected to other uses, until the funds expended in drainage became too small for effective work.

In the words of the commissioner: "The proceeds have been used for the construction of roads, bridges, public buildings, and almost every purpose other than that intended by Congress."

"States have disposed of lands in large quantities for a small consideration or granted them to railroads or other corporations. But a small proportion of the proceeds have been applied to the reclamation of the land, and the purposes of the grant have been entirely ignored and defeated." [29] After all, a considerable amount of swamp land has been reclaimed, not, it is true, mainly by the administration of the acts of 1850, but rather by the passage of general drainage laws by the states.

The states which put the swamp land in with other lands

[29] L. O. R., 1887, pp. 37, 38.

granted by the federal government disposed of it, as did Wisconsin, for example, along with the whole amount. Little or nothing was done by any of the states to fulfill the spirit of the law with respect to drainage or levee building, unless in the case of Louisiana where much money had been expended even before the granting of the land in building Mississippi River levees. A few counties to which the swamp land was granted did something in the way of reclamation.[30]

It would be a thankless and for the most part a fruitless task to trace in detail the use and the misuse of the lands granted under the Swamp Act. A few instances will suffice:

In Iowa, where the land was given to the counties, not only was open fraud practiced in the selection, but the counties bartered them for all sorts of considerations such as public buildings, bridges, and the like, purposes foreign to the intent of the United States acts granting the land.[31] They even went beyond this and in some instances bargained with an immigration company, selling the land to the company for twenty-five to seventy-five cents an acre, with the provision that the company was to put settlers on the land.[32] In other cases the land was sold by the county commissioners to themselves for mere nominal considerations.[33] Some counties gave their swamp land to railroads.[34]

Moreover, the swamp-land grants interfered with other

[30] *Iowa Land Office Report*, 1865, p. 92.

[31] *Laws of Iowa*, 1858, p. 544.

"Considerable excitement has been created in the county by the publication of a rumor, or rather something more than that, concerning the condition of certain swamp lands of Green County certified to the American Emigrant Company. In this connection it is proper to say that a difference of opinion exists among our people, as to means resorted to by the Emigrant Company to secure a favorable vote. Good men who were present in the county at the time tell us that corruption entered into the question, while others are of a different opinion. It may be that there was no 'Shenanigan' intended by the Emigrant Company, but when it foists a contract upon the county for the building of a Court House without doors or windows, we are inclined to have some harrowing doubts concerning the pristine honesty of this corporation." *Jefferson Bee* (Iowa), Dec. 22, 1871.

[32] *Report*, State Land Office, Iowa, 1879.

[33] Paulson.

[34] *Ibid.*

grants and with a multitude of private land titles. They overlapped railway lands and internal improvement grants, and cost the government big sums in indemnity.[35]

IMPORTANCE OF THE SWAMP-LAND GRANTS

The swamp-land legislation of the middle of the last century is not important, then, in its relation to the exigencies for which it was designed. Of much significance, however, is the fact that under it an area greater than the States of New York, New Hampshire, Vermont, Massachusetts, Connecticut, Rhode Island and New Jersey has passed from the ownership of the general government. A considerable portion of this area is valuable for agricultural purposes, and much of it, either immediately or after passing through the hands of various types of owners, has been occupied by settlers.

As to the influence of this legislation on the states, it was declared in Congress: "I think that the acts of 1849 and 1850, the original swamp-land acts, . . . honestly administered, . . . would have been beneficial measures. But I feel quite confident, . . . taking the whole of the public-land states together, that a very grave mistake was made in their enactment, and I think from the time of their enactment to the present day they have wrought more evil than good, and have been, in fact, a source of misfortune to most, if not all, the states to which those laws applied." [36] This judgment coincides with that of the majority of people who have given the matter any thought.

The recent tendency, however, as has been mentioned, is to relegate the task of reclamation to national initiative. The opinion that "if it is just and right to irrigate the arid lands, it is equally right and just that the government contribute toward the drainage of the lowlands," is being expressed more and more frequently, since a large extent of territory is still to be reclaimed. It is estimated that there

[35] L. O. R., 1864, pp. 16, 17.
[36] Cong. Record, 51 Cong., 2 Sess., App., p. 5.

are 79,000,000 acres of swamp and overflowed land in the United States which could be made fit for agriculture. Of this 52,700,000 acres are permanently wet and never fit for cultivation, even in favorable years; about 6,800,000 acres afford pasturage to live stock, though the forage is often of inferior quality; 14,700,000 acres are subject to periodical overflow by streams, but these at other times produce valuable crops; and 4,800,000 acres during seasons of light or medium rainfall yield profitable crops, but become wholly unproductive during the seasons characterized by a rainfall greater than normal.[37]

SUMMARY

Congress felt for many years that the public domain had little value until after it should be settled, and by that process it ceased to be public domain. Hence as public property it was worth little. With this general view prevailing it can be seen that the estimated value of the swamp land must indeed have been low. Moreover, the swamp itself was a menace, and a hindrance. Thus Congress was easily willing to give the land to the states provided only they would drain it, and use the proceeds of sales for roads and other needed improvements.

As first passed the Swamp Act donated land to Louisiana, the object being to help her in controlling the Mississippi. Soon afterward the act was made to apply to all public land states, of which there were then thirteen. Later its provisions were extended to Minnesota and Oregon, but to no others. All told 64,000,000 acres were given to the states under this grant. In few instances in the land history have the results deviated so widely from the plans. To begin with, there was wholesale fraud in choosing the land. Little better is the story of their disposal by the states. Fraud ran riot. The lands were given to railroads, or to companies of any sort for the building of a few bridges, or a pretense of constructing drainage ditches. In several states the land was given to the counties and large parts of it turned into the educational funds. The Swamp Act provided a means of getting rid of land but to a trifling extent of effecting drainage. The amount of money realized by the states out of the swamp land was small.

[37] *Sen. Doc.*, 60 Cong., 2 Sess., No. 676.

CHAPTER XV

GRADUATION OF THE PRICE OF LAND

THE DEBATE ON THE GRADUATION PRINCIPLE IN 1790

Whether all land, irrespective of its quality, was to be sold at the same price, or whether the price was to be varied to fit the land, was a question to attract early attention. During the very first debate on the land disposition under the constitution, in 1790, there was a difference of opinion in this regard. The arguments were lively, and apparently a considerable amount of information was brought to bear on the case. There were, at that time, no old and new state interests to cause friction, and hence the merits of the question presumably held first place in the controversy. It was shown that the different colonies, and afterward the states, had tried various plans. During the debate, the question was raised as to whether or not states had made a practice of selling land at one price, or at prices graded to suit the quality.

"Mr. Sedgwick answered the inquiry respecting the relative value of lands being ascertained in the several states. He said that so far as his information extended, which respected only the states of New York, New Hampshire and Massachusetts, this had invariably been the case. Every man knows there is a most essential difference in the value of lands. Those on navigable rivers may be ten times as valuable as those on the top of a mountain. This every individual is so sensible of that a difference in the price is constantly made. And why the government should not make a difference it is impossible to say; any man, by casting his eye upon a map, can at once determine that some part of the land is unspeakably more valuable than other parts.

He was certain that vesting a discretionary power in the disposal of the land would be productive of the greatest advantage to the United States, and on this principle he could not conceive why the surveyors should not determine the relative quality, that the United States may stand some chance of getting the value of this property." [1]

In favor of a fixed uniform price, it was held that after the best land had been sold the inferior lands would also, in a short time thereafter, sell for the same price. Why, then, should the government sell for less than the price fixed in one definite minimum? Again, it was urged that there was a great practical difficulty in carrying out the plan of graduating the price, since the classification must necessarily be left to the surveyors. These latter arguments together carried the day, the motion to graduate the price being lost. [2]

Not until 1820 was the matter of graduation again up for discussion in Congress. At that time it was proposed in the Senate to graduate the price on the basis of the length of time which the land had been in the market without being sold. A motion, embodying this plan, was offered by Senator Johnson of Louisiana, and was supported by the argument that in his state, as elsewhere, there was "a great deal of land which would never bring the minimum price, and that it ought, in due time, to be offered at such a price as would induce its purchase and settlement." [3] Objection was made to presentation of the amendment in connection with the cash sales bill, although some support was offered to the principle on its merits. The motion was "negatived by a large majority."

BENTON'S ADVOCACY OF THE GRADUATED PRICE

Following this defeat, Congress paid little or no attention to the graduation plan for several years, in fact, not until 1822, when Mr. Benton of Missouri, a new advocate of

[1] *Ann. of Cong.*, 1 Cong., p. 1834.
[2] *Ibid*, p. 1837.
[3] *Ibid*, 16 Con., 1 Sess., p. 486.

the pioneer, had appeared within its midst. Mr. Benton very soon became the champion of the western settlers, and one of his earliest moves was the introduction of a bill, in 1824, providing for the reduction of the price of the "refuse" lands. In introducing this bill, Mr. Benton set forth the main arguments in its support:

"He believed that a change in the manner of selling public lands was called for, both by the voice of the people and the interest of the government. By the present rule, said Mr. Benton, the good and bad land are held at the same price. The best can be got for $1.25 per acre—the worst cannot be had for less. The minimum of $1.25 per acre for all sorts of land was arbitrary and unjust. It was unjust to the people, because it prevented them from getting the inferior land at a fair price; unjust to the states, because it checked their population, and deprived them of their right of taxation; unjust to the nation, because it prevented the public treasury from receiving the money which such land was worth, and for which it would sell. The continuance of the rule would give to the United States the fabled position of the dog and the manger. The rule should be changed. The United States is a great land seller, and she should follow the practice of all other sellers; she should apportion her price to the quality of her land. When a quarter section has been offered for years at $1.25 per acre, and nobody will give that sum, it is proof that it is not worth it, and justice to the people, the states and the treasury requires that it should be offered again at a less price. The bill introduced assumes fifty cents per acre as the second minimum at which such lands should be offered; and it proposes to give away, without price, to such poor persons as may be willing to take and cultivate them, the refuse lands which will not sell for that sum."[4]

A little later a similar suggestion for graduation came from the General Land Office in a proposal to re-sell relinquished lands at a fixed proportion of the original selling

[4] *Ann. of Cong.,* 18 Cong., 1 Sess., p. 583.

price. And this, it must be admitted, was far from the general idea of graduation as applied to land of different qualities wherever found. It was rather a way out of a specific difficulty.

Alabama was among the first of the public-land states to petition Congress for a reduction in the price of land according to grade. In 1826, the legislature passed resolutions, which were forwarded in the usual manner to Congress, setting forth the unfavorable situation attendant upon the method then in vogue of selling land at auction and holding even the poorest up to the prescribed minimum price, which it was admitted was also ordinarily the auction price of even the best land. Complaint was made that speculators bought up most of the land ahead of the real settler, frightening the latter out of bidding on the land at all, at the public auction, competition being in this way stifled. As a remedy, the legislature suggested the classification of land into three grades, with prices fixed at which it might be entered by the settler. In case sales were not made at the price first set, a lower price might be accepted after a period of time. "There would," the resolutions assert, "be great propriety in ultimately reducing the quantity to be entered to forty acres and the price to twenty-five cents an acre." [5] Coupled with this was an urgent request that the government grant a preëmption right to all who located on the land prior to the time of holding the auction. Congress was urged to pass Benton's bill, which had been pending for several years.

Within a few years nearly all of the public-land states sent, through their legislatures, petitions to Congress asking that the prices of land be graduated, thus showing the West to be substantially united in regard to the advisability of such a measure. [6] Michigan alone of these states opposed graduation. Congress was slow to act. Experience had shown that great diversity of opinion was sure to develop as soon as any disposition was manifested in favor of a

[5] *Pub. Lands*, IV, p. 529.
[6] *Ibid*, VI, p. 640.

change in the land laws. It is therefore not strange that men high in the advices of party government should keep the question in the background unless it seemed to promise well as a party measure. After ignoring for some two years Benton's importunities, backed up as they were by the demands of the frontier, the House, in 1826, referred the case to the Committee on Public Lands. A little over a year later this committee brought in a report recommending a graduation to 50 cents an acre and the free granting of land not wanted at the latter price. During the same year, a similar question was referred by the Senate to its Committee on Public Lands. In this case the committee reported adversely, although a bill was presented embodying the graduation principle. The bill, after considerable debate, was laid on the table.[7] The House committee not only reported favorably, but accompanied the recommendation with arguments probably as strong as any presented on the subject at any time. Attention was directed to the fact that according to a report made shortly before by the Secretary of the Treasury, the United States government had, since organization, come into possession of 261,000,000 acres of land; that only one-thirteenth of that amount had been sold. From these premises, the committee deduced the conclusion that it would take a period of more than five centuries in which to dispose of the public domain, but they despaired of the possibility of making the sales even in so short a time, and added: "We cannot reasonably expect that, under the existing plan, the government can dispose of them [the lands] in any number of years within our power to enumerate." They continue: "To every citizen of the Union this state of things is injurious; whilst collectively they possess superabundant wealth, they are individually subject to a tax upon the conveniences and necessities of life, in the form of duties upon imports, to sustain a necessary revenue and to pay the principal and interest of the public debt. A conclusive proof of the insufficiency of the system now regu-

[7] *Cong. Deb.*, 19 Cong., 2 Sess., p. 347.

lating this great national interest is found in the fact that it has entirely failed to answer the end for which it was confessedly devised. We are told by documents accompanying the report before mentioned that the expenses on account of the public land up to January 1, 1826, including purchases, surveying and incidental expenses, amounted to almost thirty-three millions of dollars; that there had been received in cash a little more than thirty-one millions; showing a difference of near two millions of dollars between the expenditures and receipts. If to this balance is added the interest at six per cent upon the amount expended, we shall have a sum not less than fifteen millions withdrawn from the public treasury, leaving out of view the expenses annually accruing from legislating on account of these lands. It appears, therefore, to your committee that the present mode of selling the public lands has been, and will continue to be, attended with the worst results. The facts stated present the question whether the interest of the federal government, of the people of the United States, and more especially of the new states, do not require that the sales shall be accelerated in time to come, and this question seems to admit of no other than an affirmative answer." [8]

And they conclude the argument with the exhortation: "Sell public land upon the same principles that individuals sell private land and property of every sort, for what it is worth, considering its quality and locality. By adhering to a minimum you fix a price only upon the best, and leave that of less value a dead weight upon the hands of the nation, and upon the prosperity and population of the states. It appears to your committee that a scale of prices adapted to the various quality and value of lands furnishes the most reasonable and expedient system. This is the object of the many memorials before us, and is the essential proposition contained in the bill which has for some years past been under consideration in another branch of the legislature." [9]

[8] *Pub. Lands*, V, p. 448
[9] *Ibid*, p. 449.

The bill presented, in support of which these arguments were offered, provided for the reduction of land to 25 cents per acre; for the donation to actual settlers of eighty-acre tracts; and for cession to the states of land left in the market for over two years, at 25 cents per acre. There was much sentiment in favor of each of these plans, but not sufficient to carry either one through. The arguments were presented in the House in about the usual form by Mr. McHattan of Kentucky. It was held that land was a gift of God; that the United States held it at an extraordinary price; that it would serve better in reducing the public debt at a figure much below the $1.25 per acre; that settlers were poor and should be helped by the government. The bill providing for the graduation of the price was, at the end of the speech in its favor, tabled.[10]

GRADUATION FAVORED BY THE WEST, OPPOSED BY THE EAST

In the Senate the measure received more support, its main defenders being Benton together with other senators from the West. Benton, in a vigorous speech, held that the lands were ceded by the states to the national government "to be disposed of." He went over the early land history showing that Hamilton believed 25 cents to be a sufficiently high price. Benton believed that a lower price for land would bring in more money, reduce the debt, and obviate the necessity of so high a tariff on imports.[11] Senator Dickerson of New Jersey spoke for the old states. New Jersey hoped to get some money out of her share of western land. Furthermore, he believed that the plan to reduce land to 25 cents per acre after a period of offering at a higher price would amount virtually to a flat reduction to 25 cents of all land, since none would buy for a dollar and a quarter that which was destined to be worth only a quarter a little later. Senator Dickerson was willing to reduce the price to $1.00 as the minimum.[12] Mr. Webster had at one time

[10] *Cong. Deb.*, 20 Cong., 1 Sess., p. 2380.
[11] *Ibid*, p. 23 *et seq.*
[12] *Ibid*, p. 677.

favored the reduction of the minimum to $1.00. He expressed himself as favorable to the graduation bill in 1828, but, not liking all its details, voted against it as finally presented. The bill was lost by a vote of 21 to 25.[13] Thus the graduation bill was defeated in both branches of Congress. It was a sectional measure and there seemed little hope that the contending factions could get together. But one senator of the western states, Barton of Missouri, voted against the bill, while from east of the Alleghanies but two senators voted for it. During the course of the debate an alternative argument was repeatedly injected into the controversy, viz., the cession of the land to the states in which it lay.

Committee on Public Lands Favors Graduation

Very rarely has a more emphatic report been presented to Congress by one of its committees than that submitted by the Committee on Public Lands in 1832.[14] This was inspired by the report previously made by the Committee on Manufactures in which strong grounds had been taken against reduction of the price of the public land. In this report it had been shown that the public lands had not been a satisfactory source of income, but it was held that it would be unfair, unwise and impolitic to lower the price in order to accelerate sales. The Committee on Public Lands were contemptuous of the whole report, and in their criticism took a higher, at least a less materialistic, view of the whole matter. "They [the Committee on Public Lands] condemn the whole plan, idea and conception of keeping accounts and striking balances between the federal government and the federal domain. They cannot consent to bring down this government from its lofty station of parental guardianship over the people to the low level of a land speculator."[15] They go on to compare the $38,000,000 received in revenue from the public domain with the

---

[13] *Cong. Deb.*, 20 Cong., 1 Sess., p. 678.
[14] *Pub. Lands*, VI, p. 478.
[15] *Ibid*, p. 479.

$556,000,000 received from the tariff dues, yet they say all of this latter sum came in reality from the American farmer. It was argued that many of the old states wanted reduction in tariff revenue on the articles most used by them. Is it not just as reasonable that the new states should ask for a reduction in the revenue from the commodity most used by them, *i.e.,* the land? It could not diminish the real value of land already in the hands of the cultivator; it might, at most, reduce the value of land held by speculators. The use value cannot be hurt. It would not injure the values of land held by the states, or, at least, the testimony to the contrary is strong in the memorials from the states asking for a reduction of price. The committee favored the tariff, rather than the public domain, as a source of revenue. Therefore, it recommended the graduation of the price of the public lands.

Again, in 1836, a report from the Committee on Public Lands favored reduction.[16] Interest at this time, however, centered rather in distribution of the proceeds, and the report received scant consideration. In the Senate the situation was quite similar, the interest centering on still other phases of the question. Mr. Clay was back in the Senate and he and his colleague from Kentucky, Mr. Crittenden, became the champions of the distribution scheme and opponents of all favors to the settlers.

Coupled with Preëmption Bill

Following 1836 came a respite of some three or four years, when the graduation bill was revived and made the running mate of the preëmption bill. This was strictly a western pair and had the force of the West behind it, but, in the political race, graduation was beaten once more, while distribution won along with and by the aid of preëmption. "The old states want the land in the new to bring the highest possible price, that they may have annually more money packed over the mountains, to be spent among them on their wharves, lighthouses, buoys and breakwaters, and the Lord

[16] *Pub. Lands,* VIII, p. 330.

knows what; not satisfied in placing on our shoulders a protective tariff on the necessaries of life for their benefit, we must also be saddled with a high land tariff, a sort of English corn law, that they may thrive and fatten at our expense, and most generous souls! when they were kind enough to modify the tariff in 1832, to save the Union, a reduction at that time of the land revenue never entered into their imaginations; no, never." [17] Here we have a statement, by inference, of about the whole of the case. The old states feared they would lose money by a liberal policy with respect to the sale of land, and since these states had the votes they used them in maintaining what they considered their rights against the demands of the frontier.

With an interval of one year during which the graduation bill was allowed to rest, it came up in both houses in about the usual form in 1843. During that session, neither bill got farther than the committees. Two years later, a bill was introduced in the House and a hot debate ensued. Not much variety was added to the arguments already familiar. The division of opinion was mainly sectional, tempered somewhat by partisanship. On a test vote the House stood 97 for the bill and 103 against it.

Three Presidents Favor Graduation

Outside of the support given the principle of graduation in Congress, three Presidents, Jackson, Van Buren and Polk, in various messages, expressed themselves in favor of graduating the price of the public lands. The Secretary of the Treasury recommended graduation, and believed that it would increase the annual revenue from sales. The Commissioner of the General Land Office favored graduation, and this occurred not merely once—the different commissioners, during a period of years, continued the advocacy of the measure. A fair sample of the expressions from this office is that of the year 1845:

"I wish also to call your attention to the propriety of a

17 *Cong. Globe*, 26 Cong., 2 Sess., App., p. 65.

graduated reduction in the price of public lands. But few subjects of equal importance have been more earnestly pressed upon the consideration of Congress than this, and none have hitherto been less successful. The recommendations of the Executive, concurred in on several occasions by the Senate, the resolutions of legislatures, the petitions of the people, and the advocacy of the first talents of the nation have failed, as yet, to obtain the introduction of a system by which the public lands might be rated according to value." [18]

Then follows an elaborate demonstration of the hypothesis that selling at a lower price would bring, within a given extent of territory, more money into the treasury than the plan of holding all land at a uniform minimum price. Petitions from state legislatures and citizens continued. Under this pressure it is not strange that Congress was unable to let the matter drop. The usual bill was presented in 1846; it passed the Senate with a vote of 26 to 18.[19] The measure had run a trying gauntlet. Likewise, in the House, a graduation bill very similar in its provisions passed by a vote of 92 to 89.[20] There were, however, minor differences which led to amendments and the outcome was a final tabling of the bill in the House a few days later.

THE GRADUATION ACT PASSES IN 1854

The following year the Commissioner of the General Land Office, in his annual report, urged graduation as one of the changes imperatively needed in the land-disposal system.[21]

---

[18] The commissioner goes on to state that it looked like sectional jealousy of the old states against the new. A significant comment was made on the whole issue of the public land. It was assumed, the commissioner states, that the whole object of the land policy was the settlement of the unoccupied territory; that revenue was incidental, and should amount to merely enough to cover expenses of sale. A graduated price would encourage sale and settlement. The absurdity of the system in vogue was shown by the fact that the best land was bringing a very few cents above $1.25 an acre, while the poorest had to bring $1.25 or not be sold.

[19] *Cong. Globe,* 29 Cong., 1 Sess., p. 1073.

[20] *Ibid,* p. 1094.

[21] *Ibid,* 30 Cong., 1 Sess., App., p. 38.

The President also urged the measure, but nothing was done except to introduce bills. These bills—and the same condition continued until 1854—were handicapped badly by the demand for legislation much more radical. The sentiment in favor of free land to settlers was growing rapidly during these years. Why reduce the price merely when what was wanted was no price at all? But since the Homestead Bill had been defeated some three or four times, the graduation plan was resorted to as the greatest available concession to the public land states. The bill passed the House in 1854 by a vote of 83 to 64,[22] and the Senate without division.[23] By this measure a demand of the West, after a struggle extending through a period of thirty years, became a law. The question had its partisan aspects throughout, yet it was always much more clearly a sectional struggle. In the final vote in the House, 33 Democrats from the original 13 states voted against the bill while only 14 voted for it. Of the Whigs from the old states, 19 voted against the bill and 4 for it. In the new states, 45 Democrats voted for the bill, 5 against it, and of the Whigs, 16 voted aye, 5 no. Thus both parties were divided, although, in both old and new sections, the support was somewhat stronger by Democrats than by Whigs. There was, however, little margin for boasting by the Democrats, since they could not have carried the day without the support of the western Whigs.

The act as passed provided for a reduction in price of land in proportion to the length of time it had been on sale without finding a purchaser. That which had been in the market ten years was to be sold at $1.00; fifteen years at 75 cents; twenty years at 50 cents; twenty-five years at 25 cents; and thirty or more years at 12½ cents. Mr. Greeley expressed his displeasure and apprehension thus:

"We believe that no measure more fraught with vital and lasting injury to the best interests of the country has been

[22] *Cong. Globe*, 33 Cong., 1 Sess., p. 918.
[23] *Ibid*, p. 2204.

before Congress at this Session. Though ostensibly reducing the price of land in favor of settlers only, it provides no safeguards against the absorption of whole counties by individual speculators; and though professing to cede all the lands which may have remained thirty years in market to the states embracing them respectively, this is killed by providing that the lands shall first be offered for sale at 12½ cents per acre, at which price all that either are or are ever likely to be worth anything will be clutched by speculators. The natural effect of this bill will be to give us cheap lands for a few years and dear lands ever after. If the avowed object had been to create a landed aristocracy, with the great mass of the laboring population for their dependents and vassals, it would hardly be possible to have framed a bill better adapted to the purpose. How the same House could pass this and the Homestead bill we cannot understand." [24]

RESULTS OF THE ACT AND SALES BY STATES

In order to prevent the speculators from taking advantage, in a wholesale manner, of the reduced price of land it was provided that sales should be of two classes, first, to persons living upon and cultivating such land; second, to those who intended to settle and cultivate it at once. The latter provision was interpreted by the Secretary of the Interior to mean within one year as a reasonable time.[25] A year prior to this ruling Congress had amended the Graduation Act by giving the Secretary of the Interior the right to interpret its provisions. The provisions for preventing speculation in government land were hardly adequate; no limitation was placed on the amount which one person might buy. As a result the sales were very brisk.[26]

At the time of passage of the Graduation Act there were in the United States over seventy-seven million acres of land subject to sale under its provisions, at something less than

[24] *N. Y. Semi-Weekly Tribune*, April 18, 1854.
[25] *Ex. Doc*, 34 Cong., 1 Sess., No. 63.
[26] *Ex. Doc.*, 34 Cong., 1 Sess., No. 63

$1.25 per acre,[27] distributed among the states as shown in the following table:[28]

TABLE XVII

SALES UNDER THE GRADUATION ACT

	Total in each State
Ohio	70,495
Indiana	458,700
Illinois	1,384,610
Wisconsin	1,906,757
Michigan	8,785,890
Iowa	595,480
Missouri	13,850,020
Arkansas	14,212,610
Louisiana	7,806,340
Mississippi	7,602,043
Alabama	14,039,502
Florida	6,848,560
Total	77,561,007

It will be noticed that Arkansas, Alabama and Missouri had the greatest quantities of these so-called refuse lands, the three states together having well over half of the total amount in the whole country.

The greatest quantities of land sold at graduated prices by no means correspond with the location, by states, of the total amount subject to such disposal. During the year following the passage of the act the sales of public land were greatest in Iowa, Missouri, Alabama and Illinois, but in Iowa the bulk of the sales was at $1.25, leaving Missouri, Alabama and Illinois as the leading states in the sale of land which had long been in the market. The prices received tell the story: In Illinois, 33 cents per acre; in Alabama, 40 cents; in Missouri, 77 cents. These cheap lands were undoubtedly bought largely by non-resident speculators. In commenting on the failure of Congress to pass the Homestead bill, Horace Greeley speaks of "Cable's swindling

[27] *Ex. Doc.*, 34 Cong., 1 Sess., No. 13, p. 470.
[28] *Ibid.*

graduation bill" which was passed, going on to say: "The area of public lands that this act will wrest from the whole people and turn over to private monopoly (mainly non-resident) is estimated at two hundred millions of acres." [29] The same writer states three years later that land is bringing the United States but about half a dollar an acre, while in most cases the farmer is obliged to pay three dollars, and often ten, for the same land.[30]

Attempts were made from time to time by the friends of the pioneer to limit the amount of land to be had by one person at the reduced price, and to require actual settlement and cultivation as the conditions of sale. The complaints of the New York *Tribune* were referred to in the debates in Congress, and the author of the graduation bill moved an amendment safeguarding the interests of the settlers against the operations of speculators.[31] The amendment failed to pass.

Land sales had not been heavy for some years, only twice in a decade preceding the passage of this bill having exceeded two million acres a year. Within a year after the passage of the Graduation Act, approximately as much land was sold as during the eight years preceding. The Graduation Act was in effect from 1854 to the time of the passage of the Homestead Act in 1862, or about eight years. During this time there were sold at $1.00 per acre, and under, 25,696,000 acres of public land, an amount equal in area to the state of Ohio. Hence, as a means of disposing of land, the act was an important one. As to revenue, the land thus sold brought $8,207,000 or about 32 cents per acre.[32]

Thus were justified the claims of the friends of graduation that the land would sell and that it would bring in additional money.

[29] *N. Y. Semi-Weekly Tribune,* Mar. 6, 1855.
[30] *Weekly Tribune,* Feb. 13, 1858.
[31] *Cong. Globe,* 33 Cong., 2 Sess., p. 132.
[32] *L. O. R.,* 1855-1862.

Summary

A reduction in the price of land corresponding to its quality was accomplished only after a long struggle. Beginning with the first legislation on the land question it became Senator Benton's hobby some forty years later. Quite naturally the West favored reduction. What they wanted was settlers. The East, clinging longer to the idea of revenue, opposed the measure. Very properly graduation may be looked upon as a step toward free land, yet not once did the same people and factions support it as supported the free land movement; they openly stated that it would be desirable to make all land free, in small quantities to actual settlers after it had been offered for a given length of time without selling.

Although the Committee on Public Lands in the House throughout a long period favored the measure, and likewise three presidents favored it, it took till 1854 to bring the matter to a culmination. Had it not been that free land was already an avowed goal during the forties and fifties, it is reasonable to believe that graduation would have made more rapid progress. Nearly 26,000,000 acres were sold at the reduced prices, viz., $1.00, 75c, 50c, 25c, and 12½c. The average price of land sold under this act was 32 cents an acre.

CHAPTER XVI

LAND GRANTS FOR EDUCATIONAL PURPOSES

EDUCATIONAL GRANTS [1]

Common Schools.—The educational land-grant policy of the federal government has been so closely related with that pursued during the colonial period that it is deemed advisable to outline briefly the colonial educational land endowment scheme as a precedent to our American system. So strongly were the early immigrants influenced by the intellectual awakening that characterized the first half of the seventeenth century that among their very earliest undertakings was the setting aside of certain land areas in the New World for the promotion of education.

Grants by the Colonies.—The colonials were deeply impressed with the publicly endowed schools of the Old World, and were eager to use a part of the abundant supply of free land for that purpose. In addition to these incentives was that of religion. It had its particular effects in shaping the policy of the early settlers, because of the intimate relation of the church and state at that time. In England the ministry was very often endowed with a lease in perpetuity on landed property, and when the ecclesiastical powers suggested the adoption of such a plan in America the colonists readily responded by appropriating land as an endowment for the church and ministry. With this class of land grants was also associated the setting aside of landed property in the interest of education. Ministerial and school lots were usually of equal significance and very often constituted the same area; the grant provided that the land or

[1] For the Northwest Territory the best account is that by Geo. W. Knight: *History and Management of Land Grants for Education in the Northwest Territory.*

proceeds from its sale be used for the maintenance of a church and school forever.

School incomes from grants were derived from various sources. Very likely the first revenue was received in the form of rents from lands donated in perpetuity. The endowed lands were often sold and the proceeds invested, thus enabling the school to receive the yearly interest. Lands were set aside directly for the schoolmaster as a partial payment for his services. Then, too, many of the tracts allotted were sold and the net receipts turned into the school treasury in order to meet current expenses.

The school land policy of the New England colonies offers an excellent precedent for the early grants made by Congress in support of education. As it was the common procedure for towns to apply to the General Court for an assignment of land to aid them in the support of their schools, so also has the practice prevailed under our democratic form of government, in which municipal and county organizations have frequently petitioned the states and they in turn the federal government for a portion of the public domain for similar purposes.

The early history of the maintenance of schools in Massachusetts is particularly striking. As early as 1635 the town of Dorchester, Massachusetts, by an act of the General Court, came into possession of an island in Boston Harbor known as Thompson's Island, for use in maintaining its public schools.[2] Unfortunately, a few years later private interests claimed title to the island and in a trial the judge favored the plaintiff. However, in 1659 the General Court granted Dorchester 1,000 acres for educational promotion wherever it could legally be claimed.[3] Boston, in 1641, set aside Deare Island for the maintenance of a "free schoole of the towne," the income to be derived from the property in the form of a yearly rent.[4] Again, in 1660, another endowment of 1,000 acres was made.[5] Dedham, in 1642, received a tract of land

[2] *Records of the Colony of Massachusetts Bay in New England*, I, p. 134.
[3] *Ibid*, IV, p. 397.
[4] *Boston Town Records*, p. 65.
[5] *Records of the Colony of Massachusetts Bay*, IV, Part I, p. 444.

not less than 40 nor more than 60 acres for the town, the church, and the school.[6]

These early donations of land may be taken as samples of what was done substantially throughout the colonies. Other grants were made, mostly by the colonial authorities, in towns. These grants varied from 40 to 600 acres per town, and provided for the partial support of common schools.[7-17]

The peculiar conditions which confronted the possibilities of education in the colonies south of New England, such as the mode of government, the class of people, the influence of religion, and the natural conditions under which the people lived, had their particular effects in hampering the policy of land endowments. However, a number of grants were made in the face of these opposing forces. The provincial government of New Netherlands in 1658 "appropriated to the magistrates of Midwout 50 acres for the maintenance of a school, church service," [18] etc. The history of allotments in New York under the British government is very obscure. The proprietary rulers, the Penns of Pennsylvania, New Jersey and Delaware, and the Baltimores of Maryland made no land grants for the maintenance of schools. Maryland, however, in 1723, under an independent colonial rule, required that there should be established in each county at least one boarding school and that one hundred acres of land or more be donated for the welfare of each.[19]

The Virginia colony was the first to appropriate land for common schools on the western continent. In 1621 the court granted 1,000 acres of land with the services of five

[6] *Dedham Town Records*, III, p. 92.
[7] *Records of the Colony of Massachusetts Bay*, IV, Pt. I, p. 438.
[8] *Ibid*, IV, Pt. I, p. 400.
[9] *Records of the Town of Plymouth*, I, p. 124.
[10] Small, W. H., *Early New England Schools*, p. 220.
[11] *Acts and Resolves of the Province of Massachusetts Bay*, X, XI, XII.
[12] *Ibid*, XII, p. 253.
[13] *Colonial Records of Connecticut*, II, p. 176.
[14] *Ibid*, VII, p. 458.
[15] *Ibid*, VII, p. 451; VIII, p. 134.
[16] *Early Records of the Town of Providence*, III, p. 35.
[17] E. W. Clews, *Educational Legislation and Administration of the Colonial Governments*, p. 168.
[18] *Ibid*, p. 216.
[19] *Archives of Maryland*, XXXIX, p. 740.

apprentices and an overseer to cultivate it, for the maintenance of a free school.[20]

Under the proprietary rule the Carolinas and Georgia made no educational land grants. However, five years after the proprietary charter of South Carolina was forfeited, in 1719, provisions were made for a royal grant of land to support a free school at Dorchester.[21] A number of land grants were made in the southern colonies at subsequent dates.

Without making further reference to the colonial common school period, a few important cases may be noted in which land grants were fundamental in the early development of higher education, prior to American independence.

The first provisions for an American land grant in the interest of a higher school of learning was that made by the Virginia Company, it having been instructed by King James, in 1618, to reserve ten thousand acres in the territory of Henrico, Virginia, of which nine thousand acres were to be used in endowing a university, and one thousand acres for a college. The establishment of the university was to be at a future date, while, in the meantime, preparation was to be made for the building of a college.[22] Matters were very promising until the outbreak of the Indian War in 1622, when settlements were laid waste and many lives lost, thus necessitating the abandoning of educational enactments for the time.[23]

Virginia, being unable to promote her educational program, left it to Massachusetts to establish the first endowed college in 1636 at Newtown,[24] which was two years afterward renamed Cambridge,[25] and in 1640 the colonial government granted to Harvard, it being again renamed, the first American college, five hundred acres toward its maintenance.[26]

Several of the best-known colleges of the original thirteen

[20] *Records of the Virginia Company,* I, pp. 550-559.
[21] Clews, p. 465.
[22] *Records of the Virginia Company* I, pp. 220, 268.
[23] R. G. Boone, *Education in the United States,* p. 13.
[24] *Records of the Colony of Mass. Bay,* I, p. 183.
[25] *Ibid,* p. 228.
[26] *Ibid,* p. 262.

states were started with land grants. William and Mary College received 20,000 acres; Yale received 500 pounds sterling from the sale of lands; Dartmouth was the recipient of 40,960 acres; while Princeton received two acres for a campus. Colleges were started in both Georgia and South Carolina by the aid of land grants.

Thus the principle of giving land for educational purposes was well established before the adoption of the Ordinance of 1787. It was approved on the grounds of both religious freedom and democracy, on the opinion that these kindred movements were each dependent on the ability of the individual to read and think independently.[27-42]

Land Grant Provision of the Ordinance of 1787.—The Ordinance of 1787 made provision for the division of the Northwest Territory into not less than three nor more than five states, and that when a division had a population of 60,000, it should be eligible for admission into the Union. In 1802, when the eastern portion made application for statehood, Congress, in passing the act enabling the Territory of Ohio to form a constitution and state government, submitted several propositions to the people for their free acceptance or rejection. Among these was one which proposed "that Section Number 16 in every township, or where such section had been sold, granted or disposed of, other lands equivalent thereto, and most contiguous to the same, should be granted to the inhabitants of such township for

[27-42] The following citations pertain to the leading instances of land grants for the support of higher education in the colonies.
Records of the Town of Cambridge, 1630-1703, p. 33.
Clews, p. 361.
Colonial Records of Conn., V, pp. 528, 529.
Ibid, VII, p. 412.
Town Papers of New Hampshire, XII, p. 361.
Ibid, p. 159.
David Murray, "History of Education in New Jersey," *American Educational History*, VIII, No. 23, pp. 212, 227, 228.
Wickersham, J. P., *History of Education in Pennsylvania*, p. 376.
Colonial Records of Georgia, XIX, Pt. 2, p. 300.
South Carolina *Statutes at Large*, IV, pp. 674, 675.
Jol. of Cong., XII, pp. 58-61.
Laws of U. S., I, p. 573.
Ibid, pp. 495-498.
U. S. Stat. at Large, I, p. 266.
Jol. of Cong., X, pp. 96, 97.

the use of schools." [43] As a counter-concession Ohio was to exempt from taxation all property sold by the government for a period of five years after the date of sale, within which time the purchaser was expected to make final settlement. Ohio refused to agree to this compact, however, until Congress, in addition to granting school lands within the public domain, had also provided that an area equal to one-thirty-sixth of the land contained in the Connecticut, the Virginia, and the United States military reserves and the territory occupied by the Indians be reserved for the common schools within these areas. [44] This Congress consented to do in the modifying act of 1803, but in so doing provided that all the sections "appropriated for the use of schools in the state . . . be vested in the legislature of that state" and not to the particular township. [45]

This reservation of the sixteenth section of each township marked the beginning of the federal school endowment policy, also it established a precedent which has since been followed in granting indemnity land where Section 16 had already been occupied.

The usual provision was that where school sections should fall upon land already granted by virtue of any act of Congress, or claimed in consequence of an authorized foreign grant, "then should be located another section or sections in lieu thereof, for the use of schools, which location should be made in the same township, if there be any other vacant section therein, and otherwise in an adjoining township." [46]

[43] *U. S. Stat. at Large,* II, p. 175.
[44] *Ibid,* p. 225.
[45] *Ibid.*
[46] *Ibid,* II, p. 401. A large part of the indemnity lands was not located until recently. The following table shows the amount of indemnity land selections during the fiscal year 1922-1923 (L. O. R. 1923, p. 39).

State	Acres	State	Acres
Arizona	307,476	North Dakota	514
California	22,929	Oregon	369
Colorado	32,088	South Dakota	856
Florida	411	Utah	39,868
Idaho	137,035	Washington	39,303
Montana	131,262	Wyoming	8,774
Nebraska	160		
New Mexico	114,195	Total	835,240

On July 1, 1923, there were 712,471 acres pending confirmation.

In the enabling acts of North Dakota, South Dakota, Montana, Washington,[47] Utah[48] and Oklahoma,[49] the areas embraced in permanent reservations for national purposes were not at any time to be subject to school grants, nor was any land included in Indian, military or other reservations of any character to be subject to such grants until the reservations should be extinguished and the land restored to and made a part of the public domain.

Just what were the particular motives which led to the passage of the various congressional acts granting land for schools; whether they were primarily the zeal of the law-making body, interested in the promotion of education; or whether the land donated to the schools was a means of enabling Congress to dispose of the western domain more readily and at the same time get a higher price than it otherwise would have brought, is a complex question. However, the incidents connected with the granting of the 16th section for school purposes undoubtedly had their setting in colonial practices and have since been fundamental in the law establishing a fund for the maintenance of common schools.

Uniform System of Land Grants after 1848.—Until 1848 there was lack of uniformity in the time of making school land reservations. Alabama, Illinois, Missouri, Arkansas, Michigan, Florida, Iowa and Wisconsin acquired title to their school sections at the time of their admission into the Union. Indiana,[50] Mississippi[51] and Louisiana[52] were directed to reserve sections 16 for school purposes during their territorial periods. The situation in Tennessee became somewhat complicated on account of nothing having been said about the disposal of public lands at the time of its admission into the Union in 1796, and it was not until ten years afterward that the ownership of unclaimed lands within that state was definitely settled. A dispute arose as to whether the state or the nation controlled this property.

[47] *U. S. Stat. at Large,* XXV, p. 679.
[48] *Ibid,* XXVIII, p. 109.
[49] *Ibid,* XXXIV, p. 272.
[50] *Ibid,* II, p. 279.
[51] *Ibid,* II, 234.
[52] *Ibid,* II, p. 394.

In an adjustment of matters, the federal government relinquished to Tennessee all claim to an area north and east of a certain compromise line, but at the same time retained control of lands south and west of that division. In the area ceded to Tennessee, Congress required that 640 acres out of every six miles square, where existing claims would allow, should "be appropriated for the use of schools for the instruction of children." [53]

With the exceptions of the school grants to California after statehood was acquired, and to New Mexico [54] during its territorial period, Congress, after 1848, followed a uniform course of reserving school sections in the organic acts of the territories and making final grants in the acts enabling them to be admitted into the Union. Beginning with this year, 1848, section 36, as well as section 16, was granted for school purposes. The first territory to receive the added grant was Oregon. [55]

In 1836 Congress recognized that the grant of the sixteenth section was unfair to those townships in which that division was missing, due, for example, to rivers, lakes, or to inaccurate surveys, and so provided that all townships or fractional townships for which no land had been heretofore appropriated for the use of schools were to receive grants corresponding roughly to the proportional area of the township or fractional township in question.

A similar provision was made concerning the fractional thirty-sixth sections some twenty-three years afterward. [56]

An exceptional donation of public land by Congress direct to towns or villages was that provided for in an act of June 13, 1812, in which eleven towns or villages in the Territory of Missouri were granted lands for the support of schools, the grant not to exceed one-twentieth of the area of the general town or village survey. [57] As a result of this act the public schools of St. Louis procured their first landed endowment.

[53] U. S. Stat. at Large, II, p. 381.
[54] Ibid, XXX, p. 484.
[55] Ibid, IX, p. 330.
[56] Ibid, XI, p. 385.
[57] Ibid, II, p. 750.

The fact that many of the school sections had been occupied by western pioneers long before a government survey had been made or even the grant itself enacted necessitated the passage of various special preëmption laws giving to the settlers the prior right to acquire title to the property they occupied. The first preëmption act [58] affecting school lands was that of March 3, 1803, in which all reservations in the territory south of the State of Tennessee, then the Territory of Mississippi, were made subject to such claim by settlers. Michigan school lands [59] were likewise open to preëmption, and settlers occupying lands in Illinois Territory before February 5, 1813, were entitled to preëmption rights in purchasing the same. [60] The school sections of Louisiana and the Territory of Missouri in 1814, [61] as well as those of Alabama, Mississippi and Florida in 1826, were subject to similar arrangements. [62] In 1834 Congress declared that all persons residing on public lands and cultivating the same prior to the year 1829 were authorized to enter at the minimum price one quarter-section. [63] Six years afterward another law provided that every settler on public lands which were not surveyed before June 18, 1838, and who resided on the sixteenth section set apart for the support of schools, in any township, was entitled to enter at the minimum price a quarter-section. [64] Without referring specifically to other preëmption laws it is sufficient to note that as late as 1891 settlers occupying school lands unknowingly, before a survey had been made, were vested with the prior right to purchase their holdings at the regular price. In lieu of these lands other sections of equal acreage were appropriated for school purposes. [65]

Mineral Lands Excluded from School Grants.—Prior to 1866 nothing was said as to the reservation of the mineral

[58] *U. S. Stat. at Large*, II, p. 229.
[59] *Ibid*, II, p. 502.
[60] *Ibid*, III, p. 218.
[61] *Ibid*, III, p. 122.
[62] *Ibid*, IV, p. 155.
[63] *Ibid*, p. 678.
[64] *Ibid*, V, p. 382.
[65] *Ibid*, XXVI, p. 796.

lands, consequently the schools in a number of states have benefited enormously because their landed property was found to contain valuable mineral deposits. Not until two years after Nevada was granted its school land, without restrictions as to mineral reservations, did Congress reserve from sale all lands in the state that were valuable for gold, silver, quicksilver, or copper. Although no indemnity provisions were made for school sections in these reservations, Nevada accepted the school-land grants with the mineral sections excluded. Again during the year 1880 the state agreed to receive 2,000,000 acres from the federal government in lieu of the 16th and 36th sections allotted to the schools. In 1864 Congress also gave to the state and its grantees full titles, without compensation, to such school sections as had been sold or disposed of prior to the passage of the exchange bill. The state officials were authorized to select lieu lands equivalent to the area thus lost from any unappropriated, non-mineral public land in the state.[66] With the exception of the Utah [67] and Oklahoma [68] grants, in 1894 and 1906 respectively, school sections have been debarred from mineral areas in all subsequent grants to the various states. In 1910 a somewhat similar provision was instituted, Congress ordering that there be reserved the school sections of Arizona and New Mexico, which were "valuable for the development of water power or power for hydroelectric use or transmission." [69] All reservations were to be made by the Secretary of the Interior within five years after the admission of the states into the Union, and lieu lands granted equal to the areas withdrawn as mineral.

Disposal of School Land by the States.—With the exception of the direct allotment of the sixteenth section to the township organizations in Indiana [70] and Alabama,[71] Con-

---

[66] *U. S. Stat. at Large,* XXI, p. 288.
[67] *Ibid,* XXVIII, p. 109.
[68] *Ibid,* XXXIV, p. 272.
[69] *Ibid,* XXXVI, pp. 564, 575.
[70] *Ibid,* III, p. 290.
[71] *Ibid,* III, p. 491.

gress, until March 3, 1845, when Florida was admitted into the Union,[72] granted directly to all the states, excepting Michigan, school lands for the use of the townships, vesting in the state legislatures the power of appropriating to the townships such amounts of money as their particular lands brought. In the case of the Michigan grants in 1836,[73] all that was said is that "section numbered 16 of every township of public lands . . . be granted to the state for the use of schools." Subsequent grants to that of Florida were made to the various states and territories, nothing being said about the townships.

Congress exercised complete control over the school sections in the territories, and it was not until their admission into the Union that the legislatures had the power to dispose of the land. However, during the Congressional tenure the governor and legislature of each of the states and territories of Florida,[74] Michigan,[75] Arkansas[76] and Arizona[77] were given the right to lease the school lands. In the case of Mississippi[78] the right to rent was granted, but was vested in agents appointed by the various county courts; in 1885 the Wyoming county commissioners were vested with the right to lease the territorial school lands.[79]

Even with a direct appropriation of the school property to the states, they were no better off than were townships supervising their allotments or even the territories subject to Congressional provisions, since no right to sell the domain had been stipulated in any of the grants and the only thing to do was to provide for renting the lands or else letting them remain idle and wait for an increase in value. Rather than do the latter a number of the states resorted to contracting the lands to tenants, as the only means by which returns might be realized.

[72] U. S. Stat. at Large, V, p. 788.
[73] Ibid, V, p. 59.
[74] Ibid, IV, p. 201.
[75] Ibid, IV, p. 314.
[76] Ibid, p. 329.
[77] Ibid, pp. 29, 90.
[78] Ibid, III, p. 163.
[79] Ibid, XXV, p. 393.

Various systems of renting the school lands were used, the first being a lease on which the lessee was to improve a portion of the land as payment for its use. This was done in order to enable the states to realize a greater price in disposing of the lands in the future.[80] A second method was simply the payment of cash rent for a specified period.[81] Then, too, leases were made for ninety-nine years, renewable forever, to the successful bidder, who, at a public auction, was to pay a cash bonus of a certain sum per acre; the interest on this bonus at a specified rate would, therefore, be the yearly rent paid for the period.[82] Later, lands rented on a long-time lease were subject to re-valuation at certain periods, the lessee paying either interest on an increased valuation of the property or a higher money rent per acre as the case might be.[83] After giving the various tenant systems a thorough test as to practicability, state after state petitioned Congress for the authority to sell the school lands.

The legislature of Ohio was the first body to send a memorial on this subject to Congress. On February 26, 1824, it petitioned that the state be granted authority to sell the school lands in the various townships, after having obtained the consent of their habitants, and that the proceeds therefrom be invested in some permanent fund for the use of the common schools within the townships.[84] In 1827 the legislatures of Alabama and Indiana, the only two states that had their school land granted directly to the townships, sent memorials to Washington asking that the townships be given the privilege of vesting in the legislature the right to sell their property and invest the money in some profitable fund.[85] Florida[86] petitioned the same year; Missouri,[87] two years later, sent in a memorial for the right to sell.

[80] *Laws of Ohio*, 1082, p. 61; *Laws of the Indiana Territory*, 1808, p. 36; *Laws of Indiana*, 1818, p. 301; 1819, p. 57.
[81] *Laws of Ind.*, 1825, p. 93; *Laws of Illinois*, 1819, p. 107; *Laws of Ohio*, 1805, p. 230.
[82] *Laws of Ohio*, 1809, p. 109.
[83] *Ibid*, 1815, p. 418.
[84] *Pub. Lands*, III, p. 569.
[85] *Ibid*, IV, pp. 891, 957.
[86] *Ibid*, V, p. 398.
[87] *Ibid*, V, p. 603.

The principal reasons enumerated in the various memorials asking for the right to sell were that the rental system was impracticable on account of the lands being detached and scattered all over the state, thus creating an expense for their supervision in many cases greater than the returns from the lands. The class of tenants who rented the lands were persons "almost wholly destitute of pecuniary means," paying low rents or no rents at all and at the same time depleting the soil and laying waste the timberland. The petitions acknowledged that on account of the abundance of free land it was impossible to maintain such a leasing system and at the same time compete with the federal government on its terms of selling public lands.[88]

In 1826 Congress granted Ohio the privilege of selling the school lands, but required that the proceeds be invested in some productive fund and that the consent of the townships for whose benefit the land had been given should be obtained before any land could be sold.[89] Similar laws enabled Alabama [90] in 1827, Indiana in 1828,[91] and Illinois, Arkansas, Louisiana and Tennessee in 1843 to sell their school lands. The enabling acts of the states yet to come into the Union provided for the disposition of school lands.[92] However, it was not until the granting of statehood to Colorado in 1875 that a specific restriction was placed on the sale of school reservations. The Colorado enabling act required that school property be sold at a public sale for not less than $2.50 per acre.[93] All states entering the Union since that date, with the exception of Utah, have been restricted in the sale of school allotments. Washington, Montana, North and South Dakota in 1889 and Idaho and Wyoming, admitted in 1890, were required to sell their school lands at public sales at a minimum price of not less than $10.00 per acre.[94] The enabling act of Oklahoma in 1907 provided that school lands

[88] *Pub. Lands,* III, p. 570; V, p. 603.
[89] *U. S. Stat. at Large,* IV, p. 138.
[90] *Ibid,* p. 237.
[91] *Ibid,* p. 299.
[92] Iowa, for instance, in 1846. *U. S. Stat. at Large,* IX, p. 349.
[93] *U. S. Stat. at Large,* XVIII, p. 476.
[94] *Ibid,* XXV, p. 679; XXVI, pp. 216, 223.

be sold at a price not less than the value appraised by disinterested persons living in another county than that in which
the land was located.[95]

At the time restrictions were placed on the sale of school
sections, in 1875, it was also deemed wise to require that all
states entering the Union after that date create a permanent
fund from the sale of the school lands and that only the
interest derived from its investment be used to support the
public schools.[96]

Nothing more specific was said about the investment of
the school funds until 1889, when Congress, as provided for
in the enabling acts of Washington, Montana and the
Dakotas, required that the funds be safely invested,[97] and
not until the admission of Arizona and New Mexico to statehood were states required to place the school land receipts
in the hands of the state treasurer to be invested in safe
interest-bearing securities subject to the approval of the governor and the secretary of state.[98]

The salt spring land grants to certain states have been
a means of adding a considerable sum of money to the
educational account accumulated through the endowment of
federal landed property. It is unnecessary to deal with the
historical development of this grant, since that has been discussed separately. The particular feature here pointed out
is that, with the exception of California, Florida, Louisiana,
Mississippi and Nevada, all the states admitted into the
Union from 1803 to 1875 were in receipt of reserved areas
for the working of salt springs. Congress, in authorizing
the various state legislatures to sell the salt lands, provided
in the case of Ohio that the "proceeds be applied to such
literary purposes as the legislature might hereafter direct,
and to no other use, intent or purpose whatsoever." [99] The
Missouri and Indiana legislatures were directed to invest the

[95] U. S. Stat. at Large, XXXIV, p. 273.

[96] Ibid, XVIII, p. 476; XXV, p. 679; XXVI, pp. 216-223; XXVIII, p. 110;
XXXIV, p. 273; XXXVI, pp. 563-573.

[97] Ibid, XXV, p. 680.

[98] Ibid, XXXVI, pp. 564, 575.

[99] Ibid, IV, p. 79.

money derived from the sale of the salt springs and adjacent lands in a productive fund, the proceeds of which were to be forever applied for the purpose of education.[100] Other states having saline grants were permitted at various times to sell their lands and dispose of the proceeds on such terms and regulations as the legislature should direct.

Ohio,[101] Missouri,[102] Arkansas and Nebraska added the proceeds from the sales of saline lands to their permanent common school funds. Indiana[103] applied hers to a fund for graded schools. Saline grants in these five states were:

TABLE XVIII

SALINE GRANTS

State	Acreage	Date of Grant
Ohio	24,216	April 30, 1802
Indiana	23,040	April 19, 1816
Missouri	23,040	March 6, 1820
Arkansas	46,080	April 23, 1836
Nebraska	46,080	April 19, 1864

Swamp Land for School Purposes.—The educational funds derived from the sale of swamp lands granted by the federal government have been very considerable in twelve of the fifteen swamp-land states. The amount of the swamp-land fund which was granted for educational purposes varies greatly with the different states. Although the original purpose of Congress was for these funds to be used in the drainage of the swamps, most of them have been used for other purposes. Some states used a part of the fund for internal improvements, such as the building of roads and bridges, but it seems safe to say that more went for education than for any other one purpose. Thus Alabama used her entire fund for educational purposes.[104] Minnesota set aside one-half of the fund for common schools and one-half to other educational and charitable institutions.[105] Mississippi gave

---

[104] *Constitution of Alabama*, 1867, Art. XI, Sec. 10.
[100] *Ibid*, IV, 558 and *Laws of U. S.*, VIII, p. 501.
[101] *Laws of Ohio*, 1827, p. 78.
[102] *Laws of Mo.*, 1837.
[103] *Laws of Indiana*, 1834, p. 326.
[105] *Constitution of Minnesota*, 1857, Art. VIII, Sec. 2.

the fund over to the common schools with the exception of
the money received from the sale of swamp lands on the
Pearl River.[106]   Indiana [107] and Ohio [108] specified that such
funds as are left over after drainage expenses are covered
shall go to the school fund of the state. Louisiana [109] and
Florida [110] were quite indefinite as to the use which should
be made of the swamp-land funds, while Illinois [111] turned
the money over to the counties to be used for drainage levees
and "whatever is left over to go for educational purposes or
for any other purpose which the counties should decide on."
Wisconsin gave some of the fund to the common schools and
some to the state normal schools.[112]   Other states which gave
a part of the swamp-land funds for educational purposes
were Michigan,[113] Missouri[114] and Oregon.[115]

It is impossible to ascertain just the amounts of these
funds which were used for educational purposes since separate accounts have not been kept by the state auditors as
to this particular source of school revenue, but a considerable
amount has accrued in most of these twelve states, and
the greater part has usually been given to the common
schools.

*The Half Million Acre and the Five and Three Per Cent
Grants.*—Of the states receiving grants of 500,000 acres for
internal improvements five, California,[116] Iowa,[117] Nevada,[118]
Oregon [119] and Wisconsin,[120] have appropriated the receipts
from the sale of such lands to the support of common schools.
In each case, by constitutional enactment, it was provided that

[106] *Constitution of Mississippi,* 1868, Art. V.
[107] *Constitution of Indiana,* 1851, Art. VIII, Sec. 2.
[108] *Laws of Ohio,* XLIX,, p. 40; LI, p. 357.
[109] *Constitution of Louisiana,* 1845, Title VII, Art. 135.
[110] *Constitution of Florida,* 1868, Art. IX, Sec. 4.
[111] *Laws of Illinois,* 1852, p. 178.
[112] *Laws of Wisconsin,* 1856, p. 112; 1857, p. 93; 1858, p. 68.
[113] *Laws of Michigan,* 1858, p. 171.
[114] *Laws of Missouri,* 1858, p. 149.
[115] *School Laws of Oregon,* 1897, p. 47.
[116] *Constitution of California,* 1850, Art. IX, Sec. 2.
[117] *Constitution of Iowa,* 1846, Art. IX, Sec. 2.
[118] *Constitution of Nevada,* 1864, Art. IX, Sec. 3.
[119] *Constitution of Oregon,* 1859, Art. VIII, Sec. 2.
[120] *Constitution of Wisconsin,* 1849, Art. X. Sec. 2.

the proceeds derived from the sales should be paid into the school fund.

Federal money grants from the sale of public lands have done much to foster the cause of common school education. Nineteen [121] of the twenty-nine public land states were beneficiaries of the five per cent fund, using the money mainly for common schools, while Illinois received three per cent of the net receipts from the sale of public lands within the state and used it similarly. The following table will indicate the public land states which received such funds and used them mainly for common school purposes: [122]

TABLE XIX
FIVE AND THREE PER CENT GRANTS

State	Date of Grant	Per Cent	Aggregate to June 30, 1920, Inclusive
Arizona	June 20, 1910	5	$ 27,520.23
California	June 27, 1906	5	1,148,213.97
Florida [123]	March 3, 1845	5	144,061.13
Idaho	July 3, 1890	5	290,793.55
Illinois	Dec. 12, 1820	3	1,187,908.89
Iowa	March 3, 1845	5	633,638.10
Kansas	Jan. 29, 1861	5	1,127,987.59
Michigan	June 23, 1836	5	588,697.25
Montana	Feb. 22, 1889	5	565,081.10
Nebraska	April 19, 1864	5	574,157.87
Nevada	Mar. 21, 1864	5	43,476.58
New Mexico	June 20, 1910	5	142,930.23
North Dakota	Feb. 22, 1889	5	538,834.53
Oklahoma	June 16, 1906	5	65,763.81
Oregon	Feb. 14, 1859	5	755,502.27
South Dakota	Feb. 22, 1889	5	345,723.08
Utah	July 16, 1894	5	145,757.84
Washington	Feb. 22, 1889	5	429,291.98
Wisconsin [124]	Mar. 3, 1847	5	586,645.26
Wyoming	July 10, 1890	5	295,629.53

[121] See *U. S. Stat. at Large* under date of each grant.
[122] *L. O. R.*, 1921, p. 85.
[123] Common schools not specified—given for "educational purposes."
[124] See Const. of Wis., 1848. These funds for Wisconsin were: (1) for common schools; (2) Residue to academies and normal schools.

In 1841 Congress granted to Louisiana ten per cent of the net proceeds of the sales of public lands within that state independent of any other grant; the state, by a constitutional provision, set its receipts aside as a fund for the common schools.[125]

TABLE XX

FEDERAL LAND GRANTS BY SECTIONS TO STATES FOR COMMON SCHOOLS [126]

State	Date of Reservation and Grant [127]	Section	Area in Acres [128]
Alabama	March 2, 1819		
	March 3, 1903.......	16	911,627.00
Arizona [129]	May 26, 1864.......	2, 16, 32, 36	8,093,156.00
	June 10, 1910		
Arkansas	June 23, 1836.......	16	933,778.00
California	March 3, 1853.......	16, 36	5,534,293.00
Colorado	March 21, 1864		
	March 3, 1875.......	16, 36	3,685,618.00
Florida	June 15, 1844.......	16	975,307.00
	June 3, 1845		
Idaho	March 3, 1863.......	16, 36	2,963,698.00
	July 3, 1890		
Illinois	April 18, 1818.......	16	996,320.00
Indiana	April 19, 1816.......	16	668,578.00
Iowa	June 15, 1844.......	16	988,196.00
	March 3, 1845		
Kansas	January 29, 1861.....	16, 36	2,907,520.00
Louisiana	April 2, 1806.......	16	807,271.00
Michigan	June 23, 1836.......	16	1,021,867.00
Minnesota	February 26, 1857.....	16, 36	2,874,951.00
Mississippi	March 3, 1803.......	16	824,213.00
	May 19, 1852		
Missouri	March 6, 1820.......	16	1,221,813.00
Montana	February 28, 1861.....	16, 36	5,198,258.00
	May 26, 1864		
	February 22, 1889		
Nebraska	April 19, 1864.......	16, 36	2,730,951.00
Nevada	March 21, 1864.....	16, 36	2,061,967.00

[125] *Const. of La.*, 1845, Title VII, Art. 135.
[126] Bureau of Education, Department of Interior, *Bulletin*, 1922, No. 47, p. 14
[127] *U. S. Stat. at Large.*
[128] *L. O. R.*, 1922, pp. 34-39.
[129] *Report* of the State Land Office of Arizona, 1914.

TABLE XX (*Continued*)

State	Date of Reservation and Grant	Section	Area in Acres
New Mexico	September 9, 1850 July 22, 1854 June 20, 1910	2, 16, 32, 36	8,711,324.00
North Dakota	March 2, 1861 February 22, 1889	16, 36	2,495,396.00
Ohio	March 3, 1803 May 2, 1890	16	724,266.00
Oklahoma *	June 16, 1906	16, 36	1,375,000.00
Oregon	February 14, 1859	16, 36	3,399,360.00
South Dakota	March 2, 1861 February 22, 1889	16, 36	2,733,084.00
Utah	September 9, 1850 July 16, 1894	2, 16, 32, 36	5,844,196.00
Washington	March 2, 1853 February 22, 1889	16, 36	2,376,391.00
Wisconsin	August 6, 1846	16	982,329.00
Wyoming	July 15, 1868 July 10, 1890	16, 36	3,470,009.00

Total 73,155,075.00

* $5,000,000 appropriated for common schools in lieu of Indian Territory lands.

TABLE XXI

SUMMARY OF FEDERAL GRANTS FOT COMMON SCHOOLS

State	Saline acres	Swamp-lands [130] acres	One-half [131] mill. acre	5 and 3% grants in dollars	Grants by section No. acres
Alabama		439,554			911,627
Arizona				$ 27,520	8,103,680
Arkansas	46,080				933,778
California			500,000	1,148,214	5,534,293
Colorado					3,685,618

[130] Only a part of the swamp-land grants was used for educational purposes, but the larger portion of the funds which were used in, this way went to the common schools. The figures given here indicate the total acreage granted for drainage, for educational purposes and for internal improvements. See *Bulletin*, Bureau of Education, 1922, No. 47, p. 14.

[131] The proceeds from the sale of these lands rather than the land itself went into the school fund.

TABLE XXI (*Continued*)

State	Saline acres	Swamplands acres	One-half mill. acre	5 and 3% grants in dollars	Grants by section No. acres
Florida	......	20,296,443	......	144,061	975,307
Idaho	......	......	......	290,794	2,693,698
Illinois	......	1,457,708	......	1,187,909	996,320
Indiana	23,040	1,259,151	......	......	668,578
Iowa	......	......	500,000	633,638	988,196
Kansas	......	......	......	1,127,988	2,907,520
Louisiana	......	9,413,201	......	......	807,271
Michigan	......	5,679,848	......	588,697	1,021,867
Minnesota	......	4,662,967	......	......	2,874,951
Mississippi	......	3,342,641	......	......	824,213
Missouri	23,040	3,427,700	......	......	1,221,813
Montana	......	......	......	565,081	5,198,258
Nebraska	......	......	......	574,157	2,730,951
Nevada	......	......	500,000	43,477	2,061,967
New Mexico	......	......	......	142,930	8,711,324
North Dakota	......	......	......	538,835	2,495,396
Ohio	24,216	26,252	......	......	724,266
Oklahoma	......	......	......	65,764	1,385,174
Oregon	......	264,069	500,000	755,502	3,399,360
South Dakota	......	......	......	345,723	2,733,084
Utah	......	......	......	145,758	5,844,196
Washington	......	......	......	429,292	2,376,391
Wisconsin	......	3,256,612	500,000	586,645	982,329
Wyoming	......	......	......	295,629	3,470,009

GRANTS FOR AGRICULTURAL AND MECHANIC ARTS COLLEGES

Before entering upon a discussion of grants in support of agricultural and mechanic arts colleges it is essential to give a brief résumé of the general conditions and events which had to do with this, the greatest of all landed endowments, in the cause of higher education.

Early State Efforts to Establish "Colleges for Scientific Education."—Until the middle of the nineteenth century efforts to establish colleges for scientific education had been carried on solely by private initiative. A few small agricultural schools existed under the support of private donation, but nowhere could an institution for the advancement of agriculture and mechanic arts be found that received support from the state, to say nothing of the nation. However, during this period popular sentiment was leaning more and more in the direction of practical education. Numerous petitions were sent various state legislatures asking for the appropriation of means to establish agricultural schools and experiment farms as well as to establish agricultural courses in the existing educational institutions. Various societies published reports favoring state aid; everywhere there was a call for the practical application of theoretical training. But not until the year 1850 did Michigan, thus paving the way for industrial education, provide by a constitutional stipulation that "the legislature should encourage the promotion of intellectual, scientific and agricultural improvement, and as soon as practicable provide for the establishment of an agricultural school." [132]

On February 10, 1855, such a law was passed and at the same time twenty-two sections of the salt spring lands that had previously been granted to the state by the federal government were appropriated for its upkeep.[133] Two years later buildings of the Michigan Agricultural College were erected near Lansing and instruction started.[134] The same year that the Michigan law went into effect the Senate of Massachusetts passed a bill for a similar purpose, but it failed in the House. Again in 1856 the measure was presented and passed with little opposition, which fact led to the founding of the Massachusetts Agricultural College.[135] In the same year, also, the legislature of Maryland passed an act to establish and endow an agricultural college "in which the youthful student could especially be instructed in those arts and sciences indispensable to successful agriculture pursuits." [136] The general assembly of Pennsylvania, by an act of 1854, appropriated funds for building and equipping

[132] *Constitution of Michigan,* 1850, Art. 13, Sec. 11.
[133] *Laws of Mich.,* 1855, p. 279.
[134] *Report of the U. S. Commissioner of Agriculture,* 185, p. 165.
[135] *Acts and Resolves of Massachusetts,* 1856, p. 152.
[136] *Laws of Maryland,* 1856, p. 114.

the Farmers' High School, which is now the State College.[137]

The Iowa legislature in 1858 passed an act providing for the establishment of a state agricultural college and farm, and at the same time appropriated to it the proceeds of the sale of five sections of land that had been granted to the state by Congress for the purpose of erecting a capitol.[138]

As the new branch of education gained recognition locally, means for its support were not only asked from the state, but the federal government was petitioned for tracts of the public domain to be donated toward its upkeep. However, a number of the states preceded the nation as donors.

Petitions from State Legislatures Asking for State Lands.—The first state to send a petition to Congress asking for a grant of land in support of a state college of agriculture and mechanic arts was Michigan. The request was made in 1850 for 350,000 acres.[139]

In 1852 Massachusetts asked that "a national normal agricultural college" be established by means of a landed endowment, the institution to be "to the rural sciences what West Point Academy is to the military, for the purpose of educating teachers and professors for service in all of the states." [140]

The New York legislature the same year sent the following memorial to Congress asking that all the states be granted public lands for the purpose of education:

"Resolved, by unanimous consent of both House and Senate, that the public land of the federal government having been obtained by grant from individual states, or by conquest, or by purchase, and by the terms of said grants and the nature of said purchase and conquests, the joint and common property of the states are held in trust by the general government, as the common fund for the use and benefit of all the states, and should be faithfully and fairly disposed of for that purpose.

[137] *Laws of Pennsylvania*, 1854, p. 342.
[138] *Laws of Iowa*, 1858, p. 173.
[139] *Laws of Mich.*, 1850, p. 462.
[140] *Acts and Resolves of Mass.*, 1852, p. 285.

"Resolved, That while we approve of the policy that has been adopted of liberal grants to the new states for the purposes of education and internal improvement, we deem it just to the old states to share also in these grants of land for the same public purposes, and we claim for New York her just and rightful share of the domain acquired by the blood and treasure of all the states.

"Resolved, That in consideration of the grants made to the new states at the time of and since their admission into the Union, and of the many applications now made for still further appropriations for railroads and internal improvements, that our Senators and Representatives be requested to urge upon that body the propriety of making grants of land upon some equal and just principle of appropriation to all the states for the purpose of education and for other public purposes, having due regard to the grants already made and the population of the respective states." [141]

In 1853 the legislature of Illinois passed resolutions in which the representatives of that state in Congress were instructed "to use their best exertions to procure the passage by Congress of a law donating to each state in the Union an amount of public land not less in value than $500,000 for the liberal endowment of a system of Industrial Universities, one in each state." Copies of the resolutions were sent to the governor and legislature of each of the other states, and they were invited to coöperate in promoting the enterprise. [142]

Again in the early part of 1858 the legislature of Michigan sent a memorial to Congress praying for a land grant to support the agricultural college. [143] The following year the legislature of Iowa asked for a grant of land for the support of agricultural colleges and scientific agriculture. [144]

On the presentation of the various petitions of the state legislatures in both Houses of Congress they were referred to the Committee on Public Lands or else ordered to lie on

[141] *New York Senate Journal*, 1852, p. 417.
[142] *Illinois House Journal*, 1853, p. 416; *Cong. Globe*, 33 Cong., 1 Sess., p. 686.
[143] *Laws of Mich.*, 1858, p. 194.
[144] *Iowa Sen. Jol.*, 1858, p. 348.

the table and be printed. Although no immediate action resulted from the communications received from states, both north and south, from state agricultural societies, from county agricultural societies, and from individuals, yet at the same time a strong sentiment grew in favor of granting landed property to the states.[145] No doubt the real motive back of these petitions was the establishment of a practical educational system, although it was very evident that a number of the states and particularly those not having received a land grant, merely used the college as a means of obtaining a portion of the public domain. This seemed to be their best opportunity, and perhaps their only one, of receiving an endowment of public lands, since the federal government was rapidly disposing of the western domain.

The Act of 1862.—The real issue of the agricultural and mechanic arts land grant culminated in the year 1857, when the friends of the movement secured the interest and co-operation of Justin S. Morrill, a member of the House of Representatives from the State of Vermont, who, being enthusiastic in the cause of agricultural advancement, introduced a bill in the House asking that public lands be donated "to the several states which may provide colleges for the benefit of Agriculture and the Mechanic Arts." [146] The bill specified that each state be granted, for the purpose just mentioned, 30,000 acres of public land for each senator and representative in Congress to which the state was entitled. If the state did not contain sufficient public land for the grant, or none at all, it was to receive an equivalent amount of land scrip, which must be sold to private individuals who would then locate the lands in the unoccupied areas of the public land states according to the amount of scrip purchased.

The bill at the time of its presentation was immediately referred to the Committee on Public Lands and after remain-

---

[145] *Cong. Globe,* 35 Cong., 1 Sess., p. 1692.

[146] *Ibid,* p. 32. The credit for originating the idea is probably due largely to Jonathan B. Turner of Illinois. See J. H. Bailey, *Cyclopedia of American Agriculture* IV, 408.

ing in the hands of this committee four months, was reported back to the House with the strongest recommendation that it should not pass,[147] and was branded as inexpedient and unconstitutional. On being taken up by the two Houses much opposition was also encountered, yet, strictly speaking, it was a contest between the North and the South on the constitutional interpretation of the bill. At the same time a number of the members from the public land states strenuously opposed the measure on the ground that large quantities of land scrip issued to the old states would very likely be procured by land speculators and located on large tracts of the best land of the new states, and would then be held until values had increased, by which settlement and improvement would be retarded.

The bill provided that within a period of five years after its passage a college must be established. To this the objection was entered that all the scrip would necessarily have to be sold during that period, thus causing an immediate depreciation in value, and, in consequence, the public domain would be thrown entirely into the hands of the consignees of the scrip for speculative purposes.[148] After considerable discussion the bill passed the House on April 22, 1858, by a vote of 105 to 100.[149]

Although the bill passed both houses by a small majority, sufficient influence had not been brought to bear upon President Buchanan to induce him to sign the measure. He was ready with a veto in explanation of which he offered the following reasons: [150]

1.—The measure if passed would deprive the government of a great share of the revenue derived from the sale of public lands and make it extremely difficult to meet current expenses.

[147] *Cong. Globe*, 35 Cong., 1 Sess., 52, p. 1609.
[148] *Ibid*, 2 Sess., 715. The vote by sections showed in the House for the bill: North 82, South 5; against the bill: North 27, South 63. In the Senate the vote stood for the bill: North 21, South 4; against, North 4, South 17.
[149] *Ibid*, 35 Cong., 1 Sess., p. 1742.
[150] *Ibid*, 35 Cong., 2 Sess., pp. 1412, 1413.

2.—The grant would have a tendency to make the states dependent upon the federal government for support and would likely lead to extravagance, if not to corruption.

3.—It would work an injury to the new states by decreasing land values and placing the land in the hands of speculators, thus keeping out the immigrant.

4.—It was doubted as to whether the bill would contribute much to the advancement of agriculture and mechanic arts, since the state legislatures to whom the land or land scrip was entrusted could not be compelled to use the funds as specified.

5.—The grant would interfere with the existing educational institutions by creating rivalry and friction among them as to which one should receive the endowment and at the same time be creating an unnecessary duplication of school work.

6.—He believed the act to be unconstitutional.

After the President vetoed the bill, a vote was taken in the House for its reconsideration with a count of 105 to 96 favoring such action,[151] thus failing of the required two-thirds majority.

Undaunted by the veto, Representative Morrill launched forth with renewed effort for the passage of a bill similar in outline to that of the first measure, and on December 16, 1861, presented a second document for the consideration of the law-making body. After the bill had been referred to and considered by the Committee on Public Lands, it was sent back with a recommendation that it should not pass.[152] On March 5, 1862, Senator Wade of Ohio introduced a similar bill into the Senate two weeks before the rejection of the measure by the Public Lands Committee.[153]

With most of the strict constructionists fighting their own battles outside the federal chambers, the discussion primarily centered itself between the new public land states

---

[151] *Cong. Globe*, 35 Cong., 2 Sess., p. 1414.
[152] *Ibid*, 37 Cong., 2 Sess., p. 2432.
[153] *Ibid*, pp. 1935, 2187.

and the older states of the East. The issues were practically the same as before. The old states, however, made particular efforts to secure the passage of the bill, due to the fact that the enactment of the Homestead Law, then assured, would materially reduce their chance to acquire title to western lands.

The new states fought the bill insistently, predicting evil effects of land speculation and absentee landlordism,[154] and it was largely through their efforts that the amendment of Senator Lane from Kansas passed both Houses. This amendment provided that not more than 1,000,000 acres be located by the assignees in any one state, and that no such location be made before one year from the passage of the act.[155]

Other amendments were proposed which limited the amount of scrip certificates held by any one person to 640 acres,[156] and extended the time at which the act should take effect to July 1, 1864.[157] Both suggestions, however, were defeated. Although only twenty of the representatives voting for the bill in 1858 were in Congress in 1862, the measure encountered comparatively little opposition.[158]

The act granting public lands to the several states and territories, enabling them to establish colleges for the benefit of agriculture and the mechanic arts, was approved by President Lincoln on July 2, 1862. The principal features of the act were as follows: That there be granted to each state an amount of public land equal to 30,000 acres for each Senator and Representative to which the state was entitled under the 1860 census.[159]

All money derived from the sale of land or land scrip was to be invested in safe stocks constituting a perpetual fund, the interest from which was not to be less than five per cent

[154] *Cong. Globe*, 37 Cong., 2 Sess., pp. 2248, 2395.
[155] *Ibid*, pp. 2625-2628.
[156] *Ibid*, pp. 2627-2630.
[157] *Ibid*, p. 2630.
[158] *Ibid*, pp. 2634, 2770.
[159] The southern states availed themselves of the advantages of the act after 1865.

on the par value of the stock, and which was to be used for "the endowment, support and maintenance of at least one college, where the leading subjects should be, not excluding other scientific and classical studies, and including military tactics, such branches of learning as are related to agriculture and mechanic arts, in such manner as the legislatures of the states may prescribe, in order to promote the liberal and practical education of the industrial classes in the permanent pursuits and professions of life."

States containing an insufficient amount of public land within their borders were to receive, instead of the landed property, a corresponding amount of land scrip. Such scrip was to be sold and the assignee given the right of locating it upon any of the unappropriated lands open to private entry at $1.25 per acre, but in no case was it to be allotted in tracts less than a quarter-section. No land was to be located before the expiration of one year after the passage of the act; all mineral lands were excluded from entry; and no more than 1,000,000 acres were to be selected in any one state. Lands selected from those raised to double the minimum price in consequence of railroad grants counted double. Only ten per cent of the total amount received from the grant could be expended for the purchase of sites or experiment farms, the other ninety per cent to remain free from any incumbrance.

In order to receive the benefits of the act each state legislature must express acceptance of the provisions of the act within two years and establish at least one college within five years, and at the same time have full standing in the Union, "as no state in a condition of rebellion or insurrection against the government could be entitled to the benefits of the act."

It was soon found necessary to extend the time allowed for accepting the act; also to extend the privilege of establishing land-grant colleges to states just entering the Union.[160] Nevada failed to adhere to the requirements of the act,

[160] *U. S. Stat. at Large,* XIV, p. 208.

owing to peculiar conditions existing in that state, and was exempted from meeting immediate stipulations.[161] Not only Nevada, but other states, failed to establish a college within the required time,[162] and again Congress extended the period to a date not later than July 1, 1874.

The Morrill Act of 1890 and the Amendment of 1903.— Second in importance to the land, or land scrip, granted for the support of industrial education, was a bill passed by Congress August 30, 1890, and known as the Second Morrill Act. This bill provided that there should be appropriated annually to each state and territory out of the proceeds arising from the sale of public lands, "for the more complete endowment and maintenance of colleges for the benefit of Agriculture and Mechanic Arts," a sum of $15,000 for the year ending 1890 and an annual increase by an additional sum of $1,000 for a period of ten years, until such appropriation had become $25,000, after which it should remain fixed.

In 1903 a supplementary provision relative to the act of 1890 was passed by Congress, declaring that in case the annual sale of public lands were insufficient to meet this appropriation, such should be paid from the United States Treasury.

The following tables will give information concerning the amount and location of scrip lands, and the administration of the law of 1862 with later amendments.

TABLE XXII

SCRIP LANDS, AND LOCATIONS BY STATES [163]

State	Received	Located Within
Alabama	240,000	
Arizona		690
Arkansas	150,000	1,920
California		1,397,760
Colorado		238,560
Connecticut	180,000	

[161] *U. S. Stat. at Large,* XVII, p. 40.

[162] *Ibid,* p. 417.

[163] *Report* of the Pub. Land Com., specially appointed by President Roosevelt in 1903 "to make a complete survey of the public land system and to recommend changes." See *Sen. Doc.,* 58th Cong., 3rd Sess., No. 189.

TABLE XXII (*Continued*)

State	Received	Located Within
Delaware	90,000	
Florida	90,000	160
Georgia	270,000	
Idaho		160
Illinois	480,000	
Indiana	390,000	
Iowa		259,040
Kansas		874,240
Kentucky	330,000	
Louisiana	210,000	160
Maine	210,000	
Maryland	210,000	
Massachusetts	360,000	
Michigan		957,440
Minnesota		940,000
Mississippi	210,000	480
Missouri		201,120
Montana		97,440
Nebraska		1,139,200
Nevada		2,560
New Hampshire	150,000	
New Jersey	210,000	
New Mexico		3,680
New York	990,000	
North Carolina	270,000	
North Dakota		4,800
Ohio	630,000	
Oregon		70,240
Pennsylvania	780,000	
Rhode Island	120,000	
South Carolina	180,000	
South Dakota		195,040
Tennessee	300,000	
Texas	180,000	
Utah		91,200
Vermont	150,000	
Virginia	300,000	
Washington		62,400
West Virginia	150,000	
Wisconsin		1,131,200
Wyoming		3,040

TABLE XXIII. — ADMINISTRATION OF LANDS GRANTED TO AGRICULTURAL AND MECHANIC ARTS COLLEGES BY THE ACT OF 1862

STATE OR TERRITORY	INSTITUTION	LOCATION	DATE OF OPENING OF INST.	NUMBER OF ACRES ALLOTTED BY ACT OF 1862 [164]	NUMBER OF ACRES ACTUALLY RECEIVED WHERE DIFFERENT FROM ALLOTMENT [165]	RECEIPTS FROM LAND SOLD [166]	PRICE PER ACRE	NUMBER OF ACRES UNSOLD [167]	YEARLY INCOME 1917–1918 [168]	LOCATION OF SCRIP
Alabama	Ala. Polytechnic Institute	Auburn	1872	240,000*		$253,500	$1.06		$20,280	
Arizona	Arizona University	Tucson	1891	150,000*			.88	150,000	17,789	960
Arkansas	Univ. of Arkansas	Fayetteville	1872	150,000*		132,667	4.93		6,183	1,920
California	Univ. of California	Berkeley	1869	150,000*		732,485	2.25	1,402	40,484	1,397,760
Colorado	Agric. College	Fort Collins	1879	90,000*		202,784	.75	40,000	17,025	238,560
Connecticut	Agric. College	Storrs	1881	180,000*		135,000	.92		6,750	
Delaware	Delaware College	Newark	1834	90,000		83,000	1.71		4,980	
Florida	Univ. of Florida	Gairsville	1884	90,000		153,800	.90		7,790	160
Georgia	State Col. of Agr.	Athens	1872	270,000*		242,202	7.78		16,954	
Idaho	Univ. of Idaho	Moscow	1892	90,000**		700,000	1.35		43,956	160
Illinois	Univ. of Illinois	Urbana	1868	480,000		649,013	.87		32,450	
Indiana	Purdue University	Lafayette	1874	390,000*		340,000			17,000	
Iowa	Iowa State Col. of Agr. and Mechanic Arts	Ames	1868	240,000**	204,309	689,530	3.37		33,904	259,040
Kansas	State Agricultural College	Manhattan	1863	90,000*		491,747	5.97	7,686	24,877	874,240
Kentucky	State University	Lexington	1866	330,000*		144,075	.44		8,645	
Louisiana	State Univ. Agr. and Mech. College	Baton Rouge	1860	210,000**	209,920	182,313	.87		9,116	160
Maine	Univ. of Maine	Orono	1868	210,000*		118,200	.56		5,915	
Maryland	Agri. College	College Park	1859	210,000*		115,944	.55		6,543	
Massachusetts	Agri. College	Amherst	1867	360,000*		219,000	.61		7,300	
Massachusetts	Inst. of Technology	Boston	1865	Given under Massachusetts Agric. College					3,650	
Michigan	Agr. College	East Lansing	1857	240,000**	235,665	996,241	4.23	50,359	70,502	957,440
Minnesota	Univ. of Minnesota	Minneapolis	1868	120,000**	94,439	579,430	6.14		19,358	940,000

TABLE XXIII. — ADMINISTRATION OF LANDS GRANTED TO AGRICULTURAL AND MECHANIC ARTS COLLEGES BY THE ACT OF 1862 — Continued

State or Territory	Institution	Location	Date of Opening of Inst.	Number of Acres Allotted by Act of 1862 [154]	Number of Acres Actually Received Where Different from Allotment [155]	Receipts from Land Sold [156]	Price per Acre	Number of Acres Unsold [168]	Yearly Income 1917–1918 [157]	Location of Scrip
Mississippi	Agr. and Mech. Agri.	College	1880	210,000*	209,920	98,575	.47		5,915	480
Missouri	Univ. of Missouri	Columbia	1841	330,000**	277,067	365,881	1.32	47,287	18,355	201,120
Montana	State College of Ag. and M. A.	Bozeman	1893	140,000**	138,954	680,250	4.90	63,085	42,862	97,440
Nebraska	Univ. of Nebraska	Lincoln	1871	90,000**		617,131	6.86	8,396	38,005	1,139,200
Nevada	Univ. of Nevada	Reno	1886	90,000**		121,186	1.35		6,411	2,560
New Hampshire	College of Agr. and Mech. Arts	Durham	1867	150,000*		80,000	.53		4,800	
New Jersey	Rutgers Scientific School	NewBrunswick	1864	210,000*		116,000	.55		5,800	
New Mexico [169]	College of Agr. and Mech. Arts	State College	1891	150,000**						
New York	Cornell University	Ithaca	1868	990,000*	989,920	688,576	.70	141,909	34,429	3,680
North Carolina	College of Agr. and Mech. Arts	West Raleigh	1889	270,000**		125,000	.46	30,406	7,500	
North Dakota	Agr. College	Agr. College	1891	130,000**		1,323,777	10.90		73,181	4,800
Ohio	Ohio State Univ.	Columbus	1870	630,000**	629,000	524,176	.83		31,451	
Oklahoma	Agr. and Mech. College	Stillwater	1891	250,000**				250,000	37,000	
Oregon	Ore. Agr. College	Corvallis	1870	90,000**	89,908	202,664	2.28	920	10,973	
Pennsylvania	Pa. State College	State College	1859	780,000**		517,000	.66		30,000	70,240
Rhode Island	R. I. State College	Kingston	1890	120,000*		50,000	.42		2,500	
So. Carolina	Clemson Agr. Ccl.	Clemson	1893	180,000*		95,900	.53		5,754	
So. Dakota	S. D. State Col. of Agr. and M. A.	Brookings	1884	160,000**		390,941	2.44	141,138	40,285	
Tennessee	Univ. of Tennessee	Knoxville	1794	300,000*		400,000	1.33		23,960	195,040[170]

TABLE XXIII. — Administration of Lands Granted to Agricultural and Mechanic Arts Colleges by the Act of 1862 — *Continued*

State or Territory	Institution	Location	Date of Opening of Inst.	Number of Acres Allotted by Act of 1862 [164]	Number of Acres Actually Received Where Different from Allotment [165]	Receipts from Land Sold [166]	Price per Acre	Number of Acres Unsold [167]	Yearly Income 1917–1918 [168]	Location of Scrip
Texas	Agr. and Mech. Arts College	College Station	1876	180,000*		209,000			10,450	
Utah	Agr. Col. of Utah	Logan	1890	200,000**		189,657[171]	1.16	515	14,055	91,200
Vermont	Univ. of Vt. and State Agr. Col.	Burlington	1800	150,000*	149,920	135,000	.90		8,130	
Virginia	A. and Poly. Inst.	Blacksburg	1872	300,000**		344,312	1.15		20,659	
Washington	State College	Pullman	1892	90,000**	89,438	349,627	3.91	77,870	54,516	62,400
West Virginia	W. Va. University	Morgantown	1868	150,000*		115,104	.77		7,012	
Wisconsin	Univ. of Wisconsin	Madison	1849	240,000**	240,005	303,595	1.27	40	13,613	1,131,200
Wyoming	Univ. of Wyoming	Laramie	1887	90,000**	89,832	54,725	.61	74,695	16,032	3,040

164 *Bulletin*, 1920, No. 8. Department of Interior, Bureau of Education, pp. 39–40.

165 *Ibid*, pp. 79, 80.

166 *Ibid*, pp. 63, 64.

167 *Ibid*, pp. 39, 40.

168 *Ibid*, pp. 79, 80.

169 *Report of the Commissioner of Public Lands of New Mexico*, 1914, pp. 8–13.

170 *Report* of Commissioner of Public Lands of South Dakota, 1914, pp. 34–64–76.

171 This figure is given in Commissioner of Education *Report* 1917, II, 391.

* These states received scrip.

** These states got lands directly.

GRANTS FOR UNIVERSITIES, SEMINARIES, NORMAL SCHOOLS,
AND PRIVATE SCHOOLS

*The Donation of Two Townships by Ordinance of 1787
and Similar Subsequent Grants.*—In tracing the history of
the development of Congressional land grants in aid of higher
education, reference has already been made to colonial precedents and the provisions cited for the reservation of three
townships of land to support higher institutions of learning
in the Ohio Territory,—two townships having been set aside
in the tract sold to the Ohio Company in 1787 and one in
the area purchased by John Cleves Symmes the same year.
Those grants, together with those of a Colonial date, proved
to be the actual genesis of the nation's plan of establishing
institutions of advanced learning.

Other grants soon followed. In 1804 Congress, passing
an act providing for the disposal of the public lands in the
Indiana Territory which then comprised all of the northwest
section excepting Ohio, specified that there should be reserved
for the use of a seminary of learning an entire township
in each of the three districts of which Detroit, Vincennes
and Kaskaskia were the respective centers.[172]

A somewhat similar provision was made the following
year when Congress, in arranging for the disposition of
land south of the State of Tennessee, reserved "36 sections
to be located in one body by the Secretary of the Treasury
for the use of Jefferson College," and a lot not to exceed
thirty acres in the town of Natchez, to be set aside by the
governor of Mississippi for that institution.[173]

The first direct grant of land to a state for higher education was the area appropriated to Tennessee in 1806, when
Congress adjusted matters with that state in regard to the
unoccupied lands, 100,000 acres of which were granted in
one tract for two colleges, one to be located in the eastern
and the other in the western part of the state. Another

[172] *U. S. Stat. at Large,* II, 278.
[173] *Ibid,* II, p. 234.

provision of the act stipulated the setting aside of 100,000 acres in each county for the use of academies.[114] This was by far the largest allotment of land to any one state, Tennessee receiving in all over 3,500,000 acres for the cause of advanced education, or more than the combined university grants to all of the other states.

During the same year Congress reserved in the Territory of Orleans "an entire township to be located by the Secretary of the Treasury for the use of a seminary of learning." [115] Again, in 1811, it was definitely provided that this area should be located south of the Red River and that another township should be set aside north of that river for the establishment of an institution of higher learning in that region. The act also provided that in the Territory of Louisiana there should be reserved a township for a seminary.[116]

With the passage of these early reservation acts to promote the future cause of advanced learning, a national policy was soon firmly grounded in which every public land state or territory was the recipient of an area of the best public domain, and great freedom of choice was generally allowed in its selection.

Oregon and Nebraska were granted no university lands during their territorial days but received an allotment in the acts enabling them to form constitutions and be admitted into the Union. The usual grants of two townships each were made on the respective dates, February 14, 1859, and April 19, 1864.

Grants in Lieu of Saline, Swamp-Land, and Internal Improvement Grants.—After the admission of Colorado into the Union in 1876 Congress abandoned the method of granting salt spring, swamp, and internal improvement lands, and in lieu of these endowments gave to all the later states at the time of admission into the Union certain specified

[114] *U. S. Stat. at Large*, II, p. 382.
[115] *Ibid*, p. 394.
[116] *Ibid*, p. 620.

areas for the support of various institutions, of which higher education received the major portion. Only in the case of New Mexico was a part of these customary donations made during the territorial period, when in 1898 the following grants were provided: 112,702.86 acres [177] for a university, including the two townships regularly allowed each state; 100,000 acres for normal schools at Silver City and at Las Vegas; 50,000 acres for a school of mines, and 50,000 acres for a military institute.[178] These generous grants did not, apparently, cut down the grants allowed in the enabling act. The latter are shown in the following table:

TABLE XXIV

SPECIAL GRANTS FOR EDUCATIONAL INSTITUTIONS IN NEWER STATES

State	University acres	School of Mines acres	Normal acres	Scientific acres	University Prep. acres	Colored A and M acres	Military Institute
Arizona	200,000	150,000	200,000	......	......	......	150,000
Idaho	50,000	......	100,000	100,000	......	......	......
Montana	......	100,000	100,000	......	......	......	......
N. Dakota ...	40,000	40,000	80,000	......	......	......	......
New Mexico ..	200,000	150,000	200,000	......	......	......	150,000
Oklahoma ...	250,000	......	300,000	......	150,000	100,000	......
S. Dakota ...	40,000	40,000	80,000	......	......	......	......
Utah	110,000	100,000	100,000	......	......	......	......
Washington ..	......	100,000	......	100,000	......	......	......

In addition to the general grants, Oklahoma received for institutions of higher learning a grant of the thirteenth section in the Cherokee Outlet, the Tonkawa Indian Reservation, and the Pawnee Indian Reservation, together with all thirteenth-sections of the lands opened for settlement after the admission of the state, amounting altogether to 350,000 acres. The legislature of 1909 designated this grant, amounting to 1,050,000 acres as "New College Lands." [180] In the year 1899

[177] The grant provided for a donation of 65,000 acres and all saline land. These two amounts together with the two townships make the figure given. The saline grant was withdrawn in 1910 except with respect to land already selected.
[178] U. S. Stat. at Large, XXX, p. 484. 13th and 14th Ann. Report of the Com. of Pub. Lands of N. M. for the two years ending Nov. 30, 1914, p. 21.
[179] U. S. Stat. at Large, XXXVI, p. 562; XXVI, p. 217; XXV, p. 681; XXXIV, p. 275; XXVIII, p. 110.
[180] Session Laws of Oklahoma, 1909, Sec. 3, Art. 2, Ch. 28.

Alabama was allotted 25,000 acres for the use of the Tuskegee Normal and the Indian Institute and 25,000 acres for the Indian School for Girls.[181]

On a few occasions state institutions have been the recipients of special grants from Congress, such as the donation of the site on the summit of Mt. Hamilton for the Lick Observatory of the University of California;[182] a gift of 480 acres adjacent to the University of Montana for an observatory;[183] the bestowal of the campus on which stand the buildings of the University of Utah;[184] and the transference of a portion of the military reservation for an extension of the Louisiana State University and Agricultural and Mechanical College grounds.[185]

Grants to Private Institutions.—Numerous communications, petitions, and memorials were sent to Congress at different times by various committees, school trustees, and state legislatures, concerning the public lands or the money from sales thereof. They asked (1) that grants be made in support of private institutions, both sectarian and nondenominational; (2) that money derived from the sale of the public domain be divided among all the states for educational advancement; or (3) that land be granted to each state for the support of educational institutions.[186]

Apparently very few of these petitions received a favorable consideration by the committees to which they were referred. However, it is evident that though most of the applications were failures, yet they were the result of an influence which in later years culminated in the grants of university lands, as already seen, and in the endowment of other institutions as explained in a subsequent chapter.

Through the effort of private interests the following institutions received land from the federal government:[187]

[181] *U. S. Stat. at Large*, XXX, p. 837.
[182] *Ibid*, XIX, p. 57; XXVII, p. 11.
[183] *Ibid*, XXXIII, p. 64.
[184] *Ibid*, XXVIII, p. 118; XXXIV, p. 196.
[185] *Ibid*, XXXII, p. 172.
[186] *Pub. Lands*, Vols. I-VIII.
[187] *U. S. Stat. at Large*, see under dates of acts.

TABLE XXV

GRANTS TO PRIVATE COLLEGES

Name of Institution	Location	Acreage	Date of Grant
Jefferson College	Mississippi	23,040 acres	Mar. 3, 1803—Feb. 20, 1812
Vincennes University	Indiana	23,040 acres	Mar. 3, 1873
La Fayette Academy	Alabama	480 acres	May 24, 1828
Columbian College	Dist. of Columbia	Lots	July 14, 1832
Georgetown College	Dist. of Columbia	Lots	Mar. 2, 1833
Bluemont College	Kansas	160 acres	Mar. 2, 1861

The lots granted the Columbian and the Georgetown Colleges were to have a selling value of $25,000 each. Two years after the date of the Bluemont College endowment, that institution was selected as the Kansas State Agricultural College.

The table on pages 344 and 345 will indicate the lands granted by Congress directly and indirectly to the states for educational purposes:

SUMMARY

The use of land for the support of education began early in the colonial period. School lots were set aside and the income devoted to the support of the school. Not infrequently land, or the use of it was granted as part payment to the schoolmaster. In Virginia the colony provided land and the labor and equipment for its operation, the proceeds to be used for schools.

The federal government began early to appropriate land for the support of schools. The Ordinance of 1787 declared that schools should be fostered, and the Confederation at once set aside for schools section 16 of every township sold. This rule became general and was required in all public land states until, with additions of other sections, four sections per township were so reserved. This land was usually disposed of by the states, the funds being permanently invested, and only the income therefrom used.

In addition to these regular grants for common schools great amounts of "saline land" were granted for the same purpose. Of much greater importance were the swamp lands which were used for schools, as well as generous portions of the 500,000 acre grants. Provision was made for the granting of five (in one case three) per cent of the gross receipts from the sales of land to the states within which they lay. From this source important sums were derived.

Next in importance come the grants for agricultural and mechanic arts colleges. The policy had been inaugurated by several of the states. In 1862 Congress passed an act giving to each state 30,000 acres of land for each member of Congress to which the states severally were entitled. This land was to be sold and the money invested in securities as the basis of an income. Such states as had no public land or an insufficient quantity, were given "scrip" by which land might be entered elsewhere. This scrip was negotiable and was sold for the most part at a low price. Substantially all states, soon after 1862, were able to establish colleges on the basis of this federal support.

Grants of land not so liberal as those for colleges of agriculture and mechanic arts, were given to all new states, beginning with Ohio in 1787, for the support of higher learning. The Ohio grant consisted of three townships of land reserved out of the sales to the Ohio and the Symmes companies. Tennessee was given 100,000 acres. The usual grant for a state university was two townships. Beginning with 1889 the allowances were much more liberal and included support for normal, military, mining and other schools. A very few thousand acres were granted to private colleges and academies. Directly and indirectly the government gave over a hundred million acres of land for educational purposes. It is difficult to find and account for all of it.

TABLE XXVI

GRANTS TO STATES FOR EDUCATIONAL PURPOSES SUMMARIZED [188]

	Granted directly for			Grants given indirectly for Education		
	Common schools [189]	Universities, [190] seminaries, normal schools, etc.	Agricultural and mechanic arts colleges [193]	Internal [191] improvements	Saline [192]	Total
Alabama	911,627	142,160	240,000 [194]			1,293,787
Arizona	8,093,156	696,080	150,000 [194]			8,939,236
Arkansas	933,778	46,080	150,000 [194]		46,080	1,175,938
California	5,534,293	46,080	150,000	500,000		6,230,373
Colorado	3,685,618	46,080	90,000			3,821,698
Connecticut			180,000 [194]			180,000
Delaware			90,000 [194]			90,000
Florida	975,307	92,160	90,000 [194]			1,157,467
Georgia			270,000 [194]			270,000
Idaho	2,963,698	446,080	90,000			3,499,778
Illinois	996,320	46,080	480,000 [194]			1,522,400
Indiana	668,578	46,080	390,000 [194]		23,040	1,127,698
Iowa	988,196	46,080	240,000	500,000		1,774,276
Kansas	2,907,520	46,080	90,000			3,043,600
Kentucky			330,000 [194]			330,000
Louisiana	807,271	46,080	210,000 [194]			1,063,351
Maine			210,000 [194]			210,000
Maryland			210,000 [194]			210,000
Massachusetts			360,000 [194]			360,000
Michigan	1,021,867	46,080	240,000			1,307,947
Minnesota	2,874,951	92,160	120,000			3,087,111
Mississippi	824,213	69,120	210,000		23,040	1,126,373
Missouri	1,221,813	46,080	330,000			1,597,893
Montana	5,198,258	298,560	140,000			5,636,818
Nebraska	2,730,951	46,080	90,000		46,080	2,867,031
Nevada	2,061,967	46,080	90,000 [194]	500,000		2,698,047
New Hampshire			150,000 [194]			150,000

TABLE XXVI (Continued)

| | Granted directly for | | Agricultural and mechanic arts colleges[194] | Grants given indirectly for Education | | Total |
	Common schools[189]	Universities[190] seminaries, normal schools, etc.		Internal[191] improvements	Saline[192]	
New Jersey	.....	.....	210,000	.....	.....	210,000
New Mexico	8,711,324	112,703	250,000	.....	.....	9,074,027
New York	.....	.....	990,000[194]	.....	.....	990,000
North Carolina	.....	.....	270,000[194]	.....	.....	270,000
North Dakota	2,495,396	416,080	130,000[194]	.....	.....	3,041,476
Ohio	724,266	69,120	630,000[194]	.....	24,216	1,447,602
Oklahoma	1,375,000	800,000	250,000	.....	.....	2,425,000
Oregon	3,399,360	46,080	90,000	500,000	.....	4,035,440
Pennsylvania	.....	.....	780,000[194]	.....	.....	780,000
Rhode Island	.....	.....	120,000[194]	.....	.....	120,000
South Carolina	.....	.....	180,000[194]	.....	.....	180,000
South Dakota	2,733,084	416,080	160,000	.....	.....	3,309,164
Tennessee	.....	.....	300,000	.....	.....	300,000
Texas	.....	.....	180,000[194]	.....	.....	180,000
Utah	5,844,196	456,080	200,000	.....	.....	6,500,276
Vermont	.....	.....	150,000[194]	.....	.....	150,000
Virginia	.....	.....	300,000	.....	.....	300,000
Washington	2,376,391	446,080	90,000	.....	.....	2,912,471
West Virginia	.....	.....	150,000	.....	.....	150,000
Wisconsin	982,329	92,160	240,000	500,000	46,080	1,860,569
Wyoming	3,470,009	336,080	90,000	.....	.....	3,896,089

[188] This does not include swamp lands some of which were used to promote education.
[189] The area granted for common schools consists of certain specified sections as 16, 32, etc., of each township. See L. O. R., 1922, pp. 34-39.
[190] "Universities, seminaries, normal schools and others" includes: schools of mines, scientific schools, industrial schools, military institutes, reform schools, educational-charitable, and educational-penal institutions are found in only a few states. See L. O. R., 1922, pp. 34-39.
[191] The five states coming under this head all used the half-million acre grant for the benefit of the common schools.
[192] The saline grants all went into the common schools with one exception—Indiana used the lands for graded schools.
[193] For Mining and Mechanic Arts.
[194] These states received agricultural college scrip which was used for locating lands in other states.

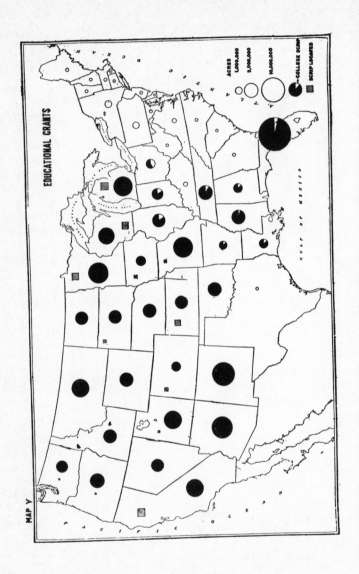

MAP V

EDUCATIONAL GRANTS

ACRES
1,000,000
5,000,000
10,000,000

COLLEGE SCRIP
SCRIP LOCATED

GULF OF MEXICO

PACIFIC OCEAN

CHAPTER XVII

THE HOMESTEAD, OR FREE LAND FOR SETTLERS

To find the origin of free grants of land by the government to the settlers, it is necessary to go back far beyond the time of the adoption of the Constitution. In the colonies, whether under the guise of the transparent fraud of the "head right,"[1] or the unenforcible stipulation of the annual quit rent, or the open offer of a gift, it was all, in the end, substantially the same thing. It meant the presentation to the settlers of the land, sometimes in large tracts, sometimes in small tracts, without money and without price. France and Spain had been liberal, even lavish, in their grants of free land to settlers. Senator Benton in his zeal for free land held that the policy was widely accepted: "I go for donations; and contend that no country under the sun was ever paid for in gold and silver before it could be settled and cultivated. . . . Were not Kentucky, Tennessee and one-third of Ohio settled in the same way? . . . Throughout the New World, from Hudson's Bay to Cape Horn (with the single exception of these United States) land, the gift of God to man, is also the gift of the Government to its citizens. Nor is this wise policy confined to the New World. It prevails also in Asia."[2] But as we have seen before, the United States early conceived the idea of deriving revenue from the public domain, and this idea proved for many years to be persistent against all opposition.

---

[1] The "head right" was the right to a certain amount of land, at first fifty acres, granted to a settler who came to Virginia. It was also allowed to the man, or company, bringing a settler.

[2] *Cong. Deb.*, 19 Cong., 1 Sess., p. 742 *et seq.*

EARLY VIEWS CONCERNING FREE LAND FOR SETTLERS

The price motive originated in the minds of men whose lives were passed in the older parts of the country. They saw land selling at good figures and believed that the fertile soil of the West was worth to the settler as much as either settler or speculator could be induced to pay for it. The man on the frontier had a different conception of values. He saw in the public domain, not farms, but the raw material out of which farms were to be made, and his imagination was keen on the subject of the making. Whether the price was two dollars, one dollar and twenty-five cents, or fifty cents, the pioneer always felt that it was at least high enough, and usually that it was too high. Hence it is only natural that the contest, mild though it was, for years between the East and West on the subject of price or no price, was bound to come. So long as the West was small in voting strength, it was useless to urge the case. Again, leadership was necessary in order that headway be made, and leadership was not always at hand. During the early years nothing more than petitions manifested the presence of a demand for free land, and these petitions were quietly and consistently, albeit respectfully, turned down.

The government was liberal with people who settled on the western land prior to the time of its coming under federal control, and no doubt this fact suggested to later pioneers the possibility of lenient treatment. Settlers along the Ohio River in 1797 asked for four hundred acres per family, agreeing to remain on the land three years before receiving title. Two years later petitions came from the vicinity of Natchez, Mississippi, asking that "vacant lands may be granted free of expense, to persons on their becoming actual settlers." [3] This petition was transmitted to Congress by the governor of Mississippi Territory, and was at once ordered to lie on the table.

Again, in 1804, a petition from Mississippi stated it to be the belief that a donation of lands to settlers would

[3] *Ann. of Cong.*, 6 Cong., 1 Sess., p. 207.

result in a great increase in population. This, together with other petitions, was referred to a committee appointed to consider matters relating to public lands. The committee formulated a letter to Albert Gallatin, Secretary of the Treasury, asking his advice. The advice of the Secretary was undoubtedly one of the main contributions on the matter of the public domain expressed during many years, but on this point of donations he was silent. In 1806 a company of pioneer farmers in Indiana, who had first ventured without authority to settle upon and improve land belonging to the government, were bold enough to ask the government for a title, and this without pay.

Although Congress was in no sense besieged with petitions for donations of land to settlers, the interest in the plan seems never to have died out. In 1812 a concerted movement of some magnitude was made in the Western States and Territories. Morrow of Ohio presented a petition from citizens of his state and moved that it be referred to the Committee on Public Lands, which was done. The petition set forth the information that the people asking for land were "poor and suffering, while thousands of acres of land, the property of the United States, are lying unoccupied; that they consider every man entitled by nature to a portion of the soil of the country; that no man ought to possess more than two hundred acres." Here was some genuine doctrine on the subject of land ownership, and in urging the reference of the petition, Mr. Morrow let it be known that the number of people involved in the case was large and that they had formed themselves into an organization called "The True American Society," a society extending its membership through western Pennsylvania and Ohio and into Illinois Territory.[4] Nothing further seems to have been heard of the organization or the petition.

A new phase was given to the question of free land in 1814 when a petition was presented "from sundry inhabitants of the several States and Territories west of the

[4] *Ann. of Cong.*, 12 Cong., 1 Sess., p. 1031.

Alleghany mountains, praying that donations of land may be granted to actual settlers on the Northwestern frontier of the United States, the better to protect the said frontier." This was referred to the Committee on Military Affairs, and, although not again heard from, similar pleas were dealt with favorably in later years. The cold treatment received by all petitioners for free land to settlers seems to have taken effect in discouraging such efforts from this time until, in 1825, Senator Benton of Missouri moved to instruct the Committee on Public Lands to inquire into the expediency of donating land to settlers, stating it as his belief that the land system then followed was favorable to the man with money, and especially to the speculator as distinguished from the settler. He believed many desirable citizens who would like to move west were prevented from doing so because of lack of money with which to purchase land. This hardly seems to harmonize with the attitude taken a few months later by his colleague, Senator Barton, in bitter opposition to the Graduation Bill providing for a reduction of the price of refuse land. This bill was submitted in December, 1825, by Senator Benton.[5] From this time until the passage of the Homestead Bill in 1862 the demand for free land to settlers was before Congress at frequent intervals. Benton made it a prime consideration, although it was to apply only to refuse lands. Could he have had his own way, it would speedily have applied to other lands as well, for, as he viewed it, "the settler, in a new country, pays the value of the best land in the privations he endures, in the hardships he encounters, and in the labor he performs."[6] Very promptly several state legislatures undertook to help Senator Benton's bill along and memorialized Congress to that effect. Illinois asked for the cession of refuse lands in order that the state might make donations to settlers.[7] Missouri made a

[5] *Cong. Deb.*, 19 Cong., 1 Sess., p. 720, *et seq.* Speeches by both Benton and Barton.
[6] *Ibid.*, 26 Cong., 2 Sess., p. 132.
[7] *Pub. Lands*, IV, p. 871.

very similar request and emphasized it by adding: "This general assembly insure your honorable bodies that the passage of such a law would, in their opinion, not only promote the strength and prosperity of this frontier state, but the happiness of thousands who, from the want of pecuniary means, are compelled to remain in an anti-republican state of dependence on rich landlords." [8] The same request was repeated in 1828. [9]

Some progress seems to have been made when in 1828 the Committee on Public Lands of the House was so far converted to the principle of the homestead as to make an emphatic report in favor of such action. A part of the report follows:

"That small tracts of eighty acres be given to the heads of such families as will cultivate, improve, and reside on the same for five years. This proposition has recommended itself to the consideration of your committee by a knowledge of the fact that there are many families who are neither void of industry nor of good moral habits, who have met with the usual share of the difficulties always accompanying the settlement of a new country, and who, living very remote from market, never expect to see the day arrive when they will be enabled to save enough, with all their efforts, from their means of support, to purchase a farm and pay for it in cash. Besides, your committee believe that such small earnings applied to the improvement and cultivation of small tracts, scattered through the public domain, would be as advantageous to the public as though they should be paid directly into the treasury. No axiom in political economy is sounder than the one which declares that the wealth and strength of a country, and more especially of a republic, consists not so much in the number of its citizens as in their employments, their capability of bearing arms, and of sustaining the burdens of taxation whenever the public exigencies shall require it. The poor furnish

[8] *Pub. Lands*, V, p. 36.
[9] *Ibid*, p. 622.

soldiers, and an experience shows that the patriotism which exists apart from an interested love of country cannot be relied upon. The affections of good citizens are always mingled with their homes and placed upon the country which contains their fields and their gardens." [10]

Two years later Arkansas asked that settlers locating within twenty-four miles of the frontier be given 160 acres of land with the requirement of five years' residence. [11] Indiana in 1827, and again in 1830 and in 1832, asked that donations be made to actual white settlers who should remain five years upon the land and make improvements as required. In these stipulations the two states anticipated the essential terms of the Homestead Act. [12]

FRONTIER DONATIONS

From 1842 to 1853 a series of acts were passed in Congress whereby donations were made to settlers in lieu of possible military service in protecting settlements from Indian attacks. Frontier settlers in Florida, Oregon, Washington, and New Mexico were given approximately 500,000 acres of land under these acts. These donations carried with them certain provisions as to time of residence and maximum number of acres to be acquired, but they differed from the Homestead Act of 1862 in that the donation was made for particular service and for undergoing dangers of the frontier, and in that it applied only to certain parts of the public domain.

The act pertaining to Florida provided for the gift of 160 acres of land, the whole amount not to exceed 200,000 acres, to any settler, who, able to bear arms, should settle within a certain prescribed territory where there was danger from Indian attack. The requirements of residence on the land were not very rigid, and were made even more liberal as the years passed. It was evidently not a plan very closely

[10] *Pub. Lands,* V., p. 449.
[11] *Ibid,* VI, p. 136.
[12] Indiana *Journal of the Senate,* 1827, p. 19; *Ibid.* 1830, p. 22.

associated with the preëmption principle, but avowedly a military measure. Over thirteen hundred entries were made under the act, and the amount of land granted exceeded the quantity first designated as the limit, there being 210,720 acres disposed of in this manner.[13]

The government was anxious to protect settlers, to prepare a territory for admission as a state in the Union, and to make salable great areas of public land. Thus the idea of reflected values was very clear in the minds of the men who enacted the law.[14] In order to insure genuine settlement and improvement of the land involved, it was provided that residence must be maintained on the land for four years, that a house must be built, and that at least five acres must be cultivated.[15]

The next frontier donation was made to settlers in Oregon. This plan was not founded on military necessity, as in the case of Florida, but was proposed as a measure of rewarding the early settlers who, going there at a time when England was trying to establish a claim, made the right of the United States tenable. This plan was developed in 1849 and in a modified form became a law in 1850.[16] The debate in Congress hinged mainly on two points: First, the propriety of granting land to settlers already on the land; second, the propriety of granting land to those who should settle in the Territory during the ensuing three years. The former point was rather readily conceded on the basis of the desirability and the attendant difficulties connected with the settlement. The latter point, though stoutly opposed, was decided favorably on much the same grounds. Oregon had been won from the Indians and the English by the settlers; they should be rewarded. Also, it was desired that the country be speedily settled, and therefore land should be offered as an inducement.

The bill as passed provided for the donation of a half

[13] Donaldson, p. 295.
[14] *Cong. Globe,* 27 Cong., 2 Sess., p. 764 *et seq.*
[15] *U. S. Stat. at Large,* V, p. 502.
[16] *Ibid,* IX, p. 496.

section of land to any single man who had settled in Oregon prior to 1850, to a married man and his wife double the amount. To those arriving between 1850 and 1853, half these amounts were offered.

Residence for four years upon the lands, and cultivation, but not to any particular extent, were required before title should issue. An interesting feature of this act was the provision that the land to which women were entitled was to be patented to them "in their own right" and not to be included with that granted the husband. Another feature peculiar to the time was the designation of "white" settlers as the beneficiaries of the act. Under this act 2,563,757 acres of land were granted to settlers.[17]

When Washington was divided from Oregon in 1853, the act granting land to pioneer settlers was made operative in the new territory, and 290,215 acres were so granted.[18]

With very little discussion Congress passed substantially the same law, granting 160 acres of land to settlers in New Mexico. Under this act [19] grants were made amounting to 20,105 acres.

Taking up again the discussion in Congress of a more general plan of donations to homesteaders Haynes of South Carolina is found explaining the methods by which other countries had granted land to settlers and showing by sharp contrast how the United States had undertaken the policy of "coining our lands into gold." The free land was, he said, the only means of building up in a wilderness great and prosperous communities. These expressions of conviction on the part of a representative of southern sentiment are of special interest in the light of later and opposite activities on the part of men from the same section. With an occasional petition for free land sent in from some frontier state, matters drifted along for a considerable number of years.

[17] Donaldson, p. 296.
[18] Ibid.
[19] U. S. Stat. at Large, X, p. 308.

A free grant of forty acres of land to the head of every family settling upon the public domain was proposed in December, 1844, by Thomasson of Kentucky. The homestead idea was linked with a graduation bill. Mr. Thomasson's purpose in the proposed change was to remove the public lands from the revenue schedule in order that receipts from sales might not serve as an excuse for breaking down the tariff system of protection.[20] On the same day Robert Smith of Illinois, in remarks on the graduation bill then before the House, expressed the opinion that the government would profit by giving away land which had been in the market ten years, provided it could thereby insure the making of such land into farms.[21] And Mr. Ficklin of the same state expressed forcibly the sentiments of the West respecting the proper use to be made of the boundless acres belonging to the government:

"Unless the government shall grant head rights, settlement rights, or donations of some kind, these prairies, with their gorgeous growth of flowers, their green carpeting, their lovely lawns and gentle slopes, will for centuries continue to be the home of the 'wild deer and wolf'; their stillness will be undisturbed by the jocund song of the farmer, and their deep and fertile soil unbroken by his ploughshare. Something must be done to remedy this evil. It is idle and senseless to continue at the present price such a wide expanse of unmitigated prairie.

"It will be kept in mind that the new states, unlike the old, pay tribute to the federal government for their land; and that the federal land officers are a sort of conduit pipe that convey the bulk of the money from the new States to the national treasury. . . .

"Notwithstanding such has been the policy of other States [that is, a nominal price, or no price, for land], yet

[20] *Cong. Globe*, 28 Cong., 2 Sess., p. 241. Senator Benton in 1828 introduced a bill providing for the granting of small tracts of land to settlers, "poor but industrious people" who should before gaining title live upon and cultivate the land.

[21] *Ibid*, p. 69.

we are told that the good old policy of donations to actual settlers, pursued more or less by all governments, whether free or despotic, is to be abandoned in the new States, and that one uniform, horizontal, unvarying price is to be demanded for all lands, whether fen, bog, marsh, prairie, or fertile plain." [22]

Later, in the discussion of the Graduation Bill, Murphy of New York offered an amendment providing for the sale of 160 acres of land to actual settlers at one mill per acre. [23] While none of these measures came to a vote during the session, the principles involved were taken up promptly when Congress next convened. On March 9, 1846, Mr. McConnell, Representative from Alabama, introduced in the House a bill providing for the "grant to the head of a family, man, maid, or widow, a homestead not exceeding one hundred and sixty acres of the public land." [24] Three days later a similar bill was proposed for a grant of one hundred and sixty acres to the head of a family "without money and without price" by Andrew Johnson of Tennessee. [25] Ficklin of Illinois introduced a bill providing for a grant of eighty acres to the head of a family, [26] and Darragh of Pennsylvania proposed an amendment similar in import. [27] Thus from every quarter came a demand for free land, not merely land which could not be sold, but any land still a part of the public domain. The campaign for homesteads was on. Congress would not accept the homestead principle but was not yet hostile toward it. The events of the next few years were needed to stir up sentiment both for and against free land.

THE FREE SOIL PARTY AND THE PUBLIC LANDS

The Free Soil Party in its efforts of 1848 put forward a strong plank in its platform in favor of free land. It read:

[22] *Cong. Globe*, 28 Cong., 2 Sess., p. 52.
[23] *Ibid*, p. 250.
[24] *Ibid*, 29 Cong., 1 Sess., p. 473.
[25] *Ibid*, p. 492.
[26] *Ibid*, p. 562.
[27] *Ibid*, p. 1077.

"*Resolved,* That the free grant to actual settlers, in consideration of the expenses they incur in making settlements in the wilderness, which are usually fully equal to their actual cost, and of the public benefits resulting therefrom, of reasonable portions of the public lands, under suitable limitations, is a wise and just measure of public policy which will promote, in various ways, the interests of all the states of this Union; and we therefore recommend it to the favorable consideration of the American people." [28]

Four years later the Free Soil Democrats put into their platform a plank similar in import but more vigorous. It declared: "That all men have a natural right to a portion of the soil; and that, as the use of the soil is indispensable to life, the right of all men to the soil is as sacred as their right to life itself."

"That the public lands of the United States belong to the people, and should not be sold to individuals nor granted to corporations, but should be held as a sacred trust for the benefit of the people, and should be granted in limited quantities, free of cost, to landless settlers." [29]

It will be observed that the basis of the argument in favor of free grants is essentially different in the two platforms. In the one it is merely implied that the undeveloped land is worth no more than the cost of developing it, hence the obvious unfairness of demanding a price for it. In the other platform the declaration that all men have a natural right to the soil is put forward as the major premise. The plan of granting but a limited portion, and to landless applicants only, is further in accordance with the doctrine that, since the sustenance of life comes from the soil, each and every individual should have a right to extract directly for himself these means of sustenance. In less lofty language the Republican Party in 1860 declared in favor of homesteads. The declaration evidently was intended to

[28] Stanwood, p. 175
[29] *Ibid*, p. 188.

cover the matter of preëmptions as well as homesteads, reading: "That we protest against any sale or alienation to others of the public lands held by actual settlers, and against any view of the free-homestead policy which regards the settlers as paupers or suppliants for public bounty; and we demand the passage by Congress of the complete and satisfactory homestead measure which has already passed the House." [30]

Thus the party alignment on the subject was clear: free homesteads became a part of the anti-slavery struggle. Had it not been for this complication, the South would evidently have favored it; as it was, they blocked its progress for a decade, but after the war declared themselves in its favor.

Had it not been for the slavery difficulty the West would surely have won, with comparatively little opposition, the privilege of settling government land free of charge. The party alignments on this, as on other things, followed the pro- and anti-slavery cleavage.

HORACE GREELEY AND THE NATIONAL REFORM ASSOCIATION

Simultaneously with the early movements in Congress for homesteads, and responsible, in some measure at least, for these movements, were the activities of an organization calling itself the National Reform Association. This association had its headquarters in New York City. Horace Greeley was its patron saint, and the columns of the *Tribune* were an open forum for its use. Mr. Greeley himself again and again over a period of years iterated and reiterated the doctrine of land reform. The principles of the association were thus stated and interpreted by him:

"1. Land Reformers do *not* complain of the present minimum price of Public Lands as too high. On the contrary, if they are to be sold evermore to whoever shall see fit to locate and pay for them we would far sooner see the price enhanced than reduced. We apprehend that a reduc-

[30] Stanwood, p. 230.

tion of the Government's selling price to three or four shillings per acre would in the long run aggravate the evils which now exist by facilitating the absorption of all the most desirable wild lands by speculators.

"2. What we *do* ask, and hold that Congress should lose no time in enacting, is simply that our Public Land System be so modified that *every person needing Land may take possession of any quarter-section not previously located, and that none other than a person needing land shall be allowed to acquire it at all.* Whether the settler shall be required to pay for his land or have it allotted to him without price, is quite a secondary subordinate consideration. We should be very willing, as a beginning, to have a quarter-section set apart to each settler thereon, allowing him (or her) forty acres thereof in perpetual occupancy without price or charge, to be extended to eighty acres to each married couple, or in case of marriage to any one not a claimant in like manner in her own right, so as to give to each family eighty acres without cost, leaving the balance of the quarter-section to be bought by that family at any time within ten years at ten shillings per acre, with legal interest added from the date of location. If said family should not see fit to buy it within the ten years, it would be proof presumptive that the eighty acres already given is as much as they need or will improve.

"3. *No Public Lands to be sold to a Speculator.* This is the essential matter—all else is but subsidiary. Let every person applying to locate land be required solemnly to affirm that he requires this land for his own use and improvement—that he fully purposes to live on it—and that he is the owner of no other land which, when added to that he now applies for, would make his entire estate exceed one hundred and sixty acres. Let this affirmation be duly recorded; and, in case it be ever proved false, let the proper officer be required to prosecute the culprit for perjury and for the present value of the property obtained by it. Only cut up land speculation by the roots and secure to every man needing Land a right to enter and improve a small portion of the Public Domain without charge, and we are quite resigned to see that Public Lands continue a source of Revenue to the Government.

"4. And yet we believe 'there is a more excellent way.' We acquiesce in this, because we admit the plausibility and force of the demand that the Public Lands shall pay their own way—that it is not just to tax a Maine farmer ten or twenty dollars in order to extinguish Indian titles, pay for surveys, etc., so as to give an Irish or German immigrant a farm for nothing. Freely admitting the force of this argument, we are ready to make way for it, though we are confident the Government would permanently increase its Revenue by giving a modicum of wild land to everyone who requires it, and looking to Duties on Imports alone for Revenue. Every new clearing in the West, every new wheat- or corn-field cut out of the Prairies, is a new source of Federal income. Every breaking-up team is a feeder to the Custom-house. So far from discouraging or impeding the creation of new farms by exacting a considerable payment for the raw material out of which a farm is made, it should be the policy of a wise government to encourage the settlement of new farms by every means in its power. The greedy youth who cut open the goose that laid the golden eggs, differed nothing in principle from the government which keeps a poor family in abject need by refusing it the lands from which it might extract a comfortable subsistence, and in so doing contribute to the Customs Revenue. The fact that a man wishing unappropriated wild land is unable to pay for it affords the very best reason for letting him have it. . . . But Land Speculation is a blight and a scourge whereof the desolating influences are not half understood. We talk of the price of Public Lands being only ten shillings per acre, when in fact the price actually paid by the settlers and improvers of those Lands average three or four times that amount. A few who care nothing for Schools, Churches, or any civilizing influences for their children, plunge boldly into the wilderness as soon as the Indian title to an inviting tract is extinguished, and seize the best locations at the minimum price, which they readily treble or quadruple in a few years, and are then ready to make another strike. But the great majority of settlers choose to locate where they shall have some sort of neighborhood . . . where they may hope soon to send their children to school, and where they can reach some kind of assemblage of Divine worship in the course of a Sunday forenoon. But wherever settlement has begun, there Land Speculation has already been busy, and has bought up with cash or covered with Bounty Warrants nearly every available acre within several miles. The settler must either go out of the world or pay the speculator's price, which is often three, five and even ten times the Government price. The Speculation is perpetually operating to scatter, to retard and barbarize our pioneer settlements, compelling each settler to wander off into the untrodden wilderness unless he is able and willing to pay five times what he should pay for his location. Banish the speculator or break up his pestilent calling, and our new lands will be settled far more compactly than they are now, since almost every one would prefer to have neighbors if he were not required to pay too much for the privilege. Then Schools, Mills, Churches, and all the incidents of civilized society would spring up where they are now precluded by the sparseness of population, and we should cease to hunt the poor Aborigines from Lands which they need and we do not. It is the unhallowed spirit of Land Speculation which drives us on to rob them and banish them from the tracts of which we have no need, and which in fact we should be far better without; since Industry is far less efficient, Happiness less general and Moral and Intellectual Progress far more difficult among a thinly scattered population than elsewhere.

". . . We have not half exhausted this momentous theme; but if we shall have induced the conservatives to understand that there is something more involved in Land

Reform than giving allotments to settlers for nothing, we have not written in vain." [31]

The striking tenets of the above creed are two: First, the plan to sell land to those who need it, and to none other; and, second, the view that free land would increase the customs receipts. The first of these views was by no means new; the second had rarely, if ever before, been set forth. The tenure proposed by the Land Reformers was in some respects unique. The homesteader, after getting his title to the land, was to have the privilege of selling to a man who, with the new purchase counted, would have not to exceed one hundred and sixty acres. In other words, the land taken from the government under the Homestead Act could never be held in quantities larger than one quarter-section per owner. Moreover, it was proposed to make the homestead inalienable except by the free consent of the owner, thus protecting it against all claims for debts and other obligations. [32] Again and again the *Tribune* made it plain that the price charged for the land was not the main object of attack. McConnell, Johnson, and Ficklin, who introduced the first homestead bills in the House, were severely criticized for not, as Greeley thought, understanding the subject which they had undertaken to handle. Mr. Greeley assumed that the bills introduced by these gentlemen were inspired by the efforts of the National Reform Association.

Whether or not this was true, their introduction followed immediately in the wake of the petitions sent in by the association: "Messrs. McConnell of Alabama and Johnson of Tennessee evidently suppose they are acting in accordance with the purpose of the National Reformers in proposing to make a gift of 160 acres of Public Lands in fee simple to every landless citizen who will claim it. But they could not be more utterly mistaken. The Reformers demand that all monopoly of, or speculation in, the Lands yet Public

[31] *N. Y. Weekly Tribune*, Jan. 24, 1852.
[32] *Ibid*, Feb. 14, 1846.

shall be stopped, henceforth and forever. They do not ask merely that landless men of to-day may be provided with a Home, but that the best possible provision shall be made for future generations also. Now this proposal to give every landless man 160 acres of Public Lands outright and leave all the lands subject to unlimited speculation and monopoly, would, if successful, afford a little present gratification and possibly relief at the expense of infinite miseries and privation in the future. Nearly all the Landless are needy; many of them are improvident; not a few are dissipated. To offer each a quarter-section of Public Lands as a free gift with liberty to sell the fee simple to anyone, would be simply enabling the speculator to obtain at second hand for a few dollars what now costs him hundreds, and thus to monopolize Counties instead of Townships." [33]

"We have before us a bill, 329 H. R., introduced by Mr. Ficklin of Illinois proposing to give to each head of a family eighty acres of Public Land on condition of settlement, cultivation, etc., said tract to be inalienable for Debt for the space of ten years, and no man to have but one tract on this basis.

"It is amazing how hard a politician can work to get round a salutary principle when it would be far more natural and every way better to embrace it at once. Mr. Ficklin has borrowed the idea of the National Reformers, and so bewitched and mangled it that its own father would not recognize—certainly would not own—it. Land Speculation and Land Monopoly are the evils which require eradication—the evil is not so much in the price of the Public Lands, which are easily obtained now if Speculators were only kept off of them. No poor settler is ever molested by the Government, even though he cannot pay the $100 asked for an 80-acre lot; but Speculation clutches all the best tracts at ten shillings per acre, and compels the actual settler to pay five to fifty times as much, holds large tracts out of use, prevents the timely erection of mills, cloth-

[33] *N. Y. Weekly Tribune*, Mar. 21, 1845.

works, etc., etc., and every way retards the settlement of the new lands. This isn't in the least guarded against by Mr. Ficklin's bill—nay, the eighty-acre tracts given away by it would soon become themselves the football of speculation; for, after raising five crops thereon, the settler (who can only so obtain it) is allowed a title in fee, and can sell to whom he pleases. The way this would work must be plain enough without further illustration." [34]

The National Reform Association never had a great membership, though it held a few national meetings, the most notable of which occurred on May 5, 1845, at New York City. The secretary of the association, a labor leader of the radical sort, Mr. Alvan E. Bovay, speaking of inalienable rights, continued: "Probably the discovery will soon be made that if a man has a right to life, he has, by inevitable consequence, the right to the elements of life, to the earth, the air, and the water." From this generalization he goes on to condemn monopoly in land. Some months before the New York meeting a petition was formulated which made its way through various channels to Congress, and became the basis of the bills above mentioned. The *Workingman's Advocate,* the leading organ of the association, again and again voiced the belief in man's right to a portion of the earth surface: "Both old parties are in favor of selling the fertile soil to mercenary wretches who might as well traffic in the life's blood of the poor." "The right of man to the soil is so obvious and clear a right." [35]

The labor leaders at the time of the National Reform Association were convinced that there was an oversupply of labor, and that the only way out of the trouble was to move to the country. A plan of uniting agriculture and industry may be mentioned in passing. It was proposed to take a township, mark off a square mile at the center, on which those not engaged in agriculture should locate. These people should have lots of at least five acres each. Outside

[34] *N. Y. Weekly Tribune,* Apr. 18, 1846.
[35] *Workingman's Advocate,* September 14 and 21, 1844.

of this central settlement the land was to be divided into farms of 160 acres each. These lots or farms were to be free to any man who wanted to work there until all were taken up. It was estimated that a township of land thus used would be able to support four to eight thousand people.[36]

During the years 1847 to 1849, inclusive, not much was done on the homestead program. The Free Soil party made its declaration in 1848, but it attracted little attention. In the same year two bills were introduced in Congress but nothing came of them.[37]

The Land Reformers seem to have become somewhat discouraged. They were still in existence, however, and in January, 1850, a petition couched in the language of this association was presented in the Senate. The petitioners objected to the system of traffic in land; asserted that tenancy was reducing the people to a condition of pauperism, misery, vice and crime; complained that European aristocracy was buying up American land while American republicans were homeless.[38] Within a few weeks of the time of the presentation of these petitions several bills and resolutions were offered for the granting of homesteads. The first was by Stephen A. Douglas, others by Daniel Webster, William H. Seward, and Sam Houston.[39]

These were substantially all alike, except that Seward's resolution was in favor of giving land to the political exiles of Europe only, though in the debate he agreed to the substance of the other measures. Here we have again, from widely separated sections of the country, from both old parties, and from one man soon to join a new party, almost a full agreement in the liberal land policy. The charge was made in the course of the debate that these distinguished men were bidding "for favor"; such a charge was, however, a mere episode in the succession of events.

[36] *Workingman's Advocate*, March 16, 1844.

[37] *Cong. Globe*, 30 Cong., 1 Sess., pp. 181, 583.

[38] *Ibid*, 31 Cong., 1 Sess., p. 196. For another petition from 1,500 citizens of Cincinnati, see *Ibid*, p. 469.

[39] *Ibid*, pp. 75, 210, 262, 263.

THE SOUTH OPPOSES FREE LAND

As it developed, the session of 1851 and 1852 gave much time and attention to homestead consideration. The start was made by a bill brought in by Andrew Johnson. It was prefaced by a statement that its purpose was to improve the "agriculture, commerce, manufactures, and other branches of industry," and it was referred to the Committee on Agriculture.[40] This committee proposed a restriction in the homestead right limiting it to those persons whose estate was worth not over $500.[41] The bill eventually passed the House by a vote of 108 to 57.[42] Although there was at the time a great deal of talk against "abolitionism," the fact is that the majority of southern Congressmen voted for the Homestead Bill, the vote of these members standing 33 to 30. The South supported this bill, but the sentiment against doing so was manifesting itself strongly. *The Courier and Enquirer* [New York City] complained that "this whole question is argued on its merits not as a political, but as a philanthropic measure. The masses in the North and West are favorable to it, as naturally they should be, inasmuch as these sections embrace nine-tenths of the needy population, for whose benefits the donations would be made. The South opposes the movement, and to our mind correctly denounces it as a fraud, and as a scheme that could proceed from no other source than demagogism itself." [43] The prominent members from the South were divided in their attitude toward the Homestead Bill—Alexander H. Stephens, for example, opposing it, while Andrew Johnson favored it. In the Senate the bill fared badly. After being adversely passed upon by the Public Lands Committee, it failed of a hearing on the floor. During a brief debate in which its friends were trying to postpone it to some definite time, Senator Mason of Virginia remarked

---

[40] *Cong. Globe,* 32 Cong., 1 Sess., p. 58.
[41] *Ibid,* p. 1317.
[42] *Ibid,* p. 1351.
[43] Quoted in *New York Semi-Weekly Tribune,* June 4, 1852.

that the support of the bill (by Mr. Hale) came from a suspicious quarter, and added: "If there were no other reason for passing it over until after the November election, that would be conclusive with me—I cannot consent to any measure which will contribute to the support of that party [the Free Soil Party]—a party which, if it ever attains its ends, can only attain them by destroying this government." [44] In the vote taken on postponement twenty-two votes were cast by Senators from slave states, and of these a solitary ballot was recorded in favor of the bill. The wide difference in the degree of sectionalism shown in the Senate and in the House would indicate strongly that the break between the North and the South was originating in the Capital rather than in the country. The veterans in politics took sides with reference to this sentiment; the recruit voted on the merits of the question. For example, in the Senate, Seward, Chase, Cass, Wade, and Sumner voted for homesteads; while Bell, Mason, and Jefferson Davis voted no. At the same time, Andrew Johnson of Tennessee and ex-Governor Brown of Mississippi voted for homesteads with as much determination as did Sumner and Wade. Moreover, the House debated the bill for several weeks, the Senate but a few minutes. The debate in the House had some points of interest. Brown of Maryland opposed the Homestead because it would offer our lands free to the European immigrant. The same objection, together with the most vigorous statement of the State Rights and strict construction view of the case, came not from the South at all but from New England. Fuller of Maine regarded the bill as unconstitutional, partial, and unjust, and in an impassioned speech declared:

"I deny the title of these petitioners, either in law or equity—I deny the authority of this Government to make the partition—I deny that this Government holds the public domain by such a tenure as that it is susceptible of any such severance and partition as is prayed for by the bill.

[44] *Cong. Globe*, 32 Cong., 1 Sess., p. 2267.

I ask by what right—by what warrant—by what title deeds
—a certain class of persons, aliens and foreigners, or citizens of a limited age—of a particular condition in their
domestic relations—of a particular condition in their
pecuniary affairs—as they chanced to be, on the 1st day
of January, 1852, appear here and claim that all, or any
portion, of the public lands—the common property of the
whole people of the United States—shall gratuitously be
set off to them, by mete and bounds, and thereafter be
held and owned in severalty, to the exclusion of a much
greater portion of the people, possessing equal rights and
equal privileges." [45]

Leading Arguments For and Against the Homestead

The leading arguments against the Homestead Bill were
its unconstitutionality, its effect on immigration and emigration, and loss of revenue. Moreover, it was charged [46] that
it would reduce the price of land already in private hands;
that it was contrary to the bounty system where land was
a reward for service; that it was especially unfair to the
railroads which had received grants; that it would make
people thriftless; that it put upon the nation duties pertaining to the states; that it would draw especially the white
laborers from the Old South to the free territories. In
addition to these objections, one Congressman at least,
John Welch of Ohio, went into the economic doctrine of
the case. He stated that the free land would be worth less
than the old land by the amount of the rent on old land.
Presumably, he meant the capitalized amount of the rent.
He even went further with his theories and expressed the
view that should labor be worth 75 cents a day on the
new land, and about 50 cents in the cities, such a discrepancy could continue only until the city laborer had
time to get to the country. [47]

[45] *Cong. Globe*, 32 Cong., 1 Sess., App. p. 386.
[46] A similar view was voiced by Jenkins of N. Y. *Cong. Globe*, 32 Cong., 1
Sess., App. pp. 429, 430.
[47] *Ibid*, p. 688.

This was the embodiment of the opposition arguments. On the affirmative side were the usual ones of philanthropy —giving to those who were poor. Moreover, the arguments which had been put forth by the Land Reformers were given a prominent place. Negatively, it was held that the price of old land would not be decreased; on the contrary, settlement always raises the price of adjoining lands. The homestead is not a gift; the five years' residence and cultivation is a real equivalent of value. The view that man had an inherent right to the soil was voiced by Galusha A. Grow, who for the following ten years was the greatest champion of the homestead measure:

"Is it not time you swept from your statute-books its still lingering relics of feudalism, wiped out the principles ingrafted upon it by the narrow-minded policy of other times, and adapted the legislation of the country to the spirit of the age, and to the true ideas of man's rights and relations to his government?

"For if a man has a right on earth, he has a right to land enough to rear a habitation on. If he has a right to live, he has a right to the free use of whatever nature has provided for his sustenance—air to breathe, water to drink, and land enough to cultivate for his subsistence. For these are the necessary and indispensable means for the enjoyment of his inalienable rights of 'life, liberty, and the pursuit of happiness.' And is it for a Government that claims to dispense equal and exact justice to all classes of men, and that has laid down correct principles in its great chart of human rights, to violate those principles in its solemn declarations in its legislative enactments?" [48]

Continuing, Mr. Grow expressed his ideas with reference to the significance of the public domain respecting the struggle of labor against capital: "The struggle between capital and labor is an unequal one at best. It is a struggle between the bones and sinews of men and dollars and cents; and in that struggle, it needs no prophet's ken to foretell

[48] *Cong. Globe,* 32 Cong., 1 Sess., App. p. 427.

the issue. And in that struggle, is it for this Government to stretch forth its arm to aid the strong against the weak? Shall it continue, by its legislation, to elevate and enrich idleness on the wail and the woe of industry?" [49]

The Senate defeated the bill in the face of a great number of petitions asking for its passage. According to the New York *Tribune*, there was a greater demand for the passage of this bill, as manifested in the "solid wall of petitions," than for any other. [50] But political conditions were critical, and the Senate could not take chances in the November election.

The next serious debate on the question came in 1854. The mutterings concerning the relation of homesteads to slavery, heard in 1852, were continued in 1854. The bill was "tinctured with Abolitionism"; it was an effort to fill up the Northwest with northern farmers, while southern farmers were prevented from settling in the Southwest because Indian titles were not extinguished. There were many that rejoiced in the bill because of this very feature. [51] One of the main subjects of debate at this session was whether or not the homestead privilege should be restricted to citizens, or "native citizens," or whether it should be extended freely to immigrants as well. Wade of Ohio moved to amend by striking out all reference to citizenship and thereby provoked a debate in which Adams of Mississippi was the main advocate of restricting the operation of the law to Americans. [52] Wade withdrew his amendment, but the provision in favor of the alien who had declared his intention of becoming a citizen was allowed to remain.

The vote in the House was a curious mixture of sectionalism and partisanship. The West had always been in favor of the measure. From time to time, the legislatures of western states passed resolutions demanding free land. For

[49] *Cong. Globe*, 32 Cong., 1 Sess., App., p. 427.
[50] *N. Y. Semi-Weekly Tribune*, Aug. 3, and 13, 1852.
[51] *Cong. Globe*, 33 Cong., 1 Sess., p. 1125.
[52] *Ibid*, p. 944 *et seq.*

example, such resolutions had recently been passed in Illinois and Ohio.[53] The western press, while not always unanimous, was strongly in favor of homesteads. A sample of press sentiment from Wisconsin reads:

"The discussion of the Homestead Bill, which recently passed the House of Representatives, has been begun in the Senate of the United States. We believe that the adoption of the principle which lies at the bottom of this wise and popular measure—the principle of freely giving, without money or price, to every man who will take it in its wild and waste state and cultivate it, a quarter-section of the public land—would constitute one of the most salutary, beneficent, important and glorious reforms that our Government has ever sanctioned. It would be a practical acknowledgment of the maxim that the soil of the country belongs to the people, and break away the barriers which prevent the landless and homeless from making for themselves an estate and a home. . . . Such a good law would operate with a democratic equality that would furnish one of the most beautiful and glorious results which flow from the existence of democratic institutions." [54]

Favorable sentiment prevailed in the House to such an extent that from the fifteen new states voting on the bill, but twelve votes were cast against it, while sixty-seven were cast in its favor. In the North Atlantic States, the vote was very much split, but in the Old South three votes only were cast in favor of the bill, while thirty-one were recorded against it. This was a prophecy of what was to follow when the Homestead bill should again become an issue. From a partisan standpoint, the division was about the same with both Democrats and Whigs—the former voting for the bill, 72 to 52; the latter likewise for it, 35 to 1⁰ The two Free Soilers voted against it.[55]

In the Senate the debate was desultory, and much of the

[53] *Ill. House Jol.*, 1853, p. 169; *Ohio Senate Journal*, 1852, 3, pp. 37, 38.
[54] *Green Bay Advocate*, Apr. 20, 1854.
[55] This analysis of the vote is taken from J. B. Sanborn's article in the *American Historical Review*, VI, 31.

time beside the mark. The criticism by the editor of the *Tribune*, though a little severe, was in point:

"That the wisest and most beneficent idea of our age—that of proffering to every citizen of our country a free home on her previously unappropriated soil—should be rejected and defeated by the present Senate, can surprise no one. From the beginning of the discussion in the Senate we have heard scarcely one manly assertion of *the right of man to cultivate the earth and enjoy the fruits of his labor,* provided he does not thereby encroach upon the natural or acquired rights of others. All has proceeded on the quiet assumption that the government is asked to give the nation's property to a class; while the idea of a landless man having any right to work, save as the more fortunate shall see fit to employ him, is treated as unworthy of consideration. Meantime, petty personal wranglings, discussions of the policy of permitting aliens to share equally with citizens in the advantages proffered to settlers by the bill, and other incidental if not trivial controversies have engrossed the time of the Senate nominally given to the consideration of the Homestead bill. Who can even affect an interest in such a squabble?" [56]

However, the Senate dodged the issue by providing a substitute bill. The substitute was not a bad bill, and had it been passed early in the session might have stood some show in the House. The main difference between the Senate and the House bills was that the former added the provision that the settler was to acquire title to the land after five years of residence and cultivation, on payment of twenty-five cents an acre, or, in case the land had been in the market twenty or more years, on payment of twelve and one-half cents an acre. [57] Having thus insured for the year the death of the movement, it was safe for all those so disposed to vote for this substitute bill. The vote against the substitute

[56] *N. Y. Semi-Weekly Tribune,* July 21, 1854.
[57] *Cong. Globe,* 33 Cong., 1 Sess., App. p. 1122.

bill was, in part, cast by the friends of the homestead principle.

There was a clear conflict between the homestead idea and the idea underlying the graduation principle. In the one the settler was to be protected against the speculator; in the other, whether by intent or not, the speculator was to be given free rein. The *Tribune* tersely called the attention of its readers to the antagonism of the two plans with the usual vigorous remonstrance against the feature of the graduation proposals which allowed any buyer to buy as much land as he chose. This, as Mr. Greeley believed, was nothing short of direct encouragement of speculation.[58]

During the session of 1857 and 1858, two homestead bills were introduced in the Senate and two more in the House. The latter failed to come to a vote; but one of the Senate bills was postponed to a definite time—January, 1859. During the course of the debate on this bill before its postponement, it was urged that the graduation of the price of the public lands down to 12½ cents an acre took the force out of the argument for the Homestead bill.[59]

The friends of the bill did their best to prevent its postponement, but were beaten by eight votes. Johnson of Tennessee, however, voted to postpone in order that he might move to reconsider.[60]

The force of southern sentiment was manifesting itself in the attitude taken by some of the most prominent men from that section, for example, ex-Governor Brown of Mississippi and Sam Houston of Texas, both of whom had been staunch friends of homesteads on all former occasions. Brown, especially, having made many declarations in its favor, voted against it.

A bill designed to aid in the matter of putting lands into the hands of settlers, and to make it difficult for speculators

---

[58] *N. Y. Semi-Weekly Tribune*, Apr. 14, 1854.
[59] *Cong. Globe*, 35 Cong., 1 Sess., p. 2425.
[60] *Ibid*, p. 2426.

to make purchases, was introduced by Mr. Grow, providing that land should not be offered for sale until fifteen years had elapsed, subsequent to its survey. This would give every opportunity for preëmption or for homestead in case the latter measure should be adopted, but its main purpose was to accomplish by other means the good results contemplated in the homestead measure.[61] A year later he made another attempt of the same character, and an amendment providing that land should not be offered for sale for ten years after it was surveyed was added to the Homestead bill.[62] Although the whole bill was doomed to defeat, the sentiment in the West was favorable to the provision, both before and after it became a part of the Homestead bill. The Chicago *Tribune* gave an opinion as to Mr. Grow's purpose in bringing the plan forward at a time when the outlook for the Homestead bill was gloomy:

"Mr. Grow of Pennsylvania, a zealous and reliable member of the House of Representatives, has the honor of bringing forward a measure for which he deserves the thanks of every western man. He proposes that hereafter all the public lands of the United States shall remain as government property fifteen years after they are surveyed, when the President may issue a proclamation and order a sale. The object to be accomplished by this measure is the occupation of fifteen years' duration, during which their own labor would enable them to become the owners, in fee simple, of the soil. It is designed as a substitute for the Homestead bill, which the South, fearing white, particularly German, emigrants, will not permit to become a law. It is supposed that Mr. Grow's bill, so just in its provisions, and so effectual in guarding the public lands from the rapacity of speculators, may be pushed through. We are sure that it will command the undivided support of the Republicans in both the Senate and the House." [63]

[61] *Cong. Globe*, 35 Cong., 1 Sess., p. 324.
[62] *Ibid*, 35 Cong., 2 Sess., p. 726.
[63] Quoted in the *Weekly Oregonian* (Portland), Apr. 10, 1858.

January, 1859, arrived and the bill, postponed to that time, was taken up. The demand of the settler was incessant.[64] For thirteen years homestead bills had been almost continuously before one or both houses of Congress. At this time its chances of passing seemed especially good because of the large number of Republicans who had gained seats in Congress and who were, almost without exception, in favor of the bill. There was little debate in the House, for, as Mr. Grow put it, the debate had already been on for years, and why prolong it? With the passage of a few sharp words, it came to vote February 1, and was carried by 120 to 76. But three votes from slave territory were recorded in its favor, one each from Kentucky, Tennessee and Missouri. From the North but one-half dozen scattering votes were cast against the bill, and these were, with one exception, Democratic.[65] Hopes were high among the friends of the bill that it would pass the Senate. The New York *Tribune* believed that Brown and Houston could still be counted on. Mr. Greeley wrote one of his best editorials urging the Senate to act without delay.[66] Western papers were enthusiastic over the prospect. The enthusiasm of the West was based on very tangible views. New settlers meant more taxes for public improvements, and settled homes in place of vacant prairies. There was always present the feeling against the unearned increment accruing to the absentee owner. The Homestead Act would put the land into the hands of settlers. It would relieve the overcrowded condition of eastern cities, a subject on which western editors were eloquent, though ignorant. Fluctuations in the course of trade were to be steadied by the rapid settlement of western land—a consummation hardly realized through the settlements which soon took place.[67]

[64] Donaldson, p. 333.
[65] *Cong. Globe*, 35 Cong., 2 Sess., p. 727.
[66] *N. Y. Weekly Tribune*, Feb. 12, 1859.
[67] The *Guardian*, Iowa, Feb. 10, 1859.

THE HOMESTEAD BILL BECOMES SEVERELY PARTISAN

Petitions poured in, but Brown and Houston had deserted the cause, as had a few others who were expected to stand by it, and a motion to set the bill aside was carried, Vice President Breckenridge giving the deciding vote. It was a close though not a rigid party vote, some six northern Democrats and two from Tennessee voting for the bill. This was about as near to passing as a bill could come and fail. That the real difficulty was the slavery question was to be seen in the balancing of the Cuban annexation plan against free land in the West. Doolittle of Wisconsin, in trying to bring the Homestead bill before the Senate, moved to postpone the Cuban bill and by so doing drew the fire of the slavery element. Toombs of Georgia stated the slavery side of the matter with great directness, accusing the northern senators of refusing to meet the Cuban issue face to face. "When is it," said he, "that this 'land to the landless' most exercises the patriotic bosoms of Free Soilers in this Senate? It is the very moment that a question comes up which they are afraid to meet." [68] To this Senator Wade responded with the much-quoted sentence: "The question will be, shall we give land to the landless, or niggers to the niggerless?" And although Cuba was not annexed, it is a clear case that the proposed annexation furnished, for the moment, the block to prevent the expansion of northern population and agriculture through the medium of free land. In addition to the slavery principle, the strict constructionists frequently fell back upon the claim that the proposed plan would be unconstitutional. This, however, would seem to have been only a subterfuge since the South was never opposed to liberal land policies which did not conflict with her other interests.

A year passed by and on March 6, 1860, Owen Lovejoy of Illinois reported from the Committee on Public Lands another of Mr. Grow's homestead bills. It soon came to vote, and although the merits of the measure were not

[68] *Cong. Globe*, 35 Cong., 2 Sess., p. 1353.

debated, there was considerable sparring between the pro-
and anti-slavery factions. Six days after being reported to
the House the bill passed by 115 to 65. In this ballot but
one vote from a free state was cast in the negative
and but one from a slave state in the affirmative. In
the Senate a bill had been introduced by Andrew Johnson
at an earlier date than that of the House bill, but the latter
gained precedence in consideration on the floor of the Senate,
and ran the gauntlet of a protracted and acrimonious debate.
From the beginning it was recognized as a sectional struggle.
Mr. Mason of Virginia tersely stated the issue in the following words: "Where does it stand now? It is brought up
as a political engine from the other wing of the Capitol,
introduced and sustained here by the compact vote of the
Opposition. What is the Opposition? A party calling themselves the Republican party. What is their purpose? To
get the control of this government, that they may act directly
on the condition of African bondage in the southern
states. . . .

"Now, Mr. President, we are indebted to the honorable
Senator from Wisconsin for lifting the veil from this
measure. It has no longer the narrow and contracted purpose of giving land to the landless, and providing homes for
men who will never occupy them; it has no longer that
diminished character of philanthropic exercise of power on
the part of this government, instituted for a very different
purpose; it is a political engine, and a potent one. It has
already received the sanction of the other branch of the
Legislature, where there is a majority—I do not know
whether a numerical—but a controlling majority of the
Opposition; and it is before us now, to be passed in the
Senate, for the purpose of effecting that great object. It
is the Emigrant Aid Society's policy upon a wider scale.
It is not to be sustained by voluntary contributions, but it is
to be purchased at the price of the public domain gratuitously
given. That is the policy of the present Homestead bill." [69]

[69] *Cong. Globe,* 36 Cong., 1 Sess., p. 1635.

The merits of the Homestead bill received little consideration. It was no doubt almost impossible to advance any argument with which the senators were not familiar. The question was clearly understood as one bearing directly on the differences of North and South. The Emigrant Aid Society, the Cuban annexation, the Kansas-Nebraska struggle, all were lugged into the controversy.

THE PASSAGE AND VETO OF THE BILL OF 1860

One serious attempt at compromise was made. The Committee on Public Lands reported a substitute bill providing that homesteads should be granted to heads of families only, and on payment of 25 cents per acre, doing away, presumably, with the constitutional objections, since it was a sale instead of a gift, and since the price charged covered substantially the cost of the land so disposed of. This plan was the work of Andrew Johnson, one of the best friends of the homestead principle.[70] As he anticipated, it caught a considerable number of southern votes, and on May 10, the substitute bill passed the Senate, 44 to 8. One of the adverse votes was cast by Hamlin of Maine; the other seven by senators from slave states.[71] After a long conference with the House, a compromise was reached and accepted by both houses, the Senate approving it by a vote of 36 to 2, the House by 115 to 51. The bill, as passed, provided for the sale at 25 cents an acre of not to exceed 160 acres of land to heads of families who should occupy the same for a period of five years. Provision was made for a modification of both the preëmption and graduation acts, making the purchase of land easier, but only on the basis of residence. It also provided for the cession to the states of all land remaining in the market for thirty years.

Thus after eight years of almost incessant effort a homestead bill was passed by both branches of Congress. It was not to the liking of its friends in many important par-

[70] *Cong. Globe*, 36 Cong., 1 Sess., p. 1649.
[71] *Ibid*, p. 2043.

ticulars, but they felt, after all, that the main point had been carried, and believed that modifications could be made from time to time.

"The House of Representatives has finally consented to take a half loaf rather than no bread with regard to the Free Homesteads. It was thought best to submit to flagrant wrong rather than subject the pioneers of Minnesota and Kansas to the calamity of being divested of the homes which are their all, yet which they are utterly unable to buy of the government in the present dearth of money, coupled with low prices of their products in those frontier regions. . . .

"We do not object to taking this as an installment, especially as it must prove a heavy blow to the present monopolists of large bodies of unimproved lands, and to the great gamblers in land warrants. We believe it will reduce the price of such lands and such warrants very materially. But, gentlemen of all parties! understand that this half loaf is accepted only for what it is, and that the friends of the Free Homestead principle will not rest till their whole object is attained." [72] So commented Greeley.

In many instances getting a bill through Congress is only two-thirds of the struggle required to enact it into law. This was one of such cases. Rumor had announced that President Buchanan would be required by his political friends to veto the bill.[73] At any rate, he vetoed it. Three days after receiving the bill the President returned it with his objections. He doubted the authority of Congress to give away lands either to individuals or to states—this bill did both. He argued that Congress undoubtedly would not claim the right to donate money to states or individuals; they cannot have a different right over land bought with money than they have over the money itself. Congress holds the land as a trustee; no trustee can report that he has disposed of the property in his care by giving it away. Furthermore, Mr. Buchanan believed that the bill discrim-

[72] N. Y. Daily Tribune, June 21, 1860.
[73] Ibid, March 19, 1860.

inated against the holder of soldiers' land warrants, rendering them cheap or worthless; that a discrimination was made
in favor of cultivators of the soil as distinguished from other
citizens; that no alien who was not the head of a family
should take a homestead, while a citizen must be the head
of a family in order to receive the privilege; that the old
states were deprived of their share of the value of the land
and would, moreover, lose through a loss of population
and a decrease in the value of their own land; that the homestead privilege would result in widespread speculation, since
capitalists would bargain with homesteaders to take up land
on shares; that much revenue would be lost; that "this bill
lays the ax at the root of our present admirable land system."
He believed that the frugal poor could buy land at the
regular price and feared the bill would introduce the dangerous doctrines of agrarianism and the "pernicious social theories which have proved so disastrous in other countries." [74]
The Senate lacked one vote of passing the bill over the veto.
The failure of the measure was a bitter disappointment to
the friends of free land. The state legislatures of the West
continued their memorials to Congress, and western governors made the subject a major consideration in their
messages. [75]

The Governor of Minnesota, in 1861, was in an opti-
mistic mood regarding the homestead prospect and hoped
"that we have witnessed the last sale of United States lands
in Minnesota." [76] The comments of Mr. Greeley on the
veto are in point: "Mr. Buchanan must be a near relative
of him whom the Yankee characterized as having 'remark-
ably winning ways to make people hate him.' The Northwest was already so unanimously averse to him that he could
only intensify its dislike into hatred; but that seems an object
worthy of his ambition. The bill which he vetoed on Sat-

[74] Richardson, pp. 608-614.
[75] E. g. Minnesota House Journal, 1859-1860, p. 30.
[76] Minn. House Jol., 1861, p. 37.

urday was not the Republican or House Free Homestead bill, it was that of the Senate, which nearly every Republican voted against on its first passage, and only acquiesced in at the last moment, *in deference to the tens of thousands in Iowa, Minnesota, Kansas, etc., who are liable to be ejected from their rude homes at any moment, because, in the present pecuniary condition of the Northwest, it is morally impossible that they should pay $1.25 per acre for the quarter-section each which is or contains their all.* The bill for their relief finally passed the Senate with but two opposing votes; in the House it had about two to one; and this bill Mr. Buchanan vetoes for reasons which apply to the Graduation and other bills which he or his party have sanctioned, but not to this. So the last hope of obtaining any good from this Congress or this Administration has vanished. Shall we ever see their like again?" [77] We never did. The next Congress was of a different character, but not to so pronounced a degree as was the new President different from the one he succeeded.

A Campaign Issue in 1860

During the political campaign of 1860, the public-land policy became an important issue. The Republicans, as noted above, declared in their platform squarely in favor of homesteads. It was a minor, though not unimportant, issue of the great campaign of 1860. Mr. Greeley declared that it was the greatest issue in the West, that it was stronger than any party. [78] He set forth clearly, and with little exaggeration in spite of his pronounced views and deep feelings, the significance of the public-land issue in the campaign.

He recounted the familiar arguments and emphasized the advantage of a balanced economic situation in which the

[77] *N. Y. Daily Tribune*, June 25, 1860.

[78] *Democrat and News*, Davenport, Iowa, Sept. 27, 1860, cited in E. D. Fite, *The Presidential Campaign of 1860*, p. 202.

fabrics of the East should be exchanged for farm products of the West. The poverty of the settler makes payment for new land impossible and speculation easy.[79]

No less positive were the utterances of Carl Schurz. In a speech on the issues of the campaign, delivered at St. Louis, he referred to the public-land situation and its relation to slavery:

" 'But,' adds the slaveholder, 'of what use to us is the abstract right to go with our slave property into the territories, if you pass laws which attract to the territories a class of population that will crowd out slavery? If you attract to them the foreign immigrant by granting to him the immediate enjoyment of political right? If you allure the paupers from all parts of the globe by your preëmption laws and homestead bills? We want the negro in the territories. You give us the foreign immigrant. Slavery cannot exist except with the system of large farms, and your homestead bills establish the system of small farms with which free labor is inseparably connected. We are, therefore, obliged to demand that all such mischievous projects be abandoned.' Nothing more plausible. Hence the right of the laboring man to acquire property in the soil by his labor is denied; your Homestead bill voted down; the blight of oppressive speculation fastened on your virgin soil, and attempts are made to deprive the foreign immigrant in the territories of the immediate enjoyment of political rights, which in the primitive state of social organizations are essential to his existence. All this in order to give slavery a chance to obtain possession of our national domain. This may seem rather hard. But can you deny that slavery for its own protection needs power in the general government? and that it cannot obtain that power except by increased representation? and that it cannot increase its representation except by conquest and extension over the territories? and that with this policy all measures are incompatible which bid fair to place the territories in the hands of free labor?" [80]

[79] N. Y. Daily Tribune. Aug. 25, 1860.
[80] Quoted in Fite, p. 250.

Mr. Lovejoy of Illinois is authority for the statement that without the pledge of the party to support the Homestead bill, the election of President Lincoln would not have been possible.[81]

THE HOMESTEAD ACT OF 1862

On the third day of the session of the new Congress in December, 1860, the House, still, of course, the old House, passed the Homestead bill by a positive majority. It was sent to the Senate and died in committee. The subject was overshadowed by more important problems, and attention was concentrated on them. Nevertheless, the project of free land was, after March 4, 1861, in the hands of its friends, and, in spite of the distracting influence of the Civil War, the party in power did not fail to redeem its pledge concerning the public domain. During the special session of Congress in the summer of 1861, a homestead bill was introduced in the House by Mr. Aldrich of Minnesota.[82] It was referred to the Committee on Agriculture, and almost at the opening of the next session of Congress was reported back.[83] It was a foregone conclusion that the Homestead bill, in some form, was to pass. Nevertheless, there were objections to it, even with the pro-slavery men no longer present in Congress. It was the belief of some of its friends that it should be postponed until after the war on account of the condition of the treasury. Justin S. Morrill of Vermont took the position that land was the basis of credit and that it was sure to be "disastrous to our public to part with any portion of our means at the present time." This view was shared by Roscoe Conkling of New York and Crittenden of Kentucky. Mr. Morrill advanced the further view that the passage of the Homestead Act at that time would make of no value the soldiers' bounty warrants.[84] These arguments were squarely met by Mr. Grow, who

[81] *Cong. Globe,* 37 Cong., 2 Sess., p. 39.
[82] *Ibid,* 1 Sess., p. 23.
[83] *Ibid,* 2 Sess., p. 14.
[84] *Ibid,* p. 136.

quoted from the Commissioner of the General Land Office to the effect that land had about ceased to be a source of revenue even then. How, therefore, could it be the *basis* of revenue? Mr. Grow went on to show that, in private hands, the land would be taxable, and therefore a source of revenue. He showed the folly of giving land warrants to the soldiers and allowing them to be sold at twenty-five or thirty cents an acre, and emphasized the fact that the soldier was given a decided advantage in the operation of the proposed law. He did not object to projection into the future of the time when the law should go into effect. The soldier argument became one of the most important of all in the debate and led Mr. Grow to say a few significant words laudatory of the men who fought the wilderness:

"But there are soldiers of peace—that grand army of the sons of toil, whose lives, from the cradle to the grave, are a constant warfare with the elements, with the unrelenting obstacles of nature and the merciless barbarities of savage life. Their battlefields are on the prairies and the wilderness of your frontiers; their achievements, felling the forests, leveling the mountains, filling the valleys, and smoothing the pathway of science and civilization in their march over the continent. While we provide with open hand for the soldier on the tented field, let us not heap unnecessary burdens upon these heroes of the garret, the workshop, and the wilderness home. They have borne your eagles in triumph from ocean to ocean, and spanned the continent with great empires of free states, built on the ruins of savage life. Such are the men whom the homestead policy would save from the grasp of speculation. By it you would secure to them all their earnings, with which to make their homes comfortable, build the schoolhouse and church, and thus contribute to the greatness and glory of the Republic." [85]

On the 28th of February the bill was put upon its passage and carried by a vote of 107 to 16.[86] Two amendments had

[85] *Cong. Globe,* 37 Cong., 2 Sess., p. 910.
[86] *Ibid,* p. 1035.

been adopted, one providing for soldiers' bounty lands, the other setting January 1 as the date when the act should go into effect. Of the votes cast against the bill, the great majority were by men still in Congress from south of Mason and Dixon's line, representing a continuation of the old opposition. It is a matter of some interest that the opinion of Andrew Jackson, a southern Democrat, to the effect that "the public lands should, as soon as possible, cease to be a source of revenue," was used throughout the long course of the homestead debates as testimony in favor of the measure.

In the Senate, many amendments, mostly pertaining to the question of military bounties, were offered and adopted.[87] On May 6 the amended bill passed the Senate, 33 to 7. The seven votes, with the exception of one from Oregon, were from slave territory and represented the last-ditch protest of the pre-war South against the plan of putting the public domain into the hands of small farmers.

The amendments of the Senate were not agreeable to the House, and after considerable parleying a compromise was reached by the conferees and promptly accepted by both houses. The compromise was very one-sided, since about everything embodied in the Senate amendments was permitted to stand. On May 20, 1862, Abraham Lincoln signed the bill and a week later reported the same to Congress. The Homestead bill had become a law.[88] Settlers finally could acquire farms of 160 acres free of all charges, except a minor fee to be paid when filing the claim. To insure permanency of settlement the law specified that before title to the land was gained the individual must live on the homestead for five years.

[87] *Cong. Globe*, 37 Cong., 2 Sess., p. 1915.
[88] *U. S. Stat. at Large*, XII, p. 392.

CHAPTER XVIII

COMMUTATION OF HOMESTEADS

The privilege of commuting, that is, of converting the homestead with a preëmption right and paying the regular price of $1.25 or $2.50 per acre for it, had been allowed in the original Homestead Act. In this act the commutation requirements were quite general. The settler was to fulfill the preëmption requirements and might do so at any time possible during the homestead period, that is to say, any time after six months following the date of filing.

During the early years of the operation of the Homestead Act the commutation privilege was not often chosen by the settler. Prior to June 30, 1880, not over four per cent of homestead entries were so handled.[1] Following this date the situation was very different. The explanation of the change is not far to seek. In the early years of the homestead law the settlers were genuine homesteaders. They settled upon the land because they wanted farms. Twenty years later the situation had changed greatly, and from that time until recently an important proportion of homestead entries was commuted. From 1881 to 1904 inclusive 22,000,000 acres out of 96,000,000 acres, or about twenty-three per cent, were so obtained.[2]

The importance of the commutation clause and its operation was, however, greater than is indicated by the statistics. It was the means whereby large land holdings were built up through a perverted use of the Homestead Act. One of the

[1] Donaldson, p. 350.
[2] *Sen. Doc.*, 58 Cong., 3 Sess., No. 180 (Report of the Public Lands Commission).

most striking instances of this was in North Dakota during the first decade of the present century, where 5,781,000 acres were commuted against 5,614,000 acres on which final proof was made. Thus the commutation privilege was used somewhat more often than the homestead principle in obtaining title to the land. The occasion for this action is quite plain. The production of wheat and flax, as well as other crops, was spreading to the west in North Dakota at a rapid rate. It was spreading over land which prior to 1900 had been government land. The land was not in the market at a dollar and a quarter, or two dollars and a half, but it could be brought into the market at those prices, a quarter-section at a time, by means of the homestead privilege, together with the right to commute. "Many instances have been recorded when a single crop has brought values sufficient to buy and improve outright the farm upon which the crop was grown. . . . These facts not only made the actual settler more or less reckless through forcing the development of his place, but, on the other hand, brought large numbers who came with the distinctive idea of speculation. Thus a veritable multitude of farmers' sons and daughters, and servant girls, as well as ne'er-do-wells, have sought lands in the Dakotas." [3] Many of these people had lived in the vicinity of these lands for years with no thought of homesteading until the increase in the price made the prospects of immediate sale at a profit a probability. Until 1899 the proportion of commuted homesteads in this state was under ten per cent. By 1903 it had risen to 60 per cent and remained near the 50 per cent division for some six years more. No sooner was the time ripe for commutation than the land was made the basis of a loan whereby it might be held as a speculation for a few years, or it was sold at once. The prices ranged during the early part of the decade from $400 to $2600 per quarter-section. [4] The sales were made to farmers who wanted large

[3] *Sen. Doc.*, 58 Cong., 3 Sess., No. 189, p. 123 (Report of the Public Lands Commission).
[4] *Ibid.*

farms, and the fact that the homestead was small in comparison with the number of acres which seem from experience to fit the grain-producing conditions of the Northwest is an important point in explaining the rapidity with which the homesteader sold out. In 1910 the average size of a North Dakota farm was 382 acres; in 1920 it was 466 acres, or almost three times the maximum size of a homestead. It was, therefore, a most logical outcome of circumstances that the homesteader should either sell his holding or buy more land, and since most of the homesteaders had little money, they were usually the sellers rather than the buyers in the reorganization transaction.

Throughout the public-land territory, as a whole, commutation was a very popular topic of discussion until the Three-year Homestead Act gave an added incentive to stay out the residence requirements rather than to pay the money. From 1910 to 1913, inclusive, the commutations were around 35 to 40 per cent of the total amount of land patented under the Homestead Act, but by 1914 it had fallen off some 75 per cent, only 650,000 acres out of 9,291,000 acres being commuted. Thus, while Congress failed to take the advice of the Land Commission of 1904 and 1905, and of various commissioners of the General Land Office, in repealing the commutation privilege of the Homestead Act, the result has been, in large measure, accomplished by the modification in the time required in residence. That the commutation privilege resulted in bringing millions of acres of prairie land into farms more rapidly than would otherwise have been done cannot be doubted.

The testimony against the commutation law and the manner in which it worked seems so convincing as to appear beyond all dispute, and yet it is not. There have been on every occasion those to uphold it. The Senate committee on public lands in 1903 brought in a strong report recommending the repeal of the commutation clause, and still a minority of the same committee were just as vigorous in its support. The minority favored commutation because it gave the homesteader a chance to escape from some calamity or misfortune. They say: "A homesteader may wish to commute because of sickness, crop failure, loss of property, inability to make a living on the land, want of school facilities, refusal of wife to live on the homestead, lack of equipment, or death of entryman and inability of his widow to carry on homestead work." [5]   All of this sounds plausible, but the chief of the special agents of the Land Office, who had every opportunity to know the facts, made a report which coincides with the usual testimony.. He says: "Commutation is the clause of the Homestead law under which citizens who are not farmers or ranchers, and who have no intention of ever becoming such, enter agricultural or valuable timber lands. . . . Actual inspection of hundreds of commuted homesteads show that not one in a hundred is ever occupied as a home after commutation. They become part of some large timber holding or a parcel of a cattle or sheep ranch. . . . They [the commuters] are usually merchants, professional people, school teachers, clerks, journeymen working at trades, cow punchers, or sheep herders. Generally these lands are sold immediately after final proof." [6]

Before 1891 residence for but six months was required before commuting was allowed. After that year fourteen months' residence was specified, but six months was allowed to elapse before the establishment of residence was actually required, leaving but eight months as the time spent on the land before commutation was permitted. During recent years the full fourteen months has been required. [7]

Another phase of commutation not yet touched upon is deserving of notice although it has but remote connection with agricultural land. This is the use made, or more accurately the abuse made, of the Homestead law as applied to the forested lands. In these districts there was hardly a possibility of complying with the spirit of the Homestead

[5] Sen. Rep., 57 Cong., 2 Sess., No. 3166, Pt. 2.
[6] Sen. Doc., 60 Cong., 2 Sess., No. 676, pp. 390, 391.
[7] L. O. R., 1907.

law, but some means of getting title to the land had, apparently, to be devised, and the preëmption law, while it existed, and later the commutation clause of the Homestead Act, were, until the Timber and Stone Act was passed, the most available means of getting land at a dollar and a quarter an acre. The fraud practiced in this connection was frequent and usually transparent. For example, "houses" were made of drygoods boxes 14 by 16 inches, and an oath taken that there was on the claim a good board house 14 by 16, with doors, windows and a shingled roof.[8] Not infrequently land worth ten or twenty thousand dollars per quarter section was through this device purchased for $400.00.[9]

LOANS TO HOMESTEADERS

Within comparatively few years after the passage of the Homestead Act it became evident that raw land, though cut up into convenient tracts, did not constitute farms. The settlers were for the most part without sufficient means and as a result distress followed fast on the trail of those who undertook to make happy homes out of wild land and enthusiasm. Even these marginal homesteaders were, however, not without their champions. Bills were introduced in Congress providing for gifts or loans of money to those who would settle on public domain, since settled it must be, and since the settling solved simultaneously two problems, that of peopling the West, and that of relieving poverty and unemployment. One of the main efforts of this kind took the form of a bill introduced in the House in 1878. It was designed for the immediate relief of needy settlers, but much more ambitious than that, it undertook "a policy which is designed to place the agricultural interests of the country where they properly belong, and that is above every other branch of the public industries." The bill proposed government loans of $500 each to homesteaders whose goods

[8] *Sen. Doc.,* 58 Cong., 3 Sess., No. 189, p. 72 (Report of the Public Land Commission).
[9] *Ibid,* 60 Cong., 2 Sess., No. 676, p. 390.

amounted in value to less than $300, the loan to be secured by mortgage on the land to run for a period of ten years, payable in installments and to draw interest at the rate of three per cent. The total amount of such loans was not to exceed $15,000,000. The main supporter of this bill appears to have been Representative H. B. Wright of Pennsylvania. His arguments were about equally directed toward relief for the unemployed laborer of the East and the unprosperous homesteader of the West. It was a plea against class legislation, the same to be accomplished by bringing into the favored class list the farmers and laborers, it being held that manufacturers, bankers and others had long been favored. Elihu Burrit was quoted: "The law that joins together man and woman in conjugal life rests on the same basis of necessity as the law that joins together labor and land. . . . There is no other country in the world where so much labor and so much land are kept asunder as in the United States." [10]

This bill and the support it received represent in a measure the interest of the laboring class in getting some form of relief outside their own field and the belief on the part of some laborers, and a few doctrinaires, in the distribution of people over the land as a means of preventing unemployment in cities and friction with capital. We are not, at least not thus far, moving in that direction.

ENLARGED HOMESTEAD ACTS

It had long been recognized that the Homestead Act did not fit conditions west of the 100th meridian. In case the land was wanted for grazing purposes a quarter-section was of little importance, being too small; if it was wanted for irrigated farming it was too much, or it was altogether out of the question because of the difficulty involved in obtaining water. Many years passed before Congress became sufficiently convinced that anything was needed in the way of new plans respecting the handling of land of this

[10] See speech by H. B. Wright delivered in the House, May 2, 1878.

kind to act farther than had been done, or was being done, in connection with desert-entry lands and Carey Act lands. However, in 1904, the Kinkaid Act,[11] increasing the size of homesteads in western Nebraska, was passed.

The Kinkaid Act.—This act applies to the State of Nebraska only and provides that in the western portion of the state, where land had long been rejected by homesteaders and preëmptors, that a homestead 640 acres in size might be taken. Under this act it was estimated that 7,000,000 acres of land were subject to entry. Within ten years after the passage of the act all but a quarter million acres of this land was entered.

The Kinkaid Act was not viewed by those who stood sponsor for it as a departure from the fundamental principles of the homestead idea. It was, in the language of the House Committee on Public Lands, an "increase in the area of the homestead above that provided by the original Homestead law . . . made with the view of compensating the homesteader, in a measure, in quantity of land for what the land lacks in quality and productiveness. The area of a homestead was originally fixed at 160 acres on the theory that this area was sufficient on which to maintain a family comfortably, and in the regions where the Homestead law first applied this was true." [12] Congress wanted to turn over to the home-making farmer these "commons" of Nebraska, on which, by might or collusion, companies herded their cattle or fenced them in. The designation of 640 acres as the proper size for this region was frankly an experiment. Major Powell in a notable report on the "Lands of the Arid Region" had suggested four times that amount as the economic unit for the holding, and the Director of the Geological Survey had said that throughout 90 to 95 per cent of the remaining public domain, 160 acres was so small as to be useless as a homestead.[13] Thus 640 acres was a com-

---

[11] *U. S. Stat. at Large,* XXXIII, p. 547.
[12] *House Report,* 58 Cong., 1 and 2 Sess., No. 2452, p. 2.
[13] *Ibid.*

promise amount. It is reported that successful homesteading has been done under the Kinkaid Act.[14]

A Similar Act Applied to Nine States.—Five years later, 1909, the Enlarged Homestead Act was passed, making it possible to take 320 acres as a homestead in nine different states and territories. In 1910 Idaho was added to the list, making ten, and two years later California and North Dakota were included. It was provided in the act of 1909 that one-fourth of the land should be cultivated; that residence should be required as on all homesteads; that the land should be non-irrigable. In the act applying to Idaho an important variation from the usual requirements was made. The homesteader may, if he can show that there is not sufficient water for domestic purposes, at the discretion of the Secretary of the Interior, be permitted to go ahead under the same regulations as in other states, but must cultivate half instead of one-fourth of the land, and instead of living on the homestead is permitted to live anywhere within twenty miles of it. He must, however, give his personal attention to the farming operations.[15] Thus, again, Congress made a notable effort to adapt the Homestead law to the conditions of the West, whereas it was first designed for the Middle West.[16]

The Geological Survey by 1913 had designated nearly 193,000,000 acres as suitable for disposition under this act. However, less than two and a half million were entered by June 30, 1921. No more conclusive proof could be required to the effect that the Enlarged Homestead Act was not solving the difficulties.

From the beginning almost every imaginable period of time to be required in residence on the homestead had been suggested. Some congressmen thought a year or two long enough; others were in favor of a longer time than five years. It was the general feeling, however, that the time should be long enough to sift out from the list of possible

[14] *L. O. R.*, 1909.
[15] *U. S. Stat. at Large*, XXXVI, p. 531; XXVII, p. 132.
[16] The arguments on the bill are mainly to be found in *House Rep.*, 60 Cong., 1 Sess., Nos. 1300, 1513 and 1555.

applicants those who wanted to gain the title to the land because of its market value from those who wanted the land as a farm and a home. At the same time it was recognized that certain hardships resulted from delay in obtaining a title. The land not only could not be sold—it could not be made the basis of a loan, and very often a loan was much desired and much needed. Until the patent was issued, the homesteader was looked upon much as is a tenant in contrast with a land owner.

The Forest Homestead Act.—"Lands in national forests are not in general open to agricultural entry, but under the act of June 11th, 1906," forest-reserve lands which are chiefly valuable for agriculture, which are not needed for public purposes, and which, in the opinion of the Secretary of Agriculture, may be occupied without injury to the forest, may be entered under the homestead laws. Application for a particular tract desired, which must not exceed 160 acres in area nor one mile in length, must be made to the Secretary of Agriculture. The land is then examined by a field agent of the Forest Service, and if his report is favorable the land is listed to the Department of the Interior, where homestead entry is allowed. The entry thereafter proceeds as would any other entry under the Homestead law, but no commutation is permitted. The law differs from all other agricultural land laws in that the land must be chiefly valuable for agriculture and that the entry may be described by metes and bounds instead of legal subdivisions of the public-land survey." [18]

THE THREE-YEAR HOMESTEAD ACT

The five years of residence was not so clearly the proper length of time to be required as to go unchallenged, even after its adoption. The tendency was in one way or another to shorten the period. Over and over, bills were introduced reducing the residence time to two years, two and a half

[17] *U. S. Stat. at Large*, XXXIV, p. 233.
[18] U. S. Geol. Survey *Bulletin* 537, p. 21.

years, or three years.[19] Nothing came of these attempts until 1912, at which time the so-called Three-year Homestead Act passed.[20] During the discussion of this act it was made plain that in the opinion of Congress, at least, the remaining public land was of such a nature that a settler under homestead conditions was not ordinarily able to make a living during the five years required in residence. It was shown that commutation of homestead entries was made increasingly difficult by departmental rulings; that desert-entry holdings required the expenditure of considerable sums of money; that preëmption was a thing of the past; that irrigation was a rich man's game; that therefore the only remaining way under which a poor man might hope for a farm from the public domain was through the five-year homestead act. The Homestead Act has been characterized as a wager in which the United States stakes a quarter-section of land that a man cannot live on it for five consecutive years. According to the trend of the discussion it was the general belief that the government was in recent years winning too many of the bets and in fairness to its citizens ought to make changes in the venture in favor of the other party. Entries were found to be falling off and emigration to Canada on the increase. In view of these beliefs, and facts, it was logical that the West should demand some relief whereby the remaining public lands might be made more attractive to settlers.[21] The Canadian argument seems to have been the most potent. The requirements of the Canadian homestead act, our old Homestead Act, and the proposed act were arranged in parallel columns and presented to Congress.[22] It was shown that in Canada residence was required but six months per year for three years. It was proposed to change our law so as to correspond in these liberal features with the Canadian law. One point, the essential one, was made, before the passage

[19] Cong. Rec., 47 Cong., 2 Sess., p. 3145.
[20] U. S. Stat. at Large, XXXVII, Pt. I, p. 123.
[21] Cong. Rec., 62 Cong., 2 Sess., p. 3685.
[22] Ibid, p. 3625.

of the act, a little less liberal to the settler than were the Canadian provisions, though in the main the act was similar: it was provided that residence should be required for seven months per year for three years. Thus the homesteader can obtain title to his land in twenty-one months of actual residence without payment of anything beyond incidental fees, whereas previously the only way of shortening the five-year period was under the commutation provisions whereby a payment of $200 was required at the end of fourteen months' continuous residence. It is, therefore, at once a question whether the additional time of the homesteader, seven months, is worth to him $200. If not, he would better take the three years, with fifteen months off, and save the $200 outlay. As a matter of fact commutations fell off at once after the passage of this act and final homestead entries increased. For example, commuted homesteads amounted to two and a half million acres a year from 1910 to 1912, but fell to two-fifths of a million acres in 1915, while in the meantime final homestead entries more than doubled, the homesteaders having elected to put in the added seven months rather than pay the $200.[23]

The Three-year Homestead Act may be looked upon as a salutary change in the public-land policy made, for the most part, to accommodate the requirements to the peculiar conditions of the arid regions as compared with the humid regions for which the first Homestead Act was clearly designed.

TABLE XXVII

ALL FINAL HOMESTEAD ENTRIES FROM THE PASSAGE OF THE HOMESTEAD ACT OF 1862 TO JUNE 30, 1923 [24]

Fiscal year ended June 30,	Number	Acres
1868	2,772	355,086.04
1869	3,965	504,301.97
1870	4,041	519,727.84
1871	5,087	629,162.25

[23] L. O. R., 1915.
[24] Ibid, 1923, p. 34.

TABLE XXVII (*Continued*)

Fiscal year ended June 30,	Number	Acres
1872	5,917	707,409.83
1873	10,311	1,224,890.93
1874	14,129	1,585,781.56
1875	18,293	2,068,537.74
1876	22,530	2,590,552.81
1877	19,900	2,407,828.19
1878	22,460	2,662,980.82
1879	17,391	2,070,842.39
1880	15,441	1,938,234.89
1881	15,077	1,928,204.76
1882	17,174	2,219,453.80
1883	18,998	2,504,414.51
1884	21,843	2,945,574.72
1885	22,066	3,032,679.11
1886	19,356	2,663,531.83
1887	19,866	2,749,037.48
1888	22,413	3,175,400.64
1889	25,549	3,681,708.80
1890	28,080	4,060,592.77
1891	27,686	3,954,587.77
1892	22,822	3,259,897.07
1893	24,204	3,477,231.63
1894	20,544	2,929,947.41
1895	20,922	2,980,809.30
1896	20,099	2,790,242.55
1897	20,115	2,778,404.20
1898	22,281	3,095,017.75
1899	22,812	3,134,140.44
1900	25,286	3,477,842.71
1901	37,568	5,241,120.76
1902	31,627	4,342,747.70
1903	26,373	3,576,964.14
1904	23,932	3,232,716.75
1905	24,621	3,419,387.15
1906	25,546	3,526,748.58
1907	26,485	3,740,567.71
1908	29,636	4,242,710.59
1909	25,510	3,699,466.79
1910	23,253	3,795,862.89
1911	25,908	4,620,197.12
1912	24,326	4,306,068.52

TABLE XXVII (*Continued*)

Fiscal year ended June 30,	Number	Acres
1913	53,252	10,009,285.16
1914	48,724	9,291,121.46
1915	37,343	7,180,981.62
1916	37,958	7,278,280.60
1917	43,728	8,497,389.68
1918	41,319	8,236,438.18
1919	32,623	6,524,759.68
1920	39,774	8,372,695.79
1921	33,889	7,726,740.44
1922	30,919	7,307,034.42
1923	22,420	5,594,258.69
Total	1,346,163	213,867,600.93

THE STOCK-RAISING HOMESTEAD ACT OF 1916

The Enlarged Homestead Act fulfilled in a measure its purpose of adapting the size of farm to be cultivated to the type of cultivation, but there remained a large area of land, in the Mountain States particularly, which is not adapted to the cultivation of any merchantable crops. This land could be used for grazing and for raising forage crops, such as kaffir corn, milo maize and some kinds of hay, which, to be worth while, must be fed to cattle rather than shipped to distant markets. More than 320 acres is necessary for such stock farming in these sections. Investigators estimated that a family might "support itself" on 640.

Hence, after considerable agitation on the part of Congressmen from the western states, and on the part of the Department of the Interior, the House of Representatives passed a bill January 18, 1915, which provided for a limit of 640 acres per homestead of lands to be designated as "stock-raising" lands. This bill failed to pass the Senate, but a bill very similar in every respect was passed and became a law December 29, 1916.

The more important provisions of this law are:

1.—That 640 acres shall be a maximum homestead.
2.—That such land must be designated by the Secretary of the Interior as "stock-raising" land.
3.—That such land to be so classified must:
   a. Have a surface such that it is good only for grazing or forage.
   b. Contain no merchantable timber.
   c. Have no convenient irrigation facilities.
   d. Have such quality that it takes 640 acres to support a family.
4.—That certain improvements rather than a certain amount of cultivation are required on these homesteads.
5.—No commutations are allowed.
6.—Coal and mineral rights are reserved.
7.—Water holes are reserved for public use—also lands on certain "trails" leading to these watering places.

No material progress was made in the administration of this law until 1918, due to failure of Congress to appropriate funds to carry on the classification of lands. But, beginning with the year 1918, 91,042 stock-raising entries had been allowed by June 30, 1923, including an area of 35,665,982.99 acres; 105,470 petitions for designation of lands as "stock-raising" and, therefore, eligible to be taken up under this law, were made, 102,516 of which were acted upon; the total amount designated through petitions, less cancellations, was 112,985,631 acres; 21,523 patents amounting to 7,141,174.71 acres were issued during the first five years of the act.[25]

The main support for this bill came from commercial clubs and general boosters of the states containing semi-arid land. It will be remembered that at the time of the passage of this bill prices were rising. Cattle and wheat were both high, and these were the leading products of the regions affected. A report by the Senate Committee on Public

[25] *L. O. R.*, 1923, p. 7.

Lands contains a summary of the arguments in favor of the act: "It believes that many settlers will take advantage of the privileges of this bill to obtain grazing homesteads, thereby adding to the development, wealth and assessment rolls of the Western states. . . . It is not desired to promote speculation in the concentration of such lands in large holdings." [26] Almost no evidence was brought forth in the debate to show that 640 acres was a suitable size for a family grazing farm in the sections for which the law was designed. The nearest approach to convincing argument was made by reference to the Kinkaid Homestead and its results. This was more apparent than real argument since Nebraska and the states interested in the new act are by no means similar. It was a case of a comparison with that which was not comparable; an analogy which was not analogous.

The leading motives back of the Grazing Homestead Act were the old familiar ones of wishes for more people in the newer states and the blind belief that small holdings always mean a greater population. Coupled closely with this desire for more people was the desire for more help in paying taxes. Outside of the states directly interested support came from different sources without a great deal of reluctance, probably mainly on the general ground of a belief in helping the small farmer and stockman. This sentiment was put into unmistakable language by Senator LaFollette of Wisconsin: "I am not one of those who believe that the nomadic stockman, the man who is getting the benefit of public property for nothing and who has had it that way for 30 or 40 years, should be continued in that privilege in perpetuity or during the rest of the existence of the United States." [27] That stockmen ought not to be given the privilege of grazing the public domain at will was a question with but one side. That the 640 acre grazing homestead was the only alternative is, however, another matter. To

[26] *Sen. Rep.* 2, Miscellaneous 11, 64 Cong., 1 Sess., No. 348.
[27] *Cong. Rec.*, 64 Cong., 1 Sess., p. 1179.

resort to a system by which thousands of families were coaxed out onto land unsuited for the purpose to which they were led to believe it adapted was a poor method of striking a blow at the predatory stockman. In the language of the Chief of the Bureau of Forestry, "it was nothing short of a crime to open this land to homestead under the act of 1916."

There were those in Congress who appreciated the situation and wanted the government to take some responsibility in deciding whether or not the land in the areas prescribed was capable of supporting a family. This of course meant shouldering a real responsibility, and those who presumably knew the most about the land were the main objectors to the assumption. Senator Mondell gave the opinion that the homesteader himself should make the decision as to the feasibility of supporting himself and family on any given piece of land. It was the method which had been followed from the beginning in the disposition of the public domain. Thus a bad system was perpetuated, and those least qualified were required to shoulder the responsibility. As a result we have a large number of sorry homesteaders; a group of stockmen bankrupt, due in part to the breaking up of the range; a great many acres of good short grass plowed up and rendered worthless for many years to come. True enough, the homesteading was obliged to await a classification of the land, but it was mainly a negative classification. That is to say, it was an attempt to prevent the homesteader from getting hold of something to which he was not entitled, such as timber, or irrigable land, land on which less than 640 acres is needed for the support of a family; but whether four times 640 acres was needed for such purpose was a matter which the homesteader must decide for himself. He has now found, through painful experiment, that it can't, under present circumstances, be done. Thus do we make another sacrifice on the altar of laissez faire.

The following table gives information as to the activities under this law, as to the states most affected and as to the proportion of total entries per year beginning with 1918.

TABLE XXVIII

ORIGINAL STOCKRAISING HOMESTEAD ENTRIES, DECEMBER 29, 1916, TO JUNE 30, 1923 [28-29]

State	Number of Entries	Acres
Arizona	2,242	995,999.17
Arkansas	3	1,120.00
California	4,115	1,634,452.38
Colorado	12,135	4,603,827.59
Idaho	4,093	1,725,085.61
Kansas	198	54,130.51
Michigan	3	1,400.00
Montana	12,317	4,149,607.14
Nebraska	343	56,666.77
Nevada	381	203,371.72
New Mexico	17,027	7,272,850.54
North Dakota	624	189,034.32
Oklahoma	241	46,868.61
Oregon	5,387	2,114,177.73
South Dakota	6,084	2,061,164.17
Utah	1,614	856,090.02
Washington	1,178	366,960.18
Wyoming	23,057	9,333,175.83
Grand Total	80,323	31,407,991.82
Year		
1918	734	236,578.08
1919	15,035	5,558,756.11
1920	20,979	8,228,749.20
1921	25,653	10,313,732.89
1922	17,922	7,070,175.54
1923	10,719	4,257,990.47

RELIEF OF SETTLERS [30]

The free-land policy as initiated by the early homestead and preëmption laws caused a great influx into new regions. People not well adapted to farming settled in districts where

[28] *L. O. R.*, 1923, p. 7.

[29] *Ibid*, pp. 73-74.

[30] This discussion is representative of relief measures granted throughout the peroid of public land disposals.

the climate and qualities of the soil were entirely unknown. As a result, in many districts it seemed as though the settlers would be obliged to abandon the undertaking. In order that such failures might be avoided Congress passed a series of acts which had for their purpose the relief of settlers upon government lands.

Crop failures, due to elements over which the settler had no control, called for a special class of legislation. Droughts, grasshoppers, and forest and prairie fires added hardships to the homesteader's already heavy burden. The complete destruction of crops often made it necessary for the pioneer to abandon his homestead and leave the district because of a lack of means of subsistence until the next year. That the settler might not be forced to relinquish his holdings under such circumstances, Congress passed a series of acts which enabled him to abandon his claim temporarily in order that he might make a living during the period of crop failure. These indulgences carried with them the extension of time on fees and commission payments on the land over the time of misfortune.

As a result of the complete destruction of crops by the grasshoppers in 1873 over large areas of the homestead districts, an act was passed in the following year allowing settlers whose crops had been so destroyed a leave of absence from their claims until July 1, 1875. The time of final proof and payment was also extended for a period of one year after the expiration of the settler's term of absence.[31] The very next Congress extended the provisions of this concession by one year more;[32] and in 1877 they were again put in force for still another year.[33]

Little legislation was passed during the eighties for the direct relief of homesteaders who could not subsist upon their claims. Their condition did not demand it, but by 1890 the general welfare of the homesteader was at such a low

[31] *U. S. Stat. at Large*, XIX, p. 55.
[32] *Ibid*, p. 59.
[33] *Ibid*, p. 405.

ebb that a joint resolution was adopted extending the time of payment on commuted homestead and preëmption claims, in case of crop failure for which the settler was in nowise responsible, for a period of not to exceed one year.[34] Four years later—1894—this extension of time was made to include all claims located under the Homestead or Desert Land Laws.[35] The term "crop failure" was not in the act. The time of payment of all homesteaders was extended.

Because of the extensive forest fires in 1894 in Wisconsin, Minnesota and Michigan, settlers in the burned district were given two years additional time for making final proof, or they or their heirs could receive title to the land by paying the minimum price, providing the law had been complied with up to the date of the fire. Furthermore, if they had not lived upon the land long enough to commute, and had lost 75,000 feet of merchantable green timber, they could obtain permission to cut the burned timber and receive a patent to their claim upon payment of $1.25 per acre.[36]

Several minor acts and resolutions have been passed since 1900 granting special dispensations as to leaves of absence and time of payments to settlers in certain states, and to restricted districts within a state. This legislation, which is no different from the more general acts mentioned, applies in most cases to homesteaders in the more newly settled territory of the states of Montana, Wyoming, Minnesota, the Dakotas, Idaho, Washington and Oklahoma.

In 1910 homesteaders on lands to be irrigated by the government were granted leave of absence until the water was turned on, with the provision that their required term of residence should not be lessened by such absence.[37]

Not only did the relief acts apply to homestead settlers, but in the years 1896, 1897, 1898, 1900 and 1901 legislation was put in force which extended the time of payment to purchasers of ceded Indian lands who had bought with the

---

[34] *U. S. Stat. at Large*, XXVI, p. 684.
[35] *Ibid*, XXVIII, p. 123.
[36] *Ibid*, XXVIII, p. 634.
[37] *Ibid*, XXXVI, p. 864.

condition of actual settlement. Each act extended the time of payment one year—except the act of 1898, which made it two years—in addition to the extension of the previous act.[38]

Relief of Settlers on Railroad Land Grants.—A very similar situation in regard to need for relief arose in connection with settlers on the railroad land grants. Complications arose due to the fact that numerous railroad grants were made which included land that had previously been subject to settlement through the homestead and preëmption laws, and the fact that the railroad grants withdrew certain of these lands from settlement except by purchase from the railroad. In the first place, it gave the roads title to lands previously preëmpted or homesteaded, and in the second place, it withdrew from entry the lands surrounding the homesteader and thus postponed the immediate settlement of his neighborhood. Both of these conditions were obviously unfair to the settler.

To relieve this situation, in 1874 Congress passed legislation entitled: "An Act for the Relief of Settlers on Railroad Lands." [39] This act entitled settlers found to have located on railroad land grants to select an equal quantity of land (not mineral) from the public domain and to receive title to the same as though they had originally settled upon it.

In 1880 another act was passed reimbursing settlers for moneys spent for fees and commissions on "void, fraudulent and conflicting claims." On land bought supposedly within a railroad grant and for which the double minimum price had been paid, if it was later found that the land did not lie within the supposed grant the excess payment, *i.e.*, $1.25 per acre, was to be returned to the purchaser.[40]

The Forty-fifth Congress (1878) provided that notices of contests must be printed in some newspaper published

[38] *U. S. Stat. at Large*, XXIX, 321, XXX, 62, XXX, p. 571, XXXI, p. 221.
[39] *Ibid*, XVIII, p. 194.
[40] *Ibid*, XXI, p. 287.

in the county, or in an adjacent county, to the one in which the land lay.[41] The next Congress gave the settler procuring a relinquishment upon a contested claim thirty days in which to make entry upon the relinquished land.[42] In 1892 it became the duty of the land register to notify the person who procured the relinquishment of the fact that the transfer had been recognized. If the person initiating the contest died before final termination, his rights and privileges accrued to his heirs.[43]

A good illustration of the statement that many of the relief acts were passed without discussion and in a matter-of-course manner is furnished by three laws exactly alike passed within short intervals of one another. Two of the acts, one a duplicate of the other, were passed by the same session of Congress within thirty days of each other. Certainly, had the subject attracted any attention whatever, the repetitions of the first act would never have appeared upon the statute book. These acts gave a settler under the preëmption laws who changed his filing to that of a homestead entry, the privilege of computing his time required to perfect his title under the homestead law from the date of his original settlement made under the preëmption laws.[44] That is to say, he could apply his residence under the preëmption laws upon his homestead entry.

The most important and longest pending relief measure, and the one which provoked the most discussion, was an amendment which granted to settlers the privilege of making out their affidavits before the clerk of the court in the county in which they resided, instead of having to appear in person at the district land office. Many of the homesteads were located some distance from the land office— probably one hundred miles in some instances. It was urged that these journeys not only required a great deal of time, but, in the case of final proof where two witnesses had also

[41] U. S. Stat. at Large, XX, p. 91.
[42] Ibid, XXI, p. 140.
[43] Ibid, XXVII, p. 270.
[44] Ibid, XIX, p. 404; Ibid, XX, pp. 63 and 113.

to appear, the trip involved an unnecessary expense upon the settler.

An act of 1864 gave those serving in the army or navy the right to make out their first affidavit—the one of entry—before their commanding officers, and also allowed persons who were prevented by reason of "distance, bodily infirmity, or other good cause" from appearing at the district land office, to make out their entry papers before the clerk of the court of their respective counties. This amendment in question merely attempted to extend these privileges to settlers in the making out of all necessary papers in connection with their homesteads. The matter dragged along, notwithstanding the fact that it passed the House twice, for a period of some ten years, but finally, in 1880, settlers on preëmption and commuted homesteads were permitted the coveted privilege of making out their affidavits before the clerk of the county court, or any court of record, in the county in which the land was situated.[45]

Ten years later—1890—the privilege was extended to applicants for the benefits of the homestead, preëmption, timber-culture and desert land laws.[46]

Immediately following the passage of this act many settlers made their affidavit before United States Court Commissioners instead of before United States Circuit Court Commissioners, and in 1894 Congress passed an act validating such affidavits.[47] This legislation was followed by the appointment of United States Court Commissioners in the territories not located within thirty miles of one another nor within thirty miles of a district land office.[48]

Besides the above named so-called relief acts, there were a number which simply pertained to minor details such as the conditions and circumstances of the making of affidavits by aliens; the refunding of fees and commissions collected

---

[45] If the land was located in an unorganized county the affidavit might be made in an adjacent country. *U. S. Stat. at Large*, XXI, p. 169.
[46] *Ibid*, XXVI, p. 121.
[47] *Ibid*, p. 227.
[48] *Ibid*, XXVIII, p. 744.

in excess of the lawfully required amount; and concerning vacancies in the office of land registers and receivers.

In recent years two minor, though important amendments in the nature of homestead relief measures have been passed. On June 5, 1900, legislation was approved to the effect that persons who had made entry under the homestead laws and had forfeited their claims were still entitled to the benefits of the Homestead law as if such entry had not been made.[49] On the following day, June 6, it became lawful for a woman who had married since filing upon a claim to retain her claim, providing she did not abandon her residence on the land after marriage and providing the man whom she married was not claiming a separate tract of land under the Homestead law.[50]

SUMMARY

In summarizing the story of the Homestead Act it would be easy to indulge in flattering commendation, or, within the bounds of truth, to criticize it harshly. Neither treatment is in accordance with the merits of the case. It was, in the first place, the inevitable culmination of a tendency, which became a struggle, covering virtually the whole period of the federal land history from the later seventeenth century to 1862, a period of nearly seventy-five years. Leniency toward the squatters, donations to defenders of the frontier, preëmption concessions, all pointed to land without price. Expediency, natural rights, class conflict, and charity were in turn, and coördinately, made the basis of the discussions and concessions. Sectional strife played a powerful, though entirely incidental, part in the development of the plan. It would have been the same in outcome ultimately with either more or less sectional trouble.

As a nation we were destined to arrive at the point of granting free land to settlers. It was at once a manifestation of the strength and weakness of a developing democracy. Immediately the democratic form of government as manifested in America was too weak to handle its public land in a way designed to bring into its treasury any considerable price for unused land. A private concern can charge what the market will bear. So can the government. But in the latter case it will bear very little, while in the former it may be a great deal. The government could not hold the price of land at any con-

[49] *U. S. Stat. at Large*, XXXI, p. 269.
[50] *Ibid*, p. 683.

siderable figure with its legislative body filled with representatives of a pioneer group convinced that land ought to be free, and aware of the fact that no drastic measures had yet been enforced against the practices of frontier settlers.

The argument that a liberal policy with respect to land would strengthen the democracy always met with a cordial response. No doubt such proved to be the case. The plan to diffuse wealth, create a land-owning, home-owning, people was part and parcel of the free land movement. The success of this portion of the program may have been real, but at best it was temporary. Where land was almost as free as water half a century ago it has risen in value to several hundred dollars per acre, and the ownership of it by those operating it has become a problem difficult of solution. Tenancy has passed the fifty per cent mark in many counties in which homesteads were the order of the day in the seventies. As an ultimate solution to the land question, or as a solution to the problem of wealth distribution it was a palliative, not a remedy.

The great weakness of the Homestead Act was, and is, its utter inadaptability to the parts of the country for which it was not designed. The idea of the farm small in acres within the semi-arid regions was tenacious, but untenable. It was even vicious in its operation. Congress was converted to the homestead principle in the large, and instructed in detail, by the people on the Missouri River frontier, backed up by the experience of the whole country, not essentially different, between Ohio and the Missouri. The frontiersmen on the plains were too few in numbers, and too unlike the earlier frontiersmen to the East of them, to compel the working out of a desirable modification of the land laws. The recent acts are improvements over the earlier ones in their application to the semi-arid states. So far as the operation of the Homestead Act in relation to forests is concerned there is hardly a mitigating feature. It was wholly inapplicable, yet it applied. It promoted perjury and profits among a large number of small adventurers. The forests were easily procured by the lumbermen and are now largely gone. In this tragedy the Homestead was a mere incident.

With all its shortcomings the Homestead Act clearly has more to its credit than any other one land act passed by the federal government. A million and a third homesteads have been taken up and carried to completion. Many failed to become farms, yet out of the number the majority remained the farm unit for some years. It was a means of peopling the wilderness, and while it was a short-sighted policy, leaving many land questions unsettled, the hope of their settlement in advance was entirely wanting. East of the hundredth meridian the Homestead was a success.

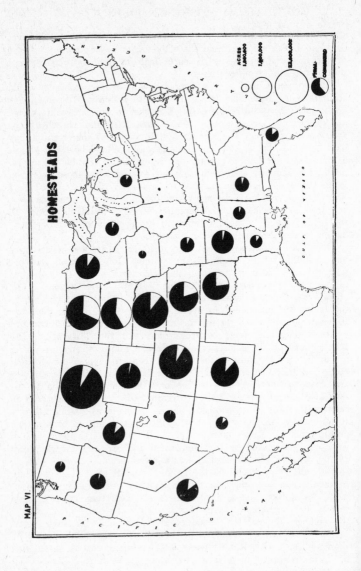

MAP VI.

HOMESTEADS

CHAPTER XIX

THE TIMBER CULTURE ACT

THE DIMINISHING TIMBER SUPPLY

During the first half and more of the nineteenth century the frontier passed westward over a region largely clothed in forests. The first efforts of the pioneer were directed toward the removal of the timber, the ax of necessity preceding the plow.

By 1866[1] it was recognized, however, that while the demand for timber was rapidly increasing, the supply was diminishing. Even in the northern parts of Michigan, Wisconsin and Minnesota, where some of the most extensive forests of the northern latitude were found, it was reported that the supply was "so diminishing as to be a matter of serious concern."

Moreover, as the frontier was now approaching the treeless regions of the plains, settlers faced a new set of conditions. The protracted droughts prevailing in this region were not only destructive in themselves, but brought with them, in addition, the ravages of the grasshopper. The difficulties which these conditions introduced, as well as the rapid diminution of the timbered area, fostered an interest in the artificial cultivation of trees.

PLANS FOR COVERING THE PLAINS WITH GROWING TIMBER

It had been found that instead of the prairie being unsuitable for tree culture, timber could readily be grown there from seed, if cultivated and protected from fires; and attention was called to the possible improvement in agri-

[1] *L. O. R.*, 1866, p. 33; *Ibid*, 1867, p. 95, and 1868.

cultural conditions which the presence of forests might bring about. For some years in the instructions from the General Land Office, surveyors general and deputies had been required to encourage United States surveyors "to plant midway between each pit and trench the seeds of trees adapted to the climate, the fact of planting and kind of seed to appear in the field notes of survey." These recommendations had fallen into disuse when, in 1866, Commissioner Wilson began to urge national legislation:

"Observation and experience appear to establish the fact that as settlements have advanced over the states of Illinois, Iowa and Minnesota, as well as certain portions of Ohio, the protection afforded to the prairies in preventing fires has resulted in increasing growth of timber, independent of the planting of orchard and shade trees and a greater regularity and more equal distribution in the fall of rain. The destructive inundations, excessive droughts and sudden changes of temperature, so well remembered by the early settlers of Iowa, and prevailing a quarter of a century ago, are diminishing every year in that prosperous state. Similar changes are noticed in the eastern portions of Kansas and Nebraska, in the vicinity of Denver, and in the valley of Salt Lake; in fact, in every locality where the improvement of settlers, even for so short a period as ten years, has resulted in adding considerably to the number of trees; attesting not only the extraordinary importance of the forest in rural economy, but the readiness of nature to second the operations of man in respect to climate, and other agencies affecting the productiveness of the soil.

"If one-third the surface of the great plains were covered with forest there is every reason to believe the climate would be greatly improved, the value of the whole area as a grazing country wonderfully enhanced and the greater portion of the soil would be susceptible of a high state of cultivation.

"It is recommended that an amendment be made to the Homestead law requiring each settler, on proving up at the end of five years, to make proof of having planted and cultivated a certain number of trees, living and at least three years old from the seed or from setting out at the time of the application for a patent. The labor of tree-planting being first enjoined as a requisite to obtain a title would fix the attention of settlers to the subject; and discovering the feasibility of the enterprise, they soon would prosecute it from the consideration of its evident advantages to themselves and the whole community. An additional inducement might perhaps be presented by a general law, offering an additional number of acres to each settler who should successfully cultivate for a given number of years a certain number of acres in forest.

"The production of a thriving forest at some point west of the 100th meridian, as it would establish the fact of its practicability, would, without doubt, contribute greatly to the value of that part of our domain. Whether an enterprise of the kind, under the auspices of the government, would be likely to realize the expectations of its projectors, would depend very much upon the character of the persons who might be charged with the duties and responsibilities of the undertaking. It is scarcely to be doubted that the artesian well system might be rendered a great success on the plains. All the conditions appear favorable."

The House of Representatives responded in 1871 by a resolution ordering that the Committee on Public Lands "be instructed to inquire into the expediency of providing by law that in all settlements hereafter made upon the public lands under the Homestead law, it shall be necessary as a condition to the perfection of the homestead that the occupant of prairie lands shall put out and cultivate some certain number of acres of timber, for a time to be fixed thereon prior to the making of his or her final proof."

The first timber-culture bill to become a law was introduced by Senator Hitchcock of Nebraska. It passed the Senate with little discussion, and that concerning details rather than the principle of the proposed act. The House treated it with even less consideration. It became a law March 13, 1873.

The Act of 1873 and Amendments

This original bill—"an act to encourage the growth of timber on western prairies" [2]—provided that any person who would plant, protect and keep in a healthy growing condition for ten years, forty acres of timber—trees not more than twelve feet apart—would receive title to the quarter-section of which the forty acres was a part. Only one quarter in any section was to be obtained in this manner.

The act provided, also, that patents should be granted to homesteaders who had been on their claims for three years and had had one acre of trees under cultivation for the last two years of that time. This, the first timber-culture act, was found wanting in many respects, as is shown by the fact that the very next year it was amended, making decided changes in some of its important requirements. [3]

The qualifications for entry under the amendments were made the same as those of the Homestead law—the head of a family, twenty-one years of age, a citizen or a person officially declaring himself about to become such—which is a marked change from the qualifications in the original act expressed in the phrase "any person." The amount of land that could be obtained under this act was limited to one hundred sixty acres to any one person. One amendment provided that timber should be cultivated for eight years instead of ten. However, the greatest change was in the method of planting and cultivating the trees. The original act required the entire forty acres to be planted in one year, which proved to be such a task as to render the law virtually void. Hence the amended act contained minute specifications for the preparation of the ground and the planting of the trees, extending over a period of four years.

Because of the devastations of grasshoppers in certain

[2] *U. S. Stat. at Large*, XVII, p. 605.
[3] *Ibid*, XVIII, p. 21.

western areas, principally Kansas and Nebraska, during the years 1874 and 1875 it was found necessary further to amend the act of 1873. The demands for modifications were great in the grasshopper district. This fact is shown by the three bills providing for the same things that were introduced in the House at the session of 1876.

An amendment passed with little discussion providing that in case trees were destroyed by grasshoppers, such destruction should not work a forfeiture of any rights of the settler, but that the time for final proofs should be extended the same number of years as was lost through the misfortune.

Furthermore, it provided that the planting of "seeds, nuts, and cuttings" would be considered a compliance with the law; and that the timber might be planted in not more than four different lots.[4] Previously the tract had to be compact. A former commissioner of the land office had allowed the planting of seeds, nuts, and cuttings, but the right to make such allowance had been questioned.[5]

THE ACT OF 1878 REDUCES REQUIREMENTS ON THE PART OF SETTLER

In the succeeding Congress—the 45th—bills, petitions and memorials were introduced asking that the number of acres of timber to be planted be reduced. The agitation resulted in the Act of June 14, 1878, which reduced the number of acres from forty to ten and prescribed the number of trees to be grown per acre as 2,700 at the time of planting and "675 living, thrifty trees" when the patent should be granted.[6]

In the discussion of this bill it was generally admitted that the timber-culture laws had not accomplished the results anticipated. Several reasons were assigned: As Senator Saunders of Nebraska put it, speaking of previous legislation,

[4] *U. S. Stat. at Large*, XIX, p. 54.
[5] *Cong. Rec.*, 44 Cong., 1 Sess., p. 1415.
[6] *U. S. Stat. at Large*, XX, p. 113.

"It is more timber, in the first place, than the settler needs, and is more than poor people can afford to put out and cultivate." [7] The gist of the whole question is well expressed in the following memorial: [8]

"To the Congress of the United States:

"Your memorialists, the Legislature of the State of Minnesota, represent that the existing law enabling citizens of the United States to enter public land under the tree-culture act, and to obtain patents to tracts of one quarter-section of the same upon proof that they have planted forty acres with trees not more than twelve feet apart, has proved to be substantially a failure, inasmuch as it is found almost impossible for the settler to plant and protect so large a tract of land for the period required by law. The trees planted twelve feet apart do not shade the land so as to keep down the growth of grass and weeds, and the task of cultivating the land becomes an endless one.

"Your memorialists recognize the question of tree-planting as one of the first magnitude to the people of the prairie regions of our country. Without tree-culture much of the territory of the United States will be uninhabitable. The necessities of the people for fuel, fencing, and shelter from the winds, all unite in demanding such legislation as will encourage the people to grow timber.

"Your memorialists would therefore ask that you amend the existing timber-culture act so as to reduce the number of acres to be planted to trees from forty acres to ten acres; providing, however, that the trees shall be planted not more than four feet apart, instead of, as at present, twelve feet apart. A change of this character would produce more trees than at present, while the timber-culture act would thereby be made a success.

"Your memorialists would also ask that parties who have entered land heretofore under the existing timber-culture act would be permitted to take advantage of the

[7] *Cong. Rec.*, 45 Cong., 2 Sess., p. 1854.
[8] *Ibid*, p. 1855.

proposed amendment on such terms as Congress may prescribe."

The principal argument urged against the bill was that it gave away the public lands on too small a pretext, one that could easily be taken advantage of by the speculator. Instances of fraud under the old law were cited as proof in support of this contention. Those favoring the amendment maintained that speculators could purchase the land outright for $200—for less than they could hire someone to cultivate ten acres of timber for eight years.

This act of 1878 marks the beginning of continued opposition to the timber-culture laws.

COMMISSIONER OF LAND OFFICE RECOMMENDS REPEAL

In his report for the year 1882, the Commissioner of the General Land Office called attention to the abuses to which the act was subject, stating that numerous fictitious entries were being made in order to hold the land out of the market, and thus sell relinquishments to the right of occupation. In his report the following year the Commissioner states:[9]

"In my last annual report I called attention to abuses flowing from this act. Continued experience has demonstrated that these abuses are inherent in the law, and beyond the reach of administrative methods for their correction. Settlement on the land is not required. Even residence within the State or Territory in which the land is situated is not a condition to an entry. A mere entry of record holds the land for one year without the performance of any act of cultivation. The meager act of breaking five acres, which can be done at the close of the year as well as at the beginning, holds the land for the second year. Comparatively trivial acts hold it for a third year. During these periods relinquishments of the entries are sold to homestead or other settlers at such price as the land may command.

"My information leads me to the conclusion that a

[9] L. O. R., 1883, pp. 7, 8.

majority of entries under the timber-culture act are made for speculative purposes and not for the cultivation of timber. Compliance with the law in these cases is a mere pretense and does not result in the production of timber. . . . My information is that no trees are to be seen over vast regions of country where timber-culture entries have been most numerous. . . . I am convinced that the public interests will be served by a total repeal of the law, and I recommend such repeal."

The sale of relinquishments became a regular occupation for many land agents. Fictitious entries were initiated for the purpose of holding the land out of market. For ten dollars and a small additional outlay for making the first necessary improvements, lands were held for one, two, or three years until the growth of the neighborhood enabled the speculator to dispose of his rights at a good profit. The next holder embarked on the same course, holding the land from market for one or more years, finally disposing of his title. In this way tracts were frequently relinquished five or six times before they fell into the hands of an actual settler, who thus found himself obliged to pay a heavy tribute to the speculator before he might be able to avail himself of the laws designed especially to provide homes for the poor. Trees were not usually planted until the settler acquired possession, when it was done without the benefits or inducements of the timber-culture law, and thus this law by delaying the coming of the settler actually delayed, too, the development of the agricultural resources of the region which it affected, and frustrated the very purpose for which it was enacted.

Under the timber-culture laws, relinquishments of entries and the making of entries for the purpose of selling relinquishments was a business of great magnitude and an unqualified abuse of the privileges of the laws. The same tracts of land were entered and relinquished over and over again. Generally in each case a new entry was filed simultaneously with the presentation of the relinquishment of the former, and this process goes on indefinitely. Meanwhile the lands are held from settlement, and remain uninhabited, unimproved and uncultivated.[10]

The timber-culture act was used for holding great tracts of land for range purposes. "Within the great stock ranges of Nebraska, Kansas, Colorado, and elsewhere, one-quarter of nearly every section is covered by a timber-culture entry made for the use of the cattle owners, usually by their herdsmen who make false land office affidavits as a part of the condition of their employment." [11] These entries could be held for thirteen years under the merest pretense of living up to the law.[12] A cattle company in Dakota had twenty-six quarter-section entries made in its interest, judiciously located along streams.

A large class of homesteaders take up adjoining quarter-sections under this act, and intend the whole for a wheat or stock farm after the lands have passed to patent. They "don't want to be bothered with brush," and argue that the law was made to be evaded.[13]

Timber-culture entries were often made by men who had already used their preëmption and homestead rights, thus getting probably 480 acres, altogether, of government land, a condition not contemplated, or favored, by the land office authorities.[14] Many other instances and methods of evasion and fraud might be given.

In 1885 the commissioner again recommended the repeal of the act, and in 1887 the same commissioner reports:

"I can truthfully say that I do not believe that one timber-culture filing in a hundred is actually made in good faith for the purpose of cultivating it to trees."

Fraud was not the only evil urged against the bill. Congress was the recipient of many petitions and memorials stating that it was impracticable and in many cases impossible to carry out the provisions of the law. Representative Pickler of South Dakota protested that "this law lays down

[10] *L. O. R.*, 1187, pp. 61-98.
[11] *Ibid*, 1885, p. 72.
[12] *Ibid*, 1885, p. 72.
[13] *Ibid*, 1884, p. 7.
[14] *Ibid*, 1883, p. 708.

rules for the growing of trees for every climate in the United States. Now it is found that it will not work. It is a failure." [15]

This sentiment is reiterated in a memorial from the legislature of the state of Washington in 1890,[16] which explains that many individual settlers in that state had expended from $500 to $1,000 in an attempt to grow timber under the law, and were no nearer to final proof than they were five or six years previously. It was inevitable that a law so easy of perversion and so little productive of good should be repealed, yet it took Congress half a dozen years to get it done.

ACT REPEALED, 1891

During the later eighties numerous bills were introduced in Congress providing for the repeal of both the timber-culture and preëmption laws. At least four of these bills passed the House but not until 1891 did such an act get through the Senate.

A bill passed the House providing simply for the repeal of the timber-culture laws, but in the Senate every portion was amended save the enacting clause. This body included an omnibus collection of land reforms in their amendments touching upon a variety of provisions ranging from the building of reservoirs in arid districts to reserving town sites in Alaska. A conference of the two houses resulted in the passage of an act entitled "An act to repeal the timber-culture laws, and for other purposes," approved March 3, 1891.[17]

To be sure, the clause, "and for other purposes," covered many things. However, as far as the timber-culture laws were concerned, it contained the following provisions:

1. All timber-culture laws were repealed.
2. Existing rights of those entered were preserved.
3. Persons who had complied with the timber-culture laws

---

[15] *Cong. Rec.*, 51 Cong., 1 Sess., p. 2352.
[16] *Ibid*, 51 Cong., 1 Sess., p. 2516.
[17] *U. S. Stat. at Large*, XXVI, p. 1095.

for four years might receive a patent for their claim by paying $1.25 per acre.

This is the last legislation concerning the timber-culture on the western prairie with the exception of a clause in an appropriation bill of 1893, to the effect that if trees planted under the timber-culture act, before its repeal, were cultivated in good faith for eight years, final proof might be made regardless of the number of trees living.

The intent of the act of 1891, which also repealed the preëmption laws, was aptly expressed by Representative Payson of Illinois, in a speech urging the passage of the bill. He said: "Ten years of continuous service has resulted in placing upon the statute books of this nation, to endure, I trust, as long as the nation shall endure, these two propositions: that not an acre of the public domain shall be taken by anybody except as the home of a poor man or for reclamation, where now there is only a desert." [18]

Summary

Why, it may be asked, did the timber-culture act fail so dismally, or, viewing it from a different angle, why did Congress make such a sad mistake, after the experience of a century, as to pass a law destined to fail? It may be of interest to note that the act was passed at the very time when there was a pronounced awakening on the whole subject of forestry and timber-culture. This sentiment found expression in a law which had for its purpose the use of the public domain, from which almost no revenue was then coming, to accomplish at a stroke a most marvelous transformation of the bleak plains of the western Mississippi Valley. Trees would grow there; manifestly the country would be benefited by their growth. Then why not let a land-hungry man cultivate a grove in exchange for a farm? It was a beautiful dream, but the substance of the dream was for the most part as unreal as such visions usually are.

It should be said further in explanation that, like the homestead law, it was made for a given type of land and applied to very different land within a short time. The Timber-Culture Act was framed when there was still some government land in Iowa, a great deal in southwestern Minnesota, and immediately to the west of the Missouri River. But by the time a few years had passed and the Timber-Culture Act got well under way its operation was crowded into

[18] *Cong. Rec.*, 51 Cong., 2 Sess., p. 3615.

the plains and into the semi-arid regions, where it would have been both impossible and undesirable to bring the trees along to the stage required by the government. The region is too dry for forests, at least of the kind then contemplated. It was one of the most complete failures, so far as accomplishing what Congress had in mind is concerned, to be recorded in the long list of unfortunate public land acts. A ride through the section of the country where land was by this means made private property fails to reveal to the traveler any of those magnificent prospects pictured by the eloquence of the Congressman.

It was another instance of a law successful in giving a large amount of land, mostly to people who did not deserve it, and bringing to the government another chapter of experience in how public domain ought not to be handled.

The land disposed of under this act is shown in the following table:

TABLE XXIX

LAND DISPOSED OF UNDER THE

TIMBER CULTURE ACT, MARCH 3, 1873 TO JUNE 30, 1921 [19]

State	Acres of final entry	Acres Commuted
Arizona	7,149	10,223
Arkansas	480	40
California	63,572	78,849
Colorado	585,243	98,180
Dakota Territory	185,467	......
Idaho	40,436	28,245
Iowa	31,988	2,331
Kansas	2,005,831	142,932
Louisiana	11,938	5,857
Minnesota	373,581	40,261
Montana	56,020	29,044
Nebraska	2,546,696	187,371
Nevada	160	......
New Mexico	12,932	7,837
North Dakota	1,226,606	120,525
Oregon	224,546	35,903
South Dakota	2,124,754	121,891
Utah	15,556	10,157
Washington	292,728	75,690
Wisconsin	40	......
Wyoming	50,543	15,288
Total	9,856,264	1,010,624

[19] L. O. R., 1921, p. 65.

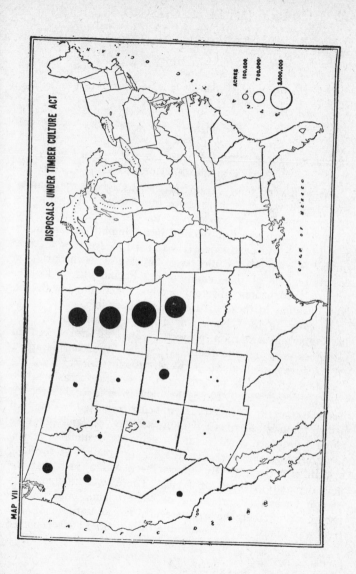

MAP VII

DISPOSALS UNDER TIMBER CULTURE ACT

ACRES
100,000
700,000
3,000,000

CHAPTER XX

THE DESERT LAND ACTS

Discovery That the Homestead Act Did Not Fit Arid Conditions

Within a very few years after the passage of the Homestead law it was evident to those familiar with its workings that it applied very awkwardly to the arid lands of the West. A quarter-section of land in the humid section might be a boon to its possessor. It was hard to see how a tract, similar in size only, could be of much use in the arid, or desert, regions of the mountain and Pacific states. Hence, proposals for some different method of dealing with the land question in these districts were inevitable.

As early as 1869 Utah was asking for land to be used in promoting irrigation projects.[1] The bill introduced in Congress covering the request received little consideration. At frequent intervals bills were brought forward asking for land to aid in irrigation. On several occasions the Committee on Public Lands brought in a favorable report, but the measures failed after being reported.[2] One bill asked for a grant of forty-eight sections of land per mile along a proposed canal.[3] But for some unaccountable reason Congress was obdurate. It was felt by many that the land system was perfect. By others there was a fear that the new demands savored of fraud. There was no unanimity of opinion as to the meaning of "desert land," and for one reason or another the grants were denied until in 1875 a trial was made. The Committee on Public Lands reported

[1] *Cong. Globe*, 40 Cong., 3 Sess., p. 781.
[2] *Ibid*, p. 1078; *Ibid*, 42 Cong., 2 Sess., pp. 120, 1965.
[3] *Ibid*, 41 Cong., 3 Sess., pp. 235, 236.

favorably a bill providing for a new plan of disposing of desert land in Lassen County, California. The bill provided that a tract of land not to exceed a section to each might be taken by certain persons who should undertake to conduct water upon it so as to reclaim all of it within two years, in which event they should receive title to the land on payment of the minimum government price.[4] It was frankly acknowledged to be an experiment. One of the main features of the bill was the privilege given to the settlers to go upon land not surveyed, and which the government hardly expected to survey, on account of its supposed worthlessness.[5] This seemed to be at least a safe beginning, but as a matter of fact Congress was dealing with a subject about which it had very little information. In the passage of the Homestead law many Congressmen knew very intimately the country to which they believed it would apply. That country had already been largely settled. The arid lands were as nature left them, and the use to which they had been put was widely different from anything provided for by federal legislation.

It took only the most superficial observation to convince one that the land laws made for the Middle West did not fit the West. President Grant made a visit to the mountain states in the autumn of 1875 and in his annual message to Congress the following December recommended the appointment of a commission to visit the West and make recommendations concerning the disposition of government land.[6] He said: "In territory where cultivation of the soil can only be followed by irrigation, and where irrigation is not practicable, the lands can only be used as pasturage, and this only where stock can reach water . . . and cannot be governed by the laws as to entries as lands every acre of which is an independent estate by itself.

"Land must be held in larger quantities to justify the

[4] *U. S. Stat. at Large*, XVIII, p. 497.
[5] *Cong. Globe*, 43 Cong., 2 Sess., p. 1787.
[6] *Cong. Record*, 44 Cong., 2 Sess., p. 32.

expense of conducting water upon it to make it fruitful or to justify using it as pasturage." While not literally exact, the substance of this judgment is in accordance with the facts.

About the time this recommendation was made by the President, the Commissioner of the General Land Office made an elaborate report in which were set forth the main conditions surrounding the land question in the West.[7] The essence of this report was that land west of the one-hundredth meridian, valuable mainly for grazing purposes, should be put upon the market and sold freely at the government price instead of being restricted to the preëmption and homestead requirements. It was his belief that on most of these western lands the homesteader could not honestly live up to the law. The report shows some appreciation of the patent fact that one farmer cannot, in many instances, finance and install an irrigation system for his own land. "For their reclamation a system necessarily expensive, because involving canals or main ditches of great length and size, is required; and, hence, associated capital must be called upon to furnish the means of success. But the security for its repayment, even the inducement to furnish it, must be found in the lands to be benefited." Here was a genuine premonition of the policies which have grown up in connection with the arid lands. The following year the commissioner, the successor to the one who made the report of 1875, elucidated the subject a little further. Speaking of large irrigation projects, he said: "Neither companies nor individuals will engage in such enterprises until they can procure titles to the lands to be irrigated, which they cannot now do." The demand was imperative. Congress might delay action; it could not refuse ultimately to act.

THE FIRST ACT PASSED

In December, 1876, a bill was introduced in the House providing for the sale of a section of land to a settler who

[7] *L. O. R.*, 1875, pp. 6-9.

would irrigate it within three years after filing. It was provided that a payment of twenty-five cents per acre was to be made at the time of filing, and of one dollar at the time of making proof of compliance with the law. This feature has been continued as a part of nearly all our desert land legislation. The bill passed the House with very little opposition. In the Senate it was referred to the Committee on Public Lands which committee made a favorable report.[8] It was the belief of the committee that the larger amount of land allowed to one settler would prove an inducement to irrigation which could not be afforded by a quarter-section as under the Homestead Act. The committee did not favor the plan of giving these lands away outright, neither did it favor sale in unlimited quantities, thinking the latter plan would result in speculation. The Senate debated the bill at considerable length, but there is hardly more than the two grains of wheat in the two bushels of chaff resulting.[9] The debate hinged mainly on details, and very little on the general principle of disposing of desert land to settlers. The bill provided that the settler should "reclaim" the land by conducting water upon it. The question was asked, "How much water?" But it passed with the reply, "Of course enough water to make it an object for people to occupy the land." Another vital point was brought out by a question from Senator Ingalls: ". . . these lands when treated by artificial irrigation become enormously productive. If that is the case, what is the reason for giving the person who takes them 640 acres when a man who takes ordinary land gets but 160 acres?" The Senator who stood sponsor for the bill replied, "Simply because it is very expensive and difficult to conduct the water to the land." It was assumed that each man would be able to look out for his own water supply. The bill became a law March 3, 1877, and applied to eleven states and territories.[10] This act resembles in several important

[8] Sen. Rep., No. 642, 44 Cong., 2 Sess.
[9] Cong. Rec., 44 Cong., 2 Sess., p. 1964.
[10] U. S. Stat. at Large, XIX, p. 377.

particulars the preëmption act requiring improvement of the
land and payment for the same at $1.25 per acre

TROUBLES BEGIN EARLY

Hardly had the measure passed before the Land Office
was recommending its repeal. That there was some demand
for the law is shown by the fact that over a quarter of a
million acres of land were entered under it within a quarter
of a year after its passage.[11] The commissioner gave the
opinion that the law was vague respecting the amount of
water to be conducted upon the land, and hence title might
be obtained with very little irrigation. On the other hand,
it would be unreasonable to enforce the law to the utmost
requiring water enough to irrigate all of the 640 acres.[12]
He believed that the law had been instigated by interested
parties and that, had the land been for sale, such action
would have been superfluous. It was the judgment of the
commissioner that the law should be repealed; that cash
sales should be resumed; and that land should be given to
those who would irrigate it. "If lands which require no
irrigation are given away to any persons who will settle
upon and improve them, why not give away the desert lands
upon the same conditions, especially when it requires so
much more to improve them?" The argument was sound
and the conclusion logical, but the feasibility of carrying
such a plan into effect was not so certain.

Congress took no action until 1891 but it must not be
assumed that the matter was entirely quiescent during the
fourteen years elapsing between desert land acts. In 1884
the Commissioner of the General Land Office spoke in no
uncertain terms.[13] Land was being entered at the rate of
half a million to a million acres a year, but only a few
thousand acres were finally patented. Considerable areas
useful for hay crops without irrigation were taken up;

[11] *L. O. R.*, 1877, p. 41.
[12] *Ibid*, pp. 33, 34.
[13] *Ibid*, 1884, p. 8.

grazing land was held by making desert entries on land bordering or including water; and whole districts were obtained by collusive entries; settlements were thus prevented. It was recommended that the desert entry act be repealed. Stockmen could and did get hold of range land by desert entry, paying the required twenty-five cents per acre. In this manner they had the land for three years and then might sell their interest in it. Large bodies of land were thus held speculatively.[14] "Hearings in contested cases and examinations by special agents have disclosed a want of any attempt to irrigate the land in many instances, that desert entries are frequently made of lands not desert in character, . . . that lands taken up under this act are often used for stock-grazing."[15]

The Surveyor General of Arizona reported, in 1887, that: "Speculators of all degrees have now turned their attention to the facilities offered by the desert land law. . . . Parties have obtained 4,000 or 5,000 acres under this law by illegal methods. . . . The desert land law as it stands fosters a wild spirit of speculation."[16] He reports that over half of those filing desert claims covering four hundred thousand acres in the aggregate were from outside of Arizona. These were men in Chicago, St. Louis, and where not, who were holding the land for speculation.

In Wyoming a great deal of so-called ditching was done by plowing a few furrows or by cutting a ditch one foot deep where eight feet were needed. Moreover, these ditches failed to follow the contour of the land with reference to the habits of water, and often they began where there was no water to be conducted and ended where there was no field to receive it; cattle companies contracted with themselves to put in the irrigating systems, and so following.[17] Special agents were appointed by the Land Office to investigate these irregular practices and it was said to be due in

14 *L. O. R.*, 1885, pp. 73-75.
15 *Ibid*, 1884, p. 8.
16 *Ibid*, 1887, p. 522.
17 *Ibid*, p. 506.

some measure to their efforts that the amount of fraud was diminished.[18] One of the first men to see that the desert-entry method devised by Congress was not only inadequate, but even of a wrong nature, was the United States Surveyor General for Idaho. In his report for 1889, after commenting on the folly of permitting private parties to file on water almost at will, he remarked: "The irrigation of the arid lands of the West should be undertaken by the government or the lands be granted to the respective states and territories upon such terms and conditions as will assure the construction of necessary canals and reservoirs for reclaiming all of the lands possible." [19]

Congress made several feints at action in response to this avalanche of testimony. Bills were introduced to amend the law, to repeal it, to grant the land to the states. But in the confusion of counsel nothing was done for some years. That is to say, no legislation was enacted. It must be admitted, however, that a great many bills and resolutions were introduced, money was spent on investigations, and it looked as though something of a signal character were about to happen. In fact, in 1888, in providing for a survey of the public lands, Congress provided that all lands selected as sites for reservoirs, canals and ditches, and all land susceptible of irrigation by such means should be withdrawn from all entry and settlement, the President, however, having the right to restore the same. This act did not attract much attention at the time, though ultimately it seemed destined to result in a virtual repeal of the desert land act.[20] Entries continued, despite this act, since the geological surveys under which the land should be withdrawn were not in many cases made promptly. Two years later a western Senator pointed out that unless the law of 1888 were repealed, two-fifths of the territory of the United States could not be settled.[21] However, the act was not repealed;

[18] L. O. R., 1888, p. 56.
[19] Ibid, 1889, p. 345.
[20] U. S. Stat. at Large, XXV, p. 527.
[21] Cong. Rec., 51 Cong., 1 Sess., App., p. 720.

yet, except in a few instances, it has not been used to preclude desert entries.

MODIFICATIONS OF THE ACT, 1891

The act of 1891 made important changes in the desert entry requirements. Preliminary to this, an act had been passed in August, 1890, restricting to 320 acres the amount of agricultural, desert entry, land which one person might acquire from the government.[22] The act of 1891 was truly an omnibus measure. It pertained to all the leading acts under which land could be obtained. Respecting the desert land policy it was stipulated that improvements amounting to $3.00 per acre, one dollar per year for three years should be put upon the land toward its reclamation; that water should be available for the entire amount; that one-eighth should be put under cultivation; that persons might associate together in a project for watering their several entries; that only citizens of the state in which the land was situated were allowed the privilege of entry.[23]

This bill, important as it was, passed Congress with very little debate. Perhaps it was generally conceded that the main features of the bill ought to pass, and since little opposition developed, the need even for advocating it was not great. Whatever important debate there was, took place in committees and conferences; nevertheless, this act, with but minor modifications, is still in force after a period of thirty-one years.

While this act seemed to make its way through Congress easily, it by no means satisfied all the demands of those interested in desert land. A plan growing strongly in favor with the western states was that of cession of the desert land to the states in which it lay. This was supported by arguments similar to or identical with those urged in favor of granting the "refuse" lands, the swamp lands, and indeed all lands to the states. The irrigation operations required

[22] *U. S. Stat. at Large*, XXVI, p. 391.
[23] *Ibid*, p. 1096.

close supervision; the states could attend to it, the federal government could not. Idaho and Wyoming took the lead in this proposal. It was shown in these memorials that the desert act failed to provide for any plan of irrigation on a large scale. The settler on his 320 acres, or even on 640 acres, could not finance the construction of great irrigation systems. The state could not help because of lack of authority to do so. Congress could hardly be expected to pass a satisfactory law for each of several states since the problems of these states were unlike. "The people of each section are the best calculated to determine the system best suited to their needs, and should be given the means of carrying it into effect." [24]

A memorial from Nebraska asked Congress to take charge of irrigation.[25] At the same time the Commissioner of the General Land Office recommended the cession to the states,[26] this because he believed that the federal government would not take the matter in hand. However, the reclamation work of the government was presaged by the withdrawal of 385,000 acres of land for reservoir sites prior to this time,[27] while the Carey Act was foreshadowed by the demands that arid land be granted to the states.

In 1903, President Roosevelt appointed a commission "to report upon the condition, operation, and effect of the present land laws, and to recommend such changes as are needed." [28]

The commission consisted of W. A. Richards, Commissioner of the General Land Office, F. H. Newell, and Gifford Pinchot. They reported on the Desert Land Act in no uncertain terms. It is shown that large landed estates are created through abuse of this measure. For example, a man and wife in the employ of a capitalist each take a desert entry claim, together a whole section of land.

---

[24] *Cong. Rec.*, 51 Cong., 2 Sess., p. 2597.
[25] *Ibid*, p. 1943.
[26] *L. O. R.*, 1891, p. 51.
[27] *Ibid*.
[28] *Sen. Doc.* 189, 58 Cong., 3 Sess.

The employer furnishes the money for the required improvements, but it does not follow that they are actually made. Stock in a projected canal company, the ownership of a pumping plant, fencing, and the like, are counted as improvements. When the patent is issued, it is soon in the hands of the employer. Another method is for the man with the money and the land hunger to take a desert claim, as does his wife, their associates doing the same. Then they incorporate, and the company takes, in addition to the land thus obtained, an assignment of 320 acres from some entryman not in the company. The same group of persons may incorporate under several different names and get as many additional half-sections. It is not unusual for a company to get hold of several thousand acres in this manner.[29]

Again, the privilege of making desert entries on unsurveyed land is an incentive to fraud. By entering the claim and paying twenty-five cents per acre, it is possible to hold these lands for many years with no further expense. Another frequent fraud is the use of the same water for irrigation on several entries, witnesses swearing that the water is available and ample.

Why, the Public Land Commission asks, should not the desert entry law require residence upon the land the same as does the Homestead Act? Why should a man have the privilege of both homestead and desert entry? Why should the desert entry of 320 acres be permitted? Furthermore, why give 320 acres to both a man and his wife, making 640 acres for the family, when irrigated land requires intensive cultivation and therefore a small acreage is enough for a farm?

"It is a fact that a very small proportion of the land disposed of under the terms of the law has actually been reclaimed and irrigated, and scrutiny of many hundreds of desert entries now passing to final proof shows that in the majority of cases these lands are not actually utilized, but are being held for speculative purposes. . . . The law

[29] *Sen. Doc.*, 58 Cong., 3 Sess., No. 189.

should render impossible the continuance of the practices by which desert lands without water, without cultivation, and without crop are passed into the possession of claimants." [30]

A cause for fraud not given by the commission because not so prominent twenty years ago as now is the value the desert lands have come to have as the basis of dry farming. Thus far no land law has been devised to fit the requirements of this use of land.

The latest effort of Congress to alleviate unfortunate conditions relating to the desert entryman was made by a law passed in March, 1915.[31] This act provides that three years' additional time may be granted the entryman who, having expended the prescribed $3.00 per acre in an effort to irrigate and cultivate the land, can show a reasonable prospect of doing so within three years' additional time. To those who have made the expenditure without prospect of getting the required water, the opportunity of getting title to the land is offered under the Homestead Act. To those failing to get water, another privilege is offered whereby the entryman may pay fifty cents per acre to the government, then expend $1.25 per acre in improvements, cultivate the land three years, and finally pay seventy-five cents additional to the government and receive title.

An act passed August 7, 1917, provides for special protection for entrymen who are in the military or naval service of the United States during times of war, i. e., the time within which he must make his reclamation is to be reckoned exclusive of the time he is in the service.

CAREY ACT GRANTS

Aside from the old law providing for the disposal of desert land, several more special expedients were tried. Scores of bills, resolutions, and petitions were continually coming up in Congress. Three main plans were proposed:

[30] *Sen. Doc.,* No. 189, 58 Cong., 3 Sess.
[31] *U. S. Stat. at Large,* XXXVIII, p. 1161.

to give the land to settlers; to give it to the state; to irrigate by federal action and sell. The western states were in favor of the more liberal policies. For the most part they felt that the land should be granted to them. If not, it should be as free as the homestead, whereas the government gave land away in the humid belt and charged for it in the arid district.

The cession of land to the states was a question that would not down, yet for the most part it was not much debated in Congress. On two occasions long speeches were made on the subject. One by Senator Dolph of Oregon,[32] the other by Senator Warren of Wyoming.[33] These were expositions of knowledge on irrigation together with arguments favoring cession of arid land to the states and territories.

More painstaking was the study put upon the question by the committees. In addition to the public land committees, Congress had organized a Committee on Irrigation of Arid Lands. This committee in the House made an elaborate report.[34] They spoke of the many memorials and petitions referred to them and of the unanimity of opinion in the West to the effect that the federal government would not undertake the work of irrigating the arid lands.

The government had, it was true, maintained bureaus, employed experts, made surveys—topographic and hydrographic—measured rainfall, gauged streams, defined irrigation and drainage areas, located reservoirs, bombarded the skies, and so on at length. All this failed to make the land habitable, and at the same time the government was following a losing policy which would ultimately result in the dissipation of the whole value of the land. Speaking of cession to the states, the committee continues: "We have arrived at the conclusion that the general government will be benefited—that it will gain rather than lose by the pro-

[32] *Cong. Rec.*, 52 Cong., 1 Sess., p. 5133.
[33] *Ibid*, pp. 6485-6506.
[34] *House Rep.*, No. 569, 52 Cong., 1 Sess.—A minority of the committee made an adverse report.

posed cession." The West was substantially united in favor of the cession, while no vigorous protest came from the East. Nevertheless, the bill failed of passage.

Two years later, 1894, a compromise measure was brought forward. It provided neither for cession outright to the states, nor for direct action by the United States. There was comparatively little debate in either house of Congress accompanying the passage of the bill, but the respective committees on public lands apparently gave the measure much care and thought.

This measure, which passed in August, 1894, is known as the Carey Act,[35] in honor of Senator Carey of Wyoming, the chairman of the Public Lands Committee. Under this act the government agreed to donate to certain states a quantity of land, not over 1,000,000 acres each, which they should cause to be settled, irrigated and, in part, cultivated; in which event the government agreed to grant patents either to the state or direct to the assignees of the state. Not much was said as to whether the state was expected to do the work of installing irrigation systems or contract with private parties for it, but the privilege of the latter plan was conferred and that plan has been followed in many cases. In some instances "irrigation districts" have been formed. The state was forbidden to lease these lands or dispose of them in any way whatsoever, except so as to secure their reclamation, cultivation and settlement, and might not sell over 160 acres to any one person.[36]

Subsequent acts and resolutions have modified in an important way the first provisions of the act. In 1896 it was provided that the state might create a lien upon the land for expenses in reclaiming it and that patents might be issued when the land was watered irrespective of its settlement.[37]

In 1908 an additional million acres was granted to

[35] U. S. Stat. at Large, XXVIII, p. 422.
[36] Thirteenth Census, V, p. 841, et scq.
[37] U. S. Stat. at Large, XXIX, p. 434.

Wyoming and two millions to Idaho,[38] and in 1911 a like additional amount to Colorado.

Altogether, provision has been made whereby ten states may withdraw a minimum of a million acres each, with an additional allowance of four million acres to certain ones, or a sum total of fourteen million acres. There had been segregated up to June, 1923, some 3,815,000 acres, or a little over one-fourth of the maximum amount subject to withdrawal, of which amount some has reverted to the government, leaving not over three million acres in a state of segregation. About one million acres have been patented to private parties.

Great hopes were expressed concerning the development to take place through the Carey Act grants. The results hardly bear them out. Not only are the lands not segregated in any such quantities as was expected, but the work of irrigation has progressed even more slowly. In 1910 the Bureau of the Census made a study of the situation and found that only 288,553 acres of Carey Act land were irrigated in 1909. This amount was a little over one-tenth of the total quantity included in the projects.[39] The 1920 Census shows 523,929 acres irrigated under this act, or about one-sixth of the land segregated for irrigation. The area of land in Carey projects decreased from 2,574,000 acres in 1910 to 1,189,000 acres in 1920, a decline of 53.8 per cent.

The state laws governing operations under the Carey Act differ much in detail, but are alike in general plan. All operations based on this law are placed under the supervision of state boards, in some instances special boards created for this purpose. All persons or corporations desiring to reclaim land under this law apply to the proper board, specifying the lands which they desire to have segregated, and describing the proposed plan of reclamation. The form of application and the items of information to be furnished

[38] *U. S. Stat. at Large*, XXXV, pp. 347, 577.

[39] *Thirteenth Census*, V, p. 839.—In 1914, the commissioner of the General Land Office estimated the amount for which water was available at 1,000,000 acres. (See *L. O. R.*, 1914, p. 27.)

by applicants are prescribed by law, by the regulations of the boards, and by the regulations of the United States Department of the Interior. If the application for segregation is approved by the state board, it is submitted to the United States Department of the Interior, and the land is withdrawn from entry pending action. If the application is likewise approved by the Department of the Interior, the land is segregated and withdrawn from all forms of entry under the public land laws. The state then enters into a contract with the applicant providing for the construction of the proposed works by him, and fixing the terms on which water rights may be sold. On its part, the state agrees to sell the lands only to parties who have entered into contract with the applicant to purchase water rights. The water rights sold must carry an interest in the works, so that when the payments for the rights are completed, the works and rights become the property of the water-rights purchasers. Under the Carey Act, as soon as any state furnishes satisfactory proof that any of the lands are "irrigated, reclaimed, and occupied by actual settlers," patents are issued to the state, and it in turn issues patents to the settlers when they have fulfilled the conditions imposed as to actual residence and improvement of the land, and have made the full payment of the purchase price. Lands are usually sold for fifty cents per acre.

When the Carey Act enterprises are completed and the lands and water rights are paid for, stock in the companies to which the enterprises are turned over is issued to the holders of the water rights, the enterprises thus becoming coöperative.

The Department of the Interior has undertaken, during the past few years, to prevent the launching of Carey Act projects under circumstances pointing to failure. Although the rewards to private enterprise in financing Carey Act projects have been precarious and few, the prize for which they play is so large that men are not lacking who are ready to try great hazards. One of the most unfortunate facts connected with the Carey Act game is that the men looking for promoters' profits use the money advanced by the settler as the major part of the stakes. Hence, if the promoters lose, they lose much of other people's money, and a little of their own. A wholesome effect would be provided by putting a much heavier financial responsibility on the promoters in the form of performance bonds.

An amendment to the Carey Act was passed January 6, 1921, which provides that unless actual construction of the reclamation work is begun within three years after the land is segregated, the Secretary of the Interior shall have the power to restore the lands to the public domain; and, further, that if the land is not actually irrigated within ten years it may be restored to the public domain. This law is designed to prevent hurried and ill-planned segregations by the states.

RECLAMATION BY THE UNITED STATES GOVERNMENT

For a quarter of a century preceding 1902 the demand that the United States take direct charge of irrigation had been almost continuously before Congress. In fact, Congress had done a good deal by way of direct appropriation for surveys, investigations by special agents, experimental artesian wells, and the like. The appropriations for these purposes varied from a thousand to a hundred thousand dollars.[40] But during these years, the argument that the United States had made a failure of forestry management; that the government was too far away; that the regions to be irrigated were too widely unlike; that it was not fair to take taxes from one set of citizens to use in developing the property of another; all these and more were used to prove that· the government should keep out of the business of establishing irrigation systems in the arid region. But the indifferent success in getting the work of irrigation done by other means kept the subject of government enterprise alive. As the prospect of action became greater, more adverse arguments were developed. It was contended that the farmers

[40] *U. S. Stat. at Large,* XXII, pp. 92, 411; XXIV, 103; XXV, p. 526.

of the East would suffer, the newly developed farms of the West would furnish competition and the prices of farm products would be depressed. The President, the Secretary of Agriculture, the Secretary of the Interior, the western members of Congress, and, to a considerable extent, the press, hastened to assure the farmer and his friends that no competition need be feared. It was held that the western farmer would have an abundant home market; that manufacturing and mining would develop in his vicinity; that he would supply goods for the Oriental trade; that few of his products would make their way to the East.[41]

In 1900 the platforms of the leading political parties contained clauses favoring reclamation of the arid lands. In each instance the language was sufficiently vague to permit anything from A to Z as a redemption of the pledge. The reclamation movement gained greatly, however, by the appearance of Theodore Roosevelt in the White House. In his first annual message to Congress, President Roosevelt said: "The pioneer settlers on the arid public domain chose their homes along streams from which they could themselves divert the water to reclaim their holdings. Such opportunities are practically gone. There remain, however, vast areas of public land which can be made available for homestead settlement, but only by reservoirs and main line canals impracticable for private enterprise. These irrigation works should be built by the National Government."[42] This put the President and his cabinet clearly on the side of government reclamation. No sooner had Congress convened than two bills were introduced providing for the reclamation by the government of arid lands. Within a short time three committee reports had been made on the subject.[43] These reports sum up the arguments pro and con and unqualifiedly recommend the passage of the bill. Likewise, both in the

[41] *Sen. Doc.*, No. 446, 57 Cong., 1 Sess. This report gives a symposium of opinions on the subject.

[42] In the preceding year, eleven reclamation bills had been introduced in Congress.

[43] *Sen. Doc.*, No. 446, 57 Cong., 1 Sess.; *Sen. Rep.*, No. 254, 57 Cong., 1 Sess. *House Rep.*, No. 1468.

Senate and the House, the debate was extended and lively. Perhaps, however, it would be more accurate to say that the bill was discussed rather than debated in the Senate, since no real opposition developed.[44]

In the House the bill was resisted, although hopelessly, by a considerable group of Congressmen. The division of opinion was not clearly on party lines. The Congress was Republican and the bill was recognized as a Republican measure, yet the opposition was mainly from members of that party also. The adverse arguments may be grouped under three heads: First, the United States has no constitutional right to go into the business of irrigating land; second, the development of irrigated farms will result in unfortunate competition with agriculture farther east; third, the expense will be enormous and will rest ultimately on the whole people of the country.

It is hardly necessary to go into the arguments of constitutionality in detail. This bogey worked out about as well and in about the same manner as usual. Rather curiously was the constitutional shelter sought on this occasion by staunch Republicans.[45] The arguments were so thoroughly refuted as to carry no weight.[46]

The second point, regarding the competition of western farming with the eastern, was taken seriously. The same arguments had been used for a full century with reference to the public domain, but the occasion for their use had been less during some fifteen or twenty years immediately preceding, thus giving them some appearance of freshness. Even so, they stood no show of carrying the day. The western men were strong in the belief that the West would not become a competitor in the grain markets of the East. All the grain and hay raised in the arid region would be needed there, while the growth of mining and commerce would make an outlet for the manufactured goods made in

---

[44] *Cong. Rec.*, 57 Cong., 1 Sess., p. 2276.
[45] *House Rep.*, No. 794, Pt. 2, 57 Cong., 1 Sess.
[46] *Cong. Rec.*, 57 Cong., 1 Sess., p. 6745.

the East. Moreover, any surplus grain in the West would probably go to the Orient. A few Congressmen took the stand that the populace would be better off with more foodstuff raised, even though a few producers suffered; hence, action should be governed with reference to the good of the larger number.

The expense argument was worked to its full capacity. A New York Congressman estimated that the plan would ultimately cost the country billions of dollars. Dalzell of Pennsylvania believed it a plan to "unlock the doors of the Treasury." Mr. Cannon of Illinois dubbed the bill a "direct grant in an indirect way." Payne of New York was of a like mind, while Hepburn of Iowa "insisted . . . that this is a thinly veneered and thinly disguised attempt to make the government, from its general fund, pay for this great work—great in extent, great in expenditure, but not great in results." Thus did the "watchdogs" of the Treasury do a considerable amount of growling, but it availed little.

The active support of the bill came from the states directly interested, and from the President and his cabinet. They had impressed both political parties with the importance and the merits of the measure. The country at large had either agreed to the plan or taken no interest in it. Twenty-five years of effort under other plans, with indifferent success, had convinced the friends of irrigation that the government should try its hand. The demand was not a sudden one; it had been developing for years, was recommended by commissioners of the General Land Office, by surveyors general, by geologists, by state legislatures, by prominent publicists, and editors. The experiment seemed destined to be tried, and there was a feeling that, if it was to be tried, why not now? The bill passed the House by 146 to 55 votes, there being 150, besides those paired, who failed to express themselves either way.[47] On June 17, 1902, the President signed the bill and it became a law.[48]

---

[47] *Cong. Rec.*, 57 Cong., 1 Sess., p. 6778.
[48] *U. S. Stat. at Large*, XXXII, p. 388.

The essential provisions of the Reclamation Act are that the national government shall set aside the money received from the sale of land, after certain deductions and reservations are made, for a "reclamation fund" to be used in developing irrigation projects. The settler shall agree to make repayment of "the cost of construction of the project,"[49] in not to exceed ten annual installments—money thus paid in to remain a part of the reclamation fund until Congress orders otherwise. In order to receive a patent for the land the settler is required (1) to make these "cost of construction" payments, (2) to reclaim at least one-half of the total irrigable area of his entry, (3) to meet the requirements of the Hometsead Act as to residence, which under these circumstances is three years.[50] However, in case water be not available, the entryman may be granted a leave of absence till such time as it shall be ready.[51] Another feature of importance is the provision that water rights may be sold to private owners of land, but in no case to non-residents or in amounts greater than 160 acres to one individual. A large number of amendatory and supplementary acts have been passed.

The greatest interest in the Reclamation Act centers around the fact that it is clearly a conscious and salutary step in the direction of a national policy of conservation. It was passed soon after the conservation principles were first prominently expounded, and embodies unmistakably the essence of those principles as applied to the use of water on the western arid lands. The purpose of the act is broad and fundamental, providing for the use of natural resources, a wide diffusion in ownership, and in consequence an opportunity to a large number of people.

During the debate on the Reclamation Act, it was pointed out by the opponents that there were nearly 600,000,000 acres of land still the property of the government, and

---

[49] Reclamation *Circular*, No. 102, p. 4, 1912, Department of Interior.
[50] *U. S. Stat. at Large*, XXXVII, p. 265.
[51] *Ibid*, XXXVI, p. 864.

that the Reclamation Service [52] might undertake to use the proceeds of the entire amount in irrigating some 75,000,000 acres. Evidently several decades will elapse before this limit is approached.

There was a widespread belief that the Reclamation Act represented the wisdom of the nation on the subject of arid lands, and that in consequence the ground would not have to be gone over again in a similar way at all soon. However, after twelve years of history, the matter came up in a way not to be ignored or slighted. During this time, some eleven thousand families, perhaps fifty to sixty thousand people, were settled on reclamation projects. [53] It will be remembered that payments for the water rights for this land were to be made in a maximum of ten installments. Estimates had been made showing the probable cost of such rights to be fifteen, twenty or forty dollars per acre. The facts showed them to cost twice these amounts. It had been supposed that crops would be grown within the first year or two, but the years stretched out beyond all expectation before the returns became important. It had been prophesied that the demand for farm produce would keep pace with the supply, the mining camps, lumber mills, and similar industries growing as rapidly as agriculture. In reality, the settlers on various governmental reclamation tracts found no market for much of the crop actually produced—alfalfa hay, for example, going begging for buyers at various times at one dollar to three dollars per ton.

Congress could not escape the responsibility of taking care, in some measure, of the people who had elected to accept the good offices of the government in getting the soil watered on reclamation projects. There was no dearth of bills introduced, and no end of demand that they pass. In 1914 relief was granted in an act extending the time of repayment to the government from ten years to twenty

---

[52] It will be noticed that the work was organized under the above heading and not within the General Land Office.

[53] *Cong. Rec.*, 63 Cong., 2 Sess., p. 12494.

years.[54] During the few months preceding the passage of this act, a vast amount of time was spent in its consideration.

The arguments brought to bear on the subject at this time were mainly concerning the question whether to leave the reclamation act unchanged except in regard to the time of repayment or to add to this modification the exaction of an interest payment of three per cent on all unpaid obligations. It was contended that the extension of time was imperatively demanded. The settlers could not pay. Should they be driven off the land or given a period of credit commensurate with their condition? Manifestly, with these alternatives from which to make a choice, there was but one outcome to be predicted: They must have additional time.

The debate on the interest proposal brought up the whole subject of the policy of handling the arid lands. Congress was reminded that the amount of land the proceeds from which had gone into the reclamation fund was but little smaller than the areas given in earlier years to the railroads. However, the significance of this comparison rather waned on the thought that in the one case the land was given away, while in the other there was no donation involved, except that of land irrigated. The money received for land and used in building irrigation works in connection with other land was, after all, merely a part of the funds belonging to the government for use in any manner, not a unique asset in any sense. The fact that the money used for reclamation purposes came from the sale of land was a mere incident, and not an important one. There was no assurance that land sales would bring in great sums of money. Thus it was clear that the government was likely to get into undertakings calling for more money than the designated source would furnish. To use the money received from the sale of land for irrigation purposes was not in any sense parallel to the granting of land as an aid to the builders of railroads.

[54] *U. S. Stat. at Large*, XXXVIII, p. 686.

The demand that interest be paid brought out some interesting economic principles. For example, the greatest advocate of reclamation in the House confessed that there had been no intention of undertaking any project of such a character as would invite private enterprise. Now private enterprise is supposed to be fairly discriminating as to the prospect of returns, and to be willing to take risks where these prospects are good. But the government apparently proposed to enter a field which was not attractive to men dependent upon getting, within a few years, returns on the money invested. Land such as the government thus proposed to irrigate was below the margin; or, in other words, land that would not pay ordinary wages and interest on labor and capital expended. The government did not propose an interest charge and justified itself in part, at least, by calling attention to the fact that the money used had not been raised by taxation but belonged to the private purse of the nation. Hence, apparently, on the ground that the necessity of getting an income on one's own money is not so pressing as on money belonging to a creditor, it was contended that the country could make no complaint worthy of consideration even though a hundred million were loaned to this enterprise. These expenditures were likened to river and harbor, good roads, and general betterment expenditures, on which interest was never charged to the beneficiaries. Neither in these cases is the principal recovered. But the arguments seem to be beside the mark, for in none of the cases cited does the value resulting from the expenditure become primarily the property of any private enterprise, while in the reclamation work it does. The real, effective argument against payment of interest was that the settlers were unable to make it.

In the meantime, the movement for rural credit legislation had become prominent, and it was the belief of several Congressmen that the demand for government loans to farmers, even without interest, could not well be resisted in the face of the fact that the government was virtually lending to farmers on the reclamation tracts many millions of dollars for long periods of time without interest.[55] There was no question about the inability of the settler to pay. Like all settlers, with few exceptions, the settler on the reclamation project was poor. His land, irrigated, was costing him thirty to a hundred dollars an acre. Added to this was the necessity of expending hundreds of dollars on an eighty-acre tract for clearing, buildings, fences, machinery, live stock, seed, and often, greatest of all, for ditches, dikes, and levelling. In very many instances the settlers are from the Middle West and have much to learn before they know intimately the problems of an irrigated country. Add to all this the necessity of a wait of several years before the majority of the farmers can hope for much return from their outlay, and it becomes plain that the probability of meeting payments amounting to from four to eight thousand dollars due the government within the first ten years is very remote. They do well, indeed, if they are able to meet their other obligations within that time.

The extension of time was destined to be made. Along with it were passed several other changes in the Reclamation Act making the situation more tolerable from the settler's standpoint. The first act provided that the payments should be made within ten years, leaving it to the Secretary of the Interior to determine the amounts of the several installments. The new act prescribed that there shall be an initial payment of five per cent, then five years shall elapse before any further payments are demanded, after which time fifteen annual payments, five per cent for the first five and seven per cent for the last ten, make up the full amount due.

One further provision requires notice. The act prescribes the reduction of each man's holding to a "farm unit," the exact size of the unit to be determined for each project by the Department of the Interior. This provision is an attempt to shut out speculators, who, it was said, were holding important positions on the projects under the old rules,

[55] *Cong. Rec.*, 63 Cong., 2 Sess., p. 12491, *et seq.*

under which each entryman might take a hundred and sixty acres.

Due to the financial stringency and low price of agricultural products, Congress passed a Public Resolution May 17, 1921, to permit the Secretary of the Interior to furnish irrigation water during the irrigation season of 1921 to water-right applicants who were in arrears for payment for operation and maintenance for more than one year. This relief was granted notwithstanding section 6 of the act of August 13, 1914, which provides that no entryman may get more than one calendar year in arrears in his payments for services rendered by the government and continue to receive the services. Since 1921 still further extension of time has been granted.

THE MOST RECENT RECLAMATION ACTION

In the summer of 1923 the Secretary of the Interior discontinued the *Reclamation Service* and in its stead established a bureau. Members of the old organization, which lasted twenty-one years, feel that the change is for the worse, and look upon it as a triumph of politics over efficient service. It should be noticed that much credit is due the Reclamation Service for the excellent engineering work done in connection with the projects. The construction of dams and canals is of a permanent character, quite in contrast with a great many made by private companies to sell.

Perhaps the greatest complaint on the part of settlers on the projects is in regard to the costs which so often exceed the estimates. The engineers make rather a poor showing in their attempted explanations of these additional charges. They found tunnels more expensive than they had anticipated; they found the water supply insufficient for the estimated acres, hence it cost more per acre on the smaller area; and almost uniformly they omitted any estimate of drainage costs. As a result, a great many projects are costing double the first figure stated. Clearly the engineers have been greatly to blame for over-estimating the water supply. They could at least have reported that they didn't know, but there is not much employment for the man who thinks a thing can't be done, while the services of the man who thinks it can be done are in demand. At all events, the engineers were optimists in the reports made prior to the location of projects. In leaving out the estimate of drainage costs they were clearly culpable, or at least somebody was. That most irrigation projects need drainage has been well known for many years.

Back of all questions as to the manner in which the government irrigation projects were handled lies the basis of the action making them possible. The whole movement was based on a "happy home" philosophy. It was discovered some forty years ago that the irrigable land would furnish homes for a few hundred thousand families. It was further discovered that this land was not being settled rapidly. In passing the Reclamation Act in 1902 as a nation we clearly forgot those things which were behind, the millions of unoccupied acres of the Mississippi Valley, consisting mostly of fertile, well-watered land needing only to be drained or cleared. Had we really been concerned over the future food supply as we pretended to be, or, being so concerned, had we calmly asked how to increase it in the cheapest and easiest manner, certain of the Reclamation projects would still be undeveloped. The former director of the Service says the fundamental object was to "make men, not money." In the fulfillment of the latter half of this object the success is undoubted. Whether we have succeeded in making men it may be too early to judge. If the results achieved are to be measured in home-making, it will be necessary eventually to determine the relative value of homes in New York City, in South Carolina, or Tennessee, and balance such value against that of the home in the arid region.

The whole matter should be put on a common sense basis.

It has been handled largely on a sentimental basis, if indeed log-rolling politics has not been an element. When we need more food we should, and will, resort to greater pains to obtain it. When we need more happy homes we should, and let us hope will, take steps toward making them obtainable. However, to explain a deficit, and undertake to predict when it will be paid, or to make clear to the American people just why it became necessary in 1902 to take up a liberal collection in order to subsidize the settlement of high cost land, when we already had a surplus of food, and at least ample space for happy homes, is a task none of those implicated have essayed.[56]

Since the Reclamation Act passed in 1902 the government has developed, to some degree, twenty-six projects. The number of acres cropped is 1,175,000. The cost of the projects thus far is about $135,000,000, of which less than one-tenth has been paid. The excuses for not paying are substantially the same as those given by the purchasers of land on credit a century ago.[57]

In the fall of 1923 a special advisory committee was appointed to report on the condition of the reclamation work and the people involved. In commenting on the report, the department interprets one of their findings thus: "The intrinsic return value of reclamation projects . . . is not established by the cost of building reservoirs, dams, and canals, but by the actual crop production of the lands under irrigation water, a principle not considered in the present reclamation law, the result of which has worked great hardship on settlers on some of the projects."[58] The committee recommended that the twenty-year time limit for making payments be abandoned, and that the payments be put on the basis of productive power of the land. It is predicted

[56] *A Survey of Reclamation*, (Nine articles reprinted from the Engineering News-Record).

[57] The main facts of the Reclamation Service are to be found in the annual reports put out by the Department of the Interior.

[58] Report of Special Advisory Committee on Reclamation.

that part of the investment will be repaid, but a part will not. "This result comes from the location of projects without recognizing the limitations of soil and climate and available markets."

The Reclamation Act and the situation developed in its operation emphasize perhaps more clearly than any other American land law and its administration the need of a comprehensive national policy. At its best it combines the spirit of the developmental and conservation views. At its worst it partakes of "pork barrel" politics. It is neither good nor bad, merely unfortunate in its conception, ill-timed, and expensive. If the plans now proposed are put into effect, the outcome will be a loan of the cost price of the works to the settlers, they to pay the interest for a period of years, after which time the principal will be cancelled.[59]

Just why there should be so much distress on the part of those responsible for Reclamation over the fact that on many projects a considerable percentage of the farms are rented is hard to comprehend. We did away with entailments long ago, and even they did not by any means insure the working of the land by the hands of the owner. A half century before the Reclamation period the innocent dispensers of the public domain were surprised and grieved to find that homesteads made their way into the hands of speculators, and were tilled by tenants. It seems hard to make people understand that private property will be private property and act as such even though it at one time passes from one party to another as a gift.

It is conceded that the riddle of the arid lands is not solved. Congress has had the matter up again and again during the past ten years. Instead of new legislation, the thought has been that better administration of existing laws was a needed and hopeful alternative.

The commissioner of the General Land Office in 1907

[59] *Report* of Special Advisory Committee on Reclamation.

gave a clear expression of the situation respecting a great deal of land to which existing laws do not even apply: "Much of the remaining public lands are semi-arid or desert in character and cannot be artificially irrigated. For these lands we have no law regulating their use or disposition. This condition has delivered the public range over to those who are powerful enough to appropriate and hold it against the weaker claimants, but mere physical force in holding the range is the least of the abuses. Monopolization of the pools, springs and streams to which the grazing herds and flocks must resort for water, and the acquisition of strips of patented lands to which title was acquired obviously to prevent access by others to the adjacent public range, is the greatest public wrong. These abuses are so universal and so far removed from decent respect for common rights that I most earnestly recommend the enactment of a comprehensive range law that will bring these vacant grazing areas under the departmental supervision and regulation. Until such laws are provided, the bulk of the public domain must continue in government ownership, but held for the use of whomsoever, by force or cunning, is able to exclude his less powerful or less artful neighbor." [60]

The following tables will indicate the progress in disposal and development of desert lands under the three acts discussed above. The first table shows the number of acres of original and final entries and the total amount received therefor under the Desert Land Act of March 3, 1877. The second table indicates the total number of acres withdrawn from entry privileges, the amount of land the states and territories asked to have segregated, and the amount of land actually segregated. According to an amendment to the Carey Act, passed March 15, 1910,[61] the states and territories may ask to have certain land temporarily withdrawn from the Public Domain, pending application to the Secretary of the Interior for segregation permanently for purpose

[60] *Report* of Secretary of Interior, 1907, p. 79.

[61] *U. S. Stat. at Large*, XXXVI, p. 237.

of reclamation, providing application for segregation is made within a year after such withdrawal. This table shows that 2,554,690 acres were thus withdrawn from the Public Domain; that the total applications for segregation up to June 30, 1921, amounted to 8,389,624, and that 3,788,626 acres were actually segregated by the states and territories. The third table gives an idea of the progress of the federal government in the business of reclamation of arid lands since the passage of the Act of June 17, 1902. In 1920 the government was prepared to irrigate approximately 2,845,000 acres and actually irrigated 2,226,000 acres, 982,000 acres of which was partially irrigated by private individuals. It was estimated by the Reclamation Service that the increase in value of 32,835 farms irrigated, together with the rise in value of adjacent lands, amounted to $500,000,000, while the total estimated expense of irrigation construction work was $130,000,000.

TABLE XXX

DESERT LAND ENTRIES—MARCH 3, 1877 TO JUNE 30, 1923 [62]

State	Original entries in acres	Final entries in acres	Total amount received
Arizona	2,522,910	334,974	$ 999,796
California	5,119,206	859,269	2,177,261
Colorado	3,216,311	692,744	1,591,065
Dakota Territory	20,021	301	5,305
Idaho	3,090,428	989,218	1,715,637
Montana	5,974,109	2,740,459	4,235,881
Nevada	611,328	143,077	285,966
New Mexico	2,153,556	230,137	869,136
North Dakota	85,279	20,094	41,440
Oregon	1,105,211	292,090	564,294
South Dakota	609,291	101,681	251,286
Utah	1,447,464	430,184	804,058
Washington	996,992	70,674	343,119
Wyoming	5,512,494	1,475,750	2,414,832
Total	32,464,599	8,380,652	$16,299,076

[62] L. O. R., 1923, p. 35.

TABLE XXXI

LAND DISPOSED OF UNDER THE CAREY ACT, AUGUST 18, 1894 TO JUNE 30, 1923 [63]

State	Segregated Acres	Cancelled Acres	Patented Acres
Arizona	13,745	....	....
Colorado	284,654	154,909	13,302
Idaho	1,321,455	392,414	658,179
Montana	246,699	81,110	99,297
Nevada	36,809	33,420	474
New Mexico	7,605	2,757	4,743
Oregon	388,877	117,859	83,919
Utah	141,815	56,306	28,866
Wyoming	1,373,448	664,926	180,842
Total	3,815,106	1,503,702	1,069,623

TABLE XXXII

STATISTICS OF RECLAMATION ACT, 1902 [64]

Government was prepared to irrigate........	1,692,000 acres (1922)
Lands actually irrigated:	
Sole water supply by Government.........	1,202,000 acres
Partial water supply by Government	1,102,000 acres [65]
Total	2,304,000 acres
Total number of farms supplied partially and wholly, (1920)	32,835
Estimated net investment in irrigation construction work since passage of act, 1902	$135,000,000
Total estimated increase in all land values due to Government irrigation work....................	$500,000,000

SUMMARY

The first real breakdown of the Homestead Act was in its attempt to cross the plains. For this task it was ill adapted. It may be objected that it broke down in its application to the forest regions. In a sense it did, but not with respect to the welfare of settlers. On the plains the Homestead was a failure from the standpoint of both

[63] *L. O. R.*, 1923, p. 41.
[64] Twenty-second *Annual Report* of Reclamation Service, pp. 1-15.
[65] Remainder supplied by private individuals under Warren Act of February 21, 1911. *Ibid*, p. 15.

individual and nation. To the credit of Congress be it said that this failure was recognized early and the Desert Land Act of 1877 passed as a modification. This act was a poor solution of the difficulties and subject to much abuse. The act of 1891, covering many features of the land situation, improved the method of disposing of desert land, yet fell woefully short of the ideal. The amount of land allowed one person—320 acres for a man and as much more for his wife— was out of all reason in the light of the requirements that it be irrigated. Fraud was invited and the challenge accepted. Land presumably intended for farms was acquired under this act for grazing.

A real attempt to better the situation was made in 1894 in the passage of the Carey Act. But the Carey Act was not an unqualified success. Under it about a million acres have been patented to private parties, but the failures have been numerous. It appeared to offer a fortune to the promoters of the projects with the result that many attempts were made on small information with too great an element of hope. The Reclamation Act, of 1902, represents a new departure in land policies. It was an attempt by the government to make land usable where and when it could not be done profitably by private enterprize. Perhaps the surprising thing about it is that the costs and failures are not greater than they really are. The undertaking shows what it means to irrigate land under difficult conditions. The government cannot put the matter on a business basis. It cannot be claimed that as a nation we did, or do, need the additional land as a source of food supply. Did the West need this development for social or economic reasons which would justify the expenditure? In more recent years we are coming to see that there are other phases of conservation than those involving the mountain and plain states. The plan should be nation-wide.

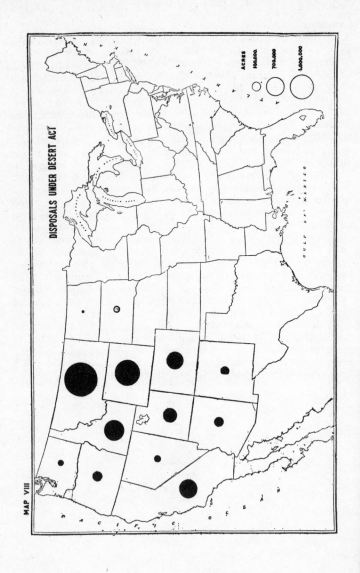

MAP VIII

DISPOSALS UNDER DESERT ACT

CHAPTER XXI

The alienation from the public forest domain of over 13,500,000 acres of timber land under the Timber and Stone Act at an average price of about $2.75 an acre is significant, not only because of the low price received in proportion to the value of the timber, but also because this considerable block of timber land was lost to the present forest reserves. This is one of the means by which the Government disposed of about four-fifths of the forest lands of the country. Under the Timber Cutting Act vast areas of the forest regions were stripped of valuable timber without any returns whatever. These are laws with good purposes but yielding poor results to the public.

EARLY HISTORY OF PROTECTION OF PUBLIC TIMBER FROM DEPREDATIONS

The influences leading to the passage of these laws had their beginnings in the problem that early confronted the Government in protecting the timber of the public domain from depredations. During the early part of the nineteenth century, the need of such protection was not evident. The forests were a liability rather than an asset to the early pioneer agricultural settlers,—the most important purchasers of our wooded potential farm lands of the humid East. The settlers' chief and most laborious problem was to clear the forests from the land. Local industrial uses were so few, transportation so poor, markets for lumber so distant, and prices so low, that the local value of timber was almost nothing.

The earliest act of Congress to protect timber against depredations was not designed to protect timber lands in general. This act of March 1, 1817, was designed to protect the live oak and red cedar forests of the Atlantic and Gulf Coast, the timber of which was so valuable for building ships for the navy in those days. Amendments or reinforcements were passed in 1820, 1822 and 1827.[1] By the act of March 2, 1831, Congress first specifically made provision against timber depredations on public lands.[2] The Supreme Court of the United States[3] construed this statute as authorizing the protection of all timber on public lands and the punishment of trespassers.[4] Attorney-General Nelson, August 11, 1843, also gave an opinion to the same effect,[5] so that by the middle of the nineteenth century it was an established principle that no timber could legally be cut from the public domain.

Under the act of 1831 the guardianship of the timber of the public lands was placed in a system of timber agencies established under the supervision of the Solicitor of the Treasury. In 1855, however, the duties of the timber agents were devolved upon the registers and receivers of the several district land offices, without any recompense for these added duties. They were instructed to seize and sell stolen timber, deposit the proceeds in the United States Treasury, and report the cases to the proper district attorneys for prosecution, unless with the approval of the land office, a compro-

---

[1] Donaldson, p. 357. An interesting sketch of the early history of our timber reservations for naval construction is given in *Exec. Doc.*, 46 Cong., 2 Sess., No. 37, pp. 9, 11, the first "Report upon Forestry," in 1877, (Washington, D C., 1878) by F. B. Hough.

[2] Donaldson, p. 357. In 1876 these provisions were embodied in section 2461, *Revised Statutes of the United States.*

[3] *United States vs. E. Briggs*, 9 How., p. 351.

[4] Donaldson, p. 357.

[5] *Ibid.*

mise payment by the depredators was effected in view of mitigating circumstances.[6] The inadequate administrative provisions authorized by Congress for enforcing the acts to protect the timber of the public domain, made these laws practically ineffective.

Before 1878 there were no specific provisions for private acquisition of timber from the public domain, nor were there any laws specifically applicable to the sale of non-agricultural timber lands. The preëmption and homestead laws presumably applied to timber lands, and also such tracts could be purchased with military or agricultural college scrip. In the West, however, were some lands on which were valuable timber and stone to which the preëmption and homestead laws could not with any reason apply, it being so obviously true that they were not adapted to agricultural use. Mining enterprises required timber, and sometimes stone, in fact could not run without them; yet there was no way of obtaining legal right to remove either from the public lands. As a result a great deal of trespassing necesarily took place.

For several years before the passage of the Timber and Stone Act of 1878 the commissioners of the General Land Office and the secretaries of the Interior had been urging action, and Congress had tried in a rather half-hearted manner to relieve the situation. In 1874 the Commissioner[7] urged the necessity of a law providing for a distinctive method of disposing of the non-agricultural timber lands. He points out four ways in which timber had commonly been obtained from the public domain (1) by theft, (2) by the Preëmption Act, (3) by the Homestead Act,[8] and (4) "the law provides

---

[6] L. O. R., 1876, pp. 19, 20.

[7] Ibid, 1874, pp. 5, 6.

[8] H. H. Schwartz, in the "Report of the National Conservation Commission, 1909." Sen. Doc., No. 676, 60 Cong., 2 Sess., III, p. 390, says that "before the timber and stone law was extended to all the public land states the commutation clause in the homestead law was the vehicle thru which timber was fraudulently acquired from the Government."

that in the discretion of the President this class of lands [timber] may be proclaimed and sold at public outcry to the highest bidder." Like the preëmption and homestead entries this last method of disposal kept the prices of the land much below its commercial value for timber. Purchasers' combinations saw to it that prices were at a minimum. Then too, since the field survey notes do not show accurately enough the exact location of the timber (pine) and non-timber lands, only the small portion of the supposed timber lands which buyers know actually to be pine and fir lands of value were sold, "while the great mass of them, receiving no bid remain with the Government as 'offered lands,' subject thenceforth to private cash purchase without settlement, and become easy prey of non-resident speculators." [9] Hence the Commissioner recommended that the privilege of preëmption and homestead entry be withdrawn from non-agricultural timber lands and that they be appraised at a fair commercial value and sold for cash as soon as possible at not less than the appraised value.

The Commissioner's chief reason for emphasizing the necessity of selling the timber lands of the public domain was to do away with timber depredations. In the absence of any law for selling the timber on the public domain, or any law applying specifically to the sale of non-agricultural timber land, and with a great demand for timber for local use and commercial speculation, the loss from depredations was large. The laws against depredations were difficult to enforce, since the administration was pitifully inadequate due to lack of a sufficient staff and funds. In emphasizing the great loss to the Government because of such wholesale depredations and

[9] *L. O. R.*, 1874-6. However, the "Report of the Public Lands Commission." *Exec. Doc.*, 46 Cong., 2 Sess., No. 46, p. 32, doesn't speak of this 4th method. It says that "until the passage of the timber and stone act there was no manner by which timber or timber lands in any of the States and Territories included in this act could be obtained except by settlement under homestead and preemption and by location of certain kinds of scrip and additional homestead rights which cost several dollars per acre."

the cause thereof the Commissioner says,[10] "Persons whose necessities require the use of timber are compelled to become either themselves depredators on the public lands, or to connive at such depredations on the part of others from whom their supplies are purchased." . . . Under this state of things timber has, in many instances, totally disappeared for miles in the vicinity of large mining centers.

The Commissioner was strongly of the opinion that the existing laws against depredations on public timber which were constantly occurring to an enormous extent, "are powerless to prevent and seemingly legally powerless to punish." He felt that no law would be found operative in fully preventing depredations, and that the practical ends to be accomplished were the prevention of waste, and returns to the Treasury for lands of this character. The wisest policy the Government can pursue in respect to the timber land of the public domain to secure these results, he concluded, "is that which will most speedily divest it of title in the same" at a fair, appraised commercial valuation for the timber thereon.[11] The Commissioner reiterates and emphasizes the same recommendations in his reports of 1875 and 1876, believing, he says, "that the greatest protection to the timber of the country now rapidly decreasing, will be found in placing it under private guardianship," [12] "as experience has shown that this is the only effectual way of preventing the waste of the timber, which involves irreparable injury to the public." [13]

[10] *L. O. R.*, 1875, p. 11. F. B. Hough in *Exec. Doc.*, 46 Cong., 2 Sess., No. 37, Report on Forestry, 1878-79, p. 8, says, "It is sufficient evidence that these early measures were ineffectual in preventing depredations upon the timber on the public lands, or of recovering something as damages after the injury had been done, when we find it stated from official sources that the total net revenue to the government for the many millions of dollars worth of timber taken amounted from the beginning of records down to January 1877, to but $154,373,74."

[11] *Ibid*, 1874, pp. 6, 9, 12.

[12] *Ibid*, 1875, p. 9.

[13] *Ibid*, 1876, p. 20.

These recommendations for the speedy outright sale of the timber lands are indeed strikingly in contrast with the general forest policy of the more advanced nations of to-day. The exact process of reasoning by which the Commissioner arrived at conclusions exactly the reverse of the general conclusions of present economists and foresters regarding the relative desirability of public compared with private ownership and management of forest land, would be most interesting and enlightening, but probably cannot be arrived at with any degree of completeness. Certain facts stand out clearly, however. *Laissez faire* was the prevailing economic concept. Individual and social economic interests were considered practically identical. The timber from the public domain was being stolen and wasted by the wholesale with no return to the Government. The land office, due to lack of appropriations and a very limited and often corrupt personnel of agents, and the strong local frontier sentiment in favor of the depredators, was almost powerless either to prevent depredations or to bring the depredators to justice. The land office knew the difficulties of the past. Apparently the officials sought primarily to avoid these, little heeding the possibility and probability of the maladjustment of distribution that would result from the concentration of timbered property. That undesirable concentration of ownership was considered a possibility, although not strongly stressed, is shown by the commissioner's statement [14] that "The question of limiting the quantity to be sold to any one person may be worthy of attention in forming legislation on the subject, though it is doubtful if any provision of that character could be made effective." In spite of previous administrative difficulties the land office seems to have greatly underestimated them and chances for fraud to be encountered in the survey, appraisal and sale of timber land. Sale of the land, one must admit, does, however, involve

[14] *L. O. R.*, 1875, p. 12

less administrative trouble than the plan of selling the timber itself as suggested by the commission in 1875.

Although bills providing for acquisition of timber from the public domain had frequently been introduced in Congress before 1878, some of which had passed the Senate or the House, none had passed both until this year when, on June 3, the Timber Cutting Act and the Timber and Stone Act were entered on the books. The debates on these bills clearly set forth the need for some provision whereby men might be legally allowed to use or acquire timber from the public domain. It was shown that at many times people had tried to buy timber or timber land from the public domain but could not do so, and thus were, in a sense, compelled to take it by trespass, trusting to the generosity of the Government that the terms would not be made too severe in settling for the depredations.[15] The frontier sentiment regarding the need of such provisions is clearly shown in memorials adopted by the legislative assemblies of the far western frontier. The Assembly of Wyoming Territory, for example, in 1878 memoralized Congress urging the necessity of a law enabling settlers "to acquire a right to utilize so much of the timber resources of the Territory as is necessary for their wants and the demands of internal improvements, both private and public." [16]

The Timber Cutting Act

The Timber Cutting Act, having as its aim the prevention of illegal depredations and the provision for the needs of the settlers, authorized citizens of certain states and territories to cut timber without charge from the mineral lands of the public domain for mining and domestic purposes. But depredations continued, even increased. In 1880 the Public Lands Commission pointed

[15] *Cong. Rec.*, 45 Cong., 2 Sess., pp. 2842, 3387, 3388.
[16] *Report* on Forestry, *Ex. Doc.*, 46 Cong., 2 Sess., No. 37, (1878-1879), pp. 9, 10.

out the inadequacy of this law, particularly the specification that free timber cutting was to be allowed only on mineral lands. "Perhaps not one acre in 5,000 in the states and territories named is mineral and not one acre in 5,000 of what may be mineral is known to be such." Hence, the benefits of the law to the miners and settlers of the frontier under strict legal interpretation were evidently of little importance. As a result there was wholesale abuse of the law by miners and lumbermen under cover of a more liberal interpretation or of the chances of escaping prosecution due to the absence of a sufficient administrative personnel.

Regarding the extensive depredations made on the public forests by large mill owners under cover of this law the Commissioner of the General Land Office has the following to say in his *Report* of 1882: "Depredations upon the public timber by powerful corporations, wealthy mill owners, lumber companies and unscrupulous monopolists . . . are still being committed to an alarming extent and great public detriment," and again in 1886, "an immense pressure is brought to bear upon the legislative and executive branches of the government to the end of securing immunity for past and unlimited privileges for future spoliations of the public timber lands, all ostensibly urged in the interest of bona fide 'agriculturists' or 'miners,' but notoriously, in fact, to forward gigantic schemes of speculation and monopoly in the remaining forests of the United States." [17]

Thus, regardless of the worthy purposes of the Timber Cutting Act, it was not only inadequate to meet the needs of the miner and settler, but it was so framed and so administered that the forest devastation was hastened. The fact also that at this time the West was experiencing a very rapid industrial development and expansion requiring an increasing amount of timber gave great impetus to such depredations.

[17] *L. O. R.*, 1886, p. 102.

THE TIMBER AND STONE ACT

The so-called "Timber and Stone Act," entitled "An Act for the sale of timber lands in the States of California, Oregon, Nevada and in the Washington Territory," was passed on the same date as the "Timber Cutting Act" and is more important in its results. In 1892 its provisions were extended to all the public land states. It provided for the sale, at not less than $2.50 an acre, to citizens of the United States or persons who had declared their intention to become citizens, of public lands valuable chiefly for timber and stone. It applied to unoccupied, unimproved, surveyed, non-mineral land that was unfit for cultivation and consequently unfit for disposal under the preëmption or the homestead laws. It was to be sold in quantities not to exceed 160 acres to each person. An affidavit was required of the entryman stating that the timber or stone was for personal use and that the purchase was not made for speculation or for any other person. [18]

Prices at Which Sales Were Made.—Although the law specifies that lands taken under this law "may be sold at the minimum price of $2.50 per acre," in administrative practice, until November 30, 1908, the maximum price asked was $2.50. Since that date, by order of the Commissioner of the General Land Office, tracts acquired have been appraised and the price fixed with reference to the amount and value of the timber and land, but at not less than $2.50 per acre. The prices received for 1923 averaged $3.68 per acre. [19]

Abuses Under the Act.—For a few years the Timber and Stone Act was apparently not made the instrument of much abuse. In speaking of the law after nearly three years of operation the Public Lands Commission in 1880 says: "The timber and stone act has not been of much practical value and furnishes but small relief to

[18] Donaldson, pp. 1084-1087.
[19] *L. O. R.*, 1923, p. 35.

settlers in the states and territories named."[20] Up to that time less than the equivalent of a township of land had been brought under its provisions. But within five years the practical effect of this law in transferring public timberlands almost directly to large corporations and timber speculators was recognized in official reports, and its repeal was strongly urged."[21] It had failed conspicuously to accomplish its purpose, as originally urged, of giving the settler, limited to his 160 acres of cultivated land, a needed wood lot to supply timber for his domestic use and of supplying local commercial use. Official reports of the Land Office, the Secretary of the Interior and reports of special commissions, reporting on the public land policy have almost unanimously condemned the law either directly or indirectly. Commissioners of the General Land Office recommended its repeal no less than twelve times between the date of enactment and 1900. In 1885, for instance, the Commissioner in his Report to the Secretary of the Interior has the following to say: "Under the timber and stone act timber worth $100 an acre is sold for $2.50. The evils are inherent in the system and can be cured only by a repeal of the law by which they are propagated." Yet the law is still unrepealed.

Numerous cases of fraudulent entries under this law have been recorded by the Land Office. The most gigantic scheme reported by the commissioner to acquire title by means of such fraudulent entries under this act is that of a large timber firm of California which a special agent of the Land Office reported (with details and many cases of specific evidence), as having fraudulently entered about 100,000 acres of the choicest and most valuable redwood lands in the Humboldt district. This case is of particular interest because of the magnitude

---

[20] Quoted in Donaldson, p. 359.
[21] *The Lumber Industry*, Part I—Standing Timber. Issued by the Department of Commerce and Labor, January 20, 1913, p. 256.

of the area involved, the brazen defiance accorded the law, and the evidence of the corruption of land office officials by means of the powerful political influence of members of the company involved.[22]

An indication of the methods used to defraud the Government is given in a letter from the chairman of the State Board of Forestry of California, containing the following: "Under the present system these forest lands are largely entered by dummies in the employ of lumbering corporations."

Recommendations for repeal of the law went unheeded by Congress and, in 1892, it was made to apply to all the public land states.[23] Congress did, however, empower the President in 1891 to set aside timber lands from the public domain for permanent National Forest Reserves. By this provision a land policy which had before considered only the disposal of the public domain was reversed, and provisions were made whereby the Government might remain a large land owner permanently.

Graduation of Price.—The situation continued about the same for several years, except that in 1908 prices were graduated, with $2.50 per acre as a minimum. This practice has increased the returns to the government slightly but has not remedied the vital defects of the law. The following quotations from the *Report of the National Conservation Commission* in 1909 show quite clearly the attitude of that body toward the Timber and Stone Act and its abuses:

"The Timber and Stone Act of June 3, 1878, was passed in order to give the home maker a timber lot to be used in conjunction with his homestead. This is evidenced by the debates in Congress at the time of the passage of the act; also by the provision that the applicant to purchase must declare 'that he does not apply to purchase the same on speculation, but in good faith to appropriate it to his own exclusive use and benefit.' As

[22] *L. O. R.*, 1886, p. 94.
[23] *U. S. Stat. at Large*, XXVIII, p. 348.

the timber of the country was cut off and destroyed by reckless lumbering and forest fires, the value of the timber land increased with great rapidity. The far-sighted lumber operators foresaw that the value of the fine timber would increase for some time in geometrical progression. They therefore followed a natural business instinct, and began to take advantage of the timber and stone act to acquire the best forests in the West. They employed cruisers, who went over and determined the value of the various legal subdivisions containing heavy stands of timber. They allowed the public to know that they would purchase certain timber land from any who might enter it under the timber and stone act. In some instances they imported shiploads and carloads of their employees and other persons, furnishing them with the necessary funds to buy. These persons entered valuable contiguous quarter sections, and transferred them wholesale to their principals. A specific instance is that in Modoc County, Cal., where more than 85 per cent of about 25,000 acres of timber land entered in one calendar year was transferred before May 1, as was shown by a search in the recorder's office of the county. Over 14,000 acres of this went to one man, and the bulk of the rest to three others."[24]

"The timber and stone act has been in force thirty years. It has brought about for $30,000,000 the sale of timber worth at a very conservative estimate over $300,000,000. The number of entries is 88,000, and they cover a total of nearly 12,000,000 acres. The Federal Government, as the steward of the people is losing yearly about $25,000,000 of the actual value of timber still being disposed of under this act, as well as the title to 1,500,000 acres of land which should be kept permanently as the property of the nation. The timber and stone act should be repealed, not only because of

[24] "Report of the National Conservation Commission," *Sen. Doc.*, 60 Cong., 2 Sess., No. 676, I, p. 87.

these facts, but also because it does not serve any useful public purpose. With its repeal there is urgent need for the sale of mature timber at its actual value and under proper restrictions, from unreserved public lands, both for the use of settlers and to supply the general need." [25]

TABLE XXXIII

TIMBER AND STONE ENTRIES, JUNE 3, 1878, TO JUNE 30, 1923 [26]

State	Acres	Amount
Alabama	37,128.44	$ 115,604.36
Arizona	2,862.80	9,071.07
Arkansas	325,064.08	710,173.59
California	2,879,465.81	7,347,419.28
Colorado	396,417.77	1,032,311.32
Florida	106,446.06	300,101.25
Idaho	1,007,717.93	2,662,298.12
Iowa	119.36	298.46
Louisiana	148,841.16	387,952.50
Michigan	148,411.91	374,015.01
Minnesota	1,402,296.64	3,532,471.71
Mississippi	17,843.49	65,815.13
Montana	663,552.75	1,727,282.25
Nebraska	97.33	268.00
Nevada	6,502.14	16,205.74
North Dakota	8,646.31	22,005.78
Oklahoma	40.00	100.00
Oregon	3,791,104.29	9,665,758.45
South Dakota	63,748.73	164,732.80
Utah	3,164.66	7,908.92
Washington	2,158,378.08	5,488,528.23
Wisconsin	80,080.62	201,862.19
Wyoming	449,691.85	1,118,118.84
Total	12,697,622.21	$34,950,303.00

SUMMARY

One of the clearest and most unfortunate failures of the government in its handling of the public domain is that in connection with the

[25] Report of the National Conservation Commission, 1909, *Sen. Doc.*, No. 676, 60 Cong., 2 Sess., I, p. 71.
[26] *L. O. R.*, 1923, p. 35.

timber supply. Although some measure of protection of the timber supply began in 1817, timber was, nevertheless, substantially a free good until near the close of the century. Timber depredations were open and flagrant. Millions of acres were alienated through the use of military and agricultural college scrip. In 1878 the Timber Cutting Act, and the Timber and Stone Act were passed. The former act was designed to aid the miner and settler. It was used as a tool by lumber companies in getting hold of great tracts of timber fraudulently. The Timber and Stone Act was of a like character. It furnished an easy means by which lumber companies obtained valuable timber, land and all, at a nominal figure. The act was improved in 1908, but has never been a measure of which to be proud.

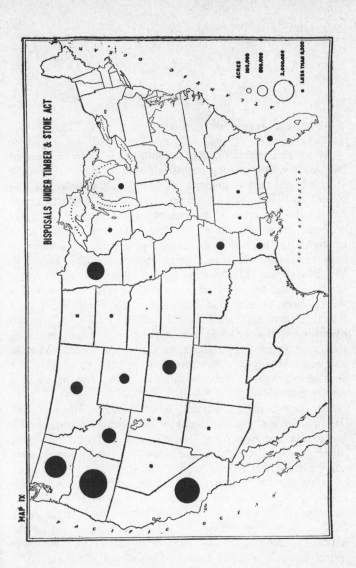

MAP IX

DISPOSALS UNDER TIMBER & STONE ACT

ACRES
100,000
500,000
2,000,000
• LESS THAN 5,000

CHAPTER XXII

THE PERIOD OF CONSERVATION, 1900-1920

About the year 1900 a great number of men prominent in politics, educators, editors, and others of public spirited character became suddenly awakened to the patent fact that the natural resources of the country could not be lavishly used, and wantonly wasted indefinitely without great danger of ultimate disaster. Like other movements there was an earlier phase to the conservation program. It was clearly appreciated by Major J. W. Powell in 1878 as shown in his report on the arid lands. The creation of national forests, a desire for which became manifest soon after the Civil War, took tangible form following an act passed in 1891, as a result of which Presidents Harrison and Cleveland set aside tracts of large proportions as forest reserves. Within six years reserves, the equivalent in area to a state the size of Michigan, were withdrawn from the disposable public domain.

The conservation period, even though lapping back thirty or more years in some of its manifestations, had a more definite beginning than can be attributed to the other periods into which the history of the public domain can be divided. Moreover, it owes its origin to the work of science. The American Association for the Advancement of Science is on record on the general subject as early as 1873, and the National Academy of Science in 1897 was directly influential in the developments of the national forestry. The conservation enterprise owes much to such men as Roosevelt, Gifford Pinchot, W. J.

McGee, and F. H. Newell, but perhaps most of all to Dr. B. E. Fernow, Dean of the Faculty of Forestry of the University of Toronto. Dr. Fernow had been a forester and conservationist in Germany, and as early as the seventies was advocating conservation measures for the United States.[1] Professors R. T. Ely, E. J. James, and Simon N. Patten were early advocates of conservation policies.

In November, 1907, President Roosevelt, at the request of the Inland Waterways Commission called a conference, mainly the governors, but including many others. In fact the meeting, held in May, 1908, turned out to be a large one, both scientific and political interests being well represented. The conference did what it was destined to do: it impressed the people of the country with the importance of conservation of the resources which had almost without exception been used with no appreciation of its ultimate limitation of supply. A set of remarkable resolutions was adopted, many of which were destined to be carried out tardily enough, but some of which resulted in prompt action. A National Conservation Commission was appointed (though not supported by Congress and therefore ineffective), and the most of the states established conservation commissions. The movement outran national boundaries and the President called a North American Conservation Congress, which convened at Washington in 1909, and later in the same year requested a meeting of the leading nations of the world at The Hague for the consideration of world resources. A National Conservation Association, a voluntary body, was organized following the failure of Congress to support the official body appointed by the President.

The most imperative need of action in our own country was in connection with the forests and coal lands of

[1] R. T. Ely, R. H. Hess, C. K. Leith, and T. N. Carver, *The Foundations of National Prosperity*, pp. 18-24.

the public domain. Mr. Roosevelt promptly withdrew 148,000,000 acres as forest reserve, and 80,000,000 acres of potential coal lands. In addition to these almost incomprehensible acreages withdrawals of great areas of potential power sites and phosphate lands were made. Altogether 234,000,000 acres, an area nearly an eighth of the United States were withdrawn from private entry and while much land in the aggregate, has been restored to entry privileges, the major portion of this vast amount is unquestionably in the hands of the government to stay. Thus the conservation program was more consciously adopted, the movement more consciously launched, than was the case with earlier programs. A National Conservation Association, a voluntary body, was organized following the failure of Congress to support the official body appointed by the President.

During this latest period the things accomplished are far short of the miraculous, and yet enough has been done already in the way of forestry and the control of minerals to characterize the period as one unlike the preceding. The recent developments in connection with the leasing of coal and oil privileges demonstrated the weakness of the administrative machinery of the government in caring for its property. The frauds in the handling of oil are no worse in kind than many that have preceded in connection with power and irrigation sites or even in the use of range land. They are simply more spectacular and more tangible with respect to personalities and the use of money.

It must not be forgotten that conservation means the practice of abstemiousness, the very antithesis of *laissez faire*. Moreover, *laissez faire* has been the dominating principle so far as a negative principle can be said to dominate, in American development. This being the case it was not to be expected that a conservation régime could be initiated in a day. It means enjoying a little less to-day in order that to-morrow's needs may be more certainly and more amply supplied.

One motive actuating the conservation movement was the belief that it furnished an effective means of preventing to a great extent the further development of monopoly. This would be true, especially respecting such resources as water power, minerals, and lumber. In connection with these resources something, at least, has been accomplished. In one important particular, however, hardly a start has been made. This is in conserving the soil. Thus far no far-reaching plan has been devised to prevent soil depletion, and worse, nothing has yet been found feasible for the control, through social action, of soil erosion. We are still "mining" the soil.

CHAPTER XXIII

FREEDOM OF THE RANGE UNTIL AFTER 1880

There had until recently always been the greatest freedom allowed stockmen in the use of the public lands for grazing or cutting hay. The practice had been universal and no complaints seem to have developed until settlement began to overtake the range cattlemen during the eighties. In the early days of the range cattle business, herding was universal. Later it was found that, with the much cheapened price of barbed wire, it was more satisfactory to fence in the range than to depend altogether on the cow-boys for guarding the stock and the grass.

FENCING THE PUBLIC DOMAIN

During the year 1883 a considerable number of letters were received at the General Land Office complaining of range fences which ran indiscriminately across section and township lines. The mail carriers reported that they could not get through this section of the country without a great deal of trouble and extra travel. The agents of the Land Office asked whether they were to give up business or use "Sharp's 45s." The settlers reported that there were hundreds of miles of fence on government land, on land suitable for farming, but that the settlers needed to be bullet proof.

In many instances, homesteads, timber claims or desert claims had been taken, but the only evidences of such

476

were the sod shanties within the enclosed districts, the shanties "holding down the claims" until patents were obtained by the cattlemen and their retinue. Signs posted on the fences at convenient intervals told the observer what he was to expect in case he molested the cattle industry. All told, it was the most unmistakable, wholesale, shameless instance of land grabbing that had yet been practiced in America. Companies with headquarters in eastern cities, and even in England, fenced in as much land as they wanted and some had the effrontery to claim in court that a man had a right to as much range as he could fence.[1]

It would be futile to attempt any very definite statement as to the extent of these enclosures. Some idea may, however, be gathered from certain approximations made in contemporary reports. Two companies in Colorado enclosed a million acres each. Other companies in Colorado, New Mexico, Nebraska and Kansas had around a quarter of a million acres each. In two counties in New Mexico three million acres were enclosed. Thirty-two cases reported to the General Land Office embraced 4,431,900 acres, while in 1888 about seven and a quarter million acres were under investigation.[2] The latter figure cannot be taken as the maximum of enclosures, neither was all the land investigated illegally enclosed, yet the report served to show roughly the amount of land on which settlement was discouraged by large holdings to which the possessor had no title at all, or a title requiring investigation. Instances of enclosures of twenty to fifty thousand acres were innumerable.[3] Enclosures of public land were made in fourteen states and territories.

The Department of the Interior did not hesitate to

---

[1] *Sen. Doc.,* 48 Cong., 1 Sess., No. 127.

[2] *L. O. R.,* 1888, p. 375.

[3] *Ibid,* 1883, 1884, 1885, 1886—By 1886 reports covering over 6,000,000 acres had been made to the land office. *Ex. Doc.,* 48 Cong., 1 Sess., No. 119.

assume the authority to declare the fencing of public domain illegal and to issue a circular to registers and receivers of United States land offices to that effect. These officers were ordered to give the notice publicity. The department proclaimed the trespassers and virtually gave settlers the right to destroy fences. However, it was one thing to proclaim and another thing to enforce. This paper defence of the settler hardly proved adequate. Congress took the matter in hand, and, in 1885, an act was passed making enclosures a punishable offense, putting the responsibility of enforcement upon certain officers and prescribing the penalties.[4]

The General Land Office was busy for some three or four years investigating enclosures. A great number of cases were taken into court and verdicts rendered.[5] For the most part, the cases were easily won by the complainants. In others, under some "color of title," the defendants won. "Color of title" was usually based on entries of a large part of the land under some one or another of the land laws. That these entries were in themselves fraudulent, was often well known but not easy to prove. There were such a multitude of abandoned homesteads, commuted homesteads, desert entry claims with no habitation or farming, and timber culture entries without visible signs of plantings, that it was impossible to make rules governing those cases involving fencing as distinguished from others.

The work of removing the fences was for the most part done within four or five years after the passage of the act of 1885. In 1890 the Commissioner of the General Land Office reported that with the exception of a few cases involving disputed title to the land, there were at that time no enclosures of the public lands of any considerable area.

[4] *U. S. Stat. at Large,* XXIII, p. 321.
[5] *L. O. R.,* 1888, 1889.

The Question of Leasing the Range Land

The enforcement of the law of 1885 meant that the lands were again free and open to all, that there was virtually no control over the land and the first comer was entitled to the grass. No one was responsible in a large way for over-grazing and the resulting destruction of the forage. As a matter of fact, however, agreements have since been entered into by cattlemen as to rights of grazing. The Public Lands Commission appointed in 1904 to investigate various public land problems has the following to say on the grazing situation: "At present the public lands are theoretically open commons, free to all citizens; but as a matter of fact a large proportion has been parceled out by more or less definite compacts or agreements among the various interests. These tacit agreements are continually being violated. The sheepmen and cattlemen are in frequent collision because of incursions upon each other's domain. Land which for years has been regarded as exclusively cattle range may be infringed upon by large bands of sheep, forced by drought to migrate. Violence and homicide frequently follow, after which new adjustments are made and matters quiet down for a time. There are localities where the people are utilizing to their own satisfaction the open range, and their demand is to be let alone, so that they may parcel out among themselves the use of the lands; but an agreement made to-day may be broken to-morrow by changing conditions of shifting interests. "The general lack of control in the use of public grazing lands has resulted, naturally and inevitably in over-grazing and the ruin of millions of acres of otherwise valuable grazing territory. Lands useful for grazing are losing their only capacity for productiveness, as, of course, they must when no legal control is exercised." [6]

Many suggestions and recommendations have been

[6] *Sen. Doc.*, 58 Cong., 3 Sess., No. 189, "Report of Pub. Lands Com.," p. xxi.

made, but up to the time of this writing no legislation has been enacted to control grazing on the range land. Undoubtedly some effective means of control must be inaugurated since, otherwise, any improvement of the range by reseeding or watering or other means at once insures heavier grazing and loss of the improvement.

The lease system seems to be the most logical method of getting the maximum of service from the range area of the public domain. It was recommended by the Public Lands Commission quoted above that the President be given authority to set aside, by proclamation, certain grazing districts as reserves, and that the Secretary of Agriculture should be given authority to classify and appraise the value of the lands and to appoint officers to have charge of the different grazing districts and to collect a moderate fee for grazing permits.[7] Definite and appropriate regulations were to be applied to each grazing district, and such regulations were to be applied "with special reference to bringing about the largest permanent occupation of the country by actual settlers and homeseekers." Thus, all land suitable for settlement should be left open to entry regardless of the grazing permit or lease.

In 1907 President Roosevelt made very similar recommendations for the control of grazing lands owned by the government.[8] First, local control, he said, should be in the hands of western men familiar with stock-raising. Secondly, there should be full local participation in the management of the range, in order to maintain a spirit of coöperation between the Government officials and the stockmen. Thirdly, the grazing fee should be small and at first almost nominal. Fourthly, such control should be taken gradually, giving ample time for grazing districts to be organized. Fifthly, the whole

[7] *Sen. Doc.*, 58 Cong., 3 Sess., No. 189, "Report of Pub. Lands Com.," p. xxi.
[8] *Ibid*, 59 Cong., 2 Sess., No. 310.

policy of control should be adjusted so as to encourage settlement by actual homeseekers.

Bills have been introduced in Congress providing for lease and fencing privileges on the public domain but all have failed of passage. This has been due in part to the fact that there has not been any adequate classification of lands made whereby the grazing lands may be distinguished from farming lands. Moreover, attempts have been made to adjust the size of homesteads to the business of grazing through the Enlarged Homestead Act of 1909 and the Stock-Raising Homestead Act of 1916. These have no doubt helped to some extent in utilizing the range lands, but they have fallen far short of expectations, since in the great majority of cases much more than 640 acres are required to support a family. In fact, the United States Department of Agriculture has estimated that from 2,000 to 4,000 acres are required in the regions of fair rainfall, and as high as 40,000 acres in the extremely arid regions of the Southwest.[9] This means that of the 300,000,000 acres[10] of agricultural land in the public domain, used chiefly for grazing, a relatively small percentage can be adapted to the homestead laws and thus remains free from control.

Besides the lack of adequate classification of public lands and the idea that adjustments of the homestead laws would suffice, certain objections have been raised to the permit or lease system.[11] It is claimed by some stockmen that they cannot afford to pay a fee, that it would mean bankruptcy. It is feared by some that under any system of control the large owners and corporations would secure a monopoly in the use of the pasture land, and the small owners would be shut out. It is claimed that young men starting in the business of stock raising would have no opportunity to build up under a lease

[9] *Yearbook*, U. S. Department of Agriculture, 1906, p. 235.

[10] *Sen. Doc.*, 60 Cong., 2 Sess., No. 676, "National Conservation Commission Report," I, p. 82.

[11] *Ibid*, 58 Cong., 3 Sess., No. 189, "Report of Pub. Lands Com.," App., p. 18.

system. Other stockmen hold the view that since they have fought out their controversies and arrived at mutual agreements as to the use of the range, it would be foolish to open the whole question for new adjustments. It is held that, although range conditions are not entirely satisfactory, it is better to continue the present system than to take any chance on the application of new methods.

But these opinions are held by a relatively small number of stockmen according to information collected by the Public Lands Commission in 1904. Of 1,400 letters received from stockmen throughout the West only 64 held the opinion that the use of the range should remain unregulated.

While the federal government is very slow to adopt a leasing system for the grazing lands, the plan is not without precedent. For example, in 1883 Texas passed an act providing for the lease of its school and asylum lands, the plan being to keep them out of the market until wanted by actual settlers. Land is leased for a maximum period of ten years to the highest bidder, providing the minimum bid is at least four cents an acre per year.[12] The lessee may fence and otherwise improve his leasehold and retain the ownership of the improvements. The amount of stock permitted upon a given leased area is limited by the state law. Wyoming has a very similar leasing system which began with an act of 1891. It has not assumed great proportions, yet a few million acres are being leased. In Colorado some two million acres are leased for approximately a quarter of a million dollars.[13] In these states the leased lands are nearly all used for grazing. In North Dakota and some other states agricultural lands belonging to the state are leased. Very similar to the leasing of grazing land by the states is the experience of several railroad com-

[12] *Sen. Doc.*, 58 Cong., 3 Sess., No. 189, Report of Pub. Lands Com., p. 35.
[13] *Report* of Colorado State Board of Land Commissioners, 1911-12, p. 5.

panies, notably the Northern Pacific and Southern Pacific, in leasing lands for grazing purposes. Furthermore, the Federal Government itself has had quite satisfactory experience in leasing lands in the National Forests for grazing purposes, as will be seen in the next section of this chapter. From reports of the Secretary of Agriculture and the state land boards and the practice of the railway companies, the lease system has much to commend it and little in the nature of objections.

The public ranges have great possibilities for pasturing live stock, and under proper regulation more and better stock might be kept, to the advantage of both stockmen and the nation. Where the regulations recommended have been tried, an increase of some thirty per cent has been realized. Cognizant of this Congress since 1910 has made annual appropriations of from ten to one hundred thousand dollars for study and experimentation in the improvement of the range forage.

GRAZING WITHIN NATIONAL FOREST RESERVES

A different situation exists in the case of grazing lands within the national forest reserves. Here the lease or permit system is applied. With the development, or at least the segregation, of great areas of national forest in the nineties, the question of grazing within them became pertinent. While over-grazing is often destructive of forests, it has been found that reasonable grazing has been of great benefit in keeping down the full growth of grass and so making the control of fires vastly easier.[14] A good forestry policy requires that the grazing be not close, since close grazing promotes erosion, one of the troubles forestry is designed to overcome.

In 1879 Congress passed an act providing for the establishment and control of national forests, in which were provisions for the use of the products. Based on

[14] *Sen. Doc.*, 60 Cong., 2 Sess., No. 676, "National Conservation Commission Report," II, p. 423.

this, the General Land Office issued in 1900 a circular of rules and regulations governing the use of the reserves for stock ranging. The earlier policy had been to prohibit grazing in national forest reserves, but much ill-feeling was developed among the stock owners who had been using the range in question and who believed that grazing the forest lands was not necessarily detrimental to the trees. By the ruling of 1900 permits for grazing were to be obtained from the Commissioner of the General Land Office.[15] The plan thus provided required of the forest officers an estimate of the number of animals which could properly be accommodated, both with respect to their own welfare and that of the forest. Preference was given to people living within the reserve, those owning farms within the reserve, and those living near, over those living at a distance.[16] Within a few years after this time, it appears that the stockmen were well satisfied with the plan. For a time they objected to paying a grazing fee, which had been required since 1905. This was only natural, since it was demanding a price for a privilege that for many years had been free. It was found, however, that the stock did better under the restrictions required by the government, and the owners soon recognized this advantage.[17] No reduction in the number of stock grazed was necessary in most cases, while in some instances it was increased.

Experiments are being made in using fences in place of herding within the forest ranges, and in most instances they have proved to be economical.[18] Fences are especially beneficial in connection with the dairy industry, and in some instances pastures for dairy cows have been made near settlements, thus keeping such cows separate from the beef cattle with their wide range.

[15] Yearbook, U. S. D. A., 1901, p. 337.
[16] Ibid, p. 347.
[17] Ibid, 1905, p. 640; 1906, p. 61.
[18] Ibid, 1908, p. 542.

During the year 1906 about 1,200,000 horses and cattle and 6,650,000 sheep and goats were grazed in the National Forest. The income from grazing fees was $850,000. In 1908 the fees reached $1,000,000, but the expenses were about the same. There is no disposition to make the forest ranges a revenue producing undertaking. The purpose is development, and to that end the rules are in favor of the settler and the small farmer and against monopoly.[19] In 1915 several hundred thousand head of milk and work animals were grazed free of charge. Over 3,500,000 head of stock crossed the Forests, feeding en route, also free of charge. In that year 31,000 individuals were holding regular grazing permits.[20]

The number of animals sustained on forest forage in proportion to the acreage available increased 50 per cent from 1905 to 1915. The actual number of persons holding permits had increased 200 per cent during this period. In his report for 1915 the Secretary of Agriculture had the following to say regarding the results obtained from regulated grazing in the forest reserves:[21] "When the regulated system was established the forest ranges, like the open public lands to-day, rapidly were being impaired. The productivity of the land for forage in most places has been restored and everywhere is increasing; the industry has been made more stable; stock come from the forests in better condition; range wars have stopped; ranch property has increased in value; and a larger area has been made available through range improvements. . . . That the forests have promoted the development of the stock industry . . . is appreciated by the stockmen and they are urging that a similar system of range regulation be extended to the unreserved public lands."

With a total area of about 161,000,000 acres in the Na-

[19] *Yearbook,* U. S. D. A., 1909, p. 92.
[20] *Ibid,* 1915, pp. 63, 64.
[21] *Ibid.*

tional Forests in 1922 we were grazing under paid permit 1,873,000 cattle, 6,512,000 sheep. Also about 68,000 horses, 36,000 goats and 2,000 hogs were grazed under these permits. Besides this hundreds of thousands of milk and work animals were grazed free of charge.[22]

It can thus be said that the policy of government regulation of grazing in the National Forests is quite satisfactory since, from all accounts, it means satisfaction to the private interests of stockmen, greatly increased production of animal products for the country as a whole, and finally, the safeguarding of tree growth in the forests.[23]

Summary

From the earliest times the public domain furnished free grazing. In the early days, or until about forty years ago, herding had been the practice everywhere. With the coming of barbed wire into general use as a fencing material about 1880 a new era was inaugurated in the cattle business. The cattlemen of the West very promptly began to substitute fences for "cowboys." They fenced in the same ranges on which their cattle had been grazing under the care of the herdsmen. Since a large part of this land was free public range it meant that public land was enclosed by the fences. Some companies fenced in a million acres each, while a hundred thousand was not uncommon. It will be recalled that at the time of the fencing the government was not selling land in any large tracts. To get hold of it through the Homestead and Preëmption provisions, whether done honestly or dishonestly was a slow process, in fact it was impracticable. A special law made fencing the public domain a punishable offense, and by 1890 substantially all fences were removed. The episode shows an unfortunate situation which was a natural result of having no adequate land policy covering the case at issue.

Removing the fence again made grazing free. Interested parties made compacts among themselves whereby claims to certain tracts were recognized. But such agreements are unstable. The Land Commission of 1904 reported a deplorable condition on the ranges,

[22] Letter from E. A. Sherman, Forest Service, to B. H. Hibbard, July 31, 1923. For 1923, permits were issued for the grazing of 1,868,979 cattle and horses, and for 6,425,299 sheep and goats, as reported by the Forest Service by letter.
[23] *Yearbook*, U. S. D. A., 1914, pp. 80, 82. Each settler is allowed to graze ten cows and work animals free of charge.

and recommended a lease system.   President Roosevelt favored the
lease.   But how to put such a plan into effect was baffling in view of
the lack of a classification of the land.   What, indeed, was grazing
land?   States have made a success of the grazing lease; the federal
government might have done so, or for that matter might do so yet,
even in spite of the ill-starred Grazing Homestead Act.

The redeeming feature of the general mismanagement of the grazing
lands is found in the plans of grazing within the national forest
reserves.   Since 1900 stock has been grazed in the national forests
under the permit system on the payment of fees.   Nearly 2,000,000
cattle, and over 6,500,000 sheep are so pastured.   Moreover, the
carrying capacity of the range land so managed is increasing.

CHAPTER XXIV

CLASSIFICATION OF THE PUBLIC LANDS

MEAGER ATTEMPTS AT CLASSIFICATION, BEGAN IN 1796

Very early in the history of the public domain an attempt was made at classifying the land. In 1796 a law provided that "every surveyor shall note in his field book the true situation of all mines, salt licks, salt springs, and mill seats which shall come to his knowledge; all water courses, over which the lines he runs shall pass, and also the quality of the lands."[1] On this and subsequent acts as a basis, surveyors have reported something as to quality of land surveyed, though most of the reports are meager enough. In 1879 an act provided for the classification of lands by a geological survey directed from the Department of the Interior, but this seems to have applied to minerals primarily and to have left out of consideration the quality of land for agricultural purposes.

"It is a curious circumstance that the method of doing that which was recognized as a necessity when the lands were so numerous has not been improved or kept abreast of the times and pursued with greater particularity when the lands have become comparatively scarce and the necessity for classification therefore the greater."[2]

Not much attention was given for a whole century to the classification subject till the Public Lands Commission appointed by the President in 1903 recommended strongly that the government classify the remaining

[1] *U. S. Stat. at Large*, I, p. 466.
[2] *Sen. Doc.*, 60 Cong., 2 Sess., No. 676, VI, p. 409.

public lands. They say: "The agricultural possibilities of the remaining public lands are as yet almost unknown. Lands which a generation or even a decade ago were supposed to be valueless are now producing large crops, either with or without irrigation. This has been brought about in part by the introduction of new grains and other plants and new methods of farming and in part by denser population and improved systems of transportation. It is obvious that the first essential for putting the remaining public lands to their best use is to ascertain what that best use is by a preliminary study and classification of them, and to determine their probable future development by agriculture.

"After the agricultural possibilities of the public lands have been ascertained with reasonable certainty, provision should be made for dividing them into areas sufficiently large to support a family, and no larger, and to permit settlement on such areas. It is obvious that any attempt to accomplish this end without a careful classification of the public lands must necessarily fail."[3]

Four Periods of Land Classification

A history of the classification of the public lands may be divided into four periods, the separation into periods being based not so much upon changes in policy relating to agricultural lands as upon policies relating to forest and mineral lands, which policies have required increasing precision in land classification for their adequate administration. In the classification of the lands of the public domain it became necessary, for instance, to recognize that the lands whose surface is suitable for agriculture or forests or may have valuable minerals beneath the surface. Because of this interrelation of uses, and because of the gradual recognition that the different classes of land require different policies, it is almost necessary in tracing the progress of the classification of agricul-

[3] *Sen. Doc.*, 58 Cong., 3 Sess., No. 189, pp. 14, 15.

tural lands in the public domain to include forest, mineral and other kinds of land, and base the separation into historical periods upon notable changes in policy concerning one or another of these more important uses.

The years prior to 1862 may be considered the first period. During these years the humid eastern states were undergoing settlement and practically all the land was esteemed primarily agricultural. The forests were still so extensive as to appear inexhaustible and to constitute an incubus to proper land utilization, rather than an asset; while the mining areas in northern Michigan, in southwestern Wisconsin and Missouri, in California and a few points in the Rocky Mountain region, even near the close of the period, were small and relatively unimportant, consequently the need of careful classification of forest and mineral land was not yet adequately appreciated. The semi-arid pastoral lands of the West had scarcely, as yet, come within the sphere of settlement. This first period, characterized by constant, careful and labored attention on the part of Congress to the great problem of proper disposal of the the humid public lands for agricultural use, reached a culmination in the passage of the Homestead Act in 1862. [4]

The second period, covering the years from 1862 to 1879, was characterized by attempts to classify and legislate for the mineral lands of the nation in a more adequate manner. The discovery of gold in California resulted in a notable migration into the Far West and the opening up of mines not only in California, but also in practically all the western states and territories. Most of these mines were located on public lands and very few on lands suitable for agricultural use. So mineral lands became more fully recognized as an important

---

[4] Senator Benton estimated that during his years of service in Congress, (1821-1851) consideration of questions affecting the public lands consumed fully one-quarter of that body's time.

and distinct class, and their proper classification and utilization received considerable attention by Congress, but not with that conspicuously successful issue which brought the previous period of agricultural legislation to a close.

The third period, extending from 1879 to about 1906, was ushered in by a general recognition of the fact that physical conditions in the western half of the United States were so different from those existing in the East that a more complete classification of the land was necessary before the remaining public domain could be properly disposed of. The mining centers that had developed in various parts of the West afforded splendid local markets for agricultural products, while the transportation of these products from the East was both long and costly, consequently a portion of the population turned to agriculture for a livelihood. Irrigated lands, therefore, became recognized as a distinct and important class; and during the period there occurred a gradual conversion of both public and professional opinion from belief in unfettered private initiative in the construction of irrigation works, through the intermediate stage of public control, to the final stage, reached in the Reclamation Act of 1902, of approval of construction by the Federal Government.

Also during this period the policy of public ownership and control of the mountain forests in the West, largely to conserve the water supply for the irrigated lands, became well established. The acts of Congress during this period further indicate that the matter of income from sale of mineral lands and protection of the public from future monopoly control received increasing consideration. It was a transition period from the policy of unrestricted individual initiative and "laissez faire," which had worked so well in the disposal of the humid agricultural lands of the East to the policy of government control of certain mineral and water resources and

even in the case of the forests, of government ownership and operation. Adequate classification of the public
lands was recognized as a preliminary to the inauguration
of this new policy.

The fourth period may be said to begin with the
awakening by the American public to the need of conserving our National resources. An exact date, therefore, is difficult to select; but perhaps the most important
even from the standpoint of land classification was the
withdrawal of large areas of valuable coal lands from
entry in 1906, and the undertaking of detailed land
classification work in that year by the United States
Geological Survey. "Since that date," to quote from a
bulletin published in 1913, "the Survey has been actively
engaged in land-classification work. The coöperative
agreement whereby certain types of information are made
available to the Land Office in its administration of individual entries and selections has already been described.
In addition coal lands are being classified and valued as
rapidly as the funds at the disposal of the Survey will
permit, and oil, gas, phosphate, and potash lands and
lands valuable for water power and reservoir sites are
being withdrawn from entry as rapidly as information
regarding them is obtained."

These lands withdrawn from entry may now, under
the provisions of an act passed in 1920, [5] be leased from
the government and operated under certain regulations
the purpose of which is to avoid waste in mining and
assure the conservation for future generations of these
gifts of nature, in so far as is compatible with present
economic conditions.

Relative to agricultural lands, the period has been
characterized by increasing general appreciation of the
fact that the original Homestead law limiting individual
entry to 160 acres was inapplicable to the vast area of
semi-arid lands in the West and required amendment, if

[5] *U. S. Stat. at Large*, XLI, p. 437.

these lands were to be transferred to private ownership and the abuses incident to unrestricted occupation by cattle, and sheep men, under sufferance by the government, were to be abated. The Enlarged Homestead Act of 1909 and the Grazing Homestead Act of 1916 had this object in view. These acts, unhappily, have been less successful than the original Homestead Act in securing the fullest utilization of the land, but are probably promoting the eventual attainment of this purpose by the circuitous and wasteful process of permitting private ownership to be acquired in small units often under fraudulent declaration of intention, which small holdings will, in most instances, be consolidated into ranches adequate in size for the support of the family.

The significant feature of this period is the fact that scientific classification of the public lands has been adopted as preliminary to their disposal or utilization, and that in this disposal or utilization the duty of conserving the national resources is clearly recognized. Dr. George Otis Smith, Director of the Geological Survey, has summarized the trend of public policy and the increasing appreciation of the importance of land classification in the following notable words:[6]

"In the latter half of the nineteenth century the spirit of the public land laws in the United States was settlement and development. With a public domain of one and a third billion acres, acquired in the preceding half century—1803-1853—by purchase, discovery, exploration, and cession, and with another third of a billion acres in Alaska constituting a later purchase, the Nation felt that it could be lavish with its lands. The wilderness called for pioneers of every type, and large premiums were held out to capital enterprise and individual initiative. Development was desired whatever the cost in lands that were intrinsically of little value without settlement. The same century that saw the creation of this national domain—an empire in itself—also witnessed the distribution of more than one-half of its acreage. This shrinkage of the national domain has naturally been coincident with national development in all lines of industry. Western prairies

[6] U. S. Geol. Survey, *Bulletin* No. 537, pp. 7, 8.

have become the world's granary, and western mountains, once wholly in public ownership, are now contributing to their private and corporate owners the profits on no small proportion of the world's output of metals and of mineral fuels.

"With advancing years, a wise nation, like a prudent man, learns to husband its resources. Land values are now recognized, the purpose in both legislation and administration has changed, and highest development alone is sought. With the most and the best of the Nation's land already alienated, the national duty is to put to its best use what remains.

"Utilization of lands for their greatest value necessitates the determination of that value, which is, briefly, land classification; and, to be adequate, land classification must be based upon first-hand acquaintance with the particular land under consideration. With a national estate including country ranging from salt-incrusted deserts to valleys knee-deep with nutritious grasses or giant forests almost impenetrable because of luxuriant undergrowth, no general statutes that may be enacted can be made so definite as not to require the exercise of well-informed judgment in their execution. To this end examination and classification of the public lands, constitute an initial step in their disposition for development and settlement. That a few decades ago settlement and development commonly outstripped classification and often far preceded even the legal disposition of the land itself is no good reason for failure to follow the more logical procedure now."

With this hasty survey of the trend of public policy relative to land classification it now appears appropriate to note briefly the more important legislative enactments and executive actions concerning classification of the public lands during each of these four periods.

THE FIRST PERIOD, 1785-1862

On May 20, 1785, Congress passed "an ordinance for ascertaining the mode of disposing of lands in the Western Territory," that had been submitted a year prior by a committee of which Thomas Jefferson was chairman. This ordinance outlined the salient features of the system of survey according to which the lands of the United States from Alabama to Ohio and westward have been measured and designated, and also most of the lands of

Canada from Ontario westward. This first land ordinance included specifications for a certain minimum degree of classification, that of the separation of mineral from agricultural land. It was provided that there should be reserved "one-third of all gold, silver, lead and copper mines, to be sold, or otherwise disposed of as Congress shall hereafter direct."[7] Likewise later laws, passed in 1800, 1807, 1816, and so on to 1841 and 1862, made more or less specific provision for the separation of mineral from agricultural lands. The intention was to derive more revenue from the more valuable lands and to keep them available for social use. Some of the leading facts pertaining to this phase of classification are outlined in the chapter on Mineral Lands.

In the classification of the agricultural land proper, or land potentially agricultural, the first legal recognition of a sub-class occurred in 1849 when an act was passed by Congress, applying exclusively to Louisiana and providing that to aid "in constructing the necessary levees and drains to reclaim swamps, and overflow lands therein ... the whole of those swamps and overflowed lands which may be, or are, found unfit for cultivation" were granted to the state.[8] This subject is dealt with in the chapter on Swamp Land. The execution of this act rested presumably on the work of the surveyors in designating land as fit for agricultural purposes or as swampy.

During this first period certain live oak and red cedar forests in the South, principally in Florida, were recognized as a separate class of the public lands and the

[7] "The mineral resources of the country at that time were but little known. Our present western precious metal regions, and the base-metal belt of the Mississippi, were almost entirely within the domain of France and Spain. The reserving clause in the ordinance of 1785 suggests the reservations as to minerals by way of royalty or sovereign dues, in some of the crown charters for colonization in America, and further shows the existing doubt as to the policy of the government in relation to holding, leasing, or selling mines and mineral lands." Donaldson, p. 306.

[8] *U. S. Stat. at Large*, IX, p. 352.

preservation of such forests in order to supply the navy with timber was provided for. The first act of this character was passed by Congress in 1817.

The Homestead Act, which is taken as marking the conclusion of this first period was intended primarily for the central humid portion of the United States, and in the West applied alike to arable, irrigable and pasturage lands, but not to timber or mineral lands.[9]

The Second Period, 1862-1879

The mining act of 1866 made "the mineral lands of the public domain, both surveyed and unsurveyed . . . free and open to exploration and occupation . . . subject also to the local customs or rules of miners in the several mining districts, so far as the same may not be in conflict with the laws of the United States.[10]

Thus to the disposal of lands primarily useful for the precious metals contained beneath the surface, the provisions of laws suitable only for agriculture, a surface use, were clumsily applied. But appreciation of the fact that different kinds of land required very different legislation in order to secure the highest utilization and that a scientific classification of the land was a prerequisite for such legislation, became quite general among the scientific men during this period, partly, no doubt, as a result of the geological and geographical surveys of the Territories, begun in 1867 under the direction of Professor Fred V. Hayden, and the survey of the Rocky Mountain region later begun under the direction of Major J. W. Powell. These surveys, carried on at first under the General Land Office, with a coöperating organization in the War Department, set a very high level of scientific work and contributed greatly toward an appreciation, not only by men of science but also by the general public, of the very diverse character of the western portion of the

[9] Public Lands Commission Preliminary *Report,* 1880, p. xxiv.
[10] *Session Laws,* 39 Cong., 1 Sess., p. 251.

United States. They "prepared land maps in which the lands of the public domain were classified into a few broad types intended to reflect their chief value. Some of these types were forest lands, irrigable lands, grazing lands, etc." [11]

The increasing realization of the need of a more accurate and adequate classification of the public lands is shown in the act of appropriation for the General Land Office in 1876. In this act it was specified that "no lands shall be surveyed under this appropriation except:

First, those adapted to agriculture without artificial irrigation.

Second, Irrigable lands, or such as can be redeemed.

Third, Timber lands bearing timber of commercial value.

Fourth, Coal lands containing coal of commercial value.

Fifth, Exterior boundaries of town sites.

Sixth, Private land claims."

It will be noted that arid grazing lands are omitted from this list, also all mineral lands except coal lands. Such mineral lands were subject to sale prior to survey.

In 1877 an act was passed providing for the disposal of saline lands. If adjudged agricultural under the homestead or other acts, lands classified as saline were to be sold at not less than $1.25 an acre. The Timber and Stone Act of 1878 required for its administration a classification of the land likely to be affected by it. This was provided for subsequently.

At the close of the second period, according to Donaldson, there existed special legislation providing for the disposal of saline, town-site lands, desert lands, coal lands, and all others as agricultural.

In April 1878, Major Powell presented to the Commissioner of the General Land Office his notable report on "Lands of the Arid Region," which report two days later

[11] Letter from W. C. Mendenhall, U. S. Geological Survey, to R. T. Ely, 1920.

was transmitted to Congress. In transmitting this report the Secretary of the Interior, Carl Schurz, explains— "Herewith are also transmitted draughts of two bills, one entitled 'a bill to authorize the organization of pasturage districts by homestead settlement on the public lands which are of value for pasturage purposes only,' and the other 'a bill to authorize the organization of irrigation districts by homestead settlements upon the public lands requiring irrigation for agricultural purposes,' intended to carry into effect a new system for the disposal of the public lands of said region." [12]

In this report Major Powell, emphasizes the great extent and importance of pasturage lands in the West, and sums up his recommendations concerning classification in the following words. "In providing for a general classification of the lands of the Arid Region, it will, then, be necessary to recognize the following classes, namely: mineral lands, coal lands, irrigable lands, timber lands, and pasturage lands. The mineral lands are practically classified by the miners themselves, and for this no further legal provision is necessary. The coal lands must be determined by geological survey. The work of determining the areas which should be relegated to the other classes —namely, irrigable, timber, and pasturage lands, will be comparatively inexpensive." [13]

In the Sundry Civil Bill, approved June 30th, 1878, following the appropriation for the surveys of the General Land Office, and for the "continuation of the Geological and Geographical Survey of the territories of the United States, under Professor F. V. Hayden," also

[12] *Ex. Doc.*, 45 Cong., 2 Sess., No. 73, "Lands on the Arid Region," p. 4. Major Powell in these bills urges the disposal of lands suitable only for pasturage in units of four sections (2560 acres) under provisions similar to those of the Homestead law, but with the land so surveyed that each unit will have access to a stream or water hole. For irrigable lands he recommends provision for "associations" of nine men or more who will construct the irrigation works needed and will then be entitled to 80 acres each of such irrigated land under provisions similar to those in the Homestead act.

[13] *Ex. Doc.*, 45 Cong., 2 Sess., No. 73, p. 45.

"Under Professor J. W. Powell; for continuation of the Geographical and Geological Survey of the Rocky mountain region," the former survey being restricted to the territory north, and that of the latter survey to the territory south of the 42nd parallel, and both surveys to the region west of the 100th meridian occurs this extraordinary provision: "and the National Academy of Science is hereby required, at their next meeting, to take into consideration the methods and expenses of conducting all surveys of a scientific character under the War or Interior Departments, and the surveys of the Land Office, and to report to Congress as soon thereafter as may be practicable a plan for surveying and mapping the territories of the United States on such general system as will, in their judgments, secure the best results at the least possible cost." [14]

Major J. W. Powell, reporting to the Secretary of the Interior on November 1, 1878, in response to the request of the acting president of the National Academy of Sciences to transmit any information available in the Department of the Interior as to surveys then in existence, after listing the classes of lands recognized under the laws, adds the following comment: "An examination of the laws . . . will show that the classes of lands mentioned above are therein recognized, and in the administration of the laws relating to these lands those belonging to each specific class must be determined; but no adequate provision is made for securing an accurate classification, and to a large extent the laws are inoperative or practically void; for example, coal lands should be sold at $10 or $20 per acre, but, the department having no means of determining what lands belong to this class, titles to coal lands are usually obtained under the provisions of statutes that relate to lands of another class, that is, by purchasing at $1.25 per acre, or by homestead or preëmption entry. An examination of the laws will

[14] *U. S. Stat. at Large,* XX, p. 230.

exhibit this fact, that for the classification contemplated therein a thorough survey is necessary, embracing the geological and physical characteristics of the entire public domain." [15]

The report of the committee of the National Academy of Sciences on Surveys of the Territories, submitted to Congress the following year, recommended the abolition of the Geological and Geographical Survey of the territories, the Geographical and Geological Survey of the Rocky mountain region, both in the Interior Department, and the Geographical Surveys West of the 100th meridian, in the War Department, and the consolidation of the activities of these surveys into a single organization, to be known as the Geological Survey. With reference to land classification this committee report states:

"The best interests of the public domain require, for the purposes of intelligent administration, a thorough knowledge of its geologic structure, natural resources, and products. The domain embraces a vast mineral wealth in its soils, metals, salines, stones, clays, etc. To meet the requirements of existing laws in the disposition of the agricultural, mineral, pastoral, timber, desert, and swamp lands, a thorough investigation and classification of the acreage of the public domain is imperatively demanded. . . .

"The Land Office shall also call upon the United States Geological Survey for all information as to the value and classification of lands. . . ." [16]

"After extended hearings before the House and Senate committees and the publication of many documents bearing upon the questions involved, Congress, in March, 1879, agreed upon a law which embodied the recommendations of the Academy of Sciences for the abolition of

[15] *U. S. Stat. at Large*, XX, p. 230.
[16] Smith, Geo. Otis, and others, U. S. Geological Survey, *Bulletin* No. 537, p. 11.

the Territorial Surveys and the establishment of the United States Geological Survey." [17]

Thus, while the classification may have been inadequate, the government was definitely committed to the plan of classifying land in substantially all cases before disposing of it.

THE THIRD PERIOD, 1879-1906

The establishment of the United States Geological Survey in 1879, is taken as marking the beginning of the third period. The Director of the Geological Survey, it is provided in the law, "shall have the direction of the geological survey and the classification of the public resources, and products of the national domain." [18]

This same act, also provided for a "Commission to codify the land laws" consisting of the Commissioner of the General Land Office, the Director of the United States Geological Survey, and three civilians. Their duties were to report to Congress "first, a codification of the present laws relating to the survey and disposition of the public domain; second, a system and standard of classification of public lands, as arable, irrigable, timber, pasturage, swamp, coal, mineral lands, and such other classes as may be deemed proper, having due regard to humidity of climate, supply of water for irrigation, and other physical characteristics; third, a system of land parcelling adapted to the economic uses of the several classes of lands; fourth, such recommendations as they may deem wise in relation to the best method of disposing of the public lands of the western portion of the United States to actual settlers." [19]

---

[17] U. S. Geol. Survey *Bulletin* No. 537, p. 12.

[18] *U. S. Stat. at Large*, XX, p. 394.

[19] *Ibid*. The commission appointed by the President consisted of J. A. Williamson, Commissioner of General Land Office, Clarence King, Director of Geol. Survey, A. T. Britton, Thomas Donaldson and J. W. Powell. The classes of land listed are practically those given in Powell's "Report on the Arid Lands."

This Commission in making its preliminary report the following year says: "In laying out its work a careful consideration of the above provisions of law led to a subdivision of the work into two principal parts. First, a codification of the present laws relating to the survey and disposition of the public domain; second, investigation looking to recommendation of new legislation." [20]

In the act which was recommended to Congress for consideration, Chapter V relates to classification of lands, the first paragraph reading—"For all purposes of surveying and sale the public lands of the United States shall be classified as arable, irrigable, pasturage, timber, and mineral, and said lands, thus classified, shall be disposed of only under acts specially applicable thereto." Then after briefly defining each class of land it practically leaves the classification to be based on "the plats and field notes of the official surveys," which however, "shall be subject to correction upon proof of error satisfactory to the commissioner of the General Land Office, and according to regulations to be prescribed by him." [21] Thus,

[20] In recommending this new legislation the commission comments on the inadequacy of existing law and need of classification of the land as follows—"There can be no doubt that much land has passed from the government into the hands of individuals in a manner and under circumstances which were not contemplated when the laws were made; that the conditions required by law have been imperfectly fulfilled by settlers and claimants, that compliance with such requirements has often been perfunctory and nominal, or even evaded altogether. It also appears that lands which should be opened to occupation and settlement are practically barred therefrom by the effect of restrictions which render their acquisition extremely burdensome and difficult. . . . A very great proportion of the lands of the West cannot become settled and pass into private ownership, because under the terms of existing laws it is not desirable to the settlers to acquire them.

"These difficulties have in the main grown out of the want of adaptation to the present public domain of the laws which were originally framed for the Northwest territory. . . . There was a kind of homogeneity in the quality and value of the land of that region. It was all valuable for agriculture and habitation, but in the western portion of our country it is otherwise. Its most conspicuous characteristic from an economic point of view is its heterogeneity. One region is exclusively valuable for mining, another solely for timber, a third for nothing but pasturage, and a fourth serves no useful purpose whatever. . . . Hence it has come to pass that the homestead and preemption laws are not suited for securing the settlement of more than an insignificant portion of the country. Report Pub. Lands Comm., 1800, pp. 5, 9; Ex. Doc., 46 Cong., 2 Sess., No. 46, p. 9.

[21] Ex. Doc., 46 Cong., 2 Sess., No. 46, p. 63.

apparently contrary to the intent of Congress in vesting the classification of land in the Geological Survey this recommendation of the Commission would vest the responsibility in the General Land Office. Yet two of the five members of the Commission were also members of the Geological Survey.

The main reason for this relinquishment by the Geological Survey of a duty apparently imposed on it by Congress is doubtless to be found principally in the fact that the hundred thousand dollars appropriated by Congress to the Survey would have been quite inadequate for so large a task; at the same time there was hesitancy on the part of a newly established bureau to appear to duplicate the work of the General Land Office, and also the criticisms by interested parties which any classification was sure to incur may have been a deterrent factor.

It is interesting to note in the recommendations of the Commission that pasturage lands were to be subject to purchase at private sale at a price decreasing from $1.25 an acre in 1881 to $1 in 1886, 75 cents in 1890, and then 12½ cents an acre each three years until a minimum price of 12½ cents was reached; provided, "that nothing in this section shall . . . interfere with settlement on said pasturage lands . . . under the homestead, homestead pasturage, or irrigation laws." The "homestead pasturage" provision recommended homestead entry on four sections, 2,560 acres, upon payment of $1,000. The policy recommended for the timber lands was sale of the timber exceeding eight inches in diameter, but retention of title to the land by the government.[22]

The first director of the Geological Survey, Clarence King, in his first report to the Secretary of the Interior, in 1880, accepts the point of view of the Public Lands Commission and states: "I have assumed that Congress, in directing me to make a classification of the public lands, could not

[22] *Ex. Doc.*, 46 Cong., 2 Sess., No. 46, pp. 63, 70, 75. Both these provisions correspond with Powell's recommendations in his "Report on the Arid Lands."

have intended to supersede the machinery of the Land Office and substitute a classification to be executed by another bureau of the government." He, therefore, concludes that "the intention of Congress was to begin a rigid scientific classification of the lands of the national domain, not for purposes of aiding the machinery of the General Land Office by furnishing a basis of sale, but for the general information of the people of the country, and to produce a series of land maps which should show all those features upon which intelligent agriculturists, miners, engineers and timbermen might, thereafter, base their operations and which would obviously be of the highest value for all students of the political economy and resources of the United States." [23]

"This interpretation," according to Mr. W. C. Mendenhall, the present chief of the Land Classification Board of the Geological Survey, "prevailed in part till about 1906, when the pressing need of the Department of the Interior for an adequate classification of mineral lands for purposes of administration led to a revival of this suspended function of the Geological Survey, not, as Director King seemed to think necessary, by superseding the machinery of the General Land Office, but by coöperation, financial and administrative, between that bureau and the Survey and by a series of orders from the Secretary of the Interior, to whom both bureaus report. These orders so define the part that each is to bear in public-land administration as to make the Survey chiefly responsible for the physical classification." [24]

The work of the Geological Survey during these years, 1879-1906, consisted largely in the preparation of topographic maps and geological maps and reports. The topographic maps, although "intended to serve primarily as bases on which to delineate and present geologic material, they have proved to be of great value for other and wider uses. Not the least of these uses is that to which they are put in land classification. The thousands of maps issued are graphic

[23] U. S. Geol. Survey *Bulletin* No. 537, p. 12.
[24] *Ibid*, p. 13.

engineering reports on the physical and cultural features of the areas they represent. They are essential to the study of drainage areas, irrigability of lands, possible power development and rights of way, and supplemental sheets now prepared give additional data on the distribution of timber and of springs, of desert and of grass land, and of cultivated and irrigated areas." [25]

In addition to the preparation of these topographic base maps of such value in land classification work, the Geological Survey has had imposed upon it by Congress several specific tasks in land classification. In 1888 it was directed to make a "special investigation of the practicability of constructing reservoirs for the storage of water in the arid regions of the United States. This work was supported for a time by appropriations, but was later discontinued by Congress after many reservoir sites had been examined and segregated and a number of reports valuable in the classification of the lands of the arid regions had been published.

"After the irrigation survey was abolished the division of hydrography was organized within the Geological Survey, at first as a part of the topographic branch and later with special small appropriations, its purpose being to continue that part of the work of the irrigation survey that involved the study of the available water resources of the Western States and Territories. As the value of this work to reclamation became manifest, Congress responded by increasing the amount of the funds annually available for this purpose until in 1903 they reached the sum of $200,000 a year.

"On June 17, 1902, the Reclamation Act [26] was passed. This act represented the culmination toward which the work of the division of hydrography had up to that time been tending. That work gave definite information as to available supplies of water and the lands on which the water could be used. The Reclamation Act authorized the construction of works for the application of these waters and the

[25] U. S. Geol. Survey, *Bulletin*, No. 537, p. 14.
[26] *U. S. Stat. at Large*, XXXII, p. 388.

reclamation of the tributary lands.[27]   But the reclamation fund is not available for general studies of water supplies; it can be used only for studies of water available for use on specific projects.   The work of the division of hydrography therefore did not cease with the organization of the Reclamation Service, but has been continued in the Geological Survey by the water-resources branch." [28]

During this third period the Geological Survey was occasionally called upon also to classify lands in Indian reservations preliminary to their disposition, and in 1895 provision was made for classification of the lands within the limits of the Northern Pacific Railroad grant in Montana and Idaho. With these exceptions, the Geological Survey devoted its energies to gathering data rather than to applying the data gathered to the classification of public lands until the year 1906.[29]

The General Land Office during these years continued its work of surveying the public domain and of examining entries or selections of public lands, excepting homestead and desert land entries.

THE FOURTH PERIOD, 1906 TO PRESENT DATE

The fourth period is characterized during its early years by numerous orders by the President, or by the Secretary of the Interior, withdrawing from entry certain classes of land pending legislation by Congress.   The early withdrawals were made mostly "by the Secretary of the Interior in the exercise of his executive discretion and without specific authority granted by Congress," and were based on court decisions concerning the powers of the Executive Depart-

---

[27] Many withdrawals of land to be included in reclamation projects were made by the Geological Survey during this period.   Lands reclaimed under the operation of the Reclamation Act must be non-mineral in character and may be entered under the Homestead law.   The enterable area is different in the different projects and in different parts of the same project, but can in no case exceed 160 acres.   No charge is made for the land, but the settler must pay his proportionate part of the cost of the irrigation works.

[28] U. S. Geol. Survey, *Bulletin*, No. 537, pp. 14, 15.

[29] *Ibid*, p. 13.

ment; but as these powers were questioned, especially by interests seeking ownership of oil lands in California, Congress passed an act in 1910 authorizing "the President of the United States to make withdrawals of public lands in certain cases." [30]

These withdrawals undoubtedly were caused immediately by the discovery of vast frauds in the alienation of valuable coal and oil lands particularly under agricultural entry; but remotely they are evidence of a change in public sentiment relative to the national domain and establishment of the belief that the natural resources therein should be conserved for the benefit of the people as a whole, both to-day and to-morrow, rather than be permitted to pass into private ownership and be exploited without regulation and for personal profit only. [31] The withdrawal of mineral lands from

[30] A section of the act provided that withdrawn lands should "be open to exploration, discovery, occupation and purchase under the mining laws of the United States, so far as the same apply to minerals, other than coal, oil, gas, and phosphate." *U. S. Stat. at Large*, XXXVI, p. 847. This provision was amended in 1912, so that withdrawn lands were open to exploration and purchase for metalliferous minerals only. "Public land withdrawals now segregate lands from all forms of entry, location, or disposition except metalliferous mineral claims, pre-existing homestead and desert-land entries and valid settlements, and oil placers on which work is being diligently prosecuted at the date of withdrawal."

[31] "In the years 1905 and 1906 the general public began to realize that large areas of valuable coal lands in the West had been obtained from the Government by means of agricultural entries. The frauds thus perpetrated were so great as to shock the public mind and to call for some immediate action to prevent further similar looting. Accordingly the President, on June 29, 1906, directed the Secretary of the Interior to withdraw from entry all valuable coal lands. The Survey had previously been making special studies of certain western coal fields and its geologists had assisted in unearthing some of the coal frauds. It was therefore prepared to submit a list of lands which should be withdrawn from entry, and on July 26, 1906, the Acting Secretary of the Interior withdrew from all forms of entry all the lands on the list submitted by the Survey. Other lists for withdrawal were prepared by the Survey during the summer and fall of 1906, and one very excellent list was prepared by the Forest Service."

"From time to time other withdrawals from coal entry were made until the spring of 1909, when many of the outstanding withdrawals were restored to their original form and made effective against all forms of entry. Soon thereafter Congress passed the withdrawal act of June 25, 1910, (U. S. Stat. at Large, 36, p. 847) and since that date coal withdrawals have prohibited all forms of entry except entries on certain classes of land which are exempted from withdrawal by that act and agricultural entries for surface rights only. The policy throughout has been to withdraw all lands on which there is a reasonable probability of the occurrence of coal, to examine these lands as rapidly as the funds available will permit, and on the information gathered

entry privilege is noted incidentally in the chapter on Mineral Lands.

Water-power Sites.—In 1908 and 1909 President Roosevelt, realizing the danger from monopoly which the private ownership of water-power sites might involve, ordered the withdrawal from entry of large areas along streams in the Rocky Mountain and Pacific States, on recommendation of the Reclamation Service.[32] These withdrawals included some good agricultural land, so that considerable popular discontent and criticism resulted. Secretary Ballinger, accordingly, soon after his appointment, ordered the restoration of all the withdrawn lands; but authorized the Geological Survey to make an investigation of water-power sites on the public domain, and upon recommendation by the Survey power-site withdrawals have been made from time to time. "It is believed that the greater number of the valuable power sites on the public domain are withdrawn from entry pending legislation by Congress for their appropriate disposal."[33]

Reservoir Sites.—In 1888 "certain tracts, especially valuable for the construction of reservoirs, were segregated" under act of Congress, as already noted. In 1910 the Geological Survey ascertained that attempts were being made to obtain possession of other reservoir sites, "not for the purpose of development, but for some inferior use of specu-

to base classifications, the lands found to be non-coal land being restored to entry and those found to contain workable coal being appraised at prices not less than the minimum prices prescribed by the statute.

"For a time the withdrawals worked great hardship. The greater part of the lands thus withheld were not good agricultural lands, but the total acreage suitable for agricultural development was large. The situation was finally relieved by the passage of three acts providing for agricultural entry upon lands withdrawn or classified as coal lands, the Government retaining title to the coal deposits and the right to prospect for and remove them." U. S. Geol. Survey, *Bulletin,* No. 537, pp. 36, 37, 45.

[32] The *Report* of the Inland Waterways Commission, 1908, contains the following statement: "Wherever water is now or will hereafter become the chief source of power, the monopolization of electricity from running streams involves monopoly of power for the transportation of freight and passengers, for manufacturing, and for supplying light, heat, and other domestic, agricultural and municipal necessities to such an extent that unless regulated it will entail monopolistic control of the daily life of our people in an unprecedented degree.

[33] U. S. Geol. *Bulletin* No. 537, p. 42.

lation"; and, accordingly, pending legislation by Congress, a number of reservoir sites were withdrawn in 1911 by President Taft, upon recommendation by the Survey.[34]

Public Water Reserves.—"In the great semi-arid grazing areas of the West watering places are few and the range is, in places, monopolized by control of the water holes. It has been common practice for a stock owner to file some form of land scrip or state selection upon all the springs in a district and thereby to exclude all other stock owners from the district as effectually as if he owned every acre of it. In most places the public range of the West is greatly overcrowded and the competition for possession of the water holes has been exceedingly bitter, with the advantage in favor of the large owner, on account of his greater ability to purchase land scrip. Exclusion from the watering places has ruined more than one stock grower and violence has not infrequently accompanied the struggle for their possession. This condition of affairs led members of the Land Office and of the Survey to urge that the watering places on the public range be retained in government ownership and thrown open to the use of all comers. The possibility of the passage by Congress of a grazing law added to the advisability of such withdrawals. . . . On March 29, 1912, public water reserve No. 1 was recommended by the Survey and approved by the President. Other public water reserves are being erected as rapidly as field data can be considered." [35]

Irrigable Land.—The importance of a careful classification of land is well illustrated in the method of handling the Carey Act tracts. The land is first withdrawn in larger amounts than is likely to be used in any given project. Following the withdrawal a classification is presumably made

[34] "Withdrawals of sites for irrigation reservoirs under the acts of June 25, 1910, (*U. S. Stat. at Large*, XXXVI, p. 847) and August, 24, 1912, (*U. S. Stat. at Large*, XXXVII, p. 497), are made in the same way as withdrawals of power sites whenever the investigations of the Geological Survey indicate that feasible locations exist. Such withdrawals are made in the interest of bona fide development and to withhold from adverse possession reservoirs required in connection with large irrigation projects, both public and private." U. S. Geol. Survey *Bulletin* No. 537, p. 187.

[35] U. S. Geol. Survey *Bulletin* 537, pp. 42, 43.

respecting irrigability, the withdrawal from entry insuring the promoter in the availability of the land suitable for a project. In case a project be undertaken such land, if any, as is restored to the public domain is assumed to be non-irrigable. The aim is to safeguard prospective settlers.[36]

Agricultural Lands.—Coincident with the carrying out of this policy of conserving the nation's resources in minerals and water remaining in the public domain, by withdrawing certain classes of land from entry, pending the enactment of adequate legislation by Congress, there developed a wide-spread appreciation of the serious injury to the pasture lands in the West by overgrazing and the need of classifying the agricultural and grazing lands in the public domain and of amending the Homestead law in a manner that would render it better adapted to the physical conditions, which are so different from those contemplated in the original act. During the period from 1906 to the present three important laws have so far been passed, the aim of which was to achieve this purpose—the Forest Homestead Act, the Enlarged Homestead Act and the Grazing Homestead Act. These later homestead acts are discussed in Chapter XVIII. The necessity for classification of the land to be taken up under these acts is obvious. It has been carried out faithfully, and with at least a fair measure of success. The work of classification pertaining to the Enlarged Homestead Act and the Grazing Homestead Act is in charge of the Geological Survey.

SUMMARY

Although as early as 1796 it occurred to those responsible for the handling of the public domain that it was desirable to know what sort of land they were selling, or giving away, it was a long time before anything significant was done about it. During the first period, 1785-1862, the main effort at classification was an attempt to reserve for special disposition one-third of the gold, silver, lead and copper mines. The intention was to derive more revenue from these more valuable lands. The intention was commendable but the results were meager.

[36] U. S. Geol. Survey *Bulletin* 537, pp. 185, 186.

During the second period, 1862-1879, a distinct advance was made. In 1876 an act provided for the survey of certain specified lands from which arid grazing land was excluded. This was presumably done on the supposition that other legislation might provide for the disposal or use of this land in some way better suited to its character. In 1878 following a report on the arid lands by Major Powell, bills were introduced providing for "pasturage districts" and "irrigation districts."

The third period, 1879-1906, of land classification is marked by the establishment of the United States Geological Survey. Among other provisions was one establishing a "Commission to codify the land laws." The outcome of this was the monumental report known as "Donaldson's Public Domain." It is said that this report has been used more than any other Congressional document. This commission recommended a classification of the public lands, to be made, however, by the General Land Office. The commission recommended the sale of the range land at graduated prices, down to 12½ cents per acre, and a "Homestead Pasturage" privilege of purchase of four sections for $1,000. The survey of land under the Geological Survey, was for many years designed mainly as a basis for geological uses rather than agricultural or mining use. However, these studies were basic with respect to agriculture, mining, power and the like, and later studies have been added to the first surveys. For example, the Reclamation Act of 1902 at once depended upon water supplies, drainage, topography, the possibilities and facts of which the survey furnished.

The fourth period, 1906 to date, is characterized mainly by a continuation of the classification begun during the previous period and the sweeping withdrawals of land from the privilege of entry under the acts in force. The administration of several recent acts under which land may be homesteaded is directly dependent upon the classification of the land which has been, or is being, made.

CHAPTER XXV

MINERAL LANDS

Early Policies Relating to Minerals

The lands of the public domain may roughly be classed on the basis of their use as farming, grazing, forest and mining. It has been fairly easy to designate land for the first three uses, but for mining, a subsurface use, it is not so easy. First, how can it be known where mineral exists? Secondly, how can it be known how extensive the deposits are? Thirdly, once these facts are known, what is the best policy in disposing of or in utilizing mineral lands of the public domain? Congress has been trying to get information on these three points for over a century.

As important mineral deposits have been discovered on the federal lands some kind of policy has been applied to the particular territory. Not till 1866 was a general law applying to mineral deposits in all lands of the public domain passed. The history of the mineral-land laws in the United States begins with a provision in the Ordinance of 1785, which reserved to the government "one-third part of all gold, silver, lead and copper mines, to be sold or otherwise disposed of as Congress shall hereafter direct."

The act passed in 1796 providing for the sale of public lands northwest of the river Ohio further reserved all salt springs and licks and a section of one square mile containing the spring. In these reservations it was apparently the intention of Congress to provide for the utilization of mineral and saline lands in a manner different from that of agricultural lands. This purpose found expression in acts passed in the year 1800 by which the surveyor-general was authorized to lease reserved saline lands and the President was authorized to employ an agent to collect information relative to the copper mines on the south side of Lake Superior, and "ascertain whether the Indian title to such lands as might be required for the use of the United States, in case they should deem it expedient to work the said mines, had been extinguished."[1] The reservation of saline lands from entry was continued in the preëmption act of 1841 and in the Homestead Act of 1862. "Salines were disposed of by special acts of Congress until 1867."[2]

In 1807, when settlement was extending farther west and the development of lead mining in Indiana Territory was under way, a provision was passed in Congress authorizing the leasing of lead mines on the public domain in that territory. This law marks the beginning of the policy of leasing mineral lands.[3]

In 1816 a law was enacted applying to all public lands so far as lead deposits were concerned. It was provided that "no permission to work the same [lead mines] shall be granted without the approbation of the President of the United States."[4] This meant in practice that certain lands were reserved and leased out. But this policy of reserving and leasing lands containing lead mines began to be reversed in 1829, when a law was passed providing for the sale outright of the reserved lead mines and contiguous lands in the state of Missouri at $2.50 per acre, i.e., they were returned to the same position as other public lands.

In 1839 the House of Representatives asked that the President "cause to be prepared a plan for disposal of the public mineral lands."[5] And six years later, December 2, 1845, President Polk said in his first annual message to Congress that "the present system of managing the mineral lands of the United States is believed to be radically defec-

---

[1] Thus Congress at this period seems to have had in mind the direct working and control of mines by the United States. *Donaldson*, p. 306.
[2] Donaldson, p. 217.
[3] C. R. Van Hise, *The Conservation of Natural Resources in the United States*, p. 98.
[4] *U. S. Stat. at Large*, III, p. 260.
[5] Donaldson, p. 307.

tive." [6] He pointed out the fact that over one million acres of public land "containing lead and other minerals" had been reserved from sale, and numerous leases had been made with a stipulated rent; and that this rent for the years 1841, 1842, 1843 and 1844 was something over $6,000, while the expenses of administering the system were over $26,000. Furthermore, he held that the system gave rise to frequent litigation between the United States and individual citizens which produced much irritation in mining regions and involved the government in heavy additional expenditures. He recommended that the leasing system be abolished, that these lands be offered on the market and sold "upon such terms as Congress in her wisdom may prescribe, reserving, however, an equitable percentage of the mineral product, and that the superintendence and management of mineral lands be transferred from the War Department to the General Land Office.[7]

The next year after these recommendations were made Congress enacted a law which provided that the reserved lead mines in the states of Illinois and Arkansas and the territories of Wisconsin and Iowa be exposed for sale as other lands, except that such lands should not be subject to preëmption until after public offering and should not be sold for less than $2.50 per acre if proof was obtained that the land contained lead ore and was so marked. By acts passed in March, 1847, the President was granted authority to sell at a minimum of $5.00 per acre in the Lake Superior district in Michigan and Wisconsin, lands "containing copper, lead and other valuable ores." [8] But in 1850 the Attorney General of the United States held that these laws did not apply to lands containing "iron ore merely." Then, since iron ore was the most important mineral content of that region, Congress passed a law that

---

[6] Donaldson, p. 307.

[7] In 1849, the Department of the Interior was created and the supervision of mineral lands was transferred to the General Land Office in that department. Donaldson, p. 308.

[8] *Ibid.*

same year ordering mineral lands in this district to be offered for sale in the same manner, at the same minimum, and with the same preëmption rights as other public lands. It has been estimated that had the government retained royalties, which have gone to individuals who obtained these lands under this law, it would have received upwards of $100,000,000 in revenue by the present time, and would, in the future, receive a total of over $1,000,000,000 more.[9]

An act was passed in 1864 providing for the disposal of coal lands on the public domain. It authorized the sale of such lands which, since the Preëmption Act of 1841 had been excluded from sale as mines, first to the highest bidder and then under preëmption at a minimum price of $25 an acre.

Most Mineral Lands of the Eastern Part of the Country Disposed of Under Agricultural Land Laws

From the period of 1785 to the discovery of gold in California in 1848 the legislation of Congress "as to survey, lease and sale of mineral lands had been for lead, copper and the other base metals and applied to the territory in the region of the Great Lakes in the now states of Michigan, Wisconsin, Minnesota, Iowa and Illinois, embracing the lead mines at Galena and the point now known as Dubuque— and the present state of Missouri."[10] But the discovery of gold at Coloma, California, in 1848 necessitated a change in the mineral laws in general. Copper, lead and iron had prior to this been the minerals for which the laws were made. "In the Ordinance of 1785 gold and silver were reserved out of abundant caution, but now gold had actually been discovered on the public domain, and legislation was necessary."[11]

Not very much legislation regarding gold and silver lands had been passed before the general mining act of 1866. However, a law of 1850 providing for survey and donations

[9] Van Hise, p. 99.
[10] Donaldson, p. 320.
[11] *Ibid*, p. 309.

to settlers specified that no mineral lands should be open to claim under the act. In 1853 provision was made "for the survey of public lands in California, the granting of preëmption rights therein, and for other purposes," excluding in express terms "mineral lands" from the Preëmption Act of 1841. Thus, up to 1866 Congress had not made any provision concerning mineral lands in California, except reserving them from preëmption and donation.[12] An act passed July 4, 1866, reserved from sale in Nevada lands valuable for mines of gold, silver, quicksilver, or copper.

Local regulations governed the location, size and possession of mining claims in the precious-metal-bearing regions prior to 1866. Districts were organized and regulations made by the miners. Such action varied from district to district. In each instance an officer was elected, known as the recorder, whose duty it was to record all notices of mining locations or claims filed with him. At first these regulations rested entirely on the consent of the miners, but they later came to be recognized by the courts as custom. State and territorial legislatures respected these rules and generally specifically recognized them in their civil codes, while Congress, by the general mining acts of 1866 and 1872, confirmed these local usages.[13]

During the first three-quarters of a century, therefore, there was apparent a general intention on the part of Congress, except for the lapses shown by the acts of 1846 and 1847 relative to the copper, lead and zinc mines, to pursue a different policy in the disposal of saline and mineral lands from that followed in the disposal of agricultural lands; nevertheless, practically all the vast mineral resources of the eastern United States, including not only the lead and zinc lands of Missouri and Wisconsin and the copper mines of Michigan, but also the vast extent of coal lands along the western slope of the Appalachians, although excluded after 1841 from sale, as mines, by the Preëmption Act, passed

[12] Donaldson, p. 311.
[13] *Ibid*, p. 321.

into private ownership under the various acts providing for the alienation of agricultural lands. Also a large portion of the iron deposits of Alabama, Michigan, Wisconsin and Minnesota were disposed of in this manner.

THE MINERAL LANDS SINCE 1866

The act of July 26, 1866, provided that "the mineral lands of the public domain, both surveyed and unsurveyed," were "to be free and open to exploration and occupation by all citizens of the United States, and those declaring their intention to become citizens, subject to such regulations as may be prescribed by law," and "subject also to the local customs or rules of miners in the several mining districts, so far as the same may not be in conflict with the laws of the United States." [14] This law further provided that a claimant might receive patents for "a vein or lode of quartz, or other rock in place, bearing gold, silver, cinnabar or copper," if the claimant "had previously occupied same according to local mining rules and had expended as much as $1,000 in labor and improvements." An interesting feature of this act was the recognition and classification of water rights for mining, agricultural, manufacturing and other purposes.

It will be observed that this law applied only to lode mining. An act passed July 9, 1870, made provision for placer mining. Land useful for such operation was thenceforth to be surveyed and sold at $2.50 an acre. For lode mining the price was $5 per acre.

The mining act of May 10, 1872, amended the act of 1866 and constituted mineral lands a distinctive class subject to special conditions of sale and affixed prices differing wholly from the requirements in these respects applied to other lands. It provided for the survey and sale of mineral lands, fixing the price of placer lands at $2.50 per acre and lode claims at $5 per acre. [15] In 1897 Congress passed an act

[14] *Session Laws*, 39 Cong., 1 Sess., p. 251.
[15] *U. S. Stat. at Large*, XVII, p. 91 *et seq*.

providing that oil lands be subject to placer mining law as to entry and patent. Similarly in 1901 saline lands were brought under the placer mining law.

Since the passage of the mining law of 1872 a few states have been excepted from the application of that law. Alabama had already been made an exception March 3, 1883, and the mineral lands of the public domain in that state are disposed of just as are agricultural lands.[16] Likewise, the mineral land laws are not applicable to Michigan, Wisconsin and Minnesota, the mineral lands in these states being disposed of in the same manner as other public lands.[17] Also Missouri and Kansas have been excepted from the general mineral land laws.[18]

THE COAL LAND LAWS

Although the acts of 1866, 1870 and 1872 were called general mineral land laws, they do not apply to coal lands. In the development of the country during the last fifty years coal has been a very great factor and the importance of the development and conservation of the coal mines on the public domain has become more and more evident. The Secretary of the Interior in his annual report for 1861, and again in 1862 and 1863, urged upon Congress the enactment of adequate laws to facilitate and regulate the utilization of the lands of the nation. In 1864 President Lincoln called the attention of Congress to the mineral lands and to the report of the Secretary of the Interior, which contained a lengthy description of the principal mining regions. The urgency of the situation as set forth in these reports led Congress to pass, in 1864, a law providing for the disposal of coal lands, setting a minimum limit upon them of $25 per acre. But Congress later considered this too high and on March 3, 1873, passed an act providing for entry of coal lands at $10 an acre where the lands were more than fifteen miles from a railroad and at $15 an acre if within that dis-

[16] *U. S. Stat. at Large,* XXII, p. 487.
[17] *Revised Statutes of the United States,* Section 2345.
[18] *U. S. Stat. at Large,* XIX, p. 52.

tance.[19] Succeeding acts extended the rectangular system of survey to the coal lands, and the entry of 160 acres for an individual, and 320 to 640 acres for an association. Since 1841 mineral lands had been excluded from regular sale to settlers.

The following table indicates the amount of coal land entered and the price received for it, by states, from the passage of the acts of March 3, 1873, to June 30, 1923:[20]

TABLE XXXIV

COAL LAND SALES AND RECEIPTS, BY STATES, 1873 TO 1923

State	Acres	Amount
Alabama	239.40	2,394.00
Arizona	6,693.35	74,997.00
California	5,535.06	81,531.30
Colorado	158,113.38	2,385,693.75
Colorado (within the Ute Reservation)	58,495.65	891,219.55
Dakota Territory	583.57	5,835.70
Idaho	3,277.41	37,911.80
Montana	64,758.47	1,219,419.39
Nevada	1,661.01	20,442.20
New Mexico	26,573.38	439,803.75
North Dakota	9,503.59	150,080.20
Oregon	10,571.96	126,552.90
South Dakota	3,623.64	39,764.80
Utah	74,070.84	2,490,334.45
Washington	64,453.51	1,035,725.20
Wyoming	113,843.87	2,866,789.36
Made in General Land Office	7.95	159.00
Total	603,006.04	$11,867,654.35

During the next three decades the fuller recognition of the vital importance of the coal deposits caused a revamping of the coal land laws. Certain definite problems had developed in connection with the disposition and utilization of such lands. There was first, the question of the advisability of withdrawing all coal lands from entry; secondly, the question of whether agricultural entries should be allowed on

[19] *Revised Stat. of the U. S.,* Sec. 2347.
[20] *L. O. R.,* 1923, p. 35.

coal lands, with the reservation of mineral rights to the United States. And finally, in case the government withdrew its coal lands from entry, how should the mines be managed? Should the government go into the mining business, or should some system of leasing to private individuals be adopted?

As to the first decisive action was taken in 1906, when the President directed the Secretary of the Interior to withdraw from entry all valuable coal lands.[21] It had been discovered by the Geological Survey that large areas of valuable coal lands in the West had been obtained from the government by means of agricultural entries. The Survey, having just previously made special studies of certain western coal fields, was prepared to submit a list of lands which should be withdrawn from entry. Beginning in 1906, the President made withdrawals from time to time as the existence of coal deposits on the public lands was discovered, or strongly suspected. Very soon, however, after the first withdrawals were made many millions of acres were restored to entry on evidence that no coal was to be found thereon.

Although the early withdrawals were made by proclamation of the President, Congress passed a withdrawal act on June 25, 1910, specifying the conditions of withdrawal. Since the withdrawals began "the policy has been to withdraw all lands on which there is reasonable probability of the occurrence of coal, to examine these lands as rapidly as the funds available will permit, and on the information gathered to base classifications, the lands found to be non-coal land being restored to entry and those found to contain workable coal being appraised at prices not less than the minimum prices prescribed by the statute."[22]

The first class of lands to be withdrawn from entry were coal lands, which withdrawals began in the autumn of 1905 and continued at intervals for several years. In accordance with acts passed in 1909 and 1910,[23] these lands were made

[21] U. S. Geol. Survey *Bulletin*, No. 537, p. 36.
[22] *Ibid*, pp. 36, 37.
[23] *U. S. Stat. at Large*, XXXVI, p. 583.

subject to agricultural entry for surface rights only, all mineral rights being reserved to the government, as well as the privileges to prospect for and remove the minerals.[24] Where the coal deposits are obviously of great value the quantity of coal available, probable cost of mining and of transporting to markets are carefully investigated by experts of the United States Geological Survey, usually only upon request, and if unencumbered by agricultural entry the land is sold in fee simple, otherwise only the sub-surface right at an appraised price. This detailed scientific classification of land and subsequent sale, not at the uniform minimum price fixed by Congress, but at a value determined by experts and varying upward to several hundred dollars an acre, marks a new departure in the history of the classification and disposal of the public lands.

[24] "The carrying out of the withdrawal policy for protecting the mineral and water resources of the public domain is in many cases rendered difficult and embarrassing by the agricultural value of the land withdrawn. If valuable water-power or reservoir sites were invariably valueless for farming, or if mineral and agricultural values could not coexist, no hardships would be imposed by and no retardation of development would result from the making of withdrawals. But some of the best farming lands in the West are underlain by coal or phosphate, and some are so situated as to be of strategic importance in power development. Any hindrance to bona fide home building or other agricultural development of the public domain is indeed unfortunate, but in order to protect the public's natural resources withdrawals resulting in such hindrance have been necessary. For certain lands the situation has been relieved by the passage of acts separating the surface right from the right to the underlying minerals. The first of these acts was that of March 3, 1909 (*U. S. Stat. at Large*, XXXV, 844), which provides that persons who have entered or selected under the non-mineral laws lands subsequently classified, claimed or reported as being valuable for coal may elect to receive patent to their land by reserving to the United States the coal deposits and the right to prospect for and mine them. The act contains a provision for the indemnification of the surface owner for damages to his estate by prospecting or mining and a further provision that the owner of the surface patent shall have the right to mine coal for his own use prior to the disposal of the coal deposits by the United States. This act granted relief only for entries or selections antedating withdrawal The act of June 22, 1910 (*U. S. Stat. at Large*, XXXVI: 583), goes a step further with regard to coal lands and provides that homestead entries, desert-land entries, and Carey Act selections may be made on lands withdrawn or classified as coal whenever it is stated in the application that the entry is made to obtain title containing a reservation of the coal to the United States. In this, as in the previous act, provision is made for damages to the surface by prospecting or mining. The act of April 30, 1912, (*U. S. Stat. at Large*, XXXVII, 496), provides for the entry or selection of withdrawn or classified oil and gas lands in the State of Utah, with a reservation to the United States of the oil or gas. The provisions of the act are similar to those of the coal act of June 22, 1910, and the classes of entries and selections permitted are the same as those in that act as amended by the act of April 30, 1912. (U. S. Geol. Survey, *Bulletin*, 537, pp. 45, 46.)

Concerning the policy of withdrawing coal lands from entry and the utilization of the land, the Geological Survey has made the following summary statement:[25] "For a time the withdrawals worked great hardship. The greater part of the lands thus withheld were not good agricultural lands, but the total acreage suitable for agricultural development was large. The situation was finally relieved by the passage of three acts providing for agricultural entry upon lands withdrawn or classified as coal lands, the government retaining title to the coal deposits and the right to prospect for and remove them."

The coal land withdrawals outstanding June 30, 1923, were:[26]

State	Acres
Arizona	141,243
California	17,643
Colorado	4,238,497
Idaho	4,761
Montana	10,460,034
Nevada	83,833
New Mexico	5,198,967
North Dakota	6,192,376
Oregon	4,361
Utah	5,087,444
Washington	692,126
Wyoming	2,437,083
Total	34,558,368

The second question in connection with coal land policies —that of the distinction between surface and subsurface rights—was inevitably connected with the policy of withdrawing coal lands from entry. This is true because much of the coal lands withdrawn were of agricultural value and the demand for the lands for farming purposes was great

[25] U. S. Geol. Survey *Bulletin* No. 537, pp. 36, 37.
[26] *L. O. R.,* 1923, p. 41.

at that time, since good lands not taken up were becoming very scarce.

Originally, the American land system, based as it was on the English system, included the mineral wealth in all cases with the surface ownership. But a change in this particular came about with the withdrawal acts of 1906 and 1907 when President Roosevelt withdrew from filing and entry privilege about 66,000,000 acres of land which presumably contained coal deposits. The occasion for such action has already been noted. Much of this land was found not to contain coal, and was restored to entry, yet the question remained as to the disposition of that part of the land retained which was valuable for agricultural purposes as well as for mining. Could the use for both purposes be conserved?

In 1910 the matter was settled by an act providing for the entry of the land under laws then operating with respect to land for farms.[27] The settler was to be given a title to the land, reserving to the government the right to dispose separately of the coal under the laws pertaining to such transactions. The settler possessing the surface right is in all cases reimbursed for loss incidental to the discovery and removal of the coal, and is to have a right at all times to dig coal for his own use.

In fact, an act was passed in 1909[28] which separated surface rights from mining rights in a limited way, namely, in the case of entrymen who had taken up supposedly nonmineral lands on which coal was later discovered. The rights of the entryman to the surface were retained and the mineral rights went to the United States. But the question of separating the surface rights from the coal right was first brought prominently to the public attention by the Conservation Commission appointed by President Roosevelt.[29] Mr. Roosevelt had withdrawn the coal lands because

[27] *U. S. Stat. at Large,* XXXVI, p. 583.
[28] *Ibid,* XXXV, p. 844.
[29] *Sen. Doc.,* 60 Cong., 2 Sess., No. 676.

he was convinced that they should not be alienated under the agricultural land laws. At the same time he did not believe that agricultural lands should be held by miners. Hence a separation of the two rights was the logical alternative. The Conservation Commission endorsed heartily the President's proposal to separate surface from mineral rights. As early as 1907 Secretary of the Interior James R. Garfield had recommended the desirability of separating mineral and surface rights.[30]

When the bill came up in Congress in 1910, the main arguments against it were that land would be taken under pretense of use for agriculture in the hope that the coal miner would have to pay damages to the owner of the surface rights, and that these damages would be worth getting.[31] Moreover, it was held that land which was valuable for coal and not for agriculture would be entered in order to recover the "damages" done by miners. These arguments did not develop much strength and the bill passed both houses without division.

As to the utilization of the coal deposits on the public domain the system of leasing to private individuals has come to be adopted. An act passed October 20, 1914, gave the Secretary of the Interior authority to lease certain coal lands on the public domain in Alaska.[32] In 1917 Congress passed a law providing for the application of the leasing system on the lands containing potassium deposits.[33] Moreover, the leasing system became the general adopted policy in 1920, when an act was passed providing for the leasing of coal lands owned by the United States.[34] The leases are "to be awarded on the basis of competitive bidding or as the Secretary of the Interior may direct."

The applications under the Federal Leasing Law from its passage, February 25, 1920, to June 30, 1923:[35]

[30] Int. Dept., *Annual Report*, 1907, p. 15.
[31] *Cong. Record*, 61 Cong., 2 Sess., p. 6040, *et seq.*
[32] *U. S. Stat. at Large*, XXXVIII, p. 741.
[33] *Ibid*, XL, p. 297.
[34] *Ibid*, XLI, p. 438.
[35] *L. O. R.*, 1923, p. 75.

State	Applications
Alabama	11
Alaska	1,265
Arizona	922
Arkansas	2
California	3,459
Colorado	1,251
Idaho	235
Kansas	1
Louisiana	145
Michigan	3
Mississippi	15
Montana	5,163
Nebraska	14
Nevada	1,133
New Mexico	1,886
North Dakota	112
Oklahoma	394
Oregon	93
South Dakota	181
Utah	3,797
Washington	129
Wyoming	5,825
Total	26,036

The policy was soon extended to lands other than coal lands. By the act of July 17, 1914, public land classified or reported as containing phosphate, nitrate, potash, oil, gas or asphaltic minerals was made subject to entry or sale for agricultural purposes just as in the case of non-mineral lands, with the provision that the mineral rights be reserved to the United States.[36]

Phosphate Lands

In 1908, also, the first withdrawal of phosphate land was made by the Geological Survey, pending provision of appropriate legislation by Congress, as it seemed important "to many students of the situation that the United States should not part with a deposit so vital to its agricultural future.

[36] U. S. Stat. at Large, XXXVIII, p. 509.

. . . Since the first withdrawal the known area of phosphate lands has been greatly increased by the explorations of the Geological Survey, and the reserves now include lands in Wyoming, Idaho, Utah, Montana and Florida.[37]

Phosphate land withdrawals outstanding June 30, 1922, were as follows:[38]

State	Acres
Florida	199,523
Idaho	720,534
Montana	287,883
Utah	302,465
Wyoming	995,049
Total	2,425,454

This withdrawal policy was, in 1908, applied to oil lands and extensive withdrawals of lands from agricultural entry, pending a determination as to their content of oil, was made in this and the following year upon recommendation of the Geological Survey.[39] However, as early as 1900 withdrawals of lands in Wyoming and California containing oil and gas were made by the General Land Office to protect oil operators from agricultural entry. In 1912 two petroleum reserves, totaling some 68,000 acres and estimated to contain 250 million barrels of oil, were created in California to assure

[37] U. S. Geol. Survey *Bulletin*, No. 537, p. 40.

[38] *L. O. R.*, 1923, p. 41

[39] "Within a short time it became apparent that the situation was only partly covered by withdrawing oil lands from agricultural entry. The inadequacy of the placer law and its inapplicability to oil lands was clearly recognized. The law was framed to apply to solid minerals; when applied to fluids, such as oil and gas, it at once led to many abuses. . . . These considerations, together with the advisability of retaining a supply of fuel oil for the use of the Navy, caused the Geological Survey to urge the suspension of all forms of entry on Government oil lands pending the enactment of new legislation by Congress. In consequence Secretary of the Interior Ballinger, on September 27, 1909, withdrew from all forms of entry, location, or disposition all public lands believed to contain valuable deposits of oil or gas. . . . Field examination has shown that certain lands so withdrawn are not valuable for their oil or gas deposits, and they have been promptly restored to public entry. In one State, Utah, the surface of the lands so withdrawn is open to agricultural entry." U. S. Geol. Survey, *Bulletin* No. 537, pp. 38, 39.

an adequate supply of fuel oil for the navy. In 1920 an act was passed authorizing the leasing of oil lands under regulations to be prescribed by the Secretary of the Interior.

Oil land withdrawals to June 30, 1923: [40]

State	Acres
Arizona	230,400
California	1,178,392
Colorado	222,977
Louisiana	466,990
Montana	1,344,640
North Dakota	84,894
Utah	1,870,608
Wyoming	1,018,761
Total	6,417,662

POTASH LANDS

Similarly it was realized that the maintenance of agricultural production in the United States was also dependent on potash, and in 1913 lands in three areas, where the existence of potash salts seemed to indicate the likelihood of future commercial exploitation, were withdrawn from entry. The Director of the Geological Survey, writing in 1913, says: "It is the present intention to recommend the withdrawal of all valuable deposits found and all lands in which there is a reasonable probability of the occurrence of valuable potash, these withdrawals to remain in force until Congress has provided more appropriate legislation than the existing placer law." [41]

METALLIFEROUS MINERAL LANDS

In 1912 certain lands which geological study indicated were likely to contain deep-seated deposits of copper and other minerals were withdrawn from entry by the President. "The deposits in this district are of such nature that no surface discovery, such as is required by the lode law,

[40] L. O. R., 1923, p. 41.
[41] U. S. Geol. Survey Bulletin, No. 537, p. 40.

can be made. As a result valid locations cannot be made upon the lands until valuable minerals have been discovered therein, either by deep drilling or deep shafting. There was danger that before either of these types of prospecting should be completed attempts would be made to obtain title to the lands by means of state selections or other non-mineral entries." [42]

SUMMARY

Although we made some effort to control the mineral resources of the country early, that is to say before the close of the eighteenth century, and tried again several times during the nineteenth century, the most distinctive accomplishments have occurred since 1905. Subsequently to 1841 mineral lands were not sold in the regular course of transactions to settlers. However, lack of accurate knowledge as to the presence of minerals made the administration of this rule very inaccurate. The price of coal land was set, in 1864, at a minimum of $25 per acre; in 1873 the minimum was reduced to $10 for land over fifteen miles from a railroad. Withdrawals of coal lands were begun in 1905. In 1909 and 1910 a more definite basis for withdrawals was provided by acts of Congress. From this time on surface rights for agricultural purposes were separated from mineral rights and disposed of on that basis. A leasing system was started in 1917 for coal lands in Alaska, and in 1920 made applicable to the United States. The lease system has since been extended to other minerals. Some eight or ten million acres of mineral lands have been withdrawn from the privilege of private entry as presumably containing oil or phosphate. Provision is made for the withdrawal of metalliferous lands, such as those containing copper, iron, or the precious metals.

[42] U. S. Geol. Survey *Bulletin*, No. 537, p. 41.

CHAPTER XXVI

RESERVED LANDS

It was estimated [1] in 1909 that of the original domain in the United States approximately 40 per cent had been disposed of to individuals and corporations; 11 per cent had been granted to states for various purposes; 23 per cent had been placed in reserve; and 26 per cent remained unreserved and unappropriated. The purpose of this chapter is to give a very brief account of the origin of the various reserves and the approximate amount of these reserves at the present time.

THE FOREST RESERVE

By far the greatest of these reservations made from the public domain is that made for the conservation of the American forests. Not until after the Civil War did any one think seriously of the necessity of conserving the supply of timber in this country. The first statement on this question that commanded attention at all was that made by Franklin B. Hough before the American Association for the Advancement of Science in 1873. He pointed out in a paper read before that body that unless steps were taken to preserve the forests the supply would disappear in a relatively short period of time.

Four years later an item of appropriation appeared in the budget of the Commissioner of Agriculture carrying authority from Congress for the Commissioner to appoint some qualified person to gather forest statistics. In 1881

[1] Van Hise, p. 294. Lands of Alaska and the Insular possessions are not included in these figures.

the forestry work was organized as a separate office under the Commissioner of Agriculture. In 1886 the office was made a division[2] and in 1897 a bureau was created in the Department of Agriculture to take care of the national forest reserve. Gifford Pinchot was made Chief of the Bureau in 1898, which position he held until 1910.[3] In 1905 its name was changed from the Bureau of Forestry to "The Forest Service,"[4] and the care of national forest reserves was transferred from the Department of the Interior to the Department of Agriculture.

It was through the efforts of a committee of the American Association for the Advancement of Science of which T. C. Mendenhall was chairman that the Secretary of the Interior was induced to recommend the passage of a law making it possible to set aside certain forest areas which should not be subject to entry under the Homestead Act, nor subject to sale in any manner. The Timber Culture Act had proved a failure and was abolished March 3, 1891, and as a "rider" on the bill abolishing this act a provision was attached giving the President authority to set aside public lands as forest reserves. The law states, "That the President of the United States may, from time to time, set apart and reserve, in any state or territory having public land bearing forests in any part of the public lands wholly or in part covered with timber or undergrowth, whether of commercial value or not, as public reservations, and the President shall, by public proclamation, declare the establishment of such reservations and the limits thereof."[5]

President Harrison started the movement by setting aside from the public domain 13,416,710 acres as national forest reserves.[6] President Cleveland followed with 25,686,320 acres. Congress made all manner of threats as to punishment of President Cleveland for what it considered high-

---

[2] *U. S. Stat. at Large,* XXIV, pp. 100, 103.
[3] Van Hise, p. 215.
[4] T. P. Ivy, *Forestry Problems in the United States,* p. 6.
[5] *U. S. Stat. at Large,* XXVI, pp. 1095, 1103.
[6] Van Hise, p. 215.

handed and unwarranted arrogance, but nothing was done about it.[7] McKinley set aside 7,050,089, and Roosevelt surpassed all with 148,346,925 acres. Reservations have been made from time to time since the end of Roosevelt's administration in 1909, but the great body of the present reserves had been set aside at that time. In fact, much of this area has been restored to the public domain from time to time as unsatisfactory for this purpose. The present area of the national forest reserves is about fifteen million acres smaller than the total of the items named above.

FORESTS AND THE PUBLIC DOMAIN

The relation of farms to the native forests throughout the whole period of American history is quite clear cut. From the beginnings of settlement until after 1850 the great proportion of farms were cleared out of forest land. Not far from 822,000,000 acres were originally forested.[8] Of this amount about five-sixths was in the eastern half of the country. A glance at a forest area map will show that until settlement reached Iowa nearly all farms were of necessity cleared out of forest land. Even the prairies of Illinois and Wisconsin were avoided until after 1850. In 1860 over 82 per cent of the two million farms were east of the Mississippi River, and of those to the west the majority were in timbered sections. For example, nearly all of the farms of Arkansas, Louisiana, Minnesota, Missouri and Texas were within timbered areas, while even Iowa, originally but one-eighth timber, was settled much more densely in the timbered area than on the prairies in 1860. It is safe to say that until after 1860, which means after the Civil War, the forests were looked upon as obstacles to be overcome in order that farming might be undertaken. Trees were cut and the logs rolled together for burning. Subsequent to the Civil War black walnut logs were burned in this manner

[7] B. E. Fernow, *History of Forestry*, p. 418.

[8] *Timber Depletion*, etc. Bulletin of Forest Service: *Report on Senate Resolution* 311 (1920), p. 32.

in Indiana. Before 1880 destruction of timber in land clearing was substantially past.[9]

During the 70's lumbering in the northern forests, *i.e.*, in the Lake States, began in earnest, and timber was cut, not for the sake of the land, but for the lumber. From 1870 the cut per year for the whole country grew enormously until the maximum was reached in 1909. In the meantime the great bulk of the timber lands under the general land laws had been bought for $1.25 per acre, preëmpted (and bought for $1.25), located with Agricultural College scrip, or taken under the Timber and Stone Act. Still there was a remnant of timber, and much more than a remnant of timber land still in national hands.

At the end of the fiscal year 1923 there were "146 national forests embracing 182,099,802 acres, of which a little over 86 per cent is public land," [10] This figure included forests in Alaska and Porto Rico. The other 14 per cent consisted of lands belonging to states or individuals but being within the boundaries of the national forests. Not quite all of this 86 per cent has been taken from the public domain, since 1,613,845 acres have been added by purchase under the act of March 1, 1911,[11] commonly called the Weeks Law. Every year some lands are added to and some are withdrawn from the national forest reserves.

The present area of national forest reserves, excluding Alaska, 161,300,000 acres, is over a twelfth of the entire area of the United States, and equivalent to about one-eighth of the original public domain, within which nearly all of the national forests lie. Without question the act permitting the withdrawals of public land from private entry was the most signal act yet performed by Congress in the direction of a national land policy. That it should have been done at an earlier date is of less importance at the present time than is the possibility of regaining public ownership of land now in private hands. Reforestation is still in its infancy.

[9] *Agricultural Yearbook*, 1922. p. 84.
[10] *L. O. R.*, 1923, p. 22.
[11] *U. S. Stat. at Large*, XXXVI, p. 961.

Thus far private enterprise has done four-fifths of the replanting, but the share of this work falling to the responsibility of the government is bound to increase. With 331,000,000 acres of cut-over and burned-over land it would be relatively easy for the nation and the states to regain ownership of great areas at small expense. While the value of these tracts would, of course, be low, there would be some hope of reforestation eventually. Cut-over land is being made into farm land very slowly, in many districts much less than one per cent a year. "No idle acres" is a good motto, but what these acres should do is quite another question. Manifestly they are not likely to be turned into arable land at a rapid rate, many of them never. To put them back into forest is the highest and best use to which they can be put. This is an expensive process, and on much old forest land would not at present appear to be worth doing. There are sub-marginal forest lands as well as sub-marginal arable lands. Public ownership of forest land is the greatest safeguard against a further shortage of timber. Moreover, while the question of monopoly in land hardly seems a real one as applied to agriculture, the concentration of ownership of timber and timber lands by private interests is clearly a prime factor in the spectacular rise in the prices of lumber during recent years.[12]

The following table gives the estimated area of the national forests on June 30, 1923, and the location by states:[13]

TABLE XXXV

AREA OF NATIONAL FORESTS ON JUNE 30, 1923, AND LOCATION BY STATES

States	Acres
Alabama	198,385
Arizona	12,220,739
Arkansas	1,470,393
California	24,291,656
Colorado	14,743,283
Florida	719,979
Georgia	680,550

[12] *Timber Depletion, etc., Report on Senate Resolution* 311.
[13] *L. O. R.,* 1923, p. 46.

TABLE XXXV (*Continued*)

States	Acres
Idaho	20,490,251
Maine	115,558
Michigan	167,492
Minnesota	1,581,014
Montana	18,839,793
Nebraska	217,808
Nevada	5,244,364
New Hampshire	870,554
New Mexico	9,607,559
North Carolina	1,730,453
Oklahoma	61,640
Oregon	15,426,362
South Carolina	137,216
South Dakota	1,275,493
Tennessee	881,763
Utah	7,986,624
Virginia	1,292,375
Washington	11,592,915
West Virginia	845,516
Wyoming	8,635,999
Total area	161,325,734

Mineral Land Reservations

The mineral land reservations are given by states in Chapter XXV, and aggregate about 43,000,000 acres, the equivalent of a state the size of North Dakota.

Indian Reservations

The Indian reservations contained an unallotted area of 35,501,661 acres June 30, 1921.[14] This area has decreased from 154,741,554 in 1880 to this figure due to the various acts passed providing for allotments to individual Indians. Approximately three-fourths of the area remaining reserved within Indian reservations—26,000,000 acres—is located in Arizona, New Mexico and Montana.

[14] *Thirteenth Census Abstract*, 1921, p. 16.

WATER POWER AND RESERVOIR SITES

The significance of water power sites is out of all proportion to the amount of land involved. As early as 1879 provision was made for the reservation of land involving access to potential water power.[15] From time to time reservations were made under this early act, but it developed that in spite of the authority vested in the government to reserve the sites they were for the most part making their way into the hands of private companies. In 1910, largely on account of complications concerning reservoir sites, new legislation was enacted, and reservations were made at a more rapid rate.[16] The temptation to file on reservoir and power sites after it became evident that the government was likely to want them in connection with projects already planned was beyond the ability of a great many private interests to resist. About 5,000,000 acres have been reserved under the various acts by which a vast amount of potential power, as well as reservoir sites, is retained in the hands of the government. No comprehensive plans have been made for its development.

NATIONAL PARKS AND MISCELLANEOUS RESERVATIONS

One of the significant developments in connection with the whole public domain is the reservation of national parks. Beginning with the Yellowstone National Park, a tract of country 55 by 60 miles, set aside in 1872, there have been reserved from time to time approximately 5,500,000 acres of land. The parks thus established are not only public playgrounds with an ever-increasing value and importance, but have a scientific value on which no price could be set. For the most part these parks are located in the Mountain and Pacific States, and are administered under the National Park Service.[17] In addition to the national parks are a consider-

[15] *U. S. Stat. at Large*, XX, p. 294.
[16] *Ibid*, XXXVI, p. 847 and XXXVII, p. 497. See also *Ibid*, XXXIX, p. 219, XL, p. 105; XX, p. 294; and *L. O. R.*, 1923, p. 16, 43.
[17] *Thirteenth Census Abstract*, p. 13; *U. S. Stat. at Large*, XXXIX, p. 535.

able number, about thirty-three, "national monuments" of historic or prehistoric interest.[18]

In addition to the above are a large number of military reservations. These are subject to a considerable amount of change from time to time. Those which seem to be fairly permanent in extent constituted somewhat over a million and a half acres in 1913. Other miscellaneous reservations, such as bird sanctuaries, and game preserves, bring the aggregate extent up to about 1,790,000 acres.

The total amount of land held in reserve, a part of it temporarily, by the United States Government is approximately 197,000,000 acres, the equivalent of two Californias.

TABLE XXXVI
SUMMARY OF RESERVATIONS

	Acres
Forest reserves	161,325,734
Coal reserves	34,558,368
Oil reserves	6,417,662
Phosphate reserves	2,425,454
Indian Reservations	35,501,661
Carey Act reserves	1,179,665
Reclamation reserves	15,500,000
Public water reserves	254,810
Miscellaneous reserves:	
Acts of June 25, 1910 and August 24, 1912	2,113,567
Reservoir site reserves	202,438
Power site reserves	2,489,507
National park reserves	7,176,774
National monuments	1,163,893
Military reservations	1,549,890
Bird and Game Reserves [19]	462,789
Forest administrative sites	19,248
Soldiers' Homes, etc.	5,818
Total	272,347,278

[18] L. O. R., 1916, p. 61.
[19] Outside of National Forests.

SUMMARY

Over a quarter billion acres, or over a fifth of the original public domain has been reserved in the interest of the public. For the most part these reservations are intended to remain the property of the government, though in part it is reserved at present to be disposed of later. The latter is true with respect to mineral reserves, water power sites, and possibly with other lands, such as certain portions of the forest reserves. Of course, not all of the mineral reserves, and power sites, will in all probability be alienated, but to dispose of them judiciously will not be contrary to the spirit of the acts under which they were reserved. A glance at the following map will show where the bulk of the reservations, forest, Indian reservations and national monuments are located. For the most part they do not occupy first class agricultural lands. On the other hand their value may be greater than that of agricultural land, and although made late in the period of public land disposal, the extent of the reservations is gratifying.

MAP X

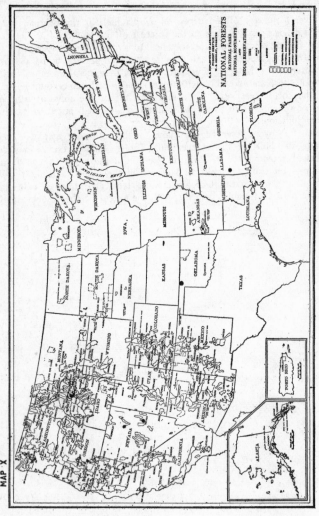

NATIONAL FORESTS
NATIONAL PARKS
NATIONAL MONUMENTS
INDIAN RESERVATIONS
1921

U.S. DEPARTMENT OF AGRICULTURE
FOREST SERVICE
W. B. GREELEY, FORESTER

CHAPTER XXVII

EFFECTS OF THE LAND POLICIES ON AGRICULTURE

Prior to the advent of the railways into the West, there was vastly less chance, than subsequently, for a liberal land policy on the part of the government to show pronounced effect in the per capita output of farm products. Until that time the physical limitations were severe; the prices of crops were sensitive to local conditions as one got away from the established highways to market. Thus no land policy could, without transportation facilities, have a very profound effect in producing a widespread glut. Of course there could be, and there were, innumerable gluts locally, and, all told, prices were bound to rule close down to the labor and capital cost of production, but widespread disturbances due to so-called overproduction were not possible before 1850, in any such sense as they have since been.

Our agricultural statistics begin with 1840, but as the railroads did not reach the Middle West till 1850, the latter date is chosen as the beginning of a forty-year period during which time the great grain fields were brought under cultivation, and during which, also, the public domain is popularly supposed to have become exhausted so far as easy use and sure results go.

In 1850 the average size of farms in the United States was 202 acres; the average production per capita of all cereals for the United States was 37 bushels. During the ten years following, the government disposed of enough land to make nearly a million more farms of the same size, but only a few more than half a million more farms were added to the number. The discrepancy in this is to be found in the fact of grants to railways and to states, as well as in sales to speculators. The per capita cereal production rose to 39 bushels—not a great change. The increase in cereal production during the decade as compared with the preceding was 43 per cent. The increase in cotton production was over 100 per cent. By this time the cotton lands had been pretty well covered so far as the public domain was concerned. The grain fields were not so completely taken up.

During the decade from 1860 to 1870 for the whole country the expansion in farm land was inconsiderable. The sales of public land were lower than at any other time since the first decade of the century. Yet the government disposed of more land than the area of North Dakota, and in the Upper Mississippi Valley the increase in farm acreage was important, though appreciably less than in the decade from 1850 to 1860. The per capita production of cereals decreased somewhat, while the production of cotton showed a marked decrease owing to the disturbance of the war. The lands that were being added to the farm acreage of the country were in the grain belt, and production of wheat and oats was expanding enormously, the increases in each of these cereals reaching 66 per cent for the ten years. Wheat is, in a large part of the country, a pioneer crop, following immediately the breaking of the new soil. Oats, while not often sown on new breaking, follow in close succession. Hence, these two grains show the first response to increased farm acreage. The wheat production rose from 5.5 to 7.5 bushels per capita and put the country definitely on an export basis.

From 1870 to 1880 the land disposed of amounted to 96,000,000 acres, or almost as much as the area of California. The number of farms increased as never before or since, the rate amounting to fifty per cent. The railroads spread with incredible rapidity into the West. Prices had ruled high during the war and for a time following, thus offering the greatest incentive to production. The price of public land in the meantime had been about wiped out by the Homestead Act. Thus labor and transportation facilities were the only limiting factors in the production of grain and live stock. The railroads furnished a solution to the transportation problem, and the invention of the self-binder and other machines made the labor question an essentially different one from what it had previously been. The government had virtually said: "Production is the basis of prosperity; here is the land; use it." Again the cereal production rose, and this time outran in proportion the increase in population. The per capita cereal production in 1870 was 36 bushels; in 1880 it was 54 bushels. The per capita production of wheat, already high in 1870, rose again, reaching nine and one-sixth bushels. The price of wheat (gold) at the close of the war was $1.53; in 1880 it was 95 cents. The western farmers were poor; they wanted more income; many voted with the Greenbackers for more dollars, yet they undertook to raise more wheat in spite of the fact that the market was dull. The average value per farm of all farm property remained substantially stationary throughout the North; the South was undergoing such changes that the corresponding figures are not comparable.

The public land disposed of from 1880 to 1890 was almost equal in extent to two Californias. The amount added to the farm area was equal to three Missouris. Of great significance is the fact that of this increase in farm acreage, well above half was in the west-north-central states, notably in Nebraska, South Dakota, and Kansas. In these three states the farm area expanded forty-nine per cent.

The per capita grain production continued to rise. The per capita wheat production for several decades was about fifty per cent above the normal consumption. Prices, as before, were low. Grain was being raised on what was virtually free land; so also were cattle on the ranges. Prices had to be low. The farmers had been coaxed to the virgin prairies by a gift of the soil, and they competed against one another until, by production beyond demand, prices of the output were kept low, and the price of the land, therefore, prevented for many years from increasing greatly.

During the forty years from 1850 to 1890 the number of acres per capita in farms for the population of the country fell from 12.7 to 9.9, a decrease of twenty-two per cent, but the significance of this vanishes at once in consideration of the fact that the number of improved acres per capita remained almost stationary, even rising a trifle, from 4.9 acres to 5 acres. Up to 1890 it had not been necessary to resort to difficult tasks in order to increase the area of improved land in proportion to population. The semi-arid regions had not become tempting to any large number of farmers. Leaving semi-arid land out of account, it may very well be said that the public domain was pretty well exhausted in 1890. A mere study of the figures showing the amount of land disposed of does not, however, suggest this date as a significant one in this respect, since even larger amounts have been taken up in very recent years than prior to that time. It is not a mere matter of area, but rather one of quality, that makes the period about 1890 a significant one. Since that time, irrigation, drainage, and "dry farming" have been terms familiar—often painfully familiar—to those interested in the public domain.

About half as much land, 107,000,000 acres, was taken from the public domain between 1890 and 1900 as during the preceding ten years. Yet during this decade the increase in farm area was greater than ever before and, in all probability, much greater than within our present boundaries it ever can be again. Two hundred and fifteen million acres were added to farms, the expansion being pronounced in all the states west of the Mississippi except in a few of the oldest. Although it seemed that no such great quantities of land would ever be taken up agriculturally again, yet between 1900 and 1910 the amount of public domain disposed of almost doubled. Prices of farm produce had risen, and risen enormously. Land that had been altogether unattractive some years earlier began to have a value. In this connection it should be noted that whereas the amounts of land taken from the public domain during the decade from 1850 to 1860 corresponded rather closely to the amounts added to farms, they are widely apart from 1900 to 1910.[1] During that time hardly over one-fifth of the area disposed of by the government appeared on the census rolls as additions to farm lands. The extraordinary increase in land alienations had been very largely through the homestead, and these mainly within the arid region. What the value of these homesteads will be and what relation they will have to farming remains to be seen. For several years the leading states in the disposal of public lands have been Montana and Colorado, in neither of which farming without irrigation is an unqualified success.

To state the time when the public lands were exhausted so far as free access to such as would normally support a family without great investment is concerned is not an easy matter. Probably 1890 will do as well as any one date, yet for twenty years later the wheat belt was being pushed farther and farther to the west in North Dakota and Kansas, in both of which there was land open to homestead. Likewise the wheat fields of the "Palouse Country" developed greatly during that time, and largely on land newly acquired from the government. Nevertheless, so far as general, mixed farming is concerned, the free government land has offered little room for expansion since 1890.

The rapid disposal of so much rich land in the West, with the attendant lowering of prices, meant hard times for many eastern farmers. The total value of all farm property was steadily increasing throughout the East until about 1870, after which time for thirty years decreases were reported in various states; for example, ten showing decreases in 1890 as compared with 1880. While between 1900 and 1910 these states responded to the general rise in price with small increases in total farm values, they showed the smallest increases of any part of the country. The same was true

[1] It must be admitted that the figures for land in farms are not entirely comparable between the censuses of 1900 and 1910. Yet the statements made stand analysis very well, the greatest discrepancies in census reports not being found in the states where homesteads are most prevalent.

from 1910 to 1920, the increase being but a little over a third as great as for the country as a whole. The different sections of the country had found their respective competitive levels. Much of the land taken up before the era of railroads became low grade or marginal land in comparison with the lands of the West. The Census Report for 1920 has a paragraph on the "Permanent Abandonment of Low Grade Land," such being found mainly in New England.

But in the West itself farm land prices were kept low by the presence of free government land nearby. The result was the most extensive kind of agriculture. Why worry about soil fertility when it was superabundant? It was labor that was scarce, and every effort was made to spread it over as great an area as possible. In the language of Jefferson: "In Europe the object is to make the most of their land, labor being abundant; here it is to make the most of our labor, land being abundant." [2] This was written in the early years of the nineteenth century, but it continued to be true for nearly another century. The public land policy, above all, gave us land so cheap as to make agriculture extensive in the extreme.

During the latter portion of the nineteenth century all prices were low, but agricultural prices were relatively lower than prices of general commodities as compared with the period just before the Civil War, and distinctly so as compared with prices for some years just before the World War. Agricultural products were higher, absolutely, in price before the Civil War than for several decades following. The general commodity price level, taking 1856-60 as the base, rose to 205 at the close of the war, stood at 135 in 1870, and at 101 in 1880, agricultural prices being below this level by ten to thirty points, the greatest discrepancy occurring about 1880. The lowest prices for farm produce were reached in 1896, although in purchasing power the farmer was somewhat better off then than in 1880. The average price of wheat in New York for the ten years

[2] Jefferson, 121.

1850 to 1859 was $1.50; from 1885 to 1899 it was 85 cents, a decrease of 44 per cent. Corn for the same years shows a decrease from 73 cents to 47 cents, or 36 per cent. Hogs in the meantime fell from $5.55 to $4.55 per hundred, 18 per cent. In all of these instances the decrease meant a relative decline in comparison with commodity prices. The relationship existing in 1856 to 1860 was regained for a period of about seven years, 1907 to 1913, during what may be called normal times. It is therefore plain that the farmer was playing a losing game so far as his income depended on selling farm produce and buying other commodities may be taken as a measure.

The same conditions, *i.e.*, abundant and cheap raw material, kept general prices low in America during the main part of the nineteenth century. Lumber was cheap, unbelievably so; iron was cheap; as a result, building costs were low. Agricultural produce was still lower in price because of the ease with which labor, no matter whether city labor, or labor originating in the country, could so easily be associated with land which costs little or nothing. The logic of the case would lead one to believe that agricultural prices would of necessity be low under such circumstances; the facts of history corroborate the conclusion. Whatever other results may be achieved, the settlement of land at a rate more rapid than the needs of the nation, or the general market, require, must of necessity lead to low prices for the produce of the land so settled. Our western farmers needed more income, and the only obvious way to get it was to raise more produce. To do this defeated its own end to some extent by forever dragging prices still lower, particularly so while increased output depended mainly on added, productive acres. In other words, while a disproportionate part of the people of the country persisted in farming, the prices of farm produce were correspondingly low.

During the decade 1910 to 1920, even under the stimulus of war prices, it was possible to increase the farm area but 8.8 per cent, the improved land area still less, 5.1 per cent, while population increased 14.1 per cent. In 1850 there were 12.7 acres per capita of total population in farms, in 1920 nine acres, and yet the improved acres for these years were 4.9 and 4.8, respectively. The highest amount per capita of improved land was in 1880 and 1890, 5.7 acres. The per capita production of cereals in 1920 was 44.6 bushels. It must be admitted that the falling off in the supply of foodstuff in proportion to population is still to come. The prediction that we were "rapidly approaching a shortage," made confidently a quarter century ago, must now be postponed at least another quarter century. Overproduction is still the cause of depression among farmers. If population continues to increase, however, the 4.8 improved acres per capita must grow smaller, and the supply of food maintained, if at all, by more intensive methods.

Negatively, it may be said that the land policies of the government have failed to keep the land permanently in the hands of tillers of the soil. It seems strange that no one, so far as can be judged, appreciated the patent fact that giving government land away could effect a wide distribution of ownership only so long as the supply of free land should last. Once exhausted, with untrammelled private ownership, it was inevitable that the forces governing prices would have full sway, and that land high in price would not be obtained without great effort. Within the lifetime of men still living much land granted without price to the settler has reached $300 and $400 per acre in selling value. At the same time, tenancy has increased in the neighborhoods of these prices from nothing at all to sixty per cent; even from virtually nothing to over forty per cent by whole states. Giving land away does not permanently revolutionize a land system.

CHAPTER XXVIII

In looking back over the history of the federal land policies, with the dreary lack of light that appears to have been shed upon them as the years have passed, a few features stand out in tolerable clearness. Whatever else may be forgotten, it should be kept in mind that as a people when we undertook to handle the public domain, there had already developed a widespread and firm belief that the wilderness was and ought to remain free to the man who should subdue it. Just how much was to be allowed to each pioneer was another question, but that some area, in the nature of a homestead, was the rightful reward of him who redeemed it from its raw state had grown up with the ideas of freedom during colonial times. Nor was the doctrine based on *a priori* reasoning alone; it was a widespread practice. Land had been free because it was abundant—superabundant. Every new colony, whether east or west of the Appalachians, wanted settlers. This was true of Massachusetts and Virginia in the seventeenth century, and of Montana and New Mexico in the twentieth.

Putting a price on land was the outcome of necessity and a matter of regret to a large number of the men who undertook to formulate the first plans. Jefferson, in 1776, had said: "I am against selling the land at all." Had it not been for the desperate state of the public finances, Hamilton would not have smitten the public land rock. Particularly after finding that the stream of revenue from this source was a small and uncertain trickle, the disposition to return to something close to free distribution was strong. However, it must be remembered that inertia works just

547

as powerfully in keeping a force in operation as in holding a body at rest. The fact that a quarter century of selling land at two dollars per acre was a matter of history, and that much land had actually been sold, was the strongest assurance against a free land policy for some years following. The purchasers of land at any given price, after having bought, will resist strenuously any attempt at a reduction of the price, and when it is a political agency in control of the policy the resistance is likely to be effective. Thus the free land policy, abandoned because of the complications and exigencies of the Revolution and the years following it, was a long time in reëstablishing itself, in spite of the fact that the forces working toward its reëstablishment were always present, usually discernible, and again and again partially victorious, until finally completely so.

To What Extent Were the Early Acts the Result of Conscious, Policies?

As one goes over the history of the public domain legislation for the first half century, say prior to 1841, the question will no doubt be brought up concerning the basis of action. Was it the result of any recognizable plan, or did the separate acts result from the sheer necessity of compromise on the part of contending forces on each separate occasion? As previously noted, a few leading men had well formulated views on the subject of land and land settlement. Among these were Jefferson, Gallatin, and several others less well known. Hamilton had views on raising revenue, and on this basis assumed a knowledge of handling the public domain. Popularly the unsettled land was viewed as a free good to the man who wanted not to exceed a few hundred acres, and something slightly above a free good as a reward for special services, it being about all the early governments had to offer on such occasions. While, therefore, there were many individuals with interesting, even excellent, ideas on how the public domain should be administered, it cannot be said that a conscious policy worthy of the name existed. It was rather a series of expedient actions put into practice from time to time which must perforce be gathered together, classified as best they may be, and called the public policies, not forgetting that from 1784 to 1900 there was a strong popular belief that the land ought to be free to the settler. This was strengthened by the still more popular belief within the confines of all new states and territories that settlement was to be desired above and beyond all other considerations.

WHAT POLICIES MIGHT HAVE BEEN FOLLOWED

What might have been is as safe as futile. There is not much at stake on the part of the critic who looks back over a program of past events and prescribes the changes that would have been better had they been appreciated and followed. Even so, it is not altogether barren of interest to inquire what might have been the policies, better than those in vogue, for the disposition of public land during the past hundred and forty years.

Some such questions as these will come to mind: Should close settlement have been prescribed and followed? Should communities have been established in an ideal, orderly fashion? Should the land have been held at a price high enough to prevent speculation, i. e., at "a sufficient price"? Should it have been free throughout the whole time? Should settlers have been kept off the land until after the surveys? Should the forests and minerals have been kept out of private hands? Should conservation have begun earlier? Should settlement have been retarded so as to keep land of a desirable, accessible quality, perhaps until now, unsettled? Had there been a few statesmen able to see the public domain in a perspective of half a century, a perspective including a vision of the development of the country with respect to industries, population, and wealth, thus relating settlement to other equally important national features, it might have put the land issue in a different light. But the *ifs* and *ands* are too numerous and prominent in the retrospective speculation here involved. Historically, that is to say, in view of what we know of the past, there can be little room for difference of opinion: It was not possible to get a view of what was destined to happen to the country for any great number of years in advance, although, looking back over the achievements, they seem to have been inevitable and natural. The imagination was not equal to the actualities. Even the few who dealt with population statistics and figured out a fairly accurate rate of increase were perfectly helpless as to what these great numbers of people were to do. Just as there is at present there was then alarm over the prospects of an inadequate food supply as soon as the supply of unoccupied land should once be exhausted.

ATTEMPTS AT A SCIENTIFIC LAND POLICY

During the century and a third over which time our legislation has extended there has been but little attempt to couple the land policies with the ultimate needs for food, or even to coördinate the demand for land wanted by settlers with any formulated doctrine concerning the most desirable rate at which land settlement should progress. The question of food hardly figured in the controversies or plans, and very naturally so, since food was abundant and cheap until within very recent years. Thus substantially the whole attention was centered on matters pertaining to settling vacant territory with the purpose of building up communities and states, and thereby extending the power and influence of the nation. Involved in this was always and ever the question of the distribution of property, it being taken for granted that a wide distribution was desirable. In the minds of the members of Congress, and they reflected the views of the people in general at least fairly well, it was believed that a wide distribution in the first instance was of profound importance, in that such distribution was likely to persist. That the constant pressure of economic law might disturb the arrangement made by political law was either not recognized at all, or was viewed as of secondary importance.

That there was an unusual opportunity, or duty, resting upon the government in making settlements over such a vast territory as the public domain hardly occurred to a member of Congress. On the contrary, there seemed to be substantially no apprehension that the settlement could be done in a wrong way, granted one thing only: the ownership of the land should, in the minds of all, be widely diffused. Every other consideration pertaining to the condition of the settler, once he got onto the land, was subordinated, or ignored. Recent students of land economics ask whether or not the Americans were acquainted with such doctrine as the Wakefield theory of colonization. In answer it must be admitted that whatever knowledge they had of plans of that character made very little impression. However, many of the most important parts of Wakefield's plan were recognized before Wakefield's time. This was particularly true of the "sufficient price" which was to prevent speculation and bring about a desirable balance between the older, industrialized, portion of the country and the frontier. It is strange that no references to Wakefield appear in the discussions of land questions in this country during the period 1834 to 1860. His main book came out in 1849, just about the time that the Homestead argument came to the front, while other writings of his had been appearing from time to time over a period of at least fifteen years previously. Probably the Americans interested in settling the West were not in a frame of mind to learn from theorists of another country. They felt themselves to be thoroughly practical, which is another way of saying that they valued their own opinions above those of any and everybody else. The feeling that the problem was before them, within sight, and that already a great deal of good history had been made, was reason enough for rejecting foreign schemes and doctrines.

The outcroppings of the central ideas of the Wakefield

system were early discernible. These were the questions of keeping settlement abreast of sales, and, the same thing in other words, the prevention of speculation in lands ahead of settlement. Washington in 1790 and 1791 refers to "timely and judicious sales," having in mind very clearly questions of settlement as opposed to revenue. There was even a suggestion that it would be well to limit the total amount of land sold per year, thereby preventing undue expansion in the matter of both settlement and speculation. The speaker of the House, Mr. Dayton, in 1796 suggested that if the $2.00 price proved to be not high enough to prevent the sale of over 500,000 to 800,000 acres of land a year it should be raised. He predicted that land would progress in value. Gallatin added that land was then selling in Ohio at four to six dollars an acre. He believed speculators could not afford to pay such prices, but that settlers could. Gallatin further expressed the view that sales in small lots, in the land districts, would result in bids at auction, by settlers, of what the land was worth. Thus, speculation would, by a sufficient price thus determined, be deterred from operating. The idea of keeping settlement and sales tied together was brought out in the same year in a motion by a member of the House that sales should be forfeited in case settlement was not promptly made.[1] Sales at the seat of government would result in lower prices bid by speculators, since they would not know the quality of the land.[2]

Mr. Morrow of Ohio, acquainted with the frontier, was convinced that a minimum price of $2.00 would serve as an effective check on speculation.

It would seem that if any man on whom responsibility devolved during the years of land policy formation should have had a disinterested, logical doctrine, Gallatin was the man. From his utterances it seems safe to infer that he did entertain the conviction that the frontier should be settled in a

[1] *Annals,* 4 Cong., 1 Sess., p. 407.
[2] *Ibid,* pp. 405-6.

systematic, compact manner, and, moreover, he mentions again and again the possibility of holding down speculation by charging a price which the speculator could not afford to pay, "fixing the price low enough to enable every industrious actual settler to become a purchaser, and leaving it sufficiently high to prevent land monopolies."[3] Among these utterances one looks in vain for a well formulated expression of a plan by which the doctrine might be put into effect. Gallatin, like the rest of the group responsible for the public debts, allowed the question of revenue to obscure his views on settlement as such. The sale of land, rather than the colonization of it, appealed to every man who during the first twenty or thirty years had to do with public finances. At one time Gallatin in discussing the question of price expressed the view that in case a reduction could be made below the $2.00 minimum, the same amount of money might be obtainable merely by giving a little more land, perhaps another 100,000 acres a year, a matter of little moment since "the difference is so trifling."

There is little or no evidence to show that there were students of Adam Smith among the men who shaped our land policies, though that distinguished writer had made some rather trenchant remarks bearing on the subject. For instance, in his chapter, "Of Colonies," Smith makes the following observations:[4] "Plenty of good land, and liberty to manage their own affairs their own way, seem to be the two great causes of the prosperity of all new colonies. . . . But the political institutions of the English colonies have been more favourable to the improvement and cultivation of this land, than those of any of the other three nations [Spanish, Portuguese, and French].

"First, the engrossing of uncultivated land, though it has by no means been prevented altogether, has been more restrained in the English colonies than in any other. The colony law which imposes upon every proprietor the obliga-

[3] *Public Lands,* I, p. 826, see also p. 167.
[4] Adam Smith, *Wealth of Nations,* Bk. IV, Ch. VII.

tion of improving and cultivating, within a limited time, a certain proportion of his lands, and which, in case of failure, declares those neglected lands grantable to any other person, though it has not, perhaps, been very strictly executed, has, however, had some effect."

In the doctrines which came to the front from about 1825, voiced by Benton, and until the time of Greeley and Grow down to the passage of the Homestead Act, substantially every sentiment expressed was either concerning the desirability of promoting settlement, or the rights of those wanting land. Restriction of the rapidity of settlement hardly entered the mind of anyone who made himself heard during half a century preceding the Civil War. The only suggestion of such a view was in connection with restriction of grants to settlers as opposed to speculators, and restriction of the amount allowed each settler. These measures would, of course, result automatically in some restriction in the general disposition of land, but not to such an extent as to constitute a planned, controlled expansion into the wilderness in accordance with the needs of the nation for a food supply and a balance between the extractive and the industrial occupations.

Might Settlement Have Been Controlled?

It is easy to say that it would have been much better had settlement progressed at a slower and more orderly pace. Compact settlements have many advantages socially, and economically. Under some circumstances it may be feasible to predetermine the rate and the bounds of settlement. Probably the conditions for such control were never more conspicuously lacking than in America during the hundred years following the Revolutionary War. The habits of the people, the attitude of the colonial governments still fresh in mind, the great abundance of land, the presence on the continent of other nations as colonizers anxious for settlers, the lack of any feeling of fear of or great respect for the federal government during the formative period and early years, the very general desire for land—all these considerations pointed to the very type of land policy which Congress devised: Cheap land, accessible to all, at a low price, or free.

That settlers were bound to move west and take up land was a fact recognized by the political leaders of the day. Speaking of the possibility of selling land to settlers, Jefferson in 1776 remarked: "They will settle the lands in spite of everybody." Some years later, Washington expressed the same opinion in response to the question of the desirability of the movement of settlers to the West: "You might as well attempt to prevent the reflux of the tide, when you had got it within your rivers." [5]

The conclusion is inevitable. Settlement could not have been controlled in the sense of holding great tracts of land back, and restricting sales, or grants, within a prescribed territory until all land designated was taken. Some sort of control through a price, such as the Wakefield "sufficient price," might conceivably have been used as a discouragement to speculation. In fact, it was, as above noted, presumably used. Could it have been used to a much greater extent? Again, this is mainly an idle and impossible question, yet it is safe to say that a price of four, or six, dollars an acre would have met with such violent opposition as to have rendered such a plan impossible at almost any time. Such a price would have been out of balance with the operations of states, and out of line with the judgment of individuals and companies having land for sale. Coupled with a credit system, it would have failed dismally. On a cash basis it would have met the combined resistance of the frontiersmen and all those who were anxious to settle the country with all speed and at all hazards. After national questions were for the time well settled, after the Homestead Act had worked out to its logical conclusion, and there remained only the semi-arid regions, wet lands, and timbered lands, it probably would have been feasible to put

[5] *George Washington: Life and Writings of* (Sparks), XII, p. 270.

a much higher price on the remaining lands and hold them off the market till someone would pay the price, or hold them forever if they were not wanted. We were, after 1900, not thinking of national prosperity in terms of expansion onto new land. Moreover, we were getting a new wisdom with respect to timber and minerals. The frontier figured far less in politics. Thus, after the bulk, and the best, viewed agriculturally, of the public domain was gone, it would have been politically possible to institute a reform respecting the balance. If possible, then why was it not done? True enough. A better statement would be that it would seem not to have been politically impossible had there been a concerted move made by an intelligent, determined body of people. The forest policy is the evidence that something was possible. With respect to agricultural lands a policy equally radical was needed, and hardly to a less degree. It was proposed, and defeated. There was no widespread understanding of the relationship of grazing land to national welfare, and without this understanding the plans made were destined to be short-sighted, individualistic, and destructive. This is what they have been. Hence, the conclusion that while, about 1900, there could conceivably have been developed a logical, rational, policy respecting the remaining public domain, sentiment was not ready to support it. There was an abundance of lip service rendered on several spectacular occasions, such as the Conservation Congresses, but the Congress of the United States was not ready for a conservation program. The main accomplishments were those made through executive authority in the withdrawal of great tracts of land from free entry.

The method by which the public domain of America was settled can hardly be called, except in the broadest sense, one of colonization. True enough, new settlements were formed, but settlements in a "body" were incidental; "companies of people" were widely and promiscuously scattered.

Schemes Resisted

By way of emphasis it may be repeated that with all the lack of constructive plans which mars the history of the disposal of our public domain, Congress did at least show great power of resistance in dealing with fantastic schemes. Land was wanted in all sorts of quantities for every sort of enterprise: educational, religious, ethical, and political. In view of the grants to transportation companies, it may be objected the resistance was strong in certain respects, only to break down pitifully in others. However, it must not be forgotten that, not Congress alone, but the whole country was converted to the use of the public domain for the promotion of internal improvements. What Congress did in this respect was a reflection of the opinions and plans of the parties involved, not the initiation of a program made out of political substance. These comments merely emphasize the fact that Congress had a few well-grounded views pertaining to the public land; they were: to bring revenue, to serve as the basis of national expansion, and, finally, and feebly, the basis of prosperity, widely diffused, for a people no longer concerned about national extension.

The Public Domain a Balance Wheel

Without doubt the public lands served as a political and economic balance wheel; but, just as a well-adjusted machine gives no outward evidence of needing a balance wheel, so the functioning of the public domain in this capacity was imperceptible. Discontented groups of people were continually moving to the West. For example, the Mormons, the Fourrierists, the Daniel Boones, Calhouns, Jacksons, and Lincolns. It is not to be inferred that these people would have, in all cases, made trouble had they remained in the older settled parts of the country. They would, however, most assuredly have made a different country of it had they not taken the alternative of moving into the sparsely settled West.

Another equally certain deduction concerning the balance-wheel nature of the public domain is seen in the attitude of labor, especially organized labor. Many theoretical economists have held that wages of common labor will usually correspond very closely with what can be made by men of this class on land; especially is the principle applicable where the land is free. No better instance of free land has been known in the western world than that of the American public domain during the century from 1790 to 1890. Until near the close of this period the laboring men not only could, but in significant numbers did, look upon the possibility of farming on the frontier as a way of escape from unfavorable conditions of employment on a wage basis. It was not necessary that many should actually leave the shops for the farm in order that employers might understand the situation. They did leave now and then on the occasion of strikes, or other troubles, and the effectiveness of such a termination of the controversy in controlling the situation cannot be doubted. At the same time, a stream does not often rise higher than its source, and, likewise, the income to the laborer on free land being low, this support for wages, though real, was correspondingly weak. Wages were greatly disturbed during the period 1830 to 1850 on account of the introduction of labor-saving machinery, as was again the case following the Civil War. The ease of escape from the city to free, or cheap, land was greater with the development of the railroads, than earlier. There was, both theoretically and practically, enough reality to the possibility of leaving the city for the frontier to serve as a mitigating influence of no small importance in labor disputes. The faith of labor in land as an outlet for numbers, or the belief that by natural right a piece of land should be free to each and all, has not impressed the labor leaders of recent years. The impressive turn of events in this respect is the movement of country people to industrial centers, with a very small counter-current toward the country.

THE INHERENT WEAKNESSES OF THE POLICIES OF THE PAST

Throughout the history of the public domain, fraud has been prevalent. It has been for the most part almost transparent fraud. The great mass of people seem willing to accommodate their consciences to the exigencies of the occasion. If the laws under which land has been taken, under which it is apparently the expectation of the government that it shall be taken, do not fit the character of the land itself, the settler, or buyer, does not feel that it is his fault. He will do as others are doing. If making a home on a claim is to stay on it one night in six months, according to the practice of claim-makers, and if the land office accepts that version, then surely the homesteader will raise his right hand and swear that the cabin on his claim is his home. If the Homestead Act is carried into the forest as the means of acquiring forest land and the officers representing the administration of the public lands require proof of agricultural operations, then surely the clearing of four square rods, the planting of half a dozen kinds of crops, and the like, will be accepted as proof of honest intentions to make a farm, notwithstanding the notorious fact that no farms are being made out of such land by such means. The abuses of the Homestead Act have been open, but they have been invited. Likewise the timber culture, the timber and stone, and the various desert land acts, though possibly not "shapen in iniquity," were for many years the basis of the wholesale breaking of at least two clauses of the decalogue.

It was probably inevitable that the affairs of the public domain should be inextricably interwoven with politics. Aside from numberless cases where temporarily the land questions were weighed against other considerations, there were two political issues to which they were strongly attached. These were the tariff, and slavery. The tariff and the public domain were yoked together to do duty as political servants of both the Whigs and the Democrats. The Whigs wanted to make the burden on the land light in order to have more weight left for the tariff to carry. The Democrats wanted to maintain the old balance in order that less tariff load would be needed. Again, the Democrats had to fight the free land movement in the interest of slave labor. So between the two there was little chance for an unprejudiced vote on land questions as such from 1830 to 1860. Since that time the public domain has played a very minor rôle in politics.

One of the most unfortunate facts concerning the whole land question is the lack of administrative force which the government has provided. How could the Homestead Act be made to fulfill its mission when no board, no commission, no officer, was charged with the duty of administering it? Of course, the Commissioner of the General Land Office was charged with administering all land laws, but he was, and is, an appointive officer, usually serving but a few years, with an enormous amount of routine work, with helpers upon whom little responsibility can be placed; and with traditions already established working against him. There is good evidence to show that many of the commissioners have performed their duties as well as they could; but there is more evidence that they could not perform them adequately. For example, they have had no means of knowing the character of the land taken in a given district. The local agent is a political appointee who is not looking for trouble, and has good reasons for continuing the *status quo*. Hence, no reform; and by the time the truth is known, it is too late to make the obviously needed changes. The land was hardly classified at all during the first century of operations, and even now not adequately. Until the classification is made to cover substantially all that settlers need to know about the land, good administration is out of the question.

THE PRESENT SITUATION

Looking at things as they are, we see that the bulk of the good land no longer belongs to the government. It is of no use to criticize the railway land grants. They were sadly mixed with fraud; they may not have been needed; but we have the railroads, and the farmers have most of the desirable railroad land, having paid little more for it than they would have paid other speculators. The forests are mainly gone into private hands. Here not so much can be said of the good outcome of a bad bargain. While the cut-over land, which was sold incidentally, the timber being the real consideration, is mainly in private hands, the government still has unknown amounts of land potentially valuable for farming. As land goes higher and higher in value, and especially as new methods of handling it are developed, these lands, now undesirable, will without doubt acquire a value. Could it be possible to take away the privilege of exploiting these lands speculatively whenever conditions are favorable for so doing, they might be made to serve a useful purpose in furnishing the basis for a normal expansion of agriculture. Particularly should the remaining public land be classified with respect to its agricultural possibilities.

The most obvious mistake in recent years is seen in connection with grazing land. Could this have been sold, leased, or given away in tracts suitable for that purpose, its usefulness might have been increased greatly and many people saved the expense and grief of a hopeless homestead. The government cannot exercise specific judgment as to the merits of a piece of land as well as can an individual with respect to what may be done in making it produce an income at a given time, due to change in prices and markets. It can, however, determine in a broad way that land with less than a given amount of rainfall, on which repeated attempts at farming have been made without success, is more valuable for grazing than for farming, and act accordingly. Then, should private initiative become insistent that a given tract should be put back into the agricultural class, it might be made a special order of inquiry and possibly a new verdict might be rendered. After land has been in use in the form of farms for some years it is bound to sell mainly on its merits, but in a wild state there is a chance for great unearned profits to be reaped from the many by the few, and likewise a chance for deep disappointments on the part of great numbers who go into regions about which salient facts are unknown. The government has in the past let facts and forces play for the stakes, with little concern for the outcome. While the government probably could not absolutely forbid the selling of land by one person to another, even though it were obvious that the buyer was making a bad bargain, there is no reason why the truth, properly told, should not act as a guide to any and all who would take the trouble to listen. Could the government have determined that much of the semi-arid land was more valuable as grazing land than as arable land and held it for that purpose during the past eight years, there would still be the possibility of changing from this to the more intensive use. To change the other way is difficult.

A Public Land Policy Still Needed

Thus far there has been no genuine land policy in and for the United States. True enough, there have been temporizing plans, some of them good for a time, and for certain sections. But a plan involving and comprehending the welfare of the whole nation, varied to fit the different parts of the country, we have not had. This does not mean that no serious attempts have been made to modify the plans so as to fit them to certain parts of the country. These attempts we have traced. Even so, such modifications of the laws as have been made in accordance with the varying conditions of the different parts of the United States have at best been compromises of political interests, rather than fitting measures for the disposal of the public domain. With the feeling that all land should be made private property as rapidly as possible, that new states should be settled with the utmost rapidity; with the general conviction that *laissez faire* is the best guide in deciding questions of conflict between government and citizen, there was little opportunity for the development of a conscious, workable, vigorous land policy. A land policy means social control over one of the greatest instruments of production, a possibility for a strong government but an impossibility for a weak government.

Wakefield had in mind a "mother country," established, but not looking to the colonies for an income. The mother country was to develop the colonies, presumably, as an indirect source of greater strength, a place from which to get raw product and to which surplus laborers might be sent. The United States lacked for at least half or three-quarters of a century the fundamental setting for the development of a Wakefield system. During more recent years there has been a feeling that the public domain was about all gone and therefore a land policy rather an anachronism than a live issue. Hardly has there been a conviction that a land policy could be needed in connection with land already in private hands. Apparently this conviction is part and parcel of the passive view which assumes that private ownership is the ultimate goal in the land struggle, and that since private property has been accomplished, the state should withdraw from the field.

That the land issue is not settled once for all by and through private ownership is demonstrated in the history of most countries of which we have knowledge, and conspicuously in the struggles going on around us to-day. Not only do Russia and Mexico furnish evidence of the persistence of the land problem long after land has once been put into private hands, but countries much more stable exhibit tendencies almost as pronounced and not greatly different in character. For example, within a quarter century there has been a virtual revolution in the land system of Ireland, supervised and financed through government; a revolution in the land ownership in Denmark, likewise managed by the government; a radical making over of the land situation in New Zealand within a period not much longer than a quarter century; Australia could be added to the list. At the present moment two of the leading countries of

Europe are apparently on the verge of land reform—England and Italy.

Land ownership must appeal to the judgment of the nation as sound, fair, and conducive to general welfare. When England granted the suffrage to the laborers in the early nineteenth century, the landlord class was apprehensive lest the ballot might be used to dispossess them of their land. A labor leader in America shared the same view.[6]

Although it seemed for three-quarters of a century following the passage of the English Reform Bill that the prediction that the laboring classes would vote the landholders out of their property would not come true, recent events suggest the possible accuracy of the prophecy.

The events of 1924 in connection with oil leases emphasize the necessity for a land policy embracing the natural treasure beneath the surface of the ground. Plans are under way for the development of such a policy.[7] Likewise the constantly recurring troubles over coal, and the helplessness of the public in resisting increases in the prices of coal, point to the necessity of some policy of social control over the necessaries of life in cases in which competition shows its inability to act as a regulator. The reservation of coal lands on the public domain is a move in the right direction. The alienation of all authority over the coal measures on which the nation is immediately dependent is bringing ominous results. A land policy respecting coal, beyond that we now have, is a probability at no very distant date.

[6] "Imagine the National Reform project to be rejected, and the whole lands of the United States to have become, as they would soon become, *private property*. Would not the same effects inevitably follow that now result from the same cause in England? Then, would not the same thing take place here, that would take place now in England, if the people there had universal suffrage, as we have? Would not the oppressed millions, when driven to the last stage of oppression, rise up and say to the land holders, 'You have unjustly used our land and our labor to amass wealth to yourselves; we will therefore have a fair and equal division, and then begin anew with equal right to the soil' ? To us it seems that the new proposition of the National Reformers is truly *conservative*." *Workingman's Advocate*, April 6, 1844.

[7] *Chicago Tribune*, April 12, 1924.

THE LAND POLICIES MOST IMMEDIATELY NECESSARY AND FEASIBLE

Without any attempt to look into the distant future, it is obvious that several things ought to be done, and, moreover, that several things can be done. From the standpoint of the nation as a whole there is crying need for a general conservation policy. This policy should be formulated and administered by those able to think in national, not sectional, terms. The food, clothing, and shelter questions are all involved. If we are able to think in national terms, we shall be able to make decisions pertaining to the best means of using the available land in developing new farms. Shall it be done by irrigating the arid lands of the West; by draining the wet lands of the Mississippi Valley; or by establishing some sort of system whereby the cut-over lands of the Lake States and the Gulf States shall be brought systematically to serve society, either by intelligent clearing or by reforestation?

The irrigation question has always been much mixed with politics, and as a result a great deal of energy and money have gone into ill-starred ventures. Irrigation should play an important rôle in the agriculture of the country, but what to do at any given time when more land is needed, or demanded, should be decided on the basis of availability of land from the standpoint of productive power in relation to cost. Had this been done in the past, the map of agricultural production would be appreciably different from what it is. The decisions have been made, on the one hand by political forces, and on the other by the private owners of land whose methods of settlement, if they are to be called such, are not made with the public welfare uppermost in mind.

The types of agriculture least suited to a *laissez faire* land policy are forestry and grazing. The former can hardly succeed without a large measure of public ownership and management. The latter might, but has not yet done so in a marked degree. While the greater part of our forest land is in private hands, and in spite of the fact that much is being done by certain private companies in producing a forest crop, the main hope of a wood supply for the future lies with the government, federal and state. There is enough land, submarginal from the standpoint of farming, on which to grow all necessary timber. The government owns a great deal of such land now and can regain the ownership of great acreages more without much cost. States can get it by offering a nominal price, and are getting much in scattered tracts through the lack of individual buyers at tax sales. Getting hold of the land on which to develop forests is but one step in the direction of a timber supply, but it is the most important step of all, since without it nothing further can be done. The most commendable act on the part of the government during the past half century was the reservation of so much forest land from private entry. The best public land policy now in operation in the United States is that of the Forest Service.

The next most crying need for a land policy is in connection with grazing land. Few people realize the extent of land suitable mainly for this purpose. A very careful estimate of the probable future use of land has been made by the United States Department of Agriculture.[8] This estimate suggests that there are likely to remain 615,000,000 acres of land usable mainly for grazing. The main part of this area is in the West; a smaller part, possibly one-third, in the form of unimproved pasture, mainly in the eastern states. Without a doubt, grazing can be carried on successfully under conditions of either state or private ownership of the land. In fact, it is done under both conditions with as good results as the general economic conditions allow. In Texas private ownership has been accomplished in many sections, the state having disposed of its holdings. In the national forests grazing is being reduced to a system satisfactory to both private enterprise and the public interests.

[8] *Yearbook*, U. S. D. A., 1918, p. 433. Article by O. E. Baker and Miss H. M. Strong.

On the great stretches of semi-arid territory the situation has been anything but satisfactory. From the standpoint of the owner of the stock the tenure has been uncertain. As the range has been treated as booty rather than as property, therefore the popular judgment of those concerned has been that a short-time view is preferable to a long-time view in range management. The Grazing Homestead Law will probably succeed in breaking up most of the free range. If such an outcome is desirable, it should have been done openly rather than by indirection. When Congress grants a homestead corresponding to an economic unit in size, as was done under the first homestead act, settlement is accomplished with comparatively little friction. When the original grant is but a third as large in extent as the local conditions prescribe, there is more friction. It does not follow that the failure to grant land in the right amounts will lead to disaster. The average farm over a large part of North Dakota is three times the size of a homestead as applied to that section, but no harm, other than a little friction in gaining title, and a few disappointed homesteaders, resulted. It was farm land which was homesteaded, and a change in size is not a calamity. In the semi-arid districts the case is quite otherwise. A good range is spoiled for a bad grain field, and the grain field cannot readily be turned back into range.

The Remaining Public Domain

Out of the 1,300,000,000 acres of public domain in the aggregate there now remain but 186,000,000. Much of this is too rough for cropping, or even for grazing. Included in this area, a little under a tenth of the area of the whole country, are mountain peaks, alkali plains, and plateaus covered with rocks. While there is some land in this remnant capable of irrigation, and still some millions of acres destined to be taken up under the Grazing Homestead Act, it must be admitted that it is a mere remnant. Undoubtedly there are still remaining rich mineral deposits, and an occasional

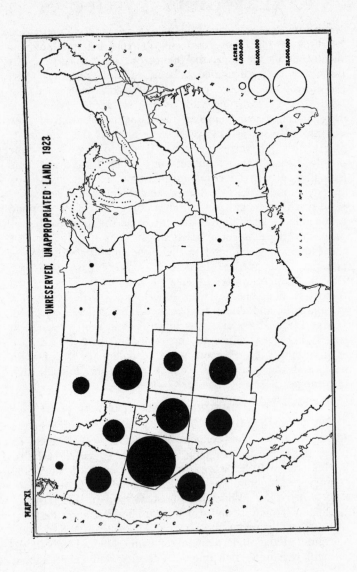

water-power site, both of which may, under existing laws, be reserved for further consideration even though the surface rights be claimed under the homestead acts. The public land now definitely reserved is greater in area than that unreserved.

ATTITUDE TOWARD FURTHER SETTLEMENT

Throughout substantially the whole period of our national history it has been the policy of the nation and the states to make it easy for settlers to get hold of land and make a start toward turning it into farms. From now on it should be made difficult for land to be taken up. Not only should this be done with respect to land belonging to the federal government but also with respect to state land, of which there are still important areas. Not only is there a considerable amount of state land at present, but there is much land falling into state hands yearly.

In the past the government and the states have paid out good money, and much of it to induce people to settle on raw land. The right to spend money in this manner has hardly been called in question. Should it be seriously proposed to spend money to get people off undesirable homesteads and other similar lands not affording a livelihood, objections would be raised at once. Just why there should be more objection to helping people to get off than on when the occasion for moving off is beyond dispute is outside the realm of logic. Precedents for giving seed wheat to certain settlers are well established; but precedents for helping them out of a bad bargain altogether, rather than to put up with it, have yet to be established. Overproduction of farm produce has been the bane of farming during the last half century, with the exception of a few years—abnormal years during the War. How to limit agricultural production is a conundrum not yet solved, but in any case the government, states included, may well cease helping to create from year to year a new crop of submarginal farmers. To get submarginal land out of the farming category, and into a use for which it is fitted, would be a worthy goal in a land policy at once desirable and attainable. Whether or not America is to be overtaken by a land reform campaign depends on the ability shown in meeting issues pertaining to land in advance of the moment when an exasperated public loses faith in the national program.

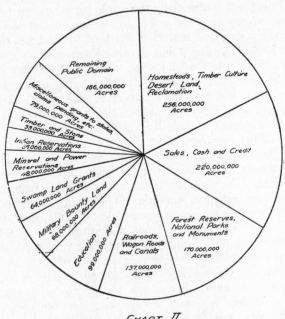

CHART II

DISPOSITION OF PUBLIC DOMAIN
Total Acreage 1,399,000,000

INDEX

571